T0189246

Lecture Notes in Computer Science 13097

More information about this subseries at http://www.springer.com/series/7409

Constantine Stephanidis ·
Vincent G. Duffy · Heidi Krömker ·
Fiona Fui-Hoon Nah · Keng Siau ·
Gavriel Salvendy · June Wei (Eds.)

HCI International 2021 - Late Breaking Papers

HCI Applications in Health, Transport, and Industry

23rd HCI International Conference, HCII 2021
Virtual Event, July 24–29, 2021
Proceedings

 Springer

Editors
Constantine Stephanidis
University of Creteand Foundation
for Research and Technology – Hellas
(FORTH)
Heraklion, Crete, Greece

Heidi Krömker
Ilmenau University of Technology
Ilmenau, Germany

Keng Siau
Missouri University of Science
and Technology
Rolla, MO, USA

June Wei
University of West Florida
Pensacola, FL, USA

Vincent G. Duffy
Purdue University
West Lafayette, USA

Fiona Fui-Hoon Nah
Missouri University of Science
and Technology
Rolla, MO, USA

Gavriel Salvendy
University of Central Florida
Orlando, FL, USA

ISSN 0302-9743   ISSN 1611-3349 (electronic)
Lecture Notes in Computer Science
ISBN 978-3-030-90965-9   ISBN 978-3-030-90966-6 (eBook)
https://doi.org/10.1007/978-3-030-90966-6

LNCS Sublibrary: SL3 – Information Systems and Applications, incl. Internet/Web, and HCI

This Springer imprint is published by the registered company Springer Nature Switzerland AG
The registered company address is: Gewerbestrasse 11, 6330 Cham, Switzerland

Foreword

Human-Computer Interaction (HCI) is acquiring an ever-increasing scientific and industrial importance, and having more impact on people's everyday life, as an ever-growing number of human activities are progressively moving from the physical to the digital world. This process, which has been ongoing for some time now, has been dramatically accelerated by the COVID-19 pandemic. The HCI International (HCII) conference series, held yearly, aims to respond to the compelling need to advance the exchange of knowledge and research and development efforts on the human aspects of design and use of computing systems.

The 23rd International Conference on Human-Computer Interaction, HCI International 2021 (HCII 2021), was planned to be held at the Washington Hilton Hotel, Washington DC, USA, during July 24–29, 2021. Due to the COVID-19 pandemic and with everyone's health and safety in mind, HCII 2021 was organized and run as a virtual conference. It incorporated the 21 thematic areas and affiliated conferences listed on the following page.

A total of 5222 individuals from academia, research institutes, industry, and governmental agencies from 81 countries submitted contributions, and 1276 papers and 241 posters were included in the volumes of the proceedings that were published before the start of the conference. Additionally, 174 papers and 146 posters are included in the volumes of the proceedings published after the conference, as "Late Breaking Work" (papers and posters). The contributions thoroughly cover the entire field of HCI, addressing major advances in knowledge and effective use of computers in a variety of application areas. These papers provide academics, researchers, engineers, scientists, practitioners, and students with state-of-the-art information on the most recent advances in HCI. The volumes constituting the full set of the HCII 2021 conference proceedings are listed in the following pages.

I would like to thank the Program Board Chairs and the members of the Program Boards of all thematic areas and affiliated conferences for their contribution towards the highest scientific quality and overall success of the HCI International 2021 conference.

This conference would not have been possible without the continuous and unwavering support and advice of Gavriel Salvendy, founder, General Chair Emeritus, and Scientific Advisor. For his outstanding efforts, I would like to express my appreciation to Abbas Moallem, Communications Chair and Editor of HCI International News.

July 2021   Constantine Stephanidis

HCI International 2021 Thematic Areas and Affiliated Conferences

Thematic Areas

- HCI: Human-Computer Interaction
- HIMI: Human Interface and the Management of Information

Affiliated Conferences

- EPCE: 18th International Conference on Engineering Psychology and Cognitive Ergonomics
- UAHCI: 15th International Conference on Universal Access in Human-Computer Interaction
- VAMR: 13th International Conference on Virtual, Augmented and Mixed Reality
- CCD: 13th International Conference on Cross-Cultural Design
- SCSM: 13th International Conference on Social Computing and Social Media
- AC: 15th International Conference on Augmented Cognition
- DHM: 12th International Conference on Digital Human Modeling and Applications in Health, Safety, Ergonomics and Risk Management
- DUXU: 10th International Conference on Design, User Experience, and Usability
- DAPI: 9th International Conference on Distributed, Ambient and Pervasive Interactions
- HCIBGO: 8th International Conference on HCI in Business, Government and Organizations
- LCT: 8th International Conference on Learning and Collaboration Technologies
- ITAP: 7th International Conference on Human Aspects of IT for the Aged Population
- HCI-CPT: 3rd International Conference on HCI for Cybersecurity, Privacy and Trust
- HCI-Games: 3rd International Conference on HCI in Games
- MobiTAS: 3rd International Conference on HCI in Mobility, Transport and Automotive Systems
- AIS: 3rd International Conference on Adaptive Instructional Systems
- C&C: 9th International Conference on Culture and Computing
- MOBILE: 2nd International Conference on Design, Operation and Evaluation of Mobile Communications
- AI-HCI: 2nd International Conference on Artificial Intelligence in HCI

Conference Proceedings – Full List of Volumes

1. LNCS 12762, Human-Computer Interaction: Theory, Methods and Tools (Part I), edited by Masaaki Kurosu
2. LNCS 12763, Human-Computer Interaction: Interaction Techniques and Novel Applications (Part II), edited by Masaaki Kurosu
3. LNCS 12764, Human-Computer Interaction: Design and User Experience Case Studies (Part III), edited by Masaaki Kurosu
4. LNCS 12765, Human Interface and the Management of Information: Information Presentation and Visualization (Part I), edited by Sakae Yamamoto and Hirohiko Mori
5. LNCS 12766, Human Interface and the Management of Information: Information-rich and Intelligent Environments (Part II), edited by Sakae Yamamoto and Hirohiko Mori
6. LNAI 12767, Engineering Psychology and Cognitive Ergonomics, edited by Don Harris and Wen-Chin Li
7. LNCS 12768, Universal Access in Human-Computer Interaction: Design Methods and User Experience (Part I), edited by Margherita Antona and Constantine Stephanidis
8. LNCS 12769, Universal Access in Human-Computer Interaction: Access to Media, Learning and Assistive Environments (Part II), edited by Margherita Antona and Constantine Stephanidis
9. LNCS 12770, Virtual, Augmented and Mixed Reality, edited by Jessie Y. C. Chen and Gino Fragomeni
10. LNCS 12771, Cross-Cultural Design: Experience and Product Design Across Cultures (Part I), edited by P. L. Patrick Rau
11. LNCS 12772, Cross-Cultural Design: Applications in Arts, Learning, Well-being, and Social Development (Part II), edited by P. L. Patrick Rau
12. LNCS 12773, Cross-Cultural Design: Applications in Cultural Heritage, Tourism, Autonomous Vehicles, and Intelligent Agents (Part III), edited by P. L. Patrick Rau
13. LNCS 12774, Social Computing and Social Media: Experience Design and Social Network Analysis (Part I), edited by Gabriele Meiselwitz
14. LNCS 12775, Social Computing and Social Media: Applications in Marketing, Learning, and Health (Part II), edited by Gabriele Meiselwitz
15. LNAI 12776, Augmented Cognition, edited by Dylan D. Schmorrow and Cali M. Fidopiastis
16. LNCS 12777, Digital Human Modeling and Applications in Health, Safety, Ergonomics and Risk Management: Human Body, Motion and Behavior (Part I), edited by Vincent G. Duffy
17. LNCS 12778, Digital Human Modeling and Applications in Health, Safety, Ergonomics and Risk Management: AI, Product and Service (Part II), edited by Vincent G. Duffy

http://2021.hci.international/proceedings

HCI International 2021 (HCII 2021)

The full list with the Program Board Chairs and the members of the Program Boards of all thematic areas and affiliated conferences is available online:

http://www.hci.international/board-members-2021.php

HCI International 2022

The 24th International Conference on Human-Computer Interaction, HCI International 2022, will be held jointly with the affiliated conferences at the Gothia Towers Hotel and Swedish Exhibition & Congress Centre, Gothenburg, Sweden, June 26 – July 1, 2022. It will cover a broad spectrum of themes related to Human-Computer Interaction, including theoretical issues, methods, tools, processes, and case studies in HCI design, as well as novel interaction techniques, interfaces, and applications. The proceedings will be published by Springer. More information will be available on the conference website: http://2022.hci.international/.

General Chair
Prof. Constantine Stephanidis
University of Crete and ICS-FORTH
Heraklion, Crete, Greece
Email: general_chair@hcii2022.org

http://2022.hci.international/

Contents

HCI in Transport

HCI in Industry and Manufacturing

Supporting Health and Well-being

How Engagement with Gamified Applications Impacts Quality of Life: A Conceptual Model

Amir Zaib Abbasi[1]([✉]), Maria Hassan[2], Umair Rehman[3], Helmut Hlavacs[4], Ding Hooi Ting[5], and Muhammad Umair Shah[6]

[1] IRC for Finance and Digital Economy, King Fahd University of Petroleum and Minerals, Dhahran, Saudi Arabia
[2] Shaheed Zulfikar Ali Bhutto Institute of Science and Technology, Islamabad, Pakistan
[3] Wilfrid Laurier University, Brantford, ON, Canada
[4] Research Group Entertainment Computing, University of Vienna, Vienna, Austria
[5] Universiti Teknologi PETRONAS, Tronoh, Malaysia
[6] University of Waterloo, Waterloo, Canada

Abstract. This study proposes a conceptual model that establishes a relationship between engagement with gamified applications, and its impact on a user's quality of life (QoL). Since gamification is rapidly gaining popularity therefore the use of such applications has become a norm. Subjective quality of life is a mental state or an individual's awareness of factors that impact major aspects of life, such as health, learning, creativity, socialization etc. Literature is sparse when it comes to investigating the impact of engagement with gamified applications, and its effect on quality of life. To address this research gap, we explore how consumer engagement with gamification cultivates an individual's perception with regards to their quality of life. We posit that consumer engagement is a higher-order formative construct, comprising cognitive, affective and behavioural dimensions, is influenced by gamified applications, leading towards an increase in subjective QoL. QoL is also a higher-order formative construct involving first-order reflective constructs such as leisure time, view of life, creativity, learning, friendship and individualistic perspective of satisfaction. This study provides an important insight to avenues of academia and practitioners by developing a conceptual model where consumer engagement in serious games acts as a predictor of users' QoL. We conclude by discussing important implications that arise from this exploration, along with its limitations and avenues for further research.

Keywords: Consumer engagement · Serious games · Gamification · Quality of life · Conceptual study

1 Introduction

The gamification is relatively an evolving strategy in the entertainment industry that is being implemented in non-gaming environment with some gaming elements and mechanics to promote behavioral learning/adaptation [1]. Hence, the gamification industry is expected to raise from $9bn to around $31bn by 2025 [2]. The concept of gamification has been studied in several contexts such as improving student's performance in education [3], providing awareness to defeat COVID-19 [4], utilizing the gamification in

C. Stephanidis et al. (Eds.): HCII 2021, LNCS 13097, pp. 3–10, 2021.
https://doi.org/10.1007/978-3-030-90966-6_1

marketing, especially in the brands settings to influence customer's brand engagement, involvement, and love [5]. Johnson, et al. [6] have highlighted the importance of using health gamified apps to derive health related behavioral change. Given the importance of health gamified apps, several gamified apps have been developed to promote positive behavioral change [1]. For instance, Zombies Run, a mobile application that is developed to motivate users to run through wrapping runs into an audio-delivered story of surviving a Zombie apocalypse [6]. Evaluating the prior studies in gamification settings, scholars have limited focus on how consumer engagement in gamified apps influence their quality of life (QoL), as study in this article.

In different research studies, GDP per capita has primarily been used to assess the quality of life (QoL). However, it is argued that per capita profits or associated measures of income are insufficient measures since they provide an incomplete understanding of QoL [7–9]. Research contends that other financial, social and physiological measures are needed along with GDP to adequately assess QoL. The idea of QoL is now exceeded the simple economist monetary view that just encapsulates standards of income; QoL now includes many different factors comprising of happiness, pleasure and welfare. In general, QoL is the capacity to which human desires and goals are fulfilled in terms of private or organizational perceptions of subjective well-being. Therefore, QoL is a primarily a way of understanding our lives and gauging our subjective wellbeing.

The major contributions provided in this study are as follows: Our first contribution includes formulating a conceptual model that assesses the relationship between engagement with gamified application and its impact on a user's QoL. We utilize the Brunnsviken Brief Quality of life scale developed by Lindner, et al. [10] and the Consumer Videogame Engagement scale by Abbasi, et al. [11] in efforts to establish this relationship. Following Earp and Ennett [12], a conceptual model aims at integrating theories from multiple disciplines by incorporating multi-level causalities. It is usually represented by a simple diagram showing a proposed causal linkage between concepts, and provides thus a visual representation of the elements of a theory. As such, it mainly summarizing the existing body of literature, proposes new research directions, and guides the formulation of hypotheses for research questions. Usually it must be followed by an empirical study to confirm the formulated hypotheses. This research is novel since there is no previous research that formalizes the relationship between these two distinct areas of research. Our study contributes to earlier studies [13, 14] as we apply the notion consumer videogame engagement in gamification context to predict the QoL among the users of gamified apps.

The second contribution that the study makes is for the benefit of practitioners and marketing specialists trying to integrate gamification through their products and services. Information regarding consumers' view of the quality of life can help them develop superior gameful experiences resulting in increased engagement that positively affects consumers view of life and other facets of QoL.

The paper brings forth a proposed conceptual model that strengthens the impact of engagement through gamified applications on self-perceived QoL. The paper first explains the concept through suitable and relevant literature on the fields of gamification, engagement, and subjective quality of life. The paper also proposes a hypothesis that can later be tested to investigate the connection between consumer engagement with gamification and its effect on QoL. The paper is then concluded with the implications of the study and how this topic can be further expanded into different areas of research.

2 Literature Review

2.1 Quality of Life (QoL)

Quality of life, abbreviated as QoL, has been defined by Ferrans and Powers [15] *"As a multi-dimensional idea that includes various distinctive dimensions and its estimation is considered as an essential factor for policy assessment."* Most would think that quality of life scales is only limited to health psychological or other illnesses. The concept of measuring This was the reason the factor of subjectivity was included in QoL scales that can be accessible to people from all walks of life [16]. There have been different subjective scales developed over the years, but there have been many with questions that only cover one construct. Such contributions have been made since the early 1960s, as mentioned by Endicott, et al. [17]. One of the many common reasons QoL scales are formed for evaluating health related issues and how such issues affect one's overall lifestyle. This notion was further analysed in the early 20th century and the need for a more expanded questionnaire was raised. This lead to many researchers in contributing further into the topic of subjective QoL with scales such as the Satisfaction with Life Scale [18], Quality of Life Inventory [19], Quality of Life Index [15], The Flanigan Quality of life Scale [9], The Quality of Life Enjoyment Scale [17] and The Brunnsviken Brief Quality of Life Scale [10], which is also proposed to be used for this study. The one thing reflected common in all the QoL scales mentioned above is the multifaceted dimensions each one of them is targeting. Work done in subjective QoL is based on how an individual perceives that what they are getting out of life and what factors are leading towards it.

One of the perspective is that the goal approach cannot be used to evaluate emotions and worries approximately QoL of a character, and hence, the subjective measurement should be considered. The subjective element of QoL examines the diverse perceptions regarding the character's lifestyle conditions. It also measures an individual's cultural and personal values using various techniques involving the ratings of happiness, wellbeing, life delight and their perception [7]. Many researchers have argued that by combining both goal and subjective measures into a single idea of QoL, we can get a real picture. Additionally, several studies are based on theories that lead toward sound dimension of an exceptional human being's existence, which includes the concept of social justice, human development, socio-economic improvement, abilities and functioning, and sustainability [9].

Within QoL, the lifestyle is primarily divided into two main domains comprising the objective and subjective factors. The objective factors include education, fitness, pleasant of surroundings, leisure, and living situations. Whereas, the subjective factor involves individuals' intellectual fitness, spiritual, emotional and cognitive, religiousness, psychological, social, private beliefs, and physical dimensions. Collectively, such dimensions explain the holistic nature of QoL. The notion of QoL is introduced and being used to assess the individual's QoL based on a particular society. Globally, the researchers have put much emphasis on developing the QoL indices to explore the individual's QoL for a particular community and society [7–9, 18, 20–23]. Few popular indices include human development index, world happiness index, Gallup-health-ways well-being and etc. [16].

As of now, there has not been any significant work done on proving that the use of gamified applications has anything to do with shaping up the perspective on the quality of life. However some work has been found [8, 24–26] which to some extent connects the use of gamified platforms related to fitness and productivity and validates the proposition to some extent that engagement through gamification might lead to change in preferred quality in an individual's life. This study contributes to QoL literature through developing a conceptual model where consumer videogame engagement plays a predicting role on QoL. Additionally, this study is different than those who studied QoL with serious games as we provide a mechanism that consumer engagement in gamified apps acts as an important predictor of QoL ensuing from the consumption of gamified apps.

The next section debates on consumer engagement in gamified apps such as serious games and its further impact on QoL.

3   Hypothesis Formation

Consumer video engagement is defined as "a psychological state that triggers due to two-way interactions between the consumer and videogame product (e.g. serious games), which generates engagement in game playing" [13]. Hookham and Nesbitt [27] acknowledged that engagement in serious game is an important factor for learning. Following this viewpoint, we perceive that when players get engaged in serious games and its narrative, they are more likely to learn the contents that are being exposed in the games. In line with the existing literature [13, 28–33], It has been perceived that engagement with gamified applications leads towards positive behavioural change. Such change occurs when internal psychological needs have been met, which according to self-determination theory are autonomy, relatedness, competence. The three basic psychological needs when fulfilled give way to intrinsic motivation which leads to user engagement [34–40]. This study posits how the engagement triggered through gamified application can lead to shape an individual's perception about the quality of life. Several studies have reported that playing the serious games have positive outcomes and learning e.g. mental health [41], personalized health [42], student education [43], health care [44, 45], health and wellbeing in elderly people [46]. In our review of earlier studies, we have found that serious games have been utilized to bring positive outcomes in individuals' live. In the same vein, we also believe that consumers' engagement in serious games may positively impact on their QoL. Our argument is in line with prior studies [46–48] who reported that serious games have unique attributes which in turn impacts on users' QoL. Therefore, we theorize and develop the conceptual model where consumers' engagement in serious games depending upon the context-specific environment can significantly improve their QoL, see Fig. 1. According to the proposed conceptual model, we posit:

H1: Subjective perception of the quality of life increases with engagement with gamified applications.

The model has been developed by adapting two scales according to the concept of gamification. To measure engagement scale of consumer videogame engagement has been adapted which contains dimensions of cognitive, affective and behavioural dimensions which have been connected with dimensions of QoL used in the Brunnsviken Brief

Fig. 1. Conceptual model

scale developed by *Lindner et al.* [10]. i.e. Leisure time, learning, creativity, friends & friendships, view of life individualistic perception of satisfaction in life. Both these scales are new in the field of research and have not been used together.

4 Conclusions

In recent years, the research on serious games and health related outcomes has gained much more importance. However, the research to date has focused on playing serious games and its associating health benefits. In contrast, our study aims to develop a conceptual model theorizing the predicting role of consumer engagement in serious games on individual's QoL. Our study fills an important theoretical gap by providing the conceptual model to predict users' QoL resulting from gamified aps.

Previously, scholars have given much emphasis on utilizing serious games to predict health-related outcomes, which collectively refer as QoL and sometimes wellbeing. Whereas, we provide a new approach for predicting health outcome i.e. users' QoL that is influenced by consumer engagement in serious games. Since the majority of QoL scales measure health-related problems and their impact on behaviour and lifestyle, this study adapts the QoL conceptualization given by Lindner, et al. [10] in which authors refer QoL as *"individual's perceived satisfaction with reference to leisure time, work, friendship, possibilities to be creative and learn new things"*. Recent literature evidence that consumer videogame engagement has been studied as endogenous variable with personality traits [49] and playful-consumption experiences [13, 14, 50] as antecedents in their study frameworks. In contrast, very little is known about the predicting role of consumer engagement in serious games and its ensuing impact on users' QoL. Hence, a notable research gap is addressed by developing the study conceptual model in gamification literature.

The results from the study can help make managers more aware of how a gamified application can impact on behavioural change which leads to a shift in the quality of life. Literature suggests that the main underlying purpose of gamification has always been long term positive behavioural change [30]. Based on this assumption, a user can only shift towards behavioural change if proper engagement with the gamified application occurs. The product of this chain reaction is often known to be reflected in a person's daily routine, may it be the regularity of exercise or picking up a healthy eating habit etc. [51]. With this process in mind, managers can create engaging applications that can provoke a user into changing his/her behaviour, in turn, creating a shift in the overall thinking and perception of life which is known as the quality of life. If data can be gathered based on QoL dimensions, managers can provide even more quality experiences resulting in more positive behaviour changes that will constantly create a change in their lifestyle.

Our study is conceptual and lacks empirical part to validate the model. Therefore, a future study is much recommended to bring new insights regarding the validation part of the conceptual model.

References

1. Tobon, S., Ruiz-Alba, J.L., García-Madariaga, J.: Gamification and online consumer decisions: is the game over? Decis. Support Syst. **128**, 113167 (2020)
2. Hass, D., Hass, A., Joseph, M.: A preliminary investigation of gamification from the young consumer's perspective. Young Consum. **22**, 413–428 (2021)
3. Zahedi, L., et al.: Gamification in education: a mixed-methods study of gender on computer science students' academic performance and identity development. J. Comput. High. Educ. **33**(2), 441–474 (2021). https://doi.org/10.1007/s12528-021-09271-5
4. Zain, N.H.M., Othman, Z., Noh, N.M., Teo, N.H.I., Zulkipli, N.H.B.N., Yasin, A.M.: GAMEBC model: gamification in health awareness campaigns to drive behaviour change in defeating COVID-19 pandemic. Int. J. Adv. Trends Comput. Sci. Eng. **9**, 1–9 (2020)
5. Xi, N., Hamari, J.: Does gamification affect brand engagement and equity? A study in online brand communities. J. Bus. Res. **109**, 449–460 (2020)
6. Johnson, D., Deterding, S., Kuhn, K.-A., Staneva, A., Stoyanov, S., Hides, L.: Gamification for health and wellbeing: a systematic review of the literature. Internet Interv. **6**, 89–106 (2016)
7. Brajša-Žganec, A., Merkaš, M., Šverko, I.: Quality of life and leisure activities: how do leisure activities contribute to subjective well-being? Soc. Indic. Res. **102**, 81–91 (2011)
8. Brustio, P.R., Liubicich, M.E., Chiabrero, M., Rabaglietti, E.: Dancing in the golden age: a study on physical function, quality of life, and social engagement. Geriatr. Nurs. **39**, 635–639 (2018)
9. Burckhardt, C.S., Anderson, K.L., Archenholtz, B., Hägg, O.: The Flanagan quality of life scale: Evidence of construct validity. Health Qual. Life Outcomes **1**, 59 (2003)
10. Lindner, P., Frykheden, O., Forsström, D., Andersson, E., Ljótsson, B., Hedman, E., et al.: The Brunnsviken Brief Quality of life scale (BBQ): development and psychometric evaluation. Cogn. Behav. Ther. **45**, 182–195 (2016)
11. Abbasi, A.Z., Ting, D.H., Hlavacs, H.: Engagement in games: developing an instrument to measure consumer videogame engagement and its validation. Int. J. Comput. Games Technol. **2017**, 1–11 (2017)
12. Earp, J.A., Ennett, S.T.: Conceptual models for health education research and practice. Health Educ. Res. **6**, 163–171 (1991)
13. Abbasi, A.Z., Ting, D.H., Hlavacs, H., Costa, L.V., Veloso, A.I.: An empirical validation of consumer video game engagement: a playful-consumption experience approach. Entertain. Comput. **29**, 43–55 (2019)
14. Abbasi, A.Z., Ting, D.H., Hlavacs, H., Fayyaz, M.S., Wilson, B.: Playful-consumption experience and consumer video-game engagement in the lens of SR model: an empirical study. In: HCI in Games (2019)
15. Ferrans, C.E., Powers, M.J.: Quality of life index: development and psychometric properties. Adv. Nurs. Sci. **8**, 15–24 (1985)
16. Ihsan, N., Aziz, B.: A multidimensional analysis of quality of life: Pakistan's context. Soc. Indic. Res. **142**, 201–227 (2019)

17. Endicott, J., Nee, J., Harrison, W., Blumenthal, R.: Quality of life enjoyment and satisfaction questionnaire: a new measure. Psychopharmacol. bull. **29**, 321–326 (1993)
18. Diener, E., Emmons, R.A., Larsen, R.J., Griffin, S.: The satisfaction with life scale. J. Pers. Assess. **49**, 71–75 (1985)
19. Frisch, M.B., Cornell, J., Villanueva, M., Retzlaff, P.J.: Clinical validation of the quality of life inventory. A measure of life satisfaction for use in treatment planning and outcome assessment. Psychol. Assess. **4**, 92 (1992)
20. Camfield, L., Skevington, S.M.: On subjective well-being and quality of life. J. Health Psychol. **13**, 764–775 (2008)
21. Cella, D.F., Tulsky, D.S.: Measuring quality of life today: methodological aspects. Oncology (Williston Park, NY), vol. 4, pp. 29–38 (1990). Discussion 69
22. Costanza, R., Fisher, B., Ali, S., Beer, C., Bond, L., Boumans, R., et al.: Quality of life: an approach integrating opportunities, human needs, and subjective well-being. Ecol. Econ. **61**, 267–276 (2007)
23. Cummins, R.A.: Fluency disorders and life quality: subjective wellbeing vs. health-related quality of life. J. Fluency Disord. **35**, 161–172 (2010)
24. de Lira, C.A.B., et al.: Engagement in a community physical activity program and its effects upon the health-related quality of life of elderly people: a cross-sectional study. Value Health Reg. Issues **17**, 183–188 (2018)
25. Hu, S., Das, D.: Quality of life among older adults in China and India: does productive engagement help? Soc. Sci. Med. **229**, 144–153 (2019)
26. Wu, Y., Kankanhalli, A., Huang, K.-W.: Gamification in fitness apps: how do leaderboards influence exercise? (2015)
27. Hookham, G., Nesbitt, K.: A systematic review of the definition and measurement of engagement in serious games. In: Proceedings of the Australasian Computer Science Week Multiconference, pp. 1–10 (2019)
28. Brigham, T.J.: An introduction to gamification: adding game elements for engagement. Med. Ref. Serv. Q. **34**, 471–480 (2015)
29. Brodie, R.J., Hollebeek, L.D., Jurić, B., Ilić, A.: Customer engagement: conceptual domain, fundamental propositions, and implications for research. J. Serv. Res. **14**, 252–271 (2011)
30. Buckley, P., Doyle, E.: Gamification and student motivation. Interact. Learn. Environ. **24**, 1162–1175 (2016)
31. Deci, E.L., Ryan, R.M.: Self-determination theory: a macrotheory of human motivation, development, and health. Can. Psychol. **49**, 182 (2008)
32. Deci, E.L., Ryan, R.M.: Motivation, personality, and development within embedded social contexts: an overview of self-determination theory (2012)
33. Deterding, S., Dixon, D., Khaled, R., Nacke, L.: From game design elements to gamefulness: defining gamification. In: Proceedings of the 15th International Academic MindTrek Conference: Envisioning Future Media Environments, pp. 9–15 (2011)
34. DomíNguez, A., Saenz-De-Navarrete, J., De-Marcos, L., FernáNdez-Sanz, L., PagéS, C., MartíNez-Herrálz, J.-J.: Gamifying learning experiences: practical implications and outcomes. Comput. Educ. **63**, 380–392 (2013)
35. Eisingerich, A.B., Marchand, A., Fritze, M.P., Dong, L.: Hook vs. hope: how to enhance customer engagement through gamification. Int. J. Res. Mark. **36**, 200–215 (2019)
36. Eppmann, R., Bekk, M., Klein, K.: Gameful experience in gamification: construction and validation of a gameful experience scale [GAMEX]. J. Interact. Mark. **43**, 98–115 (2018)
37. Hamari, J.: Do badges increase user activity? A field experiment on the effects of gamification. Comput. Hum. Behav. **71**, 469–478 (2017)
38. Hamari, J., Koivisto, J.: Why do people use gamification services? Int. J. Inf. Manag. **35**, 419–431 (2015)

39. Harwood, T., Garry, T.: An investigation into gamification as a customer engagement experience environment. J. Serv. Mark. **29**, 533–546 (2015)

40. Helmefalk, M., Marcusson, L.: Gamification in a servicescape context: a conceptual framework. Int. J. Internet Mark. Advert. **13**, 22–46 (2019)

41. Fleming, T.M., Bavin, L., Stasiak, K., Hermansson-Webb, E., Merry, S.N., Cheek, C., et al.: Serious games and gamification for mental health: current status and promising directions. Front. Psych. **7**, 215 (2017)

42. McCallum, S.: Gamification and serious games for personalized health. In: pHealth, pp. 85–96 (2012)

43. Lamb, R.L., Annetta, L., Firestone, J., Etopio, E.: A meta-analysis with examination of moderators of student cognition, affect, and learning outcomes while using serious educational games, serious games, and simulations. Comput. Hum. Behav. **80**, 158–167 (2018)

44. Lin, A.J., Cheng, F., Chen, C.B.: Use of virtual reality games in people with depression and anxiety. In: Proceedings of the 5th International Conference on Multimedia and Image Processing, pp. 169–174 (2020)

45. Ma, M., Zheng, H.: Virtual reality and serious games in healthcare. In: Brahnam, S., Jain, L.C. (eds.) Advanced Computational Intelligence Paradigms in Healthcare 6. Virtual Reality in Psychotherapy, Rehabilitation, and Assessment. SCI, vol. 337, pp. 169–192. Springer, Heidelberg (2011). https://doi.org/10.1007/978-3-642-17824-5_9

46. Nguyen, T.T.H., et al.: Impact of serious games on health and well-being of elderly: a systematic review. In: Proceedings of the 50th Hawaii International Conference on System Sciences (2017)

47. Kankaanranta, M.H., Neittaanmäki, P.: Design and Use of Serious Games, vol. 37. Springer, The Netherlands (2008). https://doi.org/10.1007/978-1-4020-9496-5

48. Cha, J., et al.: Finding critical features for predicting quality of life in tablet-based serious games for dementia. Qual. User Exp. **4**(1), 1–20 (2019). https://doi.org/10.1007/s41233-019-0028-2

49. Abbasi, A.Z., Nisar, S., Rehman, U., Ting, D.H.: Impact of HEXACO personality factors on consumer video game engagement: a study on eSports. Front. Psychol. **11**, 1831 (2020)

50. Abbasi, A.Z., Abu Baker, S.A.J.: Playful-consumption experience of videogame-play influences consumer video-game engagement: a conceptual model. Global Bus. Manag. Res.: Int. J. **9**, 9 (2017)

51. Aydın, S.Ö., Argan, M.: Understanding how gamification influences consumers' dietary preferences. J. Soc. Mark. (2021)

A Systematic Literature Review
on the Interaction Between COVID-19
and Transportation

Yan Chen[✉] and Vincent G. Duffy

Purdue University, West Lafayette, IN 47906, USA
{chen2055,duffy}@purdue.edu

Abstract. The application of human factors and ergonomics in transportation is an example of human-automation interaction. Since the year 2020, the covid-19 pandemic has become an emerging factor that interacts with transportation from epidemiological and ergonomic perspectives. This study aims at capturing the emerging trends of covid-19 related human factors in transportation through conclusions from a systematic literature review of relevant publications. Analyses of content and bibliometrics were accomplished by using tools such as VOS Viewer, Citespace, Harzing, and MaxQDA to establish the findings of emerging trends in this field. Key findings from these analyses are: (1) Since the start of the covid 19, countries over the world have administered a variety of travel-related controls in an attempt to contain or slow down the spread of the virus both domestically and internationally. (2) The enforced travel restrictions not only impacted the spread of the pandemic but also transformed people's activity and travel patterns into a new form. (3) The altered activity and travel patterns further brought changes in transportation policy design, air quality control, and industry disruptions. (4) The pandemic has motivated people to adopt new HCI technologies, and some previously HCI technologies are being challenged because of the pandemic mitigation policies.

Keywords: COVID19 · Travel network · Travel restrictions · Travel behavior · HCI

1 Introduction and Background

1.1 Human Mobility and Transportation

Human mobility is achieved through various transportation pipelines, including motor vehicles, trains, and aviation. Chapter 58 of the HFE book [1] applies human factors in designing a motor vehicle by identifying the users and evaluating the potential risks. Chapter 61 of the same book also investigated the role of human factors in aviation. Schwanitz [2] suggested changes in tunnel construction design based on the human sensation on pressure changes. In summary, the application of Human Factors in transportation aims to identify factors that impact human mobility and provide optimal policy

© Springer Nature Switzerland AG 2021
C. Stephanidis et al. (Eds.): HCII 2021, LNCS 13097, pp. 11–25, 2021.
https://doi.org/10.1007/978-3-030-90966-6_2

suggestions that facilitate human mobility, ensure a safe travel environment, and contribute to a sustainable external society. From the end of the year 2019, COVID-19 has become such an emerging factor that affects human mobility.

1.2 Human Mobility and COVID-19 Pandemic

COVID-19 Pandemic. The first clinically confirmed case of COVID-19 was identified in Wuhan, China, in December 2019. The outbreak coincided with the heavy spring festival travel season and the fact that Wuhan is one of the most important transportation hubs in China. As a result, the disease spread to peripheral areas rapidly despite the immediate lockdown of Wuhan City. The highly connected travel network between cities within China and countries out of China facilitated domestic and international human mobility and soon led to a global spread of COVID-19. On March 11, 2020, WHO ([3]) characterized the spread of COVID-19 as a pandemic based on "alarming levels of spread and severity.

Travel Controls. Since the start of the covid 19, countries worldwide have administered a variety of travel-related and other controls to contain or slow down the spread of the virus both domestically and internationally. China locked down the entire country in the early stage of the outbreak. Italy had to lock down the country shortly after the pandemic reached it. South Korea has been applying aggressive testing and mask-wearing policy throughout the pandemic. The northern European countries have maintained a normal travel and social activity policy throughout the pandemic. The US has implemented something in between the extreme lockdown and the herd-immunity philosophy. However, following the social distancing rule, schools were converted to online lecturing, most companies transformed to remote working, non-essential business ceased in-door operation. All these changes in social life expedited the formation of new travel norms.

New Travel Norms. The enforced travel restrictions not only impacted the spread of the pandemic but also transformed people's travel patterns into a new form. The travel demand reduced drastically because all activities, including learning, working, and eating, could be accomplished at home. Under the fear of the pandemic, people travel less by public transport, and the commercial aviation industry experienced harm immediately.

The arrangement of the remaining parts of this report is the following. Section 2 briefs on the objective of the report. Section 3 explains the procedure of content and bibliometrics analyses in a step-by-step manner. Section 4 illustrates the results from the content and bibliometrics analyses. Section 5 points out the future research direction.

2 Problem Statement

2.1 Literature Review

Most prior works pay attention to find the optimal transportation control measures to contain the COVID-19 pandemic while ignoring that the pandemic, in turn, has gradually transformed the transportation sector. For example, Tirachini, Alejandro, and Cats, Oded

[4] investigated the influence of several factors on reducing or increasing the COVID-19 contagion risk in public transportation, including the occupancy levels, the exposure time, the enforcement of face mask use, and the application of enhanced hygiene standards. Ortego, Jesús et al. [5] analyzed the impact of the COVID-19 pandemic on traffic congestion in 15 metropolitan areas of 13 Latin American countries. However, few studies have employed content and bibliometrics analyses to identify emerging research trends of covid-19 and transportation. Kutela, Boniphace et al. [6] presented a text mining approach to explore research themes relating to COVID and transportation. They emphasized content analysis and the geographical pattern of research themes but didn't utilize the bibliometrics analysis.

Bibliometric analysis is a statistical analysis that has been widely adopted to evaluate the timescale and citation effects among authors in academia. It could identify the research trends through citation analysis and content analysis. Guo, Fu et al. [7] utilized bibliometric analysis on affective computing researches. Gavin A. Duffy and Vincent G. Duffy [8] applied it to explore the research trends in the effects of human errors in environmental pollution. A variety of software tools have been developed to perform bibliometric analysis, such as BibExcel, CiteSpace, Pajek [7], VOS Viewer, Harzing, and MaxQDA.

2.2 Problem Statement

This report has the following three objectives. First, it summarizes the optimal travel-related restrictions under different scenarios and at various stages of the COVID-19 pandemic. Secondly, it uses content and bibliometrics analyses to identify emerging trends of covid-19 related human factors in transportation. Thirdly, it gives recommendations on transportation-related ergonomics design based on those emerging trends.

3 Procedure

3.1 Initial Keyword Search

From the initial keyword search in Google Scholar and SpringerLink, three articles, "Exploring geographical distribution of transportation research themes related to COVID-19 using text network approach" by Kutela, Boniphace et al. [6], "COVID-19 and public transportation: Current assessment, prospects, and research needs" by Tirachini, Alejandro and Cats, Oded [4], "Impact of the Covid-19 Pandemic on Traffic Congestion in Latin American Cities: An Updated Five-Month Study" by Ortego, Jesús et al. [5] were identified. These three articles were uploaded to Mendeley to manage references.

3.2 Keyword Search in Web of Science and Scopus

To collect the data for the analyses, a keyword search was conducted in the two databases: Web of Science and Scopus.

The keyword used in Web of Science was "covid and transportation", and the search yielded 532 articles in the Web of Science with a year span from 2020 to 2021. The metadata included article title, author, abstract, keywords, and references and was exported as a plain text file. Among highly cited articles and after scanning the abstracts, two articles were chosen: "Food supply chains during the COVID-19 pandemic" by Hobbs, Jill E [9] and "Population flow drives Spatio-temporal distribution of COVID-19 in China" by Jia, Jayson S et al. [10].

In the Scopus database, the keyword "covid and transportation" was searched within the article title, abstract, and keyword. The search yielded 1065 articles with a year span from 2020 to 2021. The metadata included article title, author, abstract, keywords and was exported as a.csv file.

3.3   Trend Analysis

The trend analysis is based on the search results of the Web of Science data collection.

was generated using the Web of Science analysis tool. The keyword was changed from "covid transportation" to "pandemic transportation" because there was no COVID-19 before 2020.

Shows the trend for articles involving both pandemic and transportation. The number of publications didn't exceed 20 until the year 2020, which indicates that the attack of COVID-19 was unprecedented and leads to extraordinary popularity in this research area. Besides, the number of articles in 2021 is almost two-thirds of the ones in 2020. This suggests that the research interests in this area will continue to grow in the foreseeable future (Fig. 1).

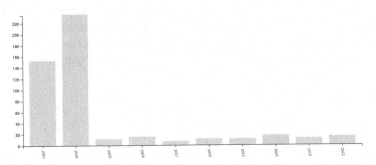

Fig. 1. Trend Diagram from 540 articles in WoS with the keyword "pandemic transportation."

3.4   Social Engagement Analysis Through Vicinitas Analytics

Vicinitas is a Twitter Analytics tool that tracks hashtags, keywords, and accounts and provides in-depth analytics on user engagement on specific topics. By comparing with another popular social topic recently and with itself (Table 1), we could see that the interaction between COVID and transportation has been actively and continuously discussed in the social network (Fig. 2).

Table 1. Measures of number of users, posts, engagement, and influence

Topic	# of Days	# of Users	# of Posts	Engagement	Influence
Covid Transportation	Ten days (Apr 18–Apr 27)	1.8k	2.0k	5.6k	77.0M
Covid Transportation	Ten days (May 24–Jun 2)	1.9k	2.1k	5.7k	139.6M
Shooting	Ten days (May 24–Jun 2)	2.0k	2.1k	3.9k	48.6M

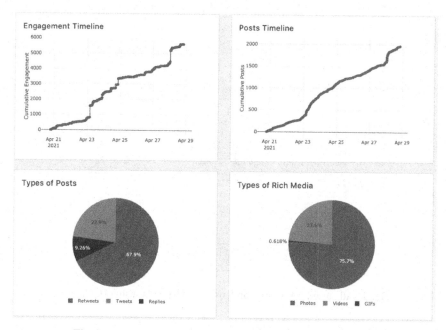

Fig. 2. Social Engagement Analysis through Vicinitas Analytics

3.5 Cluster Diagram of Key Terms

The obtained metadata from Web of Science was exported to VOSviewer, where a cluster diagram of key terms was formulated. The minimum occurrence of every keyword was set at ten.

The Scopus database was able to find 1065 articles, which is about twice as many of the ones found by the WoS database. Since there were far more occurrences of each key term, the minimum number of occurrences was set up to 50. 132 terms were generated to form the cluster diagram (Fig. 2).

3.6   Initial Key Word Search on Contribution to HCI

A keyword search was conducted on Google Scholar webpage with keywords "HCI"
AND "COVID" AND "transportation".

3.7   Advanced Key Word Search on Contribution to HCI

A keyword search was conducted on Google Scholar using the Harzing software
with keywords "International Conference" AND "Human-Computer Interaction" AND
"transportation" (Fig. 3).

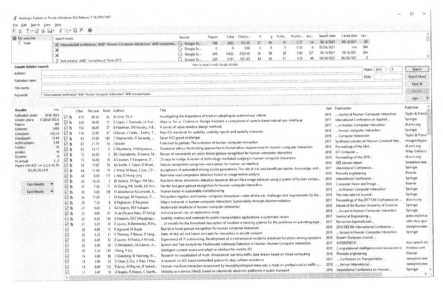

Fig. 3. Advanced key word search on Google Scholar using Harzing

3.8   Co-citation Analysis

From the metadata exported from Web of Science and Scopus, a co-citation analysis
was run to identify articles that were cited together frequently.

3.9   Word Cloud from Key References

With the chosen articles from an initial keyword search in Google scholar, SpringerLink,
and co-citation analysis from WoS and Scopus searches, a word cloud was generated
using MAXQDA to search for the most frequently used words within them. The stop word
list was imported from the MAXQDA official website with some additional customized
words after inspecting the word frequency list.

4 Results and Discussion

4.1 Content Analysis: Key Terms

The cluster diagram (Fig. 4) for key terms from WoS data was generated from 532 articles, and the minimum number of occurrences was set to ten. This cluster diagram suggested a rich amount of information. First, countries are closely connected to their dominant containment measures. For example, China has employed a lockdown policy from early on in the pandemic, and node China is close to node lockdown. On the contrary, South Korea has implemented an aggressive mask policy from the beginning of the pandemic, and node South Korea is close to mask. There was a surge of COVID-19 cases in Europe, especially Italy, in Spring 2020, researchers think one of the reasons could come from the individualism in Europeans, and the node individual is directly connected to Europe in the network. Secondly, emerging fields of study could be indicated from this diagram. For example, nodes logistic and disruption show that studies have been paying attention to the logistic disruption caused by the COVID-19 pandemic. Another interesting perspective is that the changes brought by COVID-19 may not be all bad. China has been suffered heavily from air pollution due to a large number of automobile emissions. The travel restrictions may reduce the amount of CO2 emission, thus alleviating air pollution.

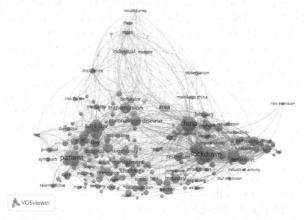

Fig. 4. Web of Science Cluster Diagram of title and abstracts data from 532 articles with a minimum of ten occurrences per keyword.

The cluster diagram (Fig. 5) for key terms from Scopus was generated from 1065 articles, and the minimum number of occurrences was set to 50. On the one hand, it shares some similarities with the cluster diagram from the WoS database. For example, China-related and air-pollution-relate nodes appear in both cluster analyses. Also, nodes patient, China, lockdown, and disease (sars cov) are still the essential words. On the other hand, this diagram differed from the previous in several places. First, the node China and the node lockdown were classified into different clusters. Secondly, the logistics-related nodes are not obviously seen in this diagram. Instead, airline-related nodes emerged. Thirdly, besides wearing a mask, social distancing was also being evaluated as a containment policy.

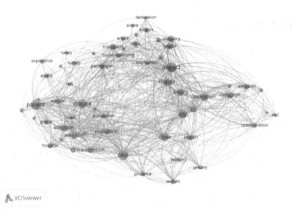

Fig. 5. Scopus Cluster Diagram of title and abstracts data from 1065 articles with a minimum of 50 occurrences per keyword.

4.2 Co-citation Analysis

A co-citation analysis (Fig. 6) based on metadata from WoS discovered 13 articles. Each of these articles was cited at least 15 times within the 532 articles found within the Web of Science. The 13 articles were formed into three clusters: (1) The clinical features of COVID-19 patients; (2) The impact of travel restrictions on the spread of COVID-19; (3) The impact of travel restrictions on air quality. One drawback in this result is that It only considered the impact of transportation on COVID-19 but not the other way around. The following papers were chosen from the 13 ones: "The effect of travel restrictions on the spread of the 2019 novel coronavirus (COVID-19) outbreak" by Chinazzi, Matteo et al. [11], "The effect of human mobility and control measures on the COVID-19 epidemic in China" by Kraemer, Moritz U. G. et al. [12], and "Temporary reduction in daily global CO_2 emissions during the COVID-19 forced confinement" by Le Quéré, Corinne et al. [13].

A co-citation analysis (Fig. 7) based on metadata from Scopus discovered 24 articles. Among the 24 articles, the following were chosen: "How did COVID-19 impact air transportation? A first peek through the lens of complex networks" by Sun, x. et al. [14], "Socially optimal lockdown and travel restrictions for fighting communicable virus including COVID-19" by Oum, Tae Hoon, and Wang, Kun [15], "The effect of COVID-19 and subsequent social distancing on travel behavior" by De Vos, Jonas [16], "The link between bike sharing and subway use during the COVID-19 pandemic: The case-study of New York's Citi Bike" by Teixeira, João Filipe and Lopes, Miguel [17], "The impact of COVID-19 partial lockdown on the air quality of the city of Rio de Janeiro, Brazil" by Dantas, Guilherme et al. [18], "Unexpected air pollution with marked emission reductions during the COVID-19 outbreak in China" by Le, Tianhao et al. [19], and "Responsible Transport: A post-COVID agenda for transport policy and practice" by Budd, Lucy and Ison, Stephen [20].

Comparing to the co-citation analysis based on WoS data, Scopus data shared three common articles. The first one is "Nowcasting and forecasting the potential domestic and international spread of the 2019-nCoV outbreak originating in Wuhan, China: a modelling study" by Wu, Joseph T. et al. [21]. The second one is "Clinical features of patients infected with 2019 novel coronavirus in Wuhan, China" by Ramanathan [22]. The third one is "The effect of travel restrictions on the spread of the 2019 novel coronavirus (COVID-19) outbreak" by Chinazzi, Matteo et al. [11]. It differed in the following ways. Firstly, there were much fewer articles that were cited together in the Scopus database. As a result, to obtain a meaningful number of articles, the minimum threshold had to be decreased from 15 to 4. Secondly, the clusters generated covered more spectrum of topics comparing with the ones from the WoS database. Besides studies on the clinical features of COVID-19 patients, the effect of transportation restrictions on COVID-19 spread, and the relationship between COVID-19 and air quality, it also identified articles that (1) investigate the reverse impact of COVID-19 on transportation

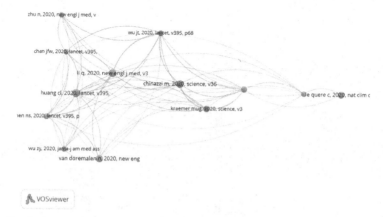

Fig. 6. Co-citation analysis of 532 WoS articles in VOS Viewer with a minimum number of 15 citations of a cited reference.

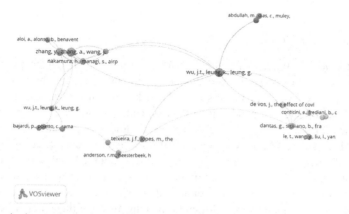

Fig. 7. Co-citation analysis of 1065 Scopus articles in VOS Viewer with a minimum number of 5 citations of a cited reference.

patterns and travel behavior, (2) study the interaction between COVID-19 and transportation from a complex network perspective, (3) indicates new transport policy in a post-covid era.

4.3 Word Cloud from Key References

With the chosen articles from an initial keyword search in Google scholar, SpringerLink, and co-citation analysis from WoS and Scopus searches, a word cloud was generated using MAXQDA to search for the most frequently used words within them. The stop word list was imported from the MAXQDA official website with some additional customized words after inspecting the word frequency list (Fig. 8).

Fig. 8. Word cloud generated by MAXQDA based on 14 key references

4.4 Lexical Search Results

Travel on Covid-19. Jia, Jayson S [10] built a human-mobility model that predicted the contagion process of COVID-19 from Wuhan city to other parts of China. This model could be employed by policy-makers to make risk assessments and allocate limited resources ahead of ongoing pandemic outbreaks. Chinazzi, Matteo [11] predicted the impact of travel restrictions on COVID-19 transmission from a similar perspective. It was concluded that the heavily enforced travel restrictions to and from the epi-center would not effectively alter the epidemic course unless coupled with a more than half reduction of transmission in the community. Oum, Tae Hoon [15] concluded that the travel restrictions via lockdown or economical penalty are necessary to contain the pandemic because individuals have difficulty in being aware of the external expense of infection risks they impose on others. Meanwhile, the strictness of the travel restriction should be higher in cities or countries with higher population density because the social burden of disease spread is more inflated in these places.

Travel Behavior Change. The enforced travel restrictions not only impacted the spread of the pandemic but also transformed people's travel patterns into a new form. Xiaoqian Sun [14] pointed out that airline is one of the industries that has been hit most because of the consequences of the pandemic wave, largely because many countries have employed country-specific lock-down policies when shutting down their borders. Because of similar reasons, the international flights have experienced much heavier hardships of the COVID-19 pandemic than domestic flights. However, many countries have surprisingly overlooked the role of domestic flights in spreading the COVID-19 virus. Jonas De Vos [16] thought that with the enforcement of social distancing, people would not only travel less but will prefer driving cars to take public transport. In order to maintain physical well-being, recreational walking and cycling might play an important growing role. Teixeira, João Filipe [17] investigated the change in ridership and duration in New York's subway and bike-sharing system, respectively. It was found that the Bike Sharing System was sturdier than the subway system, with a less significant ridership drop and an increase in the average trip duration.

Transport Policy Change. Jonas De Vos [16] suggested policymakers allocate some less-used street space to cyclists and pedestrians because of altered travel behavior. Cities in Europe and North America have already decided to turn some car lanes into sidewalks and bike lanes. Teixeira, João Filipe [17] mentioned that New York City has already launched free membership of the city bike to the critical workforce during the pandemic. Budd, Lucy [20] claimed that the emphasis in transport policy after the COVID-19 pandemic would move from demand management to awareness of the impact of individual behavior on public health so that responsible travel behavior will be encouraged or required.

4.5 Initial Keyword Search on Contribution to HCI

The following articles were selected from the initial keyword search: "Human-Automation Trust to Technologies for Naive Users Amidst and Following the COVID-19 Pandemic" by Y. Yamani et al. [23], "The Role of the Hercules Autonomous Vehicle During the COVID-19 Pandemic Use Cases for an Autonomous Logistic Vehicle for Contactless Goods Transportation" by T. Liu et al. [24].

4.6 Relevance to Human-Automation Interaction

Covid-19 has become a factor that affecting human-automation trust [23]. Since Covid-19, people started to enforce social distance measures to avoid close contact with others. These practices will in turn facilitate the adaptation and development of automated technologies. In the communication domain, to reduce disease transmission risk, more people are willing to take a chance in potential privacy information leaks and take an instance of trusting in teleconferencing tools. In the transportation domain, to achieve contact-free goods delivery, more and more people are taking a leap of faith in utilizing an autonomous logistic vehicle [24]. The pandemic altered people's travel behavior in aviation [23] and other public transport industries [17]. Policymakers in the public transport sector have to not only come up with ways to encourage people to use public transportation [16] but also ensure public health with the potential pandemic contagion risk [20]. At the same time, companies in the private sector need to develop ways to retain users who were "forced" to use automated technologies during the COVID-19 pandemic [23].

4.7 Advanced Keyword Search on Contribution to HCI

The following articles were selected because they were among the "most highly cited" using searching terms of "International Conference" AND "Human-Computer Interaction" AND "transportation": "Seven HCI Grand Challenges" by C. Stephanidis et al. [25], "Investigating the Importance of Trust on Adopting an Autonomous Vehicle" by J. K. Choi and Y. G. Ji [26], "Review of constraints on vision-based gesture recognition for human-computer interaction" by B. K. Chakraborty et al. [27], "Gender and gaze gesture recognition for human-computer interaction" by W. Zhang et al. [28].

5   Conclusions and Future Work

5.1   Contributions to HCI and Future Work

HCI Grand Challenges. Antona, Margherita et al. [25] identified seven grand challenges in the current HCI area: Human-Technology Symbiosis; Human-Environment Interactions; Ethics, Privacy and Security; Well-being, Health and Eudaimonia; Accessibility and Universal Access; Learning and Creativity; and Social Organization and Democracy. The first two are more relevant to the topic of this paper. On the one hand, the covid has forced people to use teleconference tools and autonomous vehicles. On the other hand, the pandemic has made people hesitate to take a bus or an airplane to avoid getting infected.

Trust is An Essential Factor in Adopting an Autonomous Vehicle. Choi, Jong Kyu and Ji, Yong Gu [26] conducted a survey of 552 drivers to explore what factors propel people to adopt an autonomous vehicle. The results showed that perceived usefulness and trust are predominant factors to adopt autonomous vehicles. This study also identified that trust has a negative effect on perceived risk. This finding coincides with the one in [24]. Following its conclusions, we could hypothesize that the pandemic has strengthened people's trust in HCI technologies, and the elevated trust led to more adoptions of HCI technologies.

Revolution in Facial and Gesture Recognition. Zhang, Wenhao et al. [28] proposed several algorithms, including a gender recognition algorithm utilizing facial features, a modular eye center localization approach, and a gaze gesture recognition method. These methods are not without limitations. Chakraborty, Biplab Ketan et al. [27] investigated the significant constraints on vision-based gesture recognition, including diverse contexts, multiple interpretations, spatial-temporal variations, and the complex non-rigid properties of the hand. Some covid-19 related mitigation strategies may become a new constraint for these facial or gesture recognizing algorithms. For example, if more and more people wear masks in their everyday lives, many of the current facial recognition algorithms won't perform well.

Relevant Awards. After searching the keyword "pandemic travel" on the NSF.gov website, the following NSF award was identified as a future work direction: Behavioral Risk Modeling for Pandemic Prevention and Response [29]. This direction builds a bridge that connects covid transportation transformation and Human-Computer Interaction (HCI). Human behavior contributes to the magnitude of pandemic spread, while the COVID-19 pandemic, in turn, has shaped new human travel behavior [16]. As pointed out in Sect. 4.5, the shifted travel behavior has encouraged people to take risks in new applications in the human-computer interaction field. Since transport policymakers are facing unparallel uncertainty concerning human travel behavior and compliance willingness to social distancing and mask-wearing enforcement, it is necessary to investigate the human behavior risk modelling in response to such a pandemic. It will also be interesting to evaluate the impact of more people adopting new HCI applications to prevent a future pandemic.

5.2 Conclusions

Since the start of the covid 19, countries worldwide have administered a variety of travel-related controls to contain or slow down the spread of the virus both domestically and internationally. To optimally contain a pandemic, the strictness of travel restrictions should take the population density of the area and the transmission rate in the community into account. The enforced travel restrictions not only impacted the spread of the pandemic but also transformed people's travel patterns into a new form. To avoid the risk of COVID-19, people are not only traveling less but also replacing public transport with personal cars and bikes. As a result, transport policymakers are recommended to cater to these new trends. One example could be allocating more spaces to bike lanes. Besides, social responsibility should be emphasized in public transport policy design. Lastly, the pandemic has motivated people to adopt new HCI technologies, and some previously HCI technologies are being challenged because of pandemic mitigation policies.

References

1. Salvendy, G.: Handbook of Human Factors and Ergonomics, 4th edn. Wiley, Hoboken (2012)
2. Schwanitz, S., Wittkowski, M., Rolny, V., Basner, M.: Pressure variations on a train - Where is the threshold to railway passenger discomfort? Appl. Ergon. **44**(2), 200–209 (2013). https://doi.org/10.1016/j.apergo.2012.07.003
3. Nakamura, H., Managi, S.: Airport risk of importation and exportation of the COVID-19 pandemic. Transp. Policy **96**, 40 (Sep. 2020). https://doi.org/10.1016/j.tranpol.2020.06.018
4. Tirachini, A., Cats, O.: COVID-19 and public transportation: current assessment, prospects, and research needs. J. Public Transp. **22**(1), 1–34 (2020). https://doi.org/10.5038/2375-0901.22.1.1
5. Ortego, J., Andara, R., Navas, L.M., Vásquez, C.L., Ramírez-Pisco, R.: Impact of the Covid-19 pandemic on traffic congestion in Latin American cities: an updated five-month study. In: Smart Cities, pp. 216–229 (2021)
6. Kutela, B., Novat, N., Langa, N.: Exploring geographical distribution of transportation research themes related to COVID-19 using text network approach. Sustain. Cities Soc. **67**(September 2020), 102729 (2021). https://doi.org/10.1016/j.scs.2021.102729

7. Guo, F., Li, F., Lv, W., Liu, L., Duffy, V.G.: Bibliometric analysis of affective computing researches during 1999–2018. Int. J. Hum. Comput. Interact. **36**(9), 801–814 (2020). https://doi.org/10.1080/10447318.2019.1688985

8. Duffy, G.A., Duffy, V.G.: Systematic literature review on the effect of human error in environmental pollution. In: Duffy, V.G. (ed.) HCII 2020. LNCS, vol. 12199, pp. 228–241. Springer, Cham (2020). https://doi.org/10.1007/978-3-030-49907-5_16

9. Hobbs, J.E.: Food supply chains during the COVID-19 pandemic. Can. J. Agric. Econ. Can. D Agroecon. **68**(2), 171–176 (Jun. 2020). https://doi.org/10.1111/cjag.12237

10. Jia, J.S., Lu, X., Yuan, Y., Xu, G., Jia, J., Christakis, N.A.: Population flow drives spatio-temporal distribution of COVID-19 in China. Nature **582**(7812), 389+ (2020). https://doi.org/10.1038/s41586-020-2284-y

11. Chinazzi, M., et al.: The effect of travel restrictions on the spread of the 2019 novel coronavirus (COVID-19) outbreak. Science (80-.) **368**(6489), 395–400 (2020). https://doi.org/10.1126/science.aba9757.

12. Kraemer, M.U.G., et al.: The effect of human mobility and control measures on the COVID-19 epidemic in China. Science (80-.) **368**(6490), 493–497 (2020). https://doi.org/10.1126/science.abb4218

13. Le Quéré, C., et al.: Temporary reduction in daily global CO2 emissions during the COVID-19 forced confinement. Nat. Clim. Chang. **10**(7), 647–653 (2020). https://doi.org/10.1038/s41558-020-0797-x

14. Sun, X., Wandelt, S., Zhang, A.: How did COVID-19 impact air transportation? A first peek through the lens of complex networks. J. Air Transp. Manag. **89**, 101928 (2020). https://doi.org/10.1016/j.jairtraman.2020.101928

15. Oum, T.H., Wang, K.: Socially optimal lockdown and travel restrictions for fighting communicable virus including COVID-19. Transp. Policy **96**, 94 (2020). https://doi.org/10.1016/j.tranpol.2020.07.003

16. De Vos, J.: The effect of COVID-19 and subsequent social distancing on travel behavior. Transp. Res. Interdiscip. Perspect. **5**, 100121 (2020). https://doi.org/10.1016/j.trip.2020.100121

17. Teixeira, J.F., Lopes, M.: The link between bike sharing and subway use during the COVID-19 pandemic: the case-study of New York's Citi Bike. Transp. Res. Interdiscip. Perspect. **6**, 100166 (2020). https://doi.org/10.1016/j.trip.2020.100166

18. Dantas, G., et al.: The impact of COVID-19 partial lockdown on the air quality of the city of Rio de Janeiro, Brazil. Sci. Total Environ. **729**, 139085 (2020). https://doi.org/10.1016/j.scitotenv.2020.139085

19. Le, T., et al.: Unexpected air pollution with marked emission reductions during the COVID-19 outbreak in China. Science (80-.) **369**(6504), 702–706 (2020). https://doi.org/10.1126/science.abb7431

20. Budd, L., Ison, S.: Responsible Transport: a post-COVID agenda for transport policy and practice. Transp. Res. Interdiscip. Perspect. **6**, 100151 (2020). https://doi.org/10.1016/j.trip.2020.100151

21. Wu, J.T., Leung, K., Leung, G.M.: Nowcasting and forecasting the potential domestic and international spread of the 2019-nCoV outbreak originating in Wuhan, China: a modelling study. Lancet **395**(10225), 689–697 (2020). https://doi.org/10.1016/S0140-6736(20)30260-9

22. Ramanathan, K., et al.: Clinical features of patients infected with 2019 novel coronavirus in Wuhan, China. Lancet **395**(January), 497–506 (2020)

23. Yamani, Y., Long, S.K., Itoh, M.: Human-automation trust to technologies for naive users amidst and following the COVID-19 pandemic. Hum. Factors **62**(7), 1087–1094 (Nov. 2020). https://doi.org/10.1177/0018720820948981

24. Liu, T., et al.: The role of the Hercules autonomous vehicle during the COVID-19 pandemic use cases for an autonomous logistic vehicle for contactless goods transportation. IEEE Robot. Autom. Mag. **28**(1), 48–58 (2021). https://doi.org/10.1109/MRA.2020.3045040

25. Stephanidis, C., et al.: Seven HCI grand challenges. Int. J. Hum. Comput. Interact. **35**(14), 1229–1269 (2019). https://doi.org/10.1080/10447318.2019.1619259

26. Choi, J.K., Ji, Y.G.: Investigating the importance of trust on adopting an autonomous vehicle. Int. J. Hum. Comput. Interact. **31**(10), 692–702 (2015). https://doi.org/10.1080/10447318.2015.1070549

27. Chakraborty, B.K., Sarma, D., Bhuyan, M.K., MacDorman, K.F.: Review of constraints on vision-based gesture recognition for human-computer interaction. IET Comput. Vis. **12**(1), 3–15 (2018). https://doi.org/10.1049/iet-cvi.2017.0052

28. Zhang, W., Smith, M.L., Smith, L.N., Farooq, A.: Gender and gaze gesture recognition for human-computer interaction. Comput. Vis. Image Underst. **149**, 32–50 (2016). https://doi.org/10.1016/j.cviu.2016.03.014

29. NSF Award Search: Award # 1901966 - TRAVEL: Travel to Workshop on Behavioral Risk Modeling for Pandemic Prevention and Response. https://nsf.gov/awardsearch/showAward?AWD_ID=1901966&HistoricalAwards=false. Accessed 29 Apr 2021

Improving Patient Service Quality in Physical Therapy: A Perspective of Lean

Yu-Hsiu Hung[(✉)], Mei-En Chen, and Jia-Bao Liang

Department of Industrial Design, National Cheng Kung University, Tainan, Taiwan

Abstract. The constant growth in the number of patients needing physical therapy has affected service quality and treatment effectiveness. The aim of this study was to address patient demands and service provider limitations through the perspective of lean and explore the possibility of improving the quality of physical therapy service. This study was divided into two stages. First, orthopedics referral patients in the physical therapy department were selected to conduct a customer satisfaction survey (n = 112), and service quality gaps were identified with quantitative and qualitative questions in the survey. The second stage was to develop a semi-structured interview outline based on the aforementioned results, and then to interview seven service providers in the physical therapy department about the limitations and challenges of improving the quality of service. The results showed that, quantitatively, patients' overall satisfaction was high, but, qualitatively, there were five critical service-quality demands to be improved. Five strategies were proposed for improving service quality based on the service provider's suggestions and the lean perspectives: 1) Set wayfinding lines from the department of orthopedics to the physical therapy center; 2) Reduce unnecessary motion in the environment and implement 5S; 3) Install a standing chair for patients with fractured foot; 4) Visualize the patient treatment information of the appointment system; 5) Visualize the appointment and attendance status for further improvements in reducing manpower idleness. This study proved that the lean perspective can improve the quality of physical therapy from the patients' point of view, and at the same time take into account service provider limitations.

Keywords: Physical therapy · Lean · Service quality · Patient-centered care

1 Introduction

The constant growth of the aging population in industrialized countries is causing the increasing prevalence of musculoskeletal conditions [1], and the demand for physical therapy has also increased [2]. Many physical therapists (PTs) were under great pressure due to the high volume of customers and staff shortages [3], which result in patients' longer waiting times [4, 5]. The quality and the effectiveness of treatments were affected due to a delay in treatment, which prolongs individual discomfort, resulting in deterioration of the person's condition [6].

To address these issues, more and more research has been devoted to improve the quality of physical therapy. Weitzman [7] suggests that healthcare quality can be defined

© Springer Nature Switzerland AG 2021
C. Stephanidis et al. (Eds.): HCII 2021, LNCS 13097, pp. 26–40, 2021.
https://doi.org/10.1007/978-3-030-90966-6_3

in relation to (1) the technical aspects of care, (2) the interpersonal relationship between the practitioner and the patient, and (3) the amenities of care. Service quality of physical therapy can be defined either from the viewpoint of service providers or from that of patients [8–12].

Although the patients' viewpoint complements other sources of information for the assessment of the service quality of physical therapy (e.g., knowing patients' difficulty or problem with carrying out exercises at home) [13], patients' voices were relatively underrated in existing quality improvement studies. Yet under the advancement of "patient-centered care", patients' demands are gradually valued. For example, two multidisciplinary Delphi panels were instituted including patients to develop healthcare quality indicators for the physical therapy management of patients with hip or knee osteoarthritis or rheumatoid arthritis [14]. There has been limited research on improving the quality of physical therapy services in clinical practice [6], especially at the patient perspective level. A sole emphasis on patient perspectives may neglect economic considerations, organizational issues, and cultural factors while trying to improve the quality of services, which can lead to clinical feasibility and sustainability challenges [15]. Therefore, "patient-centered care" must consider both the operational limitations of service providers and patient perspectives to improve service quality.

The underlying goal of lean is to improve value for patients through continuous improvement of the service delivery process, and doing so can also benefit other healthcare stakeholders [16, 17]. This makes the lean perspective recognizant of both the patient's perspective and the constraints of the service provider. Applying the lean perspective to medical treatment can effectively improve the speed of patient service delivery, reduce operating costs and improve quality [18], which effectively balances the needs of service providers and the satisfaction of patients [19]. The lean perspective has also been proven to be one of the methods that can improve the quality of physical therapy [9, 20]. However, this concept strongly emphasizes internal flow efficiency, while most of its implementations focus only on time-oriented aspects without delving into other aspects which customers value [19]. For example, Belter, Halsey [21] used lean methods to improve the process of orthopedic chemotherapy and increased patient satisfaction by reducing waiting time. McDermott, Kidd [22] improved diabetes day center bottlenecks at nursing stations by implementing standard referrals for screening, and setting standard clinic start times, and their findings indicated that the total patient journey time and waiting time for a treatment are reduced.

To sum up, there is limited research on improving physical therapy quality from the patient's perspective due to the lack of comprehensive consideration between the patient's demand and service provider limitations. In addition, most research on lean healthcare implementation underrated possible patient demand while focusing only on time-oriented aspects when improving the service process. Therefore, the purpose of this study is to address multiple demands of the patients and the service provider limitations through the lean perspective and explore the possibility of improving the quality of physical therapy service design. From the practical point of view, the value of this study can provide hospitals with a physical therapy quality improvement method that balances the patient's and the operational perspective. It also allows service designers to understand the limitations and difficulties of physical therapy operations when planning physical therapy services. From an academic perspective, this study can provide new insight into lean healthcare with a more diverse perspective, and provide possible solutions by adding the patient's perspective to the discussion on the improvement of physical therapy quality.

2 Literature Review

2.1 Lean Thinking

Lean Thinking is a systematic scientific management model derived from the Toyota Production System (TPS). Womack, Jones [23] defined lean thinking as continuously transforming waste into value from the customer's perspective, improving the efficiency and flow of production lines, and creating maximum benefits with the least resources through continuous improvement. Value stream mapping (VSM) is defined as a lean tool that draws the flow of customer needs and various operations required by the process, which systematically identifies waste (transportation, inventory, motion, waiting, overproduction, overprocessing, defects) and distinguishes between value-added and non-value-added operations [24]. Womack, Jones [23] suggested five improvement steps including: (1) defining value. Value is what the customer is willing to pay for. Value should be defined so as to meet the customer's needs. (2) mapping the value stream. This entails mapping the entire workflow or steps with a value stream map to identify and categorize waste in the current state. (3) creating flow. Wastes (ex. waiting, inventory...) should be removed from the value stream so that value can flow smoothly to customers without interruptions or delays. (4) using a pull system. This system lets the downstream customer pull upstream products as needed. (5) pursuing perfection. This pursuit involves a continuous process of improvement until complete elimination of waste so that all activities create value for the customer.

Lin, Gavney [25] found that the patient often complained about the waiting time in the tertiary otolaryngology clinic from comments and the previous patient satisfaction surveys. Lean Sigma principles were used to improve patient flows. The goals of the project were to streamline clinic processes and eliminate bottlenecks to reduce overall lead time from arrival to exam start, improve on-time exam starts, and decrease excess patient/staff motion. The customers in the otolaryngology clinic were identified as both external (patient) and internal (staff and providers). The distance and time of the patient's movement were visualized by VSM. The results showed the lead time from patient arrival to patient interaction with provider improved from a mean of 41 min per patient to 36 min per patient postintervention, and patient motion during a clinic encounter was a 34% reduction. McDermott, Kidd [22] conducted lean improvement studies at a diabetes day center. A literature review was performed to determine patient preferences and factors influencing satisfaction (i.e. value-adding indicators) concerning outpatient clinic visits. A key objective of the redesign was focused on improving the flow of patients through the clinic to reduce the overall patient journey time. Kaizen' workshop aimed to gather baseline data on patient flow through the clinic and information about each step in the process. The technique of VSM mapped patient flows and required that the team consider the 'ideal state', and decided that the 'ideal state' would be comprised of 10 features.

After improving bottlenecks at nursing stations, implementing standard referrals for screening, and setting standard clinic start times, research findings indicated that the total patient journey time and waiting time for a treatment were reduced.

2.2 Empirical Perspective Physical Therapy Quality

The empirical perspective is to take the best clinical physical therapy treatment as its goal, by adopting the quality indicators from the perspective of practitioners and focusing on creating good rehabilitation treatment results. For example, Leland, Lepore [8] summarized the seven quality themes needed for quality rehabilitation after fractures: objectives of care; first 72 h; positioning, pain, and precautions; use of standardized assessments; episode of care practices; facilitating insight into progress; and interdisciplinary collaboration. The goal is to maximize independence and equip the patient (and caregivers) with knowledge and skills to get home and stay home—safely. In addition, standardized treatments such as clinical treatment guidelines and adherence rates are also one of the aspects of treatment quality. For example, Riemen and Hutchison [26] pointed out that evidenced pathways for managing different surgical interventions following hip fracture are lacking. Studies found the adherence to guidelines was about 30%–48% when treating low back pain patients and vary among PTs [27, 28]. In conclusion, it can be found that the quality of physical therapy from the empirical perspective is mostly concerned with the evaluation of clinical treatment effectiveness (ex. range of motion…), provided treatment (ex. exercises, manual therapy, hydrotherapy…), standardization of treatment (ex. treatment frequency, adherence rate), and professional competence of PT (ex. communication skills, empathy…).

2.3 Patient Demand Physical Therapy Quality

Franchignoni, Ottonello [29] claimed that patient satisfaction can be considered as a patient countermeasure alternative for physical therapy quality, which is also an important indicator of the care quality in the medical sector [30]. Hills and Kitchen [31] suggested that patient demand in physical therapy is diverse, and as a result, researches have developed quality measures of physical therapy from patient demands systematically. Peersman, Rooms [32] identified high-quality physical therapy practices from the perspective of the patient including: the professional level of the PT, effective treatment, the adjustment of the treatment according to the rehabilitation outcome, the advice to avoid further health problems, the attention to patients and hygiene and privacy throughout the process. Hush, Cameron [33] found that the most consistent determinant of patient satisfaction was PT's competence (such as skills, communications…), and the second determinant was the process of care (such as adequate duration and frequency of treatment, continuity of care…) in a musculoskeletal physical therapy patient satisfaction systematic review. In addition, the type of treatment may affect satisfaction as well. For example, a study found that patients with back pain are more satisfied with exercise based physical therapy than passive therapy [34].

To summarize, most of the patient demand perspectives focus on patients' subjective experiences including: treatment, outcome, environment, accessibility, PT's professional competence, interaction with the PT, treatment time and waiting time. It is difficult to cover clinical assessments or operational constraints from the empirical perspective. Richter and Muhlestein [35] suggested that patient's perspective is greatly related to the interaction with the PT. Some empirical perspective studies mentioned the communication skills of the PT, which emphasize the information provided more than the attitude. Moreover, treatment time is not considered an important indicator from the empirical perspective, which might actually threaten the quality perceived by the patient.

3 Methods

This study was divided into two stages to explore customer perspectives and service provider constraints and suggestions to develop lean perspective solutions. In the first stage, we used a questionnaire distributed among a physical therapy center's patient. The questionnaire analysis uses the opportunity algorithm [36] to quantify the satisfaction and importance scores of each patient demand, and we also collected patient dissatisfaction from qualitative feedback. The second stage was to formulate an interview outline using the service quality gaps found in the previous stage and ask related service providers in a semi-structured interview to summarize the operational restrictions and improvement suggestions in the service process. Subsequently solutions were provided for the redesign to improve the quality of physical therapy service from the lean perspective.

3.1 Participants

The research site was a physical therapy center inside a medical center in southern Taiwan, which has 5 full-time PTs, 9 part-time PTs, 1 administrator, and 1 director. The treatment period was Monday to Friday from 9:00 to 17:00, with a one-hour break. Over 90% of the patients were by appointment. The total number of visits during the year was 14,531. Patients must be referred by orthopedic, neurologist, pediatric or orthopedic surgeons, of which about 87% were patients with musculoskeletal diseases referred by orthopedics. The PT determined the patient's treatment plan and created a treatment program based on the diagnosis and evaluation from the patient's referral physician. This study calculated the estimated number of people to be drawn based on the formula proposed by Dillman, Smyth [37], and targeted 124 orthopedic outpatients to distribute the questionnaire. Interviewees in the service provider's semi-structured interview were recruited by purposive sampling. The interviewees included 5 full-time PTs, 1 administrator, and 1 director, in a total of 7 participants. All participants had worked in the physical therapy center for more than one year.

3.2 Questionnaire

The objective of the study was to investigate the service quality gap which patients consider as important but unsatisfactory. The interview outline for the semi-structured interview of the service providers was developed from the results of the questionnaire. This questionnaire was completed in four sections as explained below:

Basic Information. The options for personal data are: age, gender, number of sessions, education level and patient diagnosis: (A) fracture; (B) arthritis; (C) soft tissue injury; (D) neck, spinal and chest disease; (E) others (self-filled by patient).

Physical Therapy Services Quality Demand. The question developed from the literature on related physical therapy patients quality assessment [11, 30, 38–40]. After several discussions with the center director, a total of 18 objects were obtained, and two questions were added for evaluating overall satisfaction (see Table 1). Patients assigned a score for each of the 18 objects on a satisfaction and importance scale. To avoid insufficient variation, a 7-point Likert scale (1: unsatisfactory or unimportant; 7: satisfactory or important). In addition to the average scores of satisfaction and importance for each quality demand, data analysis was performed using the opportunity algorithm of Ulwick [36]. A larger opportunity(OPP) score indicates that the demand is not met (i.e., a object with high importance but low satisfaction), and improvement should start from the highest OPP score, while a score of 10 or more indicates that the demand has a solid opportunity.

Overall Service Satisfaction. The overall satisfaction assessment questionnaire also used a 7-point Likert scale, but only with satisfaction scores. The purpose was to obtain an overall service quality evaluation of the patients so as to understand the impact of the physical therapy service quality demand on the overall service satisfaction.

Qualitative Feedback. In the end, the patient had a chance to write qualitative comments to further describe the service quality gap, and it was not limited to the above questions. The purpose was to allow patients to specify the cause of dissatisfaction or to supplement the gap in service quality not covered by the previous questions. This study mainly aimed to identify topics by inductive analysis, integrate similar concepts, and rank importance by number of mentions.

3.3 Semi-structured Interviews

The purpose of this semi-structured interview was to find out the service provider's operation restrictions and suggestions on the dissatisfied service quality. Therefore, an interview outline was drawn up based on the results of the questionnaire from the previous stage. Through qualitative interviews, we could understand the root causes of the gap in the quality of service delivery from front-line service providers, and find solutions. There were 7 service providers interviewed, which can be further subdivided into three types based on their duty: **Treatment executor**: the full-time PT provides insight on treating patients, and is also the most critical role in interpersonal interaction and patient satisfaction. **Administrative staff**: the administrator provides the execution of administrative operations, such as patient registration and appointments for treatment, and also receives patient complaints directly. **Operation manager: the** director provides the insight regarding management consideration and organizational revenue. The director is also responsible for assignment tasks and decision making.

The interview process was audio recorded. Researchers transcribed the interview content into text, and conducted thematic analysis by coding to distinguish the service

Table 1. Physical therapy quality demand questionnaire

No	Physical therapy service quality questions
Q1.	Directions to the center are clear
Q2.	Waiting area is comfortable and with sufficient seats
Q3.	The treatment room and treatment equipment are clean and tidy
Q4.	Air conditioning is moderate, ambient light is bright
Q5.	Staff at the counter is kind and friendly
Q6.	PT is kind and friendly
Q7.	PT listens patiently to my condition
Q8.	PT carefully evaluates and details my condition
Q9.	PT respects my privacy
Q10.	PT is professional
Q11.	Treatment methods and goals are explained in detail
Q12.	When I bring up questions during the session, I can get appropriate answers and treatment immediately
Q13.	PT answer my questions in a way I can understand
Q14.	Condition is improved after treatment
Q15.	PT recommends rehabilitation exercises after returning home
Q16.	Sufficient treatment time
Q17.	Adequate time to wait for an appointment and schedule treatment
Q18.	Clear and detailed explanations by the administrator at the counter (reservation/approval procedures)
Q19.	Willing to recommend this clinic service to relatives and friends
Q20.	Overall perception of the services

provider's operating restrictions, dilemmas and suggestions related to the patients' complaints. In order to ensure reliability, the two researchers performed coding separately, reviewed each other's codes and discussed discrepancies until the two sides reached a consensus on the topic of coding and analysis.

4 Results

4.1 Questionnaire

A total of 150 questionnaires were distributed, and 112 valid questionnaires were used in the study and analyzed. The sample consisted of 56 males and 56 females, 50% each. The average age distribution of the subjects: about 54% were less than 50 years old, and about 56% were 50 or older. According to the department's orthopedic referral patients' diagnosis data, most diagnoses were fractures and rotator cuff injuries.

The results were consistent with the responses from the questionnaire, with 60 soft tissue injuries (41%); neck, spinal and chest disease 36 times (25%); fracture 35 times (24%); arthritis 5 times; others 9 times (6%). Nearly half (48%) of the patients were treated for their first course of treatment (less than 6 sessions in a month). More than half (51%) of the patients' education level is college education. The results of the questionnaire showed that patient satisfaction was high on each question, with an average of 6.5 points (SD = 0.4), which is consistent with previous studies of patient satisfaction with physical therapy [33, 41] (see Table 2). The comments that patient wrote indicated that Q1, Q2, Q14, Q16, Q17 were the most dissatisfied service quality to them.

4.2 Semi-structured Interviews

The semi-structured interview asked the interviewees to identify operational restrictions and suggested solutions based on the five patient demand objects in the previous stage, and then summarize the countermeasures to improve service quality based on the lean perspective. (see Table 3). The following describes the respondents' suggestions and possible strategies based on the lean perspective.

Q1. Directions to the Center Are Clear. According to the patient feedback, the navigation guidelines are problematic because the center is located at B1. Most locations are already used by other units, making it difficult to adjust the spatial position. The administrator believed that the patients are mainly referred by orthopedics, and most of the orthopedic outpatient nurses should explain how to get there, but the inaccuracy in the communication process will also cause the patients to be unable to find the location. It is recommended to ask the hospital to set up a sign to the center. The director suggested that a paper map guide could be used to guide the referrals to the center. According to the lean perspective, it is necessary to reduce the time hospital staff spends on guiding the way and to decrease the probability of defects while avoiding the waste of repeated printing. Therefore, the strategy is to use a wayfinding line to allow the nurse to correctly guide the patient in a short time, and because more than 80% of the patients are referred by orthopedics, setting up a single guidance instruction from the orthopedics department can result in the most improvement.

Q2. Comfortable Waiting Area with Sufficient Seats. According to the qualitative results, patients would like to see more standing chairs added. Patients with fractured foot cannot sit on chairs of ordinary heights which make them difficult to stand up and sit down. The PT feels that most patients were suffering shoulder or upper limb injuries, and some patients with broken feet will come in a wheelchair, so this chair design is only needed by a small number of patients. The director suggested that the center can install the support chair that they can lean on. The administrator believed that the current limitation is that the waiting area is already occupied by the chairs. Setting up a support chair will lead to insufficient seats. Our study found that this type of chair can be placed next to each elevator in the building for people waiting for the elevator, and there is an elevator entrance at the main entrance of the center. Install a support chair there can be used for patients waiting for the elevator, or patients who need to wait for treatment.

Table 2. Physical therapy quality questionnaire results (n = 112)

Quality dimension	No	Importance score (SD)	Satisfaction score (SD)	Opp. score	Qualitative feedback
Environment	Q1	5.64 (1.55)	5.21 (1.55)	9.55	·Location is not easy to find (3)
	Q2	5.55 (1.27)	5.63 (1.18)	8.13	·Hard to sit for leg fractured patients
	Q3	6.46 (0.98)	6.32 (0.82)	9.82	
	Q4	6.25 (0.92)	6.35 (0.78)	9.20	
Interpersonal	Q5	6.29 (1.03)	6.52 (0.73)	8.84	
	Q6	6.63 (0.84)	6.75 (0.61)	9.55	
	Q7	6.71 (0.76)	6.71 (0.64)	9.73	
	Q8	6.68 (0.65)	6.45 (0.85)	10.09	
	Q9	6.50 (0.88)	6.56 (0.63)	9.55	
Technology	Q10	6.78 (0.55)	6.62 (0.63)	9.82	
	Q11	6.58 (0.72)	6.36 (0.88)	9.91	
	Q12	6.63 (0.71)	6.46 (0.99)	10.00	
	Q13	6.60 (0.70)	6.54 (0.70)	9.73	
	Q14	6.61 (0.73)	6.05 (1.09)	10.45	·Not fully recovered (2)
	Q15	6.71 (0.67)	6.66 (0.70)	9.82	
Time	Q16	6.43 (0.87)	6.07 (1.10)	10.09	·Wish to increase treatment time ·Time was affected by other late patients
	Q17	6.13 (1.08)	5.85 (1.33)	10.09	·Frequency insufficient (3) ·Waiting too long (3)
Administrative	Q18	6.35 (0.92)	6.39 (0.85)	9.73	
Overall	Q19	NA	6.09 (1.20)	NA	
	Q20	NA	6.19 (1.11)	NA	

Table 3. Semi-structured interviews results

No	Service provider suggestions	Strategies improving service quality
Q1	• Printed map for guidance • Improve the signs on the way to the center	• Set wayfinding lines from orthopedics to the center
Q2	• Install seats which patient can lean on to rest	• Install standing chairs beside the elevator outside the center
Q14	• Make an appointment based on the frequency information of patient treatment • Stagger the appointments based on the equipment information of patient treatment • Prediction of queue time and a notification mechanism when patient have to wait over two weeks	• Visualize the forecast waiting days through a information system • Notify PT when the administrator finds that the patient's appointment waiting time is more than two weeks • Visualize the patient treatment information of the appointment system
Q16	• Reduce interruptions during treatment • Reduce time waiting for the equipment • reduce walking and other waste in treatment	• Visualize the patient treatment information of the appointment system • Reduce unnecessary movements and implement 5S improvement
Q17	• Treat new cases according to case load quantity of the therapist • Improve "did not attend" productivity losses	• Visualize the appointment list • Visualize the status of attendance • Director response to the problem

Q14. Condition Improved After Treatment. The PT believed that the difficulty in implementing the treatment plan has caused the patient to have limited treatment effectiveness. There were two difficulties proposed by the PTs: First, "the patient has not been treated as frequently as expected." A PT said: *"There's a patient ten days apart from his first session when he came to his second session. The subsequent observation of a slow improvement may be due to this suspended treatment."* Another PT mentioned: *"Some patients I think once a week for them was enough, but they booked twice or even three times a week. While other patients that I think have to come regularly didn't get the appointment, and nobody had told me about it until I found out myself...".* The PT believed that the waiting time of some patients for more than two weeks is an abnormal situation, but the administrator did not notify her, so she recommended that the administrator should report the abnormality. Another PT suggested the need to know the patient's waiting time in advance or during treatment, so that he could communicate with the patient about home exercise. Therefore, the strategies were two stages: 1) visualize the number of waiting days beside the daily patient list for PT, so that the PT can plan treatment in advance (ex. Teach some exercises that patients can do at home); 2) The administrator can reconfirm with the therapist when appointment intervals exceed 14 days.

The second difficulty is that "some people need to use same equipment at the same time", which causes the planned treatment program to be canceled or replaced by another program. The PT mentioned in the interview: *"I promised to use Redcord for the treatment of a patient, but at some point, other patients were already using that area, so I had to give up…"*. The PT suggested that the equipment should be registered so that other PTs can be informed and make other arrangements, but PTs often does not know how long the patient will be using the equipment. The director recommended that when patients need to use the same device, the time booked should be staggered to reduce conflicts during the treatment afterward. Through the lean perspective, the strategy was the information (especially the equipment and frequency of treatment) used by PT should be logged and visualized. The administrator can make appointments for patients based on treatment plan information. This system improvement can solve the problems in follow-up treatment during the diagnosis.

Q16. Sufficient Treatment Time. In terms of increasing the treatment time, the director is facing the challenge of the center's profit and performance, of which the pressure comes from the hospital. He mentioned in the interview: *"Our department's monthly revenue is not comparable to the two operations in the surgical department. The number of treatments will be used as an indicator… The patient's single treatment income is about NT $ 288–$ 432. We must set a monthly performance for the PTs to ensure that the department will not be closed by the hospital."* The center lost an average of NT $ 80,000 per month in the previous year. The supervisor suggested that the restriction of treatment time remains unchanged, and the time that the therapist actually spends on treating patients should be increased. The scheduled treatment project should also be completed as soon as possible.

PTs believed that "waiting caused by equipment" and "treatment interrupted by administrator" often consumed their treatment time. When the equipment was used by others, PT would wait for it if it takes less then 10 min, one PT mentioned: *"There's a time the electrotherapy was occupied and we needed to wait 6 or 7 min. Me and my patient, we wait for it."* "Treatment was interrupted by administrator" is when the patient complains about the frequency of waiting for an appointment, the administrator will come in and ask if the PT can assist with the appointment. The reason is that the PT is better able to know the status of the appointment, which causes administrators who do not have treatment information to tend to go in and ask if there is a time slot for the patient. Therefore, the strategy is to allow the administrator to have sufficient treatment plan information for the appointment and reduce the time that the PT spends on dealing with the appointments or waiting for equipment. The goal is to share and present the information on equipment conflicts and treatment projects between PTs and administrator through the visualization of an information system.

In addition, some PTs suggested that the process of bending over and walking around when taking sports equipment should be improved. The strategy based on the lean perspective is to reduce the waste of walking or movement through the 5S of lean (sort, set in order, shine, standardize, sustain.) and space configuration, thereby reducing the non-value-added work of the PT during treatment.

Q17. Adequate Time to Wait for an Appointment and Schedule Treatment.
The PT believed that the difficulty lies in the fact that the caseload was too heavy.

This result is consistent with previous studies which pointed out that the PT felt that there were too many cases and insufficient manpower [3]. Because the way the center accepting new cases was fixedly receiving four new cases per week per PT regardless of the discharge rate. When the discharged rate is too low, new patients kept increasing at the same rate. The director suggested that new cases need to be queued in a waitlist if the old case cannot be closed, so as to avoid patients who cannot receive continuous treatment during the course of treatment. The director also suggested visualizing the PT's overload through the information system. Some PTs believed that it is necessary to develop uniform discharge criteria to prevent new patients from waiting too long.

The director believed that another influencing factor comes from no-shows (about 9%). Patients can take multiple appointments to meet their expected frequency of treatment, and the no-show rate, in fact, caused the PTs to be idle and therefore it interrupts the flow of patient care and reduces clinic productivity [42]. The director mentioned in the interview that *"Our patients can be divided into two categories: one is critically ill patients. In order to recover as soon as possible, they are much more cooperative. The other group is the patients who have recovered 80% but can still be better. The latter has lower compliance with the appointment time, which might cause no-shows."* He suggested that the administrator assists in formulating reservation rules through the analysis of the attendance rate of different patient types. However, the absence of existing data hinders the possibility of analysis. Therefore, the administrator suggested that the attendance of patients should be logged through an appropriate information system. The strategy of this study is to log the patient absence status into the system daily. The director can review the attendance status to reduce manpower idleness and hence decrease patient waiting time.

5 Conclusion

The purpose of this research was to find out the insufficiency of physical therapy service quality from the patient's perspective and take into consideration the cost and operational restrictions from the operator's perspective to improve the quality of physical therapy services through lean thinking. This study investigated patients through a physical therapy service quality questionnaire. Based on the two dimensions (importance and satisfaction), opportunity algorithm analysis [36] and qualitative feedback were used to identify service gaps. Physical therapy service providers were recruited to conduct semi-structured interviews to clarify operational challenges and find quality improvement measures for service gaps. Although the results showed patient satisfaction is high, there are still opportunities for improvement in the five service qualities. This study proposes five strategies to improve the quality of the physical therapy center: 1) Set wayfinding lines; 2) Install a standing chair; 3) Visualize the patient treatment information of the appointment system; 4) Improve the waste of movements and implement 5S; 5) Visualize the appointment and attendance status for further improvements in reducing manpower idleness. Hence, this study has confirmed that lean can propose solutions from the perspective of patients, while considering service provider difficulties and limitations so as to improve the satisfaction of physical therapy patients, and take into account feasibility and operational needs.

In addition, this study found that two of the qualitative responses from the patient questionnaire pointed out that the space in the treatment room was insufficient. This issue was not included in the 18 objects. It may be that the subject department has a special issue that needs to be improved. Therefore, it is suggested that future research can include patient opinions while determining the subjects of the service quality in the early stages of the questionnaire development so that the assessment questionnaire can better fit the patient perspective of each medical service department. The scope of this study was limited to the physical therapy center of a medical center, which is different from other regional hospitals and small clinics in terms of patient conditions, treatment projects, and treatment goals. The other limitation is that this study only addressed orthopedic patients in the physical therapy outpatient service. Future research may consider including inpatients or other medical conditions and diagnoses.

References

1. Woolf, A.D., Pfleger, B.: Burden of major musculoskeletal conditions. Bull. World Health Organ. **81**, 646–656 (2003)
2. Swinkels, I.C., et al.: An overview of 5 years of patient self-referral for physical therapy in the Netherlands. Phys. Ther. **94**(12), 1785–1795 (2014)
3. Lindsay, R., et al.: Workplace stressors experienced by physiotherapists working in regional public hospitals. Aust. J. Rural Health **16**(4), 194–200 (2008)
4. Deslauriers, S., et al.: Access to publicly funded outpatient physiotherapy services in Quebec: waiting lists and management strategies. Disabil. Rehabil. **39**(26), 2648–2656 (2017)
5. Laliberté, M., et al.: Operationalizing wait lists: Strategies and experiences in three hospital outpatient physiotherapy departments in Montreal. Physiother. Theory Pract. **34**(11), 872–881 (2018)
6. Boak, G., et al.: Quality improvement in physiotherapy services. Int. J. Health Care Qual. Assur. **30**(5), 424–435 (2017)
7. Weitzman, B.C., Kovner, A.R.: Health care delivery in the United States. 5th edn. Springer, Berlin (1995)
8. Leland, N.E., et al.: Delivering high quality hip fracture rehabilitation: the perspective of occupational and physical therapy practitioners. Disabil. Rehabil. **40**(6), 646–654 (2018)
9. Boak, G., et al.: Distributed leadership, team working and service improvement in healthcare. Leadership in Health Services (2015)
10. Rutten, G.M., et al.: Evaluation of the theory-based Quality Improvement in Physical Therapy (QUIP) programme: a one-group, pre-test post-test pilot study. BMC Health Serv. Res. **13**(1), 194 (2013)
11. Potter, M., Gordon, S., Hamer, P.: The physiotherapy experience in private practice: the patients' perspective. Aust. J. Physiother. **49**(3), 195–202 (2003)
12. Del Baño-Aledo, M.E., et al.: Relevant patient perceptions and experiences for evaluating quality of interaction with physiotherapists during outpatient rehabilitation: a qualitative study. Physiotherapy **100**(1), 73–79 (2014)
13. Medina-Mirapeix, F., et al.: Reliability and validity of patient reports for physical therapy quality assessment: an empirical analysis regarding the use of exercises for neck pain in Spain. J. Rehabil. Med. **38**(6), 354–359 (2006)
14. Peter, W., et al.: Healthcare quality indicators for physiotherapy management in hip and knee osteoarthritis and rheumatoid arthritis: a Delphi study. Musculoskelet. Care **14**(4), 219–232 (2016)

15. Mulgan, G.: Design in public and social innovation: what works and what could work better. Retrieved **23**(07), 2015 (2014)
16. Toussaint, J.S., Berry, L.L.: The promise of Lean in health care. In: Mayo Clinic Proceedings. Elsevier (2013)
17. Shimokawa, K., Fujimoto, T.: The Birth of Lean: Conversations with Taiichi Ohno. Eiji Toyoda, and Other Figures who Shaped Toyota Management, Lean Enterprise Institute, Cambridge (2009)
18. Harrison, M.I., et al.: Effects of organizational context on Lean implementation in five hospital systems. Health Care Manag. Rev. **41**(2), 127–144 (2016)
19. Carlborg, P., Kindström, D., Kowalkowski, C.: A lean approach for service productivity improvements: synergy or oxymoron? Manag. Serv. Qual.: Int. J. **23**(4), 291–304 (2013)
20. Doğan, N.Ö., Unutulmaz, O.: Lean production in healthcare: a simulation-based value stream mapping in the physical therapy and rehabilitation department of a public hospital. Total Qual. Manag. Bus. Excell. **27**(1–2), 64–80 (2014)
21. Belter, D., et al.: Evaluation of outpatient oncology services using lean methodology. In: Oncology Nursing Forum (2012)
22. McDermott, A.M., et al.: Restructuring of the Diabetes Day Centre: a pilot lean project in a tertiary referral centre in the West of Ireland. BMJ Qual. Saf. **22**(8), 681–688 (2013)
23. Womack, J.P., Jones, D.T., Roos, D.: The machine that changed the world: the story of lean production--Toyota's secret weapon in the global car wars that is now revolutionizing world industry. Simon and Schuster (2007)
24. Ohno, T., Toyota Production System: Beyond Large-Scale Production. CRC Press (1988)
25. Lin, S.Y., et al.: Use of lean sigma principles in a tertiary care otolaryngology clinic to improve efficiency. Laryngoscope **123**(11), 2643–2648 (2013)
26. Riemen, A.H., Hutchison, J.D.: The multidisciplinary management of hip fractures in older patients. Orthop. Trauma **30**(2), 117–122 (2016)
27. Bekkering, G., et al.: Effect on the process of care of an active strategy to implement clinical guidelines on physiotherapy for low back pain: a cluster randomised controlled trial. BMJ Qual. Saf. **14**(2), 107–112 (2005)
28. Swinkels, I.C., et al.: Physiotherapy management of low back pain: does practice match the Dutch guidelines? Aust. J. Physiother. **51**(1), 35–41 (2005)
29. Franchignoni, F., et al.: Satisfaction with hospital rehabilitation: is it related to life satisfaction, functional status, age or education? J. Rehabil. Med. **34**(3), 105–108 (2002)
30. Tennakoon, T., de Zoysa, P.: Patient satisfaction with physiotherapy services in an Asian country: a report from Sri Lanka. Hong Kong Physiother. J. **32**(2), 79–85 (2014)
31. Hills, R., Kitchen, S.: Toward a theory of patient satisfaction with physiotherapy: exploring the concept of satisfaction. Physiother. Theory Pract. **23**(5), 243–254 (2007)
32. Peersman, W., et al.: Patients' priorities regarding outpatient physiotherapy care: a qualitative and quantitative study. Man. Ther. **18**(2), 155–164 (2013)
33. Hush, J.M., Cameron, K., Mackey, M.: Patient satisfaction with musculoskeletal physical therapy care: a systematic review. Phys. Ther. **91**(1), 25–36 (2011)
34. Seferlis, T., et al.: Conservative treatment in patients sick-listed for acute low-back pain: a prospective randomised study with 12 months' follow-up. Eur. Spine J. **7**(6), 461–470 (1998)
35. Richter, J.P., Muhlestein, D.B.: Patient experience and hospital profitability: is there a link? Health Care Manag. Rev. **42**(3), 247–257 (2017)
36. Ulwick, A.W.: Jobs to Be Done: Theory to Practice. Idea Bite Press (2016)
37. Dillman, D.A., Smyth, J.D., Melani, L.: Internet, Mail, and Mixed-Mode Surveys: The Tailored Design Method. Wiley, Hoboken (2009)
38. Goldstein, M.S., Elliott, S.D., Guccione, A.A.: The development of an instrument to measure satisfaction with physical therapy. Phys. Ther. **80**(9), 853–863 (2000)

39. Beattie, P.F., et al.: Patient satisfaction with outpatient physical therapy: instrument validation. Phys. Ther. **82**(6), 557–565 (2002)

40. Medina-Mirapeix, F., et al.: Development and validity of the questionnaire of patients' experiences in postacute outpatient physical therapy settings. Phys. Ther. **95**(5), 767–777 (2015)

41. CSP. Physiotherapy Outpatient Services Survey 2012 (2013). https://innovations.csp.org.uk/innovation/oldham-first-contact-physiotherapy-service-evaluation-patient-experience. Accessed 20 Feb 2020

42. LaGanga, L.R.: Lean service operations: reflections and new directions for capacity expansion in outpatient clinics. J. Oper. Manag. **29**(5), 422–433 (2011)

Spatial-Temporal Distribution and Cross Impact of "Big Health" Policies, News and Patents

Yongxin Kong, Yuwen Wang, Guochao Peng[(✉)], and Bingqian Zhang

Sun Yat-Sen University, Panyu District, Guangzhou 510000, China
penggch@mail.sysu.edu.cn

Abstract. With the national strategy of "Healthy China 2030", China attempts to move from "disease-centered" care to "big health", aiming to promote people's health in an all-round way. National layout and local responses are key elements of realising the "big health" concept. This paper presents an exploration of the spatial-temporal distribution and cross-impact of policies, news reports and patents associated with "big health" at both national and local levels. A bibliometric analysis was carried out with data divided into three themes: disease prevention, disease cure, and health preservation. These data were retrieved from China National Knowledge Infrastructure (CNKI) and People's Database. The results show that local governments respond to national policies on "big health" rapidly and positively, and the local news reports on "big health" promptly following the central news. The change speed and range of patent output are different in the three themes of "big health". In the early and all-round development periods of "big health", national policies affect future trends and current changes of patents respectively, while local policies all affect patent output.

Keywords: "Big health" · Spatial-temporal distribution · "Big health" policies · "Big health" news · "Big health" patents · Cross impact

1 Introduction

The lives of people in China have changed significantly due to the rapid industrialization, urbanization and aging population, which result in many health problems. The prevalence of multiple chronic conditions in China is growing. People with low health literacy live an unhealthy lifestyle like smoking, excessive drinking, poor diet and lack of exercise. With more Chinese people pay increasing attention to health and fitness, the concepts of "healthy China" and "big health" are proposed.

The construction of a "Healthy China" is central to the Chinese government's agenda for national health and development, aiming to promote the health and well-being of citizens, with an emphasis on "big health" (Tan et al. 2019). To advance the construction of a "Healthy China", the Communist Party of China (CPC) Central Committee issued the "Healthy China 2030" blueprint in October 2016 (Tan et al. 2017), and promulgated an action plan in July 2019 for implementing the Healthy China initiative from 2019 to 2030 (Zhang and Gong 2019).

© Springer Nature Switzerland AG 2021
C. Stephanidis et al. (Eds.): HCII 2021, LNCS 13097, pp. 41–53, 2021.
https://doi.org/10.1007/978-3-030-90966-6_4

The disease-curing approach has been tested to its limits over recent decades, not helped by a lack of focus on disease prevention, which led to overcrowding in most sophisticated hospitals and poor access. Recognizing the importance of prevention in healthcare and health management, "big health" is put forward. "Big health" (Van Spijk 2015), an overall health concept, brings potential to address this issue, better equipping health services that cover the entire care continuum. "Big health" is divided into three themes: disease prevention, disease cure and health preservation.

The development of health over time has been investigated by numerous researchers, using health policies, news reports and patents. Health policies are the driving force for health construction and a critical factor in studying health construction status. For example, Macías-Chapula (2013) makes a comparative analysis of public health policies in different countries. Kiss, Fritz, Lakner, et al. (2020) investigate obesity policy through interdisciplinarity maps and mixed mapping of multicluster topics. Besides, news reports are the significant carrier of public opinions, and some scholars carry on research to the health news reports. Lewison (2007) studies genetically modified organisms by mass media in different countries. Kousha, Thelwall (2017) use news reports on medicine and health topics as a measure of evidence for academic research. What's more, health patents reflect technological innovation of health. Researchers study quantitative analysis of health patents (Xing et al. 2019), and the impact of open innovation in healthcare on patent activities (Orlando et al. 2020).

Several studies show that policies affect the output and quality of patents, and public opinion has an indirect effect on patents output. Scholars generally believe that policies play a positive role in patents output and fostering innovation (Gong and Peng 2018; Sharma et al. 2018; Vincenzi and Ozabaci 2017). A different research is proposed by Parra (2019). His result proves that overly protective policies lead to reduce innovation pace. Moreover, Du, Li, Guo, et al. (2019) argue the transformation of subsidy-science-technology-innovation under the influence of policies, Xia, Cao, Tan (2020) discuss that government support intensity has a moderating effect between basic research intensity and innovation performance. In terms of public opinion, the prevailing view is that the public is involved in policy making (Beierle 1998; Bijker 2003), and public opinions bring some influences in the process of making policy. McFadden (2016) considers that public perception that different from the scientific community affects scientific inquiry and innovation.

In spite of many bibliometrics analysis on health data, "big health" has not received sufficient attention. Furthermore, the few existing studies tend to explore the cross impact of policies and public opinions on patents. To fill this research gap, we represent the spatial-temporal distribution and cross-impact of "big health" policies, news reports and patents. The aim is to find the answer to the following questions: (1) What is the temporal and spatial distribution of policies, news reports and patents on "big health"? (2) How policies and news reports affect patents output in terms of "big health"?

2 Methodology

The datasets contain policies, news reports and patents data of "big health", published until the year 2020, retrieved from China National Knowledge Infrastructure (CNKI) and People's Database. The datasets of policies are retrieved by "full text = big health", and a total of 88 national policies and 957 local policies are obtained. The datasets of news and patent data are retrieved based on four topics, namely "big health", "disease prevention", "disease cure" and "health preservation". A total of 5,888 pieces of news data and 6,029 pieces of patent data are obtained.

This paper proposes the spatial-temporal distributions and cross- impact of "big health" policies, news reports and patents. Firstly, "big health" policies, news reports and patents are retrieved by three themes for analysis of different theme. The spatial-temporal distributions of "big health" policies, news reports and patents are identified among the selected data. Secondly, the cross impact of "big health" policies and news reports on patents is analyzed by three "big health" themes at a national and local level. The analysis framework is shown in Fig. 1.

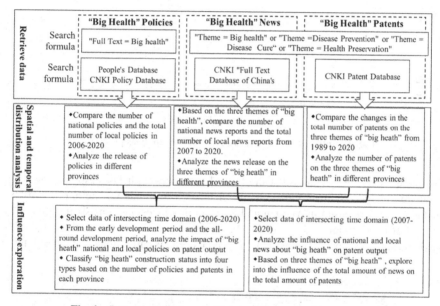

Fig. 1. Summary of data collection and data analysis processes.

3   Results and Findings

3.1   The Spatial-Temporal Distribution of "Big Health" Policies

The trend for the number of national policies on "big health" is in the shape of an inverted "V", while that of local policies is in the shape of "M" (Fig. 2). The rapid growths of national and local policies on "big health" start in the same period (i.e. 2014), which indicates that local governments respond to national policies quickly and implement various tasks effectively. The number of national policies on "big health" maintain stable after the rapid growth, while that of local policies released is continuously increasing. This shows that the macro objectives of "big health" require local governments to long-term deployment, and local governments actively respond to national policies and implement them according to local conditions. After the full deployment of the "big health" policies, the numbers of both national and local policies released are in a fluctuation period. The fluctuation period of local policies (2018–2020) is lagging behind that of national policies (2017–2019). The fluctuation period of local policies on "big health" is one year later than that of national policies, and the trend for the number of local policies on "big health" is consistent with that of national policies.

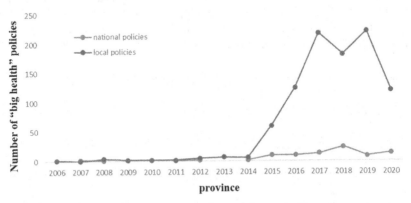

Fig. 2. Summary of data collection and data analysis processes.

Figure 3 and Fig. 4 show that the typical provinces with fast response and large fluctuation include Yunnan, Guizhou and Sichuan. The trends for the number of "big health" policies released in Yunnan and Sichuan provinces are consistent with that of the total of local policies, showing an "M" shape. The number of policies released in Guizhou is in the shape of an inverted "V", and its peak is earlier than that of the total of

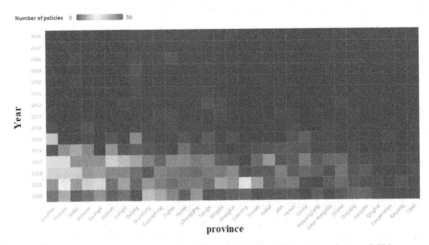

Fig. 3. Number of "big health" policies released in different provinces of China.

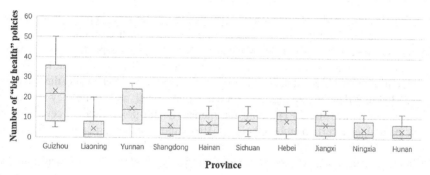

Fig. 4. Top 10 regions with maximum fluctuation of "big health" policies. (Note: The difference between the maximum and minimum number of policies in one province is called the policy fluctuation. Except for Guizhou and Yunnan with a larger median value, there is little difference in median values among other provinces.)

local policies. Therefore, Guizhou responded to national government at the fastest speed, while the response speed of Yunnan and Sichuan are consistent with that of overall local government and keeping up with the national average.

3.2 The Spatial-Temporal Distribution of "Big Health" News Reports

The trend for the total amount of central news reports on "big health" shows the shape of "M", which of local news reports shows an inverted "V" shape (Fig. 5). These results signify that both central news and local news reached their peaks in 2016, and the number of central news reports was higher in the later period, but that of local news reports was

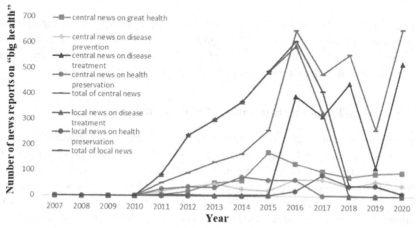

Fig. 5. Numbers of central news reports and local news reports on "big health" in subdivided theme and in total from 2007 to 2020. (Note: The red polyline represents the trend for the number of central news reports on each theme with time. The blue polyline represents the trend for the number of local news reports on each theme with time. The polylines of the same icon represent the same theme for facilitating comparative analysis.) (Color figure online)

lower. It indicates that local news reports follow the central news reports promptly but later subdivide into multiple themes. Regarding the theme "disease cure", local news reports increased continuously from 2010 to 2016 but dropped sharply to 0, while central news reports suddenly increased to the first peak in 2016. This shows that local news reports continuously reflected public opinions on disease cure. After issuing the "Healthy China 2030" in 2016, "big health" acts on the national level, and central news reported relevant national measures. Regarding the theme "health preservation", central news reports maintained a certain amount before 2016, while local news increased after 2016. This shows that the national government strongly promotes health preservation in the early stage, and the local people recognize the importance of health preservation in the later stage.

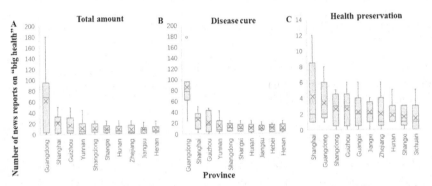

Fig. 6. Local news reports on various themes of "big heath" released by different provinces. (Note: These box charts show the top 10 regions in news reports on different themes: A. Total amount; B. On disease cure; C. On health preservation.)

We observe that the typical provinces with multi-topic reports and strong publicity efforts include Guangdong Province, Shanghai and Guizhou Province (Fig. 6). These three regions all release a larger number of news reports on disease cure and health preservation, and their numbers of news reports are among the highest in China.

3.3 The Spatial-Temporal Distribution of "Big Health" News Reports

The turning points of the number of patents on different themes of "big health" occurred around the similar time, and the trend of that was roughly the same but with different change speeds and ranges (Fig. 7). We find the following rules. (1)Turning point: The numbers of patents on disease cure and health preservation showed small spikes in 2010 and 2011 respectively, with similar peak values. The significant turning point for the number of patents on health preservation occurred in 2017; while those on disease prevention and disease cure occurred in 2019. (2) Change trend: The numbers of patents on three themes of "big health" all increase slowly, but the patents on disease cure and health preservation show a small spike. After that, they grow rapidly to remarkable peaks and then decline fast. (3) Change speed and range: Patents on disease cure have the highest growth rate and the largest increase, followed by those on health preservation and disease prevention.

The typical provinces with high numbers of patents on all three themes of "big health" include Guangdong Province, Jiangsu Province and Beijing (Fig. 8). Most significantly, the number of patents in Guangdong Province maintained and its peak value have an obvious quantitative advantage, while those in other provinces show large fluctuation and unvaried themes.

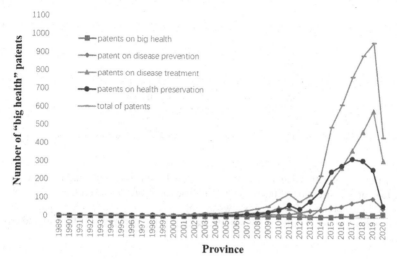

Fig. 7. Numbers of patents on various themes of "big health".

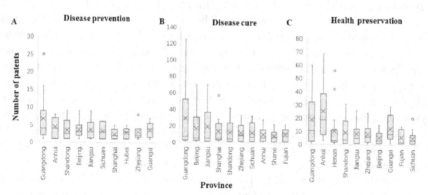

Fig. 8. Number of patents on three themes of "big health" in different provinces of China. (Note: To avoid the long tail effect, the numbers of patents from 2010 to 2020 were selected and visually analyzed, and box charts of top 10 regions in the number of patents on three themes are obtained: A: On disease prevention; B. On disease cure; C. On health preservation.)

3.4 The Effect of "Big Health" Policies on "Big Health" Patents

Since the first "big health" policy appeared in 2006, this paper selects policies and patents at the same time interval (2006–2020) for visual analysis.

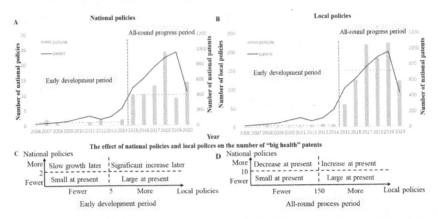

Fig. 9. The effect of national and local policies of "big health" on patent output. (Note: It shows that the temporal distribution of the number of policies and patents on "big health": A. National policies. B. Local policies. Besides, it shows the influence of national and local policies of "big health" on patent output in different periods. C. Early development period. D. All-round progress period.)

Figure 9 indicates that "big health" development process is divided into the early development period (2006–2014) and the all-round progress period (2015–2020). In the early development period, the national policies on "big health" mainly affected the future growth rate of "big health" patents, while the local policies primarily affected the current number of "big health" patents. In the all-round progress period, national policies positively influence the current change trend of the number of patents, while local policies still have positive effects on the current number of patents. These results signify that in the early development period, with a guiding role of national policies playing, scientific and technological innovation institutions began to explore into "big health" to increase patents output gradually. Local policies had more direct support for institutions, which positively affected their output of "big health" patents. In the all-round progress period, if "big health" is promoted by national policies comprehensively and vigorously, institutions will keep up with the national demands, respond quickly and improve the output of patents. The influence of local policies is similar to that in the early development period.

The number of policies reflects the government guidance and encouragement, while the number of patents presents the response of institutions and their innovation capability.

As shown in Fig. 10, the construction statuses of "big health" are classified into four types based on the number of "big health" policies and patents in each province.

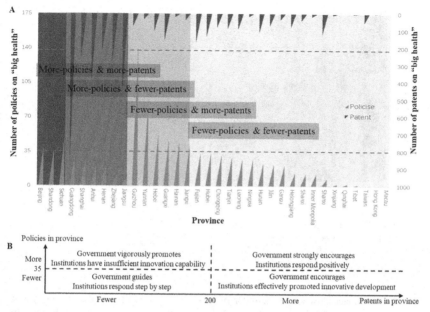

Fig. 10. Cross impact between the number of policies and patents on "big health" in different provinces of China. (Note: A. Number of local policies and local patents on "big health" in different provinces; B. Four types of construction status of "big health".)

(1) More-policies & fewer-patents type, such as Guizhou Province and Yunnan Province, indicates that the government vigorously pushes forward "big health" but the institutions are poor in innovation capability.

(2) More-policies & more-patents type, such as Beijing and Shandong Province, shows that the government strongly encourages to develop "big health" and the institutions positively answer the call.

(3) Fewer-policies & fewer-patents type, such as Hunan and Liaoning provinces, represents that the government guides the construction of "big health" and institutions address this issue step by step.

(4) Fewer-policies & more-patents type, such as Guangdong Province and Jiangsu Province, displays that innovative development is effectively accelerated by the governmental encouragement of "big health" and responses from local institutions.

3.5 The Effect of "Big Health" News Reports on "Big Health" Patents

The number of "big health" news reports denotes the importance attached by media and publicity efforts of media. In Fig. 11, the construction statuses of "big health" are grouped into four types based on the number of news reports and patents on "big health" in each province.

(1) More-news & fewer-patents type, such as Guizhou Province, indicates that the media attached great importance to "big health" but the institutions had insufficient innovation capability.

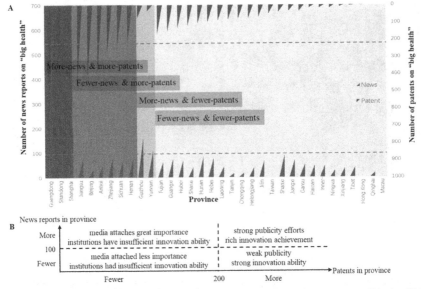

Fig. 11. Cross impact between the number of news reports and of patents on "big health" in different provinces of China. (Note: A. Number of local news and patents on "big health" in different provinces; B. Four types of "big health" construction status.)

(2) More-news & more-patents type, such as Guangdong Province and Shanghai, shows their strong publicity efforts and rich innovation achievement.

(3) Fewer-news & fewer-patents type, such as Gansu Province and Hainan Province, represents that the media neglects to report "big health" and the institutions drive innovation weakly.

(4) Less-news & more-patents type, such as Beijing, Jiangsu and Zhejiang provinces, means weak publicity but strong innovation capability.

However, there is no evidence to prove that the number of news reports on "big health" affects the number of "big health" patents (Fig. 12).

4   Discussion

As shown above, this paper provides some interesting insights into the field of "big health".

Firstly, the research results have confirmed the popular view that patent policies are the important factors to improve the growth of patent output. More importantly, this paper studies that patent output is influenced by the macro-guidance of national government and the actual support of local government. The results identified that local policies affect the number of patent output, and national policies affect the change speed and range of patents. Furthermore, this paper divides "big health" development process into the early development period and the all-round progress period. It is considered that the national policies affect the future development trend of patents in the early development

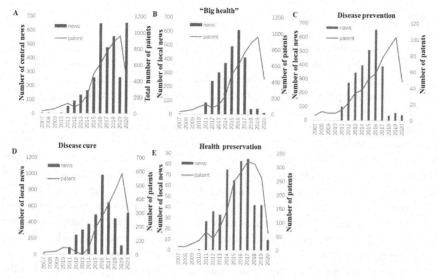

Fig. 12. Influence of central and local news reports about "big health" on patent output. (Note: A. Temporal distribution of the total number of central news reports and patents on "big health"; B. On "big health"; C. On disease prevention; D. On disease cure; E. Health preservation.)

period, and play a role in the current changes of patents in the all-round development period.

In terms of setting out policies to boost patent output of "big health", it is necessary to highlight the national planning for the future construction in the early development period and the implementation of national policies in a comprehensive way in the all-round progress periods. Besides, local policies must actively respond to national policies to improve patent output.

Secondly, it is important to note, however, that the results can't prove the influence between the number of news reports and the number of patents on "big health". As generally considered, public opinion directly or indirectly affects policy formulation, so the role of public opinion in the formulation of science and technology policies should be fully valued. The "big health" news reports that we have collected not only report the current "big health" policies and measures but also underline the issues that need to address. Those drive innovative development of "big health" and adjust research direction of "big health" patents. Therefore, "big health" news reports may indirectly affect the output of related patents. We will explore this further in our future work.

Several provinces with strong innovation capability neglect social media presence, according to the analysis of the number of "big health" news reports and patents in different provinces. Provinces with strong innovation capability need to strengthen the publicity of "big health" innovative products to increased public understanding and expand influence. Provinces with weak innovation capability need to report advanced innovative products and policy interpretation, which contributes to the institutions' motivation for "big health" innovation, public awareness of "big health" construction and output of "big health" patents.

5 Conclusion

We have demonstrated the spatial-temporal distribution of policies, news reports and patent data on "big health", and the cross impact of "big health" policies and news reports on patents. We conducted a bibliometric analysis based on datasets retrieved from CNKI and People's Database with three themes: disease prevention, disease cure and health preservation.

The major contribution of our study is identifying the trend of policies, news reports and patents on "big health". The results show that the trends of the numbers of national and local policies on "big health" are in the shape of inverted "V" and "M" respectively, indicating that local government responded to national policies quickly and positively. The trends of the numbers of national and local news reports on "big health" show the "M" and inverted "V" shape respectively, indicating that local news reports kept up with the central news promptly, with detailed views in the later period. The turning points of the number of patents on different themes of "big health" occurred at a similar time, and the change trend was roughly the same, with different change speeds and ranges.

The second major contribution of our study is presenting the typical provinces that play a crucial part in "big health" policies, news reports and patents. The provinces represented by Yunnan, Guizhou and Sichuan stand out in fast response and large fluctuation in quantity of policies. The provinces represented by Guangdong, Shanghai and Guizhou highlight multi-topic reports and strong publicity efforts on news reports. The provinces represented by Guangdong, Jiangsu and Beijing have a high number of patents.

The third major contribution of our study is revealing the impact of "big health" policies on patents through two periods. In the early development periods and all-round progress periods of the "big health", the national policies affect the future trend and current changes of patents respectively, while the local policies all affect the output of patents.

Although our study provides useful insights, it has some limitations. First, theme classification method used in this paper may neglect detailed content. In the future, we plan on experimenting with automatic keyword extraction to achieve high informativeness. Second, we can't confirm that "big health" news reports affect the output of "big health" patents. Future research may include refining the themes of policies, news and patents, analyzing their mechanism of action, revealing their operation rules.

Acknowledgements. This research was supported by the grant funded by the Key Cultivation Scheme for Young Teachers in the Sun Yat-sen University Higher Education Basic Research Program (No.: 20wkzd17).

References

Beierle, T.C.: Public Participation in Environmental Decisions: An Evaluation Framework Using Social Goals (No. 10497). Resources for the Future (1998)

Bijker, W.E.: The need for public intellectuals: a space for STS: Pre-Presidential Address, Annual Meeting 2001, Cambridge, MA. Sci. Technol. Hum. Values **28**(4), 443–450 (2003)

Du, J., Li, P., Guo, Q., Tang, X.: Measuring the knowledge translation and convergence in pharmaceutical innovation by funding-science-technology-innovation linkages analysis. J. Informet. **13**(1), 132–148 (2019)

Gong, H., Peng, S.: Effects of patent policy on innovation outputs and commercialization: evidence from universities in China. Scientometrics **117**(2), 687–703 (2018). https://doi.org/10.1007/s11 192-018-2893-5

Kiss, A., Fritz, P., Lakner, Z., Soós, S.: Linking the dimensions of policy-related research on obesity: a hybrid mapping with multicluster topics and interdisciplinarity maps. Scientometrics **122**(1), 159–213 (2019). https://doi.org/10.1007/s11192-019-03293-8

Kousha, K., Thelwall, M.: News stories as evidence for research? BBC citations from articles, Books, and Wikipedia. J. Am. Soc. Inf. Sci. **68**(8), 2017–2028 (2017)

Lewison, G.: The reporting of the risks from genetically modified organisms in the mass media, 2002–2004. Scientometrics **72**(3), 439–458 (2007)

Macías-Chapula, C.A.: Comparative analysis of health public policy research results among Mexico, Chile and Argentina. Scientometrics **95**(2), 615–628 (2013)

McFadden, B.R.: Examining the gap between science and public opinion about genetically modified food and global warming. PloS One **11**(11), e0166140 (2016)

Orlando, B., Ballestra, L.V., Magni, D., Ciampi, F.: Open innovation and patenting activity in health care. J. Intellect. Cap. (2020)

Parra, A.: Sequential innovation, patent policy, and the dynamics of the replacement effect. Rand J. Econ. **50**(3), 568–590 (2019)

Sharma, R., Paswan, A.K., Ambrammal, S.K., Dhanora, M.: Impact of patent policy changes on R&D expenditure by industries in India. J. World Intellect. Prop. **21**(1–2), 52–69 (2018)

Tan, X., Liu, X., Shao, H.: Healthy China 2030: a vision for health care. Value Health Reg. Issues **12**, 112–114 (2017)

Tan, X., Zhang, Y., Shao, H.: Healthy China 2030, a breakthrough for improving health. Glob. Health Promot. **26**(4), 96–99 (2019)

Spijk, P.: On human health. Med. Health Care Philos. **18**(2), 245–251 (2014). https://doi.org/10. 1007/s11019-014-9602-9

Vincenzi, M., Ozabaci, D.: The effect of public policies on inducing technological change in solar energy. Agric. Resour. Econ. Rev. **46**(1), 44–72 (2017)

Xia, Q., Cao, Q., Tan, M.: Basic research intensity and diversified performance: the moderating role of government support intensity. Scientometrics **125**(1), 577–605 (2020). https://doi.org/ 10.1007/s11192-020-03635-x

Xing, Z., et al.: Conversational interfaces for health: bibliometric analysis of grants, publications, and patents. J. Med. Internet Res. **21**(11), e14672 (2019)

Zhang, C., Gong, P.: Healthy China: from words to actions. Lancet Public Health **4**(9), e438–e439 (2019)

Sustainable Urban Planning and Its Connection to Environmental Health: A Literature Analysis

Michael Lambrosa[✉]

Purdue University, West Lafayette, IN 47907, USA
mlambros@purdue.edu

Abstract. The topic areas around sustainable urban planning and environmental health have grown in emphasis and research over the past few decades as part of the growing larger topic area of transportation and manufacturing in human-automation interactions. This increase has correlated with the increased attention to overall environmental health as a greater point of local and global work. With the growth and emergence of these subjects, it is pertinent to explore a possible link and connection between the two topics and their respective importance. In this study, a literature review and analysis were conducted using data from Google Scholar and Web of Science and analyzed using Vosviewer, MAXQDA, and Harzing Publish or Perish. Dual searches with the key terms "sustainable urban planning" and "environmental health" were conducted in Google scholar and web of science databases and analyzed for emergence and relevance using site trending analysis tools. Following these two topic area searches, Vosviewer, Harzing Publish or Perish, MAXQDA and Mendeley facilitated a co-citation analysis and content analysis to direct efforts to perform a larger literature review from scholarly articles over a broad range of publishing realms, home countries and authors. The results of the literature review presented results showing a possible connection between trends in both keyword topic areas and the need to analyze these emerging areas further due to their relatively new age. It is believed that future work can best push the fields of sustainable urban planning and benefit environmental health the most through definition of sustainable indicators and metrics, incorporating new technologies, and gathering and leveraging best practices. Human-computer interaction will play a pivotal role in promoting the emerging field of sustainable urban planning to a larger world audience by facilitating the creation and spread of the above future work areas.

Keywords: Sustainable urban planning · Environmental health · Vosviewer · Harzing Publish or Perish · MAXQDA · Mendeley

1 Introduction and Background

Beginning in the 1960s, environmental health began to take greater precedence and importance in public opinion and policy planning. The movement toward a healthier environment began in the western world in the areas of air, water, and ground pollution and has gradually spread into a global movement with greater emphasis and importance

© Springer Nature Switzerland AG 2021
C. Stephanidis et al. (Eds.): HCII 2021, LNCS 13097, pp. 54–67, 2021.
https://doi.org/10.1007/978-3-030-90966-6_5

in countries around the world (Goetsch, 641). The ownership of environmental health initially began with grassroots efforts to promote the overall wellbeing of the environment, a factor that is still of particular importance today. Legislatures such as the United State's Clean Air Act of 1970 and the creation of the Environmental Protection Agency (EPA) have denoted the transition from primarily independent and local environmental health champions to larger ownership of the environment on planning and governmental bodies. As the shifting responsibility of environmental health has been laid on more formal and authoritative organizations, industry and private development have been drawn into the fold of sharing the burden of promoting and upholding environmental health in a plethora of fields from air quality to hazardous waste (Goetsch, 642). Environmental health has now become such a focal point in the environmental management systems of organizations, environmental health professionals or tasks associated with these positions are often a part of these larger bodies (Brauer 31). With industry and private organizations teaming with governmental bodies, the groundwork for improving and promoting environmental health, and its greater effect on overall human health and safety, was laid.

As the overall condition of the environment and its connection to health and safety of humans in regards to air quality, water quality, ground pollution, and a host of other realms were being explored; it was found that it is not only imperative to restore the state of a deteriorated environment, but equally important to prevent the deterioration from occurring in the first place. This mindset is the concept behind environmental sustainability and has become a focal point of many large organizations' environmental management systems (Goetsch, 654). Environmental sustainability seeks to promote the sustainability of the environmental systems that will in turn facilitate overall societal health and safety (Goetsch, 654). Fundamental to environmental sustainability is the acknowledgment that human's effects on the environment are always changing and generally growing (Virgolino et al. 2020). Beginning in the 1970's the global community began to record and analyze the possible effects different manmade systems and processes would have on global environmental sustainability (Yazar et al. 2012). Among the topics discussed among agriculture, industry, and several others, urban development strikes particularly interesting importance.

As the world has moved into the 21st century, a majority of the human population now lives in cities with an ever-increasing urbanization rate (Hamid et al. 2018). Rationally, as the rate of urbanization has increased, so too has its effect on their area's respective environmental health in regions of air quality, soil pollution, water contamination, and climate among others. As urban environments are affected by the rising rate of urban development, so too are the health and safety of their residents. Adverse effects of urbanization in the forms of rapid air pollution, poor water sanitation, and contaminated ground soil can have extremely dangerous effects on the residents of urban environments. If done too quickly and without proper planning, the negative health effects of urban planning can lead to worldwide health and environmental crises brought un by urban development. With this thought in mind, organizations involved in the urbanizations of their respective environments must consider sustainable urban planning. With urbanization and environmental health growing in importance and topic strength, we should analyze the connection between sustainable urban planning and environmental health to better understand the link between these two emerging topics and use the lessons learned from analysis to influence future work.

2   Purpose of the Study

The purpose of this study is to analyze the connection between research and work done in the topic areas of sustainable urban planning and environmental health. Dissecting and relating the information and data in these areas can help to identify the benefits of sustainable urban planning and best practices in the area to best promote overall environmental health as can be affected by urban development. To collect research conducted in these fields and perform a literary analysis, the tools of VOSVIEWER, Excel, MAXQDA, and Harzing Publish or Perish were used to collect and display data from sources from the literary databases or Web of Science and Google Scholar.

3   Research Methodology

3.1   Data Collection

To perform a literary analysis of the work and research done in the topic area of sustainable urban planning and environmental health, it was first necessary to identify the databases from which to pull articles from. Web of Science and Google Scholar databases were chosen for this purpose due to their inclusion of cited references and size of search capabilities respectively. Both of these databases would allow for the ability to conduct a co-citation and content analysis using other tools later in the study. To find relevant articles in these topic areas from the chose databases, two separate keyword searches were conducted: Sustainable Urban Planning and Environmental Health. Conducting two keyword searches would facilitate the collection of two sets of literature to review and draw connections and overlaps between. Both keywords were searched in Web of Science with search parameter years set at 1990–2020 and resulted in 145,152 article results for environmental health and 10,791 article results for sustainable urban planning. Keyword searches conducted in Google Scholar through Harzing were both stopped at 450 results (*Harzing's Publish or Perish*, n.d).

3.2   Trend Analysis

With both the topics of sustainable urban planning and environmental health being relatively new fields, it was pertinent to conduct a trend analysis to establish the credibility of the emerging nature of both topics. This was accomplished by discovering the change in the number of articles published relating to both keyword searches over the past 20 years. Data from Web of Science relating to both search terms were examined for 20 year (2001–2020) growth trends and yielded the following trend graphs of articles published by year. Data from web of science was chosen for this task due to its ease of analysis and built-in tools.

Data from Fig. 1 indicates an increasing trend in the number of articles published relating to sustainable urban planning, with an increase in articles published of over

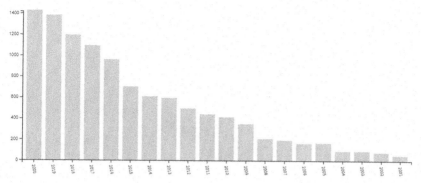

Fig. 1. Trend analysis of articles published from keyword sustainable urban planning (*web of science*, n.d.).

1,000 articles yearly between 2001 and 2020. While the number of articles published has increased every year during the rolling 20-year timespan, the increase has leveled off in years and could signal slowing growth in the work in this field.

Select	Field: Source Titles	Record Count	% of 10,791	Bar Chart
☐	SUSTAINABILITY	683	6.329 %	▪
☐	JOURNAL OF CLEANER PRODUCTION	167	1.548 %	I
☐	WIT TRANSACTIONS ON ECOLOGY AND THE ENVIRONMENT	166	1.538 %	I
☐	LAND USE POLICY	157	1.455 %	I
☐	SUSTAINABLE CITIES AND SOCIETY	154	1.427 %	I
☐	LANDSCAPE AND URBAN PLANNING	137	1.270 %	I
☐	CITIES	129	1.195 %	I
☐	HABITAT INTERNATIONAL	121	1.121 %	I
☐	PROCEDIA ENGINEERING	98	0.908 %	I
☐	IOP CONFERENCE SERIES EARTH AND ENVIRONMENTAL SCIENCE	97	0.899 %	I

Fig. 2. 10 largest publication sources of articles from keyword sustainable urban planning (*web of science*, n.d.).

Figure 2 shows the largest publication sources for articles relating to sustainable urban planning. It can be noted, perhaps unsurprisingly, that the largest number of articles were published in the source titled "Sustainability". Articles in this topic account for over 6% of all sources included in the search. Additional top 10 searches seem to fit the theme of sources related to environmental topic areas; with source titles like "Journal of Cleaner Production" and "Habitat International" underlining this.

After performing trend analysis on Web of Science data collected from the keyword search of sustainable urban planning, it was necessary to complete the same process as it related to the keyword term environmental health. Figure 3 shows the number of articles published per year relating to the keyword term environmental health for the

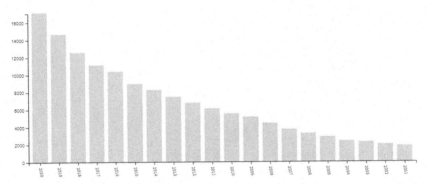

Fig. 3. Trend analysis of articles published from keyword environmental health (*web of science*, n.d.).

Select	Field: Source Titles	Record Count	% of 145,152	Bar Chart
☐	SCIENCE OF THE TOTAL ENVIRONMENT	2,351	1.620 %	I
☐	INTERNATIONAL JOURNAL OF ENVIRONMENTAL RESEARCH AND PUBLIC HEALTH	2,247	1.548 %	I
☐	ENVIRONMENTAL HEALTH PERSPECTIVES	1,742	1.200 %	I
☐	PLOS ONE	1,522	1.049 %	I
☐	ENVIRONMENTAL SCIENCE AND POLLUTION RESEARCH	1,315	0.906 %	I
☐	ENVIRONMENTAL RESEARCH	1,067	0.735 %	I
☐	ENVIRONMENT INTERNATIONAL	973	0.670 %	I
☐	CHEMOSPHERE	884	0.609 %	I
☐	ENVIRONMENTAL SCIENCE TECHNOLOGY	879	0.606 %	I
☐	JOURNAL OF CLEANER PRODUCTION	831	0.573 %	I

Fig. 4. 10 largest publication sources of articles from keyword environmental health (*web of science*, n.d.).

past 20 years (2001–2020). As was the case with sustainable urban planning articles, the number published in this topic area has increased every year for the past 20 years. A time period beginning to end increase of roughly 15,000 yearly published articles shows large growth and emergence in the topic area of environmental health. Interestingly, environmental health publication trends parallel sustainable urban planning in the overall large growth from 2001–2020 but recent relative plateaus in yearly publication over the past couple of years. This similar trend in article publication history can serve as an initial link to validate the connection between these two topic areas.

Figure 4 shows the 10 largest publication sources for the topic area of environmental health. As was seen in sustainable urban planning publication sources, many of the publication mediums are directly related to the study and promotion of the environment. The source "Science of the Total Environment" was the largest publication source accounting for 1.62% of all articles in the search field, indicating a fairly large spread of publication sources for the topic area. This large spread can be used as a tool for promoting the large breadth and concepts of the topic area, possibly containing sustainable urban planning fields.

4 Results

4.1 Co-citation Analysis

After publication trends in the topic areas relating to the keyword search terms of sustainable urban planning and environmental health were completed and validated for emergence, the results of the article search were analyzed for results and connections. To complete this, a co-citation analysis, content analysis, and word cloud generation were undertaken. The first of these processes, the co-citation analysis, was conducted to find important articles in both keyword fields and given insight into articles to further dissect for emerging and key data by analyzing the connectivity between citations in articles in the form of clusters. The co-citation analysis was performed in VOSviewer using data collected through Web of Science data from both keyword searches. Web of Science article results were used for this task because results from this database search include citations. The results from both keyword searches were limited to the latest 500 articles published as of 2020.

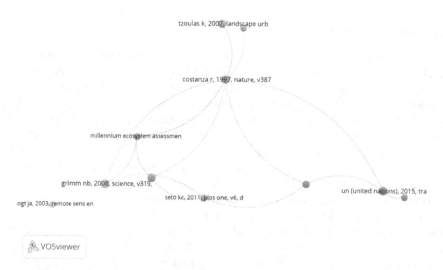

Fig. 5. Co-Citation Analysis for Sustainable Urban Planning (Vosviewer, n.d).

Figure 5 above shows a graphic figure generated from the co-citation analysis from the topic search of sustainable urban planning. The process for this keyword search was set to a minimum number of citations of a cited reference at 8 references. 13 articles met this criterion of the 29,548 cited references. The above figure can be shown to be broken down into 4 separate clusters, with each between a relatively small number of articles included in their clusters.

Fig. 6. Co-Citation Analysis for Environmental Health (Vosviewer, n.d).

Figure 6 is a graphical representation of the co-citation analysis for the keyword search of environmental health. This analysis in this topic area was limited to the number of citations of cited references at 4 references, yielding 31 articles of 31,650. The articles meeting this threshold can be broken down into 3 clusters, again with a smaller number of articles in the cluster. Usurpingly, the co-citation analysis for this topic was set at a smaller number of references for a threshold and generated more articles for results.

4.2 Content Analysis

Following completion of the co-citation analysis, a content analysis was completed on articles extracted from the previous keyword database searches. The content analysis follows a systematic process of evaluating articles in the topic areas of sustainable urban planning and environmental health for keywords and their occurrences within the title or abstracts of those articles. VOSviewer was again used to complete this procedure and used extracted Harzing metadata from Google Scholar. Google Scholar data was chosen due to its larger field of articles and metadata with which to extract terms and content. For content analysis conducted in both fields, the minimum number of occurrences for the terms was set at 10 times. The results of the content analysis will give indications of important topic areas and terms with which to direct literature reviews at.

Figure 7 is a content analysis for the search term sustainable urban planning. This content analysis was limited to terms with no less than 10 occurrences and yielded 61 terms, but after using a relevancy score of 60% for further refine search results, 31 terms were returned. The terms above are shown in occurrence frequency based on the relative size and connections between the terms are shown with links with larger links indicating stronger connections. Clusters of words are also shown with color coordination, indicating 4 separate clusters of words exist. Based on this content analysis, urban development occurred the largest number of times for keywords.

Figure 8 parallels Fig. 7 as content analysis for the topic area and term environmental health. The content analysis was limited to terms with no less than 10 occurrences and yielded 52 terms, but after using a relevancy score of 60% to further refine search results, 31 terms were returned (ironically the same as the analysis for sustainable urban planning). The terms above are shown in occurrence frequency based on the relative

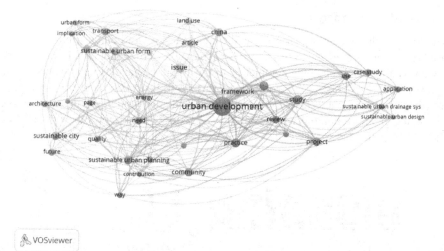

Fig. 7. Content analysis for sustainable urban planning (Vosviewer, n.d).

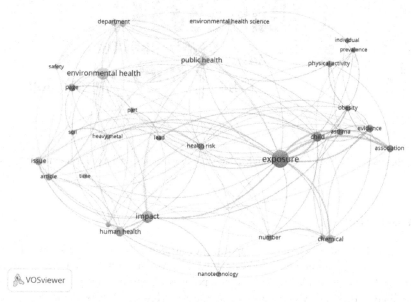

Fig. 8. Content analysis for sustainable urban planning (Vosviewer, n.d).

size and connections between the terms are shown with links with larger links indicating stronger connections. Clusters of words are also shown with color coordination, indicating 5 separate clusters of words exist. Based on this content analysis, exposure occurred the largest number of times for keywords.

4.3 Word Cloud Analysis

The final result generation process was the creation of a word cloud from all articles used for a literature review in this study. To generate a word cloud, articles used in the review as directed through the completion of the co-citation and content analysis were uploaded into MAXQDA. Keywords and terms from this article field were extracted and displayed in a word cloud format. In this data display, the larger the word in the figure, the greater the number of occurrences. Figure 9 below shows the figure of the MAXQDA generated word cloud.

Fig. 9. Word Cloud generated from MAXQDA using article generated for literature review

5 Discussion

After the collection, analysis, and reporting of articles relating to the keyword topics sustainable urban planning and environmental health, a literature review was conducted to further draw conclusions and discussion points from the available research. Articles highlighted in the co-citation analysis and searches conducted in Mendeley were sifted for content relevant to the topics and included in the deeper literature review. Discussion points on both topics are included below. Not all articles analyzed during the literature review were included in the final discussion and conclusions of this report but was limited to the most relevant and pertinent publications.

5.1 Sustainable Urban Planning

Rapid urban development beginning in the 20th century and continuing into the 21st century is a great challenge to the environmental health of urbanizing areas and their respective human and nonhuman populations (Jooste et al. 2019). With urbanization comes unique challenges, chiefly resource constraint and the need to allow for greater resource consumption for more individuals in a smaller space. This competition for consuming scarce resources often puts urban development at odds with the environment in which it is developing and can lead to great challenges in planning for the needs of their populations' resource usage (Yazar et al. 2012). This fundamental competition for consumption of resources and sustaining the environment's resources are therefore paramount to the continuing trends of urbanization. As highlighted in an article by Davis et al. this balance is all too often skewed toward the human consumption side of resource usage, with water, land, and energy resources being taken out of the environment and wastewater, polluted materials, and waste energy put back into it (Davis et al. 2016). It can also be noted that this destructive consumption pattern not only has negative side effects on the environment in the above-mentioned ways, and not surprisingly the health of the populations residing in them, but also irregularly adversely affects those of lower social standing (Davis et al. 2016). The overwhelming potential for destructive practices and effects on the environment due to poor urban development is the first highlighted note from the literature review.

A second point highlighted in the literature review on sustainable urban planning is the need to combat the potential negative effects of urbanization with sustainability-focused urban planning (Laffta et al. 2018). As humans compete with their environments for resources, it is important to systematically and holistically plan for how to best develop urban layouts for limited resource consumption and allow for their continued suitability and consumption in future generations (Rauscher et al. 2015). Examples of this can be seen in transportation systems developments with investments in environmentally and sustainability friendly mass transit systems in Tehran and building development and construction taking into consideration walkability and bicycling transportations of residents (Motieyan et al. 2018) (Rauscher et al. 2015). Not only is the current and projected scarcity of oil resources at the heart of this development, but so too is the need to curb the negative impacts of burning fossil fuels on the environment and human populations in the forms of climate change and poor air quality among others. Innovations in transportation developments are not the only strategies being implemented by the sustainable urban planning movement and only serve to highlight the movement towards the incorporation of new green technologies and methods in urban planning serving to protect and sustain the environmental health of their regions (Laffta et al. 2018As is shown in trend analysis results from article publication dates relating to sustainable urban planning, the topic and breadth of the sustainable urban planning movement continue to grow over time. The need for sustainable urban planning and the trend towards increasing technological innovations in the field are a second note from the literature review.

Urbanization has not only increased rapidly over the years but has increased at greater rates in different parts of the world. The rate of urbanization is now of particular pace in the developing world, regions where resource consumption, access to technology, and governmental planning are not as robust as their developed counterparts (Yazar et al. 2012). With this scenario, sustainability takes on another level of importance in urban planning in the developing world to prevent negative environmental health repercussions to those that inhabit these regions (Sumari et al. 2019). The last important takeaway from this literature review deals with the need to capture best practices and performance indicators of sustainability and work them into the urban planning protocols and procedures of developing countries. As underlined in a study that analyzes best practices in sustainability and their applications to developing countries like Turkey, it is necessary for community involvement, planning feedback, and monitoring are important to incorporate into urban planning practices to ensure success (Yazar et al. 2012). An example of urban planning best practices can be found in a study on urban development in Tanzania and the need for a movement towards a communicative planning approach to urban development to reduce spontaneous development and promote sustainability (Sumari et al. 2019). Another example of emerging and innovative best practices used in the field of sustainable urban planning can be seen in a case study conducted by Rauscher and Momatz on the viability of several human-automation interactive practices in Sydney Australia. This study sought to apply 3 fundamental principles for sustainable urban development (equitable for present and future generations, meets environmental protection, ensures participation of all concerned citizens) and indicators of the distribution of these principles in practice in Sydney (Rauscher et al. 2015). After applying and reviewing the principle's application through development sustainability indicators in the city, action plans for increased and future opportunities for sustainable urban planning were developed (Rauscher et al. 2015). These practices, and other best practices from additional research and works, will allow for the limiting of environmental destruction and promote environmental and human health. The need for sustainability emphasis in urban development in the developing world and the desire to capture best practices and sustainability indicators and metrics is a third takeaway from the literature review.

5.2 Environmental Health

While not as new in scope as sustainable urban planning, environmental health is still a relatively young and emerging topic in safety and health. The emergence and growth of the field can be seen in the increasing rate of publication in the field over the past 20 years as mentioned previously in the trend analysis. This growth and emergence in the field has warranted a great deal of analysis and even the advocation for the creation of harmonious integration of local and global environmental health needs (Virgolino et al. 2020). Such an idea is outlined, for example, in the proposal to create the ISAMB to analyze and fully commit to the research and analysis of the full breadth of the environmental health field. Furthermore, the ISAMB would serve to better understand not only the traditional realms of environmental health topics but also to grasp the effects environmental health has on human health (Virgolino et al. 2020). This link serves to directly connect the effects of adverse environmental conditions on human health and safety and the unprecedented emergence and emphasis of this connection.

Just as the link between environmental and human health has been emphasized and examined for connections, so too can the impact humans have on the health of the environment. One interesting example is the research done on the aquaculture industry and trends toward larger usage of terrestrial feed products in the industry (Fry et al. 2016). It is noted in this study that terrestrial agriculture products have an increase in the makeup of total input percentage for aquaculture in recent years, and the overall negative effects this trend has had on human impact on the environment. This negative impact is felt in humans the increased development of land for agriculture and very limited actual benefit this has had on potential decreased dependence on wild fisheries for feed inputs in aquaculture (Fry et al. 2016). Although not strictly "urban" in nature, this article serves as an example of the potential destructive power of human development on the environment and the lagging negative human impacts like increased water pollution from soil fertilizers that can be brought about by unchecked and irresponsible human planning.

As it is noted on the destructive abilities humans can reap on environmental health and their potential further repercussions for human health, it is important to analyze how humans can better understand and prevent damage to their environments and their residents. A study conducted on private well inspections highlights the importance and power local governments can have in determining the health of their environments and residential health (Spanier et al. 2011). This study uses information from a previously complied government report to link the adverse effects of unchecked and unhealthy well water quality on human health and points out that of several states noted for high well water nitrate levels, only 1 (Oregon) has an enforceable plan to inspect well water quality. The authors advocate for the creation of a federal plan to inspect and ensure well water quality to prevent possible negative human health complications of those drinking well water (Spanier et al. 2011). Creating a plan to inspect and enforce well water quality can serve as a first point to better understanding the root causes of contaminated well water and allow for the corrective actions to be taken to mitigate destructive practices.

6 Conclusion

Following dissection of the trends in the publication history in the areas of sustainable urban planning and environmental health, it can be noted that both topics show evidence as emerging areas of importance as related to health and safety. Both topic areas show increasing trends in their publication history and articles highlighting their incorporation with new technologies and strategies show their gaze toward future development. A case can also be made between the connection of these emerging topics and their correlation. As noted in the literature review, sustainable urban planning can have direct effects on the overall health of the environments in which they are developing and thus the health and safety of their residents. Through examples from resource consumption, agricultural land use, and well testing, environmental health can be directly influenced by the planning (or lack of) from human developers. As the area is still growing, it important to work to continue to examine and pinpoint links in sustainable urban planning and environmental health to best lead to positive change in human health and safety. Developing sustainable indicators and metrics for urban planning and development and identifying planning best practices and their leverage ability to other localities are among the important future trends in these topic areas.

7 Future Work

It is important to look to the future for effective ways to drive positive change in the realms of sustainable urban planning and environmental health. With both topics being relatively young in their concepts, the research is relatively limited and brief in their knowledge spheres. This leaves a great deal of potential in developing research plans and take ways from both areas. One such example of future work can be seen in an article from the NSF that discusses a project designed to perform a comprehensive study of the smart urban infrastructure technologies and how this advances wellbeing in cities. The project organizers discuss a comprehensive plan to analyze and create KPIs for measuring the effects of smart planning technologies in their environments and leverage best practices of these results through education and training into future sustainable urban planning (Corman 2017). Gathering best practices and developing strategies to leverage these items is an important area for sustainable urban planning in moving the field into greater use for environmental health. This study underlines three of the most important directions of future work in these topic areas: development of sustainability indicators and metrics, incorporation of new technologies and strategies, and gathering and leveraging best practices of lessons learned. The need to develop a leverageable methodology for assessing and designing urban systems and infrastructures is also explored in-depth in an article by Sahley et al. in which a skeleton of a systematic review for sustainability in urban planning is introduced (Sahley et al. 2005). The article proposes a three-prong approach to considering urban planning in regards to sustainability through 3 steps: Problem definition, inventory analysis, and impact assessment and analysis (Sahely et al. 2005). While fairly generic in scope, this process is discussed in greater detail with an example and case study for the urban water system of Toronto to show the applicability and leveragability of this process in promoting sustainable urban planning. Studies like these that dive into sustainability indicators and leveragability of best practices are important opportunities for future work in the fields of sustainable urban planning and environmental health.

While the methods and directions for driving positive and lasting benefits to society through sustainable urban planning are large and diverse in scope, the inclusion of the importance of human-computer interactions is highlighted throughout. It is critical to utilize the advantages and capabilities of human-computer interactions to fully leverage and facilitate the spread of sustainable urban planning practices and utility to promote greater environmental health. As the world develops and relies more on digital infrastructure and computer use and interaction becomes more central to daily life, it is essential to take into consideration how to incorporate these factors into the emerging and developing fields of sustainable urban planning and environmental health.

References

Brauer, R.L.: Safety and health professions. Essay. In: Safety and Health for Engineers, p. 31. Wiley, Hoboken (2016)

Corman, D.: Connecting the Smart-City Paradigm with a Sustainable Urban Infrastructure Systems Framework to Advance Equity in Communities. National Science Foundation, 16 August 2017 (2017)

Davis, M.J.M., Jácome Polit, D., Lamour, M.: Social urban metabolism strategies (sums) for cities. Proc. Environ. Sci. **34**, 309–327 (2016). https://doi.org/10.1016/j.proenv.2016.04.028

Engström, G., Gren, A.: Capturing the value of green space in urban parks in a sustainable urban planning and design context: pros and cons of hedonic pricing. Ecol. Soc. **22**(2) (2017). https://doi.org/10.5751/es-09365-220221

Fry, J.P., et al.: Environmental health impacts of feeding crops to farmed fish. Environ. Int. **91**, 201–214 (2016). https://doi.org/10.1016/j.envint.2016.02.022

Goetsch, D.L., Ozon, G.: Environmental safety. Essay. In: Occupational Health and Safety for Technologists, Engineers, and Managers, p. 658. Pearson Canada Inc., North York (2019)

Jooste, A.F., de Kock, I.H., Musango, J.K.: A systematic literature review of sustainable urban planning challenges associated with developing countries. South Afr. J. Ind. Eng. **30**(3) (2019). https://doi.org/10.7166/30-3-2247

Laffta, S., Al-rawi, A.: Green technologies in sustainable urban planning. MATEC Web Conf. **162**, 05029 (2018). https://doi.org/10.1051/matecconf/201816205029

Motieyan, H., Mesgari, M.S.: An agent-based modeling approach for sustainable urban planning from land use and public transit perspectives. Cities **81**, 91–100 (2018). https://doi.org/10.1016/j.cities.2018.03.018

Rauscher, R.C., Momtaz, S.: Sustainable urban planning. In: Sustainable Neighbourhoods in Australia, pp. 3–15 (2015). https://doi.org/10.1007/978-3-319-17572-0_1

Sahely, H.R., Kennedy, C.A., Adams, B.J.: Developing sustainability criteria for urban infrastructure systems. Can. J. Civ. Eng. **32**(1), 72–85 (2005). https://doi.org/10.1139/l04-072

Sumari, N.S., et al.: A geospatial approach to sustainable urban planning: lessons for Morogoro municipal council Tanzania. Sustainability **11**(22), 6508 (2019). https://doi.org/10.3390/su111226508

Spanier, A.J., Hoppe, B.O., Harding, A.K., Staab, J., Counter, M.: Private well testing in oregon from real estate transactions: an innovative approach toward a state-based surveillance system. Public Health Rep. **126**(1), 107–115 (2011). https://doi.org/10.1177/003335491112600115

Yazar, K.H., Dede, O.M.: Sustainable urban planning in developed countries: lessons for turkey. Int. J. Sustain. Dev. Plan. **7**(1), 26–47 (2012). https://doi.org/10.2495/sdp-v7-n1-26-47

Virgolino, A., et al.: Towards a global perspective of environmental health: defining the research grounds of an institute of environmental health. Sustainability **12**(21), 8963 (2020). https://doi.org/10.3390/su12218963

A FAHP-VIKOR Approach for Supporting the Selection of Tomography Equipment in LMIC Hospitals: A Case Study

Miguel Ortíz-Barrios[1]([⊠]), Natalia Jaramillo-Rueda[1], Antonella Petrillo[2], Zaury Fernández-Mendoza[3], and Lucelys Vidal-Pacheco[1]

[1] Department of Productivity and Innovation, Universidad de la Costa CUC, Barranquilla, Colombia
{mortiz1,njaramil,lvidal2}@cuc.edu.co
[2] Department of Engineering, University of Naples "Parthenope", Naples, Italy
antonella.petrillo@uniparthenope.it
[3] Department of Engineering, Institución Universitaria ITSA, Barranquilla, Colombia
zefernandez@itsa.edu.co

Abstract. Computerized Tomography Scanners (CT-SCAN) provide detailed cross-sectional images of the human body which are employed for the easier detection and further analysis of abnormalities concerning the functionality and structure of the skeleton, tissues, and organs. However, the appropriate CT-SCAN selection is an arduous task considering the complexity and high cost of these medical devices. This decision is even more sharpener in hospitals from Low-and-Middle-Income-Countries (LMIC) where the available budget is usually restricted and correct resource allocation should be therefore ensured while granting the greatest impact on the timeliness and efficacy of healthcare services. In this framework, multiple criteria from diverse fields need to be taken into account to satisfy the intricate requirements of users. In this regard, it is necessary to fully elicit the expectations of stakeholders as well as identify their importance in an overall decision-making context. To address these gaps, this study proposes a novel integration between the Fuzzy Analytic Hierarchy Process (FAHP) and VIKOR methods for the CT-SCAN selection problem. Initially, a Multi-Criteria Decision-Making (MCDM) model will be designed for selecting the most suitable CT-SCAN option for a particular LMIC hospital. Then IF-AHP will be applied to calculate the relative priorities of criteria and sub-criteria under uncertainty. Ultimately, VIKOR will be implemented for obtaining an overall decision-making context. To address these gaps, this study proposes a novel integration between the Fuzzy Analytic Hierarchy Process (FAHP) and VIKOR methods for the CT-SCAN selection problem. Initially, a Multi-Criteria Decision-Making (MCDM) model will be designed for selecting the most suitable CT-SCAN option for a particular LMIC hospital. Then IF-AHP will be applied to calculate the relative priorities of criteria and sub-criteria under uncertainty. Ultimately, VIKOR will be implemented for obtaining an overall appropriateness index per CT-SCAN candidate and thereby identifying the most pertinent one (s) for a specific LMIC medical institution.

© Springer Nature Switzerland AG 2021
C. Stephanidis et al. (Eds.): HCII 2021, LNCS 13097, pp. 68–82, 2021.
https://doi.org/10.1007/978-3-030-90966-6_6

Keywords: Tomography equipment · Fuzzy Analytic Hierarchy Process (FAHP) · VIKOR · Computerized Tomography Scanners (CT-SCAN) · Healthcare

1 Introduction

Computerized Tomography Scanners (CT-SCAN), as well known, is a digital radiological technique that converts analog information into numerical data that can be processed by computers [1]. From a theoretical point, the basics of CT-SCAN were introduced by the mathematician J. Radon in 1917 [2]. Only in the 1950s and 1960s some researchers, including the physicist A. Comack, developed the algorithms to reconstruct images of body sections using a finite number of projections [3]. The development of CT-SCAN revolutionized medical radiology: for the first time, it was possible to obtain high-quality tomographic images of the body's internal structures. More and more sophisticated techniques have developed and still today the CT-SCAN continues to mature [4]. CT-SCAN is now a routine clinical examination because the machines are now widespread in hospitals. It represents one of the most established diagnostic tests, often playing the role of elective method or assuming at least a position of priority of employment [5]. However, CT-SCAN is a mildly invasive exam, like other radiological tests using X-rays. In fact, the tomographic images are reconstructed from a large number of X-ray transmissions through the patient. For this reason, the researchers' goal is to improve CT-SCAN performance by reducing, for example, the measurement time. Thus, over the years there has been a technological evolution from the "first generation" CT-SCAN consisting of an X-ray tube that emitted a linear beam of X-rays, up to the "fourth-generation" tomography which had fixed sensors arranged circularly on the entire gantry ring and have been abandoned [6]. Modern tomography derive from the "third generation" but have a fundamental characteristic related to acquiring images in a spiral or continuous way. Today there are electron beam computed tomography, a new family of tomography with a high level of anatomical detail (up to 0.5 mm) [7]. In other words, it is essential to improve the technology to avoid risks to patients and to obtain high-quality images for a correct diagnosis. This awareness is the basis of the technological innovations that many researchers work on. For the above reasons, researchers try to improve the technological process of CT-SCAN according to the following main guidelines: 1) development of new systems based on different scanning principles, with the primary aim of shortening the time for measures' collection; 2) development and use of new and more improved system components to improve the image quality and increase the operational efficiency; 3) development of more efficient computing systems to reduce image waiting time and increase the flow of exams, and 4) development of application software for performing functional tests [8].

This means that a choice of a CT-SCAN should take into consideration various parameters including technical characteristics and costs. The equipment chosen should always represent the best of their production in terms of technology [9]. In addition, an important feature is that the patient dose reduction should be guaranteed. In other words, the purchase of a CT-SCAN is not easy and requires careful cost-benefit analysis as there are several factors to consider (i.e. CT SCANNER PRICE; SLICE COUNT; DOSE OPTIMIZATION; etc.). This decision is even more sharpener in hospitals from Low-and-Middle-Income-Countries (LMIC) where the available budget is usually restricted and correct resource allocation should be therefore ensured while granting the greatest impact on the timeliness and efficacy of healthcare services [10].

Thus, this study tries to answer the following question: *How to select the best CT-SCAN?* It is clear that this is a Multi-Criteria Decision-Making (MCDM) problem. Indeed, the economic criterion should not be applied as the only criterion since the most economically advantageous offer does not always represent the most adequate one from a technical and patient health point of view. Thus, the present study proposes a multi-criteria approach, based on a novel integration between the Fuzzy Analytic Hierarchy Process (FAHP) and VIKOR methods. The present research is an extension of our previous research in which AHP and TOPSIS are applied to define the most appropriate tomography equipment [11].

The rest of the paper is organized as follows: Sect. 2 outlines related work on the topic trying to summarize the state of the art; Sect. 3 explains the proposed methodological approach applied in the study; Sect. 4 summarizes the results of the model and the main results. Finally, in Sect. 5 the main conclusions and future developments are highlighted.

2   Related Work

Choosing a new medical technology such as a new CT-SCAN is a hard decision because of the many factors to consider [12]. There are many manufacturers of CT SCAN (i.e. CANON, PHILIPS, SAMSUNG, SIEMENS, etc.) that offer different technical solutions considering also maintenance contracts or warranty plans. Thus, it becomes important to choose suitable criteria in a given context with certain characteristics (social, economic, structural, etc.). Considering the importance of the issue, we investigated Scopus, the largest abstract and citation database of peer-reviewed literature to analyze the state of art on this issue. The Boolean operators AND and OR were used. In detail, the following string: (TITLE-ABS-KEY (medical AND equipment) AND TITLE-ABS-KEY (analytic AND hierarchy AND process) OR TITLE-ABS-KEY (vikor) OR TITLE-ABS-KEY (mcda)) was employed. The investigation returned **62** documents. An overview of these documents is analyzed below. The first interesting aspect to note is the number of publications over the years as shown in Fig. 1. Another interesting aspect to highlight is the type of documents published. In detail, it emerges that most of the documents are articles (37; 59.7%) followed by conference paper (22; 35.5%), book chapter (2; 3.2%), and conference review (1; 1.6%). The analysis of the documents shows that the most covered research areas are: Engineering (24.2%); Medicine (24.2%), and Computer Science (20%).

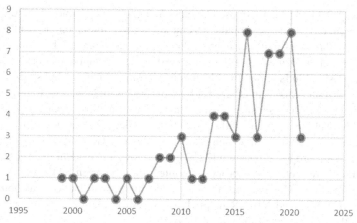

Fig. 1. Documents by year (source: Scopus)

Furthermore, the 5 most productive countries are Iran (11.2%) followed on an equal footing by China, Czech Republic, Italy, and United Kingdom (9.6%) as shown in Fig. 2.

Fig. 2. Documents by country/territory (source: Scopus)

Among the 62 selected documents, we have identified those most cited in the scientific community (updated data of June 2021). The first one is the publication by Hsu et al. [13] with 68 citations in which is proposed an AHP model to select medical waste firms and then reduce the potential risks for hospitals. An interesting point of view, aligned with our research has been proposed by Pecchia et al. [14] with 61 citations. In their paper, AHP is used to elicit user needs for a new CT scanner for use in a public hospital. In 2015, AHP and Delphi methods were used by Ivlev et al. [15] (43 citations) as a tool to select medical devices under uncertainty. Previously, in 2014, Ivlev et al. [16] (38 citations) investigated the application of AHP, multi-attribute utility theory, and elimination and choice expressing reality to manage medical equipment. The research remains very theoretical and with few practical implications. Other researches in line with our proposal have been proposed by other authors. For example, in 2020, Hummel et al. [17] applied AHP to assess medical technologies in development. Recently, a Fuzzy AHP Fuzzy in the renewal of healthcare technologies was developed by Domínguez and Carnero [18]. While Ozüdoğru [19] applied AHP to define biomedical device purchase of a private hospital in Istanbul. Finally, it is interesting to mention the studies by Kirá-lyová et al. [20] and Shamsan et al. [21] both published in 2017. The first one applied AHP to select a PET/CT scanner for the department of nuclear medicine. The second one proposed ANP and Monte Carlo simulation to select CT scanners. In general, the literature analysis has shown that many studies apply the AHP method in problems similar to the present proposed research [22, 23]. However, it is evident that there is a lack of bibliographic references that propose an integration between FAHP and VIKOR or some other methods. Our research tries to cover this gap. In fact, in our opinion, the integration of FAHP and VIKOR methods is useful to obtain an optimized result by combining the advantages of the two methods.

3 Proposed Methodology

The objective of this study is to identify the most suitable CT-SCAN option for a particular LMIC hospital through the integration of the Fuzzy Analytical Fuzzy Hierarchical Process (FAHP) and VIKOR methods. The proposed methodology is comprised of three phases (refer to Fig. 3):

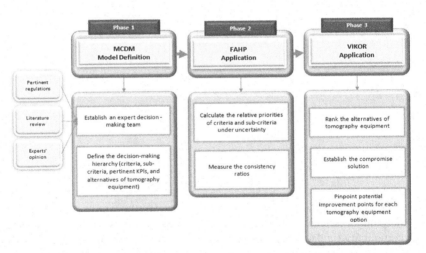

Fig. 3. The proposed methodology for the selection of the most suitable tomography equipment in a particular LMIC hospital.

– *Phase 1 (MCDM model definition):* A group of experts is selected based on their experience in the use of biomedical technology. Then, criteria and sub-criteria are determined with the participation of the decision-making team, the relevant scientific literature, and the pertinent regulations.

- *Phase 2 (FAHP application):* Fuzzy AHP is applied to calculate the relative priorities of criteria and sub-criteria under uncertainty.
- *Phase 3 (VIKOR application):* In this last phase, VIKOR is implemented to line up the tomography equipment options from the highest to the lowest suitability measure. The results of the worst and ideal solution are also incorporated in this study. Finally, the alternative with the highest suitability measure is selected, which would represent the best CT-SCAN option for a particular LMIC hospital.

3.1 Fuzzy Analytic Hierarchy Process (FAHP)

The Fuzzy Analytic Hierarchy Process (FAHP) is one of the most commonly used MCDM methods. It combines the Analytic Hierarchy Process (AHP) with Fuzzy Logic [24] and its main objective is to deal with the uncertainty associated with human judgments which is not covered in AHP. The paired comparisons in FAHP are represented by triangular fuzzy numbers [25] denoting different levels of importance:

Table 1. Correspondence between linguistic terms and fuzzy triangular numbers in FAHP

Reduced AHP scale	Fuzzy triangular number	Definition
1	[1, 1, 1]	Equally important
3	[2, 3, 4]	More important
5	[4, 5, 6]	Much more important
1/3	[1/4, 1/3, 1/2]	Less important
1/5	[1/6, 1/5, 1/4]	Much less important

The FAHP algorithm is divided into the following phases:

- **Phase 1.** By using the fuzzy triangular number scale (TFN) described in Table 1, paired comparisons between criteria and sub-criteria are performed. The result of this process is a matrix of fuzzy judgments $\tilde{B}^k (b_{ij})$ represented in Eq. 1:

$$\tilde{B}^k = \begin{bmatrix} \tilde{b}_{11}^k & \tilde{b}_{12}^k & \cdots & \tilde{b}_{1n}^k \\ \tilde{b}_{21}^k & \tilde{b}_{22}^k & \cdots & \tilde{b}_{2n}^k \\ \cdots & \cdots & \cdots & \cdots \\ \tilde{b}_{n1}^k & \tilde{b}_{n2}^k & \cdots & \tilde{b}_{nn}^k \end{bmatrix} \tag{1}$$

$\tilde{b}_{ij}$ symbolizes the *kth* decision-maker's preference of *ith* criterion/sub-criterion over *jth* criterion/sub-criterion.
- **Phase 2.** The geometric mean of all paired comparisons is obtained using Eq. 2. In this case, K represents the total number of decision-makers participating in the selection process.

Taking into account the above considerations, the initial fuzzy judgment matrix is updated as shown in Eq. 3.

$$\tilde{b}_{ij} = \sqrt[k]{\tilde{b}_{ij}^1 * \tilde{b}_{ij}^2 * \cdots * \tilde{b}_{ij}^k} \tag{2}$$

$$\tilde{B} = \begin{bmatrix} \tilde{b}_{11} & \cdots & \tilde{b}_{1n} \\ \vdots & \ddots & \vdots \\ \tilde{b}_{n1} & \cdots & \tilde{b}_{nn} \end{bmatrix} \tag{3}$$

– **Phase 3.** Estimate the geometric average of the fuzzy comparisons ($\tilde{r}_i$) for each criterion by employing Eq. 4.

$$\tilde{r} = \left(\prod_{j=1}^{n} \tilde{b}_{ij} \right)^{1/n}, i = 1, 2, \ldots, n \tag{4}$$

– **Phase 4.** Set the fuzzy weights of each criterion and sub-criterion by implementing Eq. 5.

$$\tilde{w}_i = \tilde{r}_i \oplus (\tilde{r}_1 \oplus \tilde{r}_2 \oplus \cdots \oplus \tilde{r}_n)^{-1} = (lw_i, mw_i, uw_i) \tag{5}$$

– **Phase 5.** Defuzzify ($\tilde{w}_i$) by utilizing the Center of Area procedure outlined in Eq. 6. The outcome is a non-fuzzy number (M_i) which is further normalized via Eq. 7. Lately, consistency ratios (CR) are calculated to verify the reliability of the decision-making process. If CR $< 10\%$, the matrix is then considered as consistent; otherwise, paired judgments need to be revised by the decision-makers.

$$M_i = \frac{lw_i + mw_i + uw_i}{3} \tag{6}$$

$$N_i = \frac{M_i}{\sum_{i=1}^{n} M_i} \tag{7}$$

3.2 Vlsekriterijumska Optimizacija I Kompromisno Resenje (VIKOR)

VIKOR is a method that is implemented to solve a decision-making problem with non-commutative decision criteria. This technique ranks a set of alternatives taking into account their proximity to the ideal scenario, which is denoted by predefined criteria [26]. VIKOR introduces a ranking index that describes the closeness of each alternative to the ideal solution [26, 27]. The VIKOR algorithm is described below:

– **Phase 1.** An array set of t tomography equipment options represented as $(T^{(1)})$, $(T^{(2)}),\ldots, (T^{(t)})$ is defined. Each alternative $(T^{(i)})$ is described by a set of decision criteria (n). This is described in Matrix A (Eq. 8). The measure of each sub-criterion SC_j is here denoted by sij:

$$
A = \begin{array}{c} (T^{(1)}) \\ (T^{(2)}) \\ (T^{(3)}) \\ \vdots \\ (T^{(t)}) \end{array} \begin{bmatrix} SC_1 & SC_2 & \cdots & SC_n \\ s_{11} & s_{12} & \cdots & s_{1n} \\ s_{21} & s_{22} & \cdots & s_{2n} \\ s_{31} & s_{32} & \cdots & s_{3n} \\ \vdots & \vdots & \vdots & \vdots \\ s_{t1} & s_{t2} & \cdots & s_{tn} \end{bmatrix} \tag{8}
$$

– **Phase 2.** Identify the best s_j^* and worst s_j^- measures for each sub-criterion by employing Eqs. 13–14 respectively.

$$
s_{ij} = \begin{cases} max_i s_{ij} \ for \ benefit \ cirteria \\ min_i s_{ij}, \ for \ cost \ criteria \end{cases}, i = 1, 2, \ldots, m \tag{9}
$$

$$
s_{ij}^- = \begin{cases} max_i s_{ij} \ for \ benefit \ cirteria \\ min_i s, \ for \ cost \ criteria \end{cases}, i = 1, 2, \ldots, m \tag{10}
$$

– **Phase 3.** Compute the S_i and R_i measures by applying Eqs. 11–12. The weights (w_j) of sub-criteria SC_j are those obtained with the Fuzzy AHP method.

$$
S_i = \sum_{j=1}^{n} \frac{w_j\left(s_j^* - s_{ij}\right)}{s_j^* - s_j^-}, \tag{11}
$$

$$
R_i = max_j \left(\frac{w_j\left(s_j^* - s_{ij}\right)}{s_j^* - s_j^-} \right) \tag{12}
$$

– **Phase 4.** Obtain the values of Q_i using Eqs. 13–14. In the Eq. 13, v denotes the weight of the maximum group utility [28]; while $1 - v$ describes the individual regret contribution.

$$
Q_i = v \frac{S_i - S^*}{S^- - S^*} + (1 - v) \frac{R_i - R^*}{R^- - R^*} \tag{13}
$$

$$
S^* = min_i S_i, \ S^- = max_j S_j, \tag{14}
$$

$$
R^* = min_i R_i, \ R^- = max_j R_j, \tag{15}
$$

- **Phase 5.** Order the tomography equipment alternatives according to the S_i, Q_i, and R_i measures.
- **Phase 6.** Provide a compromise solution including the best ranked alternative considering the ranking list Q_i whereas satisfying the ensuing conditions:

  • Acceptable advantage (represented by the Eq. 16 and Eq. 17)

$$Q\left(T^{(2)}\right) - Q\left(T^{(1)}\right) \geq DQ, \tag{16}$$

$$DQ = \frac{1}{(t-1)}. \tag{17}$$

Here $Q\left(T^{(2)}\right)$ is the tomography equipment with the second greatest priority in the ranking list Q_i.
  • Adequate stability in the decision-making process: the tomography equipment $\left(T^{(1)}\right)$ must be also the best in the list of classifications S_i and R_i.

If some of the conditions are not met, choose one of these solutions:

• $\left(T^{(1)}\right)$ and $\left(T^{(2)}\right)$ if there is no adequate stability in the decision-making process.
• $\left(T^{(1)}\right)$, $\left(T^{(2)}\right)$,..., $\left(T^{(t)}\right)$ if there is no acceptable advantage as outlined in Eq. 18.

$$Q\left(T^{(t)}\right) - Q\left(T^{(1)}\right) < DQ \tag{18}$$

4 Results and Discussion

An MCDM model integrated by 5 criteria and 17 sub-criteria was proposed based on the outputs derived from the decision-making team, the associated regulations, and the pertinent literature. The global (GW) and local weights (LW) are enlisted in Table 2. According to the results obtained from FAHP, the CT DOSE (SF6) obtained the highest global score (0.40581) which denotes the importance of ensuring minimum risk of radiation to the patient while crafting the images. In fact, a high risk of radiation is linked to greatest likelihood of developing cancer [29]. CT-SCAN with the lowest radiation dose is then preferred considering the need for lessening the cumulative effect of radiation in patients with frequent imaging requirement for their diagnosis and treatment. Furthermore, in Fig. 4 where the global weights of the criteria are shown, it can be interpreted that the most important criterion for the hospital when acquiring tomography equipment is PATIENT SAFETY (0.54576). Recently, there has been an increasing trend towards implementing patient-centered approaches targeting ameliorated adverse events stemming from the healthcare processes [30, 31]. In this regard, technology managing uncertainties during imaging is pretty much appreciated to reduce the intricate radiation risks.

Table 2. Global and local weights of decision elements

CRITERION	GW	LW
IMAGING PERFORMANCE (C1)	**0.12471**	
Transaxial Resolution (SF1)	0.03566	0.28593
Rotation Speed (SF2)	0.03249	0.26051
Imaging Software (SF3)	0.00672	0.05391
Image Resolution (SF4)	0.02899	0.23246
Resolution Cuts (SF5)	0.02085	0.16719
PATIENT SAFETY (C2)	**0.54576**	
CT Dose (SF6)	0.40581	0.74356
Patient Monitoring (SF7)	0.07039	0.12897
Contrast (SF8)	0.06957	0.12747
TECHNOLOGY ADVANCEMENT (C3)	**0.12332**	
Maintenance (SF9)	0.05842	0.47375
Data Warehousing (SF10)	0.02319	0.18804
Energy Use (SF11)	0.04171	0.33821
TECHNICAL CONFIGURATION (C4)	**0.09792**	
Processing Software (SF12)	0.04182	0.42710
Interoperability (SF13)	0.04704	0.38148
Automatic management (SF14)	0.02361	0.19142
FINANCIAL PROFILE (C5)	**0.10829**	
Unit cost (SF15)	0.01784	0.16480
Payment facility (SF16)	0.06867	0.63415
Cost of maintenance (SF17)	0.02177	0.20105

The consistency indices of all the matrices (Table 3) were acceptable (CR ≤ 0.1). The results then confirm the high level of reliability of the decision-making model [32, 33]. The VIKOR method was later applied to rank the tomography equipment alternatives $(T^{(1)})$, $(T^{(2)})$, and $(T^{(3)})$. The S_j and R_j measures are depicted in Table 4 while Fig. 5 presents the ranking based on the Q_j values ($v = 0.5$).

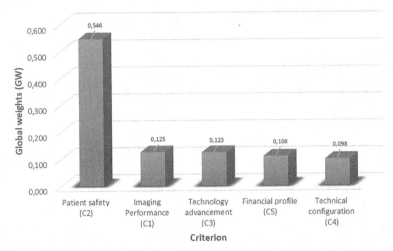

Fig. 4. Global weights of criteria considered in tomography equipment selection.

We then evaluated the two VIKOR conditions [34, 35]: a) Acceptable advantage, b) Adequate stability. As $0.333 - 0.095 < 0.5$, there is no acceptable advantage between $\left(T^{(2)}\right)$ and $\left(T^{(3)}\right)$. However, upon assessing this statement in $\left(T^{(1)}\right)$ Vs. $\left(T^{(2)}\right)$, the derived mathematical expression is $1.000 - 0.095 > 0.5$ which denotes a significant advantage of $\left(T^{(2)}\right)$ over $\left(T^{(1)}\right)$. On the other hand, the tomography equipment $\left(T^{(2)}\right)$ was not found the best in the S_i classification. Therefore, it is indistinct to select either $\left(T^{(2)}\right)$ or $\left(T^{(3)}\right)$ as a compromise solution for the showcased hospital.

Table 3. Consistency ratios for Fuzzy AHP matrices.

Matrix	Consistency ratio (CR)
Criteria	1.86%
Imaging Performance	5.62%
Patient safety	9.99%
Technology advancement	0.09%
Financial profile	0.11%
Technical configuration	0.20%

Table 4. Ranking of alternatives based on S_j and R_j values.

Alternatives	Sj	Rank	Rj	Rank
$\left(T^{(1)}\right)$	0.559	3	0.406	3
$\left(T^{(2)}\right)$	0.048	2	0.048	1
$\left(T^{(3)}\right)$	−0.073	1	0.286	2

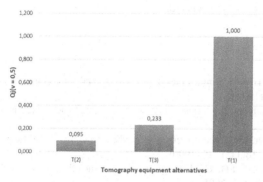

Fig. 5. Ranking of tomography equipment options based on Q_j ($v = 0.5$).

Ultimately, an important outcome for CT-SCAN designers is the identification of the weakest features related to their particular tomography offer. For instance, in $\left(T^{(1)}\right)$, it is advised to reduce the radiation dose (in Mega Hit Units - MHU) to protect frequent patients from a latent risk of developing cancerous cells. Also, it is recommended to propose a more attractive advance payment percentage so that budget-restricted hospitals can find it as an effective way of resource allocation.

5 Conclusions and Future Work

This research showed an MCDM approach based on FAHP and VIKOR supporting the selection of the most suitable CT-SCAN especially for low-and-medium-income hospitals where high effective decisions are needed considering a multifactorial practical environment. In particular, 5 criteria and 17 sub-criteria were identified as potentially affecting this decision. Definitively, the financial criterion should not be considered as the only criterion since the most economically beneficial offer does not always ensure the most suitable one from a technical and healthcare perspective.

The FAHP-VIKOR application showed that *patient safety* is the most important criterion with a global weight of 54.57% while the other criteria evidence low importance between 9% and 12%. On a different tack, as there is no adequate stability in the decision-making process, the compromise solution is integrated by $\left(T^{(2)}\right)$ and $\left(T^{(3)}\right)$ with Q_i equal to 0.095 and 0.333 correspondingly.

This research will permit hospitals and medical centers from different regions to make right decisions regarding technology purchasing, an aspect that is essential to establish an exact diagnosis and upgrade patients' health, quality of care, and sustainability of healthcare health institutions considering restricted budgets. The solution here proposed is useful for supporting chest CT scans required during the current Covid-19 pandemic. Future work will consider environmental criteria within the decision hierarchy as well as the application of new-generation methods like Best and Worst Method (BWM), Combined Compromise Solution (CoCoSo), and intuitionistic fuzzy approaches. Also, it is expected to implement this methodology in high-income countries to undertake comparative studies and determine which changes need to be incorporated to effectively respond to the new healthcare scenario.

References

1. Hounsfield, G.N.: Historical notes on computerized axial tomography. Can. Assoc. Radiol. J. **27**(3), 135–142 (1976)
2. Harper, C.: CT scanners: the industry behind the science. Radiol. Technol. **51**(2), 199–202 (1979)
3. Stytz, M.R., Frieder, O.: Three-dimensional medical imaging modalities: an overview. Crit. Rev. Biomed. Eng. **18**(1), 1–25 (1990)
4. Wesolowski, J.R., Lev, M.H.: CT: History, technology, and clinical aspects. Semin. Ultrasound CT MRI **26**(6), 376–379 (2005)
5. Mackie, T.R.: History of tomotherapy. Phys. Med. Biol. **51**(13), R24, R427–R453 (2006)
6. Evseev, I., Klock, M.C.L., Paschuk, S.A., Schulte, R.W., Williams, D.C.: Computerized tomography with high-energy proton beams: tomographic image reconstruction from computer-simulated data. Braz. J. Phys. **34**(3A), 804–807 (2004)
7. Sittig, D.F., Ash, J.S., Ledley, R.S.: The story behind the development of the first whole-body computerized tomography scanner as told by Robert S. Ledley. J. Am. Med. Inform. Assoc. **13**(5), 465–469 (2006)
8. Huda, W., Nickoloff, E.L., Boone, J.M.: Overview of patient dosimetry in diagnostic radiology in the USA for the past 50 years. Med. Phys. **35**(12), 5713–5728 (2008)
9. Holmberg, O., Malone, J., Rehani, M., McLean, D., Czarwinski, R.: Current issues and actions in radiation protection of patients. Eur. J. Radiol. **76**(1), 15–19 (2010)
10. Silva, H.P., Viana, A.L.D.: Health technology diffusion in developing countries: a case study of CT scanners in Brazil. Health Policy Plan. **26**(5), 385–394 (2011)
11. Barrios, M.A.O., De Felice, F., Negrete, K.P., Arenas, A.Y., Petrillo, A.: An AHP-topsis integrated model for selecting the most appropriate tomography equipment. Int. J. Inf. Technol. Decis. Mak. **15**(4), 861–885 (2016)
12. Jamshidi, A., Rahimi, S.A., Ait-Kadi, D., Ruiz, A.: A comprehensive fuzzy risk-based maintenance framework for prioritization of medical devices. Appl. Soft Comput. **32**, 322–334 (2015)
13. Hsu, P.-F., Wu, C.-R., Li, Y.-T.: Selection of infectious medical waste disposal firms by using the analytic hierarchy process and sensitivity analysis. Waste Manag. **28**(8), 1386–1394 (2008)
14. Pecchia, L., Martin, J.L., Ragozzino, A., Mirarchi, L., Morgan, S.P.: User needs elicitation via analytic hierarchy process (AHP). A case study on a Computed Tomography (CT) scanner. BMC Med. Inform. Decis. Mak. **13**(1), 2 (2013)
15. Ivlev, I., Vacek, J., Kneppo, P.: Multi-criteria decision analysis for supporting the selection of medical devices under uncertainty. Eur. J. Oper. Res. **247**(1), 216–228 (2015)

16. Ivlev, I., Kneppo, P., Bartak, M.: Multicriteria decision analysis: a multifaceted approach to medical equipment management. Technol. Econ. Dev. Econ. **20**(3), 576–589 (2014)
17. Hummel, M.J.M., Van Rossum, W., Verkerke, G.J., Rakhorst, G.: Assessing medical technologies in development: a new paradigm of medical technology assessment. Int. J. Technol. Assess. Health Care **16**(4), 1214–1219 (2000)
18. Domínguez, S., Carnero, M.C.: Fuzzy multicriteria modelling of decision making in the renewal of healthcare technologies. Mathematics **8**(6), 944 (2020)
19. Ozüdoğru, A.G.: Determination of Biomedical Device Selection Criteria I [Biyomedikal Cihaz Seçiminde Kriterlerin Önem Düzeylerinin Belirlenmesi]. In: 2018 Medical Technologies National Congress, TIPTEKNO 2018 8596889 (2018)
20. Királyová, E., Steklá, M., Donin, G.: Selection of a PET/CT scanner for the department of nuclear medicine. In: 2017 E-Health and Bioengineering Conference, EHB 2017 7995428, pp. 329–332 (2017)
21. Shamsan, A., Alzu'bi, A., Aqlan, F.: Selection of CT scanners using analytic hierarchy process and Monte Carlo simulation. In: 67th Annual Conference and Expo of the Institute of Industrial Engineers 2017 pp. 1997–2002 (2017)
22. Hajdau, C., Spiridonica, A.-M.: AHP - Based weighting of criteria for medical equipment selection. In: 2015 E-Health and Bioengineering Conference, EHB 2015 7391519 (2016)
23. Cho, K.-T., Kim, S.-M.: Selecting medical devices and materials for development in Korea: the analytic hierarchy process approach. Int. J. Health Plan. Manag. **18**(2), 161–174 (2003)
24. Meshram, S.G., Alvandi, E., Singh, V.P., Meshram, C.: Comparison of AHP and fuzzy AHP models for prioritization of watersheds. Soft. Comput. **23**(24), 13615–13625 (2019). https://doi.org/10.1007/s00500-019-03900-z
25. Chen, T.: Enhancing the efficiency and accuracy of existing FAHP decision-making methods. EURO J. Decis. Processes **8**(3–4), 177–204 (2020). https://doi.org/10.1007/s40070-020-00115-8
26. Zhang, J., Li, L., Zhang, J., et al.: Private-label sustainable supplier selection using a fuzzy entropy-VIKOR-based approach. Complex Intell. Syst. (2021)
27. Gupta, R., Kumar, S.: Intuitionistic fuzzy scale-invariant entropy with correlation coefficients-based VIKOR approach for multi-criteria decision-making. Granul. Comput. (2021). https://doi.org/10.1007/s41066-020-00252-08
28. Yang, W., Pang, Y., Shi, J., Wang, C.: Linguistic hesitant intuitionistic fuzzy decision-making method based on VIKOR. Neural Comput. Appl. **29**(7), 613–626 (2016). https://doi.org/10.1007/s00521-016-2526-y
29. Vonder, M., Dorrius, M.D., Vliegenthart, R.: Latest CT technologies in lung cancer screening: protocols and radiation dose reduction. Transl. Lung Cancer Res. **10**(2), 1154–1164 (2021). https://doi.org/10.21037/tlcr-20-808
30. Ortíz-Barrios, M.A., Escorcia-Caballero, J.P., Sánchez-Sánchez, F., De Felice, F., Petrillo, A.: Efficiency analysis of integrated public hospital networks in outpatient internal medicine. J. Med. Syst. **41**(10), 1–18 (2017). https://doi.org/10.1007/s10916-017-0812-6
31. Ortiz Barrios, M., Felizzola Jiménez, H.: Reduction of average lead time in outpatient service of obstetrics through six sigma methodology. In: Bravo, J., Hervás, R., Villarreal, V. (eds.) AmIHEALTH 2015. LNCS, vol. 9456, pp. 293–302. Springer, Cham (2015). https://doi.org/10.1007/978-3-319-26508-7_29
32. Ortiz-Barrios, M., Miranda-De la Hoz, C., López-Meza, P., Petrillo, A., De Felice, F.: A case of food supply chain management with AHP, DEMATEL, and TOPSIS. J. Multi-Criteria Decis. Anal. **27**(1–2), 104–128 (2020). https://doi.org/10.1002/mcda.1693
33. Ortiz-Barrios, M., Cabarcas-Reyes, J., Ishizaka, A., Barbati, M., Jaramillo-Rueda, N., de Jesús Carrascal-Zambrano, G.: A hybrid fuzzy multi-criteria decision making model for selecting a sustainable supplier of forklift filters: a case study from the mining industry. Ann. Oper. Res. (2020). https://doi.org/10.1007/s10479-020-03737-y

34. Ortíz-Barrios, M., Neira-Rodado, D., Jiménez-Delgado, G., Hernández-Palma, H.: Using FAHP-VIKOR for operation selection in the flexible job-shop scheduling problem: a case study in textile industry. In: Tan, Y., Shi, Y., Tang, Q. (eds.) ICSI 2018. LNCS, vol. 10942, pp. 189–201. Springer, Cham (2018). https://doi.org/10.1007/978-3-319-93818-9_18
35. Ortíz-Barrios, M., Nugent, C., García-Constantino, M., Jimenez-Delgado, G.: Identifying the most appropriate classifier for underpinning assistive technology adoption for people with dementia: an integration of Fuzzy AHP and VIKOR Methods. In: Duffy, V.G. (ed.) HCII 2020. LNCS, vol. 12199, pp. 406–419. Springer, Cham (2020). https://doi.org/10.1007/978-3-030-49907-5_29

Implementation of Lean Six Sigma to Lessen Waiting Times in Public Emergency Care Networks: A Case Study

Miguel Ortiz-Barrios[1]([✉]) [ID], Dayana Coba-Blanco[1] [ID], Genett Jiménez-Delgado[2] [ID], Valerio A. P. Salomon[3] [ID], and Pedro López-Meza[4]

[1] Department of Productivity and Innovation, Universidad de la Costa CUC, 080002 Barranquilla, Colombia
{mortiz1,dcoba3}@cuc.edu.co
[2] Department of Industrial Engineering, Institución Universitaria ITSA, Barranquilla, Colombia
gjimenez@itsa.edu.co
[3] Department of Production, Universidade Estadual Júlio de Mesquita Filho, Av. Ariberto P. Cunha 333, Guaratinguetá, SP 12516-410, Brazil
valerio.salomon@unesp.br
[4] Department of Maritime and Port Administration, Corporación Universitaria Reformada, Barranquilla, Colombia
p.lopez@unireformada.edu.co

Abstract. Emergency Care Networks (ECNs) are integrated healthcare systems comprised of emergency departments (EDs). ECNs are called to be the primary response of healthcare authorities to deal with the expected uptick in the future demands for emergency care during the current Covid-19 pandemic. Lean Six Sigma (LSS) has been proposed to address this challenge since it allows managers to detect factors contributing to the extended waiting times (WT) throughout the patient journey. The suggested framework follows the DMAIC cycle that was initiated with the project charter definition; in the meantime, a SIPOC diagram was drawn to analyze the emergency care process and pinpoint critical process variables. Following this, a nested Gage R&R study was undertaken to study the measurement system performance; subsequently, a normal-based capability analysis was carried out to determine how well the ECN process satisfies the specifications. The next step was to identify the potential causes separating the ECN nodes from the desired target. Afterwards, improvement strategies were devised to lessen the average WT. After suitable data collection, a before-and-after analysis was performed to verify the effectiveness of the implemented strategies. Ultimately, a control plan containing an I-MR control chart was designed to maintain the improvements achieved with the LSS implementation. The results revealed that the average WT of the showcased node passed from 190.02 min to 103.1 min whereas the long-term sigma level increased from -0.06 to 0.11. The proposed framework was validated through a case study including the involvement of a medium-sized hospital from the public sector.

Keywords: Emergency Care Networks (ECNs) · Healthcare · Lean Six Sigma (LSS) · Waiting times (WT) · Covid-19

© Springer Nature Switzerland AG 2021
C. Stephanidis et al. (Eds.): HCII 2021, LNCS 13097, pp. 83–93, 2021.
https://doi.org/10.1007/978-3-030-90966-6_7

1 Introduction

Healthcare, as an essential service and determinant of the quality of life, has become one of the main targets of public agendas at a global level, which demands an ever more significant investment of resources to guarantee coverage and service quality, especially in developing economies. This is evident through the average Gross Domestic Product (GDP) presented in countries like Colombia (7.2%) and Mexico (5.5%) based on the data provided by the Organization for Economic Co-operation and Development (OECD). On the other hand, the growing demand for patients as a result of the Covid-19 pandemic requires the implementation of interventions and the continuous quality improvement of healthcare processes to respond to the needs of timely diagnosis and treatment of patients. In this regard, the ECNs have been projected as an essential strategy to strengthen the provision of emergency care services while ensuring quality, opportunity, and efficiency in the use of resources [1]. The scientific literature has identified different advantages of emergency networks, such as the potential to improve the quality of care and underpin significant organizational changes in the health system [2].

However, ECNs face challenges not yet widely addressed at the research level, such as improvement in waiting times, which is more important in emergency services than in any other component of the health system [3]. Long waiting times generate blockages in access to patients, overcrowding, and user dissatisfaction, with a negative impact on the efficiency and service costs in the health system. These problems have motivated researchers to develop specific interventions towards providing a solution to address the future challenges of ECNs [4–6].

Lean Six-sigma (LSS) is proposed to bridge this gap as it is a methodology supporting the managerial decision-making process by identifying the waste factors or *muda* that affect the waiting times in ECNs. In addition, it identifies the relevant technical, economic, and administrative strategies that generate value for patients [7]. LSS methodology has evidenced a growing evolution in recent years with wide application in different healthcare units such as gynecology departments, clinical laboratories, and emergency departments. Also, different aims have been pursued like reducing the appointment lead-time, patient flow, and waiting times, but relatively few studies have focused on the reduction of WT in public ECNs. In a similar vein, more studies evidencing improvements, practical implications, and the development of LSS-oriented policies in the health sector are needed [3], especially in ECNs where this approach may also promote innovation, knowledge, and cooperation among the different ECN stakeholders [8–10]. This article then proposes the use of LSS methodology to reduce waiting times in public ECNs and provides a case study for laying the groundwork for implementation in the wild.

The remainder of this paper is organized as follows. Section 2 presents the literature review of LSS applications in healthcare and ECNs. Section 3 describes the proposed methodology whereas Sect. 4 presents the LSS application in a public ECN. Finally, conclusions and future works are presented in Sect. 5.

2 Literature Review

Lean Six Sigma is defined as an integration of Lean Manufacturing (LM) and Six Sigma methodologies oriented towards reducing losses, minimizing process variability that originates quality deviations, and generating value for the stakeholders [11]. LM focuses on the factors affecting the organizational system efficiency in terms of process flows, times, quality, and costs [12]. In the meantime, Six Sigma helps to foster continuous process improvement focused on reducing the variability that generates errors or defects through comprehending the root causes of variations and proposing improvement strategies [13]. The LSS provides healthcare managers with an evidence-based methodological framework for effective decision-making. Indeed, substantial growth in the number of LSS-based studies is evidenced in the scientific literature.

For a better understanding of the evidence base related to this topic, a more recent literature review (January 2009 – June 2021) was developed by scanning the search code "emergency care networks" AND "lean six sigma" in the Scopus database. After a detailed screening, only 13 articles published in indexed journals were identified, mainly in Medicine, Health Sciences, Computer Science, Engineering, and Multidisciplinary (refer to Fig. 1).

The first studies applying LSS in emergency departments focused on improving patient flow, waiting times, length of stay, and customer satisfaction [3, 14–17]. The results revealed the effects of the LSS programs on waiting times and the quality of care in emergency services. These interventions must be supported by a solid organizational culture while being potentiated by strong leadership and collaborative work.

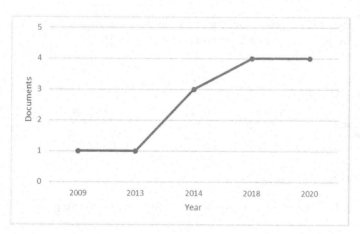

Fig. 1. Documents by year – LSS-studies focused on ECNs (source: Scopus).

Other studies have presented the applications of the Lean philosophy and the benefits of its combination with Six Sigma in the health sector, as well as the most influencing factors in the implementation of this methodology [18–21]. In this regard, it is necessary to highlight the leadership of healthcare managers and the work team training as critical factors for the successful implementation of LSS programs.

The most recent studies include the integration of Lean thinking with Six Sigma, Discrete Event Simulation, and the Design of Experiments in emergency departments [22] for reducing the patient's length of stay (LOS) and determining the optimal number of resources for the expansion of services in response to the growing demand of patients, with substantial improvements in the average LOS and the downtime of human resources. For the specific case of ECNs, the studies have focused on the design of in-time and economically sustainable ECNs using methodologies such as Lean Six Sigma, Discrete Event Simulation, and collateral payment models with good progress on reducing the average waiting time through the optimization of cooperation flows of emergency networks [6]. These works have also generated other challenges: the development of multicriteria models to support decision-making for evaluating and improving emergency departments and networks, optimizing resources, and propel collaborative environments [23, 24].

Considering the reported literature, the evidence from research aiming at improving waiting times for ECNs is scarce. More LSS applications are then required for designing ECNs adapted to the complexities and dynamics of the Covid-19 context characterized by increased demand, and the need for a high quality of care with optimal use of available resources. In this sense, the main contribution of this study is the application of LSS to lessen the WT experienced by patients in ECNs so that a practical methodological framework can be provided for ensuring the timely provision of the emergency care services during the Covid-19 outbreak.

3   Methodology

To reduce the waiting time experienced in the public emergency care network, the following five-phase methodology is proposed (See Fig. 2).

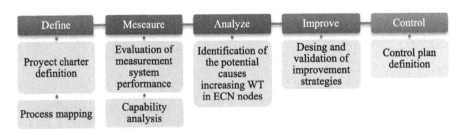

Fig. 2. Proposed methodology for reducing waiting times in the public ECN

To reduce the waiting time experienced by patients within an ECN node, we seek to eliminate the non-value-added activities along with the emergency care and transferring process. The level of intervention in each ED as well as the optimization of operating processes is of vital importance to this aim [6]. The methodological approach adopted in this manuscript considers the DMAIC cycle (Define, Measure, Analyze, Improve, and Control) which is integrated by the following components [25]:

Define: It begins with the definition of the objectives, scope, and timeline of the project as outlined in the project charter. This document also details the WT problem by providing the appropriate statistical measures. In addition, the ECN node processes are characterized by a SIPOC graphic.

Measure: The objective of this phase is to estimate the current state of the WT, determine the reliability of the data, and undertake the capability analysis to verify the compliance with the standard WT.

Analyze: The data collected from the emergency care process are analyzed to identify the main causes deviating the ECN node from the desired performance. This section seeks to reduce the WT gap between the real behavior versus the standard, by using industrial engineering tools such as the cause-and-effects analysis, Pareto diagram, Experimental design, 5WH, and LM.

Improve: In this step, improvement strategies are devised and implemented in the practical ECN scenario. The results obtained in the *"Measure"* step are compared with those achieved through the strategies to decide whether the WT gap has been reduced.

Control: Ultimately, the monitoring of enhanced WT improvements is supported by a control plan considering I-MR control charts.

4   Results

This section presents the step-by-step application of the LSS approach in a 2-level ECN node with an installed capacity of 11 beds available for emergency care. This hospital admits approximately 28120 patients per year and is part of a regional ECN in a low-and-middle-income country. Firstly, a six-sigma group integrated by six experts was established to underpin the LSS application. The team was led by two black belts with significant background in the implementation of LSS projects. After initial diagnosis, the mean WT was estimated to be 190.02 min with a standard deviation of 101.33 min which provides evidence of non-compliance with the target (30 min at most). The showcased ECN node then requires profound changes to lessen the WT and subsequently tackle the delayed diagnosis problem while minimizing the likelihood of developing more serious symptoms and using more complex healthcare services such as hospitalization, surgery, and intensive care.

Following this, a project charter was set taking into account the above context. In this respect, several profits for the stakeholders (i: increased quality of care; ii: diminished mortality rates, iii: reduction of operational costs, iv: increased patient satisfaction) and four performance indicators (process sigma level, defects per million of opportunities, mean waiting time, and operational cost per patient) were stated. Furthermore, the project goals were presented to the sponsor and ethical committee to obtain formal before kick-off. A SIPOC graph was then derived to elucidate the principal phases of the emergency care process during the Covid-19 outbreak and the interrelations with other units within the hospital (Fig. 3). With this application, diverse and complex pathways, as well as non-valued process steps throughout the Covid-19 patient journey, were further identified.

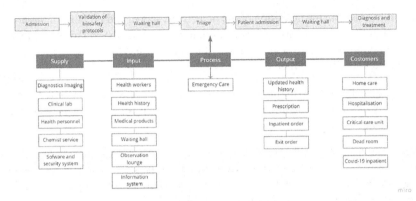

Fig. 3. SIPOC graphic for the emergency care process in the showcased node

This is consistent with the findings described in Nuñez-Pérez et al. [26] and Bones et al. [27] where the heterogeneity assumption of patient pathways is fully supported.

The most recent waiting times referring to the case study hospital (n = 28,120 patients) were collected using the Decision Support Software deployed by the Software unit. After suitable data cleaning, the six-sigma group implemented a normality test where an Anderson-Darling test provided sufficient evidence to accept the normality hypothesis of WT data on the selected (AD = 0.292; p-value = 0.606).

To verify how far the emergency care process is with respect to the desired WT, the six sigma group applied a normal-based capability analysis (Fig. 4). The exploratory analysis revealed a process with a Cpu of –0.52 which points out that the ECN node is not capable of satisfying the maximum accepted WT. Given the negative nature of CPu, big interventions are then needed to improve the hospital performance within the ECN operation. This is also evidenced through the short-term sigma level (-0.06) which, in the meantime, expresses that 941,482 in every 1,000,000 patients admitted in this hospital will have to wait for more than 30 min.

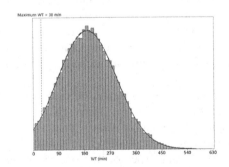

Fig. 4. Capability graph for the WT in the showcased hospital

Given the output obtained from the capability analysis, it is evident that serious intervention needs to be carefully crafted to address the WT problem. Therefore, it is necessary to investigate the causes behind the low performance to alleviate the burden faced by Covid-19 patients and hospitals in overcrowded wards and delayed emergency care provision. In this respect, a cause-and-effect analysis was emanated to map the problem tree associated with the particular WT context (Fig. 5). As such, the prospective causes were determined with the support of the Six-sigma group to provide clinicians and administrators with a solid framework for decision-making. As stated in the motivation of the study, the WT problem in ECNs has been poorly addressed and has the risk of increasing in the future. Analysis of Variance (ANOVA) (alpha level = 5%) tests were deployed for verifying these causes in the real scenario. For instance, the results provided good support to conclude that the turnaround time *for the delivery of diagnostic images to the ECN* node was estimated as statistically significant to the *increased WT experienced by Covid-19 patients* (*p-value* = 0.000). There is also proof of an important influence of the clinical lab delays upon the WT in the emergency department associated with the showcased hospital (*p-value* = 0.000).

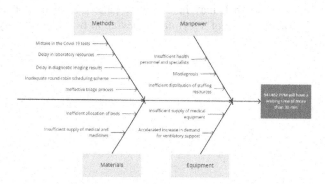

Fig. 5. Cause-and-effect analysis for the WT problem in the ECN node

Accordingly, the six-sigma group crafted improvement scenarios for minimizing the WT perceived in the ECN node. In summary, four scenarios were defined and implemented: i) Adoption of visual control techniques to better discriminate the ED specimens, ii) Reconfiguration of roles and responsibilities for phlebotomists, iii) Definition of the optimal batch sized considering the minimum specimen transportation time, and iv) Definition of an optimal scheduling policy minimizing the % of late imaging reports.

After a 2-month rolling out, the new WT was analyzed using Minitab 17® software to define whether the proposed strategies were effective to deal with the above-mentioned problem. The outcomes, described in Fig. 6, revealed that the Cpu is now −0.46 which denotes a slight improvement in the WT experienced by Covid-19 patients; indeed, 917,223 out of 1,000,000 patients (Reduction: 24,259 PPM) will have to wait for more than 30 min thereby evidencing the need for more effective strategies decreasing the WT at a more significant degree. These findings are validated by the long-term sigma level (0.11) which provided enough support for developing new DMAIC cycles increasing the ED response against the current outbreak.

Lately, it was necessary to establish a control plan sustaining the improvements achieved through the implementation of the 1st DMAIC cycle [28]. In this sense, the

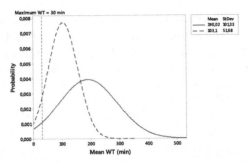

Fig. 6. The contrast between the initial WT performance and the new process status after improvement

first decision was to formally ingest these strategies within the ISO 9001 system of the ECN node followed by the design of an I-MR chart supporting the WT monitoring (Fig. 7). Thereby, the black belt may have a wide panorama of the emergency care process and react timely in case of a significant deviation from the recently enhanced WT performance.

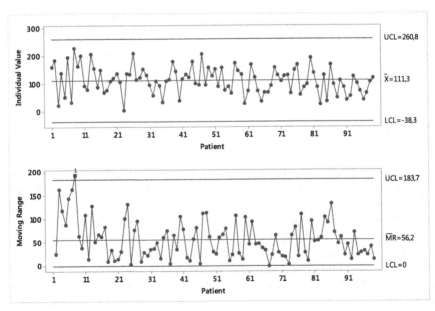

Fig. 7. I-MR control chart for monitoring the WT after project finalization

5   Conclusions and Future Work

This work proposes the implementation of Lean Six Sigma (LSS) to Emergency Care Networks (ECNs). Despite being a consolidated methodology, with several successful cases on industrial engineering and management, LSS was sparsely implemented in ECN, as presented in the literature review. This is the major contribution of this paper: to present that LSS concepts and tools may be very useful for other sectors, as healthcare management.

LSS was completely implemented in an ECN of a regional hospital from a low-and-middle-income country. This implementation followed the DMAIC cycle, with Design, Measure, Analyze, Improve, and Control results presented in Sect. 4. In the specific case study, the LSS application resulted in the reduction of 24,259 PPM while the mean WT passed from 190.02 min to 103.1 min which is the first step to the continuous improvement of this indicator during the current Covid-19 outbreak.

The main delimitation of this work is on the showcased hospital. Therefore, the first subject for future research is the application of LSS in extremes cases, as lowest-income and highest-income countries. Still, on this issue, multi-case studies on LSS applied to other centers of healthcare management, as long-term treatments. Finally, the adoption of other industrial management methodologies as Balanced Scorecard or Project Management to reduce waiting times in ECNs is another interesting source for new researches.

References

1. Mann's, B.J., Wasylak, T.: Clinical networks: enablers of health system change. CMAJ **191**(47), 299–305 (2019)
2. Brown, B.B., Patel, C., McInnes, E., et al.: The effectiveness of clinical networks in improving quality of care and patient outcomes: a systematic review of quantitative and qualitative studies. BMC Health Serv. Res. **16**, 360 (2016). https://doi.org/10.1186/s12913-016-1615-z
3. Al Owad, A., Karim, M.A., Ma, L.: Integrated lean six sigma approach for patient flow improvement in hospital emergency department. Adv. Mater. Res. **834–836**, 1893–1902 (2014). https://doi.org/10.4028/www.scientific.net/AMR.834-836.1893
4. Sklar, D.P., et al.: The future of emergency medicine: an evolutionary perspective. Acad. Med. **85**(3), 490–495 (2010)
5. Ortíz-Barrios, M., McClean, S., Jiménez-Delgado, G., Martínez-Sierra, D.E.: Integrating lean six sigma and discrete-event simulation for shortening the appointment lead-time in gynecobstetrics departments: a case study. In: Duffy, V.G. (ed.) HCII 2020. LNCS, vol. 12199, pp. 378–389. Springer, Cham (2020). https://doi.org/10.1007/978-3-030-49907-5_27
6. Ortiz-Barrios, M., Alfaro-Saiz, J.-J.: An integrated approach for designing in-time and economically sustainable emergency care networks: a case study in the public sector. PLoS ONE **15**(6), e0234984 (2020). https://doi.org/10.1371/journal.pone.0234984
7. Azevedo, J., et al.: Improvement of production line in the automotive industry through lean philosophy. Proc. Manuf. **41**, 1023–1030 (2019). https://doi.org/10.1016/j.promfg.2019.10.029
8. Abu-Laban, R.B., Drebit, S., Svendson, B., Chan, N., Ho, K., Khazei, A., et al.: Process and findings informing the development of a provincial emergency medicine network. Healthc. Manag. Forum **32**(5), 253–258 (2019)
9. Christenson, J.: A network to improve emergency patient care by facilitating practitioners to effectively support practitioners. Healthc. Manag. Forum **27**(3), 132–135 (2014)
10. Ahmed, A., Page, J., Olsen, J.: Enhancing Six Sigma methodology using simulation techniques: literature review and implications for future research. Int. J. Lean Six Sigma **11**(1), 211–232 (2019)

11. DeFeo, J., Moret, D.: Lean Six Sigma, Lean & Six Sigma: A Definitive Guide. Juran Institute (2019). https://www.juran.com/blog/guide-to-lean-and-lean-six-sigma/

12. Jimenez, G., et al.: Improvement of productivity and quality in the value chain through lean manufacturing – a case study. Proc. Manuf. **41**, 882–889 (2019)

13. Kuo, A.M.-H., et al.: A healthcare lean Six sigma system for postanesthesia care unit workflow improvement. Qual. Manag. Healthc. **20**(1), 4–14 (2011)

14. Dickson, E.W., Anguelov, Z., Vetterick, D., Eller, A., Singh, S.: Use of lean in the emergency department: a case series of 4 hospitals. Ann. Emerg. Med. **54**(4), 504–510 (2009). https://doi.org/10.1016/j.annemergmed.2009.03.024

15. Johnson, P.M., Patterson, C.J., O'Connell, M.P.: Lean methodology: an evidence-based practice approach for healthcare improvement. Nurse Pract. **38**(12), 1–7 (2013). https://doi.org/10.1097/01.NPR.0000437576.14143.b9

16. Vermeulen, M.J., et al.: Evaluation of an emergency department lean process improvement program to reduce length of stay. Ann. Emerg. Med. **64**(5), 427–438 (2014). https://doi.org/10.1016/j.annemergmed.2014.06.007

17. Richardson, D.M., et al.: Using lean methodology to decrease wasted RN time in seeking supplies in emergency departments. J. Nurs. Adm. **44**(11), 606–611 (2014). https://doi.org/10.1097/NNA.0000000000000133

18. Improta, G., Cesarelli, M., Montuori, P., Santillo, L.C., Triassi, M.: Reducing the risk of healthcare-associated infections through lean six Sigma: the case of the medicine areas at the Federico II university hospital in Naples (Italy). J. Eval. Clin. Pract. **24**(2), 338–346 (2018). https://doi.org/10.1111/jep.12844

19. Terra, J.D.R., Berssaneti, F.T.: Application of lean healthcare in hospital services: a review of the literature (2007 to 2017). Production **28** (2018). https://doi.org/10.1590/0103-6513.20180009

20. Suman, G., Prajapati, D.R.: Statistical analysis of the researches carried out on lean and six sigma applications in healthcare industry. Int. J. Qual. Eng. Technol. **7**(1), 1–38 (2018). https://doi.org/10.1504/IJQET.2018.094667

21. Patri, R., Suresh, M.: Factors influencing lean implementation in healthcare organizations: an ISM approach. Int. J. Healthc. Manag. **11**(1), 25–37 (2018). https://doi.org/10.1080/20479700.2017.1300380

22. Gabriel, G.T., et al.: Lean thinking by integrating with discrete event simulation and design of experiments: an emergency department expansion. PeerJ Comput. Sci. **6** (2020). https://doi.org/10.7717/PEERJ-CS.284

23. Pegoraro, F., Alves Portela Santos, E., de Freitas Rocha Loures, E.: A support framework for decision making in emergency department management. Comput. Ind. Eng. **146** (2020). https://doi.org/10.1016/j.cie.2020.106477

24. Ortiz-Barrios, M., Alfaro-Saiz, J.: A hybrid fuzzy multicriteria decision-making model to evaluate the overall performance of public emergency departments: a case study. Int. J. Inf. Technol. Decis. Mak. **19**(6), 1485–1548 (2020). https://doi.org/10.1142/S0219622020500364

25. Scala, A., et al.: Lean six sigma approach for reducing length of hospital stay for patients with femur fracture in a university hospital. Int. J. Environ. Res. Public Health **18**(6), 1–13 (2021). https://doi.org/10.3390/ijerph18062843

26. Nuñez-Perez, N., Ortíz-Barrios, M., McClean, S., Salas-Navarro, K., Jimenez-Delgado, G., Castillo-Zea, A.: Discrete-event simulation to reduce waiting time in accident and emergency departments: a case study in a district general clinic. In: Ochoa, S.F., Singh, P., Bravo, J. (eds.) UCAmI 2017. LNCS, vol. 10586, pp. 352–363. Springer, Cham (2017). https://doi.org/10.1007/978-3-319-67585-5_37

27. Jones, B., McClean, S., Stanford, D.: Modelling mortality and discharge of hospitalized stroke patients using a phase-type recovery model. Health Care Manag. Sci. **22**(4), 570–588 (2018). https://doi.org/10.1007/s10729-018-9446-6

28. Ortiz Barrios, M., Felizzola Jiménez, H.: Reduction of average lead time in outpatient service of obstetrics through six sigma methodology. In: Bravo, J., Hervás, R., Villarreal, V. (eds.) AmIHEALTH 2015. LNCS, vol. 9456, pp. 293–302. Springer, Cham (2015). https://doi.org/10.1007/978-3-319-26508-7_29

Design Opportunities of Digital Tools for Promoting Healthy Eating Routines Among Dutch Office Workers

Sibo Pan[1], Xipei Ren[2(✉)], Steven Vos[1,3], and Aarnout Brombacher[1]

[1] Eindhoven University of Technology, Eindhoven, The Netherlands
[2] Beijing Institute of Technology, Beijing, China
x.ren@bit.edu.cn
[3] Fontys University of Applied Science, Eindhoven, The Netherlands

Abstract. Eating healthier at work can substantially promote health and well-being among knowledge workers. However, little has been investigated on designing digital tools and interventions specialized in improving workday eating routines. This paper presents a user-centered contextual inquiry based on mixed-methods with an online questionnaire and a semi-structured interview. This study aimed to understand knowledge workers' eating experiences and identify design opportunities and application strategies of digital tools to improve current practices. The questionnaire feedback from 54 Dutch knowledge workers revealed that their concerns over productivity, health and nutrition, energy support, and well-being could be decisive in shaping their eating routines at work. Furthermore, the results of 12 interview sessions suggested a set of expected digital features to encourage healthy eating at work, including health knowledge access, goal setting and self-tracking, technology-assisted health programs, and social support. Additionally, our findings also indicated that these digital features should be integrated into the office setting to offer personalized feedback and contextualized health interventions. Based on these findings, we derive design opportunities for workplace digital tools to promote healthy eating and discuss their potential contributions and future work to improved office vitality.

Keywords: Healthy eating · Office vitality · Digital health · Contextual inquiry · User-centered design

1 Introduction

According to World Health Organization, an unhealthy eating is among the major risk factors for a range of chronic diseases, including cardiovascular diseases, cancer, diabetes, and suboptimal conditions linked to obesity [1]. Healthy eating habits can be influenced by many different aspects of life, such as the socioeconomic status, the accessibility of healthy foods, the self-efficacy for healthy eating, and the daily work [2, 3]. Particularly, eating healthy at work can substantially improve individuals' physiological and mental well-being. Office environments and work routines offer good settings to

© Springer Nature Switzerland AG 2021
C. Stephanidis et al. (Eds.): HCII 2021, LNCS 13097, pp. 94–110, 2021.
https://doi.org/10.1007/978-3-030-90966-6_8

apply healthy eating interventions [2]. Increasingly, public health researchers investigated opportunities for promoting healthy eating routines among knowledge workers using e.g., tailored health program [4], social supports [5], worksite changes [6], and digital technologies [7].

Many newly developed digital technologies can track eating behaviors and provide health interventions using ubiquitous digital tools such as sensors and mobile apps. For instance, Fitocracy Macros [8] tracks macronutrients in the diet and helps users achieve healthy eating goals. Similarly, MyFitnessPal [9] allows users to track nutritional values of diets through scanning the barcode of selected foods and searching the database. In addition, several monitoring devices focus on enabling the automated tracking of eating-related activities, such as upper body and arm motion during intake [10], chewing [11], and swallowing [12]. Besides, some digital health applications support recording photos of the food to estimate the nutrients components [13, 14]. However, when applying those digital tools to the workday routine of an office-based employee it can be very challenging to generate desired outcomes for the health promotion [15]. For instance, besides the technical advantages, knowledge workers may find the wearable sensors are too obtrusive to long-term use [16]. Also, the workers may abandon the self-tracking and management app, which require too much effort to keep using in work routines [17].

To promote healthy eating among office workers, there is an urgent need to understand this specific context's challenges and opportunities to design and develop dedicated digital tools. In this paper, therefore, we take a user-centered and context-specific view [18, 19] to qualitatively understand the context and explore the user requirements for enlightening the office diet digital tools' future design. We carried out this project in the Netherlands, where the majority of full-time knowledge workers work for eight-hour per day and five days per week and have at the minimum one meal in the office during the day [20]. This situation makes the workplace an essential setting for the intervention design to promote healthy eating.

2 Related Work

2.1 Interventions to Promote Healthy Eating at Work

Many interventions have been introduced into office settings and their effectiveness on promoting healthy eating has been widely evaluated. For instance, Campbell and colleagues [4] tailored a health program for female workers and examined the effects of such interventions. Park et al. [5] researched cultural and social supports for food choice and eating patterns of South Korean employees. A systematic review by Engbers et al. assessed the effectiveness of worksite health promotion programs on physical activity and eating with environmental modifications to indicate health risks to office-based employees [6].

There have been a variety of dietary interventions investigated to promote healthy eating among office workers. Some research has focused on encouraging fruit and vegetable intake at work [21]. For example, the '6-a-day' worksite study in Denmark [22] implemented changes over eight months among staffs from five workplaces, focusing on improving the taste and the preparation of fruit and vegetables. Additionally, some projects have explored the relationship between food prices and dietary improvements.

For instance, research evidence has shown that reducing the price of healthy food and offering more healthy foods can increase the consumption of these foods [21, 23]. Several other studies have focused on providing tailored interventions to promote the healthy eating change for individual workers, such as using the customized health-promoting emails [24].

2.2 Digital Health Technologies for Healthy Eating Routines

The rapid advance of digital technologies offers many advantages to promote healthy eating routines. Data collected from health tracking applications can be used to support self-reflection on eating behaviors and improve self-awareness of eating decisions [25, 26]. There have been various digital health tools developed to improve the daily eating practices. For instance, Eat & Tell [27] is a mobile application designed to facilitate the collection of eating-related data through automated tracking and self-report. Fitocracy Macros [8] tracks macronutrients and helps users achieve fitness goals. MyFitnessPal [9] supports the user to acquire the nutritional values of the chosen foods (e.g.,) by extracting the information based on the barcode from the food packages.

Some ubiquitous sensors and wearable devices have also been increasingly developed to create new opportunities for monitoring data related to eating behaviors. For example, some studies [28–32] utilize the ear-pad sound sensors to capture the food breakdown in the chewing cycles as the sound data, which is then distilled through the particular pattern recognition algorithms to distinguish different types of food. Moreover, Bi et al. [33] developed a wearable system based various sensors, consisted of an electromyograph, a video fluoroscopy, and a stethoscope microphone, to monitor food intake behaviors automatically through analyzing the sound. Similarly, the interruption of breathing has been collected by a wireless chest-belt for detecting the short apneas due to the food intake process [34]. Additionally, many previous studies analyze eating-related images to capture nutrients elements [14] and eating activities [35–38].

2.3 User-Centered Approaches to Understand Contextual Factors

Eating activities, particularly in public settings, can be influenced by the socio-cultural contexts significantly. According to Hofstede [39], people with different cultural backgrounds may hold different values on six dimensions, including *individualism, masculinity, long-term orientation, power distance, uncertainty avoidance,* and *indulgence.* Such varied cultural values could determine people's eating patterns to some extent. For instance, in highly individualistic countries (e.g., the Netherlands), people do not mind to eat at different time slots [40]. Whereas people in collectivistic countries (e.g., China) tend to eat together in the social context [41].

However, health interventions and digital technologies are commonly designed for general usage without a deep understanding of the socio-cultural contexts, which might limit their effectiveness. Particularly, it comes as a surprise that little research has been done to identify design opportunities of digital tools for promoting healthy eating routines dedicated to the context of the office work. In this study, we take a user-centered and context-specific view [18, 19] to qualitatively understand the context and explore the user requirements of office diet digital tools for enlightening the future design of digital health.

We set out this project in the societal context of the Netherlands to mainly understand how Dutch workers eat at the office work and what digital health technologies are expected to improve their eating routines.

3 Methods

We set out a user-centered contextual inquiry involving an online questionnaire based on the format of sentence completion [42] and a semi-structured interview [43]. The Ethical Review Board approved this project at Eindhoven University of Technology, the Institutional Review Board of Partners Healthcare: reference ERB2020ID8. Before each type of study, participants were reminded about the study's goals and that all information would be kept confidential and in a secure location. Participation in both the questionnaire and the interview studies was fully voluntary, and the participants did not receive any incentive.

3.1 Study Design

The Sentence-Completion Questionnaire. The questionnaire study's goal was to understand the context and gather some assumptions for the semi-structured interview. This study was advertised and spread via social media posts (e.g., on Facebook, Twitter), emails, and word of mouth to recruit respondents. People who (1) engaged in office-based knowledge work for more than 6 h per day, (2) had been working in the Netherlands for more than six months, and (3) without a special diet were included. The study candidates who matched our inclusion criteria were presented with a consent description of the questionnaire and agreement to participate in the study to start the survey. Afterward, they would start to fill in the sentence completion tasks one by one for each category. In the end, questions were asked related to demographics, e.g., age, gender, level of education, and occupation.

The questionnaire study was aided with sentence completion [42] tasks to encourage office workers to disclose their concealed experiences and opinions. As a semi-structured projective technique, the sentence completion task is designed with unfinished sentences. As such, the respondent has the freedom to interpret and complete the sentence based on their wish [42]. The sentence completion technique has been widely applied in HCI and design studies and proved effective in assessing user experiences, behavioral motives, and expectations towards new technology [44]. In our questionnaire, all the sentence completion tasks were designed based on the first-person perspective [45]. E.g., *"In my workdays, I normally have lunch at _____."* By doing so, we aim at supporting the respondents to think along with our questions and engage in reflecting on their daily practices related to eating and using technologies in their office work. To consolidate our questionnaire, we circulated a draft to two external researchers to review items and suggest improvements for wordings. In this study, the questionnaire was implemented using SurveyMonkey. All the questionnaire responses were anonymized and exported from the SurveyMonkey platform as an Excel sheet that was only accessible by the research team for data analysis.

The Semi-Structured Interview. The interview study was set out to identify design opportunities of digital tools that can enhance office-based employees' eating routines and find out strategies to apply digital health into the workday eating routines in the societal context of the Netherlands. We recruited participants by spreading information via word of mouth, taking a snowball sampling approach. Initially, we asked people we knew who had similar characteristics to our target subjects. We then asked them to pass the information to their social contacts. During recruiting, we screened study candidates based on identical inclusion criteria as the questionnaire study. Prior to the study, we explained the study's procedure and purpose to participants in detail and obtained the consent upon their voluntary participation. They were also given the opportunity to withdraw at any point in the study.

All the interviews were semi-structured [43] with a set of open-ended questions. The benefits of adopting semi-structured interviews are engaging participants in sharing their opinions based on the interview guidance to obtain in-depth and reliable insights into research questions [46]. This interview protocol was drafted by the first authors and reviewed and discussed by all the co-authors. All interview sessions were conducted by the first author. Each session was organized in two parts: We began by inquiring about their recent experiences with office eating routines. E.g., *"How do you like your eating routine during workdays?" "Have you and your organization done anything to improve your office eating routine? And why?"* and *"What would you expect in the future to aid the eating aspect of your workdays?"* We then discussed opportunities to design digital tools for enhancing their office eating routines with two open-ended questions: *"How do you think to use digital technologies to improve eating routines at work?"* and *"What food-related features do you expect in the future technology?"* During the interview, we left enough space for participants to elaborate on their opinions freely. Besides, we asked them to explain some interesting statements that emerged from the discussion. The interview took around 18- to 39-min per session and was audio-recorded and transcribed later for qualitative analysis.

3.2 Qualitative Data Analysis

The questionnaire and interview data were analyzed respectively by thematic analysis following deductive coding [47]. Specifically, our data analysis was proceeded as following: To begin with, one researcher (the first author) divided the responses of the questionnaire and interview transcripts into labeled statements through repeated reading. Next, the researcher measured the labeled statements using affinity diagrams [48] to identify recurring clusters and emergent themes. According to the member check approach [49, 50], all the identified themes and clusters were reviewed, discussed, and revised through several iterations with all the members from the research team (all the co-authors) to validate the qualitative analysis.

4 Results

4.1 Participants' Description

The questionnaire study was conducted over a period of one month. A total of 86 responses were received, and 32 were excluded due to incomplete demographics information. Therefore, data from the 54 respondents (gender: 36 females and 18 males, age: M = 32.95, SD = 9.84) were eventually used for analysis. The characteristics of the respondents are summarized in Table 1.

Table 1. The demographics of the questionnaire respondents (N = 54).

Characteristics	Category	N	Percentage
Age	18 to 29	32	59.26%
	29 to 59	21	38.89%
	60 +	1	1.85%
Gender	Male	18	33.33%
	Female	36	66.67%
Working years	0 to 5 years	35	64.81%
	5 to 20 years	11	20.37%
	20+ years	8	14.81%
Education	Secondary level	2	3.70%
	Bachelor	15	27.78%
	Master and above	37	68.52%

For the interview study, 17 knowledge workers from various office-based jobs were recruited to participate. Eventually, five participants dropped out due to unexpected changes in their agenda that conflicted with the interview holding time. Therefore, we report results from interviews with the remaining 12 participants (gender: 10 females and 2 males, age: M = 39, SD = 11.52). The characteristics of the interview participants are summarized in Table 2. We labeled them as P1 to P12.

Table 2. The demographics of the interviewees (N = 12).

ID	Sex	Age	Education level	Working years	Working hours/day	Type of occupation
P1	F	26	MBO 1	0.5	8	Secretary
P2	F	53	HBO 2	35	8	Secretary
P3	F	44	HBO 2	20	8	Secretary

(continued)

Table 2. (*continued*)

ID	Sex	Age	Education level	Working years	Working hours/day	Type of occupation
P4	F	26	Bachelor	3	8	Secretary
P5	M	27	Master	2	8	Junior researcher
P6	F	30	PhD	8	8	researcher
P7	M	52	HBO 2	30	8	Administrator
P8	F	54	HBO 2	32	8	Office Worker
P9	F	25	Master	1	8	Administrator
P10	F	40	HBO 2	22	8	Secretary
P11	F	46	HBO 2	26	8	Administrator
P12	F	45	HBO 2	15	7	Human resource

1 MBO: vocational training; 2 HBO: bachelor's degree in applied science.

4.2 Workers' Considerations that Lead to Current Eating Routines

In general, most participants (43 out of 54) chose to have their lunch around 12:00 in noon with occasional snacking as beneficial micro-breaks [51] in the work routine. This situation is in line with the recommendations of lunch and snack breaks, according to Gronow and Jääskeläinen [52]. For the majority of office-based jobs in the Netherlands, it is common to embed an unpaid time slot into the work schedule as a lunch break [53]. It has also been suggested that having snacks regularly can replenish needed energy and nutrition in the work routine [54]. Additionally, we received a variety of reasons behind the patterns of their workday eating routines, which can be classified into the following aspects, including productivity, health, energy support, and wellbeing (Table 3).

Well-Being. Many respondents (n = 45) valued eating-related activities in the working context as meaningful to physical, social, and mental well-being. For instance, they believed that social interactions during lunch could bring various benefits, such as "*relief from work*", "*exchange ideas on the project*", "*improve collaboration and social relationships*", and "*improve the joyfulness*". Moreover, sharing food with colleagues was also deemed beneficial to promote social dynamics.

Productivity. 28 respondents expressed their concerns over maintaining productivity in eating routines with the following decisions: short-time lunch at the workstation (n = 28), eating alone (n = 13), choosing light and convenient food (n = 23). Their reasons behind these eating patterns were, e.g., "*saving time for work*", "*keeping the mind clear in the afternoon*", "*to become fitter and healthier*".

Health. 24 participants indicated their needs for high-quality food and health-promoting activities during the lunch breaks, such as having lunch with balanced nutrition and eating outside of the workplace for a physical and mental break. Moreover, 19 respondents believed that eating fruits as office snacks could be an effective way to improve their

Table 3. Considerations that lead to current eating routines among Dutch office workers.

Consideration	Defined example
Wellbeing (n = 45)	*"My colleagues and I like to share our snacks with each other. The most important thing [from sharing the snack] is that it brings us a casual ambiance in the work routine and regular social-based breaks."* *"I have fixed time slots to eat some snacks in the office. These short breaks are relieving."* *"When I eat, I also prefer walking for a while to refresh my mind and body."*
Productivity (n = 28)	*"I don't like to spend much time for lunch because I have a tight schedule. And it's very convenient to take lunch at my desk."* *"Eating in my office doesn't influence my work that much, so it is my first choice."* *"I often buy fast/easy food in advance or buy some in the supermarket nearby. Then I don't need to pay attention about what I need to eat and save my time to keep working."*
Health (n = 24)	*"I think it is healthy to leave my workspace and have a physical break at lunch."* *"Because I like to have lunch with co-workers, so we keep a certain schedule when to eat and this is good for health"* *"We discuss food and share our cooks, which is enjoyable and let us be more aware of our diet and health."* *"I try to eat more healthy food, such as nuts, yogurt and fruits (like apple/banana). I don't want to let the eating part in my work unhealthy."*
Energy support (n = 11)	*"During working time, I eat more chocolate and cookie a lot. I can eat more when my colleague share some to me."* *"When I skip my lunch, I prefer to eat some chocolate or candy to support energy to my body in a fast way."*

health conditions. Several participants (n = 6) also considered a small portion of nuts as healthful.

Energy Support. 11 respondents indicated food intake behaviors in the work routine were essential as an energy supplement of their workdays, particularly some energy-boosting snacks (e.g., chocolate, cookie, candy, muffin.). A few (n = 3) further stressed the necessity of having energy drinks (e.g., coffee) to keep up their work performance.

4.3 Expected Features of Digital Tools for Promoting Healthy Eating

After the qualitative analysis of the interview study, 259 selected quotes were used, which can be categorized under four main themes (see Table 4) as technological features of digital tools for promoting healthy eating at office work, including *support accessing relevant knowledge, enable planning and goal setting, combine with health programs,* and *facilitate social supports.*

Table 4. Aspired features of digital tools to improve eating routines.

Feature	Defined example
Support accessing relevant knowledge	*"I used to learn a lot of health knowledge in my job as a sport coach. So, I know what healthy foods are."* (P2) *"I learn nutrient knowledge online. As my knowledge grow, I will try to improve my eating practices."* (P4) *"Some online scientific videos help me know why I must to eat healthy. I also want to know more information about healthy food and eating."* (P12) *"Years ago, I wanted to lose some weight, so I got some useful knowledge about healthy eating. Now, I try again to eat healthy, but I cannot find the information anymore."* (P6)
Enable planning and goal setting	*"Setting health goal is useful. I will be motivated for a long period."* (P7) *"I have an eating schedule on my computer screen. I can see what I eat for each day of the next week, I change the modify the schedule at the end of each week like playing a puzzle game."* (P12) *"I prefer to take notes on my phone about what I want to cook for the next week. It can help me prepare my grocery shopping lists."* (P5) *"I hope some technologies can help me decide what foods to eat. For example, it can recommend me the type of lunch and snacks and calculate calories accordingly."* (P2)
Combine with health programs	*"Swimming helps me to be more aware of keeping my eating routine healthy and regular."* (P5) *"I do physical exercises once or twice per week. This helps me pay attention to take healthier and more balanced food."* (P1) *"I try to not waste any opportunity to have a mini break during my working hours and eat something during such a mini-break is relaxing."* (P12) *"I know doing more physical activity is good, but I don't know how to arrange it with my busy agenda other than reminding myself to walk for a while after my lunch."* (P9)

(*continued*)

Table 4. (*continued*)

Feature	Defined example
Facilitate social supports	*"I like eating lunch with others. When I eat alone, I normally eat very fast, which I know is not so healthy. But chatting with others help me eat slowly."* (P5) *"I feel good when my colleagues see my lunch delicious, and we often share cooking experiences during lunch."* (P4) *"I like eating lunch together so that we can chat and share interesting information."* (P2) *"My colleague and I like sharing food with each other. This gives us a short time for chat and have a rest."* (P2) *"My colleague sitting next to me likes to share snacks with me, and this made our eating time and routine identical. The good result is I became more aware of eating fruits."* (P4) *"When any colleague celebrates a birthday, we are so happy to have some cakes and snacks together."* (P3) *"I am very encouraged to see some Instagramers sharing their healthy eating experiences frequently."* (P4)

Support Accessing Relevant Knowledge. During the interviews, most participants expressed their interests in obtaining knowledge for improving healthy eating behaviors. Spontaneously, some of them tried to find relevant information from the third party in order to enrich their 'knowledge base'. For instance, P4 used to read informative articles of some nutritionists she followed on Facebook; P9 subscribed magazine called Health to gain information about diet advice; P12 watched scientific videos about healthy eating via an online platform called Game changer; P2 was a P.E. teacher in a university, she could use university's online library to learn more about the relationship between healthy eating and physical vitality. They believed that the increase in eating-related knowledge served as a motivational factor that contributes to fostering their healthy eating behavior and attitude change. Therefore, they expected tools such as a digital platform that would help them learn the desired knowledge systematically. In this study, our participants stated several aspects of knowledge that could be meaningful to improve the workday eating routine, including the influences of (un)healthy eating and the recommendations for healthy ingredients of office food.

Enable Planning and Goal Setting. We found that some participants created eating goals as a strategy to, e.g., prevent potential chronic disorders, improve well-being, lose weight. In general, these goals were described in two kinds: 1) to eat more regularly to support a healthy daily routine; 2) to eat with more balanced nutrition for a healthier lifestyle. To aid these kinds of goal-settings, some participants expected digital tools similar to activity tracking applications (e.g., Fitbit), which could easily allow the user to set healthy eating goals. They also preferred this system to provide some suggestions for supporting the user to reach health-promoting goals. For instance, from this study, we learned that some interviewees (P1, P3, P5, P12) wanted an app to generate a grocery shopping list and recipes according to their goals and personal eating habits.

Combine with Health Programs. We learned that almost all interviewees easily connected their healthy eating practices with other health promotion means, such as physical activity. Examples include running (P3, P8, P10, P11), yoga (P2, P4, P6, P8), swimming (P5, P7), boxing (P1), cycling (P7). They pointed out that the underlying reason was that a good eating routine alone might not be enough to improve their health conditions. It would be beneficial to maintain healthy eating while increasing physical exercises in the daily routine. Additionally, some participants literally combined eating with some relaxation breaks to add micro health benefits to their work routine. Nevertheless, our interviewees found it is challenging to keep up their engagement in multiple health-promoting activities, especially during a hectic workday. To address this problem, one suggestion received during our interviews was to facilitate a structured health program consisted of multiple activity plans (e.g., healthy eating, relaxation, physical activity) to guide the office workers to improve their health step by step. Furthermore, some participants recognized digital technologies, such as virtual coaches, reminders, or rewarding mechanisms, could be applied to encourage office workers to adhere to these kinds of health programs.

Facilitate Social Supports. According to the interview results, social interactions with colleagues can play a crucial role in supporting healthy eating routines among Dutch office workers. Most interviewees (P1 – 2, P4 – 5, P7, P9 – 12) suggested the dual benefits of committing to eating-related social activities. On the one hand, they indicated that eating together with, e.g., colleagues could strengthen social bonding and enhance mental well-being during work. On the other hand, having lunch together or sharing foods with each other was also deemed as an effective way to increase the self-awareness of eating healthy. For example, P5 recalled that he sometimes compared his eating behaviors with coworkers' during lunch and tried to make some improvements afterward, such as slowing down his chewing speed. Moreover, some workers (P2, P4, P8, P9) described their experiences that sharing snacks (e.g., cakes, fruits.) frequently with colleagues made them more conscious about their office's healthiness snacks. Although the workday eating routines were loosely connected to those social activities, our participants expected the digital tools could further leverage social mechanisms to augment such peer supports. For example, P4 suggested developing an online health-promoting community within her department so that they could share their experiences and achievements as well as help each other. P12 described an intelligent system that could help colleagues with similar eating-related health goals create a mutual support team to enhance goal commitment.

4.4   Strategies to Apply Digital Tools into Workday Eating Routines

Our interview participants indicated that both technology and eating routines in the office could be largely affected by various contextual determinants, such as the workflow and the office environment. All the participants believed that the digital tools' technological features should be adapted according to the everyday context to improve the office eating routines. Their feedbacks were selected as 116 quotes and analyzed into two major aspects (see Table 5), namely: *Integrate health-promoting digital applications into the office context* and *Provide system feedback according to individual differences.*

Table 5. Recommended strategies to apply digital tools into workday eating routines.

Strategy	Defined example
Integrate health-promoting digital applications into the office context	*"I can track my eating behaviors. But I am not motivated to do so when I am working, because I can easily forget to put information into the technology."* (P1) *"People may not commonly be motivated to change their eating habits, as we don't see the benefits for office people."* (P4) *"I like following schedules without extra effort. When I am busy with work, I don't have time to think about my eating routine and health. If the technology can combine eating activities with my agenda, I think I will be more likely following it."* (P7) *"I don't have time to remember when I need to log my eating information. I hope the eating behaviors and food content could be tracked in some easy ways."* (P11)
Provide system feedback according to individual differences	*"If future technology can learn my routine and situation in a positive manner, maybe I will try to follow its advice."* (P2) *"When I eat some unhealthy food, I hope the technology can give me some very constructive tips to combat my unhealthy behaviors."* (P1) *"I hope the food-tracking app could learn my preference over time and could be changed based on my different needs in different periods."* (P4)

Integrate Health-Promoting Digital Applications into the Office Context. From the interview, many participants expressed their concerns about overusing any digital tools to improve eating patterns because the use of nonworking-related technologies may increase their task load and distract their daily work. Some participants suggested that health-promoting technologies should be designed and implemented in combination with both the digital and physical infrastructure in the workplace. On the one hand, the majority of our participants indicated that some health-related features provided by the mobile applications could be expanded further into different workplace software platforms. One suggestion received was embedding breaks with suggested foods into workers' outlook calendar to prompt and encourage healthy eating activities. On the other hand, participants expected improving eating routines at work as a simple behavior change without requiring too much effort. Therefore, they looked forward to more pervasive systems in the workplace that could be integrated into the office facilities, e.g., food trays in the company canteen, snack machine at the coffee corner. As such, they hoped the system could collect, analyze and give feedback on workers' eating-related practices unobtrusively without violating the privacy concern.

Provide System Feedback According to Individual Differences. From this interview study, we learned that one general reason behind the low acceptance of digital tools for healthy eating was the lack of valuable suggestions and guidance based on divergent individual characteristics. To increase digital technology adoption for office eating routines, firstly, many participants wanted a more personalized service system. For instance, they expected the digital system to behave like a personal health specialist that could learn individual's daily routine over time and provide customized suggestions according to his or her health- and work-related status. Secondly, several participants said that they did not want to be bonded up with a digital tool for healthy eating entirely during the workday. Therefore, they suggested that the system should allow them to easily subscribe/unsubscribe different functions due to their subjective opinions or working conditions.

5 Discussion, Conclusions, Future Work

Healthy eating can contribute to the overall health and vitality of office-based knowledge workers [55]. The rapid advance of digital health technologies can play a crucial role in improving the workday eating routines. In the office context, knowledge workers can be very busy with their tasks at hand throughout the day and should keep their performance following the implicit and explicit workplace rules [56]. Obviously, these office-related factors can potentially create barriers for utilizing digital health technologies in general and adhering to the health interventions during the daily work. This study was conducted as the user-centered contextual inquiry, based on the sentence-completion survey and semi-structured interviews, to identify design opportunities of digital tools to promote healthy eating routines in the Dutch office context. The survey results indicated that the formation of workday eating routines could be mainly attributed to workers' considerations in well-being, productivity, health, and energy support. Moreover, the promotion of healthy eating at work could be facilitated by several strategies, such as the easy access to relevant knowledge, eating goal and planning support, the integrated workplace health programs, and social supports between coworkers. These findings emphasize the opportunities of embodying contextual elements to encourage healthy eating routines, which are in line with a number of previous studies. For instance, a literature review by Nestle and colleagues [57] indicated that gaining nutrition knowledge could motivate users to choose a healthier diet based on various food products. Hargreaves et al. [58] conducted a focus-group study and found that well-planned eating can improve the quality of individuals' diet and the healthfulness of dietary habits. A review study about social influence on eating by Higgs and Thomas [59] revealed that appropriate healthy eating actions are impacted by the comparison with other eating partners' behaviors. As described in the previous section, based on our findings, we gained some valuable insights into technology features and application strategies of digital health to aid the workday eating routines for our target users.

The findings of this study may need to be cautiously interpreted due to the following limitations. Firstly, the study was conducted with a small number of people (54 participants in the online survey and 12 participants in the interview study), which might not be adequate to quantitatively prove the eating behavior in the workplace context. As an exploratory study, we took the user-centered perspective and applied the qualitative user research approach, including the online questionnaire based on sentence-completion tasks [42] and the semi-structured interviews [43]. Therefore, our study's main goal is to identify design opportunities for the digital tools that can be applied further to promote healthy eating routines in the office work. Secondly, the findings were not representative of office eating characteristics and expected digital tools features globally. Different regions may have very varied working culture and food culture [60], it is valuable to understand experiences and requirements in one particular cultural context. We believe our approach can be used to understand the other eating patterns, related behaviors as well as possible expectations of digital tools in the workplace context in other countries.

As the study results were discussed and synthesized as design implications for future work, we look forward to developing a high-fidelity interactive prototype based on the design opportunities derived from this study and investigating its potential in workplace healthy eating promotion by conducting user studies, such as the lab-based comparative evaluation and the co-design workshop, to validate our approach and improve our system. Afterward, we plan to consolidate our prototype and implement the data infrastructure to facilitate our design's full user experiences. Eventually, we plan to conduct a longitudinal field study based on our finalized prototype to examine our design 's effectiveness for promoting healthy eating and office vitality.

Acknowledgment. We thank all participants who volunteered to take part in the studies. The first author is being sponsored by China Scholarship Council. This work was supported in part by the NWO Creative Industry KIEM Grant KI18054.

References

1. World Health Organization. https://www.who.int/topics/diet/en/
2. Brug, J.: Determinants of healthy eating: motivation, abilities and environmental opportunities. In: Family Practice (2009). https://doi.org/10.1093/fampra/cmn063
3. Swan, E., Bouwman, L., Hiddink, G.J., Aarts, N., Koelen, M.: Profiling healthy eaters. Determining factors that predict healthy eating practices among Dutch adults. Appetite **89**, 122–130 (2015)
4. Campbell, M.K., et al.: Effects of a tailored health promotion program for female blue-collar workers: health works for women. Prev. Med. (Baltim) **34**, 313–323 (2002)
5. Park, S., Sung, E., Choi, Y., Ryu, S., Chang, Y., Gittelsohn, J.: Sociocultural factors influencing eating practices among office workers in urban South Korea. J. Nutr. Educ. Behav. **49**, 466–474 (2017)

6. Engbers, L.H., van Poppel, M.N.M., Paw, M.J.M.C.A., van Mechelen, W.: Worksite health promotion programs with environmental changes: a systematic review. Am. J. Prev. Med. **29**, 61–70 (2005)
7. Chang, K.S.-P., Danis, C.M., Farrell, R.G.: Lunch line: using public displays and mobile devices to encourage healthy eating in an organization. In: Proceedings of the 2014 ACM International Joint Conference on Pervasive and Ubiquitous Computing, pp. 823–834. ACM (2014)
8. Higgins, J.P.: Smartphone applications for patients' health and fitness. Am. J. Med. **129**, 11–19 (2016)
9. Evans, D.: MyFitnessPal. Br. J. Sport Med. **51**, 1101–1102 (2017)
10. Junker, H., Amft, O., Lukowicz, P., Tröster, G.: Gesture spotting with body-worn inertial sensors to detect user activities. Pattern Recognit. **41**, 2010–2024 (2008)
11. Amft, O., Stäger, M., Lukowicz, P., Tröster, G.: Analysis of chewing sounds for dietary monitoring. In: Beigl, M., Intille, S., Rekimoto, J., Tokuda, H. (eds.) UbiComp 2005. LNCS, vol. 3660, pp. 56–72. Springer, Heidelberg (2005). https://doi.org/10.1007/11551201_4
12. Amft, O., Troster, G.: Methods for detection and classification of normal swallowing from muscle activation and sound. In: 2006 Pervasive Health Conference and Workshops, pp. 1–10. IEEE (2006)
13. Martin, C.K., Nicklas, T., Gunturk, B., Correa, J.B., Allen, H.R., Champagne, C.: Measuring food intake with digital photography. J. Hum. Nutr. Diet. **27**, 72–81 (2014). https://doi.org/10.1111/jhn.12014
14. Almaghrabi, R., Villalobos, G., Pouladzadeh, P., Shirmohammadi, S.: A novel method for measuring nutrition intake based on food image. In: 2012 IEEE I2MTC - International Instrumentation and Measurement Technology Conference Proceedings, pp. 366–370 (2012). https://doi.org/10.1109/I2MTC.2012.6229581
15. Pan, S., Ren, X., Brombacher, A., Vos, S.: Designing technology to encourage healthy eating at work. In: Proceedings of the 9th International Conference on Digital Public Health, p. 131 (2019)
16. Neil, D., Lapierre, N., Bal, H., Perrault, S., Parker, D., Reilly, D.: Limber: exploring motivation in a workplace exergame. In: Proceedings of the ACM Conference on Computer Supported Cooperative Work CSCW, pp. 239–242 (2013). https://doi.org/10.1145/2441955.2442013
17. Lazar, A., Koehler, C., Tanenbaum, J., Nguyen, D.H.: Why we use and abandon smart devices. In: Proceedings of the 2015 ACM International Joint Conference on Pervasive and Ubiquitous Computing - UbiComp 2015, pp. 635–646 (2015). https://doi.org/10.1145/2750858.2804288
18. Holtzblatt, K.: Contextual design. In: Human-Computer Interaction, pp. 71–86. CRC Press (2009)
19. Holtzblatt, K., Wendell, J.B., Wood, S.: Rapid contextual design: a how-to guide to key techniques for user-centered design. Ubiquity **2005**, 3 (2005)
20. Jastran, M.M., Bisogni, C.A., Sobal, J., Blake, C., Devine, C.M.: Eating routines. Embedded, value based, modifiable, and reflective. Appetite **52**, 127–136 (2009). https://doi.org/10.1016/j.appet.2008.09.003
21. Quintiliani, L., Poulsen, S., Sorensen, G.: Healthy eating strategies in the workplace. Int. J. Work. Heal. Manag. **3**, 182–196 (2010)
22. Lassen, A., Thorsen, A.V., Trolle, E., Elsig, M., Ovesen, L.: Successful strategies to increase the consumption of fruits and vegetables: results from the Danish '6 a day' Work-site Canteen Model Study. Public Health Nutr. **7**, 263–270 (2004)
23. French, S.A., et al.: Pricing and promotion effects on low-fat vending snack purchases: the CHIPS Study. Am. J. Public Health. **91**, 112 (2001)
24. Sternfeld, B., et al.: Improving diet and physical activity with ALIVE: a worksite randomized trial. Am. J. Prev. Med. **36**, 475–483 (2009)

25. Wing, R., Hill, J.: Successful Weight Loss Maintenance (2001). https://doi.org/10.1146/ann urev.nutr.21.1.323
26. Parker, A.G., Grinter, R.E.: Collectivistic health promotion tools: accounting for the relationship between culture, food and nutrition. Int. J. Hum. Comput. Stud. **72**, 185–206 (2014). https://doi.org/10.1016/j.ijhcs.2013.08.008
27. Achananuparp, P., Abhishek, V., Lim, E.P., Yun, T.: Eat & tell: a randomized trial of random-Loss incentive to increase dietary self-tracking compliance. In: ACM International Conference on Proceeding Series, 2018-April, pp. 45–54 (2018). https://doi.org/10.1145/3194658.319 4662
28. Päßler, S., Fischer, W.J.: Food intake monitoring: Automated chew event detection in chewing sounds. IEEE J. Biomed. Heal. Inform. **18**, 278–289 (2014). https://doi.org/10.1109/JBHI. 2013.2268663
29. Amft, O., Kusserow, M., Tröster, G.: Bite weight prediction from acoustic recognition of chewing. IEEE Trans. Biomed. Eng. **56**, 1663–1672 (2009). https://doi.org/10.1109/TBME. 2009.2015873
30. Liu, J., et al.: An intelligent food-intake monitoring system using wearable sensors. In: Proceedings - BSN 2012: 9th International Workshop on Wearable and Implantable Body Sensor Networks, pp. 154–160 (2012). https://doi.org/10.1109/BSN.2012.11
31. Amft, O.: A wearable earpad sensor for chewing monitoring. In: Proceedings of IEEE Sensors, pp. 222–227 (2010). https://doi.org/10.1109/ICSENS.2010.5690449
32. Päßler, S., Fischer, W.: Acoustical Method for Objective Food Intake Monitoring Using a Wearable Sensor System. Presented at the (2012). https://doi.org/10.4108/icst.pervasivehea lth.2011.246029
33. Bi, Y., Lv, M., Song, C., Xu, W., Guan, N., Yi, W.: AutoDietary: a wearable acoustic sensor system for food intake recognition in daily life. IEEE Sens. J. **16**, 806–816 (2015). https:// doi.org/10.1109/JSEN.2015.2469095
34. Dong, B., Biswas, S.: Wearable diet monitoring through breathing signal analysis. In: Proceedings of the Annual International Conference of the IEEE Engineering in Medicine and Biology Society, EMBS (2013). https://doi.org/10.1109/EMBC.2013.6609718
35. Kim, H.-J., Kim, M., Lee, S.-J., Choi, Y.S.: An analysis of eating activities for automatic food type recognition. In: Proceedings of the 2012 Asia Pacific Signal and Information Processing Association Annual Summit and Conference, pp. 1–5. IEEE (2012)
36. Amft, O.: Automatic dietary monitoring using on-body sensors: detection of eating and drinking behaviour in healthy individuals. ETH Zurich (2008)
37. Thomaz, E., Essa, I., Abowd, G.D.: A practical approach for recognizing eating moments with wrist-mounted inertial sensing 1029–1040 (2015). https://doi.org/10.1145/2750858.280 7545
38. Zhang, S., Ang, M., Xiao, W., Tham, C.K.: Detection of activities by wireless sensors for daily life surveillance: eating and drinking. Sensors **9**, 1499–1517 (2009)
39. Hofstede, G.: Dimensionalizing cultures: the hofstede model in context. Online Read. Psychol. Cult. **2**, 1–26 (2011). https://doi.org/10.9707/2307-0919.1014
40. De Castro, J.M., Bellisle, F., Feunekes, G.I.J., Dalix, A.M., De Graaf, C.: Culture and meal patterns: a comparison of the food intake of free-living American, Dutch, and French students. Nutr. Res. **17**, 807–829 (1997). https://doi.org/10.1016/S0271-5317(97)00050-X
41. Stajcic, N.: Understanding culture: Food as a means of communication. Hemispheres **28**, 1–10 (2013)
42. Kujala, S., Walsh, T., Nurkka, P., Crisan, M.: Sentence completion for understanding users and evaluating user experience. Interact. Comput. **26**, 238–255 (2014). https://doi.org/10.1093/ iwc/iwt036

43. Kallio, H., Pietilä, A., Johnson, M., Kangasniemi, M.: Systematic methodological review: developing a framework for a qualitative semi-structured interview guide. J. Adv. Nurs. **72**, 2954–2965 (2016)

44. Soley, L., Smith, A.L.: Projective Techniques for Social Science and Business Research. Southshore Press, Mastic Beach (2008)

45. Kujala, S., Nurkka, P.: Sentence completion for evaluating symbolic meaning. Int. J. Des. **6**, 15–25 (2012)

46. Gillham, B.: Research Interviewing: The Range of Techniques: A Practical Guide. McGraw-Hill Education (UK) (2005)

47. Braun, V., Clarke, V.: Using thematic analysis in psychology. Qual. Res. Psychol. **3**, 77–101 (2006)

48. Kawakita, J.: The original KJ method. Tokyo Kawakita Res. Inst. **5** (1991)

49. Birt, L., Scott, S., Cavers, D., Campbell, C., Walter, F.: Member checking: a tool to enhance trustworthiness or merely a nod to validation? Qual. Health Res. **26**, 1802–1811 (2016). https://doi.org/10.1177/1049732316654870

50. Koelsch, L.E.: Reconceptualizing the member check interview. Int. J. Qual. Methods **12**, 168–179 (2013). https://doi.org/10.1177/160940691301200105

51. Geurts, M., van Bakel, A.M., van Rossum, C.T.M., de Boer, E., Ocké, M.C.: Food consumption in the Netherlands and its determinants. Natl. Inst. Public Heal. Environ. 1–69 (2017)

52. Gronow, J., Jääskeläinen, A.: The daily rhythm of eating. Eat. Patterns. A Day Lives Nord. People 91–124 (2001)

53. Tucker, P., Folkard, S.: Working time, health, and safety: a research synthesis paper. Conditions of Work and Employment Series No. 31 (2012)

54. Deuster, P.A., Kemmer, T., Tubbs, L., Zeno, S., Minnick, C.: The Special Operations Forces Nutrition Guide 225 (2012)

55. Health Canada: Eating Well with Canada's Food Guide: A Resource for Educators and Communicators. Publications Health Canada (2011)

56. Reinhardt, W., Schmidt, B., Sloep, P., Drachsler, H.: Knowledge worker roles and actions—results of two empirical studies. Knowl. Process Manag. **18**, 150–174 (2011)

57. Nestle, M., et al.: Behavioral and social influences on food choice. Nutr. Rev. **56**, 50–64 (2009). https://doi.org/10.1111/j.1753-4887.1998.tb01732.x

58. Hargreaves, M.K., Schlundt, D.G., Buchowski, M.S.: Contextual factors influencing the eating behaviours of African American women: a focus group investigation. Ethn. Heal. **7**, 133–147 (2002). https://doi.org/10.1080/1355785022000041980

59. Higgs, S., Thomas, J.: Social influences on eating. Curr. Opin. Behav. Sci. **9**, 1–6 (2016). https://doi.org/10.1016/j.cobeha.2015.10.005

60. Silva, T.H., Vaz De Melo, P.O.S., Almeida, J., Musolesi, M., Loureiro, A.: You are what you eat (and Drink): Identifying cultural boundaries by analyzing food and drink habits in foursquare. In: Proceedings of the 8th International AAAI Conference on Weblogs and Social Media, ICWSM 2014, pp. 466–475 (2014)

Automation in Healthcare Systematic Review

Raquel L. Ruiz$^{(\boxtimes)}$ and Vincent G. Duffy$^{(\boxtimes)}$

Purdue University, West Lafayette, IN 47906, USA
{ruiz142,duffy}@purdue.edu

Abstract. Systematic reviews are an essential tool to help healthcare providers and medical practitioners stay up to date on the latest evidence and practices within their field. In recent years, developments have arisen in automating these systematic reviews. While automated systematic reviews are not currently in widespread use in the medical field, they present a way to increase the output of systematic reviews. This study is a literature review of how the automating of systematic reviews is currently being integrated into the healthcare system. This literature review will be relying on tools such as Web of Science, Harzing's Publish or Perish, VOSviewer, CiteSpace, and MAXQDA to collect and analyze article data sets based on keywords "automating systematic reviews" and "healthcare systematic reviews". Co-citation and content analyses were performed on data sets to determine which articles were most relevant. These analyses showed that automating systematic reviews is developing more within fields outside of the medical field. However, researchers are beginning to take an interest in the applications of an automated systematic review to use in the medical field. The healthcare sector has been more hesitant to adopt automation and often continues to rely on traditional methods. Automation technology is quickly advancing but currently lacks the ability to apply critical thinking of how literature is relevant to current practice, more easily understood by clinician experience, attitudes, and values.

Keywords: Systematic review · Healthcare · Automation · Bibliometric analysis · Harzing · VOSviewer · CiteSpace · MAXQDA

1 Introduction and Background

1.1 Systematic Reviews in Healthcare

A systematic review is a summary of primary research on a specific topic to collect information and reduce bias. It "typically involve[s] a detailed and comprehensive plan and search strategy", "reducing bias by identifying, appraising, and synthesizing all relevant studies" [1]. With ever-increasing advancements in medical technology, practices, and knowledge, medical practitioners need to be well informed of the most recent evidence. Systematic reviews offer medical practitioners a collection of primary studies to assist them with decision-making. Not only are systematic reviews useful for obtaining up-to-date information, but they are also used when developing new clinical practice guidelines [2]. Systematic reviews are relied upon for the prevention of errors, patient satisfaction and safety, improving the quality of care, and saving lives. Deaths from

© Springer Nature Switzerland AG 2021
C. Stephanidis et al. (Eds.): HCII 2021, LNCS 13097, pp. 111–124, 2021.
https://doi.org/10.1007/978-3-030-90966-6_9

healthcare errors are estimated to be over 250,000 a year, with many likely unreported. Based on these numbers, healthcare errors are the 3rd leading cause of death in the United States [3]. Challenges arise for busy healthcare clinicians to fully access information of similar and relatable trials which may be applicable to quality and safety improvements specific to their areas of practice. Reviews are rapidly added, making it difficult to keep up to date [4]. Many of these reviews may not be fully updated or amended when new data arises. As healthcare advancements rapidly change, healthcare clinicians have less time to research, evaluate, educate, and adopt new evidence-based practices. Inadequate reporting can create poor interpretation and critical analysis of systematic reviews. While they have many drawbacks, they are still more advanced in comparison to traditional "opinion reviews that cite evidence selectively to support a viewpoint" [5]. Finally, concerns with validity exist within these trials as limitations and bias, whether transparent or unrecognized, along with sample populations and targeted responses to questions may lack relevance to current clinical practice. Systematic reviews require extensive evaluation and time to increase the likelihood of being applicable to current practice [5].

1.2 Systematic Review Automation

With evidence-based publications arising at rapid rates, healthcare guidelines are continuously requiring revisions to be up to date. Significant delays in literature review for application in clinical practice make achieving improved patient outcomes difficult to achieve. A proposed solution is developing and adopting automation tools to search, gather, and more effectively and efficiently group and analyze publications [4]. Automation can serve by increasing the speed of data acquisition and generate valid, up-to-date recommendations for best practices. Using artificial intelligence within automation can serve to solve complex problems and accelerate advancements in health-related practice and treatments [6]. In addition, automation may reduce the risk of bias in the grouping of publications or omission of other relevant publications that do not serve the interests of the reviewer. While automation may lead to greater efficiency, concerns arise with "the extent to which an innovation is in line with current values and practices" [4]. Other challenges with automation include the need for high relatability and transparency which requires critical thinking and experience [7].

2 Purpose of Study

The purpose of this study is to conduct a literature review on how automation is being integrated into the healthcare systematic review process. Automated data collection has been gaining attention from both large and small businesses in the past decade. While it has made progress in the healthcare sector, there is still hesitation to fully implement an automated systematic review for medical practices. This study will look at how automating healthcare systematic reviews are perceived by the medical community and understand why there is hesitation in fully automating this process within the medical field. This study uses programs such as Web of Science, Harzing's Publish or Perish, VOSviewer, CiteSpace, and MAXQDA. The program Zotero was used to create the citations and reference list [8].

3   Methodology

3.1   Data Collection

Data was initially collected from doing a keyword search within the Web of Science database. This search was later refined with a larger data pool using the program Harzing's Publish or Perish to conduct a keyword search in both the Web of Science and Google Scholar databases. Both databases were used since each has its advantages and disadvantages. Web of Science offers data on the title, authors, source, abstract, and cited references, but only allows 500 articles per data set. Google Scholar does not include data on cited references but offers up to 1000 articles in a data set from a larger amount of articles. Since cited references are required for co-citation analysis, the data from Google Scholar cannot be used. However, the larger data set from Google Scholar is preferable for cluster analysis. The keywords used in the data collection were "automating systematic reviews" and "healthcare systematic reviews".

3.2   Trend Analysis

The trend analysis was conducted using data from the Web of Science along with analysis tools provided within the program. All data was collected between the years 1980 and 2021.

Figure 1 shows the number of articles published per year that were found using a keyword search of "automating systematic reviews". This graph shows that interest in this topic first began in 1993, but gained interest in the 2010s. The year 2021 shows a significant decrease in article publication due to the year not being completed. Based on the increasing trend of prior years, it can be predicted that the year 2021 will have an even greater amount of published articles than the years prior.

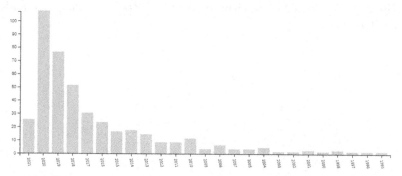

Fig. 1. Trend analysis of data from the articles on automating systematic reviews [9]

Figure 2 is created with the same data as Fig. 1, but it shows how many articles are written in each field. This graph shows that most articles that have the keyword "automating systematic review" are from the computer science information systems field. There is a significant decrease in articles of over 20 articles between the computer science information systems field and the remaining fields. This graph also shows the field of health care sciences services is ranked 7th for this keyword search with 24 articles. The information from Fig. 2 can suggest that most of the development of automating systematic reviews are occurring within the computer science information systems field and from there, being applied to other fields.

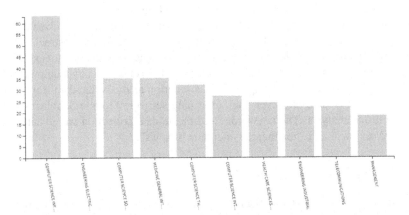

Fig. 2. Trend analysis of data from the articles on automating systematic reviews organized by field [9]

Figure 3 is created with the same data as Fig. 1 and Fig. 2 but has refined the keyword search to only include articles within the medical field. This decreased the articles in the data set from 416 articles to 35 articles. This graph shows the year 2019 was the peak of when articles with the keyword "automating systematic review" were published. This contradicts the trend of increasing published articles in Fig. 1. The lower amount of published articles in 2020 could have been due to resources being put towards the COVID-19 pandemic.

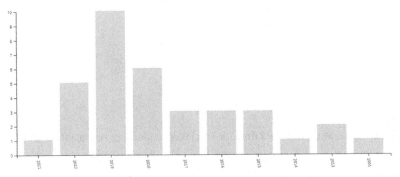

Fig. 3. Trend analysis of data from the articles on automation of systematic reviews in the medical field [9]

Figure 4 is a graph of the number of articles published per year that were found using a keyword search of "healthcare systematic reviews". This graph shows a trend of an increase in published articles. The year 2020 had the largest amount of published articles. This lowers the likeliness of the explanation for the decrease in articles in the year 2020 for Fig. 3 to be true.

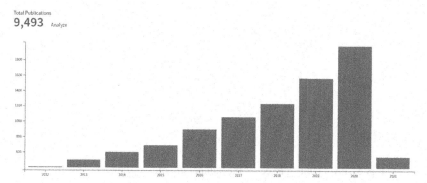

Fig. 4. Trend analysis of data from the articles on healthcare systematic reviews [9]

Figure 5 is a pivot table showing the results of an analysis of the sum of articles per author. Figure 5 was created from data collected using a keyword search of "automating systematic reviews in healthcare" conducted with Harzing's Publish or Perish from the Google Scholar database. A pivot table is a tool that can convert 65,000 rows of data into a summarized table [10]. The author with the largest number of articles is James Thomas, with nine articles. Most of the articles he has published are on the topic of automation and computer assistance. While not directly in the medical field, his articles show interesting perspectives on automation. One such article is "On the use of computer-assistance to facilitate systematic mapping" [11]. The author with the second largest amount of published articles is Paul Glasziou who began working on the topic of automating systematic reviews when the topic gained popularity. One of his earlier publications is "The automation of systematic reviews" [12].

4   Results

4.1   Co-citation Analysis

The co-citation analysis was conducted with the program VOSviewer with data extracted from the article search in the Web of Science. Specifically, the data used to make Fig. 3 was used to create Fig. 5. The exported data included the title, authors, source, abstract, and cited references. Co-citation analyses are used as a way to adequately identify the relationships and structure between research areas [15]. The basis of the co-citation analysis is the higher amount of co-citations between authors there is, the stronger the relationship of the authors is [16]. The VOSviewer creates a cluster map with the imported data that shows the articles that we cited the most. The links between the authors show

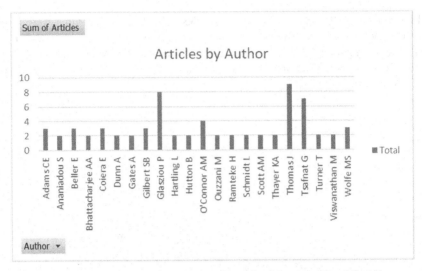

Fig. 5. Pivot table in Excel of the number of articles per author [13, 14]

which articles have been cited together. Limits can be set for the minimum number of citations for each article. Another program that can perform a co-citation analysis is CiteSpace. This program uses the same data as the VOSviewer, but a unique output it has is a citation burst. A citation burst is a way that makes "it possible to find the articles that receive particular attention from the related scientific communities in a certain period of time" [17]. Not only is it able to perform co-citation analyses, but it is also able to assist in "identifying betweenness centrality between pivotal points in scientific articles, which indicates the significance of the nodes in a network" [17]. CiteSpace is able to identify co-cited articles by choosing different nodes [17].

VOSviewer Analysis. Figure 6 is a co-citation cluster map of the data from the keyword search for "automating systematic reviews" within the medical field. The minimum number of co-citations was set to 10. Figure 6 contains 2 clusters, 44 links, and has a total link strength of 244. The article with the largest citations was "Using text mining for study identification in systematic reviews: a systematic review of current approaches" [18] with 22 citations. The article with the second largest citations was "Systematic review automation technologies" [19] with 21 citations. The earliest article within this cluster is from 2009, with most of the other articles from the mid to late 2010's. This appears to follow the article publication trend from Fig. 4.

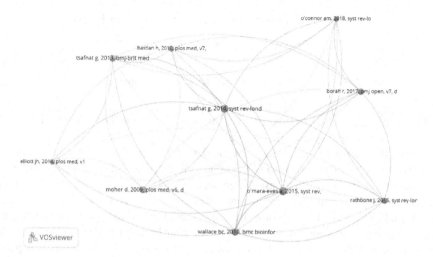

Fig. 6. Co-citation analysis for automating systematic reviews in the medical field [20]

CiteSpace Analysis. Figure 7 is a cluster burst created with CiteSpace using the data from the keyword search "healthcare systematic reviews". There are 5 bursts within Fig. 7 that show the main keyword per cluster.

Figure 8 is a list of references from the data in Fig. 7 with the strongest citation burst. The top reference is "Grading Quality of Evidence and Strength of Recommendations: A Perspective" [21].

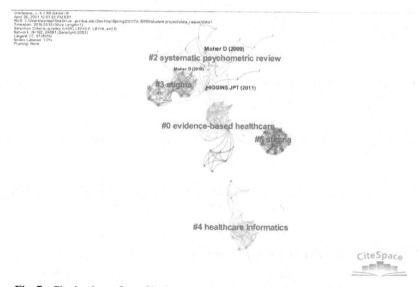

Fig. 7. Citation burst from CiteSpace on data for healthcare systematic reviews [22]

Top 1 References with the Strongest Citation Bursts

References	Year	Strength	Begin	End	2016 - 2019
Moher D, 2009, PLOS MED, V6, P0	2009	4.74	**2016**	2017	▬▬

Fig. 8. References from Fig. 8 with the strongest citation bursts [22]

Figure 9 is a cluster burst created with CiteSpace using the data from the keyword search for "automating systematic reviews" within the medical field.

Figure 10 is a list of references from the data in Fig. 9 with the strongest citation burst. The top reference happens to be the same as Fig. 8, "Grading Quality of Evidence and Strength of Recommendations: A Perspective" [21]. The second top reference is "Seventy-Five Trials and Eleven Systematic Reviews a Day: How Will We Ever Keep Up?" [23]. Figure 8 and Fig. 10 show that while there has been a significant increase in articles written for automating systematic reviews for healthcare, the most referenced article is from 2009. Technology has increased significantly since this paper was published; however, Fig. 8 and Fig. 10 suggest that there is still a lack of research and integration on this topic within the medical field.

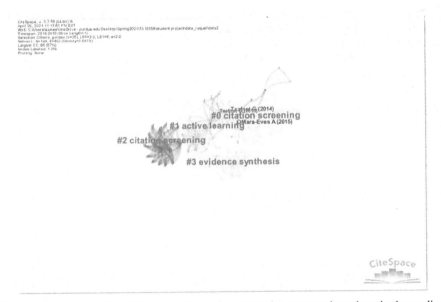

Fig. 9. Citation burst from CiteSpace of data for automating systematic reviews in the medical field [22]

Top 2 References with the Strongest Citation Bursts

References	Year	Strength	Begin	End	2016 - 2019
Moher D, 2009, PLOS MED, V6, P0	2009	1.87	**2016**	2017	▬▬
Bastian H, 2010, PLOS MED, V7, P0, DOI 10.1371/journal.pmed.1000326, DOI	2010	1.8	**2017**	2019	▬▬

Fig. 10. References from Fig. 8 with the strongest citation bursts [22]

4.2   Co-authorship Analysis

A co-authorship analysis is used as "a proxy of research collaboration" "that links different sets of talent to produce a research output" [24]. It is a useful analysis to understand where articles are coming from and what social networks have an interest in specific research topics. Co-authorship also allows the "relations between these groups and changes in time" between these groups to be analyzed [25].

Figure 11 is a cluster map of a co-authorship analysis for the data from the keyword search for "automating systematic reviews" within the medical field. Figure 11 contains 4 clusters, 41 links, and has a total link strength of 84. The authors with the most connections are James Thomas, Paul Glasziou, and Guy Tsafnat. These results are confirmed with the trend analysis in Fig. 5 since these authors have the most published articles so they will most likely have the largest co-authorship within this keyword search. Together Fig. 4, Fig. 5, Fig. 11 suggest that more authors have taken interest and begun to publish papers.

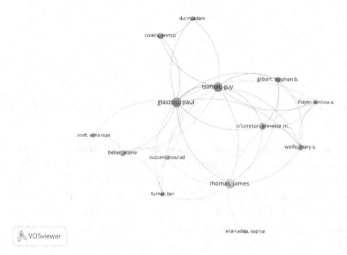

Fig. 11. Co-authorship analysis on data for automating systematic reviews in the medical field [20]

4.3   Content Analysis

Comparable with co-citation analysis, content analysis is conducted with the program VOSviewer. However, it uses data collected from Google Scholar using the program Harzing's Public or Perish [13]. Since content analysis does not require cited references in the data, data from Google Scholar can be used. The advantage to using data from Google Scholar is the ability to export a larger data pool compared to Web of Science. Content analyses are used to organize and interpret the data from imported articles to gain reasonable results and understanding from the set of articles [26].

Figure 12 is a content analysis cluster map produced from the data collected from the keyword search for "systematic review in healthcare". The data set was collected from Google Scholar and contains 980 articles. The minimum occurrence was set to 20 which resulted in 51 keywords but only the 60% most relevant keywords which is 31. Figure 12 contains 5 clusters, 287 links, and has a link strength of 1918. The keywords with the largest connection are "systematic review" with 692 occurrences, 'healthcare" with 177 occurrences, and "systematic literature review" with 121 occurrences.

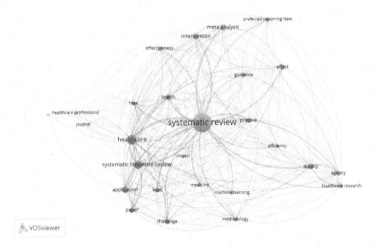

Fig. 12. Cluster analysis on data for automating systematic review in healthcare [20]

Figure 13 is a content analysis cluster map produced from the data collected from the keyword search for "automating systematic review" in the medical field. This data set was exported from the Web of Science and contains 35 articles. Figure 9 has 3 clusters, 78 links, and a total link strength of 1112. The minimum number of articles was set to 20 occurrences and 16 keywords met this condition. The top keywords from this content analysis cluster are systematic review, automation, and study. These keywords had occurrences of 84, 83, and 72, respectively. Both Fig. 12 and Fig. 13 show that the articles within the data sets used focus on automation and systematic reviews.

4.4   Content Analysis from MAXQDA

MAXQDA performs a similar content analysis as VOSviewer, however, MAXQDA uses a smaller set of data and is able to examine this data in greater detail. MAXQDA also allows the user to manually remove stop words from being analyzed within the data. MAXQDA is also able to visualize results into a word cloud, which can be an effective way to communicate the most common words within articles [27].

Figure 14 is a word cloud created from a data set collected from Web of Science using a keyword search of "healthcare automation". This word cloud shows that the top three keywords found in the articles in the data set are "systematic", "automation", and "review". Figure 14 shows that recent articles having to do with "healthcare automation" are beginning to focus on systematic reviews.

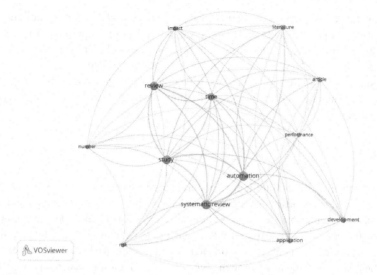

Fig. 13. Cluster analysis on data for automating systematic reviews in the medical field [20]

Fig. 14. Word Cloud from MAXQDA [28]

5   Conclusion

A systematic review of literature is critical for the advancement of healthcare practice, safety, and improved patient outcomes. The healthcare sector has been more hesitant to adopt automation and often continues to rely on traditional methods. Challenges exist in both traditional and advanced technology methods. Shortcomings with traditional methods include significant delays in the collection of relevant and relatable data, a potential bias that may result in omitting or overuse of selected articles and keeping up to date with the rapid additions of research literature. Automation technology is quickly advancing but currently lacks the ability to apply critical thinking of how literature is relevant to current practice, more easily understood by clinician experience, attitudes, and values. Developing and utilizing further advancements in technology, including artificial intelligence may lead to maximizing the full potential of systematic literature reviews. Understanding and addressing concerns of healthcare clinicians such as ensuring technology is well-matched with current practice and values, is vital for acceptance and trust of automation.

6   Future Work

Advancements in artificial intelligence, natural language processing, and machine learning have created more advanced algorithms that can enhance the efficiency and quality of automated systematic reviews. This complex ecosystem can provide interconnections of numerous techniques in artificial intelligence to solve complex problems within the automation process. This may lead to faster activity, more accurate, and less expensive results. Machine learning is a promising type of artificial intelligence that may accelerate quality outcomes [29]. Funding challenges have led to delays and fragmented development. Collaboration of automated tools are critical towards overcoming this barrier. In 2015, the International Collaboration for the Automation of Systematic Reviews was founded to exchange data and develop more efficient toolkits. Members include a wide variety of interdisciplinary professions such as software engineers, librarians, statisticians, experts in artificial intelligence, linguists, and researchers [29]. The NSF is also currently funding the University of Arkansas System with an award for collaborative research on automated knowledge discovery in reliability and healthcare from complex data with covariates [30]. This award has already helped produce publications such as "Flexible methods for reliability estimation using aggregate failure-time data" [31] and "Comparison study on general methods for modeling lifetime data with covariates" [32].

References

1. Uman, L.S.: Systematic reviews and meta-analyses. J. Can. Acad. Child Adolesc. Psychiatry **20**(1), 57–59 (2011)
2. Gopalakrishnan, S., Ganeshkumar, P.: Systematic reviews and meta-analysis: understanding the best evidence in primary healthcare. J. Fam. Med. Prim. Care **2**(1), 9–14 (2013). https://doi.org/10.4103/2249-4863.109934
3. Anderson, J.G., Abrahamson, K.: Your health care may kill you: medical errors. Stud. Health Technol. Inform. **234**, 13–17 (2017)
4. Arno, A., Elliott, J., Wallace, B., Turner, T., Thomas, J.: The views of health guideline developers on the use of automation in health evidence synthesis. Syst. Rev. **10**(1), 16 (2021). https://doi.org/10.1186/rs.3.rs-23742/v2
5. Maggio, L.A., Sewell, J.L., Artino, A.R., Jr.: The literature review: a foundation for high-quality medical education research. J. Grad. Med. Educ. **8**(3), 297–303 (2016). https://doi.org/10.4300/JGME-D-16-00175.1
6. O'Blenis, P.: Past, Present, and Future: Automation in Systematic Review Software. https://blog.evidencepartners.com/past-present-and-future-automation-in-systematic-review-software. Accessed 25 Apr 2021

7. Marshall, I.J., Wallace, B.C.: Toward systematic review automation: a practical guide to using machine learning tools in research synthesis. Syst. Rev. **8**(1), 163 (2019). https://doi.org/10.1186/s13643-019-1074-9
8. Zotero. Corporation for Digital Scholarship. https://www.zotero.org/
9. Web of Science. https://apps-webofknowledgecom.ezproxy.lib.pur-due.edu/WOS_General Search_input.do?product=WOS&search_mode=General-Search&SID=7EKUw7yEVcCG VrUwOlu&preferencesSaved=
10. Alexander, M., Jelen, B.: Pivot Table Data Crunching. Pearson Education (2001)
11. Haddaway, N.R., et al.: On the use of computer-assistance to facilitate systematic mapping. Campbell Syst. Rev. **16**(4), e1129 (2020). https://doi.org/10.1002/cl2.1129
12. Tsafnat, G., Dunn, A., Glasziou, P., Coiera, E.: The automation of systematic reviews. BMJ **346**, f139 (2013). https://doi.org/10.1136/bmj.f139
13. Anne-Wil, H.: Harzing's Publish or Perish. https://harzing.com/resources/publish-or-perish
14. Persson, O.: BibExcel. https://sites.google.com/site/bibexcel2015/
15. Jeong, Y.K., Song, M., Ding, Y.: Content-based author co-citation analysis. J. Informetr. **8**(1), 197–211 (2014). https://doi.org/10.1016/j.joi.2013.12.001
16. Andrews, J.E.: An author co-citation analysis of medical informatics. J. Med. Libr. Assoc. **91**(1), 47–56 (2003)
17. Zhou, W., Chen, J., Huang, Y.: Co-citation analysis and burst detection on financial bubbles with scientometrics approach. Econ. Res.-Ekon. Istraživanja **32**, 2310–2328 (2019). https://doi.org/10.1080/1331677X.2019.1645716
18. O'Mara-Eves, A., Thomas, J., McNaught, J., Miwa, M., Ananiadou, S.: Using text mining for study identification in systematic reviews: a systematic review of current approaches. Syst. Rev. **4**(1), 5 (2015). https://doi.org/10.1186/2046-4053-4-5
19. Jan van Eck, N., Waltman, L.: VOSviewer. Leiden University's Centre for Science and Technology Studies. https://www.vosviewer.com/
20. Ansari, M.T., Tsertsvadze, A., Moher, D.: Grading quality of evidence and strength of rec-ommendations: a perspective. PLOS Med. **6**(9), e1000151 (2009). https://doi.org/10.1371/journal.pmed.1000151
21. Chen, C.: CiteSpace. Drexl University. http://cluster.cis.drexel.edu/~cchen/citespace/
22. Bastian, H., Glasziou, P., Chalmers, I.: Seventy-five trials and eleven systematic reviews a day: how will we ever keep up? PLOS Med. **7**(9), e1000326 (2010). https://doi.org/10.1371/journal.pmed.1000326
23. Kumar, S.: Co-authorship networks: A review of the literature. Aslib J. Inf. Manag. **67**, 55–73 (2015). https://doi.org/10.1108/AJIM-09-2014-0116
24. Peters, H.P.F., Van Raan, A.F.J.: Structuring scientific activities by co-author analysis. Scientometrics **20**(1), 235–255 (1991). https://doi.org/10.1007/BF02018157
25. Bengtsson, M.: How to plan and perform a qualitative study using content analysis. NursingPlus Open **2**, 8–14 (2016). https://doi.org/10.1016/j.npls.2016.01.001
26. Lohmann, S., Heimerl, F., Bopp, F., Burch, M., Ertl, T.: Concentri cloud: word cloud visual-ization for multiple text documents. In: 2015 19th International Conference on Information Visualisation, pp. 114–120 (2015). https://doi.org/10.1109/iV.2015.30
27. Kuckartz, U.: MAXQDA. VERBI Software. https://www.maxqda.com/
28. Beller, E., et al.: Making progress with the automation of systematic reviews: principles of the International Collaboration for the Automation of Systematic Reviews (ICASR). Syst. Rev. **7**(1), 77 (2018). https://doi.org/10.1186/s13643-018-0740-7
29. Award Abstract #1635379 Collaborative Research: Automated Knowledge Discovery in Reli-ability and Healthcare from Complex Data with Covariates. NSF. https://www.nsf.gov/awa rdsearch/showAward?AWD_ID=1635379&HistoricalAwards=false

30. Karimi, S., Liao, H., Fan, N.: Flexible methods for reliability estimation using aggregate failure-time data. IISE Trans. **53**(1), 101–115 (2021). https://doi.org/10.1080/24725854.2020.1746869

31. Liao, H., Karimi, S.: Comparison study on general methods for modeling lifetime data with covariates. In: 2017 Prognostics and System Health Management Conference (PHM-Harbin), Harbin, China, July 2017, pp. 1–5 (2017). https://doi.org/10.1109/PHM.2017.8079122

User Perceptions of Security and Privacy Risks with Contact Tracing Apps

Hervé Saint-Louis[✉] ⓘ and Bob-Antoine Jerry Ménélas

Université du Québec à Chicoutimi, Chicoutimi, QC G7H 2B1, Canada
Herve_saint-louis@uqac.ca

Abstract. This article explores Canadians' response to their federal government's release of the COVID-19 Tracing app for smartphones in 2020 during the pandemic. Researchers and industry have proposed cellphone-based contact tracing to help contain the spread of SARS-COV-2 virus in people during the COVID-19 pandemic. However, the efficacy of contact tracing requires a certain threshold of participants and for people to enable specific access to communication ports on their mobile devices. Privacy and confidentiality concerns over users' data on their personal devices have existed for years. Rightfully, industry watchdogs have raised concerns about the long-term consequences of contact tracing. As well questioning the potential confidentiality risks, privacy experts have also raised questions about whether contact tracing can curb the spread of the SARS-COV-2 virus. The uncertainty of this technology and pre-existing privacy concern could affect the adoption by the public. It is unknown how people perceive their security regarding contact tracing during the COVID-19 pandemic. This article presents early theoretical work and survey data taken from an ongoing study on participants' perceptions of security and privacy perceptions of the COVID Alert contact-tracing app released in several Canadian provinces and territories during the 2020–2021 pandemic.

Keywords: Contact tracing · Security · Canada · COVID-19 · COVID alert

1 Introduction

This study explores Canadians' response to their federal government's release of the COVID-19 Tracing app for smartphones in July 2020 during the pandemic. Researchers and industry have proposed cellphone-based contact tracing to help contain the spread of SARS-COV-2 virus in people during the COVID-19 pandemic. However, the efficacy of contact tracing requires a threshold of 60% of participants [1] and for people to enable specific access to communication ports on their mobile devices [2]. Privacy and confidentiality concerns over users' data on their personal devices have existed for years [3–6]. Rightfully, industry watchdogs have raised concerns about the long-term consequences of contact tracing [7, 8]. As well questioning the potential confidentiality risks, privacy experts have also raised questions about whether contact tracing can curb the spread of the SARS-COV-2 virus [9]. The uncertainty of this technology and pre-existing privacy concern could affect the adoption by the public.

© Springer Nature Switzerland AG 2021
C. Stephanidis et al. (Eds.): HCII 2021, LNCS 13097, pp. 125–139, 2021.
https://doi.org/10.1007/978-3-030-90966-6_10

It is unknown how people perceive their security regarding contact tracing during the COVID-19 pandemic. Do they differentiate between academic projects such as the DP3T and proposals such as Apple and Google's joint decentralized contact tracing architecture? Are there concerns in random samples of individuals of contact tracing or are the security concerns localized with users with high levels of information security literacy? This article presents preliminary data exploring users' perceptions of security risks related to cellular-based contact tracing.

Contact tracing during epidemics and pandemics is a practice used for centuries as far back as the Middle Ages' Black Plague, in the 19th century with the cholera outbreak in London, and with the AIDS epidemic worldwide [10]. Used as recently as the 2003 SARS epidemic, contract tracing was performed by epidemiologists and their staff [11]. The responsibility to trace and locate potentially infected individuals as well as protecting their privacy rested mainly with health experts, not the public. While the involvement of exposed individuals was always required [12], the level of voluntarism was limited.

We frame contact tracing through cellphone-based sensors as an emerging digital practice no longer mediated by expert health professionals and experts. It is one that has shifted epidemiology from institutional structures and experts to end users with agency over the health process and success of the practice. However, contact tracing probably intrudes into one of the most personal digital technologies tied with individuals' identities. Thus, it entrusts security to what could be considered one of the weakest links in the chain—people. This is an important human-centered security risk mediated by technology and promoted by policymakers, security developers, and health professionals without clear buy-in from the public.

With cellphone-based contact tracing apps like the one released by the Canadian government in July 2020, the public now had a role to play by being encouraged to download the COVID Alert app released by federal authorities. Many responsibilities were left to the public to facilitate the efficacy of this infection control practice. Canadians had to download the app, enable it, but also self-report any infection diagnostic given to them by health authorities. Without their support, the efficacy of this infection mitigation practice was squandered.

Yet, an initial qualitative evaluation into Canadians' perceptions of the COVID Alert app demonstrated some concerns by members of the public on social media [13]. We could observe fear of privacy-lacking feature and state surveillance in social media posts by Canadians. Historical concerns from Canadians about contact tracing found new life online.

Our study was conducted throughout Canada, including provinces that have not enabled the COVID Alert app. We seek to understand their perceptions of security and privacy with the COVID Alert app released by the Canadian government. We seek to understand participants' perceptions of the following.

a) Understand participants' use of the COVID Alert app.
b) Understand and evaluate their perceptions of the COVID Alert app.
c) Understand how health authorities, policymakers, and security developers can facilitate the adoption of cellphone-based contact tracing apps based on the Canadian approach.

This article presents early theoretical work and survey data taken from an ongoing study on participants' perceptions of security and privacy perceptions of the COVID Alert contact-tracing app released in several Canadian provinces and territories during the 2020–2021 pandemic.

2   Background

Contact tracing has been used as far back as in medieval times during the Black Plague when infected households were "marked". John Snow used it in the 19th century by to track the cholera outbreak in London [10]. Contact tracing is part of several infection control practices. Other mitigating practices against infectious diseases include screening, vaccination, isolation, quarantine, social distancing, and use of protective gear and apparel such as face masks [14]. It is based on the analysis of the circle of contacts of people. To do this, tracers assess who was connected to or in contact with an infected person in order to determine the clusters and routes of infection.

There are several types of contact tracing. They include active contact tracing where health officials warn contacts provided by the index of exposure, hiding the identity of the latter [12]. Tracers advise contacts to undergo and seek testing. Limiting contact tracing is the second type of contact tracing [12]. Tracers notify individuals who might be unaware of infection risks. It is mostly used when the population is large. Then, there is voluntary contact tracing where tracers encourage the index to identify all contacts [12].

Contact tracing methods include interviews, narrowcasting, where tracers ask a sample at risk populations to get tested [15]. Next, there is real-time detection which is a combination of ambient technology (CCTV, facial recognition, signal tracking (of cell phones) [15]. These are intrusive approaches. Finally, we have sensor-based tracing mostly based smartphone censors [15].

Sensor-based smartphone detection was first used in the 2014–2016 Ebola epidemic in West Africa [16]. It is a process that includes the registration of contacts, the contact detection of infected individuals and finally, an infection report. Limits to sensor-based social tracing include the necessity of having a participation in the population of at least 60% [1]. Sensors have limited ranges and often report false positives [15]. Finally, this method excludes older phones that do not meet the minimum technical requirements. Thus, there is a possibility that disadvantaged populations reliant on older cellular technologies who could be at greater risk of infection cannot be reached by sensor-based approaches.

3   Related Works

Research on contract tracing with smartphones is not new. The social tracing of Ebola was one of the first use cases of contact tracing through smartphones [17, 18]. Recent research on app-based contact tracing has focused mainly on the COVID-19 pandemic offering insights into its history. Ahmed et al. [19] offer a survey of contact tracing apps asking questions about their security, privacy, and data management features. They compare centralized apps where the data and operations are performed on a central server, sending data to client apps on users' phones; decentralized apps where all operations are performed on users' phones and provide, theoretically the most confidentiality and anonymity; and finally, they look at hybrid architectures where part of the operations are distributed to users' smartphones. Bengio et al. [9] investigate the privacy limits of decentralized contact tracing apps, demonstrating that even with such systems, user identification is possible. Nguyen et al. [15] also explore the technological aspects of the sensors used in contact tracing.

Issues surrounding ethics [20, 21], personally identifiable traces [22], or the debate between civil liberties, legal concerns about the privacy of contact tracing apps [23], social alienation [16], the social acceptance of contact tracing apps [24], and public health [2] are also addressed by the literature.

The issues presented in this article mirror to some extent, concerns voiced by the COVID-19 Exposure Notification App Advisory Council created by the Canadian federal government to advise on the app and ensuring that public health policy objectives are meat. The Council's focus, in it just-released report has been on measuring social and economic determinants of adoption of the app, to analyze the COVID Alert app as a government service and a public health utility [25].

4 Methods

This questionnaire relies on online interviews hosted through the LimeSurvey account of our university (University of Quebec At Chicoutimi)'s LimeSurvey's account. The questionnaire seeks to uncover respondents' perceptions of the COVID Alert app. There are four main question blocks. The first one seeks relates to demographic data about respondents. It aims to understand their social contexts and to determine their digital literacy levels. The second section attempts to understand respondents' use of the COVID Alert app. The third section attempts to understand respondents' perceptions of the COVID Alert app. The third section seeks to provide data for policymakers and health authorities on the use of contract tracing apps. Finally, the last section seeks to understand respondents' security and privacy concerns about the COVID Alert app.

The questionnaire has 25 twenty-five questions including four sub-questions. Question 6 asked respondents if they had downloaded and activated the COVID Alert app. Respondents who indicated that they had were prompted to answer a sub-question asking to what prompted them to install it. Respondents who answered negatively were asked what would encourage them to install the app. Question 9 asked respondents if they had removed the app since installing it. A sub-question asked those who answered positively what prompted them to remove the app. Question 13 asks if respondents they have received a COVID Alert notification felt better informed about their health risks. Those who answer "no" saw see an extra open-ended sub-question asking them to describe other reasons why they felt the app was useful or not. Questions are either based on multiple-choice designs, Likert scales, or are open-ended. The multiple choice and the Likert scales questions allow us to perform statistical analyses on all respondents' responses. We performed coding analyses on the open-ended questions to seek repeating patterns of responses. These responses after the first coding analysis can further analyzed qualitatively or quantitatively.

The identity of respondents and their personal emails are unknown to the researchers as these people information are not asked in the survey nor elsewhere. Ergo, researchers do not know the identities of respondents who self-declare having received a COVID Alert notification. None of the questions asks respondents if they have had COVID-19 or not. Thus, no personal health data is being shared with researchers.

The interview was publicized online and through local Saguenay and Toronto media (academic newsletters, email announcements). Most of the recruitment was be performed online through social media (Facebook, Twitter, and LinkedIn). We sought at least 200 respondents but reached about a hundred. Respondents were given a link to the online survey where they were able to choose the language they want to answer in (from French and English). Both versions of the survey ask the same questions and are thus analogous to one another. All adult Canadian residents could participate in the survey.

We had chosen not to eliminate results from the province of Alberta and the Yukon Territory were not being blocked although at the time of writing this document, their governments had not authorized the use of the COVID Alert app within their political boundaries. As the COVID-19 pandemic progresses, these governments could easily change their policies and adopt the federal government's app. No respondents from those provinces answered our survey. Data on residents of the two Canadian jurisdictions who do not use the COVID Alert app was considered of interest to this research and could have been significant. The survey results obtained cover responses between December 28, 2020, to February 10, 2021. Ethics approval was obtained from our university's IRB. The number of respondents to this initial survey is small, and thus not representative of trends and perceptions of the Canadian population to the COVID Alert app.

Ninety-two respondents answered our survey. $N = 57$, 67.06% were women. $N = 74$, 87.06% of respondents were from the Province of Quebec while $N = 11$, 12.94% were from Ontario. While we attempted to recruit respondents nationally, announcements of this initial survey did not collect data from all Canadians systematically. We are fully aware that this skews results, making them more regional than national.

5   Results

In this section we present our survey results by looking at respondent demographics and their digital literacy; their motivations for using the COVID Alert app; their perceptions about the app; we observe public policy concerns raised by respondents; and we examine their security and privacy concerns.

5.1   Demographics and Digital Literacy

Nine out of ten of the ninety-two respondents who answered out initial survey were aged fifty-five and under. While we surmise that older respondents probably responded less to the survey because of lower familiarity with smartphones and apps, this group is the most at risk for negative COVID-19 implications following an infection from SARS-COV-2. As we will see below, it could be possible that the low response rate is not necessarily due to a lack of digital literacy with smartphones but a lack of expressed need to use the

Table 1. Age of participants.

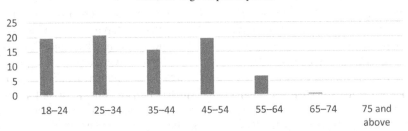

COVID Alert app to mitigate infection due to limited activity and external excursions (Table 1).

To understand their digital literacy to see if there were any correlations with their usage or lack of, of the COVID Alert app, we asked respondents how they used their phones daily. Respondents could select as many options as possible. Most respondents (N = 73, 85.88%) mentioned that they used their phones to speak, send text messages (N = 82, 96.47%), to surf the internet (N = 76, 89.41%), for productivity (defined as using emails, agendas, and banking) (N = 75, 88.24%), and to watch videos or listen to music (N = 59, 69.41%). These activities are standard with smartphone usage. A minority reported that they used their smartphones to play games (N = 28, 32.94%), and for creative works (defined as recording podcasts, making videos, and photography) (N = 30, 35.29%). Playing games and creative works necessitate more active and sustained use of smartphones and may require more digital literacy than most other activities, safe for productivity.

5.2 Respondents' Motivation for the Use of the COVID Alert App

Most respondents (N = 61, 74.39%) had downloaded and activated the COVID Alert app on their smartphones. When asked what prompted them to install the app, they offered various open-ended responses that we coded under several labels. These labels were obtained from a third pass coding effort where at first, we identified several labels for respondents' answers. In the second pass, we regrouped similarly themed answers. We regrouped themes a second time after a third qualitative coding analysis. The final themed categories for respondents' answers are the following; (1) safety, prevention, protection of others or loved ones; (2) advertising and news; (3) civic duty, social consciousness, will to flatten the curve; (4) public health, government, employer request and recommendations; (5) curiosity and need to be informed if infected; (6) personal network recommendation, replication practice; (7) utility; (8) and trust with remaining privacy concerns partly assuaged. The labels for the themes seem wide but they are the result of the grouping done in the second and third pass qualitative coding. For example, in the first coding pass, safety and prevention were grouped together whereas the protection of others and loved ones was a separate category. Similarly, advertising and news were separate categories until the third coding pass. While we initially distinguished between curiosity and need to be informed, we decide to regroup them during the third coding pass as they conveyed aspects of the same motivations and were often used conjointly when coding certain responses. Responses were not limited to one category, as can be seen in Table 2.

Table 2. Motivation for the Use of the COVID Alert App

Codes	Percentages
(1) Safety, prevention, protection of others or loved ones	N = 14, 25%
(2) Advertising and news	N = 8, 14.29%
(3) Civic duty, social consciousness, will to flatten the curve	N = 21, 37.5%
(4) Public health, government, employer request and recommendations	N = 9, 16.07%
(5) Curiosity and need to be informed if infected	N = 6, 10.71%
(6) Personal network recommendation, replication practice	N = 2, 3.58%
(7) Utility	N = 2, 3.58%
(8) Trust with remaining privacy concerns partly assuaged	N = 3, 5.36%

Civic duty, social consciousness and will to flatten the curve appears as the most frequently cited motivation for respondents downloading the app (37.5%). Personal safety and that of others are the second most cited motivations (25%) given by respondents. Motivations pertaining to the public good appear to be important for respondents. Other motivations such as recommendations from authorities (16.07%) support this reading into a public good impetus. Motivations related to the security of personal data did come up (5.36%) but were not as significant in this section of the survey.

Respondents who did not download the app were also asked about what would encourage them to install the app. We obtained fewer responses (15) but they two important themes surfaced. N = 7, 46.67% of respondents who indicated that they had not installed the app, cited that nothing could encourage them to download the COVID Alert app. While not citing exact motivations, these respondents seem to have antagonistic views towards the COVID Alert app and possibly contact tracing. Similarly, N = 5, 33.33% of respondents mentioned that the COVID Alert app framework was either too new for their older phones or incompatible with their devices' operating system. Now these respondents clearly would like to use the app but are excluded because of their technological barriers. Two respondents did mention that they did not see a need to download the app because of limited public exposure. In the word or P29 "I don't have internet on my cell phone. As retirees, my wife and I, don't hang out with anyone and stay at home. When I have to do errands, I group them together and follow all the sanitary instructions."

Very few respondents (N = 4, 4.88%) mentioned that they received COVID-19 alert through the COVID Alert app indicating that they had been in contact with a self-reported infected person. According to the responses, only one person reported an infection with SARS-COV-2. We asked respondents if they had removed the app since installing it. N = 6, 7.32% answered that they had. When prompted as to why they had removed the app, the few answers we received were very insightful. We did not code the five responses, but each was detailed and explain possible flaws in the COVID Alert app and how respondents perceived its utility. P48 wrote that the app was useless. P72 mentioned that the app was affecting the battery of the phone. The respondent wrote, "I deleted it the first time because I felt it was draining my battery. I often do more than 2 days on a charge despite my fairly intense use of my cell [...], but with this application open all day, I was losing a lot of battery life. I then re-installed it and only activate it when I go to public places. P79 did not feel the need to download the app. The respondent wrote, "My partner downloaded it and he's been the only person I've been around for months. So I did not see the point of downloading this application for my case." P88 wrote, "When installing the application, I kept receiving the notification to activate my position (GPS). As I was (and still am) at home most of the time, I only activated my GPS when I went out (e.g., grocery shopping). Tired of this notification, I deleted the application. A report indicating the low effectiveness of the app if too few people were activating it ironically prompted me to remove it as well." P102 wrote, "The app was not at all responsive to changes in the region (colour ranges) and I wasn't getting notifications of COVID cases, so I concluded that either people were not downloading it or that they weren't positive on it—so the app lost its usefulness." Concerns over low usage of COVID Alert in the Canadian population appear to discourage some respondents from downloading the app. Coupled with respondents who do not feel overtly exposed, and that the app is more a burden than helpful, the low level of engagement with the COVID Alert app's engagement failure with some Canadian becomes a self-fulfilling prophecy. As fewer people download the app, fewer people feel the utility and effectiveness of the app.

5.3   Respondents' Perceptions of the COVID Alert App

In this section, we look at respondents' perceptions to the COVID Alert app by asking them about if they find it effective for COVID-19 prevention; if they find the app useful; if they feel safer after having installed it on their phones; if they felt better informed if they had received a notification; if they can think of any reason why COVID Alert had been useful or not; and if they have recommended the app to other people. In Table 3, we observe that respondents are People are more neutral and agree that the COVID Alert app appears to be effective. It should be noted that this is a rather positive observation.

In Table 4 we observe that respondents do not feel safer after having downloaded the app.

In Table 5, we observe that respondents did not recommend others to use the app.

We can surmise that COVID Alert does not create strong perceptions and reactions in respondents and that the app exists in people's smartphones but because of its passive and dormant nature, its lack of interaction and feedback with respondents means that it can be perceived neutrally and if we draw from the responses of those who removed the app, it could be seen as useless. This is an interesting predicament as the very utility and success of the app requires it to be as unobtrusive as possible. Lack of feedback on the infection in nearby residents indicates a certain level of success in the fight against COVID-19.

Table 3. The COVID Alert is effective for COVID-19 prevention.

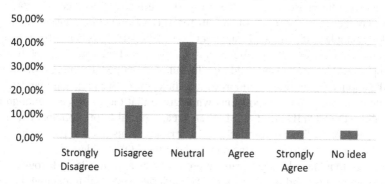

Table 4. I feel safer after having installed the app on my smartphone.

Table 5. I have recommended the used of the COVID Alert app to other people.

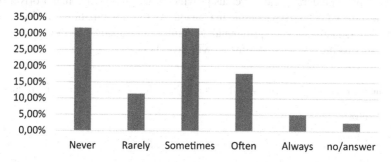

5.4 Respondents and Public Policy

In this section we attempted to draw data from respondents that could prove useful for Canadian and international public health policy makers. Our initial focus was on how Canadian authorities communicated with the public about the COVID Alert app. The main messaging has been done by the federal government which is not the one deemed to be closest to people.

First, we asked respondents how they would have liked to be informed about the COVID Alert app. While several respondents had no response or opinion to share, some had very strong views on the matter. P17 wrote, "No trust that the government keeps our personal data. No matter what they say." P52 added, "No information would have convinced me of the interest of this application." P95 expressed worries about the app by writing, "I would like to know not only its usefulness, but also the potential dangers."

Some participants seemed more positive about the app yet blamed authorities for not doing enough to promote the usage of COVID Alert. P22 wrote, "[I] t's not a bad idea but rather requires a critical mass of people to be using it to make sense, which I suspect is not the case. This really should be a mandatory thing as part of having cell coverage in the first place—in the same way you can't opt out from Amber Alerts, you should not be able to opt out from having this app active and for reporting your status if tested positive. Otherwise, it really doesn't work as effectively as it could." P47 added, "I would say there have been ads of various forms (e.g., on public transit, social media, etc.) asking people to download the app, but I don't think this has been effective. I don't believe enough has been done to effectively promote use of the app." P55 felt that usage of the app should be compulsory, adding, "I would have hoped that more citizens would install the application in order to improve its efficiency, or even make it mandatory…".

While there were more respondents who agreed that there had been enough information about the COVID Alert app in their area, a plurality of participants (41.33%) disagreed, as seen in Table 6. Similarly, 44% or respondents felt that provincial governments were best suited to inform the public about the COVID Alert app versus 29.33% who preferred that the federal government promotes the app, and 25.33 favoured municipal health authorities and municipalities. The federal-provincial-municipal dichotomy is important in Canada. Health is a provincial responsibility but the federal government and sets national standards when transferring funding for health to provinces. The interplay between federal policies versus provincial ones has been a major driver of the fight against the COVID-19 pandemic in Canada. As for municipalities and local health authorities in Canada, they are provincial "creatures" in Canada, and thus take as much responsibility as provincial governments will give them.

Table 6. There has been enough information about the COVID Alert app in my area.

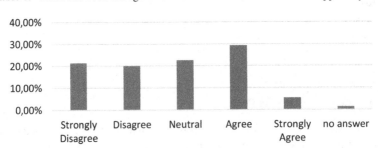

5.5   Respondents' Security and Privacy Concerns About the COVID Alert App

Respondents' responses about the usable security aspects of COVID Alert are perplexing. While a plurality of responders (45.21%) found the app convenient, safe, and confidential, another 42.47% had no opinion, as seen in Table 7. A significant number of respondents seem to have no direct interaction with the app and a lack of feedback allowing them to determine the efficacy of the app.

Table 7. My experience using COVID Alert was as convenient, safe, and confidential.

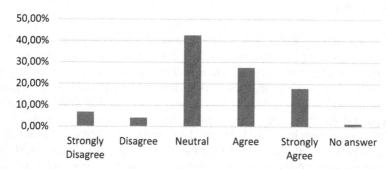

A minority of respondents (N = 7, 9.59%) estimated that the app collects and shares personal information with health authorities. This, as we know, is a serious concern in social tracing endeavours. Doubts persist as N = 20, 27.40% of respondents are unsure or do not know if the app collects any personally identifiable data about users, regardless of clear indications by federal authorities and health agencies that it does not. Yet, many respondents (N = 38, 52.05%) believe these indications by authorities.

But this positive outlook should not be celebrated just yet as N = 13, 17.81% of respondents believe that all data collected by the app is kept in a centralized database against N = 16, 21.92% who believe that it does not, and N = 37, 50.68% who does not know or is unsure. There appears to be a contradiction between these results and those about whether the app shares personal identifiable data to health authorities. Many of the same respondents (52.05%) who did not believe that app shared personally identifiable data about them were not as certain about the location of a centralized database which in essence would amount to the same outcome, in terms of personally identifiable data being shared and collected.

Similarly, N = 25, 34.25% of respondents felt that health authorities could trace the origin of a voluntary COVID-19 report through the app against N = 19, 26.03% who felt that this was possible sometimes, and N = 25, 34.25% who felt that that this never happened or did so only rarely, as seen in Table 8.

Table 8. Health authorities can trace the origin of a voluntary COVID-19 report.

6 Discussion

Digital literacy in respondents does not seem to deter the downloading of the COVID Alert app in respondents. As discussed above, our results showed high usage of their smartphones for several intensive activities such as surfing the internet, productivity, gaming, and creative works. Other activities such as phone calls, and texting require an awareness of notifications, call, and contact management, which would prepare users of the app to be able to interact and respond to exposure warnings effectively. Because most of the respondents in the study are aged 55 and under, low digital literacy cannot be used to explain the level of interaction of the study's respondents with COVID Alert.

Support for the COVID Alert app rested on its efficacy in the public. Without a perception of value in its users, they can mistrust the app. This mistrust thus can affect other segments of the population who perceive utility in terms of how many Canadian residents use the app. Thus, they can withdraw their own participation in this contact tracing endeavour. For example, P105 wrote, "The effectiveness of this app largely depends on the number of people who download it and mention that they have been infected. The government should therefore lead a campaign to encourage people to download it." P82 added "My level of confidence and my responses are moderate in terms of the level of security that I consider provided by this application, not because of the application itself, but rather since the effectiveness of this type of application lies in the fact that 'a significant proportion of the population must also use the application, which does not appear to be the case." P71 wrote, "I believe in the effectiveness of this application; however, many people do not use it, or forget to use it when a positive diagnosis is made. So, I cannot rely on this application to feel better protected and alerted in the event of a spread." Efficacy of the COVID Alert app is thus based not only on how people interact with it and how many positive results it broadcasts, but also how many users use the app.

It appears that people think the app is safe in that it respects privacy. However there were some usability issues such as the battery drain. Moreover, it seems that the app should have been sold as a utility capable of helping to achieve targeted containment. Seen this way, we think people would have seen a usefulness in the app which probably would have had a better impact on its acceptance.

Issues of trust are variably intertwined with issues of efficacy. For example, P50 relates that "I lost confidence in the application after having to enter my tracking code following a positive COVID screening test only to realize that my spouse did not even receive an exposure alert. It is obvious that our two cell phones were nearby for more than 15 min while the application was active on both phones." While examples such as P50's story could be flukes and at best anecdotes, the success of the COVID Alert app rests, unfortunately on such personal stories of users interacting of failing to interact with the app.

Paradoxically, an app designed to be passive and as unobtrusive as possible can be judged by users by standards that define other apps where extensive interaction and notifications can make it appear that the app is "doing something". P53 argued this when writing, "It [the app] seems unpopular. I would have liked to see a map with areas where COVID cases are known. There is still too much confidentiality. I take the example of lice: it is not a lack of hygiene that spreads the problem, but a lack of communication. Like COVID: it's accidental/unintentional (at least in most cases)." P77 suggested more features to increase interaction with the app and its appeal. "It would be nice if we occasionally won stuff (4K TV, trip to the South [after the pandemic…], gold, bitcoins, etc.)." P86 made further suggestions writing, "Perhaps links to help us detect symptoms or other tools for prevention."

The COVID Alert contact tracing app was designed to do one thing well, which is to warn Canadian residents of nearby exposure risks to infections. But apps have a different meaning with our people, and it is normal for them to expect this app to behave like other apps on their smartphones. When the app does not seem to act like other apps, users in our survey found started questioning its utility and efficacy.

7 Conclusion

In order to understand the scope of the COVID-19 Alert App that was launched by the Canadian federal government to deal with the COVID-19 pandemic, it seemed relevant to us to understand the perception of Canadian residents in terms of performance and privacy. This paper presents the first data that we collected through a survey that was carried out between December 28, 2020, and February 10, 2021.

Although the survey was open to everyone, only ninety-two persons participated in the survey. Of these, 57 were from Quebec while the remaining 11 were from Ontario. Although limited, the information collected suggested a level of resentment with the app. While some saw usability and efficacy issues, others raised questions about privacy. An important barrier to the apps' adoption seems to be the perception of a lack of engagement by the general populace by some of our respondents. This in turn discourages usage of the app by respondents who find such an app beneficial. A classic game theory challenge occurs as the fewer people perceive the app to be used, the fewer people want to use it. The particularity of this situation seems to us, an interesting avenue to explore in subsequent research on the adoption of the COVID Alert social tracing app.

References

1. Flanagan, W.F.: Equality rights for people with AIDS: mandatory reporting of HIV infection and contact tracing. McGill Law J. **34**(3), 53–602 (1989)
2. Armbruster, B., Brandeau, M.L.: Contact tracing to control infectious disease: when enough is enough. Health Care Manag. Sci. **10**(4), 341–355 (2007). https://doi.org/10.1007/s10729-007-9027-6

3. Bengio, Y., et al.: Inherent privacy limitations of decentralized contact tracing apps. J. Am. Med. Inform. Assoc. **28**(1), 193–195 (2021)

4. Dubov, A., Shoptawb, S.: The value and ethics of using technology to contain the COVID-19 epidemic. Am. J. Bioeth. **20**(7), W7–W11 (2020)

5. Guinchard, A.: Our digital footprint under Covid-19: should we fear the UK digital contact tracing app? Int. Rev. Law Comput. Technol. **35**(1), 84–97 (2021)

6. Kitchin, R.: Civil liberties or public health, or civil liberties and public health? Using surveillance technologies to tackle the spread of COVID-19. Space Polity **24**(3), 362–381 (2020)

7. van Kolfschooten, H., de Ruijter, A.: COVID-19 and privacy in the European Union: a legal perspective on contact tracing. Contemp. Secur. Policy **41**(3), 478–491 (2020)

8. Nguyen, K.A., Luo, Z., Watkins, C.: Epidemic contact tracing with smartphone sensors. J. Locat. Based Serv. **14**(2), 92–128 (2020)

9. Roche, S.: Smile, you're being traced! Some thoughts about the ethical issues of digital contact tracing applications. J. Locat. Based Serv. **14**(2), 71–91 (2020)

10. Rowe, F., Ngwenyama, O., Richet, J.-L.: Contact tracing apps and alienation in the age of COVID-19. Eur. J. Inf. Syst. **20**(5), 545–562 (2020)

11. Trang, S., Trenz, M., Weiger, W.H., Tarafdar, M., Cheung, C.M.: One app to trace them all? Examining app specifications for mass acceptance of contact-tracing apps. Eur. J. Inf. Syst. **29**(4), 415–428 (2020)

12. Saint-Louis, H.: User perceptions of security risks related to contact tracing technologies. In: 2020 SERENE-RISC Workshop, Montreal (2020)

13. Ferretti, L., et al.: Quantifying SARS-CoV-2 transmission suggests epidemic control with digital contact tracing. Science **368**(6491), 1–7 (2020)

14. Crossler, R.E., Bélanger, F.: The mobile privacy-security knowledge gap model: understanding behaviors. In: Proceedings of the 50th Hawaii International Conference on System Sciences, Honolulu (2017)

15. Mancini, C., Thomas, K., Rogers, Y., Price, B.A., Jedrzejczyk, L., Bandara, A., Nuseibeh, B.: From spaces to places: emerging contexts in mobile privacy. In: UbiComp 2009: Proceedings of the 11th International Conference on Ubiquitous Computing, New York (2009)

16. Boyles, J.L., Smith, A., Madden, M.: Privacy and Data Management on Mobile Devices. Pew Research Center, Washington (2012)

17. Barkuus, L., Dey, A.: Location-based services for mobile telephony: a study of users' privacy concerns. In: Proceedings of the INTERACT 2003, 9TH IFIP TC13 International Conference on Human-Computer Interaction, Zurich (2003)

18. Simpson, E., Conner, A.: Digital Contact Tracing to Contain the Coronavirus: Recommendations for States. Center for American Progress, Washington, D.C. (2020)

19. European Commission: COMMISSION RECOMMENDATION of 8.4.2020 on a common Union toolbox for the use of technology and data to combat and exit from the COVID-19 crisis, in particular concerning mobile applications and the use of anonymised mobility data. Brussels: European Commission (2020)

20. Tognott, E.: Lessons from the history of quarantine, from plague to influenza A. Emerg. Infect. Dis. **19**(2), 254–259 (2013)

21. Piret, J., Boivin, G.: Pandemics throughout history. Front. Microbiol. **11**(631736) (2020)

22. COVID-19 Exposure Notification App Advisory Council: Interim report on social and economic determinants of app adoption, retention and use. Government of Canada, Ottawa (2021)

23. Sacks, J.A., et al.: Introduction of mobile health tools to support Ebola surveillance and contact tracing in Guinea. Global Health: Sci. Pract. **3**(4), 646–659 (2015)

24. Danquah, L.O., et al.: Use of a mobile application for Ebola contact tracing and monitoring in northern Sierra Leone: a proof-of-concept study. BMC Infect. Dis. **19**, 810 (2019)
25. Ahmed, N., et al.: A survey of COVID-19 contact tracing apps. IEEE Access **8**, 134577–134601 (2020)

The Role of IoT in the Fight Against Covid-19 to Restructure the Economy

Abhishek Sharma[(✉)] [iD]

Swinburne University of Technology, Melbourne, Australia

Abstract. In the current Covid-19 situation, people all over the world must begin to adhere to social distancing guidelines. However, ensuring that people follow these social distancing guidelines has proven to be a difficult challenge for the government. To combat this issue, authorities have implemented IoT solutions such as remote health monitoring and contact tracing techniques to effectively manage the spread of coronavirus. To address this issue in depth, the current paper provides a comprehensive review of how IoT applications have aided the healthcare, education, home, entertainment, transportation, hospitality, and retail sectors of an economy. Additionally, the risk and challenges posed by the widespread adoption of IoT solutions are also addressed. Finally, the paper suggests ways to mitigate existing challenges associated with the implementation of IoT solutions.

Keywords: Covid-19 · IoT privacy · IoT applications · Pandemic

1 Introduction

The global pandemic of COVID-19 epidemic began in December 2019 in the Chinese city of Wuhan. Since then, the outbreak has spread to over 200 countries, with 175,231,926 confirmed cases and a death toll of 3,778,632 to date (Worldometers 2020). The virus began to gain international attention in the Hubei province of China after its widespread effects began to emerge in other countries such as India, USA, and Europe (Cucinotta and Vanelli 2020; Yousif et al. 2021; Zwitter and Gstrein 2020). Even now, densely populated countries (such as India, Brazil, and the United States) appear to be dealing with massive infections and rising death tolls on a daily basis (Singhal 2020; Wang et al. 2020a). As a result of the increase in infections, governments worldwide have imposed social distancing guidelines, which have influenced how people perform their daily tasks (Bentlage et al. 2020; Jahmunah et al. 2021; Yousif et al. 2021). To address these problems, IoT technologies such as contact tracing applications, remote health tracking techniques, and many others have been implemented to fight against the pandemic.

Since its inception, IoT technologies have proven to play a critical role in a variety sectors of an economy (Jie et al. 2013; Lee and Lee 2015). However, its major implementation has proven to be useful in lockdown situations where face-to-face interactions are limited and risky (Siddiqui et al. 2021; Yousif et al. 2021). Some of its applications are used to prevent the virus from spreading (e.g., contact tracing, quarantine monitoring, temperature screening, etc.), while others are used to help people

© Springer Nature Switzerland AG 2021
C. Stephanidis et al. (Eds.): HCII 2021, LNCS 13097, pp. 140–156, 2021.
https://doi.org/10.1007/978-3-030-90966-6_11

adjust to the new normal that the pandemic has created (e.g., Virtual education, smart gym, contactless housekeeping services) (Jahmunah et al. 2021; Kumar et al. 2020; Siddiqui et al. 2021; Stavropoulos et al. 2020; Yousif et al. 2021). On a broader scale, IoT solutions in Covid-19 scenarios have proven to be effective in the sectors of healthcare, education, transportation, hospitality, and retail industries. These applications include GPS tracking, face mask detection, RFID, and NFC technologies that are embedded in wearable/portable devices that can be used in everyday situations (Jahmunah et al. 2021; Siddiqui et al. 2021; Stavropoulos et al. 2020; Yousif et al. 2021). Though IoT technologies have helped in the fight against the spread of Covid19, long-term use of these technologies poses significant risks to a user's privacy (Angst and Agarwal 2009; Cho et al. 2020; Jung and Park 2018). As a result, as an emerging field of study, an in-depth examination of how IoT solutions are effective in real-world scenarios and their privacy concerns in widespread adoption needs to be addressed. Therefore, the current paper discusses the significance and privacy issues of IoT solutions in the seven key sectors of an economy (such as healthcare, education, home, entertainment, transportation, hospitality, and retail) in the fight against the Covid-19 pandemic.

The paper is structured in six sections as follows. Section 1 introduces the topic and provides an overview of the main goals of this paper. Next, Sect. 2 provides an idea of the key objectives of this study, along with the discussions on the role of IoT technology in previous literature. Next, in Sect. 3, a brief discussion of the methodology used in this study to conduct this review is provided. Next, in Sect. 4, key selected literature on the role of IoT solutions in relation to Covid-19 are reviewed. Later, Sect. 5 briefs a summary of the challenges associated with adopting IoT solutions in Covid-19. Lastly, in Sect. 6, suggestions for mitigating the challenges posed by the large-scale implementation of IoT solutions are highlighted, followed by the concluding remarks of the paper.

2 Background

The COVID-19 pandemic has increased the level of uncertainty in an individual's lifestyle. However, within the current new normal situation, IoT (i.e., Internet of Things) and AI (i.e., Artificial Intelligence) are expected to play a crucial role in everyone's lifestyles (Javaid and Khan 2021; Kamal et al. 2020; Lotfi and Elmisery 2019; Yousif et al. 2021). The majority of the COVID-19 challenges are expected to be met by IoT solutions. Officials are now employing IoT solutions to combat the COVID-19 challenges, either as an alert system or as a warning/penalty mechanism (Jahmunah et al. 2021; Siddiqui et al. 2021; Yousif et al. 2021). For example, IoT technologies can notify officials about an increase in the density of people present in a specific location (Jahmunah et al. 2021; Yousif et al. 2021). Furthermore, it has been observed in several instances that people are using wearable devices (such as IoT-Q bands and proximity tracing) to track people who are in quarantine while adhering to social distancing guidelines (Jahmunah et al. 2021; Seshadri et al. 2020; Singh et al. 2020; Stavropoulos et al. 2020). In addition, delivery-based drones and disinfectant-based drones are used in the hospitality and tourism industries to monitor safe contactless services (Jahmunah et al. 2021; Siddiqui et al. 2021; Yousif et al. 2021).

Despite the fact that these IoT solutions are beneficial, their scalability, dependability, and privacy concerns are all major barriers to widespread adoption (Jahmunah et al. 2021;

Kamal et al. 2020; Mbunge 2020). Furthermore, these IoT solutions have been found to be questionable in most cases when it comes to providing adequate security solutions to the community while avoiding major breaches of privacy. As a result, the current paper provides a review of the key IoT technologies that are being used to address the challenges posed by Covid-19 in this new normal situation. Several reviews in the literature address various aspects of IoT. However, only a few studies have depicted the key challenges of IoT applications and are able to provide a brief idea on how to address its privacy concerns. As a result, the current study focuses on discussing the application of key IoT solutions in various economic sectors and providing answers to the following research questions:

(a) Identification of critical IoT applications that aid in the management of COVID19-related issues.
(b) Providing a more in-depth review of the privacy and security issues raised by IoT applications used in the Covid-19 pandemic.
(c) Identifying and recommending key strategies for mitigating the existing challenges posed by IoT solutions.

3 Methodology

To meet the above-mentioned objectives, an extensive literature review search is conducted upon designated databases such as EbscoHost, ProQuest and Google Scholar. Based on this review, articles are chosen that correspond to the key sectors and their contributions to COVID-19 through IoT technologies. Several keywords shown in Table 1 below were selected to conduct this review.

Table 1. Search results from designated databases

Keywords	EBSCOhost	Google Scholar	ProQuest
IOT AND COVID AND Healthcare	41	5,400	413
IOT AND COVID AND Transportation	2	3,510	229
IOT AND COVID AND Education	17	6,690	374
IOT AND COVID AND Retail	6	2,580	129
IOT AND COVID AND Entertainment	252	1,820	69
IOT AND COVID AND Hospitality	136	990	58

The purpose of this review was better to understand the impact of IoT-based technologies within COVID-19. The industry sectors and the implementations of IoT chosen are not exhaustive. It is chosen based on the initial search results obtained from the designated databases, which are primarily based on previous studies conducted upon the role of IoT solutions within the Covid-19. Furthermore, the key sectors selected within this review are depicted in Fig. 1 below.

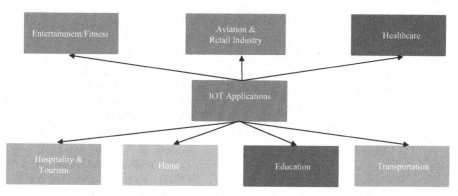

Fig. 1. IoT applications within different sectors

Based on the sectors selected for this review, the following subsections details how IoT technologies and solutions have been shown to be useful in each of these sectors of an economy.

4 Role of IoT Solutions in Covid-19

4.1 Healthcare

Even before the Covid-19 pandemic, IoT had made several positive contributions to the healthcare industry by transforming the way patients are monitored. However, its major contributions were visible during the Covid-19 pandemic. With personalized solutions designed to monitor each patient thoroughly, IoT has always ensured that it can track a patient's health status and generate alerts on any unusual detections of attacks. Moreover, smart solutions used during the COVID-19 pandemic, such as wearable sensors, drones, and robots, have improved the way patient monitoring is done in a time-efficient manner as per social distancing guidelines (Behar et al. 2020; Javaid and Khan 2021; Kumar et al. 2020; Seshadri et al. 2020). Therefore, based on the number of search results and recommendations made by previous studies, a review of how IoT solutions have benefited the healthcare sectors is presented in Table 2 below.

4.2 Aviation and Retail Industry

The aviation and retail sectors are primarily oriented with a customer-centric approach. However, due to several lockdowns and social distancing constraints in the Covid-19 situations, retailers and aviation industries have struggled to maintain sustainable profits (Choi 2021; Drljača et al. 2020; Serrano and Kazda 2020; Siddiqui et al. 2021). In addressing these issues, IoT solutions are effective in improving consumer experiences for target audiences while adhering to social distancing guidelines (Drljača et al. 2020; Shankar et al. 2021; Wang et al. 2020b). Furthermore, most security checkpoints and service points within the aviation and retail sectors have been automated by IoT technologies (Braithwaite et al. 2020; Drljača et al. 2020). Therefore, based on the number

Table 2. Role of IoT applications in healthcare sectors

Domain	Applications of IoT	Related literature
Healthcare	Contact tracing	Reichert et al. (2020), Dar et al. (2020), Cho et al. (2020), Ahmed et al. (2020), Javaid and Khan (2021), Mbunge (2020), Riemer et al. (2020), Siriwardhana et al. (2020)
	Wearable sensors	Seshadri et al. (2020), Ates et al. (2021), Al-Emran and Ehrenfeld (2021), Sun et al. (2020), Ding et al. (2020), Weizman et al. (2020), Quer et al. (2021), Stojanović et al. (2020), Krishnamurthi et al. (2021), Siriwardhana et al. (2020)
	Remote health monitoring	Behar et al. (2020), Watson et al. (2020), Annis et al. (2020), Naik et al. (2020), Massaroni et al. (2020), De Morais Barroca Filho et al. (2021), Izmailova et al. (2020)
	Emergency services	Kamal et al. (2020), Bai et al. (2021)
	Hospital bed management	Pecoraro et al. (2021), Pecoraro et al. (2020), Jena et al. (2021), Manoj et al. (2019), Javaid and Khan (2021)
	Hygiene management (automated hand hygiene systems)	Omoyibo et al. (2020), Lotfi and Elmisery (2019)

of search results and recommendations made by previous studies, a review of how IoT technologies have benefited the aviation and retail industries is presented in Table 3 below.

4.3 Entertainment and Fitness

Several lockdowns and social distancing guidelines have been implemented around the world during the pandemic. As a result of these circumstances, entertainment and fitness activities (such as gym, clubs, theatres, and travel) have almost lost their presence in the current world (Siddiqui et al. 2021; Yousif et al. 2021). However, IoT solutions such as wearable equipment and smart gyms have helped people to access sports centres and other leisure activities in this pandemic to make life easier within easing limitations (Siddiqui et al. 2021; Yousif et al. 2021). This technology can be used in conjunction with a pandemic or regulatory rules since it reduces face-to-face encounters, limits gathering with other people, and reduces the risk of coronavirus exposure in any social gathering setting. Therefore, based on the number of search results and recommendations made by previous studies, a review of how IoT solutions have helped the entertainment and fitness sectors of an economy is presented in Table 4 below.

Table 3. Role of IoT applications in aviation management & retail sectors

Domain	Applications of IoT	Related literature
Aviation management & retail Industry	Social distancing	Huynh (2020), Barrios et al. (2021)
	Self-checkout/self-service kiosk	Shankar et al. (2021), Wang et al. (2020b), Marabelli et al. (2021), Shin and Kang (2020), Siddiqui et al. (2021)
	Automated boarding pass control	Drljača et al. (2020), Serrano and Kazda (2020)
	Automated security checkpoints	Drljača et al. (2020), Braithwaite et al. (2020)

Table 4. Role of IoT applications in entertainment & fitness sectors

Domain	Applications of IoT	Related literature
Entertainment/fitness	Smart gym	Bentlage et al. (2020), Siddiqui et al. (2021)
	Online gym classrooms	Nyenhuis et al. (2020), Yousif et al. (2021)

4.4 Transportation

COVID-19 has greatly influenced the transportation industry (Umair et al. 2021; Yousif et al. 2021). In addition, IoT solutions have changed the way contact tracing is carried out within the transportation industry (Darsena et al. 2020). In most cases, officials have been seen inquiring about people who have recently travelled to hotspot zones and keeping a close eye on close contacts (Brinchi et al. 2020; Jung and Agulto 2021). Consequently, government officials have begun to use IoT solutions to avoid face-to-face contact. Therefore, based on the number of search results and recommendations made by previous studies, a review of how IoT solutions have helped the transportation sectors of an economy is presented in Table 5 below.

4.5 Education

The pandemic has caused a reform in the educational system by reducing face-to-face instruction and on-campus learning. Students and teachers have now been forced to adapt to online learning facilities (Daniel 2020; Schneider and Council 2020; Yousif et al. 2021). In this situation, IoT solutions have made it possible for students to learn and communicate effectively with their teachers and family members. Although online education has established a better route for interactive teaching methods, it remains questionable how virtual studies can improve learning conducted through laboratories (Besser et al. 2020; Marek et al. 2021). Therefore, based on the number of search results and recommendations made by previous studies, a review of how IoT solutions have

Table 5. Role of IoT applications in transportation sectors

Domain	Applications of IoT	Related literature
Transportation	Transport monitoring	Darsena et al. (2020), Brinchi et al. (2020)
	Smart vehicles	Gupta et al. (2020), Golpîra et al. (2021)
	Traffic monitoring & management	Favale et al. (2020), Parr et al. (2020), Fernández-Caramés et al. (2020), Jung and Agulto (2021), Umair et al. (2021)
	Incident management	Wang et al. (2020a), De Tantillo and Christopher (2021), Krishnan et al. (2021)

helped the education and communications sectors of an economy is presented in Table 6 below.

Table 6. Role of IoT applications in education sectors

Domain	Applications of IoT	Related literature
Education	Distance learning & virtual studies	Schneider and Council (2020), Daniel (2020), Lassoued et al. (2020), Marek et al. (2021), Churiyah et al. (2020), Dietrich et al. (2020), Giovannella (2021), Chen et al. (2020), Yousif et al. (2021), Chandra (2020)
	Face recognition	Cabani et al. (2021), Ting et al. (2020), Yousif et al. (2021)

4.6 Home

The global pandemic has significantly altered how people live their lives and work. The terrible consequences of these lockdowns were undoubtedly apparent within the education sectors of an economy. As education shifts away from traditional platforms towards online/virtual classrooms, parents are forced to devote more time to monitoring and motivating their children to continue their education (Chandra 2020; Siddiqui et al. 2021). E-learning/conferencing demands high-speed digital technologies and continuous internet connections. Additionally, to ensure that internet technologies are delivered continuously, businesses are ensuring that apps such as Zoom, Microsoft Teams, Canvas, and Skype are included in cloud services (Çaldağ et al. 2021; Lieux et al. 2021). However, as a result of these unprecedented changes in lifestyles, parents were discovered to be under severe stress as they had to handle work from home as well as other household responsibilities. To address some of these issues, smart home services are being installed to reduce anxiety and stress in the household activities (Sequeiros et al. 2021; Yousif et al. 2021). Therefore, based on the number of search results and recommendations made by previous studies, a review of how IoT solutions have helped household sectors of an economy is presented in Table 7 below.

Table 7. Role of IoT applications in household sectors

Domain	Applications of IoT	Related literature
Home	Working/studying from home	Hermanto et al. (2021), Ford et al. (2020), Wilczewski et al. (2021), Feng and Zhou (2020)
	Emotional well-being management	Lades et al. (2020), Ripp et al. (2020), Restubog et al. (2020), Thomaier et al. (2020), Wu et al. (2020), Kanekar and Sharma (2020), Sequeiros et al. (2021)

4.7 Hospitality and Tourism Industry

The global tourism and hospitality industry has been greatly impacted by the COVID-19 pandemic and strict travel restrictions (Pillai et al. 2021; Sharma et al. 2021). The hotel industry was the first to be severely impacted by the epidemic and is still expected to take the longest to recover, with over 3 million hotel-related jobs lost (Pillai et al. 2021; Shin and Kang 2020). While there have always been risks associated with travel and tourism, the primary concern for most tourists when visiting places or hospitality properties is a health risk (Shin and Kang 2020). In this regard, IoT solutions have consistently provided services that can track and monitor persons who are travelling or are in quarantine. Therefore, based on the number of search results and recommendations made by previous studies, a review of how IoT solutions have helped hospitality and tourism sectors of an economy is presented in Table 8 below.

5   Challenges of IoT Solutions

IoT solutions have grown exponentially in the current era of digital technology. However, implementing these IoT solutions is not simple. Scalability along with privacy and security issues, are two major concerns that must be addressed before it can be implemented on a larger scale (De Morais Barroca Filho et al. 2021; Xu et al. 2020b; Yousif et al. 2021).

IoT solutions used in healthcare sectors rely heavily on these IoHT devices, which track and monitor crucial patient information and store it in cloud services (Al-Aswad et al. 2021; Jahmunah et al. 2021). Each IoT device is supposed to contain several sensors. With so much data flowing every second, disruptions in LTE/4G/5G networks

Table 8. Role of IoT applications in hospitality and tourism sectors

Domain	Applications of IoT	Related literature
Hospitality & tourism	Facial check-in services	Lau (2020), Xu et al. (2020a), Pillai et al. (2021)
	Contactless housekeeping services	Jiang and Wen (2020), Pillai et al. (2021), Zeng et al. (2020)
	Online food delivery	Mehrolia et al. (2020), Ali et al. (2021), Chang and Meyerhoefer (2021), Kim et al. (2021), Pillai et al. (2021), Rummo et al. (2020)

could place patients in critical condition (Siriwardhana et al. 2020). Furthermore, IoT networks must focus more on data encryption to provide end-to-end security for their users. Moreover, Yousif et al. (2021) state that IoT devices present several security challenges when connected to other devices of varying versions and complexities.

As a result, before IoT technologies can be used on a broader scale in post-pandemic stages, privacy and security concerns must be adequately addressed. Further, it could be argued that the adoption of IoT solutions will be limited unless security and privacy are guaranteed. Therefore, a brief on security & privacy issues related to IoT solutions are showcased in Table 9.

Table 9. Risk & challenges of IoT solutions

IoT solutions	Risks & challenges	Related literature
Contact tracing apps	Permission of users and justification of information to users	Cho et al. (2020), Liu et al. (2020), Mbunge (2020)
Wearable sensors	Wearable devices increase the risk of confidential data being hacked or lost	Ghaffari et al. (2021), Homayounfar and Andrew (2020), Nasiri and Khosravani (2020)
Smart camera devices connected to a wireless network	Misuse of surveillance by spying on others or interested parties, ethical concerns about privacy	Capuder et al. (2020), Uddin et al. (2019)
IoT smart homes/mobile apps	Malicious attacks, Risks to sensitive data	Prange et al. (2019), Sovacool and Del Rio (2020)
Online teaching	Associations with adaptability, Lack of motivation, Technical obstacles	Besser et al. (2020), Gill et al. (2020), Hutchison et al. (2020)
Self-checkout/self-service kiosk	Increased theft and higher installation costs	Lee and Leonas (2020), Putra (2020)

Although some IoT solutions are not yet sufficiently mature to be utilized on a broad scale, it has demonstrated a great potential for tackling the pandemic. This review is expected to provide additional validation and assist in the future development of these applications, allowing them to be deployed in a larger context with confidence.

6 Mitigating the Challenges Posed by IoT Solutions in Covid-19

With the increased reliance on IoT solutions within the Covid-19, its growth in the coming years is expected to skyrocket. However, the adoption of IoT solutions will be limited unless its security and privacy are assured. The challenges of developing scalable IoT networks are apparent; however, solutions to these issues are discussed in a limited amount of literature that discusses how IoT solutions can be successfully deployed. As a result, noteworthy solutions to these challenges of IoT solutions are presented in the below Table 10.

Table 10. Solutions to the existing challenges of IoT solutions

IoT implementation challenges	Solutions	Related literature
Interoperability & data security	IoT solutions with lightweight security algorithms	Shah and Engineer (2019), Goyal and Sahula (2016), Ahmed et al. (2019), Kamal et al. (2020)
Adaptive & predictive analysis	IoT networks based on artificial intelligence	Kamal et al. (2020), Akbar et al. (2017)
Developing security architecture	Implementation of generic layering system that consists of: - Perception layer, Network layer, Support layer and Application layer	Yousif et al. (2021), Leloglu (2016)
Improving privacy & security	Integrating Blockchain technology with IoT networks	Dorri et al. (2017), Kamal et al. (2020), Reyna et al. (2018), Al-Aswad et al. (2021)

7 Conclusion

The importance of IoT technologies has grown dramatically over the last decade. However, the best of its applications can be seen in the Covid-19 situation. Several IoT solutions (e.g., contact tracing) have provided much-needed assistance in managing the COVID-19 outbreak, whereas others are being deployed as experimental trials. Although the majority of these IoT solutions have shown promising results in the current pandemic situation, their large-scale implementation is still uncertain due to security and privacy concerns.

As a result, this review summarizes the key applications of these IoT solutions in seven key economic sectors. Furthermore, it elaborates on the key challenges associated with the implementation of key IoT solutions in various sectors of the economy. Finally, the review offers solutions to the key challenges of IoT technologies that arise during large-scale implementation.

References

Ahmed, N., et al.: A survey of Covid-19 contact tracing apps. IEEE Access **8**, 134577–134601 (2020)

Ahmed, S.F., Islam, M.R., Nath, T.D., Ferdosi, B.J., Hasan, A.T.: G-TBSA: a generalized lightweight security algorithm for IoT. In: 2019 4th International Conference on Electrical Information and Communication Technology (EICT), pp. 1–6. IEEE (2019)

Akbar, A., Khan, A., Carrez, F., Moessner, K.: Predictive analytics for complex IoT data streams. IEEE Internet Things J. **4**(5), 1571–1582 (2017)

Al-Aswad, H., El-Medany, W.M., Balakrishna, C., Ababneh, N., Curran, K.: BZKP: blockchain-based zero-knowledge proof model for enhancing healthcare security in Bahrain IoT smart cities and COVID-19 risk mitigation. Arab J. Basic Appl. Sci. **28**(1), 154–171 (2021)

Al-Emran, M., Ehrenfeld, J.M.: Breaking out of the box: wearable technology applications for detecting the spread of COVID-19. J. Med. Syst. **45**(2), 1–2 (2021). https://doi.org/10.1007/s10916-020-01697-1

Ali, S., Khalid, N., Javed, H.M.U., Islam, D.M.: Consumer adoption of online food delivery ordering (OFDO) services in Pakistan: the impact of the COVID-19 pandemic situation. J. Open Innov. Technol. **7**(1), 10 (2021)

Angst, C.M., Agarwal, R.: Adoption of electronic health records in the presence of privacy concerns: the elaboration likelihood model and individual persuasion. MIS Q. **33**(2), 339–370 (2009)

Annis, T., et al.: Rapid implementation of a COVID-19 remote patient monitoring program. J. Am. Med. Inform. Assoc. **27**(8), 1326–1330 (2020)

Ates, H.C., Yetisen, A.K., Güder, F., Dincer, C.: Wearable devices for the detection of COVID-19. Nat. Electron. **4**(1), 13–14 (2021)

Bai, J., Xu, T., Ji, A.-P., Sun, W., Huang, M.-W.: Impact of COVID-19 on oral emergency services. Int. Dent. J. **71**(1), 27–31 (2021)

Barrios, J.M., Benmelech, E., Hochberg, Y.V., Sapienza, P., Zingales, L.: Civic capital and social distancing during the Covid-19 pandemic. J. Public Econ. **193**, 104310 (2021)

Behar, J.A.: Remote health diagnosis and monitoring in the time of COVID-19. Physiol. Measur. **41**(10), (2020)

Bentlage, E., et al.: Practical recommendations for maintaining active lifestyle during the COVID-19 pandemic: a systematic literature review. Int. J. Environ. Res. Public Health **17**(17), 62–65 (2020)

Besser, A., Flett, G.L., Zeigler-Hill, V.: Adaptability to a sudden transition to online learning during the COVID-19 pandemic: understanding the challenges for students. Scholarsh. Teaching Learning in Psychology (2020)

Braithwaite, I., Callender, T., Bullock, M., Aldridge, R.W.: Automated and partly automated contact tracing: a systematic review to inform the control of COVID-19. Lancet Digit. Health **2**(11), (2020)

Brinchi, S., et al.: On transport monitoring and forecasting during COVID-19 pandemic in Rome. Transp. Telecommun. **21**(4), 275–284 (2020)

Cabani, A., Hammoudi, K., Benhabiles, H., Melkemi, M.: MaskedFace-Net–A dataset of correctly/incorrectly masked face images in the context of COVID-19. Smart Health **19**, 100144 (2021)

Çaldağ, M.T., Gökalp, E., Alkış, N.: ICT-based distance higher education: a necessity during the era of COVID-19 outbreak. In: Arpaci, I., Al-Emran, M., A. Al-Sharafi, M., Marques, G. (eds.) Emerging Technologies During the Era of COVID-19 Pandemic. SSDC, vol. 348, pp. 365–385. Springer, Cham (2021). https://doi.org/10.1007/978-3-030-67716-9_23

Capuder, T., Sprčić, D.M., Zoričić, D., Pandžić, H.: Review of challenges and assessment of electric vehicles integration policy goals: Integrated risk analysis approach. Int. J. Electr. Power Energy Syst. **119**, 105894 (2020)

Chandra, Y., Online education during COVID-19: perception of academic stress and emotional intelligence coping strategies among college students. Asian Educ. Dev. Stud. **10**(2), 229–238 (2020)

Chang, H.H., Meyerhoefer, C.D.: COVID-19 and the demand for online food shopping services: empirical evidence from Taiwan. Am. J. Agr. Econ. **103**(2), 448–465 (2021)

Chen, E., Kaczmarek, K., Ohyama, H.: Student perceptions of distance learning strategies during COVID-19. J. Dental Educ. **85**, 1190–1191 (2020)

Cho, H., Ippolito, D., Yu, Y.W.: Contact tracing mobile apps for COVID-19: Privacy considerations and related trade-offs. arXiv preprint arXiv:2003.11511 (2020)

Choi, J.H.: Changes in airport operating procedures and implications for airport strategies post-COVID-19. J. Air Transp. Manag. **94**, 102065 (2021)

Churiyah, M., Sholikhan, S., Filianti, F., Sakdiyyah, D.A.: Indonesia education readiness conducting distance learning in Covid-19 pandemic situation. Int. J. Multicult. Multirelig. Underst. **7**(6), 491–507 (2020)

Cucinotta, D., Vanelli, M.: WHO declares COVID-19 a pandemic. Acta Bio-Medica Atenei Parmensis **91**(1), 157–160 (2020)

Daniel, S.J.: Education and the COVID-19 pandemic. Prospects **49**(1–2), 91–96 (2020). https://doi.org/10.1007/s11125-020-09464-3

Dar, A.B., Lone, A.H., Zahoor, S., Khan, A.A., Naaz, R.: Applicability of mobile contact tracing in fighting pandemic (COVID-19): issues, challenges and solutions. Comput. Sci. Rev. **38**, 100307 (2020)

Darsena, D., Gelli, G., Iudice, I., Verde, F.: Safe and reliable public transportation systems (SALUTARY) in the COVID-19 pandemic. arXiv preprint arXiv:2009.12619 (2020)

De Morais Barroca Filho, I., Aquino, G, Malaquias, R.S., Girão, G., Melo, S.R.M.: An IoT-based healthcare platform for patients in ICU beds during the COVID-19 outbreak. IEEE Access **9**, 27262–27277 (2021)

De Tantillo, L., Christopher, R.: Implementing the national incident management system at schools of nursing in response to COVID-19. J. Prof. Nurs. **37**(2), 255–260 (2021)

Dietrich, N., et al.: Attempts, successes, and failures of distance learning in the time of COVID-19. J. Chem. Educ. **97**(9), 2448–2457 (2020)

Ding, X., et al.: Wearable sensing and telehealth technology with potential applications in the coronavirus pandemic. IEEE Rev. Biomed. Eng. **14**, 48–70 (2020)

Dorri, A., Kanhere, S.S., Jurdak, R., Gauravaram, P.: Blockchain for IoT security and privacy: the case study of a smart home. In: 2017 IEEE International Conference on Pervasive Computing and Communications Workshops (PerCom Workshops), pp. 618–623. IEEE (2017)

Drljača, M., Štimac, I., Bračić, M., Petar, S.: The role and influence of industry 4.0 in airport operations in the context of COVID-19. Sustainability **12**(24), 10614 (2020)

Favale, T., Soro, F., Trevisan, M., Drago, I., Mellia, M.: Campus traffic and e-learning during COVID-19 pandemic. Comput. Netw. **176**, 107290 (2020)

Feng, Y., Zhou, W.: Is working from home the new norm? An observational study based on a large geo-tagged Covid-19 twitter dataset. arXiv preprint arXiv:2006.08581 (2020)

Fernández-Caramés, T.M., Froiz-Míguez, I., Fraga-Lamas, P.: An IoT and blockchain based system for monitoring and tracking real-time occupancy for COVID-19 public safety. In: Engineering Proceedings, p. 67. Multidisciplinary Digital Publishing Institute (2020)

Ford, D., et al.: A tale of two cities: software developers working from home during the Covid-19 pandemic. arXiv preprint arXiv:2008.11147 (2020)

Ghaffari, R., Rogers, J.A., Ray, T.R.: Recent progress, challenges, and opportunities for wearable biochemical sensors for sweat analysis. Sens. Actuators 332, 129–447 (2021)

Gill, D., Whitehead, C., Wondimagegn, D.: Challenges to medical education at a time of physical distancing. Lancet 396(10244), 77–79 (2020)

Giovannella, C.: Effect induced by the Covid-19 pandemic on students' perception about technologies and distance learning. In: Mealha, Ó., Rehm, M., Rebedea, T. (eds.) Ludic, Co-design and Tools Supporting Smart Learning Ecosystems and Smart Education. SIST, vol. 197, pp. 105–116. Springer, Singapore (2021). https://doi.org/10.1007/978-981-15-7383-5_9

Golpîra, H., Khan, S.A.R., Safaeipour, S.: A review of logistics internet-of-things: current trends and scope for future research. J. Ind. Inf. Integr. 22, 100194 (2021)

Goyal, T.K., Sahula, V.: Lightweight security algorithm for low power IoT devices. In: 2016 International Conference on Advances in Computing, Communications and Informatics (ICACCI), pp. 1725–1729. IEEE (2016)

Gupta, M., Abdelsalam, M., Mittal, S.: Enabling and enforcing social distancing measures using smart city and its infrastructures: a COVID-19 use case. arXiv preprint arXiv:2004.09246 (2020)

Hermanto, H., Rai, N.G.M., Fahmi, A.: Students' opinions about studying from home during the COVID-19 pandemic in Indonesia. Cypriot J. Educ. Sci. 16(2), 499–510 (2021)

Homayounfar, S.Z., Andrew, T.L.: Wearable sensors for monitoring human motion: a review on mechanisms, materials, and challenges. SLAS Technol. 25(1), 9–24 (2020)

Hutchison, K., Paatsch, L., Cloonan, A.: Reshaping home–school connections in the digital age: challenges for teachers and parents. E-Learn. Digit. Media 17(2), 167–182 (2020)

Huynh, T.L.D.: Does culture matter social distancing under the COVID-19 pandemic? Saf. Sci. 130, 104872 (2020)

Izmailova, E.S., Ellis, R., Benko, C.: Remote monitoring in clinical trials during the Covid-19 pandemic. Clin. Transl. Sci. 13(5), 838–841 (2020)

Jahmunah, V., et al.: Future IoT tools for COVID-19 contact tracing and prediction: a review of the state-of-the-science. Int. J. Imaging Syst. Technol. 31(2), 455–471 (2021)

Javaid, M., Khan, I.H.: Internet of Things (IoT) enabled healthcare helps to take the challenges of COVID-19 pandemic. J. Oral Biol. Craniofacial Res. 11(2), 209–214 (2021)

Jena, K.K., Bhoi, S.K., Prasad, M., Puthal, D., A fuzzy rule-based efficient hospital bed management approach for coronavirus disease-19 infected patients. Neural Comput. Appl. 1–22 (2021).https://doi.org/10.1007/s00521-021-05719-y

Jiang, Y., Wen, J.: Effects of COVID-19 on hotel marketing and management: a perspective article. Int. J. Contemp. Hosp. Manag. 32(8), 2563–2573 (2020)

Jie, Y., Pei, J.Y., Jun, L., Yun, G., Wei, X.: Smart home system based on IoT technologies. In: 2013 International Conference on Computational and Information Sciences, pp. 1789–1791. IEEE (2013)

Jung, Y., Agulto, R.: A public platform for virtual IoT-based monitoring and tracking of COVID-19. Electronics 10(1), 12 (2021)

Jung, Y., Park, J.: An investigation of relationships among privacy concerns, affective responses, and coping behaviors in location-based services. Int. J. Inf. Manage. 43, 15–24 (2018)

Kamal, M., Aljohani, A., Alanazi, E.: IoT meets COVID-19: status, challenges, and opportunities. arXiv preprint arXiv:2007.12268 (2020)

Kanekar, A., Sharma, M.: COVID-19 and mental well-being: guidance on the application of behavioral and positive well-being strategies. Healthcare **8**, 336 (2020)

Kim, J.J., Kim, I., Hwang, J.: A change of perceived innovativeness for contactless food delivery services using drones after the outbreak of COVID-19. Int. J. Hosp. Manag. **93**, 102758 (2021)

Krishnamurthi, R., Gopinathan, D., Kumar, A.: Wearable devices and COVID-19: state of the art, framework, and challenges. In: Al-Turjman, F., Devi, A., Nayyar, A. (eds.) Emerging Technologies for Battling Covid-19. SSDC, vol. 324, pp. 157–180. Springer, Cham (2021). https://doi.org/10.1007/978-3-030-60039-6_8

Krishnan, R.S., Kannan, A., Manikandan, G., Sri Sathya, K.B., Sankar, V.K., Narayanan, K.L.: Secured college bus management system using IoT for Covid-19 pandemic situation. In: 2021 Third International Conference on Intelligent Communication Technologies and Virtual Mobile Networks (ICICV), pp. 376–382. IEEE (2021)

Kumar, S., Raut, R.D., Narkhede, B.E.: A proposed collaborative framework by using artificial intelligence-internet of things (AI-IoT) in COVID-19 pandemic situation for healthcare workers. Int. J. Healthc. Manag. **13**(4), 337–345 (2020)

Lades, L.K., Laffan, K., Daly, M., Delaney, L.: Daily emotional well-being during the COVID-19 pandemic. Br. J. Health. Psychol. **25**(4), 902–911 (2020)

Lassoued, Z., Alhendawi, M., Bashitialshaaer, R.: An exploratory study of the obstacles for achieving quality in distance learning during the COVID-19 pandemic. Educ. Sci. **10**(9), 232 (2020)

Lau, A.: New technologies used in COVID-19 for business survival: insights from the hotel sector in China. Inf. Technol. Tour. **22**(4), 497–504 (2020). https://doi.org/10.1007/s40558-020-00193-z

Lee, H., Leonas, K.: Millennials' intention to use self-checkout technology in different fashion retail formats: perceived benefits and risks. Cloth. Text. Res. J. **39**(4), 264–280 (2020)

Lee, I., Lee, K.: The Internet of Things (IoT): applications, investments, and challenges for enterprises. Bus. Horiz. **58**(4), 431–440 (2015)

Leloglu, E.: A review of security concerns in Internet of Things. J. Comput. Commun. **5**(1), 121–136 (2016)

Lieux, M., Sabottke, C., Schachner, E., Pirtle, C., Danrad, R., Spieler, B.: Online conferencing software in radiology: recent trends and utility. Clin. Imaging **76**, 116–122 (2021)

Liu, J.K., et al.: Privacy-preserving COVID-19 contact tracing app: a zero-knowledge proof approach. IACR Cryptol. Eprint Arch. **2020**, 528 (2020)

Lotfi, A., Elmisery, A.M.: Sensor network in automated hand hygiene systems using IoT for public building. Emerg. Trends Intell. Comput. Inform. Data Sci. Intell. Inf. Syst. Smart Comput. **1073**, 463 (2019)

Manoj, R., Kumarasami, R., Joseph, J., George, B., Sivaprakasam, M.: Continuous weight monitoring system for ICU beds using air-filled mattresses/pads: a proof of concept. In: 2019 IEEE International Symposium on Medical Measurements and Applications (MeMeA), pp. 1–5. IEEE (2019)

Marabelli, M., Vaast, E., Li, J.L.: Preventing the digital scars of COVID-19. Eur. J. Inf. Syst. **30**(2), 176–192 (2021)

Marek, M.W., Chew, C.S., Wu, W.-C.V.: Teacher experiences in converting classes to distance learning in the COVID-19 pandemic. Int. J. Dist. Educ. Technol. **19**(1), 40–60 (2021)

Massaroni, C., Nicolò, A., Schena, E., Sacchetti, M.: Remote respiratory monitoring in the time of COVID-19. Front. Physiol. **11**, 635 (2020)

Mbunge, E.: Integrating emerging technologies into COVID-19 contact tracing: opportunities, challenges and pitfalls. Diabet. Metab. Syndr. Clin. Res. Rev. **14**(6), 1631–1636 (2020)

Mehrolia, S., Alagarsamy, S., Solaikutty, V.M.: Customers response to online food delivery services during COVID-19 outbreak using binary logistic regression. Int. J. Consum. Stud. **45**, 396–408 (2020)

Naik, B.N., Gupta, R., Singh, A., Soni, S.L., Puri, G.: Real-time smart patient monitoring and assessment amid COVID-19 pandemic–an alternative approach to remote monitoring. J. Med. Syst. **44**(7), 1–2 (2020)

Nasiri, S., Khosravani, M.R.: Progress and challenges in fabrication of wearable sensors for health monitoring. Sens. Actuators **312**, 112105 (2020)

Nyenhuis, S.M., Greiwe, J., Zeiger, J.S., Nanda, A., Cooke, A.: Exercise and fitness in the age of social distancing during the COVID-19 pandemic. J. Allergy Clin. Immunol. **8**(7), 2152 (2020)

Omoyibo, M.O., Al-Hadhrami, T., Olajide, F., Lotfi, A., Elmisery, A.M.: Sensor network in automated hand hygiene systems using IoT for public building. In: Saeed, F., Mohammed, F., Gazem, N. (eds.) IRICT 2019. AISC, vol. 1073, pp. 463–476. Springer, Cham (2020). https://doi.org/10.1007/978-3-030-33582-3_44

Parr, S., Wolshon, B., Renne, J., Murray-Tuite, P., Kim, K.: Traffic impacts of the COVID-19 pandemic: statewide analysis of social separation and activity restriction. Nat. Hazards Rev. **21**(3), 04020025 (2020)

Pecoraro, F., Clemente, F., Luzi, D.: The efficiency in the ordinary hospital bed management in Italy: an in-depth analysis of intensive care unit in the areas affected by COVID-19 before the outbreak. PLoS ONE **15**(9), e0239249 (2020)

Pecoraro, F., Luzi, D., Clemente, F.: The efficiency in the ordinary hospital bed management: a comparative analysis in four European countries before the COVID-19 outbreak. PLoS ONE **16**(3), e0248867 (2021)

Pillai, S.G., Haldorai, K., Seo, W.S., Kim, W.G.: COVID-19 and hospitality 5.0: redefining hospitality operations. Int. J. Hosp. Manag. **94**, 102869 (2021)

Prange, S., von Zezschwitz, E., Alt, F.: Vision: exploring challenges and opportunities for usable authentication in the smart home. In: 2019 IEEE European Symposium on Security and Privacy Workshops (EuroS&PW), pp. 154–158. IEEE (2019)

Putra, H.Y.: Fraud detection at self checkout retail using data mining. In: 2020 International Conference on Information Technology Systems and Innovation (ICITSI), pp. 211–216. IEEE (2020)

Quer, G., et al.: Wearable sensor data and self-reported symptoms for COVID-19 detection. Nat. Med. **27**(1), 73–77 (2021)

Reichert, L., Brack, S., Scheuermann, B.: Privacy-preserving contact tracing of Covid-19 patients. IACR Cryptol. Eprint Arch. **2020**, 375 (2020)

Restubog, S.L.D., Ocampo, A.C.G., Wang, L.: Taking control amidst the chaos: emotion regulation during the COVID-19 pandemic. J. Voc. Behav. **119**, 103440 (2020)

Reyna, A., Martín, C., Chen, J., Soler, E., Díaz, M.: On blockchain and its integration with IoT. Challenges and opportunities. Future Gener. Comput. Syst. **88**, 173–190 (2018)

Riemer, K., Ciriello, R., Peter, S., Schlagwein, D.: Digital contact-tracing adoption in the COVID-19 pandemic: IT governance for collective action at the societal level. Eur. J. Inf. Syst. **29**(6), 731–745 (2020)

Ripp, J., Peccoralo, L., Charney, D.: Attending to the emotional well-being of the health care workforce in a New York City health system during the COVID-19 pandemic. Acad. Med. **95**(8), 1136–1139 (2020)

Rummo, P.E., Bragg, M.A., Stella, S.Y.: Supporting equitable food access during national emergencies—the promise of online grocery shopping and food delivery services. JAMA Health Forum, American Medical Association (2020)

Schneider, S.L., Council, M.L.: Distance learning in the era of COVID-19. Arch. Dermatol. Res. **313**(5), 389–390 (2020). https://doi.org/10.1007/s00403-020-02088-9

Sequeiros, H., Oliveira, T., Thomas, M.A.: The impact of IoT smart home services on psychological well-being. Inf. Syst. Front. 1–18 (2021).https://doi.org/10.1007/s10796-021-10118-8

Serrano, F., Kazda, A.: The future of airport post COVID-19. J. Air Transp. Manag. **89**, 101900 (2020)

Seshadri, D.R., et al.: Wearable sensors for COVID-19: a call to action to harness our digital infrastructure for remote patient monitoring and virtual assessments. Front. Digit. Health **2**, 8 (2020)

Shah, A., Engineer, M.: A survey of lightweight cryptographic algorithms for IoT-based applications. In: Tiwari, S., Trivedi, M.C., Mishra, K.K., Misra, A.K., Kumar, K.K. (eds.) Smart Innovations in Communication and Computational Sciences. AISC, vol. 851, pp. 283–293. Springer, Singapore (2019). https://doi.org/10.1007/978-981-13-2414-7_27

Shankar, V., et al.: How technology is changing retail. J. Retail. **97**(1), 13–27 (2021)

Sharma, G.D., Thomas, A., Paul, J.: Reviving tourism industry post-COVID-19: a resilience-based framework. Tour. Manag. Perspect. **37**, 100786 (2021)

Shin, H., Kang, J.: Reducing perceived health risk to attract hotel customers in the COVID-19 pandemic era: focused on technology innovation for social distancing and cleanliness. Int. J. Hosp. Manag. **91**, 102664 (2020)

Siddiqui, S., Shakir, M.Z., Khan, A.A., Dey, I.: Internet of Things (IoT) enabled architecture for social distancing during pandemic. Front. Commun. Netw. **2**, 6 (2021)

Singh, V., Chandna, H., Kumar, A., Kumar, S., Upadhyay, N., Utkarsh, K.: IoT-Q-Band: a low cost internet of things based wearable band to detect and track absconding COVID-19 quarantine subjects. EAI Endorsed Trans. Internet Things **6**(21), 163997 (2020). https://doi.org/10.4108/eai.13-7-2018.163997

Singhal, T.: A review of coronavirus disease-2019 (COVID-19). Indian J. Pediatrics **87**(4), 1–6 (2020)

Siriwardhana, Y., Gür, G., Ylianttila, M., Liyanage, M.: The role of 5G for digital healthcare against COVID-19 pandemic: opportunities and challenges. ICT Express **7**(2), 244–252 (2021). https://doi.org/10.1016/j.icte.2020.10.002

Sovacool, B., Furszyfer, D., Rio, D.: Smart home technologies in Europe: a critical review of concepts, benefits, risks and policies. Renew. Sustain. Energy Rev. **120**, 109663 (2020). https://doi.org/10.1016/j.rser.2019.109663

Stavropoulos, T.G., Papastergiou, A., Mpaltadoros, L., Nikolopoulos, S., Kompatsiaris, I.: IoT wearable sensors and devices in elderly care: a literature review. Sens. Actuators **20**(10), 2826 (2020)

Stojanović, R., Škraba, A., Lutovac, B.: A headset like wearable device to track Covid-19 symptoms. In: 2020 9th Mediterranean Conference on Embedded Computing (MECO), pp. 1–4. IEEE (2020)

Sun, S., et al.: Using smartphones and wearable devices to monitor behavioral changes during COVID-19. J. Med. Internet Res. **22**(9), e19992 (2020). https://doi.org/10.2196/19992

Thomaier, L., et al.: Emotional health concerns of oncology physicians in the United States: fallout during the COVID-19 pandemic. PLOS ONE **15**(11), e0242767 (2020). https://doi.org/10.1371/journal.pone.0242767

Ting, D.S.W., Carin, L., Dzau, V., Wong, T.Y.: Digital technology and COVID-19. Nat. Med. **26**(4), 459–461 (2020)

Uddin, H.: IoT for 5G/B5G applications in smart homes, smart cities, wearables and connected cars. In: 2019 IEEE 24th International Workshop on Computer Aided Modeling and Design of Communication Links and Networks (CAMAD), pp. 1–5. IEEE (2019)

Umair, M., Cheema, M.A., Cheema, O., Li, H., Lu, H.: Impact of COVID-19 on IoT adoption in healthcare, smart homes, smart buildings, smart cities, transportation and industrial IoT. Sens. Actuators **21**(11), 3838 (2021)

Wang, Y.X., Chen, Z., Wang, D., Wang, Y.: Providing uninterrupted care during COVID-19 pandemic: experience from Beijing Tiantan Hospital. Stroke Vasc. Neurol. **5**(2), 180–184 (2020). https://doi.org/10.1136/svn-2020-000400

Wang, Y., Xu, R., Schwartz, M., Ghosh, D., Chen, X.: COVID-19 and retail grocery management: insights from a broad-based consumer survey. IEEE Eng. Manage. Rev. **48**(3), 202–211 (2020)

Watson, A.R., Wah, R., Thamman, R.: The value of remote monitoring for the COVID-19 pandemic. Telemed. e-Health **26**(9), 1110–1112 (2020)

Weizman, Y., Tan, A., Fuss, F.: Use of wearable technology to enhance response to the Coronavirus (COVID-19) pandemic. Public Health **185**, 221–222 (2020)

Wilczewski, M., Gorbaniuk, O., Giuri, P.: The psychological and academic effects of studying from the home and host country during the COVID-19 pandemic. Front. Psychol. **12**, 644096 (2021). https://doi.org/10.3389/fpsyg.2021.644096

Worldometers 2020: Worldometer: Coronavirus Cases. Viewed 3 Mar 2021

Wu, A., et al.: Supporting the emotional well-being of health care workers during the COVID-19 pandemic. J. Patient Saf. Risk Manag. **25**(3), 93–96 (2020). https://doi.org/10.1177/251604352 0931971

Xu, F.Z., Zhang, Y., Zhang, T., Wang, J.: Facial recognition check-in services at hotels. J. Hosp. Mark. Manag. **30**(3), 1–21 (2020)

Xu, H., Zhang, L., Onireti, O., Fang, Y., Buchanan, W.J., Imran, M.A.: BeepTrace: blockchain-enabled privacy-preserving contact tracing for COVID-19 pandemic and beyond. IEEE Internet Things J. **8**(5), 3915–3929 (2021). https://doi.org/10.1109/JIOT.2020.3025953

Yousif, M., Hewage, C., Nawaf, L.: IoT technologies during and beyond COVID-19: a comprehensive review. Future Internet **13**(5), 105 (2021)

Zeng, Z., Chen, P.-J., Lew, A.A.: From high-touch to high-tech: COVID-19 drives robotics adoption. Tour. Geogr. **22**(3), 724–734 (2020)

Zwitter, A., Gstrein, O.: Big data, privacy and COVID-19 – learning from humanitarian expertise in data protection. J. Int. Humanit. Action **5**(1), 1–7 (2020). https://doi.org/10.1186/s41018-020-00072-6

Designing a Smart Shirt to Support Adolescents' Sitting Posture Based on Strain Textile Sensors

Qi Wang, Xin Zhou, Weiwei Guo[✉], and Xiaohua Sun

Tongji University, Shanghai, China
{qiwangdesign,weiweiguo,xsun}@tongji.edu.cn

Abstract. Due to the schoolwork and long-time electronic devices use, teenagers have longer time in sedentary behavior and their good postures are continuously attracting attentions. Wearable technology based on IMUs or computer vision technology based on cameras have been widely explored. Smart textile sensing technology which has great potential in body postures monitoring is one of the fields that has developed rapidly in recent years. This article focuses on teenagers' sitting posture, following the approach of research through design, we identified the problems and challenges, tested multiple textile samples, performed the locations analysis, and finally proposed a smart shirt integrated with six stretchable textile strain sensors. The resistance of each textile sensor will change linearly through the length change. Together with the classification model in MatLab, the smart shirt can distinguish inappropriate postures with an accuracy rate of 99.1%. We also proposed a feedback design and performed a wizard-of-oz field study to see how the smart shirt may help the teenagers to maintain good postures and how do the participants value the usability. The results demonstrated the system can help the participants facilitate maintaining good postures heir posture in sedentary work.

Keywords: Strain textile sensor · Sitting posture · Smart shirt · Wearable system

1 Introduction

Nowdays, adolescents tend to have high sedentary time due to the school work, traffic time and electronic devices use. A recent study based on 300 adolescents samples in China shows their average daily sedentary time on school days is 565.77 min, while on rest days, the average daily sedentary time has also reached to 544.61 min [1]. Teenagers are in a critical period of bone development, and the habits formed at this stage will greatly affect later life. While bad postures are threatening adolescents' health, for example, bad postures may lead to nearsightedness, scoliosis, etc. The poor sitting posture may impact their vision, bone development and sleep quality, they may even develop myopia, cervical and spinal diseases. From a physiological point of view, the human spine supports the body and bears most of the body pressure. When sitting in a correct posture, the spine maintains its natural physiological curvature, allowing the intervertebral and surrounding muscle tissue to bear the most suitable pressure.

© Springer Nature Switzerland AG 2021
C. Stephanidis et al. (Eds.): HCII 2021, LNCS 13097, pp. 157–169, 2021.
https://doi.org/10.1007/978-3-030-90966-6_12

Therefore, it is essential to maintain a relatively correct sitting posture and the self-correction method has gradually become a trend. Normally the posture monitoring system consists of two parts: firstly, the user's sitting posture is monitored by computer vision or sensor technology, then a reminder is issued to the user to motivate them to adjust and correct their sitting posture. Regarding the wearable posture sensing technologies, inertial measurement units (IMU) based solutions have been widely explored [2] E-textile solutions received increasingly attentions. Smart textiles have the functions of electronic components and the characteristics of textile. While with the rapid development of smart textiles [3], textile-based solutions show great potential on the aspects of comfort and weaability which are crutial to daily use.

In this article, we proposed a novel smart shirt based on strain textile sensor networks and the system is capable of classifing 8 wrong sitting postures that adolescents tend to develop in sedentary work. We investigated the performance and user experience of the system including a visual feedback, and we presented the results that the smart shirt has great potential to help the participants improve their sitting posture.

2   Related Works

Sitting posture detection mainly involves two key aspects. The first part is the standard, which is the fundamental of the sitting posture detection research, the second one is the method of posture detection, that is, how to effectively collect the sitting posture data and how to process the collected signals to achieve accurate classification results.

2.1   Sitting Posture Standards and Classification

In the discussion of the standard classification of sitting posture, Vasileios Korakakis et al. surveyed 544 physical therapists regarding the best sitting and standing postures, to select the most correct sitting posture from the professional perspective of the physical therapist. And 97.5% of the physical therapists reached an agreement that the spine perpendicular to the chair surface without bending the back is the best one [4]. Martins et al. [5] classified the sitting postures that may appear in office scenes into sitting upright, hunched, leaning forward, leaning backward, leaning backward without backrest, leaning left, leaning right, right leg crossed, and left leg crosse. Based on previous research, we can found that the correct sitting posture standards reached consensus while wrong postures standards are differentiated mainly because of different scenarios. Therefore, in this study, the basic correct sitting posture standards will be used as the basis for judgment to conduct the user research, to collect data and carry out the classification of the target sitting posture.

2.2   Wearable Posture Monitoring Methods

The wearable systems usually involved multiple sensors attached to specific body segments. In previous studies, IMUs were mostly used, for example, Du et al. [6] proposed a smart garment embedded two IMUs to support office workers maintain good posture in sedentary work. Due to the limitations of wearability and flexibility and rapid develoents of advanced materials, smart textiles-based solutions show great possibilities. For example, Esfahani et al. [7] proposed a smart undershirt that consists of 11 textile sensors to track upper body motions. Skach et al. [8] proposed smarty pants with embedded textile pressure sensors, and it can recognize 19 different postures. Liu et al. [9] developed a system that can reconstruct the elbow joint by strain textile sensors. However, few studies have addressed the scenario of adolescents'sitting posture monitoring.

3   Design Process

3.1   Textile Sensor Selection

The first step is the performance test of the textile sensor. Based on the desk research, we focused two kinds of strain textile sensors. One is the conductive PPY (polypyrene) textile, three different samples are numbered as A, B, and C with different parameters. The other one is the elastic conductive fabric woven from silver fiber and elastic fiber which is numbered as sample D (see Fig. 1a). The characteristics of the resistance change are also different.

This research adopts a fixed tensile experiment, using Arduino to control a stepper motor (see Fig. 1b), and connecting the slide rail for reciprocating movement, the sensor to be measured is fixed on the slide rail and stretch within the specified moving distance interval. The textile sensor was connected to the Arduino analog signal port to read the resistance signal change. The Arduino serial port displays the resistance curve change, and we recorded the value of the signal.

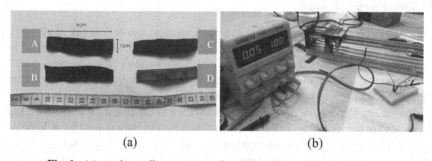

(a)   (b)

Fig. 1. (a) stratin textile sensor samples; (b) tensile experiment platform

The resistance change curve is as shown in the Fig. 2. Among them, the vertical axis represents the resistance value, and the coordinate is converted into a period according to the reciprocating motion, that is, each period unit represents a stretch and recovery of the sensor. The blue line in the figure is the actual resistance value, and the red curve is an ideal linear change curve drawn by taking the highest value and the lowest value of the resistance change. According to the above actual and ideal resistance change curves, it can be found that the resistance change curves of material A and material B have greater interference during the repeated stretching process, and exhibit poor linearity.

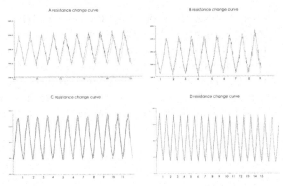

Fig. 2. Resistance data of four materials during the fixed length tensile test (Color figure online)

Among them, material C and material D showed a better linearity. And material D has the best repeat stability, and the resistance value fluctuates in a smaller range during the repeated tensile test. Therefore, in the follow-up process of this research, material D will be selected for sensor implementation.

Regarding the conductive properties of stretched fabric, factors include the length and width of a single piece of sensing fabric. In the subsequent tests, it can be found that the 10 cm length of the material D performed better than the 5 cm length in repeat stability and sensitivity. Besides, considering that the sensor with a length of 10 cm can monitor a wider range, the material D with a length of 10 cm will be used as the strain textile sensor in the following study.

3.2   Target Sitting Postures

In this study, we will refer to the prementioned articles, and follow the physiological comfort and rationality, and make the reference formulation of "standard sitting posture" according to the subdivision of teenagers in their main sitting posture scenes.

In this study, through observations and interviews, we recorded the common sitting postures of adolescents in the above-mentioned sitting situation, and summarized them as the target sitting postures that need to be identified in the research. There are 8 types namely: lean to the right, lean to the left, lean forward, lean back, hunch back, bend over the table, support the cheek on the right, and on the left. In the follow-up stages, the 8 postures and the correct sitting posture, a total of 9 sitting postures (shown in Fig. 3) will be used as the targets to classify.

3.3   Prototype Implementation

After selecting the stretched textile with mechanical properties that meet the requirements, the second stage is to initially apply it to the target scene to observe whether the corresponding changes can be detected, and to find the most suitable sensor placements.

We prepared a highly stretchable shirt as testing garment, which is called the body-fitting shirt in the following text and it will support the sensor deployment experiments.

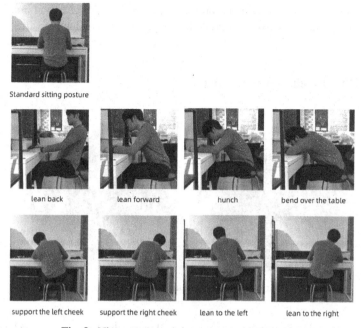

Standard sitting posture

lean back   lean forward   hunch   bend over the table

support the left cheek   support the right cheek   lean to the left   lean to the right

Fig. 3. Nine common sitting postures of teenagers.

Besides, the stretched length of the material needs to be measured. The fixed points can be used as a mark, and the distance can be observed and recorded.

In this research, we used a combination of empirical judgments based on references and experiments to try different schemes. Based on the layout plan in previous studies and the stretching distance measurement carried out in the material test, we selected the position with larger variation as the possible layout area. A total of 6 placement positions were selected: vertebrae C5 to T2 and L1 to L3 for spine monitoring, the areas of the teres minor and infraspinatus on the upper back where the bending deformation is most obvious, and the lower back abdomen and external oblique muscles on both sides. Subsequently, we connected all the sensors by snaps to the body-fitting shirt as shown in Fig. 4.

Fig. 4. Sensor resistance reading circuit connection.

In the second iteration, the final prototype (see Fig. 5) is designed and implemented by sewing all the textile sensors on predefined locations by conductive yarns, which is the basis for data collection and classification model construction in real scenes.

3.4 Signal Collection and Processing

Fig. 5. Prototype clothing circuit sewing inside and outside.

When each sitting posture is executed, it will cause the resistance of each sensor in different placements to change. As shown in Fig. 6, when the user's body is tilted to the left (including left tilt and left cheek support), the back muscles are stretched, and the sensor located in the area of the teres minor and infraspinatus on the right side of the upper back (green line in the waveform diagram) Indicates), and the sensor 6 located at the external oblique muscle on the right side of the lower back (indicated by the gray line in the waveform diagram) receives the greatest stretch, and its resistance increases accordingly. Among them, in the sitting posture with the cheek resting on the left, the distortion of the back is slightly greater than that of the left tilt, so the resistance change is more obvious.

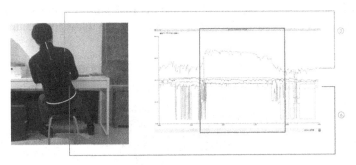

Fig. 6. The sensor's resistance change of the left-leaning sitting posture.

When the user's body is tilted to the right (including right tilt and right cheek support), as shown in Fig. 7, the sensor 1 located in the area of the teres minor and infraspinatus on the left side of the upper back (indicated by the blue line in the waveform), And the sensor 4 (indicated by the yellow line in the waveform diagram) located at the external oblique muscle on the right side of the lower back received the greatest stretch, and its resistance increased accordingly. Among them, the muscle stretching and the corresponding resistance changes in the sitting posture with the cheek supported are more obvious.

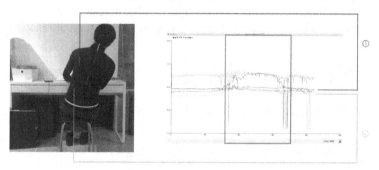

Fig. 7. The sensor's resistance change of the right-leaning sitting posture. (Color figure online)

When sitting in a hunched posture (see Fig. 8), the sensor located at the spine has the greatest deformation, so the resistance signals of the sensor 2 and 5 increase at the same time. Besides, sensors in other parts are also deformed, the sensitivity of sensor 4 is higher and it can be observed from the waveform diagram that the sensor signal values at these three positions have increased significantly.

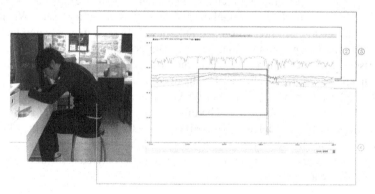

Fig. 8. The sensor's resistance change of the slouch sitting posture.

In this research, Matlab software is used to apply the automatic classification algorithm to generate a model that can classify the 9 sitting postures. According to the classification principle and Matlab algorithm model generation requirements, we provided a training data set. The data sets contain classification standards and its corresponding multiple sets of training data.

After the circuit was connected, a participant wore the suit and executed the 9 target postures. When each action was performed, the participant continuously adjusted his sitting posture in the interval of the setting postures for 15 s. During the collection process, the collection frequency of the Arduino Mega board is set to 500 Hz, so each sitting posture can collect about 7,500 items of data.

After the training data was imported into Matlab, we adopted different models. In this study, KNN (K = 1 and K = 5), Naive Bayes, decision tree, SVM (Support Vector Machine) are the four most commonly used machine learning classification algorithms for data learning and model training. The specific parameter settings are shown in Table 1.

Table 1. Algorithms and parameters used to train the model.

No	Algorithm	Parameter
1	KNN	K = 1
2	KNN	K = 5
3	Naive Bayes	Default
4	Support Vector Machines	RBF, C = 1, Degree = 3
5	Decision tree	Max split number = 100

We divided the data set, 70% were used as the training set of the sitting posture classification model, and the other 30% were used as the validation set. For a trained model, the evaluation and comparison of the following indicators are usually used, which are accuracy (Accuracy), precision (Precision), recall (Recall), and F-1 value. The KNN algorithm (K-Nearest Neighbor) has the highest accuracy result. When the K value is 1, the accuracy of prediction and judgment is 99.1%, that is, when the model classifies the validation dataset. Compare the data containing the 6 resistance signal characteristics with the training set, select the nearest neighbor for classification, and the classification accuracy reaches 99.1%. Its overall performance, that is, the F-1 score is also the highest. Compared with other types of algorithm models, the KNN (K = 1) model exhibits the best performance. Therefore, in the subsequent part of this research, the KNN classification model will be used as a tool for sitting posture classification. Then we exportd the trained model in Matlab to Arduino through Simulink, so that the sensor signal detected on Arduino can be classified by the derived algorithm model, and return the classification result.

3.5 Feedback Design and Implementation

This research also aims to build a complete posture detection system including textile sensor and feedback, so they can make adjustments to the correct postures.

The target scenes are mostly classrooms and homes, the user's main activities are reading, writing, and having classes. Therefore, the feedback modalities are designed according to the user's environment: in the classroom environment, the feedback carriers are mainly wearable modules; in the home environment, the carriers of feedback are wearable modules and visual feedback on APP.

The feedback based on the wearable module can be divided into two parts. One type is the haptic by vibration motors, three vibration motors are respectively arranged on the left, right sides of the lumbar spine and the middle position of the spine.

The working mode of vibration is that when the wearer's body is in a sitting posture that tilts to the right (right cheek support, right tilt), the vibration module located on the left side of the lumbar spine will give a short vibration prompt. When the body is in a sitting posture tilted to the left (left cheek support, left tilt), the vibration module located on the right side of the lumbar spine will give a short vibration prompt. When the body is in a sitting posture tilted back and forth, the module located in the middle of the spine gives a short vibration prompt.

The second type of wearable feedback is the visual feedback which was realized by sewable LEDs. As mentioned in the previous studies, visual feedback is the best for the user's guidance. At the same time, too complex visual feedback may cause interference. Therefore, we choose to guide the user to correct the sitting posture through weak LED light feedback.

Mobile APP will be used as another main feedback channel for the following considerations:

(1) indicative feedback with more clear and indicative contents to support the users adjust their postures;
(2) display long-term posture data so that users can get more comprehensive personal health information;
(3) social support, target groups mentioned they would be more motivated to participate when their friends around them were doing the same thing.

The specific sitting posture adjustment feedback interfaces (see Fig. 9) are as follows: When the user sits in a wrong way, the avatar will appear in the corresponding state simultaneously, specifically when the user has four wrong sitting postures: forward, backward, hunchback, and prone writing. A prompt to adjust the sitting posture appears in the interface, as well as a background adjustment auxiliary scale circle. (The ring scale does not correspond to the actual angle, and serves to magnify the deviation of the user's sitting posture).

Fig. 9. APP interface for posturing reminding.

4   Evaluation

In this study, based on the realized design prototype, and considering the rationality of the test resources, we deployed different methods. For the wearable monitoring and feedback part, we focus on effectiveness and user experience evaluation. Participants are invited to have a short-term use, comprehensive evaluation and analysis of the use reactions were summarized. Regarding the APP interface, we focus on the usability evaluation.

4.1   Effectiveness Test of the System

In this section, the goal of the experiment is to verify the feasibility and effectiveness of the system in the real environment and evaluate the user's experience.

Here, a comparative observation experiment method was adopted, by controlling the working state of the system under test as a variable factor, we observed the different states of users when they performed the same task as an objective evaluation of the effect of the system. At the same time, we collected information about subjective feelings in the form of questionnaires and interviews. The scene was set to simulate teenagers' daily home/classroom environment. Therefore, before the test, a quiet and closed venue was searched to eliminate external interference factors, a set of desks and chairs was prepared for performing learning tasks, and the entire process of the experiment was recorded through video equipment.

Participants. Since the smart long-sleeve shirt has a size limit, three users aged from 19 to 23 (M = 22.3, SD = 2.31) with similar heights (M = 161 cm, SD = 1 cm) and weights (M =, SD =) were selected when recruiting volunteers for the study.

The detailed participants information:

Participant 1: A 19-year-old freshman with a height of 161 cm and a weight of 49 kg. He has not used a sitting posture correction device before. The task was writing.
Participant 2: A 23-year-old graduate student with a height of 162 cm and a weight of 46 kg. He has never used a sitting posture correction device before. The task was to use a computer.

Participant 3: A 23-year-old graduate student with a height of 160 cm and a weight of 44 kg. The selected task was reading books.

Procedure. This study followed a fours phases design (see Table 2), in each condition the smart shirt was worn and and different variables were controlled. Each condition lasts for 30 min. The first condition would be the baseline stage, that is, without any sitting posture reminder, the preset task was executed, and the sitting posture data of the user's natural state wascollected for comparison. In the second stage, the wearable feedback module was activated, that is, when the user's sitting posture was wrong, the vibration module and the LED module would give corresponding reminders. In the third stage, the mobile phone was placed on the desktop, the APP feedback was also provided together with the wearable feedback module. Finally, in the last stage, only APP interface was available.

Table 2. 4 stages of the experiment.

Stage 1	Stage 2	Stage 3	Stage 4
No feedback 30 min	Wearable 30 min	Wearable + APP 30 min	APP 30 min

Data collection after the test: After the test, subjective evaluation and objective data extraction are taken to comprehensively evaluate the effectiveness of the system. Users are asked to fill in the evaluation questionnaire after use; and after the questionnaire fill-in session, the users are interviewed with an open mind. In the objective data part, by observing the video of the user's test process, and cooperating with the detection of changes in the data detected by the clothing, calculate the user's correct sitting posture and various incorrect sitting posture time distributions, as well as the number of sitting errors. Among them, the number of sitting errors is calculated as the user changes from one sitting posture to another incorrect sitting posture, which is recorded as the number of sitting errors once; the correct sitting posture time refers to the length of time in the right sitting posture.

Results. The number of incorrect sitting postures detected by the smart shirt of the three users are 98 times, while the number of times calculated from actual observation are 103 times, recognition rate of the system for incorrect sitting postures is 95.1%. Among the sitting postures that have not been successfully recognized, the main ones are left and forward. The reason is that when the user occurs this type of sitting posture, the back straight state puts less stress on the sensor.

In this study, the Intrinsic Motivation Scale was used as a questionnaire to evaluate the system experience. The scale is based on the user's experience of wearing and operating, and the user's sense of enjoyment and completion Six aspects are evaluated (Interest/Enjoyment, Perceived Competence, Effort/Importance, Pressure/Tension, Value/Usefulness, Relatedness).

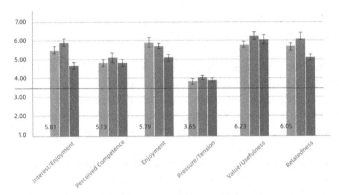

Fig. 10. The scores of IMI questionnaire.

Figure 10 shows the IMI scores. The highest point is the value/usefulness subscale, which reached a score of 6.23. In the interview, all the participant said they felt that their state has become better when using the system. Participant 1 also mentioned that sitting in a right way can improve the working efficiency, especially when they are tired. It is verified that the system can prompt the user to maintain a good physical posture, thereby making the user feel the value from the psychological level. In terms of negative factors, users gave a high score on the sense of pressure, reasons could be when the two types of feedback modes are turned on at the same time, the user would feel nervous and uncomfortable.

5   Limitations

In this research, a prototype of the sitting posture monitoring interactive system was designed and evaluated. In the process of design practice, the following points can be further optimized:

1. In the early stage of design, more feasible types of textile sensors can be tested. Due to the resource limitation in this study, the materials tested are similar. In the follow-up research, we will test more kinds of materials, such as conductive fibers, to explore better solutions.
2. In this research, the user experience evaluation was mainly obtained by simulating the normal scenes of adolescents. The prototype of this study was used to verify the feasibility of the overall design concept, more evaluations regard to comfort and aesthetics are needed.

6 Conclusion

This study focused on the posture health problems of adolescents, an interactive sitting posture monitoring smart clothing based on strain textile sensor was proposed and verified through the usability and effectiveness test. Our system demonstrates the feasibilities of textile sensing technology in realtime sitting postures classifications. The results also showed that the system can help the participants facilitate preventing bad postures in sedentary work.

References

1. Yang, J., Wu, M., Qiu, F., Li, A., Jiang, J., Zhu, T.: Research on health-related sedentary behaviors of children and adolescents aged twelve to 17. Chin. J. Rehabil. Theory Pract. **26**(12), 1365–1372 (2020)
2. Wang, Q., Markopoulos, P., Yu, B., Chen, W., Timmermans, A.: Interactive wearable systems for upper body rehabilitation: a systematic review. J. NeuroEng. Rehabil. **14**, 20 (2017)
3. Shi, J., et al.: Smart textile-integrated microelectronic systems for wearable applications. Adv. Mater. **32**, 1901958 (2020)
4. Korakakis, V., et al.: Physiotherapist perceptions of optimal sitting and standing posture. Musculoskelet Sci. Pract. **39**, 24–31 (2019)
5. Martins, L., et al.: Intelligent chair sensor. In: Iliadis, L., Papadopoulos, H., Jayne, C. (eds.) EANN 2013. CCIS, vol. 383, pp. 182–191. Springer, Heidelberg (2013). https://doi.org/10.1007/978-3-642-41013-0_19
6. Du, J., Wang, Q., de Baets, L., Markopoulos, P.: Proceedings of the 11th EAI International Conference on Pervasive Computing Technologies for Healthcare, PervasiveHealth 2017, pp. 235–243 (2017)
7. Esfahani, M.I.M., Nussbaum, M.A.: A "smart" undershirt for tracking upper body motions: task classification and angle estimation. IEEE Sens. J. **18**, 7650–7658 (2018)
8. Skach, S., Stewart, R., Healey, P.G.T.: Smarty pants: exploring textile pressure sensors in trousers for posture and behaviour classification. In: Proceedings, vol. 32, p. 19 (2019)
9. Liu, R., Shao, Q., Wang, S., Ru, C., Balkcom, D., Zhou, X.: Reconstructing human joint motion with computational fabrics. In: Proceedings of the ACM Interactive, Mobile, Wearable and Ubiquitous Technologies, vol. 3, pp. 1–26 (2019)

Research on the Design of Mobile Infusion Devices for Children Based on Emotionalization

Xueqing Zhao, Wei Yu$^{(\boxtimes)}$, and Xin Liang

School of Art Design and Media, East China University of Science and Technology, No. 130, Meilong Road, Xuhui District, Shanghai, People's Republic of China

Abstract. The purpose of this study is to effectively obtain the emotional needs of children and their families during the infusion process, explore the design strategies of children's mobile infusion equipment from the emotional perspective, and improve the emotional experience of children and their families during the children's infusion process. Firstly, this study conducts research on the children and their families through user interviews and questionnaires, and maps out the flow chart of infusion for children by combining the results of the research and field observations. Through the analysis of the pain points and opportunity points in the process, the needs of the children and their families are extracted respectively, and then they are preliminarily analyzed, integrated and classified according to the three levels of emotional thinking. Secondly, in order to analyze and filter the requirements more deeply, this study introduces the Kano model, classifies the classified emotional design requirements into Kano attributes, and then uses the Better-Worse coefficient formula to calculate the user satisfaction index of each design requirement. And on this basis, we conduct a four-quadrant analysis of the requirements to obtain the importance ranking of the emotional requirements of the children and their families. Finally, based on the results of the above needs analysis, this study explores the design principles and strategies of children's mobile infusion equipment at the visceral, behavioral and reflective levels, and discusses the innovative ideas of children's infusion equipment in emotional expression. This study bridges the gap of emotional care for children and their families in the field of pediatric infusion, provides a reference for the design of children's mobile infusion equipment, and also provides a reference for the design optimization of future pediatric medical products.

Keywords: Emotional design · Infusion equipment for children · Kano model

1 Introduction

With the development of social economy, people have put forward higher-level requirements in various fields closely related to the growth and health of children, and the demand for products has risen from the most basic material needs to a deeper level of psychological needs. However, the reality has generally fallen short of expectations, especially in some areas such as children's health care, which are less profit-driven and still need to be strengthened. Infusion in children is a rapid and effective method of

C. Stephanidis et al. (Eds.): HCII 2021, LNCS 13097, pp. 170–185, 2021.
https://doi.org/10.1007/978-3-030-90966-6_13

intravenous drug delivery, and is the most common form of treatment in pediatric clinics and an important area of medical care for children. Children's cooperation with physicians during intravenous infusion directly affects the safety and efficiency of infusion therapy [1]. As a special group of patients, children are quite different from adults in terms of emotional performance, emotional regulation, and emotional perception [2]. The long infusion process is an extremely difficult stage for children to endure, and children are prone to rejection, irritability, crying, and other negative emotions, which not only affect the smooth implementation of infusion therapy, but also cause parents' anxiety, and therefore require special psychological and emotional care. The survey found that most hospitals in China currently do not have dedicated children's infusion areas or use infusion equipment specifically for children; besides meeting the basic functional needs of infusion, infusion places and related equipment for children lack emotional and humanized care for this special group [3]. In addition, the emotions of the child's family, who are also involved in the entire infusion process, are often overlooked. Therefore, this study will start from this background, combine emotional design thinking and use the Kano model to gain insight into the emotional needs of children during infusion, while incorporating and paying attention to the emotional needs of accompanying persons, so as to help children accept and adapt to infusion treatment with a more positive mindset. This has an important role in improving the quality of infusion care, enhancing the satisfaction of children and their accompanying persons, and reducing doctor-patient disputes.

2 Emotional Design and Kano Model

2.1 Emotional Design Overview

Emotion is an innate human need. With the continuous enrichment and enhancement of material and spiritual aspects, emotion gradually draws people's attention and becomes a new concept derived from the joint action of various factors [4]. Emotional design is one of such concepts, proposed by American cognitive psychologist Donald Norman, which states that the human emotional system consists of three distinct but interconnected levels, each of which influences people's experience of the world in a particular way: the visceral level, the behavioral level, and the reflective level [5]. The visceral level refers to people's intuitive experience, including the user's feelings about the product in terms of shape, color, sound, material and smell, that is, the first impression of the product; the behavioral level refers to usability, that is, the user's experience of using the product functions, such as fluency and efficiency when operating the product; the reflective level is the highest level of emotional design, which is the user's deep-seated feelings, comprehension, reflection and recognition of the product, its usage, embedded culture and meaning of existence, etc.

The design of the product should not only meet the user's needs for the basic functions of the product, but also allow them to obtain psychological and emotional satisfaction in the use. The use of emotional design concepts when designing products can make the design more warm, and thus arouse the emotional resonance of users [6].

2.2 Combining of Emotional Design Thinking and Kano Model

The Kano model is a structured questionnaire analysis method proposed by Noriaki Kano [7], which is a powerful tool to quantify, classify and rank user needs, reflecting the non-linear relationship between user needs and user satisfaction. After nearly forty years of development, the Kano model has provided effective guidance on both user satisfaction and the degree of product feature improvement, and has been widely used in product design, service quality research, and user needs identification [8]. Therefore, this study combines the hierarchical framework of emotional thinking with the Kano model to explore user needs in order to explore users' psychological needs at a deeper level and enhance their emotional experience.

3   The Current Situation of China's Children's Infusion Industry

According to our survey, not all regular public hospitals in China have infusion rooms for children. On the contrary, many children still share infusion rooms with adults, and infusion equipment for children, such as mobile infusion stents, medicine packaging and needle equipment, is almost the same as adults'. First of all, in terms of space, with the exception of a few general hospitals, most hospitals have infusion rooms that lack independent space for children, and problems usually exist such as poor air circulation and narrow space available for individuals. Especially during the outbreak of seasonal diseases, infusion rooms are crowded, chaotic and noisy, which makes children unable to enjoy a quiet and healthy medical environment during infusion. Secondly, in terms of the pertinence of the products, with the exception of the difference in drug dosage, the medical products used by children are almost the same as those used by adult patients which are cold in color in appearance, do not match the human-machine relationship. They lack physical and psychological care for children, and lack comfort, safety, fun, flexibility and emotion.

The lack of distinction between children's and adults' infusion space and products has aggravated children's fear of infusion. During our visits to hospitals around Shanghai, we find that crying and resistance often appear in the infusion rooms. 83% of children under the age of 12 have crying problems or show resistance, avoidance, and impatience during infusion. And the younger the child is, the worse the emotional control is. This undoubtedly brings a huge burden to the accompanying persons. According to the visits, we find that each child has at least one person to accompany, and sometimes even grandparents and parents will accompany the child to the doctor together. As the participants in the whole infusion process of children, the accompanying personnel also have great anxiety and pressure. On the one hand, it comes from the children's negative emotions. On the other hand, it is also affected by the lack of emotional care of hospital equipment. Admittedly, the emotions of the accompanying personnel are often ignored in the infusion process and related studies. Therefore, based on the emotional needs of children and their escorts, exploring the design strategies of mobile infusion equipment will not only relieve children's tension, strengthen children's cooperation, but also relieve the pressure of escorts to a large extent which has profound research significance.

4 User Needs Analysis Based on Emotional Thinking and Kano Model

4.1 The Acquisition of Emotional Needs

In order to obtain users' emotional design needs for mobile infusion devices, first, this study conducts user interviews with 32 groups of children under 12 years old and their parents. And these children have all had infusion experience and had negative emotions

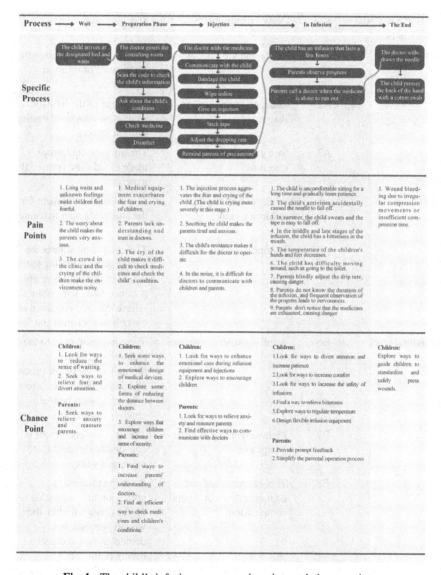

Fig. 1. The child's infusion process, pain points and chance points.

during the infusion process. In addition, we draw up a flow chart of children's infusion based on the interview results, combined with literature search and field observation, and dig out and analyze the pain points and chance points in the process of children's infusion (see Fig. 1).

We brainstorm the above results, refine the opportunity points into specific functional requirements for the children and their parents. Combining the opinions of professional

Table 1. Emotional design needs of children.

Levels of emotional requirements	#	Design requirements	Specific instructions
Visceral level	A1	Bright and vibrant colors	The colors are applied to the appearance of infusion equipment
	A2	Cute and funny cartoon shapes	The shape of the infusion equipment adopts interesting cartoon images
	A3	Safe and comfortable materials	The infusion equipment is made of safe and comfortable materials
	A4	Product sizes to fit children's body	The infusion equipment fits the children's man-machine size
	A5	Thermostatic systems	The equipment adjusts the temperature according to the nature of the medicine and patients' body temperature to relieve the cold condition of the children's hands and feet
Behavioral level	B6	A full-on voice conversation	The equipment talks to the children with voice throughout the whole process, alleviating the fear of direct communication between children and doctors
	B7	Lightweight and flexible equipment	The infusion equipment is convenient for children to move and walk
	B8	Timing reminders and demonstrations of wound compression	After the infusion, a corresponding animation is used to bring children the wound hemostasis demonstration and give a timing reminder

(continued)

Table 1. (*continued*)

Levels of emotional requirements	#	Design requirements	Specific instructions
Reflective level	C9	Entertainment and educational activities	The equipment provides entertainment and educational activities such as children's picture books, audio books, cartoons, etc.
	C10	Encouraging health games	The equipment provides games to divert children's attention
	C11	Accompanying virtual character design	Virtual partners to accompany children with infusions can increase children's sense of security and companionship

medical staff, we retain the medically reasonable and safe parts, and classify them according to the three levels of emotional thinking, and finally obtain the emotional design requirements of the children and their parents (see Tables 1 and 2).

Table 2. Emotional design needs of children's parents.

Levels of emotional requirements	#	Design requirements	Specific instructions
Visceral level	D1	Clear and concise information interface	The information interface style is concise and clear
	D2	A interface with beautiful pictures and coordinated colors	
	D3	Cleanliness of equipment	The equipment is always kept clean
Behavioral level	E4	Precautions before infusion	The equipment informs parents about the precautions related to the children's infusion in advance
	E5	Doctors' profile description	The equipment increases parents' understanding and trust in doctors by providing relevant information

(*continued*)

Table 2. (*continued*)

Levels of emotional requirements	#	Design requirements	Specific instructions
	E6	Online Archives of Children	The archives include visit records, allergen records, etc., to break the information occlusion between different hospitals and facilitate communication between parents and doctors
	E7	Feedback of children's status	It provides more detailed feedback on the physical conditions of children such as body temperature
	E8	Online verification of medicines	It makes it easy for parents to check and verify drug information at any time
	E9	Prevention of misuse of children and parents	The infusion equipment has a safety design to avoid misoperation by parents and children
	E10	Infusion monitoring of children	Parents can remotely observe the children's situation when they leave to go through the formalities
	E11	Monitoring and feedback of infusion rate and estimated time	The equipment monitors and alerts the infusion rate and estimated time of infusion, and visualizes the data
	E12	One-Click Call to Doctor	
Reflective level	F13	Parent-child interactive games	Games allows parents and children to participate together, increasing parent-child interaction
	F14	Future tracking	After the infusion, parents obtain precautions such as taboos, and answers to questions about the children's conditions online

4.2 Collection and Reliability Resting of Kano Questionnaire

The Kano questionnaire in this study is divided into two parts. The first part is aimed at children under 12 years of age, who have all experienced infusions and have had negative emotions during the infusion process. And the second part of the survey is aimed at the children's accompanying persons. The expression form of each question in the questionnaire is shown in Fig. 2. A total of 78 sets of questionnaires are distributed both online and offline, and 70 valid questionnaires are collected. Because the children under the survey are all under 12 years old and have weaker understanding and cognitive abilities, they complete their responses with the explanation and assistance of the researchers and their parents. Using SPSS 22.0 software to analyze the reliability of the questionnaire, it is found that the Cronbach's α value of both forward and reverse questions is greater than 0.8, indicating that the survey results of the questionnaire have good reliability.

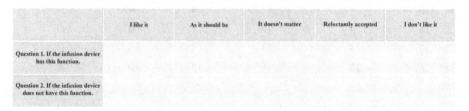

	I like it	As it should be	It doesn't matter	Reluctantly accepted	I don't like it
Question 1. If the infusion device has this function.					
Question 2. If the infusion device does not have this function.					

Fig. 2. The Kano model questionnaire form.

4.3 Kano Attribute Classification of Emotional Needs

Based on the positive and negative questioning results of the Kano model questionnaire, five types of requirements can be finally derived: attractive requirements (A), one-dimensional requirements (O), must-be requirements (M), indifferent requirements (I), reverse requirements (R) (see Table 3). We classify the emotional needs attributes of children and their families according to the Kano model evaluation table, and the results are shown in Tables 4 and 5.

Table 3. Kano model evaluation table

Customer requirement		Negative question				
		Like	Must-be	Neutral	Live with	Dislike
Positive question	Like	Q	A	A	A	O
	Must-be	R	I	I	I	M
	Neutral	R	I	I	I	M
	Live with	R	I	I	I	M
	Dislike	R	R	R	R	Q

Table 4. Kano attribute classification results of the emotional needs of children.

#	Attractive requirements (A)	One-dimensional requirements (O)	Must-be requirements (M)	Indifferent requirements (I)	Reverse requirements (R)	Kano properties
A1	15	33	20	2	0	O
A2	18	32	16	4	0	O
A3	8	14	41	7	0	M
A4	16	15	30	9	0	M
A5	26	13	18	13	0	A
B6	21	12	7	28	2	I
B7	11	37	16	5	1	O
B8	18	8	12	28	4	I
C9	18	29	16	7	0	O
C10	17	33	11	9	0	O
C11	28	12	18	12	0	A

Table 5. Kano attribute classification results of the emotional needs of children's parents.

#	Attractive requirements (A)	One-dimensional requirements (O)	Must-be requirements (M)	Indifferent requirements (I)	Reverse requirements (R)	Kano properties
D1	32	19	12	7	0	A
D2	33	15	19	3	0	A
D3	1	29	39	1	0	M
E4	14	7	14	35	0	I
E5	26	2	11	31	0	I
E6	27	20	14	9	0	A
E7	15	9	15	31	0	I
E8	15	17	12	26	0	I
E9	11	19	36	4	0	M
E10	26	16	13	13	2	A
E11	13	31	21	5	0	O
E12	11	23	27	9	0	M
F13	14	12	11	30	3	I
F14	26	10	20	14	0	A

4.4 User Satisfaction Results and Importance Ranking of Emotional Design Requirements

The Better-Worse coefficient calculation method is proposed by the scholar Berger et al. It is used to indicate the degree of user satisfaction as well as dissatisfaction when a certain type of demand increases or decreases. The calculation method [9] is:

$$Better = (O + A)/(M + O + A + I) \tag{1}$$

$$Worse = (O + M)/(M + O + A + I) \times (-1) \tag{2}$$

The Better coefficient represents the degree of user satisfaction when a certain requirement is met, and the Worse coefficient represents the degree of dissatisfaction of the user when a certain requirement is not met. In order to calculate the user satisfaction index of each emotional need, the classification results of Tables 4 and 5 are brought into the Better-Worse formula, and the satisfaction results of the children and accompanying persons are obtained, as shown in Tables 6 and 7.

Table 6. User satisfaction index of emotional design needs of children.

#	Kano properties	Better	|Worse|
A1	O	0.69	0.76
A2	O	0.71	0.69
A3	M	0.31	0.79
A4	M	0.44	0.64
A5	A	0.56	0.44
B6	I	0.49	0.28
B7	O	0.70	0.77
B8	I	0.47	0.30
C9	O	0.67	0.64
C10	O	0.71	0.63
C11	A	0.57	0.43

Table 7. User satisfaction index of emotional design needs of children's parents.

#	Kano properties	Better	|Worse|
D1	A	0.73	0.44
D2	A	0.69	0.49
D3	M	0.43	0.97
E4	I	0.3	0.3
E5	I	0.4	0.19
E6	A	0.67	0.49
E7	I	0.34	0.34
E8	I	0.46	0.41
E9	M	0.43	0.79
E10	A	0.62	0.43
E11	O	0.63	0.74
E12	M	0.49	0.71
F13	I	0.39	0.34
F14	A	0.51	0.43

According to the above results, in order to more intuitively see the importance of various emotional needs on the children and their families, the Better value is used as the vertical coordinate, and the absolute value of the Worse value is used as the horizontal coordinate. Scatter plots are established respectively, as shown in Figs. 3 and 4.

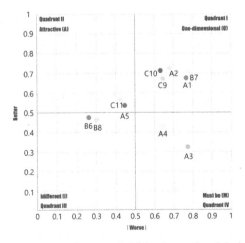

Fig. 3. Four-quadrant diagram of children's emotional design needs

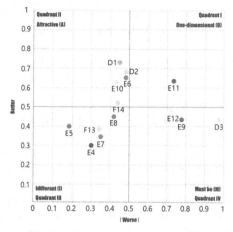

Fig. 4. Four-quadrant diagram of the emotional design needs of children's families

It can be seen from the figure that the first quadrant is the one-dimensional require-ment. When the user's one-dimensional requirements are met, the user will be more satisfied. On the contrary, if the one-dimensional requirements are not met, the user will be even more dissatisfied. The one-dimensional requirements of children mainly include A1, A2, B7, C9, and C10, which are the requirements for the appearance and color of infusion equipment at the visceral level, the requirements for flexibility of infusion equipment at the behavioral level, and the requirements for emotional encouragement and recreational activities at the reflective level. And the one-dimensional requirement of parents is mainly E11, which is the needs for monitoring and reminding functions of infusion progress at the behavioral level. Meeting the above needs is especially impor-tant for infusion equipment design to improve the satisfaction of children and parents. The second quadrant is the attractive requirements. When the attractive requirements are met, the user's satisfaction will increase. However, when the attractive requirements are not met, the user's satisfaction will not decrease. The attractive requirements of children mainly include A5 and C11, which are the need for constant temperature at the visceral level and the need for companionship such as virtual characters at the reflective level. In addition, the attractive needs of parents are D1, D2, E6, E10, F14, which are the demands for simple, beautiful and clear interface design, online archives of children, infusion monitoring for children and later tracking, etc. Such design is conducive to enhance the charm of infusion equipment, and bring surprise experience to children and their families. The third quadrant is indifferent needs, which are not urgent and unneces-sary needs. The indifferent needs of children are mainly B6 and B8, which are the needs for voice conversation and wound compression demonstration functions. Moreover, the indifferent needs of children's families are mainly E4, E5, E7, E8 and F13, which are the needs for precautionary tips before infusion, doctor's introduction, feedback on chil-dren's status, online medication verification and parent-child interactive games, etc. Such functions do not have an impact on the satisfaction of children and their families. The fourth quadrant is the must-be requirements, which are the most basic user needs to be met by the product. The must-be requirements of children are A3 and A4, which are the visceral needs for proper human-machine size and safe and comfortable materials. The must-be requirements of children's families are D3, E9 and E12, which are the needs for cleanliness of the device, safety to avoid misuse, and the need to call the doctor with one button. Such functions are the basic functions that children and parents think should exist and need to be focused on.

5   The Design Principles of Children's Mobile Infusion Equipment

In the extraction of the emotional needs of children and their families in the infusion process, we find that children's needs for infusion equipment are mainly concentrated on the visceral and reflective levels, mainly for sensory experience and emotional reflection and expression. Compared with children, the accompanying persons are more inclined to the behavioral level of the infusion equipment, which puts forward a higher level of demand for the ease of use of the equipment. In this regard, we combine the above conclusions and the ranking results of the importance of various emotional needs in the survey, and propose the following design principles for children's infusion equipment:

5.1   Visceral Level

Reasonable Ergonomics
Since the physiology of children differs greatly from that of adults, the design of children's infusion equipment must make a reasonable ergonomic analysis of the product, and fully consider the children's human-machine size, use process and behavior habits, etc. In addition, the special physiological reactions of children during infusion should also be paid attention to. For example, the temperature of children's hands and feet will gradually decrease during infusion, and taking appropriate measures such as intelligent temperature control can enhance the emotional experience of children during infusion. Moreover, attention should also be paid to the rationality of the use of medical and nursing staff, and the human-machine interaction between the equipment, the child and the doctors should be handled so that the doctors can treat the child under comfortable conditions as much as possible.

Safe and Comfortable Material
Tactile sensation is the most direct means of human perception of objects, and material is an important part of the product manufacturing process. The nature of the material itself can cause the user's emotional resonance with the product [10], and a good sense of touch can enhance the affinity of the infusion device and close the distance between the patient and the infusion device. Therefore, materials for children's infusion equipment should be selected with particular care, and materials with high safety performance that give parents peace of mind and children's comfort should be chosen. On the one hand, physical quantities such as strength and wear resistance should be considered, and on

the other hand, the affinity of the material and its emotional relationship with the child should also be considered.

Interesting Appearance and Proper Color Matching

Infusion devices for children should try to adopt relatively round and soft shapes, avoiding sharp and rigid shapes. At the same time, attention should be paid to the vivid and interesting appearance of the design. In the appearance design, designers should also pay attention to the suitability of colors. Generally speaking, colors with higher brightness and purity are relatively more popular with children. Appropriate color matching and vivid and interesting appearance of the equipment are conducive to bringing a good first impression to the children, laying a relaxing and pleasant atmosphere for the infusion process afterwards, which can effectively alleviate the adverse emotions of the children in the infusion treatment.

5.2 Behavioral Level

Safety and Reliability Principles

The principle of safety and reliability is the top priority of infusion equipment, which is also the must-be requirement that parents pay attention to. Many safety risks exist during infusion. The doctors may make operational errors due to non-cooperation of children, personal fatigue, lack of concentration and so on. At the same time, parents' unauthorized adjustment of the drug drip rate or children's misuse may also cause safety problems. Therefore, the design of warning feedback, protection mechanisms and prevention of misoperation mechanisms should be involved. In addition, children have strong curiosity and poor self-discipline ability, and they are prone to disobey the command and move involuntarily during infusion. So the edges of the equipment should be chamfered to avoid the occurrence of children bump injury and other accidents. In short, the safe and reliable design is conducive to building trust in the infusion equipment for children and their families.

Usability Principle

The principle of ease of use should be emphasized in the design process of children's infusion equipment, so that the product functions can be effectively brought into play. Firstly, the interface needs to be clear, so that it can accurately guide the users' control. Next, the users' human body size, characteristics, operating habits and space should also be taken into full consideration. Finally, usability principle requires functional simplification of the operation process of the children's family members. For instance, the monitoring and reminding of infusion speed and time can effectively avoid the frequent observation and judgment on the progress of infusion. And the online archive can clearly record key information such as past illnesses and allergens of children, which plays an effective prompting role. It can break the information barriers between different hospitals, reduce the number of parents' judgments, and simplify the operation process. The usability principle of the infusion equipment can establish a direct relationship between the behaviors and expectations of children and their accompanying personnel, so that they can obtain joy and satisfaction during use.

5.3 Reflective Level

Gamification and Entertainment Experience
Infusion therapy is a very long process for children. In view of children's feelings of helplessness, fear, impatience and other emotional manifestations during infusion, the motivating and educational gamification design can be applied to infusion equipment. For example, nurturance games can issue virtual courage coins based on the children's medical performance, so that they can exchange virtual animals online to establish their own animal tribes, which motivates the children. Other entertainment educational designs such as virtual image accompanying, audio books, etc. are all conducive to attracting children's attention and increasing children's participation and trust in infusion equipment, so that children can receive treatment in a relaxing and happy atmosphere.

Follow-Up and Feedback After Infusion
Infusion therapy is just one part of the treatment. After leaving the hospital, the children still need to go through a period of recovery. By proposing precautions such as taboos and training suggestions, and answering parents' questions online, the tracking and feedback of the condition can be achieved, which can not only show the emotional care for the children and their families, but also be conducive to improving users' satisfaction and loyalty to the infusion equipment.

6 Conclusion

This study introduces emotional design thinking into the design of children's mobile infusion devices. By combining the emotional design framework with the Kano model, we establish an emotional needs analysis and screening model, explore the emotional needs of two groups of people during children's infusion from the perspective of the subjective feelings and experiences of children and their families, and propose design principles and strategies for children's mobile infusion devices as a result. This study helps to deeply explore the potential emotional needs of children, and pay attention to the needs of potential users in children's medical products which are the children's families. This study explores the design approach of children's medical products from an emotional perspective, and make up for the lack of research on the emotions of children and their accompanying persons in children's medical design, and provides a reference basis for the design optimization of future children's medical products to enhance the emotional experience of children and their families during medical visits.

References

1. Pang, H., et al.: Design and application of multi-functional infusion device for children. Chin. Nurs. J. **54**(08), 1274–1276 (2019). CNKI:SUN:ZHHL.0.2019-08-037
2. Wang, X., Yan, X., Jiang, X.: Research on the design of home medical appliances for children with chronic diseases based on emotional cognition. Packag. Eng.
3. Jin, W., Li, H., Xing, Y.: Children's infusion products based on empathic design. Packag. Eng. **04** (2017)

4. Li, L.: Study of emotional expression in visual communication design. Packag. Eng. **42**(06), 345–348 (2021). https://doi.org/10.19554/j.cnki.1001-3563.2021.06.051

5. Norman, D.A., et al.: Design Psychology: Emotional Design. CITIC Press, Beijing (2012)

6. Fu, F., Gao, S., Ma, J.: Emotional design in medical supplies for the elderly from a smart pillbox. Technol. Innov. Appl. **36**, 26–28 (2019)

7. Yu, S., Ceng, Q.: Design study on functional improvement of office desk based on Kano model. Packag. Eng.

8. Lu, M., Zhou, B., Tan, M.: Research on the use requirements of urban signage system based on Kano model. Packag. Eng.

9. Sauerwein, E., et al.: The Kano model: how to delight your customers. In: International Working Seminar on Production Economics, vol. 1, no. 4 (1996)

10. Wu, J.: The application of emotional design in food packaging. Packag. Eng. **41**(02), 284–286+290 (2020). https://doi.org/10.19554/j.cnki.1001-3563.2020.02.044

Experimenting with a Prototype Interactive Narrative Game to Improve Knowledge and Beliefs for the HPV Vaccine

Anna Zhu[1], Muhammad Amith[2], Lu Tang[3], Rachel Cunningham[4], Angela Xu[5], Julie A. Boom[4,6], and Cui Tao[2(✉)]

[1] Southern Methodist University, Dallas, TX, USA
[2] School of Biomedical Informatics, The University of Texas Health Science Center at Houston, Houston, TX, USA
cui.tao@uth.tmc.edu
[3] Department of Communication, Texas A&M University, College Station, TX, USA
[4] Texas Children's Hospital, Houston, TX, USA
[5] St. Johns High School, Houston, TX, USA
[6] Baylor College of Medicine, Houston, TX, USA

Abstract. Narratives can have a powerful impact on our health-related beliefs, attitudes, and behaviors. The human papillomavirus (HPV) vaccine can protect against human papillomavirus that leads to different types of cancers. However, HPV vaccination rates are low. This study explored the effectiveness of a narrative-based interactive game about the HPV vaccines as a method to communicate knowledge and perhaps create behavioral outcomes. We developed a serious storytelling game called Vaccination Vacation inspired by personal narratives of individuals who were impacted by the HPV. We tested the game using a randomized control study of 99 adult participants and compared the HPV knowledge and vaccine beliefs of the Gamer Group (who played the game, n = 44) and the Reader group (who read a vaccine information sheet, n = 55). We also evaluated the usability of the game. In addition to high usability, the interactive game slightly impacted the beliefs about the HPV vaccine over standard delivery of vaccine information, especially among those who never received the HPV vaccine. We also observed some gender-based differences in perception towards usability and the likelihood of frequently playing the game. A narrative-based game could bring positive changes to players' HPV-related health beliefs. The combination of more comprehensive HPV vaccine information with the narratives may produce a larger impact. Narrative-based games can be effectively used in other vaccine education interventions and warrant future research.

Keywords: Serious games · Narratives · Vaccine · Human papillomavirus · Education · Public health · Vaccine Information Statement

© Springer Nature Switzerland AG 2021
C. Stephanidis et al. (Eds.): HCII 2021, LNCS 13097, pp. 186–201, 2021.
https://doi.org/10.1007/978-3-030-90966-6_14

1 Introduction

Storytelling is one of the oldest and most universal ways of sense-making and communication. Stories trigger emotional reactions, increase engagement, and increase persuasion effectiveness [1]. Storytelling has been incorporated into health applications [2]. Utilizing stories of individuals impacted by HPV and HPV-related cancers, we developed a story-based game to improve the awareness of the HPV vaccine among young adults. Human papillomavirus (HPV) causes many life-threatening cancers, and the most effective preventive measure is through vaccination. However, HPV vaccination rates are lagging behind projected national goals [3]. Effective vaccine education that includes persuasive personal stories can positively influence an individual's decision to vaccinate by emphasizing the risks of HPV and the importance of vaccination [4–6]. Unfortunately, vaccine education is often time-consuming, and health care providers are limited in their ability to spend an extended amount of time providing detailed vaccine education [7].

The standard practice for informing parents about the HPV vaccine is through provider recommendation, provider conversation, and the Vaccine Information Statement (VIS) documents. VISs are federally mandated documents provided by the Centers for Disease Control and Prevention (CDC). VISs are distributed to patients before vaccine administration as part of the informed consent process. An interactive fictional game could serve as a possible intervention tool to supplement the HPV VIS to engage patients during their visit wait time. We used the HPV VIS as a standard baseline for informing patients about the vaccine and HPV.

1.1 Related Studies

We identified four published studies that implemented serious games for health that were related to HPV or the HPV vaccine. Amresh et al. (2019) created a platformer style game to facilitate communication about HPV between parent-child pairs and to promote vaccination [8]. It found that adolescents and their parents had vastly different expectations for the game and that any such game should be generalizable to a wide variety of demographics, making the ideal game genre a puzzle-based game. Additionally, the study concluded that any such game should be relatively short as adolescents have a short attention span.

Cates et al. (2017) developed a video game for preteens eligible to receive the HPV vaccine [9]. The game took the form of a secret garden, in which players planted a garden and used a potion that represented the HPV vaccine to make sure the plants grew up healthy. After playing the game, preteens demonstrated more curiosity and interest in the vaccine. The study concluded that a serious video game can be effective in promoting HPV vaccination awareness, decreasing stigma, and promoting communication between children and parents regarding the vaccine.

Darville and colleagues assessed the impact of avatar customization on risk perception of HPV and intention to get the HPV vaccine among college-age men [10]. The game simulated the spread of an infectious virus and allowed participants to be vaccinated and quarantined in order to stop the spread of the disease. The study found that customization of avatars did not have a statistically significant effect on the impact of the game, but customization of an avatar to reflect one's ideal self did. The largest effect occurred among college-age men.

An educational game, *FightHPV*, was designed to communicate information about HPV and its prevention using fictional characters and a puzzle for each level of knowledge [11]. Players were encouraged to play the game with the use of leaderboards and achievements to increase competitiveness and appealing characters and animation. The majority of participants enjoyed the game and *FightHPV* had a statistically significant impact on improving HPV knowledge.

1.2 Approach

Walter Fisher's *narrative paradigm* suggest that stories are more potent method in persuading an audience instead of debate [12, 13]. Furthermore, he states it is natural for humans to use stories to communicate ideas and beliefs. Medical sciences rely heavily on logic and reason that is supported through statistical data, which may not directly appeal to the individualized human experience [14]. Research has demonstrated that most health consumers are unable to make sense of the statistical probabilities of health information [15, 16].

Health communication research have noted the potential of narratives stories health behavior change [17–20]. The National Cancer Institute endorses the use of vaccine decision stories in embedding positive vaccine messages, particularly in targeting young adult women [21]. On the other hand, the anti-vaccine movement has been effective with anti-vaccine messages, especially through the story telling by celebrities [14].

Interaction fiction is defined as "works of fiction which call the reader to interact with them explicitly upon by means of queries or replies, to take an active role in the story, and deliberately change the development of plot, character, setting, or language along with the author" [22]. Examples of interaction fiction games range from the text-based multi-user dungeon (MUD) games of the mid-to-late 20th century to Depression Quest [23], a game that kindled the Gamergate controversy in 2014 [24], and Kim Kardashian: Hollywood [25]. We assume that interactive fiction games for health could increase user motivation, identification, and immersion that could translate to personal cues to actions. Also, our serious gaming approach is an extension of health communication that wields both visual imagery and storytelling - that can have the potential effect on intention to vaccinate and perception of risk [14].

Compared to the previous studies, our study employs the use of interactive narratives to approximate a relatable and personal experience towards HPV and the HPV vaccine. Other studies focus on metaphorical games that aim at educating the user on the virus' mechanism. In addition, this study conducts a randomized control experiment to analyze the effectiveness of a serious game for health to improve beliefs and knowledge of the HPV vaccine among users. We used validated surveys to measure usability, HPV vaccine knowledge, and HPV-related health beliefs. This study poses the following research questions:

RQ1. How would the Gamer group evaluate the usability of the game? Will such evaluation differ based on demographic characteristics such as gender and, previous knowledge and experience of the HPV and HPV vaccines?

RQ2. Is the interactive narrative game more effective in promoting health beliefs than the standard vaccine information method?

RQ3. Is the interactive narrative game more effective in improving knowledge outcomes than the standard vaccine information method?

2   Materials and Methods

2.1   Game Development

We created a game called Vaccination Vacation. We started this project with the narratives compiled from the experiences of real-life patients infected with HPV [26]. Game characters were created with inspiration from these narratives. A storyline was created to connect all the characters and embed HPV-related knowledge. After the storyline was developed, a script was written, and the game flow was created to ensure the overall story was coherent and well-connected. Finally, characters and scenes were drawn using digital tools and pieced together in GameMaker Studio 2 [27] to create a functioning game. Game development was completed in the Fall of 2018.

The story involves a doctor, played by the user, who creates a machine to target cells and uses it to treat people with HPV related cancers while on vacation. The player encounters different patients and engages in conversations with them about HPV vaccines. The game also includes an action component where the player uses the machine to attack the cells of HPV-related cancers inpatients (Fig. 1). The patient information displayed will show the age and gender of individuals and the kind of cancers that HPV can cause. The player has to convince some patients (males and females of different ages) to get the vaccine by choosing what to say to these patients from many facts about the HPV and HPV vaccine provided in the game. The player also has to answer questions from patients about the HPV and the HPV vaccines (Fig. 2). If the player answers a question incorrectly, he will have to answer it again to ensure both the player and the non-player patient know the right answer.

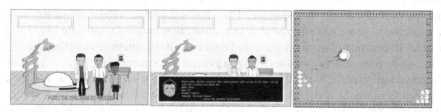

Fig. 1. Scenes from Vaccination Vacation. The doctor meets the patient (l) and the game displays information about the patient (m). Action aspect of the game involves attacking cells related to HPV-causing cancers (r).

2.2   Experimental Procedure

A posttest only control group design experiment was conducted to examine the effectiveness of the game. The study was approved by the Internal Review Boards of The

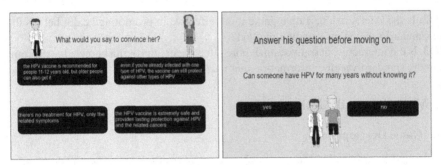

Fig. 2. Scenes from Vaccination Vacation where the doctor convinces the patient about the HPV vaccine.

University of Texas Health Science Center at Houston and Texas A&M University in College Station (HSC-SBMI-18-0746 and IRB2018-1157D). Afterward, participants were recruited from an undergraduate research participant pool at Texas A&M University. The experiment was conducted online using Qualtrics. After giving consent, participants first answered a set of questions about their demographic information such as age, sex, year in college, HPV vaccine status, etc. Next, participants were randomly assigned to either the experiment group to play the game (Gamer group) or the control group to read a Vaccine Information Statement (VIS) document for HPV (Reader group). Afterward, they either played the game or read the VIS. Finally, they completed a survey questionnaire that measures their knowledge of HPV vaccines [28] and health beliefs about HPV vaccines [29, 30]. The perceived system usability was also measured in the Gamer group [31, 32]. Data collection was conducted in November and December of 2019.

2.3   Measurements

System Usability. The System Usability Survey (SUS) scale was administered to measure the overall usability of the game. The SUS is a simple, validated assessment to measure users' perceived effectiveness and satisfaction in using a software [31, 32]. It includes 10 questions that produce a score between 0–100 to quantify usability. The final score can be compared to baselines to give a general assessment of the game's usability. The first question of the SUS (*"I think that I would like to use this game frequently"*) was excluded from the SUS overall computation since we envision the game as a clinical tool to help providers inform patients, and we envision users are unlikely to play the game multiple times. The SUS score was computed using the standard procedure for the remaining nine items [33].

HPV Vaccine Beliefs. We utilized the Carolina HPV Immunization Attitudes and Beliefs Scale (CHIAS) that was modified for young adults under the age of 25 [29]. This validated survey measured inclination towards or against the HPV vaccine based on several factors of their beliefs: *Perceived Harms, Risk Denial, Perceived Barriers, Perceived Effectiveness, and Perceived Uncertainty*. This survey has 17 items on a four-point Likert scale. Lower values for this survey correspond to a positive propensity towards the HPV vaccine, while the higher values correspond to a negative propensity towards the HPV vaccine.

HPV Knowledge Test. We measured knowledge of the HPV and HPV vaccine using a validated HPV knowledge test, which contains 14 True-or-False questions reflecting basic knowledge of HPV and the HPV vaccine [28]. A knowledge score was computed for each individual who took the HPV knowledge test based on the percentage of correct responses.

2.4 Data Analysis

RStudio and Stata v15 were used for data analysis. To answer RQ1, we conducted a one-sample t-test to compare participants' evaluation of the game's usability to the baseline of 68, the average usability for software [34]. We also examined differences in SUS scores between genders, ethnicity, and awareness of the HPV and the vaccine using t-tests.

Independent samples t-tests were used to compare HPV-related health beliefs from the two groups (RQ2). In addition, we assessed the effect of the intervention on beliefs based on specific characteristics of the participants – whether they had heard of the virus, the HPV vaccine, or had the HPV vaccine prior, gender, ethnicity, etc.

To answer RQ3, an independent samples t-test was conducted to compare the knowledge scores of the Gamer group and the Reader group. For the Gamer group, demographic variables and game usability questions were taken into consideration. For the Reader group, only the background questions were taken into consideration. Correct answers for each question were calculated for each group, gamer and reader, and a grade was calculated for each question. Afterward, an average of the grades was calculated for each group was calculated and compared. The questions with low scores and questions that had low scores for both groups were determined to see how the information could be improved.

3 Results

In total 108 participants completed the online experiment. However, 9 participants in the Gamer group were excluded from data analysis. These 9 participants spent less than 251 s in completing the study and were considered outliers who were unlikely to have played the game and completed the surveys. Among the remaining 99 participants, 44 were in the Gamer group and 55 were in the Reader group. Table 1 shows a breakdown of the participants' characteristics.

For RQ1, the final SUS score of the game was 73.6 ($\sigma = 18.5$), which is higher than the average of 68 ($\sigma = 12.5$) reported in earlier studies [34], even though the difference was not statistically significant ($t(43) = 1.80$, $p = 0.08$). According to researchers, this score would be classified as "Good" suggesting that usability is acceptable [35]. There was no statistically significant difference in the SUS scores based on ethnicity, previous knowledge about HPV/HPV vaccines, or HPV vaccination status.

Table 1. Participant characteristics.

	Gamer (n = 44)	Reader (n = 55)
Age (standard deviation)	19.9 (0.20)	19.9 (0.22)
Gender		
Male	22 (50%)	26 (47.3%)
Female	22 (50%)	29 (52.7%)
Ethnicity		
Asian	3 (6.8%)	4 (7.3%)
Black	2 (4.6%)	1 (1.8)%
Hispanic	9 (20.5%)	11 (20%)
White	30 (68.2%)	39 (70.9%)
College year		
Freshman	4 (9.1%)	6 (10.9%)
Sophomore	21 (47.7%)	27 (49.1%)
Junior	10 (22.7%)	11 (20%)
Senior	9 (20.5%)	11 (20%)
Heard of HPV		
Yes	36 (81.8%)	46 (83.7%)
Maybe	2 (4.6%)	3 (5.5%)
No	6 (13.6%)	6 (10.9%)
Heard of HPV vaccine		
Yes	34 (77.2%)	44 (80%)
Maybe	1 (2.3%)	4 (7.3%)
No	9 (20.5%)	7 (12.7%)
Taken the HPV vaccine		
Yes	19 (43.2%)	29 (52.7%)
Maybe	14 (31.8%)	10 (18.2%)
No	11 (25%)	16 (29.1%)

There was no significant difference in the overall usability perception of the game between men and women based on an independent-sample t-test calculation ($t(41) = 0.88$, $p = 0.38$); however, a one-sample t-test revealed an almost significant difference between men's SUS score and the average perceived usability ($M = 76$) reported in previous studies ($t(21) = 2.10$, $p = 0.05$). Furthermore, there were gender differences with specific usability items of SUS: SUS2 (complexity: I found the game unnecessarily complex), SUS5 (perceived integration: I found the various functions in the game were well integrated), and SUS10 (difficulty to learn: I needed to learn a lot of things before I could get going with the game). Female gamers indicated higher perceived complexity of the game (M = 2.41) than the male gamers (M = 1.73). Females also indicated higher rating for their perceived integration of the game (M = 3.91) than the male gamers (M = 3.32), and they perceived the game to be difficult to learn (M = 2.32) than the males (M = 1.68). Table 2 below summarizes the breakdown of the SUS Score based on various variables among those that played the game (n = 44).

Table 2. System Usability Scale breakdown table. *p < 0.05, **p < 0.10. Unaware are individuals who do not know HPV, or HPV vaccine, and never had the HPV vaccine prior.

	SUS score	Frequency
All (n = 44)	73.6 (18.5)	44
**SUS Score was higher than the average usability of 68, t(43) = 1.80, p = 0.08*		
Gender		
Male (SD)	76.0 (17.9)	22
Female (SD)	70.1 (19.2)	22
Usability perception is different between male gamers and females, t(41) = 0.88, p = 0.38		
Male perceived usability higher than the average of 68, t(21) = 2.10, p = 0.05		
Female perceived usability higher than the average of 68, t(21) = 0.51, p = 0.62		
SUS1		
Male (SD)	1.5 (0.86)	22
Female (SD)	2.55 (1.18)	22
Male and female interest in frequently playing the game, t(42) = −3.35, p = 0.00		
SUS2		
Male (SD)	1.73 (0.94)	22
Female (SD)	2.41 (1.33)	22
**Male and female perceived the game to be complex, t(42) = −1.96, p = 0.06*		
SUS5		
Male (SD)	3.32 (1.32)	22
Female (SD)	3.91 (0.75)	22
**Males and females perceived the game to be well integrated, t(42) = −1.82, p = 0.08*		

(continued)

Table 2. (*continued*)

	SUS score	Frequency
SUS10		
Male (SD)	1.68 (0.99)	22
Female (SD)	2.32 (1.21)	22
**Males and females perceived the game to be difficult to learn, t(42) = −1.91, p = 0.06*		
Ethnicity		
White	72.2 (19.2)	30
Hispanic	71.3 (17.7)	9
Black	73.6 (2.0)	2
Asian	86.1 (24.1)	3
Perception of usability differencing based on the ethnicity of the gamer, p = 0.35		
Heard of HPV		
Yes	74.5 (18.5)	35
Maybe	79.2 (9.8)	2
No	66.2 (21.2)	6
Perception of usability differing based on hearing about HPV virus, p = 0.73		
Heard of HPV vaccine		
Yes	73.7 (18.7)	33
Maybe	72.2 (0)	1
No	73.1 (19.7)	9
Perception of usability differing based on hearing about the HPV vaccine, p = 0.85		
Taken HPV vaccine		
Yes	77.3 (18.1)	18
Maybe	74.8 (13.4)	14
No	65.9 (23.4)	11
Perception of usability differing based on taking on the HPV vaccine, p = 0.18		
Unaware		
No	74.5 (18.5)	35
Yes	69.4 (19.2)	8
Perception of the usability differing based on completely being unaware of HPV and the HPV vaccine, p = 0.49		

RQ2 asked if the game and the VIS influenced participants' HPV Vaccine Beliefs differently. Table 3 presents survey ratings for CHIAS collected from both the Gamer group and the Reader group of the study. A set of independent-sample t-tests indicated no significant differences between the two groups.

Table 3. CHIAS Ratings between Gamers and Readers. N.B. Low CHIAS rating indicates a high propensity for the HPV vaccine, and a high CHIAS rating indicates a low propensity toward the HPV vaccine.

	CHAIS rating	Frequency
Harms		
Gamers (SD)	3.45 (0.71)	44
Reader (SD)	3.39 (0.70)	55
Harms factor rating differing between the gamer and reader group, p = 0.67		
Barriers		
Gamers (SD)	3.73 (0.90)	44
Reader (SD)	3.79 (0.88)	55
Barriers factor rating differing between the gamer and reader group, p = 0.77		
Effectiveness		
Games (SD)	3.20 (0.72)	44
Readers (SD)	3.19 (0.89)	55
Effectiveness factor rating differing between gamer and reader group, p = 0.99		
Uncertainty		
Gamers (SD)	3.23 (0.91)	44
Readers (SD)	3.47 (0.85)	55
Uncertainty factor rating differing between gamer and reader group, p = 0.19		
Risk Denial		
Gamers (SD)	3.75 (0.67)	44
Readers (SD)	3.98 (0.79)	55
Risk Denial factor differing between gamer and reader group, p = 0.12		

RQ3 asked if the game and the VIS were likely to lead to significant differences in participants' HPV knowledge. The Gamer and Reader groups were first filtered to remove any participants who did not answer every question (n = 5) and the Gamer group was further filtered to only include participants who played the game for 251 s and over (n = 94). An independent-sample t-test did not find any significant differences between the Gamer and Reader group. (See Table 3 for the differences between the Gamer group and the Reader group.) However, among participants who never had the HPV vaccine, there was a slight difference between the Gamer group and the Reader group (t(45) = 1.93, p = 0.06).

We further explored the detailed results of the knowledge test (See Table 4). Overall, the average knowledge score was about the same between the two groups and the Gamer group did a little bit better than the Reader group. There were three questions where both the gamer and reader group did not perform well: Q48 (HPV can cause HIV/AIDS), Q55 (HPV usually doesn't need any treatment), and Q62 (HPV vaccines are most effective if given to people who have never had sex). We saw that for a majority of questions that were included in both the game and VIS, the gamer performed better than the reader group, showing that the game could be more effective than the pamphlet regarding those questions. (See Table 5 for the common questions and the proportion of gamers or readers who answered correctly.) However, the overall difference between gamers and readers was not significant ($t(10) = 1.53$, $p = 0.156$).

Table 4. Knowledge Score breakdown between the reader and gamer group. Aware are individuals who have known or may know HPV, HPV vaccine and who had or may had the HPV vaccine prior. Unaware are individuals who do not know HPV, or HPV vaccine, and never had the HPV vaccine prior. **$p < 0.10$.

	Knowledge score	Frequency
Group		
Gamers (SD)	0.81 (0.10)	40
Readers (SD)	0.79 (0.10)	54
Knowledge score differing between reader and gamer groups, $p = 0.64$		
+never had vaccine		
Gamers (SD)	0.82 (0.07)	22
Readers (SD)	0.77 (0.09)	25

**Knowledge score between reader and gamer groups who never had the HPV vaccine, $t(45) = 1.93$, $p = 0.06$

Table 5. Questions that appear in both the game and VIS. Gamer Group Score is the proportion of gamers who correctly answered the question. Reader Group Score is the proportion of readers who correctly answered the question.

Questions	Gamer Group Score	Reader Group Score
Q41 (HPV can cause cervical cancer)	0.9250	0.9444
Q42 (a person could have HPV for many years without knowing it	0.9750	0.9259
Q44 (HPV is very rare)	0.9750	0.9259

(continued)

Table 5. (*continued*)

Questions	Gamer Group Score	Reader Group Score
Q63 (men cannot get HPV)	1.0000	0.9815
Q52 (there are many types of HPV)	0.9250	0.9444
Q64 (HPV can cause genital warts)*	0.9250	0.7778
Q53 (HPV can be cured with antibiotics)	0.9000	0.8148
Q54 (most sexually active people will get HPV at some point)*	0.4750	0.7222
Q57 (one of the HPV vaccines offers protection against genital warts)*	0.8500	0.5556
Q60 (HPV vaccines offer protection against most cervical cancers)*	0.8250	0.5741
Q61 (The HPV vaccines require three doses)	0.8750	0.7407
*Questions with larger differences	Difference between gamer and reader groups, t(10) = 1.53, p = 0.156	

4 Discussion

We developed an interactive narrative game, called Vaccination Vacation, to inform and affect participants' knowledge and beliefs of the HPV vaccine and the HPV. This game leverages interactive fiction, which is different from what other HPV games offer, for storytelling in an interactive way. The game was used as an experimental intervention for a randomized control group study, with the control group reading a VIS document for the HPV vaccine (standard protocol in a clinical environment). Surveys for usability, health beliefs, and attitudes toward the HPV vaccine, and an HPV vaccine knowledge test were administered to the participants. The study is the first to implement a control study to investigate the effect of narrative health games on beliefs and knowledge. If effective, this game could serve as a fun complement to federally-mandated VIS given at the time of vaccination for each patient, especially in instances where the VIS is underutilized by some of the patients [36].

The usability of the game is crucial to adoption by the user and analyzing a game's usability can shed light on whether the game itself poses a barrier. The composite SUS score settled any concerns that usability may have hindered the operational use of the game. With a SUS score of 74, higher than the average of 68 recorded in previous studies, the game's usability is deemed to be better than average or "good," according to usability experts. This means most of the players had relatively low issues with the game and were able to play the game.

Gender seems to be a factor in perceived usability, as males perceived the game to have high usability than females based on their mean SUS score. Yet, male gamers were less likely to plan to play the game frequently compared to females. It is possible that women are more drawn to games that involve identifying with avatars than the competitive aspect of games [37]. The narrative format of Vaccination Vacation does not provide any competitive feature. However, the narrative roleplaying feature may be appealing to female players than male players. There were additional factors that differentiated males and females with the game, like females indicating that the game was complex, less integrated, and they had difficulty learning to play the game compared to the males. We assume that perhaps interactive narrative games or the look and feel may have the interest of female gamers than males. Another explanation is that males were more likely to be gamers [38, 39] and have some familiarity with playing various video games, which might explain the higher usability ratings over female players. This may be an important finding that could encourage health game developers to consider the target audience based on gender. The gender differences for games open up more questions for future researchers to investigate and possibly draw upon. Moreover, this may signify the utility in using narrative-based games to a young female population, especially a population that is impacted by adult onset of cervical cancer, a cancer that is caused by HPV infection.

Between the Gamer group and the Reader group, there seemed to be no indication of whether interactive narrative games can have an impact on health beliefs. We believe this is due to the limited scope of the prototype game to focus on personal narratives. While we administered health belief surveys to assess the effect of the game, previous studies in this area have looked at directly mapping behavioral health models into a game, which was not considered in this prototype. Future goals will need to combine both the direct mapping of health behavior theory and narratives to study and improve the outcome of the narrative health games.

While not statistically significant, better knowledge gain was observed with those that played the game than those that read the Vaccine Information Statement for the HPV vaccine. What was conclusive is that the game appears to have better knowledge increases than the Reader group among those that never had the HPV vaccine, albeit marginally significant results. Overall, there is minimal evidence to support the claim that the game can produce better knowledge gains than reading brochures and flyers. We can surmise that if the game-based approach is better, particularly among those not initiated with the HPV vaccine, that it could be an educational supplement to inform individuals before receiving the HPV vaccine, which is needed to impart information about the benefits of the HPV vaccine and increase the vaccination rates among the public [4–6]. Nonetheless, some researchers have declared that knowledge by itself is not enough to affect the vaccination intention [40–43], as there might be other factors that contribute towards people's decisions [44–46]. As an informational tool, games could serve as a more engaging and immersive piece to reach out to individuals.

We tallied 11 questions that the game addressed. Eight of the questions produced better results than the paper-based method with the participants, but only three were significant – HPV can cause genital warts, one of the HPV vaccines offers protection against genital warts, HPV vaccines offer protection against most cervical cancers. The latter question is an important message that health professionals promote and which is the main driver for getting the HPV vaccine – that will protect against viruses that lead to life-threatening cancers. In any case, future work with the game will need to address every facet of the HPV vaccine and virus-related knowledge.

Future studies would need to assess the possibility of vaccination uptake as a result of playing the game. In some instances, the game and the paper-based method had a similar impact on beliefs, which says a few things: If the game is as good as the paper-based method, could the game be an alternative to informing patients, and if the game were to embed more comprehensive intervention in affecting beliefs can the game be more effective in modifying the beliefs of the user towards cues to action? The main limit of this interactive narrative game is the strict adherence in using narratives to communicate some information about the HPV vaccine. Incorporation of additional information about the HPV vaccine or narratives that address some of the gaps in health beliefs may improve the effectiveness of the game.

5 Conclusion

Interactive narrative games are akin to role-playing games or an electronic version of the "choose your own adventure" novels. We developed a prototype serious game that employs interactive narratives to communicate health information about the HPV vaccine and the virus that it targets. The result of our randomized control experiment indicated that the impact of health beliefs is compatible with the standard method. The perceived usability of the game indicated some receptiveness of the game by participants, especially among females. While the game exhibited minor advantages over the standard practices of informing patients, improvements are needed to expand the scope of information, tailoring for male and female players, and directly mapping certain health belief factors into the game. We presume this would enhance the overall effectiveness of any serious game for health that employs interactive narrative. We also presume that our study offers some best practices to conduct controlled experiments for serious gaming of vaccines.

References

1. Murphy, S.T., Frank, L.B., Moran, M.B., Patnoe-Woodley, P.: Involved, transported, or emotional? Exploring the determinants of change in knowledge, attitudes, and behavior in entertainment-education. J. Commun. **61**, 407–431 (2011)
2. Lugmayr, A., Sutinen, E., Suhonen, J., Sedano, C.I., Hlavacs, H., Montero, C.S.: Serious storytelling – a first definition and review. Multimed. Tools Appl. **76**(14), 15707–15733 (2016). https://doi.org/10.1007/s11042-016-3865-5
3. Nahme, E., Patel, D.A., Oppenheimer, D.M., Elerian, N., Lakey, D.: Missed opportunity: human papillomavirus vaccination in Texas. The University of Texas System (2017)
4. Fokom Domgue, J., Chido-Amajuoyi, O.G., Yu, R.K., Shete, S.: Beliefs about HPV vaccine's success at cervical cancer prevention among adult US women. JNCI Cancer Spectr. **3**, pkz064 (2019). https://doi.org/10.1093/jncics/pkz064
5. Shelal, Z., et al.: Knowledge matters and empowers: HPV vaccine advocacy among HPV-related cancer survivors. Support. Care Cancer **28**(5), 2407–2413 (2019). https://doi.org/10.1007/s00520-019-05035-1
6. Suk, R., et al.: Public knowledge of human papillomavirus and receipt of vaccination recommendations. JAMA Pediatr. **173**, 1099 (2019). https://doi.org/10.1001/jamapediatrics.2019.3105

7. Zimet, G.D., Rosberger, Z., Fisher, W.A., Perez, S., Stupiansky, N.W.: Beliefs, behaviors and HPV vaccine: correcting the myths and the misinformation. Prev. Med. **57**, 414–418 (2013). https://doi.org/10.1016/j.ypmed.2013.05.013

8. Amresh, A., Chia-Chen, A., Baron, C.T.: A game based intervention to promote HPV vaccination among adolescents. In: 2019 IEEE 7th International Conference on Serious Games and Applications for Health (SeGAH), pp. 1–6. IEEE, Kyoto, Japan (2019). https://doi.org/10.1109/SeGAH.2019.8882459

9. Cates, J.R., et al.: Developing a serious video game for preteens to motivate HPV vaccination decision-making: "land of secret gardens." J. Adolesc. Health **60**, S8–S9 (2017). https://doi.org/10.1016/j.jadohealth.2016.10.038

10. Darville, G., et al.: Customization of avatars in a HPV digital gaming intervention for college-age males: an experimental study. Simul. Gaming **49**, 515–537 (2018). https://doi.org/10.1177/1046878118799472

11. Ruiz-López, T., et al.: FightHPV: design and evaluation of a mobile game to raise awareness about human papillomavirus and nudge people to take action against cervical cancer. JMIR Serious Games **7**, e8540 (2019). https://doi.org/10.2196/games.8540

12. Fisher, W.R.: Narration as a human communication paradigm: the case of public moral argument. Commun. Monogr. **51**, 1–22 (1984)

13. Fisher, W.R.: The narrative paradigm: an elaboration. Commun. Monogr. **52**, 347–367 (1985)

14. Cunningham, R.M., Boom, J.A.: Telling stories of vaccine-preventable diseases: why it works. J. South Dakota State Med. Assoc. **6** (2013)

15. Lipkus, I.M., Samsa, G., Rimer, B.K.: General performance on a numeracy scale among highly educated samples. Med. Decis. Making **21**, 37–44 (2001)

16. Schwartz, L.M., Woloshin, S., Black, W.C., Welch, H.G.: The role of numeracy in understanding the benefit of screening mammography. Ann. Internal Med. **127**, 966–972 (1997)

17. Larkey, L., Hecht, M., Slater, M., Helitzer, D., Kreuter, M., Lopez, A.: A model of narrative as culture-centric health promotion. Society for Behavioral Medicine (2008)

18. Kreuter, M.W., et al.: Narrative communication in cancer prevention and control: a framework to guide research and application. Ann. Behav. Med. **33**, 221–235 (2007)

19. Hinyard, L.J., Kreuter, M.W.: Using narrative communication as a tool for health behavior change: a conceptual, theoretical, and empirical overview. Health Educ. Behav. **34**, 777–792 (2007)

20. Cappella, J.N., Hornik, R.C.: The importance of communication science in addressing core problems in public health. In: Distinctive Qualities in Communication Research, pp. 89–102. Routledge (2009)

21. National Cancer Institute: HPV Vaccine Decision Narratives: Encouraging Informed HPV Vaccine Decision-making. https://ebccp.cancercontrol.cancer.gov/programDetails.do?programId=22620324. Accessed 01 May 2021

22. Niesz, A.J., Holland, N.N.: Interactive fiction. Crit. Inq. **11**, 110–129 (1984)

23. Quinn, Z.: Depression Quest. The Quinnspiracy (2013)

24. Stuart, B.: #GamerGate: the misogynist movement blighting the video games industry. https://www.telegraph.co.uk/culture/culturenews/11180510/gamergate-misogynist-felicia-day-zoe-quinn-brianna-wu.html. Accessed 01 Apr 2020

25. Glu Mobile: Kim Kardashian: Hollywood. Glu Mobile (2014)

26. Cunningham, R.M., Boom, J.A.: Vaccine-Preventable Disease - Human Papillomavirus (HPV) Special Edition. Texas Children's Hospital (2016)

27. YoYo Games: GameMaker Studio 2. (2018)

28. Marlow, L.A.V., Zimet, G.D., McCaffery, K.J., Ostini, R., Waller, J.: Knowledge of human papillomavirus (HPV) and HPV vaccination: an international comparison. Vaccine **31**, 763–769 (2013). https://doi.org/10.1016/j.vaccine.2012.11.083

29. Dempsey, A.F., Fuhrel-Forbis, A., Konrath, S.: Use of the Carolina HPV Immunization Attitudes and Beliefs Scale (CHIAS) in young adult women. PLoS ONE **9**, e100193 (2014). https://doi.org/10.1371/journal.pone.0100193

30. McRee, A.-L., Brewer, N.T., Reiter, P.L., Gottlieb, S.L., Smith, J.S.: The Carolina HPV Immunization Attitudes and Beliefs Scale (CHIAS): scale development and associations with intentions to vaccinate. Sex. Transm. Dis. **37**, 234–239 (2010)

31. Brooke, J.: SUS: a retrospective. J. Usab. Stud. **8**, 29–40 (2013)

32. Brooke, J., et al.: SUS-a quick and dirty usability scale. Usab. Eval. Ind. **189** (1996)

33. Lewis, J.R., Sauro, J.: Can I leave this one out? The effect of dropping an item from the SUS, vol. 13, p. 9 (2017)

34. Sauro, J., Lewis, J.R.: Quantifying the User Experience: Practical Statistics for User Research. Morgan Kaufmann, Burlington (2016)

35. Bangor, A.: Determining what individual SUS scores mean: adding an adjective rating scale, vol. 4, p. 10 (2009)

36. Frew, P.M., Chung, Y., Fisher, A.K., Schamel, J., Basket, M.M.: Parental experiences with vaccine information statements: implications for timing, delivery, and parent-provider immunization communication. Vaccine **34**, 5840–5844 (2016)

37. Van Bauwel, S.: Women gamers. In: The International Encyclopedia of Gender, Media, and Communication. Wiley, Hoboken (2020)

38. Borgonovi, F.: Video gaming and gender differences in digital and printed reading performance among 15-year-olds students in 26 countries. J. Adolesc. **48**, 45–61 (2016)

39. Desai, R.A., Krishnan-Sarin, S., Cavallo, D., Potenza, M.N.: Video-gaming among high school students: health correlates, gender differences, and problematic gaming. Pediatrics **126**, e1414–e1424 (2010)

40. Bennett, A.T., et al.: Human papillomavirus vaccine uptake after a tailored, online educational intervention for female university students: a randomized controlled trial. J. Women's Health **24**, 950–957 (2015)

41. Juraskova, I., Bari, R.A., O'Brien, M.T., McCaffery, K.J.: HPV vaccine promotion: does referring to both cervical cancer and genital warts affect intended and actual vaccination behavior? Women's Health Issues **21**, 71–79 (2011). https://doi.org/10.1016/j.whi.2010.08.004

42. Perez, G.K., Cruess, D.G., Strauss, N.M.: A brief information–motivation–behavioral skills intervention to promote human papillomavirus vaccination among college-aged women. Psychol. Res. Behav. Manag. **9**, 285 (2016)

43. Richman, A.R., Maddy, L., Torres, E., Goldberg, E.J.: A randomized intervention study to evaluate whether electronic messaging can increase human papillomavirus vaccine completion and knowledge among college students. J. Am. Coll. Health **64**, 269–278 (2016)

44. Gerend, M.A., Shepherd, J.E.: Predicting human papillomavirus vaccine uptake in young adult women: comparing the health belief model and theory of planned behavior. Ann. Behav. Med. **44**, 171–180 (2012)

45. Hopfer, S.: Effects of a narrative HPV vaccination intervention aimed at reaching college women: a randomized controlled trial. Prev. Sci. **13**, 173–182 (2012)

46. Juraskova, I., O'Brien, M., Mullan, B., Bari, R., Laidsaar-Powell, R., McCaffery, K.: HPV vaccination and the effect of information framing on intentions and behaviour: an application of the theory of planned behaviour and moral norm. Int. J. Behav. Med. **19**, 518–525 (2012)

HCI in Transport

Injury Prevention for Transportation Safety: A Bibliometric Analysis

Ali Alkhaleefah[✉], Quirinus Renardo[✉], and Vincent G. Duffy[✉]

Purdue University, West Lafayette, IN 47907, USA
{aalkhale,qrenardo,duffy}@purdue.edu

Abstract. Transportation accident is one of the most common forms of accidents. Transportation accidents can be caused by a distracted driver, speeding, pedestrians' influence, and alcohol influence. Accidents can lead to injuries, and transportation injuries accounted for around 38% of work-related injuries. Therefore, finding a way to prevent injury caused by transportation accidents can help in reducing fatalities and increase safety. This paper demonstrates a bibliometric analysis of scientific papers on injury prevention and transportation safety. Keywords used to help analyze the relationship between articles such as "Injury," "Transportation," and "Safety." The analyses were conducted using VOSViewer, MAXQDA, Harzing's Publish or Perish 7, BibExcel, CiteSpace, Vicinitas, and Mendeley. By approaching these keywords in this article, promising transportation safety techniques and illustrating the connectivity between articles can improve the gap between transportation safety and the status quo. The articles themselves were collected from multiple databases such as Web of Science, SpringerLink, Scopus, and Google Scholar. Key findings from this paper are that to reduce accidents that caused injuries, protecting both drivers and pedestrians, such as creating pedestrian refuge islands and installing single-lane roundabouts and proper education about transportation safety, is necessary.

Keywords: Injury · Transportation · Safety · Harzing · MAXQDA · VOSViewer · Mendeley · Bibliometric analysis

1 Introduction and Background

Every day we lose thousands of people who are killed and injured on the roads. Road traffic injuries cause the main issue for public health and affect unprotected users of the road. Therefore, road traffic injury prevention must be organized with different interest parties such as law enforcement, road infrastructure companies, and mobility planning. According to the World Health Organization, over 16 000 people die from all types of crashes and injuries. The risk factor in road traffic is a function of four elements, including exposure, underlying probabilities of an impact, probabilities of damage, and the result of a crash (World Health Organization 2004).

Our article aims to learn about various trends in research addressing injury prevention for transportation safety by conducting a bibliometric analysis of articles in the last

© Springer Nature Switzerland AG 2021
C. Stephanidis et al. (Eds.): HCII 2021, LNCS 13097, pp. 205–218, 2021.
https://doi.org/10.1007/978-3-030-90966-6_15

19 years (2002–2021). Search terms and databases are identified in the first section, and a keyword search is performed on Vicinitas to obtain trend and engagement information. Next, Harzing Publish or Perish through Google Scholar is used to extract data from 980 articles, used with VOS Viewer to form a network cluster based on author and citation. In the consequent sections, Wordcloud.com and MAXQDA are used to upload and parse relevant articles for generating a word cloud visualization of frequent keywords appearing in the papers. In the following sections, leading tables are generated, and CiteSpace analysis gives a visual summary of co-citation analysis. Finally, future work and insights are discussed to suggest potential improvements in the area.

2 Purpose of Study

Injury Prevention for Transportation, an integral aspect of road safety, needs to be well analyzed by deriving previously written articles. Here, we conduct a bibliometric analysis of papers on transportation injuries and ways to prevent them. The study aims to identify the current status of accidents that caused injuries and provide a basis for further research on this topic.

3 Methodologies

3.1 Data Collection

The research started with collecting data. This process is done by searching for three keywords on different databases. The keywords used in this search were "Injury," "Transportation," and "Safety." Next, those keywords were used on four other databases. For this paper, Web of Science, Scopus, SpringerLink, and Google Scholar were used as the databases. For Google Scholar, a software called Harzing's Publish or Perish was required to get the metadata. Harzing is a powerful software that can extract articles and metadata from 6 databases, Crossref, Google Scholar, PubMed, Microsoft Academic, Scopus, and Web of Science. For this paper, Harzing will only be used for Google Scholar. However, Harzing is limited to only 1,000 results from Google Scholar. The three keywords were used in Google Scholar for this paper. Web of Science, SpringerLink, and Scopus were accessible through the Purdue Library Databases website. Articles and metadata related to the topic were extracted from the three databases. Important information such as title, author, abstract, and citations was all part of the collected metadata. This collected metadata was then utilized using Vosviewer. This software tool can generate different analyses, such as co-citation analysis and content analysis.

3.2 Bibliometric Analysis

Bibliometric Analysis has been extensively applied to examine models of scholarly publication and evaluate research results (Guo et al. 2020). Using bibliometrics can compare the timescale and the discipline citation outcomes between researchers and organizations (Bornmann et al. 2015). MAXQDA is another tool used in this paper. MAXQDA helped in generating a word cloud from collected articles and also being able to select/deselect words on the word cloud to remove any unnecessary words. The extended lexical search was also conducted using MAXQDA. Bibexcel is another software used to generate leading tables and pivot charts. The pivot chart was generated using Microsoft Excel using data from Bibexcel. Both the leading table and pivot chart helped in identifying leading authors for this paper. A tool used for bibliometric analysis was Vicinitas. Vicinitas helped generate an engagement graph for keywords data from Twitter. Cluster analysis and citation burst were generated using CiteSpace. Cluster analysis helped identify which articles have similarities, and citation burst helped identify which articles were cited the most. Lastly, Mendeley was used to help generate a Chicago-style citation for all the references used in this paper.

4   Results

The research for this paper started with collecting data out of the four chosen databases. It was decided to collect data from Web of Science, Scopus, SpringerLink, and Google Scholar. The keywords used for the data collection were "injury," "transportation," and "safety." Table 1 illustrates the results of data collection. It shows what databases are used, number of articles found, and keywords used.

Table 1. Table of databases, number of articles, and keywords.

Database	Number of articles	Keywords
Web of Science	1,299	Injury and Transportation and Safety
Scopus	3,269	Injury and Transportation and Safety
SpringerLink	22,000	Injury and Transportation and Safety
Google Scholar (through Harzing's Publish or Perish)	980	Injury and Transportation and Safety

4.1   Trend Analysis

Trend analyses were conducted through Web of Science, Scopus, and Vicinitas. In addition, publication years and categories were analyzed to see the trend for the topic. The keywords used on the search were "Injury and Transportation and Safety."

Figure 1 shows the trend analysis for the keywords search, "Injury and Transportation and Safety" on Web of Science. The bar graph shows the result of the past 20 years, spanning from 2002 to 2021. A surge of search happened around 2015 and kept rising until 2020 (2021 was low due to the writing of this paper taking place in early 2021). Before 2015 the topic trend was often going up and down but seeing that the topic was

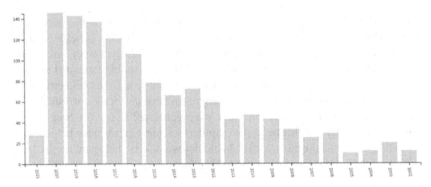

Fig. 1. Trend analysis of articles on Web of Science for keywords "Injury and Transportation and Safety."

Select	Field: Web of Science Categories	Record Count	% of 1,300	Bar Chart
☐	PUBLIC ENVIRONMENTAL OCCUPATIONAL HEALTH	452	34.769 %	
☐	TRANSPORTATION	424	32.615 %	
☐	TRANSPORTATION SCIENCE TECHNOLOGY	238	18.308 %	
☐	ENGINEERING CIVIL	188	14.462 %	
☐	ERGONOMICS	177	13.615 %	
☐	SOCIAL SCIENCES INTERDISCIPLINARY	172	13.231 %	
☐	MEDICINE GENERAL INTERNAL	57	4.385 %	
☐	ENGINEERING INDUSTRIAL	45	3.462 %	

Fig. 2. Analysis of categories on Web of Science.

generally rising is a good thing since people/researchers were paying more attention to transportation injury and safety.

Figure 2 shows the analysis of categories from the Web of Science. From this table, "public environmental occupational health" was the number one category regarding the keyword search of "Injury and Transportation and Safety." Transportation-related categories were also in the top eight listed categories.

Figure 3 shows the trend analysis conducted through Scopus. The graph shows documents by year from 2000 until 2021. Although having more results in several articles than Web of Science, the trend analysis was pretty similar to the one on Web of Science. The trend was going up and down since 2000. A difference compared to Web of Science was from 2016 to 2019, with a decline in documents.

Figure 4 shows the analysis of categories from Scopus. Three main categories were building up this graph, engineering with 30.1%, medicine with 21.7%, and social sciences with 20.4%. Those categories were expected to be on top because this paper's topic relates to engineering, medicine, and social sciences to understand people's behavior better.

Figure 5 shows the Vicinitas analysis for engagement and influence. Vicinitas gathered data from Twitter for the last ten days to create a word cloud and engagement

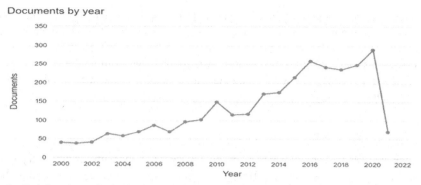

Fig. 3. Trend analysis of articles on Scopus for keywords "Injury and Transportation and Safety."

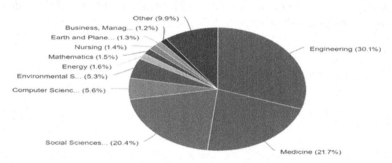

Fig. 4. Analysis of categories on Scopus.

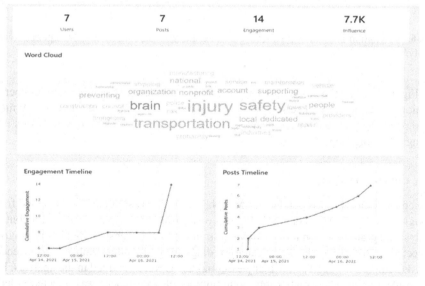

Fig. 5. Engagement and influence analysis on Vicinitas.

timeline. The keywords used were "Injury and Transportation and Safety." The analysis shows that about seven users, 7 posts, 14 engagements, and 7,7000 influences were related to the keywords. The engagement was also on the rise for the search, with a spike during the last day. Vicinitas also shows posts for 10 days, with 43.2% being tweeted and 54.1% retweeting. The word cloud generated contain words such as injury, safety, transportation, and brain.

4.2 Co-citation Analysis

Citation analysis was conducted to examine the degree of connectivity between pairs of papers/articles (Fahimnia et al. 2015). Link strength was observed to determine how impactful and vital the papers were. This co-citation analysis was conducted using VOSViewer. VOSViewer used the metadata collected from Web of Science using keywords, "Injury and Transportation and Safety," and only 500 articles were collected. The 500 articles were selected in terms of date of publication (the 500 latest articles). The result of the analysis is shown below.

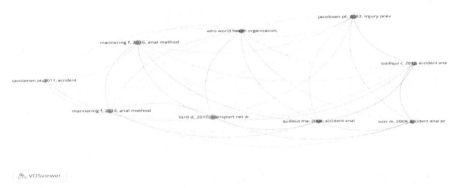

Fig. 6. Co-citation analysis from VOSViewer using keywords, "Injury and Transportation and Safety."

Figure 6 shows the co-citation analysis from VOSViewer. The minimum number of citations of a cited reference was set on 20, and out of 17,258 cited references, 9 meet the threshold. Thus, the 9 papers had 41, 35, 28, 24, 23, 22, 20 citations with total link strength ranging from 74 to 28.

4.3 Content Analysis

The content analysis was conducted through VOSViewer using the data collected from Google Scholar through Harzing's Publish or Perish. VOSViewer generated a content analysis diagram based on terms extracted from the title and abstract field of previously collected articles. To set the content analysis diagram, a minimum number of occurrences was determined to specify how many essential terms were included in the analysis. For this content analysis, a smaller minimum number of occurrences was selected to have more important terms in the analysis diagram.

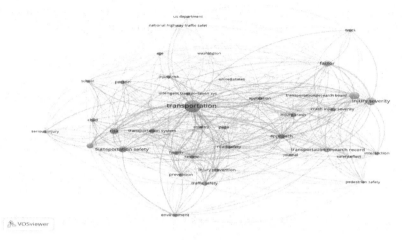

Fig. 7. Content analysis from VOSViewer using keywords, "Injury and Transportation and Safety."

Table 2. Keywords and occurrences from VOSViewer for Google Scholar search.

Keyword	Occurrences
Transportation	478
Injury severity	205
Model	181
Risk	125
Transportation safety	122

Figure 7 shows the content analysis done by VOSViewer using the data collected from a keyword search of "Injury and Transportation and Safety" on Google Scholar via Harzing. The minimum number of occurrences of a term was set at 20, and out of the 6,887 terms, 68 meet the threshold. Table 2 also shows the top 5 terms with the most occurrences. "Transportation" is the top term with 478 occurrences, followed by "injury severity" with 205, "model" with181, "risk" with 125, and "transportation safety" with 122 occurrences.

4.4 Content Analysis from MAXQDA

Word Cloud. The content analysis was conducted through MAXQDA. First, a word cloud of keywords was generated. For this word cloud, 100 keywords with at least 20 minimum frequencies were selected for the word cloud. Some of the top keywords were safety with 299 frequencies, vehicle with 297 frequencies, traffic with 290 frequencies, driving with 284 frequencies, and drivers with 280 frequencies. Based on the word cloud, a quick analysis can be conducted on what is related to the topic of this paper, injury prevention and transportation safety. For example, some of the causes of transportation safety could be placed on speed, noise, behavior, drinking, and age (Fig. 8).

Fig. 8. Word cloud generated from MAXQDA

Extended Lexical Search. The extended lexical search was conducted using the most important and impactful words found during content analyses and from the word cloud. Some example keywords were selected to conduct the following extended lexical search.

Vehicle. The word vehicle was one of the important words among articles for this paper. One of the most interesting and important relationships found during this lexical search was between alcohol and drugs with vehicle transportation. It was determined that there is a strong relationship between motor vehicle deaths and the blood alcohol levels of drivers (Brauer et al. 2016a, b). Drinking and vehicle accidents are not something new, but it is still something of a concern. Drunk driving is one of the deadliest traffic-related deaths in the United States. Back in 2016, 28% of traffic-related deaths were caused by alcohol-impaired driving (CDC 2014). In another article, some ways to reduce drunk driving and to improve safety were mentioned. One solution is a device that can detect a driver's inattention and affect the driver to take a break (from driving) (Allsop et al. 2020).

Safety. Safety was also one of the most mentioned words during the analyses. Safety (transportation safety) is important because the leading cause of severe injuries among teenagers is injuries sustained in traffic (Bojesen et al. 2020). Some believed that cellular phone calls are to blame in most transportation collisions. Drivers who use cellular phones are more at risk of being involved in motor vehicle collisions and should consider road safety precautions (Redelmeier et al. 1997).

Transportation. It was common to see the word transportation across the articles. For example, one article mentioned transportation in relation to transportation risk behaviors and that reducing transportation risk behaviors can prevent crashes and injuries (Yellman et al. 2020). Another interesting founding was focused on work-related transportation.

Back in 2013, around 4,628 work-related fatalities were reported, and out of those 4,628 fatalities, 1,740 were transportation-related cases which are about 38% (U.S. Environmental Protection Agency et al. 2016). This just shows that transportation safety is important in all aspects of life.

Injury. The *injury* was another common word found among articles. Considering it was one of the top words, as shown in the content analysis, it was an important word. One of the more common causes of transportation injury happened while lane changing, and younger male drivers were the most common to blame (Adanu et al. 2021). Therefore, the driving training program can be more focused on young drivers to build confidence and skills to prevent such transportation accidents and injuries (Adanu et al. 2021). Another common injury is pedestrian and motor vehicle crashes, and some ways to control that are by having sidewalks, single-lane roundabouts, and pedestrian refuge islands (Retting et al. 2003).

Drivers. Drivers are one of the most important factors when it comes to injury prevention in transportation. Drivers are essential in that protecting the driver can help reduce injuries caused by transportation accidents. Drivers can be more protected by using driver's aid pre-collision systems such as forward collision warning, pre-crash brake assist, and autonomous pre-crash brake (Kusano et al. 2012).

4.5   Cluster Analysis

The cluster analysis was conducted using CiteSpace. First, the metadata was extracted from Web of Science using keywords search "Injury and Transportation and Safety." Then, CiteSpace generated a cluster analysis that contained different clusters where similar papers were grouped under the same cluster. Figure 9 shows the cluster analysis generated through CiteSpace. The top three clusters were land use, multivariate spatial crash frequency model, and large truck crashes.

4.6   Citation Burst

CiteSpace also generated citation bursts. Citation bursts analysis shows us which references have the most substantial surge of citations. Figure 10 shows the top 4 references with the strongest citation bursts. The strongest was Siddiqui, with a strength of 2.86, followed by DiMaggio with 2.28. WHO came third with 2.19 strength and Wei with 1.99 strength.

4.7   Leading Table

The leading table was generated through BibExcel. Extracted metadata from Google Scholar was uploaded to BibExcel. The leading table was created to show leading authors in decreasing order (highest to lowest). Table 3 shows the leading table of authors. Table 3 shows the leading table of authors with Khattak as the highest author with 18 articles, followed by Abdel-Aty with 16 articles, and Lee with 9 articles.

Fig. 9. Cluster analysis generated through CiteSpace using data from Web of Science.

Top 4 References with the Strongest Citation Bursts

References	Year	Strength	Begin	End	2016 - 2019
Siddiqui C, 2012, ACCIDENT ANAL PREV, V45, P382, DOI 10.1016/j.aap.2011.08.003, DOI	2012	2.86	**2016**	2017	
DiMaggio C, 2013, PEDIATRICS, V131, P290, DOI 10.1542/peds.2012-2182, DOI	2013	2.28	**2016**	2017	
WHO, 2013, GLOB STAT REP ROAD S, V0, P0	2013	2.19	**2016**	2017	
Wei F, 2013, ACCIDENT ANAL PREV, V61, P129, DOI 10.1016/j.aap.2012.05.018, DOI	2013	1.99	**2016**	2017	

Fig. 10. Citation burst table generated from CiteSpace.

A pivot table was also generated using the data received from the leading table. The pivot table was constructed in Microsoft Excel using the pivot table function. Figure 11 shows the pivot table with the same information from the leading table of authors and descending order.

Table 3. Leading table of leading authors from BibExcel.

Author	Articles
Khattak, A.J	18
Abdel-Aty, M	16
Lee, J	9
Eluru N	9
Fan W	8
Huang H	8
Lord D	7

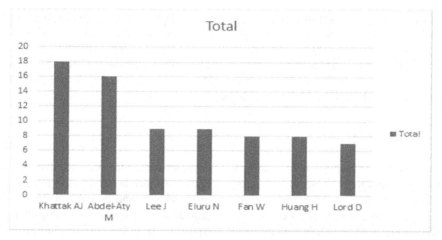

Fig. 11. Pivot table of leading authors from BibExcel.

5 Discussion

Bibliometric analysis conducted for this paper shows that a lot of research was conducted relating to transportation safety and injury prevention. Numerous papers were written with the same topic idea, as shown in the trend analysis and the engagement diagram. Transportation accidents can be caused by distracted drivers, speeding, alcohol use, and pedestrians' influence. However, it was found that 28% of most transportation accidents were related to alcohol use (CDC 2014). The age and gender of the driver was also a factor in transportation accident with younger inexperienced male drivers accounted for more transportation accidents (Adanu et al. 2021). In addition, they distracted driving, especially by using cellular phones, as a factor in most transportation accidents (Redelmeier et al. 1997). All of these factors play a part in causing accidents that can lead to injuries and fatalities. Among teenagers, it was discovered that the most severe injuries happened due to transportation accidents (Bojesen et al. 2020). All of this information was gathered through the review of articles, and by knowing the factors that caused transportation accidents, finding a solution to it is a must.

A driving training program could be a potential solution and should be focused more on younger and novice drivers to build confidence and skills (Adanu et al. 2021). This does not mean that the driving training program is only for young drivers, but it can also be effective for all kinds of drivers. Reducing transportation risk behaviors such as not wearing a seat belt, drunk driving, and using the cellular phone through safety campaigns can help in preventing crashes, injuries and save lives (Yellman et al. 2020). All of these actions can help in reducing injuries and increase transportation safety.

However, it was also determined that pedestrians play a part in transportation safety. In 2018, an increase of three percent of fatal traffic accidents involved pedestrians (Goguen 2019). Traffic volume, resident population, and land are some of the causes of traffic-pedestrian injury collisions (Wier et al. 2008). Some ways to reduce vehicle-pedestrian collisions are installing sidewalks, single-lane roundabouts, signal phasing, increase lighting, pedestrians refuge islands, and advanced stop lines (Retting et al. 2003). Regarding transportation safety, autonomous vehicles were observed as less risk than human-operated vehicles. That may reduce the fatalities in transportation but still need more examinations for passengers' protection since autonomous vehicles are perceived as a risker. In contrast, autonomous vehicles are perceived as less unsafe than human-operated vehicles (Hulse et al. 2018).

6 Conclusion

The bibliometric analysis layout the trends in articles during the past two decades on injury prevention for transportation safety. Despite the multiple efforts and suggestions on improving transportation safety and reducing accidents and injuries, more time is needed to ensure that the safety measures are adequate to prevent injuries. Transportation safety is one of the key safety engineering, both work-related and not. Multiple articles mentioned ways to improve safety and reduce accidents that can lead to injuries and fatalities. Implementing transportation safety from a very young age can be beneficial and recommended. Continued emphasis on safety with the increase of age could be an effective way to reduce risks (Yellman et al. 2020). The keywords found help enhance transportation safety by analyzing the connection among the articles discovered. These findings will decrease the mortality and morbidity correlated with transportation safety and reduce accidents by implementing new analyses on education, including autonomous vehicles, redesigning the refuge islands for pedestrians, and establishing roundabouts for a single lane. As observed in the results, the keywords search trend displays a surge and keeps increasing due to increased awareness of transportation safety. In addition, there are keywords conducted in extended lexical search that show the most effective and impactful words determined during content analyses.

7 Future Work

There is a lot of range of research in this area for the future. For example, researchers have been developing new methods that apply injury prevention for transportation to mitigate accidents. The National Science Foundation (NSF) website has many funded proposals related to this work. We found two such proposals using the search terms "injury prevention" and "transportation safety." The first proposal titled "A Smart Service System for Traffic Incident Management Enabled by Large data Innovations (TIMELI)" by Iowa State University intends to develop large scale data analytics to decrease the number of road accidents within proactive traffic control and reducing the influence of different events that do happen through early exposure, response, and traffic management and control (NSF 2016). The second proposal titled "EAGER: A Systems Approach to Predicting and Preventing Accidents During Operations," awarded to the Massachusetts Institute of Technology, emphasizes building on a new design of accident causation called STAMP System-Theoretic Accident Model and Processes and a new hazard analysis system (STPA or System-Theoretic Process Analysis) to work on that design. STAMP increases current accident causality to cover more complicated reasons than just part failures and chains of failure issues (NSF 2018).

References

1. Adanu, E.K., Lidbe, A., Tedla, E., Jones, S.: Factors associated with driver injury severity of lane changing crashes involving younger and older drivers. Accid. Anal. Prev. **149**, 105867 (2021). https://doi.org/10.1016/j.aap.2020.105867
2. Allsop, R.: Drink driving as the commonest drug driving—A perspective from Europe. Int. J. Environ. Res. Public Health **17**(24), 1–14 (2020). https://doi.org/10.3390/ijerph17249521
3. BibExcel. https://homepage.univie.ac.at/juan.gorraiz/bibexcel/. Accessed 03 June 2021
4. Bojesen, A.B., Rayce, S.B.: Effectiveness of a school-based road safety educational program for lower secondary school students in Denmark: a cluster-randomized controlled trial. Accid. Anal. Prev. **147**(September), 105773 (2020). https://doi.org/10.1016/j.aap.2020.105773
5. Bornmann, L., Marx, W.: Methods for the generation of normalized citation impact scores in bibliometrics: which method best reflects the judgements of experts? J. Inform. **9**(2), 408–418 (2015). https://doi.org/10.1016/j.joi.2015.01.006
6. Brauer, R.L.: Transportation, Chap. 14. In: Safety and Health for Engineers. Wiley (2016)
7. Brauer, R.L.: Human behavior and performance in safety, Chap. 31. In: Safety and Health for Engineers. Wiley (2016)
8. Burnham, J.F.: Scopus database: a review. Biomed. Digit. Libr. **3**, 1 (2006). https://doi.org/10.1186/1742-5581-3-1
9. CDC: Impaired Driving: Get the Facts. Transportation Safety (2014). https://www.cdc.gov/transportationsafety/impaired_driving/impaired-drv_factsheet.html
10. CiteSpace. http://cluster.cis.drexel.edu/~cchen/citespace/. Accessed 03 June 2021
11. Fahimnia, B., Sarkis, J., Davarzani, H.: Green supply chain management: a review and bibliometric analysis. Int. J. Prod. Econ. **162**, 101–114 (2015). https://doi.org/10.1016/j.ijpe.2015.01.003
12. Goguen, D.: Car Accidents with Pedestrian. NOLO (2019). https://www.nolo.com/legal-encyclopedia/car-accidents-with-pedestrians-30113.html
13. Google Scholar. https://scholar.google.com/. Accessed 03 June 2021
14. Guo, F., Li, F., Lv, W., Liu, L., Duffy, V.G.: Bibliometric analysis of affective computing researches during 1999–2018. Int. J. Hum.–Comput. Interact. **36**(9), 801–814 (2020). https://doi.org/10.1080/10447318.2019.1688985
15. Harzing's Publish or Perish. https://harzing.com/resources/publish-or-perish. Accessed 03 June 2021
16. Hulse, L.M., Xie, H., Galea, E.R.: Perceptions of autonomous vehicles: relationships with road users, risk, gender and age. Saf. Sci. **102**, 1–13 (2018). https://doi.org/10.1016/j.ssci.2017.10.001
17. Kusano, K.D., Gabler, H.C.: Safety benefits of forward collision warning, brake assist, and autonomous braking systems in rear-end collisions. IEEE Trans. Intell. Transp. Syst. **13**(4), 1546–1555 (2012). https://doi.org/10.1109/TITS.2012.2191542
18. MAXQDA. https://www.maxqda.com/. Accessed 03 June 2021
19. Mendeley. https://www.mendeley.com/?interaction_required=true. Accessed 03 June 2021
20. National Science Foundation (n.d.). https://nsf.gov/awardsearch/showAward?AWD_ID=1632116. Accessed 22 Apr 2021
21. National Science Foundation (n.d.). https://www.nsf.gov/awardsearch/showAward?AWD_ID=1841231. Accessed 22 Apr 2021
22. Redelmeier, D.A., Tibshirani, R.J.: Association between cellular-telephone calls and motor vehicle collisions. N. Engl. J. Med. **336**(7), 453–458 (1997). https://doi.org/10.1056/nejm199702133360701
23. Retting, R.A., Ferguson, S.A., McCartt, A.T.: A review of evidence-based traffic engineering measures designed to reduce pedestrian-motor vehicle crashes. Am. J. Public Health **93**(9), 1456–1463 (2003). https://doi.org/10.2105/AJPH.93.9.1456

24. SpringerLink. https://link.springer.com/. Accessed 03 June 2021
25. Van Eck, N.J., Waltman, L.: Software survey: VOSviewer, a computer program for biblio-metric mapping. Scientometrics **84**(2), 523–538 (2010). VOSViewer. https://www.vosviewer.com/
26. Vicinitas. https://www.vicinitas.io/. Accessed 03 June 2021
27. Web of Science. https://apps.webofknowledge.com. Accessed 03 June 2021
28. Wier, M., Weintraub, J., Humphreys, E.H., Seto, E., Bhatia, R.: An area-level model of vehicle-pedestrian injury collisions with implications for land use and transportation planning. Accid. Anal. Prev. **41**(January), 137–145 (2008). https://doi.org/10.1016/j.aap.2008.10.001
29. World Health Organization, Peden, M.M.: World report on road traffic injury prevention. World Health Organization, Geneva (2004)
30. Yellman, M.A., Bryan, L., Sauber-Schatz, E.K., Brener, N.: Transportation risk behaviors among high school students—Youth risk behavior survey, United States, 2019. MMWR Suppl. **69**(Suppl-1), 77–83 (2020). https://doi.org/10.15585/mmwr.su6901a9

A Causal Model of Intersection-Related Collisions for Drivers With and Without Visual Field Loss

Bianca Biebl[1]([✉]) [ID], Severin Kacianka[2] [ID], Anirudh Unni[3], Alexander Trende[4] [ID], Jochem W. Rieger[3] [ID], Andreas Lüdtke[4], Alexander Pretschner[2] [ID], and Klaus Bengler[1] [ID]

[1] Chair of Ergonomics, Technical University of Munich, Boltzmannstraße 15, 85747 Garching, Germany
bianca.biebl@tum.de
[2] Chair for Software and Systems Engineering, Technical University of Munich, Boltzmannstraße 3, 85747 Garching, Germany
[3] Department of Psychology, University of Oldenburg, Ammerländer Heerstraße 114-118, 26129 Oldenburg, Germany
[4] OFFIS – Institute for Information Technology, Escherweg 2, 26121 Oldenburg, Germany

Abstract. Causal models allow us to reconstruct traffic accidents, predict the likelihood of future accidents and implement counter measures to prevent them. For drivers with impairments like visual field loss, naturalistic data on crash causes is however scarce due to their current prohibition to drive. This paper presents an approach to deriving a causal model for the prediction of crash risks for current non-drivers. The applied use case focuses on a collision with an overlooked crossing vehicle in an intersection. Based on the combination of crash analyses for normal sighted drivers and models of information processing and human errors, a general structural causal model for crash risks in this use case was developed. The application of this model to drivers with visual field loss on the side of the approaching vehicle revealed four causal factors with an increased risk of occurring: faulty anticipation of location and timing of hazards; inadequate guidance of gaze movements; adverse scanning patterns; and cognitive overload. These elevated crash risks can guide the development of assistive technologies for drivers with visual impairments in the future.

Keywords: Interface for disabled and senior people · Mobile HCI and automobiles · Causal model · Visual impairments · Crash prediction

1 Theoretical Background

The incidence of strokes increases from approximately 3.5% to 13% for persons above the age of 65 [1]. With demographic change, it can thus be expected that a growing number of people exhibit impairments due to strokes or other age-related illnesses. Since approximately 90% of all driving-related information is presented visually, deficits

© Springer Nature Switzerland AG 2021
C. Stephanidis et al. (Eds.): HCII 2021, LNCS 13097, pp. 219–234, 2021.
https://doi.org/10.1007/978-3-030-90966-6_16

within the visual domain are especially detrimental for maintaining individual mobility [2]. In many countries, a loss of vision within the central to mid peripheral field of view prohibits driving [3, 4]. Besides difficulties concerning longitudinal and lateral guidance, this can be justified with challenges in visual scanning of the driving scene, hazard detection and the resulting risk for collisions in some drivers with visual field loss [5–7]. However, the actual impact of visual field loss on accident risk is difficult to estimate, since driver license regulations limit naturalistic driving data for this user group. In other areas, we can build on an ample body of literature concerning previous crashes and their causes in order to predict traffic accidents and develop compensatory measures like trainings or assistive technologies. The usage of naturalistic data for crash prevention is evident in many current regulations. A review of the effect of alcohol on driving skills by the National Highway Traffic Safety Administration (NHTSA) [8], for example, has shown that different attentional, visual, cognitive and psychomotor skills are susceptible to be impaired at different blood alcohol concentration levels. Implicit causal models on human errors and accident risks consequently suggest that driving under the influence of alcohol can cause accidents. The reported increase of crash risks with higher blood alcohol concentration supports this notion [9]. Based on these deliberations, countermeasures were derived to dissect the causal connection of alcohol and real-world crashes, e.g., by setting a maximum blood alcohol concentration limit, implementing sobriety checkpoints and developing intervention training programs [10]. Concerning driving with visual field loss, on-road and simulator studies as well as prospective long-term studies indicate an increased risk for collisions [11–13]. While some influencing factors like e.g., extent, location and side of the visual deficit are discussed, reports on specific causes for the increased accident risk are scarce. Contrary to driving under the influence of alcohol, there is little crash data for drivers with visual impairments to derive such causal factors.

This paper presents an approach to predicting crash causes for current non-drivers or users of new technologies. This identification of increased risk factors is based on crash analyses of normal sighted drivers with theoretical considerations on divergent challenges for drivers with visual field loss. The extracted factors can then serve as a basis for the derivation of appropriate features for assistance systems to promote inclusive mobility in the future. Different locations and extents of blind areas within the visual field can be expected to have different impacts on driving performance, driving challenges and optimal compensatory strategies [14]. The causal crash analysis presented in this paper will focus on impairments that mainly concern areas outside of the central visual field, which encompasses both smaller scotomas and larger deficits up to a complete loss of vision in the left or right visual hemifield (so-called homonymous hemianopia, HH). Within the scope of this paper, we will focus on the latter to allow for a unified and comprehensible depiction of the related processes. As a worst-case approach, it can nevertheless be assumed that the identified crash risks are also applicable, albeit reduced, for smaller blind spots.

2 Methods

2.1 Structural Causal Models

We analyzed human behavior with a focus on drivers with visual limitations to derive structural causal models (SCMs; see Pearl et al. [15] for a gentle introduction), because SCMs offer us a unified mathematical framework to express and draw conclusions on causal relations. SCMs consist of (1) a graphical model where nodes represent random variables and edges express the causal connections between them, and (2) structural equations that describe the exact mechanism between two nodes. Two main advantages of using SCMs are that they can be tested against real-world data and allow us to automatically reason about causal relations. Given the model's propriety, SCMs furthermore allow likely causes of an outcome to be predicted (and thus mitigated) a priori, as well as crash reasons to be analyzed ex post.

The formation and combination of SCMs follows a defined set of rules and definitions. Formally, an SCM M is a tuple,

$$M = (U, V, F) \tag{1}$$

where U is a set of exogenous variables, V is a set of endogenous variables, and F associates with each variable $X \in V$ a function that determines the value of X given the values of all other variables [15].

For every SCM, we can create a graphical causal model with the semantics that an edge $A \to B$ denotes that A causes B. This means that a structural equation $f \in F$, which determines the value of B, has A as an input. Figure 1 depicts one such abstract causal model with four endogenous variables (C1, C2, C3, and O) and at least four exogenous variables. Exogenous variables are considered influences that are not further explicable and by convention not shown in the graphical model. In this model, the value of the outcome variable O is determined by a function that takes three causal variables, C1, C2 and C3, as input:

$$\text{Outcome} = f_{\text{outcome}}(\text{cause 1, cause 2, cause 3}) \tag{2}$$

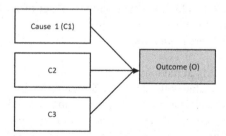

Fig. 1. SCMs offer us a simple graphical way to express the idea that different variables can cause a certain outcome.

It is important to note that although such structural equations inherently have no direction, modelers can decide on the direction of causality based on theoretical considerations. As such, while a respective correlation between O and C1, C2 and C3 can be found in data, we might want to express our assumption that C1, C2 and C3 cause O and not the other way around (see Fig. 1).

In practice, several causal models might exist targeting the same use case from different perspectives. Experimental studies and expert judgments often focus on investigating single causes in order to allow for a clean methodological approach that controls for confounding variables. When investigating an accident or designing a system however, we want to take all relevant causes into account. Kacianka et al. [16] have shown that it is in principle possible to use SCMs to join a causal model of a technical systems and a causal model of humans respectively. Furthermore, Beckers and Halpern [17] have shown that causal models can be abstracted and thus allow us to join models of different levels of abstraction in a mathematically sound manner. One method for the combination of multiple SCMs as long as they are compatible was proposed by Alrajeh et al. [18]. According to the authors, two models M1 and M2 have a hierarchical, compatible relationship, if they agree on the causal dependence of a variable O. This hierarchy is also given if the causal dependence of O in M1 is represented in more detail than in M2 by including mediating variables. For example, while model M1 notes:

$$C1 \rightarrow C2 \rightarrow C3 \rightarrow O \tag{3}$$

model M2 might represent the causal dependence of variable O as:

$$C1 \rightarrow O \tag{4}$$

Two models are then compatible and can be combined, if it holds that one model dominates another model for each variable. For the integrated SCM, the dominating model is used to represent the causal dependence. In cases where the models themselves might not be compatible, it is often possible to provide strict but falsifiable assumptions under which they are compatible. If they are proven not to be compatible, however, any conclusions drawn from a joint model must be reevaluated. Based on these mathematical foundations, the model development for the applied use case in this paper roughly followed the methodology implicitly given by Alrajeh et al. [18]:

1. Convert data from multiple crash analyses into a set of n SCMs, each of which describes some part of the outcome (i.e. the collision).
2. Show that all n SCMs are *compatible.*

   a. Choose an SCM M_n at random and add it to the set of compatible SCMs (CS).
   b. If M_n is not compatible with any M in CS, change M_n to make it compatible with M (following Alrajeh et al. [18], it will be compatible with all other SCMs). This process is not deterministic and depends on the models' order. If the required changes to M_n are impossible or exceed plausibility, starting with model M_n as first instance of CS is an option that might improve results.

3. When all SCMs are compatible, combine them to the joint SCM M*.
4. Once individual models are combined to M*, we can reason over accident causes that span the source models.

Based on this joint model for crash causes in normal sighted drivers, we can evaluate differences in causal dependencies for drivers with visual field loss. We therefore considered each node of M* regarding a causal dependency on visual abilities with a focus on the impact of HH on each node.

2.2 Use Case

For all drivers, intersections present a safety-critical situation with great potential for crashes. Even though they constitute only a small percentage of the entire road infrastructure, between 30 and 40% of all crashes are located at or near intersections [19–21]. According to a report on intersection-related crash factors by the German Federal Highway Research Institute (BASt) [22], oversight of other road users is the main reason for accidents when drivers are turning or crossing. Similarly, a report by the NHTSA [19] states that the main cause for intersection-related crashes is a failure to recognize certain situations or objects, most commonly because of inadequate scene surveillance. Further analyses on prevalent courses of accidents and their causes show very heterogeneous results, which might result from differences concerning the levels of abstraction, choice of the use cases considered and selection of parameters. According to information processing models, the selection and execution of actions to avoid accidents begins with the uptake of relevant information [23]. As such, the perception of an approaching hazard can be regarded as a fundamental and frequently reported cause for collisions, which is why the SCM derived in this paper will regard a collision due to overlooking a conflicting crossing vehicle as outcome. It can be assumed that this use case is also suited for revealing additional challenges for drivers with HH, since relevant information for detecting a vehicle approaching from the blind side is presented in the affected peripheral field of view.

Currently, the availability of published reports on crash factors in different situations and especially in the addressed use case is scarce. Most literature on traffic accidents focuses either on methodologies for crash and safety modeling, experimental investigations of singular parameters or the descriptive prevalence and severity of crashes. While potentially useful for the scope of this paper, the latter hereby often concerns specific maneuvers and intersection characteristics rather than human errors. In total, we identified three reports with potential for the integration into a joint SCM: grand scheme reviews of intersection-related crashes by the BASt [22] and the NHTSA [19] and an analysis of the need for driver assistance systems by Lange [24].

3 Results

3.1 Model Development

We built three SCMs based on reports by Vollrath et al. [22], Choi et al. [19] and Lange [24]. The vast majority of causal factors in these reports are expressed as direct causal influences on the intersection-related crash. In other words, these models talk about different aspects of the same outcome (the collision) and are therefore compatible. To give an example, Vollrath et al. [22] provide model M1 with the link that the misdirection of attention (MoA) is a cause for collisions, so MoA → Col. Choi et al. [19] provide model M2 with the link from distraction to collision, so Dis → Col. These two models are compatible, because MoA ∉ M2 and Dis ∉ M1. This means that M1 dominates M2 regarding MoA and M2 dominates M1 regarding Dis.

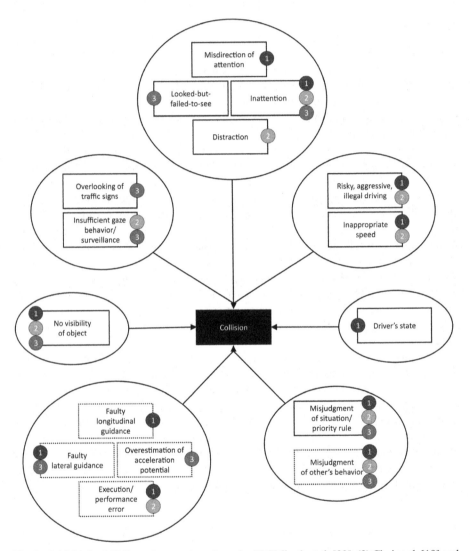

Fig. 2. Initial joint SCM based on crash analyses by (1) Vollrath et al. [22], (2) Choi et al. [19] and (3) Lange [24]. All factors related to a failure to perceive relevant information from the surrounding are represented with a rectangle. Dotted lines mark factors that are related to a latter processing of this information. Circles represent a first clustering of individual factors for further analyses.

Next to this simple form of a compatible aggregation of causal factors, some nodes within the three SCMs referred to similar risk factors but mentioned specific use cases or levels of detail (e.g., a misjudgment of the *situation* or the *priority rule*; insufficient *gaze behavior* or *surveillance*; misjudgment of others' *speed* or *actions*). In order to enhance generalizability and readability of the model graph, such factors were summarized in one overarching node. Within the report by Vollrath et al. [22], some crash risks were expressed with a mediating additional node (a. lack of consideration of others; b. faults in longitudinal guidance) between the specific causes (a. driver's state/inattention/misdirection of attention/misjudgment of situation; b. no visibility of object) and the collision. These specifics of the SCM based on Vollrath et al. [22] were not included in the joint model, since they did not suit the abstraction level of the other two SCMs and therefore did not allow for a bijective allocation of all reported factors to the hierarchical levels within the joint SCM. In order to ensure easier comprehension of the joint model, we clustered different factors into categories according to their respective domain (see circles, Fig. 2). Nevertheless, each square in Fig. 2 should be interpreted as an individual cause for the outcome (collision).

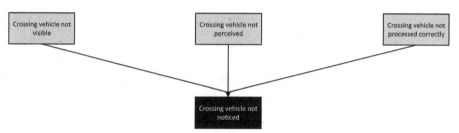

Fig. 3. Lowest hierarchical level of the adapted SCM based on driving error classifications by Hacker [25] and Weber et al. [26].

In a second step, we aimed to adapt this general joint model to the addressed use case and enrich it with theoretical models on the causal interrelation of factors. All nodes related to the failure to perceive relevant information are marked with a solid rectangle in Fig. 2 and were integrated into the adapted SCM. Nodes regarding latter aspects of information processing, response selection or execution are marked with a dotted line (see Fig. 2). These were not included in the adapted SCM in detail but instead summarized as a faulty processing of perceived information as one of three main sources of driving errors. According to this classification suggested by Hacker [25] and Weber et al. [26], oversight of a crossing vehicle can be ascribed to information not being visible, the driver not using the perceptually available information or the driver not using it correctly to derive or implement action goals and programs (see Fig. 3). Lack of visibility was directly transferred from the initial model in Fig. 2. Many other nodes from the initial model could not be attributed to one of these three collision causes indefinitely. Speeding might, for example, prohibit a timely and appropriate amount of surveillance of the scene (influence on perception; second node in Fig. 3) or go along with an overestimation of one's own deceleration potential (influence on further processing; third node in Fig. 3). We focused the exploration of causal interrelations on the most prominent aspect for our use case, which was a lack of perception of the crossing vehicle (second node in Fig. 3).

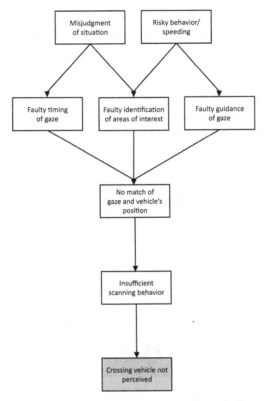

Fig. 4. An SCM for insufficient scanning behavior.

One reported aspect that combines different reasons for a missing perception of the vehicle is inadequate surveillance of the scene in combination with insufficient scanning behavior. Since a correct visual exploration of the driving scene is vital for detecting a crossing vehicle, we segmented these nodes from Fig. 2 into pertinent subfactors (see Fig. 4). The execution of sufficient scanning movements requires the driver's knowledge of the time and place of relevant information. According to the SEEV model by Wickens [27], this identification of relevant areas for a redirection of attention at each moment is influenced by bottom-up and top-down information. The latter concerns the anticipated bandwidth and value of information within an area of interest, which rests upon a mental representation of the task and scene ahead. Since the anticipation of relevant information requires a basic understanding of the intersection (e.g., concerning general layout, regulations and priority rules), a prior misjudgment of the situation was included as an input variable for a faulty timing or location of scans. According to Wickens [27], the value of information depends its relevance for a task and the importance of this task for the driver. A tendency for risky driving with a reduced desire to cover all potential hazards exhaustively can therefore affect the identification of task-relevant areas of interest. Risky driving with an inappropriate speed might furthermore inhibit drivers from executing the required gaze movements to cover all identified areas of interest sufficiently and in time. Such an inadequate guidance of scans was added as a third input for a mismatch between the hazard's current location and gaze position. Generally, gaze guidance to a certain location at a certain time point must be adapted to the current physiological, situational or pathological requirements either deliberately or subconsciously. Uptake of information with peripheral vision might for example not suffice to identify details like small traffic signs due to its reduced visual acuity. Similarly, drivers with glasses must adapt their gaze movements to ensure that all relevant information falls into the corrected field of view.

Next to an intentional neglect of the scanning task due to risky driving, unintentional (partial) neglect can arise from attention deficits (see Fig. 5). According to the reviewed crash analyses, these include general inattention, misdirection of attention and distraction by other tasks. Reduced attention to the driving scene (e.g., due to interactions with a mobile phone) can also be regarded as one aspect of the driver state represented in the initial joint model. Other exemplary driver states with an impact on attentional capabilities are monotony or fatigue [28, 29]. While attention to the scanning task is relevant for performing appropriate gaze movements, it is also crucial for a conscious perception of the sensorily acquired information. As mentioned earlier, a faulty processing of perceived information was not the focus of the SCM derived for our use case. However, one notable aspect of information processing for the perception of a crossing vehicle is called "looked-but-failed-to-see". This phenomenon describes users fixating an object without noticing it consciously. According to Koustanaï et al. [30], the main driver-related factors contributing to this phenomenon are the driver's attentional demand and an inappropriate visual search strategy and/or mental processing. In more detail, the authors argue that a scanning strategy might be appropriate for the majority of cases, but cause relevant information to be overlooked in situations that arise less frequently. Next to its influence on the conscious perception of information, the scanning strategy is also crucial for appropriate gaze behavior and was therefore included as another input variable for sufficient scanning (see Fig. 5). Nodes in Fig. 4 mainly concern the calculation and performance of singular gaze movements to a relevant area. Within the driving context and especially in intersection scenarios, however, drivers must scan multiple areas of interest in different parts of the visual field for relevant information. An inappropriate scanning strategy might therefore result in an inefficient sequence of gaze movements with a potential neglect of individual areas.

The two partial SCMs in Figs. 4 and 5 focusing on scanning and attention respectively were combined into one final SCM (see Fig. 6).

3.2 Causal Differences for Drivers with Peripheral Visual Field Loss

The joint SCM in Fig. 6 depicts relevant causes for an intersection-related collision due to overlooking a crossing vehicle. This model based on data from normal sighted drivers presents the foundation for the identification of crash factors with an increased risk of occurrence in drivers with visual impairments. For this purpose, each node must be evaluated against the backdrop of theoretical or experimental findings of vision-related challenges. Using counterfactuals, we have a formal method of analyzing this SCM in a mathematically sound way. A counterfactual is a sentence in the form "If A were true, then B would have been true" and as such, a way to reason about a state of the world

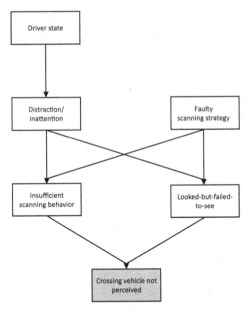

Fig. 5. An SCM focusing on slips of attention.

that is counter to the actual factual world but theoretically possible. In our case, we have a model that describes the factual world for normal sighted drivers, and we would now like to ask the counterfactual question "If the driver had HH, would X have the same probability of leading to a collision". In an SCM, this can be done by removing all the inbound edges into a node and then fixing the value of a node.

Elevated risk factors are marked in yellow in Fig. 6 with the letters (a) to (f). Letter (g) in blue represents a risk factor that additionally arises from a visual field loss. Since the visibility of hazards (Fig. 3; left grey node) is context-bound, one must not expect differences between normal sighted and visually impaired drivers in this high-level factor. The processing of information (Fig. 3; right grey node) is also not altered since visual field loss itself only concerns the ability to take up information. Challenges in perception (Fig. 3; middle grey node) will be elaborated hereinafter.

One of the main differences between drivers with HH and normal sighted drivers is the ability to perceive relevant information in all parts of the visual field (a, Fig. 6). Swan et al. [31] report that deficient gaze detections in drivers with HH can be categorized into a lack of scans to the blind side, an execution of scans with inadequate magnitude, looked-but-failed-to-see errors and scan-across movements without detecting the object. Since the difficulties in perceiving relevant information may also affect recognition of the priority rule or the general layout of the intersection ahead, there is also a greater risk of the driver misjudging the intersection scenario (b, Fig. 6). To evaluate the causal factors for insufficient gaze behavior, we must consider the differing requirements and characteristics of the scanning task for visually impaired and normal sighted drivers. Biebl and Bengler [32] note that scanning is aggravated for drivers with HH due to a lack of bottom-up information. According to the authors, this missing bottom-up

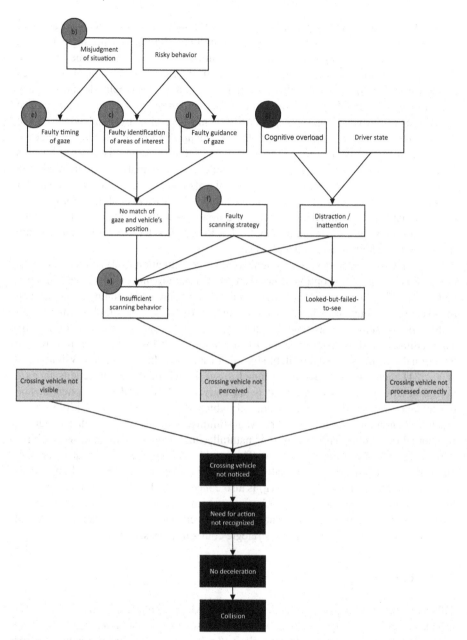

Fig. 6. An SCM of a collision with an overlooked crossing vehicle in an intersection. Factors with an increased risk of occurring in drivers with visual field loss are marked yellow with letters (a) to (f). Letter (g) in blue marks a variable that is not part of the causal model for normal sighted drivers, but an additional increased crash risk for drivers with HH. (Color figure online)

information on approaching hazards aggravates the identification of relevant areas of interest, since attention is not pulled to salient stimuli (c, Fig. 6). The missing peripheral guidance of scans in combination with a requirement for larger scans on the blind side [32, 33] furthermore aggravates the execution of appropriate gaze movements to an area of interest (d, Fig. 6). As a result, drivers with HH show a smaller amplitude and accuracy of scans [6, 7, 34, 35]. It can be assumed that the compensation of these challenges also affects the timing of gazes (e, Fig. 6), since drivers must perform larger and more frequent scans to the blind side to identify relevant information. An altered timing of gazes is also evident in reports on slower gaze movements and belated first fixations of hazards in studies with drivers with HH [5, 6, 36]. Parallel to the adaptation of individual gaze movements, the scanning strategy (f, Fig. 6) must also be accommodated to account for the increased risk of missing hazards on the blind side. Bowers et al. [33] for example mention that drivers with HH tend to make a first scan to the blind side with a second scan later on instead of the common look left – look right – look left pattern to account for the increased crash risk on the blind side.

Since HH is a visual and not a cognitive disorder, attention itself is most likely not affected. However, the adoption of compensatory scanning movements takes cognitive and visual effort due to the continuous top-down generation of scanning strategies and the execution of numerous large gaze movements. Especially in complex situations, it is therefore reasonable to assume that drivers experience cognitive overload (g, Fig. 6). The additional task of compensating for the visual field loss could therefore reduce attentional resources usually available for other aspects of the driving task. While Swan et al. [31] mention that looked-but-failed-to-see is one of the main deficits in gaze detection among drivers with HH, it is currently not clear whether this phenomenon occurs more frequently compared to normal sighted drives. Koustanaï et al. [30] mention that this phenomenon is promoted if relevant stimuli arise in the periphery due to reduced perceptual thresholds. This threshold is naturally further reduced when no visual input is received in parts of the visual field. This could, however, be compensated for with appropriate foveal fixations. Alternatively, a secondary increase in the looked-but-failed-to-see phenomenon through (f) and (g) is also conceivable. Lastly, risky behavior is not directly affected by visual field loss as long as no comorbid deficits in executive functions are present. It could furthermore be argued that drivers who recognize their deficits tend to drive more cautiously as part of a strategic compensatory scheme.

4 Discussion

This paper presents an approach to developing SCMs to predict crash risks for new user groups or new technologies. Based on crash analyses for current drivers and models on human behavior and human errors, we derived relevant reasons for intersection-related collisions with an overlooked crossing vehicle. The resulting model was then used to extract aspects that are altered and at higher risk for drivers with visual field loss on the side of the approaching vehicle. The analysis showed that limitations of visually impaired drivers have an impact on the following aspects:

- Identification of location and timing of relevant information

- Guidance and timing of gaze movements
- Scanning strategy/pattern to cover all relevant areas.

The compensation of these challenges can furthermore lead to:

- Cognitive overload and the reduction of attentional capabilities.

These factors presented in Fig. 6 as nodes marked with letters (a) to (g) are regarded to be causally dependent on the driver's visual ability. Formally, this means that the structural equations for these nodes must have an input that reflects this visual deficit. To provide automatic reasoning about the exact impact of HH on these nodes, we would need a more intricate understanding of how visual abilities affect them, concerning both the mechanisms and severity of impact. However, the analysis of collision risks presented in this paper already shows that visually impaired drivers are confronted with specific challenges that must be overcome either by adopting compensatory strategies or with the support of an assistive technology. Since fully autonomous vehicles will not be available for some years to come, and a driver is still required to monitor the system or take over control in critical situations, these challenges should be considered when designing assistive and automated systems. It may not be applicable to assume that the identical human-machine interface and features of assistance systems can support drivers of all cognitive, visual or motoric abilities in the same manner. As such, drivers with visual impairments might benefit more from systems that assist scanning and reduce workload compared to normal sighted drivers. Concerning the scanning task, this could entail information on the general layout and regulations of the scene ahead, location and timing of potential hazards, as well as guidance of gaze movements and scanning patterns. Concerning workload, features to reduce visual and cognitive resources are advisable for drivers with visual field loss. It is also interesting to note the nodes that are not causally dependent on the driver's visual ability. For example, while technology that alerts drivers of cars that are currently not visible will probably decrease the number of accidents, it should do so regardless of the driver's visual ability.

The specific challenges of drivers with visual field loss should be considered when evaluating assistive technologies developed for normal sighted drivers concerning their usability for new user groups. It must be assumed that such features may not always be as valuable for drivers with visual impairments. A human-machine interface based on vision might for example be overlooked if presented within the blind field. As a secondary visual task, it could furthermore aggravate scanning and increase cognitive and visual workload. The implementation of assistive technologies should therefore consider characteristic challenges of the targeted user group to design effective systems that target causal crash factors while considering individual information needs.

5   Conclusion

This paper presents a theoretical approach to predicting collision risks for current non-drivers on the use case of drivers with visual impairments in an intersection scenario. The analysis of crash causes builds on SCMs for normal sighted drivers in combination with common models on information processing and human errors. The derived SCM provides an initial basis for the derivation of guidelines for assistive systems to prevent collisions within the presented use case. It must be considered that the selection of risk factors provided in crash analyses is highly dependent on the type of the investigated intersection and the level of abstraction of the results. Therefore, it cannot be assumed that the identified risk factors are exhaustive. For a validation and weighting of the derived crash factors, we suggest a large-scale on-road study with visually impaired and normal sighted drivers to analyze collision scenarios and their causal factors systematically.

Acknowledgement. This work was supported by the Deutsche Forschungsgemeinschaft (DFG) under grant no. RI1511/3-1 to JWR, LU1880/3-1 to AL and BE4532/15-1 to KB ("Learning from Humans – Building for Humans") and PR1266/3-1 to AP ("Design Paradigms for Societal-Scale Cyber-Physical Systems").

References

1. Johnson, C.A., Keltner, J.L.: Incidence of visual field loss in 20,000 eyes and its relationship to driving performance. Arch. Ophthalmol. **101**, 371–375 (1983)
2. Shaheen, S.A., Niemeier, D.A.: Integrating vehicle design and human factors: minimizing elderly driving constraints. Transp. Res. Part C: Emerg. Technol. **9**, 155–174 (2001). https://doi.org/10.1016/S0968-090X(99)00027-3
3. Prevent Blindness. State Vision Screening and Standards for License to Drive (2020). https://lowvision.preventblindness.org/2003/06/06/state-vision-screening-and-standards-for-license-to-drive/
4. European Council of Optometry and Optics. Visual standards for driving in Europe: A consensus paper (2007)
5. Alberti, C.F., Goldstein, R.B., Peli, E., Bowers, A.R.: Driving with hemianopia V: do individuals with hemianopia spontaneously adapt their gaze scanning to differing hazard detection demands? Transl. Vis. Sci. Technol. **6**, 11 (2017). https://doi.org/10.1167/tvst.6.5.11
6. Bahnemann, M., et al.: Compensatory eye and head movements of patients with homonymous hemianopia in the naturalistic setting of a driving simulation. J. Neurol. **262**(2), 316–325 (2014). https://doi.org/10.1007/s00415-014-7554-x
7. Bowers, A.R., Mandel, A.J., Goldstein, R.B., Peli, E.: Driving with hemianopia, I: detection performance in a driving simulator. Investig. Ophthalmol. Vis. Sci. **50**, 5137–5147 (2009). https://doi.org/10.1167/iovs.09-3799
8. Moskowitz, H., Florentino, D.: A review of the literature on the effects of low doses of alcohol on driving-related skills. Washington, DC (1988)
9. Compton, R.P., Berning, A.: Drug and alcohol crash risk. J. Drug Addict. Educ. Erad. **11**(1), 29–46 (2015)
10. Shults, R.A., et al.: Reviews of evidence regarding interventions to reduce alcohol-impaired driving. Am. J. Prevent. Med. **21**, 66–88 (2001). https://doi.org/10.1016/S0749-3797(01)00381-6
11. Papageorgiou, E., Hardiess, G., Mallot, H.A., Schiefer, U.: Gaze patterns predicting successful collision avoidance in patients with homonymous visual field defects. Vis. Res. **65**, 25–37 (2012). https://doi.org/10.1016/j.visres.2012.06.004
12. Bro, T., Andersson, J.: The effects of visual field loss from glaucoma on performance in a driving simulator. Acta Ophthalmologica (2021). https://doi.org/10.1111/aos.14765

13. Kwon, M., Huisingh, C., Rhodes, L.A., McGwin, G., Jr., Wood, J.M., Owsley, C.: Association between glaucoma and at–fault motor vehicle collision involvement among older drivers: a population-based study. Ophthalmology **123**, 109–116 (2016). https://doi.org/10.1016/j.oph tha.2015.08.043

14. Patterson, G., Howard, C., Hepworth, L., Rowe, F.: The impact of visual field loss on driving skills: a systematic narrative review. Br. Irish Orthoptic J. **15**, 53–63 (2019). https://doi.org/10.22599/bioj.129

15. Pearl, J., Glymour, M., Jewell, N.P.: Causal Inference in Statistics: A Primer. Wiley, Hoboken (2016)

16. Kacianka, S., Ibrahim, A., Pretschner, A., Trende, A., Lüdtke, A.: Extending causal models from machines into humans. In: Electronic Proceedings in Theoretical Computer Science, pp. 17–31 (2019). https://doi.org/10.4204/eptcs.308.2

17. Beckers, S., Halpern, J.Y.: Abstracting causal models. In: Proceedings of the AAAI Conference on Artificial Intelligence, pp. 2678–2685 (2019). https://doi.org/10.1609/aaai.v33i01.33012678

18. Alrajeh, D., Chockler, H., Halpern, J.Y.: Combining experts' causal judgments. Artif. Intell. **288**, 103355 (2020). https://doi.org/10.1016/j.artint.2020.103355

19. Choi, E.-H.: Crash factors in intersection-related crashes: an on-scene perspective. Washington, DC (2010)

20. Gerstenberger, M.: Unfallgeschehen an Knotenpunkten, Dissertation. Technical University of Munich, Munich (2015)

21. Tay, R., Rifaat, S.M.: Factors contributing to the severity of intersection crashes. J. Adv. Transp. **41**, 245–265 (2007). https://doi.org/10.1002/atr.5670410303

22. Vollrath, M., Briest, S., Drewes, J.: Ableitung von Anforderungen an Fahrerassistenzsysteme aus Sicht der Verkehrssicherheit. Bergisch Gladbach (2006)

23. Wickens, C.D., Hollands, J.G., Banbury, S., Parasuraman, R.: Engineering Psychology and Human Performance, 3rd edn. Psychology Press, Upper Saddle River (2000)

24. Lange, C.: Wirkung von Fahrerassistenz auf der Führungsebene in Abhängigkeit der Modalität und des Automatisierungsgrades, Dissertation. Technical University of Munich, Munich (2006)

25. Hacker, W.: Fehlhandlungen und Handlungsfehler: Defizite der psychischen Handlungsregulation. In: Hacker, W., Sachse, P. (eds.) Allgemeine Arbeitspsychologie: Psychische Regulation von Tätigkeiten, 3rd edn. Hogrefe Verlag, Göttingen (2014)

26. Weber, S., et al.: Was können Fahrerassistenzsysteme im realen Unfallgeschehen leisten? Köln (2010)

27. Wickens, C.D.: Noticing events in the visual workplace: the SEEV and NSEEV models. In: The Cambridge Handbook of Applied Perception Research, vol. II, pp. 749–768. Cambridge University Press, New York (2015). https://doi.org/10.1017/CBO9780511973017.046

28. Boksem, M.A.S., Meijman, T.F., Lorist, M.M.: Effects of mental fatigue on attention: an ERP study. Cogn. Brain Res. **25**, 107–116 (2005). https://doi.org/10.1016/j.cogbrainres.2005.04.011

29. Fahlman, S.A., Mercer-Lynn, K.B., Flora, D.B., Eastwood, J.D.: Development and validation of the multidimensional state boredom scale. Assessment **20**, 68–85 (2013). https://doi.org/10.1177/1073191111421303

30. Koustanaï, A., Boloix, E., van Elslande, P., Bastien, C.: Statistical analysis of "looked-but-failed-to-see" accidents: highlighting the involvement of two distinct mechanisms. Accid. Anal. Prev. **40**, 461–469 (2008). https://doi.org/10.1016/j.aap.2007.08.001

31. Swan, G., Xu, J., Baliutaviciute, V., Bowers, A.R.: Hemianopic field loss and failures of awareness in simulated driving. Investig. Ophthalmol. Vis. Sci. **61**, 3511 (2020). https://doi.org/10.22599/bioj.129

32. Biebl, B., Bengler, K.: I spy with my mental eye – analyzing compensatory scanning in drivers with homonymous visual field loss. In: Black, N.L., Patrick Neumann, W., Noy, I. (eds.) IEA 2021. LNNS, vol. 221, pp. 552–559. Springer, Cham (2021). https://doi.org/10.1007/978-3-030-74608-7_67

33. Bowers, A.R., Ananyev, E., Mandel, A.J., Goldstein, R.B., Peli, E.: Driving with hemianopia: IV. Head scanning and detection at intersections in a simulator. Investig. Ophthalmol. Vis. Sci. **55**, 1540–1548 (2014). https://doi.org/10.1167/iovs.13-12748

34. Wood, J.M., et al.: Hemianopic and quadrantanopic field loss, eye and head movements, and driving. Investig. Ophthalmol. Vis. Sci. **52**, 1220–1225 (2011). https://doi.org/10.1167/iovs.10-6296

35. Zihl, J.: Visual scanning behavior in patients with homonymous hemianopia. Neuropsychologia **33**, 287–303 (1995)

36. Coeckelbergh, T.R.M., Brouwer, W.H., Cornelissen, F.W., van Wolffelaar, P., Kooijman, A.C.: The effect of visual field defects on driving performance: a driving simulator study. Arch. Ophthalmol. **120**, 1509–1516 (2002). https://doi.org/10.1001/archopht.120.11.1509

Reducing Driver's Cognitive Load with the Use of Artificial Intelligence and Augmented Reality

Kweku F. Bram-Larbi[1], Vassilis Charissis[1]([⊠]) [iD], Ramesh Lagoo[2], Shu Wang[3], Soheeb Khan[1], Samar Altarteer[4], David K. Harrison[1], and Dimitris Drikakis[5] [iD]

[1] School of Computing, Engineering and Built Environment, Glasgow Caledonian University, Glasgow, UK

[2] Research and Development, Core Lab + Ltd, Glasgow, UK

[3] Research and Development, Volkswagen, Beijing, China

[4] School of Design and Architecture, Dar Al-Hekma University, Jeddah, Saudi Arabia

[5] Defence and Security Research Institute, University of Nicosia, Nicosia, Cyprus

Abstract. Multiple infotainment sources can significantly overload the driver's cognitive load and increase the collision probabilities. Current solutions provided have attempted to alleviate this issue with the centralization of infotainment devices to single touchscreen devices in the dashboard area. Yet this solution still requires the driver to take the eyes from the road and concentrate on operating the secondary tasks unrelated to the driving process. The paper presents a prototype Augmented Reality Head-Up Display (AR HUD) system that superimposes a selected number of infotainment data on the vehicle's windshield only when this is safe for the driver. The selection of infotainment data and projection timing is calculated by a prototype Artificial Intelligence (AI) Co-Driver that aims to reduce the driver's cognitive load. The proposed system was evaluated by 50 users against a typical touchscreen dashboard system. This work presents and discusses the subjective feedback related to the cognitive load that the users perceived during the trials. The paper concludes with a future plan for improving both the AI and AR HUD elements to perform in an urban environment.

Keywords: Cognitive load · Augmented Reality · Virtual Reality · Driver distraction · Head-Up Display · Artificial Intelligence · Simulation

1 Introduction

Driving distraction has been extensively studied and analysed to define the reasons that cause this problem aiming to provide viable solutions [1]. In a nutshell, the driver distraction could be attributed to the driver's temporary focus on an irrelevant to the driving, object or event. If these objects or events are external to the vehicle environment they are limited solutions that could be applied to maintain the driver's focus on the primary objective. However, in-vehicle distractions such as infotainment systems, present the highest hazard of distraction and potential collision [2, 3].

The automotive industry responded to this issue by centralising the infotainment systems to a single interactive screen. Yet the screen is located again in the lower -

© Springer Nature Switzerland AG 2021
C. Stephanidis et al. (Eds.): HCII 2021, LNCS 13097, pp. 235–245, 2021.
https://doi.org/10.1007/978-3-030-90966-6_17

central section of the dashboard/Head -Down Display (HUD), which requires the driver to take the eyes of the road and focus towards the lower section of the vehicle's cabin.

To alleviate this issue, contemporary studies have focused mainly either on the presentation of this data and interaction with various touch-screens, and vehicles sensor capabilities [2, 4]. The transient state of the continuously changing traffic conditions, however, and the sheer volume of infotainment data provided, require a more agile solution that does not rely only upon the software and hardware provision from each vehicle.

To this end, the augmentation of human responses with the use of emerging technologies such as Augmented Reality (AR) and Artificial Intelligence (AI) aims to enhance the user's spatial and situational awareness [5].

Additionally, Head-Up Displays (HUDs) have become a focal point of research in the automotive industry, bearing the promise of augmenting spatial awareness and reducing the driver's reaction times [2–4]. Recent developments in vehicular electronics have identified HUD interfaces as an increasingly feasible alternative to dashboard-bound touchscreens and other HDD devices, as they manage to maintain the driver's gaze on the road [2–4].

Such systems would not only require the deployment of sensory equipment on the vehicle itself but would be benefited by inter-vehicle communication facilities to enable a bird's-eye view of road traffic conditions. Our previous research in Human-Machine Interaction regarding AR HUD systems has proved that such interfaces significantly enhance driver's spatial and situational awareness resulting in faster responses and collision avoidance [2–4].

In this work, we present a custom AR/AI HUD interface that aims to augment human senses and improve driver responses in challenging collision scenarios. The latter are designed based on information provided by the local traffic authorities and simulated in the Virtual Reality Driving Simulator (VRDS) which entails a real-life vehicle, full surround 3D stereoscopic projection CAVE environment, surround audio and vibrotactile devices to increase driver's immersion. To evaluate the augmentation of human senses and responses, the proposed AR/AI HUD system has been contrasted to a typical HDD and evaluated by 50 users. Finally, the paper presents and discusses the results of users' mental and physical workload as well as their collision avoidance performance through the comparative study.

2 Driver Distractions and Cognitive Load

During driving, various vehicular systems, and external stimuli could contribute to driver distraction [6]. Multiple attempts to categorise the source and intensity of these distractions have formulated several models [2, 7–10]. Typically the distraction is attributed to (a) visual/audio, (b) manual and (c) cognitive elements.

The Cognitive Load Theory (CLT) attempts to quantify the driver distraction issue based on the principle that the human cognitive load capacity is limited and as such should be utilised for the main task rather than being segmented in multiple secondary or parallel tasks [7]. In particular, during driving or other similar complex activities, human attention and mental resources must be concentrated on the main task to avoid increased collision probability as illustrated in Fig. 1.

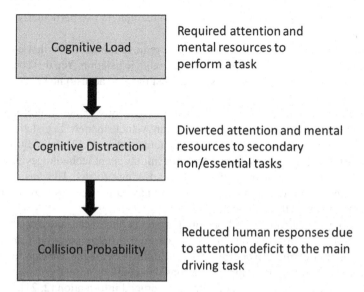

Fig. 1. Diagram depicting the human attention and mental resources that affect cognitive load, distraction and collision probability; adaptation from [11].

The contemporary vehicular infotainment systems require driver's attention through visual, audio, manual and cognitive means reducing significantly the remaining cognitive load capacity that is not adequate to perform the driving task. As such the collision probabilities are increased particularly under challenging traffic flow and weather conditions [4, 12–14]. Additional distractions that could further burden the cognitive load are the internal communications between driver and passengers [3, 15, 16]. This particular work is concerned with the provision of infotainment in a fashion that is timely presented to the driver. This was deemed essential to optimally exploit the human mental resources for the driving task whilst avoiding the driver's isolation from the typical infotainment interactions that he/she is accustomed to. The latter observation and required connectivity necessities are described in detail in the following section.

3   Current Solutions

Current solutions provided by automotive manufacturers incorporated the vast majority of the infotainment systems in a homogenous interface ecosystem and positioned in one specific place within the vehicle cockpit which is typically located in different heights in the middle of the dashboard.

Although this provided an overall control of these devices the amount of incoming information increased exponentially through the years resulting in a highly attention-demanding environment that could increase significantly the cognitive workload of the driver [2, 3]. Previous studies have identified these User Interfaces (UI) as one of the most prominent reasons for driver distraction [17, 18]. Further user familiarization with these interfaces could arguably reduce the distraction effects for some drivers, yet interfaces that serve secondary tasks should be discreet and simple to use particularly whilst the vehicle is in motion.

An alternative simple solution would be to remove the elements that could cause distractions, either physically or ban their use through legislation. Yet, this could deprive contemporary drivers of a plethora of systems that they are accustomed to continuously using.

This lack of in-vehicle connectivity could consequently create several issues with the acceptability and usability of current and future vehicle models. Legislative attempts are either circumvented or ignored by a large number of users [2]. In addition, drivers result in improvising solutions to transfer such infotainment technologies within their vehicles which would be incompatible with the driving process. This has occurred in the early stages of introducing mobile phone and navigation devices retrospectively in older vehicle models with detrimental effects [2].

Various other applications and operating systems have been introduced to block, or mute external communications and send automated responses whilst driving [19, 20]. The isolation of the driver from external influences might enhance temporarily the driver's attention yet on multiple occasions this could upsurge the driver's anxiety, feeling disconnected and deprived of potentially crucial information [2, 21].

In addition, contemporary drivers are accustomed to deciding each application's activities and as such prohibitive or predetermined systems are not favourable. As such, the automotive manufacturers are inclined to maintain or in some cases increase the infotainment applications and activities with the caveat of introduction pages that present the potential issues and request from the driver/user to read and accept the conditions under which will use the infotainment system. While these applications mitigate the direct use of mobile phones and other infotainment devices, they still pose a major distraction issue [22, 23].

4 Proposed Solution

The proposed system couples a prototype AR HUD with direct manipulation, gesture-recognition interface and auditory signals enabling the driver to interact efficiently and timely with the incoming information released by the system in appropriate intervals. An embedded AI system identifies the urgency of the information and time to read/respond to the driver. Additionally, it operates as a filtering mechanism and through interrupt strategies regulates the pace of information released to the driver, when it is deemed safe. The information is superimposed in the vehicle's windscreen through the AR HUD projection.

The AR HUD solution was deemed essential to minimise the time required off-the-road, for the driver to visually inspect and interact with the infotainment system on the vehicle's dashboard. The proposed UI enables the driver to interact with the information through the proposed multimodal gesture recognition interface in safely provided intervals as illustrated in Fig. 2.

The proposed UI is designed to receive, contain, distil and release infotainment data in appropriate time intervals aiming to minimise the driver distraction and reduce the cognitive load imposed by these attention-seeking applications. Previous work on direct

Fig. 2. Driver's AI/AR HUD and gesture recognition for controlling infotainment sources.

manipulation and adaptive UI was employed to support the development of the presented prototype system [22–25].

As such the interface was limited to only three main symbols namely (a) home, (b) navigation and (c) mobile phone communication which includes both phone calls and text messages as illustrated in Fig. 2.

The selection of data and their release to the driver has been tasked to an Artificial Intelligence (AI) agent which is currently under development and adaptation for different AR HUD systems [25–27]. The particular AI system plays the role of an artificial co-driver which is concerned with the collection, prioritisation and distribution of information to the driver only when this complies with the safety rules and reduced collision probabilities. Adhering to the human-machine collaboration concept, this hybrid approach utilises the AI co-driver to support the driver and minimise the unnecessary intrusion caused by the multiple infotainment sources [4, 28–30].

During the simulation, the driver is intentionally distracted by the infotainment system which attempts to create a cognitive overload, reducing his/her capacity to efficiently and timely respond to the collision challenges.

5   Experiment Requirements

The proposed AI/AR HUD system was evaluated against a typical HDD touch screen in the in-house VR Driving Simulator laboratory. The provision of information in different intervals during driving in a local motorway (M8) and moderate traffic flow was designed to test the driver's attention and gradually result in a cognitive overload scenario.

5.1   Driving and Accident Scenario Design

Following previous driving scenarios that emulate rear collision accident situations, the lead vehicles brakes abruptly challenging the driver to respond swiftly and either stop the vehicle or perform an avoidance manoeuvre [2, 4, 12]. Just before the abrupt braking event, the driver receives a mobile text message regarding a hypothetical meeting that changed location. In addition, the navigation systems present fresh information related to traffic ahead and alternative routes that the driver might consider to avoid a traffic jam.

5.2   Participants

The participants for the evaluation experiment were 50 volunteers with valid driving licences. The sample was composed of users spanning a variety of ages, professions and genders. On the latter, the distribution was 41 male and 9 female.

5.3   VR Driving Simulation

The experiment took place in the built for purpose Virtual Reality Driving Simulation (VRDS) laboratory that utilises a real-life vehicle (Mercedes A-Class 2003 model)

Fig. 3. The Virtual Reality Driving Simulator laboratory (VRDS Lab) in action.

and a fully immersive CAVE environment as illustrated in Fig. 3. The latter employs a 5.1 surround audio system connected to vibrotactile devices that simulate the road imperfections and the vehicle engine, gearbox and tyres' vibrations.

The simulation software is also custom-built offering a photorealistic representation of the local motorways' network between Glasgow, Edinburgh and Stirling in Scotland. The VR environment was developed as a closed circuit (the motorway exits were blocked from construction activities) to avoid having users driving in random directions within the large area of the simulation which was 28 miles of motorway roads (Fig. 4).

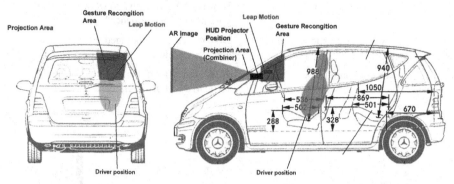

Fig. 4. Schematic of the Virtual Reality Driving Simulator laboratory (VRDS Lab) and the relevant equipment used for the experiment.

6   Evaluation and Results

6.1   Task Load Index AR/AI HUD vs HDD

A customized version of Hart and Staveland's NASA Task Load Index (TLX) method was used to access the AI/AR HUD with contactless gestures perceived in 7-point scales namely; mental demand, physical demand, temporal demand, performance, effort, and annoyance [31]. The TLX used, assesses the user's workload on five graduations in increments of very high, high, medium, low and very low. The task load index was scored lower on all scales by the vast majority of the users as presented in Fig. 5 (Table 1).

The evaluation presented that the *mental demand* perceived by the users was very low by 22% and low by 54%. The 12% of the users that responded that the system required a medium mental effort to operate suggested that further familiarization could have probably alleviated this issue.

In turn, the *physical demand* to operate the system was rated as 12% very low and 42% low. Yet, 46% of the users found the physical effort to be medium (38%), high (6%) and very high (2%). This result could be largely attributed to the actual driving simulator hardware which for this experiment had to be composed of existing off-the-shelf components (i.e. Leap Motion) and other peripherals which were not originally designed for in-vehicle interaction with custom UIs, which was confirmed by the majority as an issue in the debriefing session after the simulations.

Table 1. Task load index for user experience and cognitive load

7-point scale questions		
A.	Mental demand	How mentally demanding was the task?
B.	Physical demand	How physically demanding was the task?
C.	Temporal demand	How hurried or rushed was the pace of the task?
D.	Performance	How successful were you in accomplishing what you were asked to do?
E.	Effort expended	How hard did you have to work to accomplish your level of performance?
F.	Annoyance experienced	How insecure, discouraged, irritated, stressed, and annoyed were you?
G.	Overall preference	Please rate your preference comparing the HUD to the HDD interface

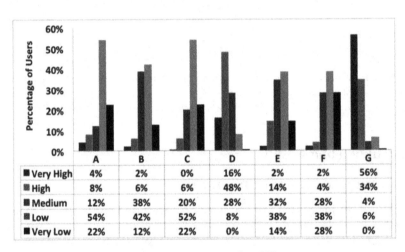

	A	B	C	D	E	F	G
Very High	4%	2%	0%	16%	2%	2%	56%
High	8%	6%	6%	48%	14%	4%	34%
Medium	12%	38%	20%	28%	32%	28%	4%
Low	54%	42%	52%	8%	38%	38%	6%
Very Low	22%	12%	22%	0%	14%	28%	0%

Fig. 5. Task Load Index results of 50 users.

The temporal demand required was rated as 22% and 52% very low and low respectively. The AR projection of the information promptly by the AI co-driver, provided additional time to respond and maintain the eyes on the road, resulting in better collision avoidance manoeuvres.

This was also confirmed by the user-perceived performance which was assessed as high and very high by 64% of the users whilst using the HUD with contactless gestures.

In terms of minimising the stress, 59.18% accepted that HUD was very useful in reducing stress for interaction with infotainment while driving as illustrated in Fig. 5. In total 90% of the users responded that they preferred the AR HUD system to the typical HDD.

7   Conclusions

This work presented the current issues of driver distraction and cognitive load occurred by the contemporary attention-demanding infotainment systems. The latter contributes to the increased collisions and fatality rates. Adhering to the above observations the paper describes the development rationale of a prototype system that employs AI and AR HUD technologies aiming to curb driver distraction by controlling the incoming infotainment data.

In contrast to previous attempts, the particular system doesn't deflect completely the incoming information, but distils, prioritises and presents the main information to the driver when it is considered safe by a dedicated AI Co-driver designed in conjunction with the AR HUD system. The released information is superimposed on the vehicle's windshield maintaining the driver's eyes on the road. The information is concentrated in the simplified AR UI which the driver could operate through a gesture recognition interface. The cognitive load to operate the system was evaluated in contrast to an existing HDD touchscreen, by 50 users.

The evaluation was performed in the VRDS laboratory. The results were promising and offered an indicative appraisal of the system's functionality and future. A tentative plan for future work would entail the further development and tuning of the AI and AR HUD parts of the proposed system, to perform in an urban environment and facilitate additional interrupt strategies and timely provision of infotainment data.

References

1. Young, K., Regan, M.: Driver distraction: a review of the literature. In: Faulks, I.J., Regan, M., Stevenson, M., Brown, J., Porter, A., Irwin, J.D. (eds.) Distracted Driving, pp. 379–405. Australasian College of Road Safety, Sydney, NSW (2007)
2. Lagoo, R., Charissis, V., Harrison, D.K.: Mitigating driver's distraction: automotive head-up display and gesture recognition system. IEEE Consum. Electron. Mag. **8**(5), 79–85 (2019). https://doi.org/10.1109/MCE.2019.2923896
3. Wang, S., Charissis, V., Lagoo, R., Campbell, J., Harrison, D.K.: Reducing driver distraction by utilising augmented reality head-up display system for rear passengers. In: IEEE International Conference on Consumer Electronics (ICCE), Las Vegas, USA (2019). https://doi.org/10.1109/ICCE.2019.8661927
4. Charissis, V., Papanastasiou, S.: Human-machine collaboration through vehicle head-up display interface. Int. J. Cogn. Technol. Work **12**(1), 41–50 (2010). https://doi.org/10.1007/s10111-008-0117. Cacciabue, P.C., Hollangel, E. (eds.) Springer, London
5. Kim, S., Dey, A.K.: Augmenting human senses to improve the user experience in cars: applying augmented reality and haptics approaches to reduce cognitive distances. Multimed. Tools Appl. **75**, 9587–9607 (2015). https://doi.org/10.1007/s11042-015-2712-4
6. Fernández, A., Usamentiaga, R., Carús, J.L., Casado, R.: Driver distraction using visual-based sensors and algorithms. Sensors **16**, 1805 (2016). https://doi.org/10.3390/s16111805
7. Sweller, J.: Cognitive load during problem solving: effects on learning. Cogn. Sci. **12**, 257–285 (1988)
8. Engström, J., Markkula, G., Victor, T., Merat, N.: Effects of cognitive load on driving performance: the cognitive control hypothesis. Hum. Factors **59**(5), 734–764 (2017). https://doi.org/10.1177/0018720817690639

9. Victor, T.W., Engström, J., Harbluk, J.: Distraction assessment methods based on visual behavior and event detection. In: Regan, M., Lee, J., Young, K. (eds.) Driver Distraction: Theory, Effects and Mitigation, pp. 135–165. CRC Press, Boca Raton, FL (2008)

10. Engström, J., Johansson, E., Östlund, J.: Effects of visual and cognitive load in real and simulated motorway driving. Transp. Res. Part F: Traffic Psychol. Behav. **8**(2), 97–120 (2005). https://doi.org/10.1016/j.trf.2005.04.012

11. Jahagirdar, T.: Modeling and measuring cognitive load to reduce driver distraction in smart cars. Master thesis, Arizona State University (2015)

12. Charissis, V., Papanastasiou, S., Chan, W., Peytchev, E.: Evolution of a full-windshield HUD designed for current VANET communication standards. In: IEEE Intelligent Transportation Systems International Conference (IEEE ITS), The Hague, Netherlands, pp. 1637–1643 (2013). https://doi.org/10.1109/ITSC.2013.6728464

13. Okumura, H., Hotta, A., Sasaki, T., Horiuchi, K., Okada, N.: Wide field of view optical combiner for augmented reality head-up displays. In: 2018 IEEE International Conference on Consumer Electronics (IEEE ICCE) (2018)

14. Charissis, V., Naef, M., Papanastasiou, S., Patera, M.: Designing a direct manipulation HUD interface for in-vehicle infotainment. In: Jacko, J.A. (ed.) HCI 2007. LNCS, vol. 4551, pp. 551–559. Springer, Heidelberg (2007). https://doi.org/10.1007/978-3-540-73107-8_62

15. Barker, J.: Driven to distraction: children's experiences of car travel. Brunel University, UK (2009). https://doi.org/10.1080/17450100802657962

16. Wang, S., Charissis, V., Harrison, D.K.: Augmented reality prototype HUD for passenger infotainment in a vehicular environment. Adv. Sci. Technol. Eng. Syst. J. **2**(3), 634–641 (2017)

17. Grahn, H., Kujala, T.: Impacts of touch screen size, user interface design, and subtask boundaries on in-car task's visual demand and driver distraction. Int. J. Hum.-Comput. Stud. **142**, 102467 (2020)

18. Khan I., Khusro S.: Towards the design of context-aware adaptive user interfaces to minimize drivers' distractions. Mob. Inf. Syst., Article ID 8858886, 23 (2020). Special Issue: Personal Communication Technologies for Smart Spaces, Hindawi

19. Shabeera, H.A., Wahidabanub, R.S.D.: Averting mobile phone use while driving and technique to locate the mobile phone used vehicle. In: International Conference on Communication Technology and System Design 2011 (2011). Proc. Eng. **30**, 623–630 (2012). Elsevier Ltd. https://doi.org/10.1016/j.proeng.2012.01.907

20. Khandakar, A., et al.: Portable system for monitoring and controlling driver behavior and the use of a mobile phone while driving. Sensors **19**(7), 1563 (2019). https://doi.org/10.3390/s19071563

21. Charissis, V., et al.: Employing emerging technologies to develop and evaluate in-vehicle intelligent systems for driver support: infotainment AR HUD case study. Appl. Sci. **11**(4), 1397 (2021). https://doi.org/10.3390/app11041397

22. Bram-Larbi, K.F., Charissis, V., Khan, S., Lagoo, R., Harrison, D.K., Drikakis, D.: Intelligent collision avoidance and manoeuvring system with the use of augmented reality and artificial intelligence. In: Arai, K. (ed.) FICC 2021. AISC, vol. 1363, pp. 457–469. Springer, Cham (2021). https://doi.org/10.1007/978-3-030-73100-7_32

23. Labský, M., Macek, T., Kleindienst, J., Quast, H., Couvreur, C.: In-car dictation and driver's distraction: a case study. In: Jacko, J.A. (ed.) HCI 2011. LNCS, vol. 6763, pp. 418–425. Springer, Heidelberg (2011). https://doi.org/10.1007/978-3-642-21616-9_47

24. Wang, J., Wang, W., Hansen, P., Li, Y., You, F.: The situation awareness and usability research of different HUD HMI design in driving while using adaptive cruise control. In: Stephanidis, C., Duffy, V.G., Streitz, N., Konomi, S., Krömker, H. (eds.) HCII 2020. LNCS, vol. 12429, pp. 236–248. Springer, Cham (2020). https://doi.org/10.1007/978-3-030-59987-4_17

25. Tchankue, P., Wesson, J., Vogts, D.: The impact of an adaptive user interface on reducing driver distraction. In: Proceedings of the 3rd International Conference on Automotive User Interfaces and Interactive Vehicular Applications (AutomotiveUI 2011), pp. 87–94. Association for Computing Machinery, New York, NY, USA (2011). https://doi.org/10.1145/2381416.238 1430

26. Bram-Larbi, K.F., Charissis, V., Khan, S., Harrison, D.K., Drikakis, D.: Improving emergency vehicles' response times with the use of augmented reality and artificial intelligence. In: Stephanidis, C., Duffy, V.G., Streitz, N., Konomi, S., Krömker, H. (eds.) HCII 2020. LNCS, vol. 12429, pp. 24–39. Springer, Cham (2020). https://doi.org/10.1007/978-3-030-59987-4_3

27. Bram-Larbi, K.F., Charissis, V., Khan, S., Lagoo, R., Harrison, D.K., Drikakis, D.: Collision avoidance head-up display: design considerations for emergency services' vehicles. In: 2020 IEEE International Conference on Consumer Electronics (ICCE), pp. 1–7, Las Vegas, NV, USA (2020). https://doi.org/10.1109/ICCE46568.2020.9043068

28. Rothkrantz, L., Toma, M., Popa, M.: An intelligent co-driver surveillance system. In: Acta Polytechnica CTU Proceedings, vol. 12, p. 83 (2017). https://doi.org/10.14311/APP.2017.12.0083

29. Frank, M., Drikakis, D., Charissis, V.: Machine-learning methods for computational science and engineering. Computation **8**, 15 (2020)

30. Charissis, V., Papanastasiou, S.: Artificial intelligence rationale for autonomous vehicle agents behaviour in driving simulation environment. In: Aramburo, J., Trevino, A.R. (eds.) Robotics, Automation and Control, pp. 314–332. I-Tech Education and Publishing KG, Vienna, Austria, EU (2008). ISBN 953761916-8I

31. Galy, E., Paxion, J., Berthelon, C.: Measuring mental workload with the NASA-TLX needs to examine each dimension rather than relying on the global score: an example with driving. Ergonomics **61**, 517–527 (2017)

Research on Autonomous Vehicle Delivery System Based on Service Design Theory

Chao Fang and Lei Liu[✉]

Southeast University, Nanjing, China
liulei@seu.edu.cn

Abstract. With the development of e-commerce models in the domestic market, the demand for package delivery service has increased. It's imminent to design an package delivery system to solve the problems of large demand, numerous classifications, and low user satisfaction in package delivery service. Due to the low user cost, remote controllability and other features, autopilot technology is suitable for package delivery system and has become a hot spot for theoretical research and commercial applications. This paper presents a new model of autonomous vehicle delivery service as a solution to the optimization program, which will be suitable for small area of the cities. The user relationship in the system has been resigned, the service process has been updated, and the service blueprint has been analyzed, then the service model based on time requirements of the users has been proposed. The ant colony algorithm was used for route planning of the autonomous vehicle as to the technical support, and a simulation was performed. The prototype interfaces of main functional modules in the delivery model were produced. A survey has been done to analyze the usability of the delivery model based on a questionnaire. Furthermore, the paper presents the benefits and the limitations of this kind of system.

Keywords: Service design · Autonomous vehicle delivery · Blue print · Interface prototype

1 Introduction

The Internet economy has led to the rapid development of online shopping in China, and the demand for package delivery from users is increasing day by day. However, problems such as work overload of the delivery staff, random placement of packages without permission by users, and non-delivery home happen constantly [1]. With the addition of smart hardware such as package stations and package cabinets in the community can only provide some convenience for users to pick up their packages, the "Last mile" problem of package delivery in the small area of the cities still exists. Autonomous driving technology has been used in autonomous vehicle delivery service because of its low user cost, remote operation, and high convenience [2]. Especially under the background of the epidemic in 2020, autonomous vehicle delivery is particularly important. However, there are still limitations of the current autonomous vehicle delivery service. For example, users

© Springer Nature Switzerland AG 2021
C. Stephanidis et al. (Eds.): HCII 2021, LNCS 13097, pp. 246–260, 2021.
https://doi.org/10.1007/978-3-030-90966-6_18

often feel upset because of the less-selective delivery time, the size of bigger packages and unreasonable human-computer interaction interface when they are willing to try the delivery service by an autonomous vehicle, which may reduce the satisfaction [3] (Fig. 1).

Fig. 1. Autonomous vehicle delivery scenario

In this paper, the current autonomous vehicle delivery service model has been analyzed based on the concepts and thoughts of service design, and the usability science tools of service design have been used to summarize the existing problems of the service process and pain points of the users. A kind of new service model with time requests has been proposed by the "service provider-unmanned vehicle-user" cycle in the system, which could be one of the optimization solutions of autonomous vehicle delivery problems. In the route planning, time windows, when the customer is available, would be considered based on the ant colony algorithm. The prototype interfaces of main functional modules have been redesigned based on service design theory to improve user experience and we want to verify the feasibility of the service model.

2 Related Work

2.1 Service Design Concepts and Tools

Service design is a planned and organized design of human, infrastructure, communication and other related factors involved in a service process to improve user experience and service quality [4]. Service design can be tangible or intangible, and always follow the five design principles: user-centric, co-creation, sequentiality, physical presence and integrity [5]. The tools and methods used in service design usually integrate the methods of product design and interaction design, which provides many methods for service visualization design. The user experience map and service system diagram are commonly used to analyze problems in service design [6]. The service blueprint and service flowchart are widely used by service plans [7]. The service system is under the guidance of the service design concepts, including the relationship between service providers,

Fig. 2. Five principles of service design

users, software/hardware, service scenarios and other supporting resources, and provides a service interface between service providers and users as a delivery medium for services (Fig. 2).

In this paper, The service blueprint and service flowchart were mainly used to analyze the autonomous vehicle delivery service. Through user behavior, front-end behavior, back-end behavior, and support process parts, the visual boundary, internal interaction line and external interaction line are determined, so that the service process can be dynamically displayed [8]. The user and service experience process can be visualized by the service blueprint, which could be positive on improving service quality, service efficiency and user satisfaction.

2.2 Vehicle Route Planning Algorithm

To maximize the efficiency of autonomous vehicle delivery and optimize the service process, it is necessary to study the route planning of autonomous vehicle delivery to provide specific delivery service. If there is only one vehicle starting from the delivery point, completing the users' delivery service in the set order and returning to the delivery station, we call this the classic traveling salesman (TSP) problem. If the user has a time window requirement during the delivery, the problem becomes a traveling salesman problem with the time window (TSPTW) [9]. Some of the most common algorithms used for route planning are described: Dijkstra, A*, ANT colony algorithms, genetic algorithms and hybrid genetic algorithms [10]. When solving the Traveling Salesman Problem with time window (TSPTW), it is necessary to provide the time window list of the users, and the route results output according to the time requirements. In this paper, we solve the routing problem based on the ANT colony algorithm because of its good robustness [11].

3 Service Concept

3.1 Users' Relationship Model

In the "service provider-autonomous vehicle-user" cycle model proposed in this paper, there are two types of users in the system, namely service providers and users. Service providers including delivery staff and backstage management staff, they have different division of responsibilities. The staff at the package station are mainly user-oriented and providing users with package loading and delivery service, they are the direct deliverers of the service. The backstage management staff are responsible for controlling the operation of the entire system, monitoring the status of the delivery service, they are the indirect deliverers of the service. The users relationship model in the autonomous vehicle delivery system is shown in Fig. 3. Among them, the autonomous vehicle, as the hardware carrier of the delivery service, connecting the users and the service providers.

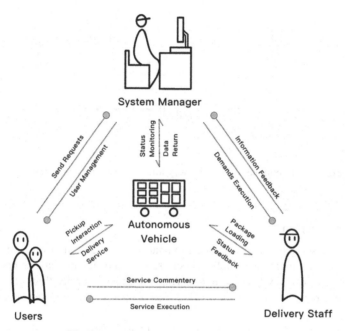

Fig. 3. System users role relationship model

3.2 Service Flowchart

According to literature research, the current stage of the autonomous vehicle delivery service process is described: after the package arrives at the station, the user receives the notification of picking up the package, then the user chooses autonomous vehicle delivery with a fixed time. When the package is loaded by the staff, the autonomous vehicle starts delivering to the location designated by the user, only one piece at a time, which could cause low delivery efficiency due to the uncertainty of delivery time. And the high empty-load rate of one delivery may result in waste of resources and low user experience quality.

Based on the service design concept, the current autonomous vehicle delivery service process could be updated and described: the pick-up time of the users is increased, the delivery route is planned according to the time requirements of the users to optimize the delivery efficiency and increase the loading rate. With the time window selection function, the autonomous vehicle delivery service process is updated as follows: After the package arrives at the station, the user receives the pickup notification, and the user could select the delivery time freely through the mobile application. After the backstage management staff reviews the requirements, the system plans the route according to the time window of the users, then the staff loads the packages, and the autonomous vehicle delivers to the designated location. The service process is shown in Fig. 4.

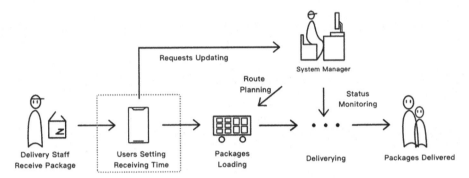

Fig. 4. Autonomous vehicle delivery flowchart with time requirements

3.3 Service Blueprint

In this part, the service blueprint is used to analyze the users, the front and back staff behaviors of the autonomous vehicle delivery service at different phases, combing with the analysis of the users' relationship model and the updated service flowchart, as shown in Fig. 5. The delivery service is divided into 3 phases, pre-service, in-service and after-service.

In the pre-service phase, the users know about the delivery mode and service content of the autonomous vehicle. The delivery staff conduct service training and divide regional classification, the backstage management staff classify the user population personas. The system function modules, system information architecture, and autonomous vehicle manufacturing should be the supporting processes.

In the service, the users update time requirements and wait for the packages delivered to come to the door. The delivery staff carry out the packages loading to the autonomous vehicle, the backstage management staff check the requirements and monitor the real-time delivery status to ensure safety. The system provides route planning for the autonomous vehicle which could meet the time window of the users. The supporting processes need system updating, data returning and system operation to ensure the stability of the system.

In the after-service phase, the users make service commentary, provide feedback on the problem in delivering period. The delivery staff handle the abnormal packages and check the status of autonomous vehicles, the backstage management staff integrate the information system data. The supporting processes need to ensure system data recording and turning.

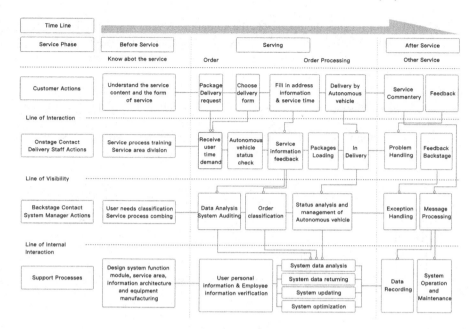

Fig. 5. Blueprint of autonomous vehicle delivery service

3.4 Service Model Description

Combining the previous analysis of the users' relationship model, service flowchart and service blueprint, it is proposed that the service content is the free setting of the users' pick-up time. The autonomous vehicle delivery service model designed in this paper is based on the service design concept and supported by the ant colony algorithm to provide route planning. The specific service model process links have been sort out as shown in Fig. 6. The specific service process can be described as follows:

(1) The users' pickup requests are sent to the backstage operation center of the autonomous vehicle delivery system. The users can set the delivery time on the mobile application and fill in the address information. The time requirements can be organized by the system automatically and push to the delivery staff at the package station.

(2) Demands received, the delivery staff at the package station will sort the packages, scan and load the packages according to the system guidelines.

(3) When packages loaded, the autonomous vehicle receives instructions and delivery route information from the system, locates according to its GPS and sensors, then follows the set route to the first user to finish the delivery task, when the status information and delivery process are updated in real-time. The users in the system could view the status information via mobile applications or PC.

(4) After the autonomous vehicle arrives at the specific location set by the first user, the system will send a notification to the user, and the user could use a pick-up code or scan the QR code to complete the operation.

(5) When the user finishes the operation, the autonomous vehicle will send the confirmation notification to the user, and the system will push notifications to the delivery staff and backstage management staff for data statistics. After that, the autonomous vehicle will continue to finish the other delivery tasks.

(6) If the user cannot pick-up the package or delay, the backstage management staff could update and adjust the route planning information according to the actual situation.

(7) When the autonomous vehicle finishes the whole delivery process in sequence according to the planned route, it returns to the package station.

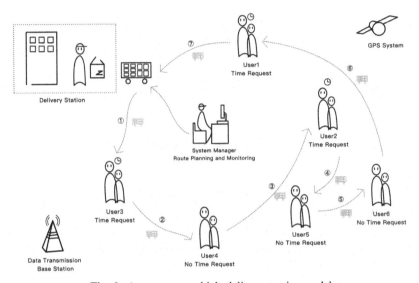

Fig. 6. Autonomous vehicle delivery service model

As shown in the figure above, the autonomous vehicle departs from the package station, completes the users' delivery tasks in turn according to the users' time window requirements, and finally returns to the delivery station.

4   Implementation

4.1   Route Planning Based on ANT Colony Algorithm

In this section, the implementation method of autonomous vehicle delivery technology will be explained. The ANT colony algorithm has been chosen to make the route planning for delivery service. The minimum delivery time ($MinT$) has been set as the objective function, the constraint function is the time window ($E_i < TW < L_i$) of the users. Besides, the traveling salesman problem with time window (TSPTW) can be described as: an autonomous vehicle starts from the starting point, returning back after completing the delivery task at each point in turn, and visiting each point only once in the whole process. The formula for calculating the delivery time during the delivery process is:

$$T = \sum_{i=1}^{k}\sum_{j=1}^{k} t_{ij}x_{ij} + \sum_{i=1}^{k} SvT \tag{1}$$

In formula (1), t_{ij} represents the delivery time of each route, $x_{ij} = 1$ if the autonomous vehicle travels from user i to user j, and 0 otherwise, SvT represents the service time of each point. i, j represent a single delivery user point separately, $i = (0, 1, 2, \ldots\ldots, C), j = (1, 2, \ldots\ldots, C, C + 1), i = 0, j = (C + 1)$ represents the package station, C is the collection of customer points. In the delivery process, the autonomous vehicle delivery sequence needs to meet the users' time window requirements to ensure that the delivery time is within the users' demand time. The restrictions is:

$$E_i \leq TW \leq L_i \tag{2}$$

The flowchart of the autonomous vehicle route planning based on ANT colony algorithm is shown in Fig. 7.

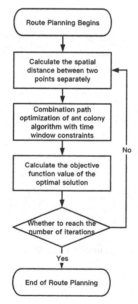

Fig. 7. Flowchart of vehicle route planning model based on ant colony algorithm

4.2 Planning Process

In the daily life scenario of autonomous vehicle delivery, there are various delivery needs. According to the model set up in the previous article, some users have time requirements, and autonomous vehicle needs to deliver the packages to the user point within the specified time range, otherwise, secondary delivery may be carried out, which will reduce user satisfaction, and the whole delivery efficiency will be affected. Therefore, during the delivery, the planning should be designed according to the time windows of the users, the users who have time requirements should be given priority in delivery order. Users who have no time requirement should be inserted into the existing delivery sequence according to the general planning route and the distance in space. The solution steps of the ANT colony algorithm are shown in Fig. 8.

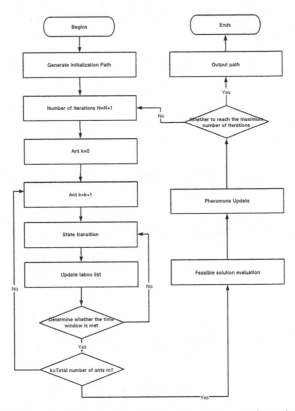

Fig. 8. Flowchart of route planning algorithm that meets time window

Step1: Initialization parameters, set the delivery point location data, time window data, initial pheromone matrix and other parameters, and the maximum number of iterations.
Step2: Randomly generating the number of ants = m, constructing paths one by one according to the transfer formula, using the objective function to calculate the cost of each ant, and getting the initial solution.
Step3: Calculating the time window, determining whether the time window is met, if it is met, go on Step4, otherwise go back to Step2.
Step4: Update pheromone.

Step5: When the new solution generated is better than the current optimal solution, accept the current new solution as the current optimal solution, otherwise go to Step6.
Step6: If reaching the upper limit of the number of iterations, outputting the current optimal solution and go to Step7, otherwise go back to Step2.
Step7: Outputting the global optimal solution and end the program.

4.3 Test and Validation

An area of Southeast University is selected to test and valid for autonomous vehicle delivery. As shown in Fig. 9, the blue point represents the starting point of the delivery process, the red points represent the users with time window, and the yellow points with no time requirements, in total 9 points. There is operating time for the user to pick up the package of each point. ArcGIS software was used to obtain the coordinate data of each point in the map, and the time window data is shown in Table 1. *ID* represents the serial number of the point, *STime* represents the start time of the time window, *DTime* represents the end time of the time window, *SvTime* represents the operation time of the users.

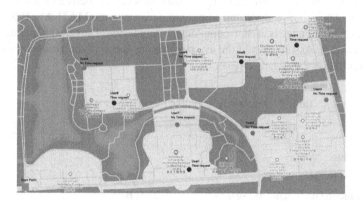

Fig. 9. Location information of delivery points

As shown in Table 1, the tenth point is the starting point, which represents the package station, and the starting point is the ending point of the delivery. Points 1, 4, 5, and 8 have a time window, the remaining points have no requirements. When solving the model, delivery priority is given to points with a time window, and then the overall route is planned.

Table 1. Experimental setting of delivery points information data

ID	X(m)	Y(m)	STime(s)	DTime(s)	SvTime(s)
1	118.819121	31.887092	40	20	30
2	118.82204	31.888036	0	0	45
3	118.824483	31.888819	0	0	15
4	118.823371	31.890442	90	30	30
5	118.821412	31.89007	200	50	15
6	118.819435	31.88999	0	0	10
7	118.819169	31.88823	0	0	10
8	118.816906	31.888819	300	100	15
9	118.815879	31.889869	0	0	10
10	118.813854	31.886309	0	0	0

With the time window constraint, the autonomous vehicle delivery route is planning based on the ANT colony algorithm solution process, and the MATLAB_R2017b software MATLAB language is used to complete the simulation. The relevant parameters are shown in Table 2. Assuming that the average driving speed of the autonomous vehicle is $V = 7.2$ km/h $= 2$ m/s.

Table 2. Ant colony algorithm related parameters table

Parameter name	Parameter value
Number of ants	$m = 50$
Pheromone importance factor	$Alpha = 1$
Heuristic function importance factor	$Beta = 3$
Pheromone volatilization factor	$Rho = 0.85$
Constant coefficient	$Q = 100$
Maximum number of iterations	$NC\_max = 50$

The result of the autonomous vehicle delivery route is 10 -> 1 -> 2 -> 4 -> 3 -> 5 -> 7 -> 8 -> 6 -> 9 -> 10, as shown on the map in orange lines in Fig. 10.

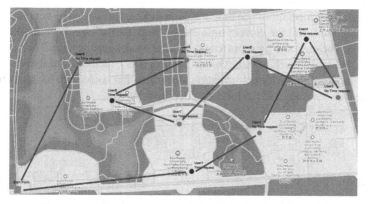

Fig. 10. Autonomous vehicle delivery route planning results

5   Interface Prototype Design

After completing the model construction and technical realization of the autonomous vehicle delivery system based on the service design concept. In this section, some human-computer interaction interface prototype was designed for users. A good interaction interface can help the users reduce operation errors and improve operational efficiency, which can bring an emotionally pleasant experience as well [12]. The interface prototype design is based on the concepts of service design, the characteristics of human's perception of external information have been considered. Two main functional modules can be described as the "time selection part" and the "delivery status viewing part", as shown in Figs. 11 and 12.

(1) Time selection part

When users are in this functional module, they have more choices to pick-up time. The information presented in the left interface includes the current package size information

Fig. 11. Time selection part interface prototype

and the timetable information. The time selection function is divided by hour, the optional time is highlighted, and the current time status "peak period" has been marked, which could provide convenience for users to choose time for delivery service. The information presented in the right interface is the confirmation of users, including the delivery address and time selection. The twice confirmation of information could help the users improve their cognitive characteristics and reduce operational errors.

(2) Delivery status viewing part

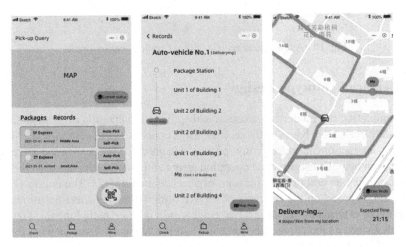

Fig. 12. Delivery status viewing part interface prototype

When users are in this functional module, they can easily get the status information of the current delivery process. Adding this function of real-time viewing for users could help them enhance the immersive experience. The information presented in the left interface including "convenient entry for map", "my packages" and "delivery records", buttons including "Auto-pick" and "Self-pick", which means the users have more choice for picking up packages. The global scanning function can provide users with direct feedback when picking up packages. The delivery status information in the middle interface is expanded in timeline with context, the users can view the current location of the autonomous vehicle. The right interface is mainly the map mode of the middle, presenting the delivery information in a visualization way, which could increase the sense of fun to use the function for users and enhancing the user experience.

6   Survey

To verify the usability of the autonomous vehicle delivery system based on the service design concepts, a survey has been done in this section. A network questionnaire on the service model was conducted, and a total of 51 valid questionnaires were collected. The results are described as follows: the average age of users is 28.3 years old. 21.4% of the users have already tried autonomous vehicle delivery service, but they are all dissatisfied with the current service model, 68.3% of the users expressed their willingness to try the delivery service, with 78.9% of the users said that the ability to select time is very important.

When asked if they are willing to use the autonomous vehicle delivery service proposed in this paper, 77.2% of the users expressed their willingness or they need the service. The reasons for not using or unwilling to can be summarized as "worrying about the safety of packages and personal information" (47.8%). These answers usually come from older users who are not sensitive to new technologies. There are also 54.6% of respondents who said that the autonomous vehicle delivery can be used for takeaway, and they said they need this feature very much.

7 Conclusion and Future Work

This paper proposed a new autonomous vehicle delivery model that meets the time requirements of users based on the service design concepts. Route planning algorithm has been used as the technical support of the model. The interactive prototypes of core functions were finally designed to improve user experience. Besides, a certain area of Southeast University is selected for test and simulation, and the conclusion route is calculated. However, there are still some problems to be solved, such as the improvement of route planning algorithm and other needs of the users when using the autonomous vehicle delivery service.

A performed survey showed that the proportion of users are willing to try or experience autonomous vehicle delivery service and agree with the time selection function, which reflects that the practical significance of the research on this subject. In the open question of the survey, they put forward new functional requirements for the autonomous vehicle delivery, such as delivering takeaways in a small area.

The autonomous vehicle delivery service model based on the service design concepts proposed in this paper provides a new idea for the delivery model to some extent, which provides a solution for the current stage of autonomous vehicle delivery as well. How to use autonomous vehicles to develop more flexible, low-cost and suitable models is the future research direction.

References

1. Li, Z., Zhou, W., Hu, F.: Research on the collaborative development path of express delivery and e-commerce in the central Yunnan urban economic circle under the background of smart cities. Mod. Bus. **8**(10), 26–28 (2019)
2. Ran, B., Qin, J.: Product design of unmanned vehicles applied to smart logistics services. Packag. Eng. **42**(06), 37–45 (2021)
3. Liu, S., Li, Q., Cheng, L.: Research on unmanned distribution logistics service system based on unmanned driving technology. China New Telecommun. **23**(01), 73–74 (2021)
4. Zomerdijk, L.G., Voss, C.A.: Service design for experience-centric services. J. Serv. Res. **13**(1), 67–82 (2010)

5. Wang, G.S.: Service Design and Innovation. China Construction Industry Press, Beijing (2015)
6. Xin, X.Y., Cao, J.Z.: Location service design. Packag. Eng. **39**(18), 43–49 (2018)
7. Verma, R., Teixeira, J., Patrício, L., et al.: Customer experience modeling: from customer experience to service design. J. Serv. Manag. **23**(3), 362–376 (2012)
8. Wang, Y.H., Lee, C.H., Trappey, A.J.: Service design blueprint approach incorporating TRIZ and service QFD for a meal ordering system: a case study. Comput. Ind. Eng. **107**, 388–400 (2017)
9. Lin, G. Q.: Research on Vehicle Routing Problem with Time Window Based on Hybrid Genetic Algorithm, pp. 18–19. Shandong University (2017)
10. Fu, M., Li, J., Deng, Z.: A practical route planning algorithm for vehicle navigation system. In: 5th World Congress on Intelligent Control and Automation, vol. 6, pp. 5326–5329, IEEE (2004)
11. Li, X.J., Yang, Y., Jiang, J.Y., Jiang, L.M.: Application of ant colony optimization algorithm in logistics vehicle scheduling system. Comput. Appl. **33**(10), 2822–2826 (2013)
12. Jonathan, A., John, M., Robb, W.: The effective UI Team. Effective UI: The Art of Building Great User Experience in Software, pp. 150–205. O'Reilly Media (2010)

A Systematic Literature Review on Injury Prevention in Transportation Sector

Jathin Katikala[1]($\boxtimes$) and Vincent G. Duffy[1,2]

[1] School of Industrial Engineering, Purdue University, West Lafayette, IN, USA
{jkatikal,duffy}@purdue.edu
[2] Department of Agricultural and Biological Engineering, Purdue University, West Lafayette, IN, USA

Abstract. Accidents caused by vehicles of transportation domain are the leading cause of death worldwide. Nearly 75% of road deaths happen in developing countries. The road traffic accident rate caused by four-wheeled vehicles is the highest among the reported statistics on road traffic accidents. Standing motorized scooters' popularity has been continuously increasing in major cities of the USA and surge of traumatic injuries is observed in many hospitals. This report will analyze bibliometric data using tools like Harzing's Publish or Perish, VOSviewer, MAXQDA, Mendeley, BibExcel, and CiteSpace to provide a systematic literature review of publications on the above-mentioned subject. Analysis is performed on articles considered from a variety of outlets, including Google Scholar, Web of Science, SpringerLink, ResearchGate, and a few chapters from Salvendy's Handbook of Human Factors and Ergonomics, Fourth Edition. A co-citation analysis was performed to identify the most significant publications in the literature. This article also discusses how potential studies like usage of autonomous vehicles, usage of virtual reality, reducing human intervention, and increasing human-computer interaction can avoid accidents in the transportation industry.

Keywords: Injuries · Prevention · Transportation · Autonomous vehicles · Human-computer interaction · Technology · Bibliometric analysis · Harzing · VOSviewer · MAXQDA · Mendeley

1 Introduction

The transportation sector plays one of the most crucial roles in maintaining a smooth flow of day-to-day activities in the world. Rollover crashes are responsible for a considerable number of injuries and fatalities that we are considering in this article. There are a wide number of reasons for the cause of rollover crashes like surroundings being dark without sufficient lighting, rainy climate, improper overtaking by truck vehicles, the age of the vehicle, traffic volume at that instant, the number of lanes on the road, the speed limit, terrain of the road (Anarkooli et al. 2017). There is also a huge soar in the popularity of standing motorized scooters in many major cities in the United States of America. Since the safety regulations are poorly defined for the riders, many hospitals are experiencing

© Springer Nature Switzerland AG 2021
C. Stephanidis et al. (Eds.): HCII 2021, LNCS 13097, pp. 261–277, 2021.
https://doi.org/10.1007/978-3-030-90966-6_19

a massive rise in traumatic injuries associated with standing motorized scooters. Recent findings have pointed that there has been an exponential rise in emergency department visits due to standing motorized scooter-related trauma in hospitals (Kim and Campbell 2021).

Accidents caused by vehicles of transportation domain are the leading cause of death worldwide. Nearly 75% of road deaths happen in developing countries. The road traffic accident rate caused by four-wheeled vehicles is the highest among the statistics that are reported on road traffic accidents (Al Turki 2014). Some of these accidents are caused due to lack of sufficient knowledge on new technology by drivers. This issue is clearly emphasized in (van der Laan 1997) and techniques to assess the acceptance of technology are discussed in detail. According to a survey by National Highway Traffic Safety Administration, 93% of traffic accidents are caused due to human error. Ground falls are the most common cause of injury in these crashes. Injuries associated with ground-level falls have become a serious global problem. More than 60% of traumatic brain injury cases in old-aged people are the result of falls (Kim et al. 2021). According to research, injuries due to crashes are the leading cause of death among American teenagers. American teenagers drive cars, motorcycles, and bicycle. In most states, teenagers can obtain an unrestricted driver's license at the age of just 16 years ("Differences in Transportation-Related Injury" n.d.). The Commission for Global Road Safety believes that it is quite crucial to stop this preventable and horrific rise in road injuries. We will discuss how increasing human-computer interaction and increase in usage of autonomous vehicles can prevent the injuries in accidents in detail in later sections.

2 Purpose of Study

The objective of this study is to conduct a systematic literature review of studies on the topic of injuries and crashes in the transportation sector from a Human automation perspective. Other examples that illustrate the bibliometric analysis methodology in this style are shown in the literature (Duffy and Duffy 2020). Bibliometric analysis, including scientific methodologies, provides a systematic and overall analysis in showing how critical it is to prevent injuries in crashes. Bibliometric analysis methods including MAXQDA, VOS Viewer, Publish or Perish-Harzing, Mendeley, BibExcel were used in this study for data collection, content analysis, trend analysis, and co-citation analysis. Based on these bibliometric data analyses, results and conclusions can be drawn, nudging future studies in the right direction to avoid injuries in motor vehicle crashes.

3 Research Methodologies

3.1 Data Collection

The first stage of the research involved gathering data for analysis by searching three keywords through many databases, including SpringerLink, Google Scholar, Scopus, and Web of Science. More findings were found in Google Scholar than in any other database. By logging into the library system and accessing the relevant database and conducting a keyword search, Purdue Libraries was able to access Web of Science, Scopus, and SpringerLink.

(SpringerLink n.d.). Harzing's Publish or Perish (Harzing's Publish or Perish n.d.) can be used to extract papers from Google Scholar. Harzing's Publish or Perish can search for articles and retrieve bibliometric data from a variety of databases, including Crossref, Google Scholar, Scopus (Scopus n.d.), Pubmed, and others. However, access to the other databases which are not affiliated with Purdue requires an external subscription and is limited to only 1000 articles in a search.

I used "Injury Prevention", "Automation" and "Transportation" to search for the articles that talk about the topics that are related to our required keywords in Google Scholar. This search was done on Harzing's Publish or Perish initially. The search resulted in 1000 results and the corresponding bibliometric metadata was extracted to analyze like co-citation analysis and co-author analysis. Explanation of these analyses in much detail is in the later sections. The second search was on the Web of Science, Scopus, and SpringerLink databases through Purdue Library as mentioned above. The metadata from Web of Science ("Web of Science" n.d.) includes the author, article title, keywords, abstract, and citations for every article. This kind of metadata is not available in Harzing's metadata for the corresponding search. The same keywords were used again to look up the articles that correspond to our topic of discussion in the search. This search resulted in around 5,800 articles. The metadata of these articles is collected to do the systematic literature review.

3.2 Data Analysis

The first study was a pattern analysis using data from the Web of Science database. Web of Science has in-built tools to analyze the data obtained from the database. The data point corresponding to the year 2021 would be corrupt and was excluded. It is because the year 2021 has just begun and that data point might deviate from the original trend. This exclusion aids in better understanding the trend and to eliminate the corrupt data point of the year 2021 in the trend.

The following figure shows the trend analysis for injury prevention in the last 24 years. We can observe that the issue of injury prevention was quite prevalent even back in 1996. There was a steady rise in the trend from 1996 to 2015 in the number of articles published every year. There was a slight dip in the curve between 2015 to 2018 but the peak is observed in 2019. A similar pattern emerged on examining the data from Harzing's (Fig. 1).

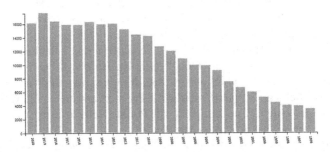

Fig. 1. Trend analysis of articles on injury prevention

The following figure depicts the top sources of titles for injury prevention. The in-built tools of the Web of Science were used for this research (Fig. 2).

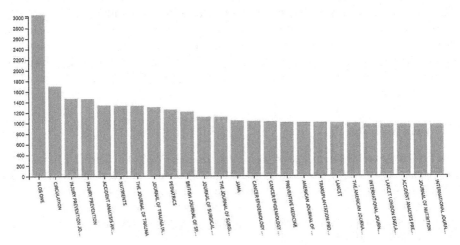

Fig. 2. Source titles analysis for injury prevention

The following figure shows a country-wise filter on the number of articles published on injury prevention. It can be observed that the USA has published the highest number of articles when compared to other regions of the world. It can be interpreted that the USA faces more issues of injuries in motor vehicle crashes or at workstations than other countries (Fig. 3).

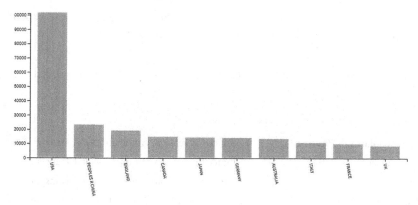

Fig. 3. Analysis of the number of articles published by a region on injury prevention

After the initial analyses to understand the criticalness of injury prevention, other analyses were performed to provide a more robust systematic review of literature on injury prevention in the transportation sector. The VOSviewer software was used to conduct the next step. It is a tool that can generate cluster diagrams of co-author analysis, co-citations analysis, and keywords analysis (Kurniawan and Duffy n.d.). The databases used for the analyses were Web of Science and Google Scholar through Harzing's Publish or Perish. Extracted the bibliometric data from these databases to perform the analyses as mentioned above. One important aspect to be considered when examining the cluster diagrams is the size of the bubbles for each author. The size of each bubble represents the number of his or her publication and the connecting line between authors or citations represents the co-citation links.

MAXQDA software was used to perform the next step. MAXQDA ("MAXQDA" n.d.) is another tool that helps us in visualizing the keywords in the set of collected articles. The same keywords are then used in MAXQDA to do an extended lexical search. MAXQDA can perform a lexical search across multiple articles at the same time. CiteSpace is another software which is used to perform citation bursts. Further analysis is shown on the collected bibliometric metadata to extract authorship information into leading tables and was further visualized using pivot charts using Microsoft Excel. The next step was performed using "Mendeley" to retrieve some articles that are relevant to "injury prevention", "automation" and "transportation" and generate a Chicago-style citation. Mendeley ("Mendeley" n.d.) is a managing software that is equipped with some amazing features regarding citations and references.

4   Results

4.1   Keyword Search

As mentioned previously, the research started with data collection by searching 3 keywords in various databases: Scopus, Web of Science, Google Scholar, and SpringerLink. The Google Scholar database is accessed using Harzing's Publish or Perish program, while the other databases are accessed by logging into a Purdue account and using the

Purdue Library function. Table 1 below illustrates the database and the corresponding number of articles obtained from the keywords in each database, respectively.

Table 1. The number of articles in each database was generated with the mentioned keyword search

Database	Number of articles	Keywords used
Google Scholar	560	Injury Prevention, Automation and Transportation
Web of Science	220	Injury Prevention, Automation and Transportation
Scopus	380	Injury Prevention, Automation and Transportation
SpringerLink	1135	Injury Prevention, Automation and Transportation

4.2 Co-citation Analysis

Bibliometric data with citation information is needed to perform co-citation analysis. "The degree of connectivity between pairs of papers is examined using citation analysis" (Fahimnia et al. 2015). VOSviewer creates clusters from pairs of papers that are cited together. This research method is used to evaluate the most important paper for them by measuring the number of times the papers are cited. The more co-citations two documents receive, the higher their co-citation strength. This technique is also quite often used for identifying the intellectual structure of a research domain. Bibliometric data was extracted from Web of Science in a text file and is inputted into the VOSviewer to perform full count analysis. The keywords used in Web of Science are "Injury Prevention" and "Transportation". The counting method used to generate the desired diagram was "Full counting" (Fig. 4).

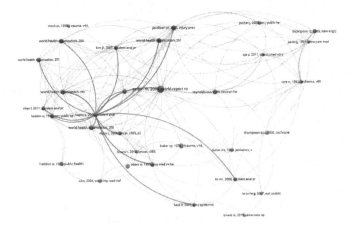

Fig. 4. Co-citation cluster map

The parameters used to obtain the Co-citation analysis are:

1. Minimum number of citations of a cited reference: 5.
2. Out of the 12958 cited references, 33 meet the threshold.
3. Out of the 33 items in the network, the largest set of connected items consisted of 32 items.

The results of the co-citation cluster diagram are as follows (Tables 2 and 3):

Table 2. Results of co-citation analysis from VOSviewer

Type	Number of them available
Items	32
Clusters	4
Links	154
Total Link Strength	199

Table 3. Results of authors, year of publication, number of citations, and link strengths

Authors	Year of publication	Citations	Link strength
Peden M et al.	2004	18	34
Jackobsen P et al.	2003	7	24
Kopits E et al.	2005	6	21
Thompson D C et al.	1992	6	15
Sacks JJ et al.	1968	6	14
Kim J K et al.	2007	5	15
Haddon W et al.	1968	5	12

4.3 Co-authorship Analysis

The next step in the analysis is to use the bibliometric data to generate co-authorship cluster diagrams from VOSviewer. The metadata obtained from Web of Science is fed into the VOSviewer in a text file. CoAuthorship networks are powerful tools that are utilized to "assess collaboration trends and to identify leading scientists and organizations" (Fonseca et al. 2016). The keywords used in Web of Science are "Injury Prevention" and "Transportation". The counting method used to generate the desired diagram was "Full counting" (Fig. 5).

Fig. 5. Co-authorship cluster map

The parameters used to obtain the Co-authorship analysis are:

1. Maximum number of authors per document: 5
2. Minimum number of documents of an author: 3
3. Minimum number of citations of an author: 0
4. Out of 912 authors, 13 meet the threshold (Table 4).

Table 4. Results of co-authorship analysis from VOSviewer

Type	Number of them available
Items	13
Clusters	9
Links	4
Total Link Strength	10

4.4 Co-occurrence Keyword Analysis Using VOSviewer

The next step in the analysis is to use the bibliometric data to generate Co-occurence keyword analysis cluster diagrams from VOSviewer. The Co-occurrence analysis operates by searching for words that are commonly used in the selected articles (Krishnan 2015). A co-occurrence keyword analysis would help us capture the relationships between words that "co-occur" together in articles (Martínez-Ruiz et al. 2015). The bibliometric data from 560 articles that were generated via Harzing's Publish or Perish using keywords like "injury prevention", "automation" and "transportation". The extracted data was exported to VOSviewer in RIS file format and this metadata is to generate a visualized bibliometric network or a cluster diagram that displays the most frequently used words. The counting method used to generate the desired diagram was "Full counting". The title and abstract fields were used to extract the keywords (Fig. 6).

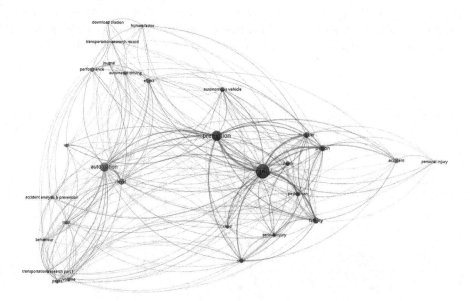

Fig. 6. Co-occurence keyword analysis cluster map

As we can see, "injury" is the most occurred word in our articles. The second most occurred word is "prevention". They are accompanied by the word "automation" in the third place. The parameters used to obtain co-occurence keyword analysis are:

1. Maximum number of occurrences of a term: 5.
2. Out of the 2714 terms, 49 meet the threshold.
3. Number of terms to be selected: 29 (29 keywords were selected as 60% most relevant items) (Table 5).

Table 5. Results of Co-occurence keyword analysis from VOSviewer

Type	Number of them available
Items	29
Clusters	4
Links	249
Total Link Strength	1299

4.5 Content Analysis from MAXQDA

Word Cloud. A group of nine papers and, two chapters from the Handbook of Human Factors and Ergonomics were chosen from a pool of hundreds of articles to create a word cloud. The two chapters that are considered for the analysis are chapter 25, "Occupational Health and Safety Management" and chapter 53, "Design for Children". All prepositions, numbers, symbols, and terms that are unrelated to the issue of injury prevention in the transportation sector were removed from a stop list to acquire substantive words (Fig. 7).

Fig. 7. Word cloud generated based on nine articles and two chapters from HFE

We can see that "injury" is the most frequently word used in the considered set of articles and chapters. Other words that stand out are "injuries", "prevention", "road" and "traffic".

The parameters used to obtain the word cloud are:

1. Minimum frequency of each word: 4
2. Limit on the number of words in the word cloud: 200 (Table 6).

Table 6. Frequency of the words and word lengths for the words present in the above word cloud

Word	Word length	Frequency	Rank	Documents	Documents %
Injury	6	564	1	8	57.14
Injuries	8	319	2	9	64.29
More	4	229	3	12	85.71
Crashes	7	223	4	6	42.86
Analysis	8	221	5	12	85.71
Research	8	205	6	11	78.57
Data	4	204	7	12	85.71
Study	5	203	8	12	85.71
Model	5	191	9	6	42.86
Crash	5	181	10	6	42.86
Severity	8	172	11	7	50.00

Extended Lexical Search. Based on the analyses as mentioned earlier and the created word cloud, multiple key terms were selected for an extended lexical search using MAXQDA software over the nine selected articles and two chapters from The Handbook of Human Factors and Ergonomics. Some of the key terms are "injury", "injuries", "prevention", "road" and "traffic".

As we can see, "injury" is the most frequently occurred word adhering to our subject of interest – "Injury Prevention". The words "Injuries" and "prevention" are the adhering to our topic as well. Since our theme is in the transportation sector, we can also see that the words "road", "traffic", "motorcycle," and "bicycle" are also occurred, adhering to our theme of interest.

There are many research articles in our chosen nine, that speak significantly about risk factors for severe injury in cyclists involved in traffic crashes (Boufous et al. 2012). There is also another research article that mainly focused on the severity and the injuries and crashes caused by cyclists running through the red-light at the junctions (Pai and Jou 2014). There is another research article that solely focused on the enormity of bicycle crashes and injuries in which the author tries to emphasize the need to account for bicycle crashes as they are always neglected (Juhra et al. 2012; Heesch et al. 2011; Dettori and Norvell 2006). There are a couple of articles that focused on motorcycle crashes as injuries in motorcycle crashes are quite severe and more than 30% of crashes result in death casualties. The articles also focus on the effectiveness of protective clothing to prevent injuries to riders (Vanlaar et al. 2016; de Rome et al. 2012).

4.6 Keyword Cluster Analysis Using CiteSpace

The keyword cluster analysis using CiteSpace is quite similar to using VOSviewer as shown above. The current cluster analysis performed is more oriented towards the articles corresponding to injury prevention and transportation sector chosen from the Web of Science database. The primary purpose of this analysis is to figure out which type of injuries are most common in the transportation sector and where the research is being focused. The following figure shows the topic of focus in the form of a cluster using CiteSpace software (Fig. 8).

Fig. 8. Cluster Analysis using CiteSpace

From the above-displayed figure, we can see the focused areas which are being calculated based on the highest frequency of occurrence in various sources. "Injury Prevention" is the most frequently occurred topic. The "Knee injury prevention" is the 5th most frequently occurred word. This can be observed even in the chosen articles where the author speaks about the severity of knee injuries and how the injuries can be averted. One other topic of focus is the "training load".

4.7 Leading Tables in BibExcel and Visualization of Pivot Charts

BibExcel was used to further analyze the bibliographic metadata. The input data to the BibExcel was obtained from Harzing's Publish or Perish ("Harzing's Publish or Perish" n.d.). Metadata of around 600 articles were extracted into an ISI format file and then imported into BibExcel. BibExcel is a software tool designed to assist a user in analyzing bibliographic data, or any data of a text natured file. The idea is to generate data files that can be imported onto Excel later or any other software which can consume tabbed data records to analyze further.

All the 600 results were thoroughly scrutinized for bibliographic information once the input file was imported in BibExcel. This resulted in finding information about the number of articles related to our specific topic. The results were arranged in descending order and are copied into Microsoft Excel, where we create a pivot table and obtain the pivot chart shown below. The top 20 results are displayed in the following table (Table 7 and Fig. 9).

Table 7. The results obtained from the BibExcel

Author name	Number of articles
Litman T	5
Dellinger AM	5
Mohan D	4
Morency P	4
Ferguson SA	4
Mock C	3
Dannenberg AL	3
Dickerson AE	3
Braver ER	3
McAndrews C	3
Shults RA	3
Anderson C	3
Sleet DA	3
Lee J	3
Sleet D	3
Gilchrist J	3

5 Discussion

Humanity has excelled a lot since the industrial revolution. Some fantastic discoveries happened along the path and the motorization of vehicles is one of those. Motorized vehicles have become a part of day-to-day human life. Humanity has a direct dependency on vehicles so much that the world cannot sustain without using motor vehicles for even a single day (Lehto et al. 2012). Motorized vehicles have become an essential part of life as the school bus, vanpool to go to an office, the post mail van, shipping of raw materials and finished goods to and fro from a company. Hence, one should maintain healthy

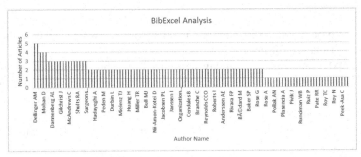

Fig. 9. Results of BibExcel on leading authors are organized in descending order in a Pivot Chart

conscience while using motor vehicles or even bicycles in public. Our findings indicate that many high school students riding with a driver who had been drinking alcohol self-reported that drinking was the cause of the accidents resulting in injuries. One should also consider the job design of seats associated with children in motor vehicles, as discussed in one of the articles that we focused on (Reddell et al. 1992; Rice and Cosby 2009).

The article (Kim et al. 2021) emphasizes the point that men were more likely than women to present to the ED with severe head injuries and men in the head injury group were also more likely than women to have suffered significant injuries. The overall incidence of fall-related injuries is higher in the older adults in women than in men. However, the mortality rate associated with such injuries was much lower in women than in men. The article (de Rome et al. 2012) emphasized the significant impact of nonfatal motorcycle crashes on the physical, emotional, and social wellbeing of riders. This article focused on how well protective clothing helps a rider during a motor vehicle crash.

By this review, we can get a sense of how important it is to consider injury prevention in motor vehicle crashes based on the mortality rate and the severity of injuries as discussed in the set of articles. This report provides a systematic literature review on injury prevention in the transportation sector. Firstly, a trend analysis was carried out to understand the importance of this topic. The trends show that this topic is no longer in primitive stages and that significant research has been made and continues further to prevent injuries in motorized vehicle crashes. Secondly, a co-citation analysis was performed to understand how many people are working on this topic and how many articles have been influential in shaping the research and raising a voice about the topic in this domain. This analysis was performed in the VOSviewer ("VOSviewer" n.d.) software after extracting bibliometric information from various databases like Google Scholar ("Google Scholar" n.d.), SpringerLink, Scopus, and Web of Science. Co-authorship analysis is performed with the same metadata that was extracted from the previously mentioned databases. Content analyses were carried out during the subsequent steps. Next, a keyword co-occurrence cluster was generated in VOSviewer after extracting content information from Google Scholar using the Harzing Publish or Perish software. Since the keyword search used for this stage in the analysis was a generic topic, this analysis helped identify the area this report would address. A content analysis in the form of a word cloud was done in MAXQDA once the topic was identified and a select number of research articles were collected from different sources. Results from the previous analysis shows that topics such as "injury", "prevention", "transportation" and "automation" are highly referenced in all these articles and occurred multiple times in the articles. After that, a cluster analysis of the content on CiteSpace gave more insight into the fact that "injury" was highly used in many research articles. Lastly, BibExcel was used to find the leading authors who are actively participating and conducting research in this domain.

6 Conclusion

Firstly, we discussed the issue of rollovers and the severity of the injuries. The major factors for rollover are related to driver-specific attributes (e.g., age, gender, etc.), the surrounding environment (e.g., land use, weather condition, access point), vehicle features (e.g., vehicle type, vehicle age), roadway conditions (e.g., shoulder width, horizontal curvature, terrain), crash-specific characteristics (e.g., time of the crash, injury severity), and traffic conditions (e.g., light-vehicle traffic, heavy-vehicle) (Anarkooli et al. 2017).

We also discussed the exponentially growing issue of injuries while driving standing motorized scooters. Through the analyses mentioned in the article, we can understand the significance of injury prevention in transportation sector. We also identified some of the key factors that cause injuries in the transportation sector and can focus the research on how to sustain these incidents. National Science Foundation (NSF) has shown keen interest in funding projects like "Programming safety into self-driving cars" which can improve the safety by implementing optimized artificial intelligence algorithms. Innovations in optimizing the human-computer interactions have shown significant promise in mitigating injuries caused in accidents of transportation sector.

7 Recommendation for Future Work

Although this report addresses the importance of injury prevention in motorized vehicle crashes and provides a systematic literature review on the same, there still is a lot of research that could be pursued in some of the specific topics. A lot of future research has been funded in Malaysia on studying the factors mentioned above to come up with creative solutions to reduce or even stop the rollovers of motorized vehicles. Future research work can focus on how to prevent the riders to drive these scooters when they are intoxicated as this one of the main reasons why riders prefer to drive these scooters. There are no laws implemented to restrict the riders to drive them when they are intoxicated in the current world (Kim and Campbell 2021).

Fatalities in traffic accidents reduced notably due to recent advancements in safety technologies. To reach greater heights in advancements in safety, the automobile industry has invested in developing autonomous vehicles and minimize human intervention which is one of the most significant causes of accidents (Choi and Ji 2015). Autonomous vehicles could improve safety by increasing the human-computer interaction. Autonomous vehicles can help elderly people by having computers do the major tasks (Bimbraw 2015). One other domain to focus future research is training in virtual safety. Training children in immersive virtual reality to teach the necessary pedestrian skills is empha-sized in (Dixon et al. 2020). Training in virtual reality could really help young drivers to gain sufficient knowledge and might reduce traffic accidents. Research to develop driver assistance and intuitive driver-car communication can improve driving safety (Eyben et al. 2010).

References

1. Anarkooli, A.J., Hosseinpour, M., Kardar, A.: Investigation of factors affecting the injury severity of single-vehicle rollover crashes: a random-effects generalized ordered probit model. Accid. Anal. Prev. **106**(September), 399–410 (2017). https://doi.org/10.1016/j.aap.2017.07.008
2. Boufous, S., de Rome, L., Senserrick, T., Ivers, R.: Risk factors for severe injury in cyclists involved in traffic crashes in Victoria, Australia. Accid. Anal. Prev. **49**(November), 404–409 (2012). https://doi.org/10.1016/j.aap.2012.03.011
3. Dettori, N.J., Norvell, D.C.: Non-traumatic bicycle injuries a review of the literature. Sports Med. **36**, 7–18 (2006)
4. Differences in Transportation-Related Injury (n.d.)
5. Duffy, G.A., Duffy, V.G.: Systematic literature review on the effect of human error in environ-mental pollution. In: Duffy, V.G. (ed.) HCII 2020. LNCS, vol. 12199, pp. 228–241. Springer, Cham (2020). https://doi.org/10.1007/978-3-030-49907-5_16
6. Fonseca, E., de Paula Fonseca, B., Sampaio, R.B., de Arajo Fonseca, M.V., Zicker, F.: Co-authorship network analysis in health research: method and potential use. Health Res. Policy Syst. **14**(1), 1–11 (2016). https://doi.org/10.1186/s12961-016-0104-5
7. Fahimnia, B., Sarkis, J., Davarzani, H.: Green supply chain management: a review and biblio-metric analysis. Int. J. Prod. Econ. **162**, 101–114 (2015). https://doi.org/10.1016/j.ijpe.2015.01.003
8. Google Scholar (n.d.). https://scholar.google.com/. Accessed 27 Apr 2021
9. Harzing's Publish or Perish (n.d.). https://harzing.com/resources/publish-or-perish. Accessed 27 Apr 2021
10. Heesch, K.C., Garrard, J., Sahlqvist, S.: Incidence, severity and correlates of bicycling injuries in a sample of cyclists in Queensland, Australia. Accid. Anal. Prev. **43**(6), 2085–2092 (2011). https://doi.org/10.1016/j.aap.2011.05.031
11. Juhra, C., et al.: Bicycle accidents - do we only see the tip of the iceberg?: A prospective multi-centre study in a large German City combining medical and police data. Injury **43**(12), 2026–2034 (2012). https://doi.org/10.1016/j.injury.2011.10.016
12. Kim, S.H., Kim, S., Cho, G.C., Lee, J.H., Park, E.J., Lee, D.H.: Characteristics of fall-related head injury versus non-head injury in the older adults. BMC Geriatr. **21**(1), 1–11 (2021). https://doi.org/10.1186/s12877-021-02139-4
13. Kim, W.C., Campbell, A.R.: Common injury patterns from standing motorized scooter crashes. Curr. Surgery Rep. **9**, 1–5 (2021). https://doi.org/10.1007/s40137-021-00283-9
14. Krishnan: How to use words co-occurrence statistics to map words to vectors (2015). https://iksinc.online/2015/06/23/how-to-use-words-co-occurrence-statistics-to-map-words-to-vectors/
15. Kurniawan, J., Duffy, V.G.: Systematic review of the importance of human factors in incorporating healthcare automation, pp. 1–18 (n.d.)
16. Lehto, M.R., Lafayette, W., Cook, B.T.: Miller engineering, and ann arbor, Chap. 25. In: Management of Occupational Safety. Handbook of Human Factors and Ergonomics (2012)
17. MAXQDA (n.d). https://www.maxqda.com/. Accessed 27 Apr 2021

18. Martínez-Ruiz, V., Jiménez-Mejías, E., Amezcua-Prieto, C., Olmedo-Requena, R., De Dios LunaDel-Castillo, J., Lardelli-Claret, P.: Contribution of exposure, risk of crash and fatality to explain age- and sex-related differences in traffic-related cyclist mortality rates. Accid. Anal. Prev. **76**, 152–158 (2015). https://doi.org/10.1016/j.aap.2015.01.008

19. Mendeley (n.d.). https://www.mendeley.com/?interaction_required=true. Accessed 27 Apr 2021

20. Pai, C.W., Jou, R.C.: Cyclists' red-light running behaviours: an examination of risk-taking, opportunistic, and law-obeying behaviours. Accid. Anal. Prev. **62**, 191–198 (2014). https://doi.org/10.1016/j.aap.2013.09.008

21. Reddell, C.R., Congleton, J.J., Huchingson, R.D., Montgomery, J.F.: An evaluation of a weightlifting belt and back injury prevention training class for airline baggage handlers. Appl. Ergon. **23**(5), 319–329 (1992). https://doi.org/10.1016/0003-6870(92)90293-5

22. Rice, V.J.B., Cosby, B.: Introduction: how designing for children is different from 2 principles of designing for children is different from designing, Chap. 53, pp. 1640–1653 (2009)

23. de Rome, L., Ivers, R., Fitzharris, M., Haworth, N., Heritier, S., Richardson, D.: Effectiveness of motorcycle protective clothing: riders' health outcomes in the six months following a crash. Injury **43**(12), 2035–2045 (2012). https://doi.org/10.1016/j.injury.2011.10.025

24. Scopus (n.d.). https://wwwscopuscom.ezproxy.lib.purdue.edu/search/form.uri?display=basic#basic. Accessed 27 Apr 2021. SpringerLink (n.d.). https://link.springer.com/. Accessed 27 Apr 2021

25. Al Turki, Y.A.: How can saudi arabia use the decade of action for road safety to catalyse road traffic injury prevention policy and interventions? Int. J. Injury Control Saf. Promot. **21**(4), 397–402 (2014). https://doi.org/10.1080/17457300.2013.833943

26. Vanlaar, W., Hing, M.M., Brown, S., McAteer, H., Crain, J., McFaull, S.: Fatal and serious injuries related to vulnerable road users in Canada. J. Saf. Res. **58**(September), 67–77 (2016). https://doi.org/10.1016/j.jsr.2016.07.001

27. VOSviewer (n.d.). https://www.vosviewer.com/. Accessed 27 Apr 2021

28. Web of Science (n.d.). https://www.webofknowledge.com/. Accessed 27 Apr 2021

29. Bimbraw, K.: Autonomous cars: past, present and future. In: 2015 12th International Conference on Informatics in Control, Automation and Robotics (ICINCO), pp. 191–198 (2015). https://www.scitepress.org/Papers/2015/55405/55405.pdf

30. Choi, J.K., Ji, Y.G.: Investigating the importance of trust on adopting an autonomous vehicle. Int. J. Hum.-Comput. Interact. **31**(10), 692–702 (2015). https://doi.org/10.1080/10447318.2015.1070549

31. Dixon, D.R., Miyake, C.J., Nohelty, K., Novack, M.N., Granpeesheh, D.: Evaluation of an immersive virtual reality safety training used to teach pedestrian skills to children with autism spectrum disorder. Behav. Anal. Pract. **13**(3), 631–640 (2019). https://doi.org/10.1007/s40617-019-00401-1

32. Eyben, F., et al.: Emotion on the road-necessity, acceptance, and feasibility of affective computing in the car. Adv. Hum.-Comput. Interact. (2010). https://doi.org/10.1155/2010/263593

33. van der Laan, J.D., Heino, A., de Waard, D.: A simple procedure for the assessment of acceptance of advanced transport telematics. Transp. Res. Part C: Emerg. Technol. **5**(1), 1–10 (1997). https://doi.org/10.1016/S0968-090X(96)00025-3

Bibliometric Analysis on the Safety of Autonomous Vehicles with Artificial Intelligence

Hak Jun Kim[✉] and Vincent G. Duffy[✉]

School of Industrial Engineering, Purdue University, West Lafayette, IN 47907, USA
{kim3001,duffy}@purdue.edu

Abstract. The objective of the study was to look at the trend and advancement of Artificial Intelligence, Transportation, and Safety research through bibliometric analysis. The review retrieved data in Web of Science using specific terms related to Artificial Intelligence, Transportation, and Safety. VOSViewer, CiteSpace, and MAXQDA were utilized to conduct the citation analysis and content analysis of the Web of Science data set and 8 selected documents including 6 research articles and 2 chapters from the textbook Occupational Safety and Health for Technologists, Engineers, and Managers. Articles from GoogleScholar using Harzing's Publish or Perish software and Web of Science database were used. The citation analysis creating a co-occurrence map discovered several keywords within clusters that were suggested to be subtopics of the general topic. Performing content analysis using the 8 selected documents has shown the most occurring keywords to be similar to those discovered in the citation analysis. The articles utilized bibliometric analysis tools to have further insight on the contributing journals and keywords drawn from multiple sources and methods of Artificial Intelligence and Transportation research. Articles from the Citespace citation burst and VOSViewer co-citation analysis were used to further support the necessity of automation and safety in artificial intelligence and transportation.

Keywords: Artificial Intelligence · Transportation · Artificial intelligence safety · Bibliometric analysis · Citespace · Harzing · VOSViewer · MAXQDA · Vicinitas

1 Introduction and Background

1.1 Artificial Intelligence in Transportation and Ethics

Transportation in modern times has drastically shifted towards a higher dependency on automation following innovation, regulation, and consumer demand. With the recent boom in interest in driver assistance for vehicles driven on public roads, safety has become a significant issue as technology pushes for fully automated systems.

Artificial Intelligence (AI) is the ability of a computer program or a machine to think, learn, and make decisions like humans [10]. Some aspects of AI that are currently

© Springer Nature Switzerland AG 2021
C. Stephanidis et al. (Eds.): HCII 2021, LNCS 13097, pp. 278–289, 2021.
https://doi.org/10.1007/978-3-030-90966-6_20

in use are machine learning and deep learning which are utilized to train the AI for certain automation tasks. Programs are trained with large data sets which are processed and a correlation between the data set and outcome allows the program to think and perform human actions. Implementing this concept with data from road vehicles enables the vehicle to respond to data through numerous sensors and respond accordingly in real-time.

The automotive industry has drastically embraced the use of AI to further innovate and appeal to consumers. Currently, four degrees of autonomy in AI are being heavily pursued: Level 0, Level 1, Level 2, Level 3, and Level 4. Level 0 autonomy indicates a complete lack of autonomous control. Level 1 autonomy indicates the vehicle has individual elements to facilitate its driving such as assisted cruise control and blind-spot monitoring. Level 2 autonomy indicates the vehicle is theoretically able to drive without any operator input but reliability is a significant concern and requires constant input from the operator. Level 3 autonomy indicates the vehicle is able to control itself without operator input for longer periods of time with more confidence. Level 4 autonomy indicates the vehicle can drive by itself without operator input but some conditions such as weather may not be compensated [11]. Level 5 autonomy is not widely pursued as the industry is still experiencing a lack of confidence with Level 4 autonomy.

Although there is a push for autonomous vehicles, most vehicles driven on public roads are still driven without much assistance. One of the most significant challenges currently is that much effort has gone into developing automated systems to improve efficiency and safety than has gone into interaction with people and autonomous systems at an infrastructure level [4]. With a higher level of autonomy, the question of ethics is brought up as the system must make decisions with little to no operator input. Ethics heavily references the conscience, morality, and legality. Legality is a set of rules defined on paper and can be managed by the AI based on if the condition and action are considered legal or not. Morality refers to the values that are subscribed to and fostered by society in general and individuals within society [4]. One challenge faced today with AI is how morality is determined through training the AI.

1.2 Overview of Plan for Bibliometric Analysis

The bibliometric analysis aims to show the relationship between AI, transportation, and safety through the use of trend diagrams, cluster analysis, pivot chart, word cloud, content, and co-citation analysis. The analysis will be performed through software applications including Mendeley [10], MaxQDA [9], Harzing's Publish or Perish [7], Citespace [2], and VOSViewer [18] to summarize key aspects of new research in this popular area and identify the safety issues that are forming the basis for further research in AI, transportation, and safety.

2 Research Methodology

2.1 Data Collection

Bibliometric analysis used multiple databases to collect references. Web of Science (WoS) [18], Scopus, and GoogleScholar databases were used through Harzing's Publish or Perish software as shown in Table 1. Additional references were collected through ResearchGate.

The topic of "Artificial Intelligence and Transportation" was searched by keywords "Artificial Intelligence", "Transportation", and "Safety". The WoS database was used for multiple analyses such as content and co-citation analysis. Due to the specifics of the searched keywords, "Safety" was omitted if the search results did not allow certain analysis to be performed correctly. Table 1 shows the different databases used with the searched terms and their results.

Table 1. Database search with corresponding search terms and results

Database	Search terms	Results
Scopus	"artificial intelligence" AND "transportation" AND "safety"	724
Web of Science	"artificial intelligence" AND "transportation" AND "safety"	123
Web of Science	"artificial intelligence" AND "transportation"	791
Google Scholar	"artificial intelligence" AND "transportation" AND "safety"	109,000
Harzing's Publish or Perish	"artificial intelligence" AND "transportation" AND "safety"	893

2.2 Trend Analysis

Trend analysis of a given search allows further insight into whether the topic of focus is gaining interest. The analysis is based on the results of the WoS database which provides different analyses such as Publication Year, Funding Agencies, Source, etc. Publication Year shows the increasing volume and momentum of articles on the topic.

Figure 1 shows the Publication Year trend for articles found with the topics "Artificial Intelligence", "Transportation", and "Safety" from the WoS database. Starting from 2017 and onwards, the number of publications increases dramatically. The increase every year since 2017 suggests that there will be more articles published in 2021 than 2020 running in line with the increasing push for autonomous vehicles by consumers and regulation. The number of articles published in 2020 compared to 2019 was 13 more and suggests 2021 may see upwards of 40 or more articles published directly related to the safety of AI and transportation.

2.3 Emergence Indicator

Determining the impact and engagement of AI and its effect on transportation and safety shows what is focused on by the public. This data can be used to estimate how much safety

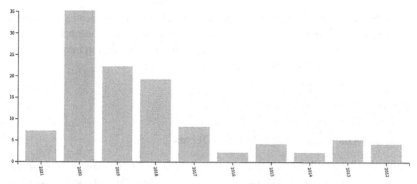

Fig. 1. Trend analysis in publication year of "Artificial Intelligence", "Transportation", and "Safety" containing articles (as of May, 2021)

is prioritized in AI and transportation. Vicinitas [17] downloaded hashtag or keyword-related tweets over a certain period (10 days) and performed various analyses to show impact and engagement. Impact and engagement are determined by the users, posts, engagement, and influence. Users are determined by the total number of unique users who posted tweets. Posts are determined by the total number of tweets. Engagement is determined by the total number of likes and retweets received by the posts. Influence is determined by the sum of the number of followers of each user who posted tracker-matching tweets.

In Vicinitas, the terms "AI", "car", and "safety" were searched. The term "Artificial Intelligence" and "Transportation" was too long and resulted with close to zero results. The terms "AI" and "car" were used as replacements and resulted in significantly more results. In the period of 10 days, 156 users, 10 posts, 372 engagements, and 909.8k influences were made.

The word cloud generated in Vicinitas showed the highest occurring terms in the tweets searched for previously as shown in Fig. 2. There are some key terms that indicate rising awareness of not only autonomous vehicles, but the safety concerns surround them. Apart from the term "safety", infrastructure, deaths, risk are terms that may be key leading terms to suggest safety as an emerging topic with AI and transportation. Due to the timeframe of only 10 days, it is difficult to gauge how much these terms have been more exposed to over a long period of time. Deaths being part of the word cloud in moderate

Fig. 2. Word cloud from Vicinitas search of tweets in the past 10 days containing "ai", "car", and "safety"

size and infrastructure suggests that to increase safety and lower deaths, infrastructure may need to be prioritized as consumers are less willing to ride autonomous vehicles that sacrifice passengers in favor of saving pedestrians and regulation may need to create solutions such as better infrastructure [1].

3   Results

3.1   Content Analysis Based on Leading Terms

Search results from Publish or Perish were saved as a WoS export for use in cluster analysis on the most frequently used and related terms. Publish or Perish searched through GoogleScholar for "Artificial Intelligence", "Transportation", and "Safety". The search resulted in 830 articles and of which 123 terms occurred at least 10 times. The 123 terms were further filtered for the 60% most relevant terms which resulted in 74 terms. The cluster analysis of the most frequently used terms is shown in Fig. 3.

Table 2. Top 15 leading terms after filtering unrelated terms

Term	Occurrences	Relevance
Artificial Neural Network	59	0.87
Prediction	44	0.59
Intelligent Transportation	34	0.86
Big Data	30	0.63
Communication	28	0.99
Smart City	27	1.35
Intelligent System	27	0.72
Intelligent Transportation Systems	26	2.14
Driver	23	0.92
Neural Network	23	0.59
Robot	22	0.80
Performance	22	0.72
IoT	21	1.29
Road Safety	21	0.74
Car	21	0.48

The rate of occurrences from the 830 articles shows more detail in how the cluster is generated. Table 2 shows the rate of the occurrences. Surprisingly, the terms searched originally in Publish or Perish were not found in the table of 15 most occurring terms. The most occurring term was Artificial Neural Network which many autonomous control applications use. Neural networks learn to carry out predictions which is the second most occurring term in the content analysis. However, neural networks that are used for perception systems are limited by insufficient feedback of uncertainty [13]. A neural network's prediction is mostly dependent on the quality of the data used to learn from. This brings attention to the aspects of automation and safety such as ethics and morality as the data and regulation will allow more control over decisions being made in the public with passengers and pedestrians.

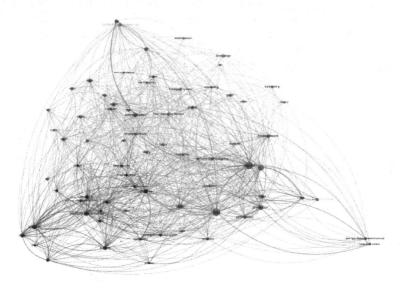

Fig. 3. Cluster analysis in VOSViewer based on metadata captured from search result with "Artificial Intelligence" AND "Transportation" AND "Safety"

Table 3. Top 5 leading cited references from co-citation analysis

Cited reference title	Citations	Total link strength
Traffic Flow Prediction With Big Data: A Deep Learning Approach	4	8
Deep Architecture for Traffic Flow Prediction: Deep Belief Networks With Multitask Learning	3	7
ImageNet Classification with Deep Convolutional Neural Networks	4	4
Grand Challenges in Transportation and Transit Systems	3	4
A Comparative Survey of VANET Clustering Techniques	4	3

3.2 Co-citation Analysis

Co-citation analysis was performed in addition to the content analysis, which is the frequency of articles appearing together in the reference section of another article. The top

5 leading terms determined from the content analysis were considered when performing co-citation analysis, but the WoS database was preferred due to it only using peer-reviewed articles. The articles used in the co-citation analysis were from the previously exported WoS database search result. The set of data was used to create a cluster map of the co-citation analysis as shown in Fig. 4. A minimum of 3 cited references resulted in 16 co-citations out of 5,397 cited references.

The leading cited references from the co-citation analysis showed that references were more for technical articles on AI techniques and less about the safety concerns when these techniques are implemented. Although safety is being addressed, the content analysis' leading terms in Table 2 and leading cited references in Table 3 suggest that safety is not emphasized enough and the current concern is about the AI itself.

Fig. 4. Co-citation analysis of WoS articles with a minimum of 3 cited references

Table 4. Top 13 leading authors among 1780 authors and number of co-citations and total citations

Cited author	Documents	Citations
Wang, F. Y	14	3127
Zhang, Y	11	463
Zhang, J	8	1527
Yang, L	7	339
Sun, Y	7	89
Liu, X	7	295
Wang, Y	7	932
Ning, B	5	549
Wang, X	5	172
Chowdhury, M	5	220
Das, S	5	75
Zhang, L	5	597
Zhang, S	5	252

In addition to using VOSViewer for co-citation analysis, Citespace and BibExcel were used to create a pivot chart and citation burst. The pivot chart was generated using BibExcel to summarize the leading co-authors which matches the values in Table 4 as shown in Fig. 5.

Citespace was used to perform a citation burst which detected a burst event which provided evidence that a particular publication was associated with a surge of citations.

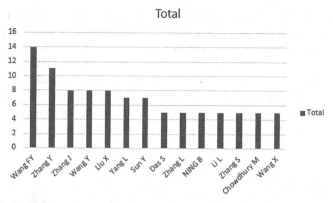

Fig. 5. Pivot chart of leading co-authors processed from WoS data with BibExcel

Figure 6 shows the citation burst results from the WoS database results. Fagnant, D.J. resulted with the strongest burst in publications between 2018 and 2020. A strong burst suggests it has also been an extraordinary degree of attention from the scientific community of its respective focus. However, Fagnant's result was not shown in Fig. 5 or Table 3 which suggests that the article received extraordinary attention from a higher system level view. Most of AI, transportation, and safety related articles resulted in more technical terms such as neural network rather than policy or barriers as shown in Table 2. The strong burst and low or non-existent co-author analysis suggest that the automation and safety aspects have not assimilated with a higher level of concern such as at a governing or economic level. This suggests that there is more potential for better regulation to further define the boundaries of ethics and safety of AI in vehicles being driven.

Top 5 References with the Strongest Citation Bursts				
References	Year	Strength	Begin	End 2018 - 2020
Fagnant DJ, 2015, TRANSPORT RES A-POL, V77, P167, DOI 10.1016/j.tra.2015.04.003, <u>DOI</u>	2015	1.62	**2018**	2018
Kingma DP, 2014, 14126980 ARXIV, V1412, P6980	2014	1.53	**2018**	2018
Bostrom N, 2014, SUPERINTELLIGENCE PA, V0, P0	2014	1.53	**2018**	2018
Ma XL, 2015, TRANSPORT RES C-EMER, V54, P187, DOI 10.1016/j.trc.2015.03.014, <u>DOI</u>	2015	1.59	**2019**	2020
Fu R, 2016, 2016 31ST YOUTH AC ...... OF AUTOMATION (YAC), V0, P324, <u>DOI</u>	2016	1.47	**2019**	2020

Fig. 6. Citation burst of WoS data using Citespace

3.3 Content Analysis with MAXQDA

The articles selected for systematic literature analysis were used to perform further content analysis with MAXQDA. The MAXQDA software allows analysis through visual means such as word clouds [9]. Word clouds are collections of words varying in size depending on the number of occurrences and can suggest what themes the articles are under.

Articles were imported into MAXQDA and a word cloud was generated. Irrelevant words such as conjunction words were removed to create a word cloud that could represent the best summary of the articles. The most occurring words were vehicle, autonomous, safety, and control as shown in Fig. 7. An interesting relationship between these terms is that for autonomous control to occur safely, the underlying governing strategies must take the risks and safety into consideration [16]. There are multiple types of governing strategies such as no-response, prevention-oriented, control-oriented, toleration-oriented, and adaption-oriented. All these strategies ultimately work to control risk at varying degrees.

Fig. 7. Word Cloud for articles in the reference section within the MAXQDA SW

4   Discussion

4.1   Automation and Robots

The Sociotechnical systems theory aims to minimize potential problems associated with automated systems and the environment such as passengers in non-automated systems and pedestrians. The most challenging aspect of automation in the case of driving is the variance control or how the system is able to control the unexpected events that can be introduced. Perfect road and traffic conditions would decrease the chances of an unexpected event but in reality, that is nearly impossible.

The article by Fagnant, Daniel J. through the Citespace citation burst supports this by suggesting that governing bodies are needed to expedite the adoption of autonomous driving systems [4]. Autonomous control introduces impacts to society such as monetary savings from lower running costs. Cutting travel time also impacts society as the traffic times experienced in large metropolitan areas are no longer relevant. These impacts create large cuts in costs to the consumers. Despite all of these cuts in cost for consumers, autonomous vehicles will still require the utmost attention to safety while offering to consumers at a reasonable price. Fagnant suggests that governments must intervene to support areas such as the underlying technology that drives autonomous systems to expedite the development and adoption rate. This is supported by the fact that communication standards and protocol between existing infrastructure and connected and autonomous vehicles have not been defined yet [11]. Other articles researched in the previous sections exposed the safety concerns, which depend on the collected data and regulation.

The article by Yisheng Lv through the VOSViewer co-citation analysis supports the push for regulation and infrastructure to increase the rate of adoption of autonomous driving systems [8]. Traffic flow prediction is dependent on accuracy and timing and plays a significant role in a successful intelligent transportation system. Current infrastructure may need to support more sensors to supply more data which results in a higher probability of accurate predictions. Regulation and infrastructure changes lead by governing bodies are required to expedite the adoption of these autonomous driving systems.

4.2 Safety and Ethics

Safety is the most significant concern with autonomous control systems for vehicles on public roads. AI aims to reduce the risks by learning from real-world data. The relationship between machines and humans together on the road via autonomous vehicles, passengers, and pedestrians is not so binary. Decisions must be made by the AI at the moment that creates the least amount of damage, but what is considered the least amount of damage by the AI? Ethics is defined as the application of morality within a context of the cultural and professional values and social norms. AI can be trained with more relevant data but it is difficult to decide a binary outcome when the environment has unexpected variables that may not have been learned previously.

There are other ways of determining ethics when deciding the risks. AI learns from the given data. Specific ethical behavioral tests commonly used by professionals can be correlated with the types of behaviors seen on the road to set more defined boundaries between what is right or wrong. However, it is significant to distinguish between what is legal and ethical. Consumers and AI algorithms have different priorities with the former prioritizing passenger lives over pedestrians. Regulations may be needed to further define what is considered legal and ethical as there is a social dilemma with autonomous systems interacting with humans.

4.3 Recent Works

Current applications of AI in transportation are making significant progress towards a fully automated infrastructure but safety is still a major concern. The project "Formal Reinforcement Learning Methods for the Design of Safety-critical Autonomous Systems" addresses the limitations of current AI-centered methods for autonomous vehicles [3]. The project addresses the safety concerns by proposing an approach that uses both formal methods for verification about the uncertainty of data-driven models. The project proposes to develop a new reinforcement learning method that could be useful in more generic applications that can satisfy safety specifications. AI only relies on the data that is used to learn from it. The priority for a good result is good data, but innovation in the underlying technical details which is the algorithm is also necessary to learn the data more efficiently and produce better results. Although safety is still a concern, the project suggests that not only is regulation necessary to define the boundaries of legal and ethical, but the AI itself must improve to produce desired results that are in line with safety regulations and the public opinions of autonomous vehicle safety.

5 Conclusion

Transportation automation with AI is one of the few trends that is receiving numerous attentions from the public and government. However, it is crucial to understand the safety aspects of AI when used in an environment that involves live passengers and pedestrians. Sociotechnical systems theory is key with AI to set more defined boundaries of what AI should be able to do. Safety is a significant factor that is currently being focused on but should increase aggressively as the risks and ethics of AI in transportation is still immature. The boundaries of what is legal and ethical is still a controversial opinion as AI and consumer opinions prioritize different things such the latter prioritizing passenger lives first. A regulation should be encouraged to help define and push the limits of ethics and morality to allow safety to be at its maximum efficiency. The regulation is also needed to advance automation by defining communication standards and infrastructure to allow unequipped vehicle drivers to interact with assisted driving behavior safely.

References

1. Bonnefon, J.F., Shariff, A., Rahwan, I.: The social dilemma of autonomous vehicles. Science **352**(6293), 1573–1576 (2016). https://doi.org/10.1126/science.aaf2654
2. Citespace. http://cluster.cis.drexel.edu/~cchen/citespace/. Accessed 18 Apr 2021
3. Jain, R., Nuzzo, P.: Formal Reinforcement Learning Methods for the Design of Safety-critical Autonomous Systems, National Science Foundation (2019). https://nsf.gov/awardsearch/showAward?AWD_ID=1839842&HistoricalAwards=false
4. Fagnant, D.J., Kockelman, K.: Preparing a nation for autonomous vehicles: opportunities, barriers and policy recommendations. Transp. Res. Part A: Policy Pract. **77**, 167–181 (2015). https://doi.org/10.1016/j.tra.2015.04.003
5. Goetsch, D.L.: Occupational Safety and Health for Technologists, Engineers, and Managers, Chap. 26, pp. 587–598. Pearson Education, London (2018)
6. Goetsch, D.L.: Occupational Safety and Health for Technologists, Engineers, and Managers, Chap. 23, pp. 526–535. Pearson Education, London (2018)
7. Harzing's Publish or Perish. https://harzing.com/resources/publish-or-perish. Accessed 18 Apr 2021
8. Lv, Y., Duan, Y., Kang, W., Li, Z., Wang, F.: Traffic flow prediction with big data: a deep learning approach. IEEE Trans. Intell. Transp. Syst. **16**, 865–873 (2014). https://doi.org/10.1109/tits.2014.2345663
9. MAXQDA. https://www.maxqda.com/. Accessed 18 Apr 2021
10. Mendeley. https://www.mendeley.com/?interaction_required=true. Accessed 18 Apr 2021
11. Papadoulis, A.: Evaluating the safety impact of connected and autonomous vehicles on motorways. Accid. Anal. Prev. **124**, 12–22 (2019). https://doi.org/10.1016/j.aap.2018.12.019
12. Preuk, K., Stemmler, E., Schießl, C., Jipp, M.: Does assisted driving behavior lead to safety-critical encounters with unequipped vehicles' drivers? Accid. Anal. Prev. **95**, 149–156 (2016). https://doi.org/10.1016/j.aap.2016.07.003
13. Schwarting, W., Alonso-Mora, J., Rus, D.: Planning and decision-making for autonomous vehicles. Annu. Rev. Control Robot. Autonom. Syst. **1**(1), 187–210 (2018). https://doi.org/10.1146/annurev-control-060117-105157

14. Singh, A.R., Singh, H., Anand, A.: Vulnerability assessment, risk, and challenges associated with automated vehicles based on artificial intelligence. In: Hura, G.S., Singh, A.K., Siong Hoe, L. (eds.) Advances in Communication and Computational Technology. LNEE, vol. 668, pp. 1323–1337. Springer, Singapore (2021). https://doi.org/10.1007/978-981-15-5341-7_100

15. Skarbek-Zabkin, A., Szczepanek, M.: Autonomous vehicles and their impact on road infrastructure and user safety. In: The 11th International Science and Technical Conference Automotive Safety, pp. 1–4 (2018). https://doi.org/10.1109/AUTOSAFE.2018.8373343

16. Taeihagh, A., Lim, H.: Governing autonomous vehicles: emerging responses for safety, liability, privacy, cybersecurity, and industry risks. Transp. Rev. **39**(1), 103–128 (2019). https://doi.org/10.1080/01441647.2018.1494640

17. Vicinitas. https://www.vicinitas.io/. Accessed 18 Apr 2021

18. VOSViewer. https://www.vosviewer.com/. Accessed 18 Apr 2021

19. Web of Science. https://apps.webofknowledge.com. Accessed 18 Apr 2021

The Influence of Cognitive Psychology on Automotive HMI Design and Evaluation

Jin Lu[1], Zaiyan Gong[1(✉)], Jun Ma[1], and Ming Sun[2]

[1] HVR Lab, Tongji University, Shanghai, China
gongzaiyan@ammi.cn
[2] Northeastern University, Shenyang, China

Abstract. The automotive HMI system has become a flourishing topic in the field of human-machine interaction and user experience. In driving scene, it's important to reduce the burden of drivers when doing interactive tasks due to the driving distraction, which belongs to the research category of cognitive psychology (CP). This study deduced four HMI design and evaluation dimensions from CP: 1. perceivability of elements, 2. comprehensibility of elements, 3. memorability of elements, 4. rationality and fluency of system feedback. In these dimensions, twelve HMI key guidelines for touch screen were defined based on CP theory and international guidelines and standards, which are about the size and contrast of icons and texts, the pattern and color of icons, the quantity and arrangement of information in the interface, and appropriate feedbacks. The results are strong references for automotive HMI design and evaluation.

Keywords: Cognitive psychology · Automotive HMI · Design and evaluation guidelines

1 Introduction

Cognition, which describes the acquisition, storage, transformation and use of knowledge, contains a large number of mental processing processes. As a related concept, cognitive psychology (CP) is usually synonymous with cognition, referring to the various mental activities mentioned above [1]. Essentially, cognitive psychology is information-processing theory: 1. how to pay attention to and select information; 2. understanding and storing information; 3. using information to make decisions and guide external behavior [2, 3]. The purpose of CP is to explain how people process information when they complete cognitive activities. Whether people are doing simple or complex tasks, they all need cognition, and the cognitive load, the used amount of working memory resources, is related to the complexity of the task.

One of the typical representations of complex tasks is human-machine interaction, which has become an important part of people's daily activities due to the development of hardware and software. For users, the interaction process with machine can be divided into three stages: perception, cogitation and reaction (see Fig. 1), which completely corresponds to the three parts in the information-processing theory [4, 5]. It proves that

© Springer Nature Switzerland AG 2021
C. Stephanidis et al. (Eds.): HCII 2021, LNCS 13097, pp. 290–304, 2021.
https://doi.org/10.1007/978-3-030-90966-6_21

the process of human-machine interaction is a typical complete cognitive process. It can be seen that cognitive psychology has a crucial guiding significance for the design and evaluation of human-machine interaction.

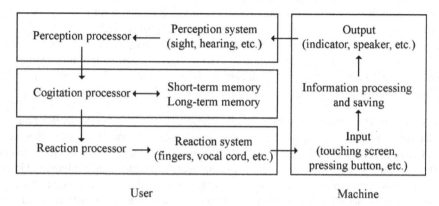

Fig. 1. Human-machine Interaction model.

In the field of human-machine interaction, automotive human-machine interface (HMI) is a flourishing topic. What's more, in-vehicle is a special scenario of interaction which puts safety first. When people do interactive tasks in driving, their attention is occupied by driving and interactive tasks at the same time. This creates a risk of driving distraction and making mistakes. Human error is not random. It results from basic human abilities and physical skills combined with the features of tools being used, the tasks assigned, and the operating environment [6]. For example, if a driver feels a bit cold while driving, he wants to reduce the air volume of the air conditioner, but he cannot quickly find the button to control the air volume among a large number of colorful buttons. When he uses more attention to find the button, if the car in front brakes suddenly, he may not be able to react and eventually cause a car accident. So automotive HMI experience designers need to consider not only aesthetics, what's more important is users' cognition. Similarly, cognitive psychology theory should be an important basis for evaluating automotive HMI.

Based on the research of CP theory and automotive HMI experience, this paper shows how CP influents automotive HMI and concludes suggestions for design and evaluation of in-vehicle HMI from the perspective of CP.

2 Theory and Method

2.1 Deducing Dimensions of CP Influencing System Design and Evaluation

The emergence of modern cognitive psychology was in 1956. The content involved attention, perception, learning, memory, language, problem solving, reasoning and thinking [7]. It's a consensus that cognition is a form of information processing in human brain [2]. Atkinson and Shiffrin proposed Atkinson-Shiffrin model about steps of memory which was popular in field of CP [8]. It was the earliest widely recognized information processing model describing short-term memory and long-term memory. Baddeley developed a working memory model to supplement the previous memory theory [9]. Although Gallistel and King thought that we need a more complex model to explain human mind, information processing theory, comparing human information processing with computer operations, is still a basic theory in CP [10]. In fact, Herbert A. Simon has made a clear explanation about this process through various of experiments: 1. how to pay attention to and select information; 2. understanding and storing information; 3. using information to make decisions and guide external behavior [3]. Several dimensions of how CP influences system design and evaluation can be deduced from this process.

How to Pay Attention to and Select Information. If we treat people as information processing systems, the inputs are called physical symbols, including what they see, what they hear, what they touch, and etc. For example, on pages of book, different letters are different symbols that can be seen by eyes. In people's daily behavior, a large number of symbols enter the sense organs at all times. Only a few of these symbols cause central nervous activity. Human brain needs the ability to filter information in order to process it, so people have the ability of controlling attention [7]. Experiments show that the effect of attention control mechanism is to limit perception of the secondary information [8]. In complex systems with many elements, making the main elements more perceptible makes it easier for users to assign attention to them, which decreases user's cognitive burden [9]. A good system should allow users to achieve their goals with the least cognitive burden. In summary, this part is about perceivability of elements.

Understanding and Storing Information. In order to recognize and understand information, people build symbol structure by finding the relationship between various symbols. What's more, to process the newly input information, it is necessary to use the stored knowledge to connect the old information with the new information [1]. People's understanding of things is essentially the understanding of relationships. For instance, when a person looks at a graph, his vision processes each part of the graph first, and then looks at the relationship between them. When an image is recognized, it is stored in short-term memory. Although short-term memory input and output are fast, the capacity is very limited [10, 11]. Therefore, strengthening the relationship between system elements can make them more understandable. Meanwhile, the number of system elements should be limited not to exceed the user's memory capacity. Making the system more understandable and memorable is also to reduce user's cognitive burden during operation. In summary, this part is about comprehensibility of elements and memorability of elements.

Using Information to Make Decisions and Guide External Behavior. The information output by the system being operated is called feedback. System feedback is not only the input of the system to users, but also the response to people's behavior, which is different from other kinds of information in the system. So that it not only applies to the cognitive principles mentioned above, but also needs to let people know the influence of his behavior at the appropriate time and in the appropriate way. As a form of communication between user and system, effective feedback needs to be successfully perceived and correctly understood within the effective time. In summary, this part is about the rationality and fluency of system feedback.

Over all, when using the principles of CP to guide the design and evaluation of a system, it can be divided into several dimensions: perceivability of elements, comprehensibility of elements, memorability of elements, rationality and fluency of system feedback.

2.2 The Intersection of Automotive HMI and CP Theory

Automotive HMI system is a branch of user experience and belongs to information technology which can be perceived from dimensions of usefulness and usability [12]. Usefulness means whether the system provides the features users need. The definition of usability is how easy and pleasant these features are to use. It includes learnability, efficiency, memorability, errors and satisfaction [13]. These two dimensions are also recognized by the latest ISO files [14]. On the emotional aspect, user experience elements are composed of symbolic value, aesthetics, and motivation [15]. By definition, CP theory mainly focuses on usability and concerns little about those emotional elements. Automotive HMI can be analyzed from three interactive modalities: touch screen, voice interaction and physical buttons. This paper will focus on the touch screen.

Interactions between a driver and a screen must be simple, non-distracting, and easily interrupted, so the driver's attention can quickly return to the road. At this interface, the most basic elements are icons and text. Icon is an effective form of displaying and interacting with information. They can reduce the complexity of the system and hence make it easier to learn by giving an immediate impression to users, especially first time, that the system is easy to use [16]. Text is a key element that determines whether users can fully understand the system. Because the meaning of graphics to individuals may not be exactly the same, while the meaning of clear text descriptions is almost the same for everyone. Then, multiple sets of texts and icons are arranged in an orderly manner to form a page. The touch screen can be evaluated from all the CP dimensions deduced above. For example, the size of icons and text should ensure that they are easy to be seen by human eyes, the icon design needs to allow users to recognize the correct meaning, icons and texts on the screen can be remembered by users in a short time, clear feedback should be given to users to eliminate anxiety and etc. More specific content will be expanded later.

Through studying CP, designers can make automotive HMI more in line with the information processing method of the human brain, thereby improving in-vehicle user experience and driving safety.

2.3 Research Method

To get the most prominent problems of using the touch screen, 24 HMI users were invited to participate in the survey and answer questionnaire. The participants consisted of 12 male and 12 female, whose ages ranged from 20 to 45 years old.

All the participants were asked to experience 6 HMI prototypes used in production vehicles at a simulation driving platform. (See Fig. 2.) They had to complete 15 basic interactive tasks such as adjusting the temperature of air conditioner, switching songs, set navigation destination and etc. on the prototypes while doing simulation driving at a stable speed. After the experience, each participant completed a satisfaction questionnaire of experience. With the results, the recorder counted some common problems as well as insights. For example, more than 50% of users cannot adjust the temperature of air conditioner successfully with one click while using System C because the button was too small. Generally, the problems are mainly related to the size and contrast of icon and text, the pattern and color of icon, the number and arrangement of icon and text, and the perception of system feedback.

Fig. 2. Simulation driving platform.

Through analyzing these problems and insights from the perspective of CP theory, combining the international guidelines and some HMI experimental results [17–23], a series of automotive HMI design guidelines and evaluation methods has been summarized in the following chapters.

3   CP-Derived HMI Design and Evaluation

3.1   Perceivability of Elements

In vehicles, users visually perceive screen content, mainly icons and texts. Perceivability of screen content means that elements on the screen need to be easily seen and recognized by users. This dimension concerns the size of icons and texts and the contrast between elements (including background).

Size of Icons and Texts. According to CP theory, it is necessary to specify the minimum size of icons and text in car HMI design. If icons are too small, users will pay more attention on the behavior of trying to see the icons when reading the information on the screen. The process of attention distribution is a serial process in the brain, rather than parallel process, which means that when users spend more attention trying to see the smaller icons, they will reduce the amount of attention allocated to driving. The icons on the dashboard of vehicle A are typical counterexamples. (See Fig. 3.) Some of their sizes are so small that users can hardly see them clearly when driving.

Fig. 3. Dashboard of vehicle A.

In this dimension, some standards of size are recommended to ensure that the elements on the screen can be quickly recognized by glance. You's experiment results show that the minimum icon size should be 9 mm and the icon size between 12 mm and 18 mm is recommended in central console interface design [20]. Icons that are much smaller than this standard are undesirable in car HMI design. Suitable text size makes users recognize text messages more easily and pay enough attention to driving. Under normal circumstances (the screen is about 0.5 m away from driver's eyes), the minimum height of the text is recommended to be 4.5 mm [18].

Contrast Between Elements (Including Background). The principles of contrast between elements also come from serial processing of the human brain, which is similar with the size impact. Furtherly, cognitive psychology experiments show that contrast difference can change the importance of elements [3]. For example, if change a few characters in a line of black words to red, the user's attention will be more distributed to the red words. This phenomenon is called Von Restorff effect [21]. In the vehicle B interface, the contrast between icon and background, icon and icon are both too low. The blue icons blend with the blue background, and it is not easy for users to identify each function since the graphs of icons blend with the background of icon. (See Fig. 4.) This design greatly increases the user's attention required to complete interactive tasks in the driving scene. In car HMI design, the contrast between the element and the background should be sufficient, and important content should have a higher contrast with other content for users to perceive.

In this dimension, sufficient color contrast ratios are suggested to use because insufficient contrast makes icons and text blend with the background. When the element is relatively small, it prefers a contrast ratio of 7:1 or higher. Also, the contrast between elements can emphasize important information [17]. The contrast ratio standard for large icons, text, and other images must be at least 4.5:1 [22]. This requirement applies to any displayed items that convey information. However, if redundant information is provided (such as an icon and text that convey the same meaning), only one element needs to meet contrast guidelines. These results comply with ISO 15008, ensuring legibility and compliance with accessibility standards [23]. Based on IDX & Tongji (2020) Baidu Apollo

Fig. 4. Vehicle B main interface.

Central Control Visual Basic Research Project, the generally optimal contrast interval is 3:1–7:1. (See Fig. 5.)

Fig. 5. Generally optimal contrast interval.

According to the above analysis, the following guidelines should be considered for car HMI design and evaluation from the perspective of CP theory:

1) Make sure the icons and texts have minimum size for users to perceive, not smaller than the results from experiments.
2) The contrast between the element and the background should be sufficient. Different sizes of elements follow the corresponding contrast standard.
3) Important content should have a higher contrast with other content for users to perceive.

3.2 Comprehensibility of Elements

Although icons can reduce the complexity of the system, the premise is that the user can correctly understand the meaning of each icon. The main reasons that affect the result of understanding are the pattern and color of icons.

Pattern. Many users expressed that it's hard to understand the patterns of widgets on the main interface of vehicle C (See Fig. 6.) because there is no consistency between them and the pattern design is too complex. Although the functions of two widgets are both about setting, the patterns are greatly different, which increases the difficulty to understand the relationship between them. Maintaining the consistency of the icon pattern is important because people's understanding of things is mainly the understanding of relationships between them, and confirming that two things have the same components is one of the ways to understanding relationships [3]. Therefore, for car HMI, consistent patterns can make people aware of the correlation between the functions of each icon more easily. In addition, the icon pattern design should keep up with mainstream cognition, such as IOS or Android style. This kind of relationship is also one of the ways to reduce the user's learning and memory costs. (See Fig. 7.)

Fig. 6. Vehicle C main interface.

Fig. 7. Apple Carplay interface.

However, people are always working on discovering the regularity of the world around them. In the experiment, the experts clearly told the subjects that the stimulation was random and irregular, but they still wanted to find a certain regularity [3]. It can be concluded that in HMI design, not all icons with similar functions need to be consistent. For example, the consistency of icons for similar functions of the driving module and the entertainment module will give users the hint that two different modules have the same priority while they should be distinguished.

Color. In CP theory, color is another impact showing the relationship between elements. Generally, not all content on an interface is endowed with interactive features. In UX design, using different brightness is a common way to distinguish interactivity. (See Fig. 8.) The mainstream cognition that users have developed is: when there are elements with obvious different brightness on the interface, the elements with high brightness are interactive, and the elements with low brightness are not interactive. For car HMI design, the most important role of color is also to distinguish interactivity, which allowing users to understand the interactivity of elements at a glance, improving the success rate of the first interaction and reducing unnecessary driving distraction due to false tapping.

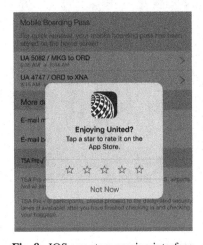

Fig. 8. IOS app store scoring interface.

According to the above analysis, the following guidelines should be considered for car HMI design and evaluation from the perspective of CP theory:

1) Maintain the consistency of the patterns of similar function icons in the same module, avoid the consistency of icons in different modules.
2) Icon pattern design is better to keep up with mainstream cognition, such as current IOS or Android style. Intricate patterns that users haven't seen aren't suitable for car HMI.
3) Use different patterns or colors to help users understand the interactivity of elements at a glance.

3.3 Memorability of Elements

In the driving scene, users cannot keep looking at the screen for a long time to operate the vehicle system. They need to remember the content for a short time after glancing at the screen. The difficulty for users to remember the elements on the screen is mainly depends on the number and arrangement of the elements.

Number of Elements. The driving scene is one of the scenes where users mainly use short-term memory in CP theory. In the related theories of short-term memory, the unit of memory is called chunks. Whether it is visual information or auditory information, chunks remain in short-term memory for less than 1 s. Short-term memory output and input are relatively fast, and the capacity is very limited, usually about 6 chunks [1]. The function of short-term memory is to keep the information needed in the work. In car HMI design, characteristic of short-term memory is an important basis for designing the text length and number of icons or widgets. Therefore, design principles about the number of elements are emphasized. Take vehicle D function interface for example (See Fig. 9.), each icon with the explanatory text can be seen as a chunk. 12 chunks have far exceeded the capacity of short-term memory. User can't remember all the chunks at one glance so that they have to review the screen multiple times to choose and tap the icon they want while driving, which increasing driving distraction and decreasing driving safety. In general, the number of widgets or main function icons on the interface should be around 6, arranging from 4–8, within the short-time memory capability of ordinary users.

Fig. 9. Vehicle D function interface.

About limiting text length: Text items using the Roman alphabet must not exceed 120 characters, including punctuation and spaces [19]. (Note for reference: The preceding sentence is 101 characters.) Text items in Japanese must not exceed a total of 31 Roman characters, kana, or kanji combined. The aim of the limitation is for drivers to understand tasks or system states by glancing at the screen. The ideal time is within 2 s. As to Chinese characters, on the recommended interface template, line length of the task transmission text is 7–9 words, within 13 words [18]. (See Fig. 10.)

Arrangement of Elements. The principles of the arrangement are all from a concept in CP theory, which is "sequential pattern" [3]. In short, it's easier for users to remember ordered elements because of the obvious relationship. In general perception, people's

Fig. 10. Recommended interface template.

reading order is from left to right, top to bottom. In car HMI design, using the arrangement that meets user's reading habits will expose the relationship of elements to users so that people can understand a chunk through the help of understanding the relationship between it and the previous chunk or the next chunk. In the vehicle E main interface (See Fig. 11.), icons are arranged in a geometric manner in order to create a unique style. However, in the actual driving scene, few users thought this arrangement was easy to read. They had to spend more time to find a specific icon in this interface than in others. This is a situation that does not conform to CP theory, which needs to be avoided.

Fig. 11. Vehicle E main interface.

Orderly layout of information can avoid trouble to the driver due to layout changes in different driving scenarios, which helps the driver reduce memory costs through position association [18]. The widget layout information density is recommended 3*2, and can be adjusted between 4*1–4 *2. What's more, two commonly used reading modes, Z pattern and F pattern are recommended for typesetting. (See Fig. 12.)

According to the above analysis, the following guidelines should be considered for car HMI design and evaluation from the perspective of CP theory:

1) The number of widgets or main function icons on the interface should be around 6, within the short-time memory capability of ordinary users.
2) The line length of the task transmission text should be as short as possible, appropriately around 7–9 words (Chinese).

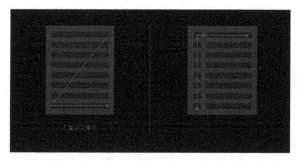

Fig. 12. Recommended typesetting template.

3) The arrangement of interface content should be in line with people's general perception, which is Z pattern or F pattern. Avoid irregular alignments.

3.4 Perceivability and Fluency of System Feedback

Feedback of a system is mainly composed of visual feedback, auditory feedback and tactile feedback. Through appropriate feedbacks, users can know the results of operation directly without double checking which costs more time and attention. The "appropriate feedback" depends on the rationality and fluency.

Rationality of Feedback. Although successful feedback is essential in driving scenarios, this topic is rarely mentioned by international standards or design principles. Only Baidu has a standard for status color [18]. In combination with the relevant GB 4094 signal color regulations, the status color definition needs to be combined with relevant laws and regulations and users' habitual thinking. For instance, the successful color system is mainly the green color torch, and the warning color system is mainly the red color torch with dangerous information. (See Fig. 13.)

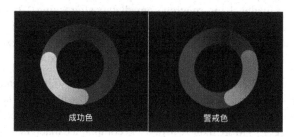

Fig. 13. Suggested status color range. (Successful color left, warning color right)

From the perspective of CP theory, the function of feedback is to convey information to the human brain: one interaction process has been completed, and the result is success (or failure). Thus, users can process the information obtained from the feedback and start the next interactive operation. The whole process is like Human-machine Inter-action model. (See Fig. 1.) It can be seen that with appropriate feedback, users don't need to allocate more attention to proactively confirming the operation result to get the information guiding the next operation.

In a feedback process, the status color change is essentially the contrast change, which is visual. But in some scenarios, such as complex road conditions, it's inconvenient for users to look at the screen, so the visual feedback information may not be conveyed to them. Therefore, auditory and tactile feedback are as important as visual feedback in car HMI. Multi-modal feedback is the most appropriate and can ensure that users can get effective information in all scenarios. What's more, similar with the principles in Sect. 3.1, sufficient contrast, volume & tone and vibration level are important for users to perceive the feedbacks. Otherwise, users can hardly perceive feedbacks, even if they exist, like the tapping feedback of vehicle F, which has too little change in contrast. (See Fig. 14).

Fig. 14. Tapping feedback of vehicle F

Fluency of Feedback. Due to the characteristics of human brain serial-processing, human brain does one thing in 0.25 s [3]. If system responds within 0.25 s, the user's brain can receive and process feedback information immediately after taking 0.25 s to command to complete an interactive task. Since user behavior is often determined by system feedback, it's better to make sure that system response times after user input (for example, the time between a tap and the resulting ripple animation) do not exceed 0.25 s.

Fluency is not only reflected in the reaction time, but also in the animation effects, especially for gesture interaction. When users swiped left with a three-finger gesture on the vehicle G screen to switch pages, the new page would appear directly without any animation. (See Fig. 15.) More than 70% of users complained that it makes them feel that the system is stuck. The main reason is about user's cognitive expectations [24]. When users did on-screen gesture control in automotive HMI systems, they would expect the animation effects which were similar to smart phone systems that had been well designed in terms of gesture interaction. What's more, survey results show that animation meeting users' cognitive expectations helps them memorize complex interactions.

According to the above analysis, the following guidelines should be considered for car HMI design and evaluation from the perspective of CP theory:

Fig. 15. Three-finger gesture interaction in vehicle G.

1. All user operations require feedbacks, preferably containing visual, auditory and tactile, with sufficient contrast, volume & tone and vibration level.
2. Make sure that system response times after user input do not exceed 0.25 s.
3. The visual effects need to correspond to the operation method, such as sliding-the screen follows the movement of the finger, which meets users' cognitive expectations.

4   Conclusions and Discussions

This study explains the relationship between cognitive psychology and automotive HMI in detail and defines twelve guidelines for automotive HMI design and evaluation based on the CP theory and internationally recognized standards. Four dimensions were deduced, which are perceivability of elements, comprehensibility of elements, memorability of elements, rationality and fluency of system feedback. One of the implications is to provide a reliable basis for evaluating HMI, which has not been systematically summarized. In addition, with strong theoretical basis, designers can make automotive HMI more in line with the information processing method of the human brain, thereby improving in-vehicle user experience and driving safety.

The results and implications from this study have to be viewed under consideration of the limitations. With the current twelve guidelines, HMI designers can avoid most errors about cognition when designing systems but can hardly make systems reach very high level, which needs more targeted experiments and tests with larger sample size to get more specific results for design practice. What's more, in the future work, voice interaction and physical buttons also need to be discussed to complete the study of the impacts of cognitive psychology on automotive HMI.

References

1. Matlin, M.W.: Cognitive Psychology. Wiley, New York (2014)
2. Piccinini, G., Scarantino, A.: Information processing, computation, and cognition. J. Biol. Phys. **37**(1), 1–38 (2011). https://doi.org/10.1007/s10867-010-9195-3
3. Simon, H.A.: Information processing models of cognition. Ann. Rev. Psychol. **30**(1), 363–396 (1979)

4. Parasuraman, R., Sheridan, T.B., Wickens, C.D.: A model for types and levels of human interaction with automation. IEEE Trans. Syst. Man Cybern. - Part A: Syst. Hum. **30**(3), 286–297 (2000). https://doi.org/10.1109/3468.844354

5. Johannsen, G.: Human-machine interaction. Control Syst. Robot. Autom. **21**, 132–162 (2009)

6. Leveson, N.: Engineering a Safer and More Secure World, vol. 273. MIT, Cambridge (2011)

7. Eysenck, M.W., Keane, M.T.: Cognitive Psychology: A Student's Handbook. Taylor & Francis, New York (2005)

8. Treisman, A.M., Riley, J.G.: Is selective attention selective perception or selective response? A further test. J. Exp. Psychol. **79**(1p1), 27 (1969)

9. Ratey, J.J.: A user's guide to the brain: perception, attention, and the four theatres of the brain. Vintage, pp. 114–115 (2001)

10. Baddeley, A.D., Hitch, G.J., Allen, R.J.: Working memory and binding in sentence recall. J. Mem. Lang. **61**(3), 438–456 (2009)

11. Gallistel, C.R., King, A.P.: Memory and the Computational Brain: Why Cognitive Science Will Transform Neuroscience, vol. 6. Wiley, New York (2011)

12. Davis, F.D.: Perceived usefulness, perceived ease of use, and user acceptance of information technology. MIS Q. **13**(3), 319–340 (1989)

13. Nielsen, J.: Usability 101: Introduction to Usability. Nielsen Norman Group (2012). https://www.nngroup.com/articles/usability-101-introduction-to-usability/. Accessed 4 Jan 2016

14. ISO 9241-210:2019: Ergonomics of human-system interaction—Part 210: human-centred design for interactive systems (2019)

15. Thüring, M., Mahlke, S.: Usability, aesthetics and emotions in human–technology interaction. Int. J. Psychol. **42**(4), 253–264 (2007)

16. Rogers, Y.: Icons at the interface: their usefulness. Interact. Comput. **1**(1), 105–117 (1989). https://doi.org/10.1016/0953-5438(89)90010-6

17. Human Interface Guidelines, Apple Developer. https://developer.apple.com/design/human-interface-guidelines/carplay/overview/introduction/

18. Design Principles, Baidu in-vehicle ecological open platform. http://chelianwang.baidu.com/homepage/openPlateform/design.html

19. Design for Driving, Google Developers. https://developers.google.com/cars/design

20. You, F., et al.: Icon design recommendations for central consoles of intelligent vehicles. In: Ahram, T., Taiar, R., Gremeaux-Bader, V., Aminian, K. (eds.) Human Interaction, Emerging Technologies and Future Applications II, vol. 1152, pp. 285–291. Springer, Cham (2020). https://doi.org/10.1007/978-3-030-44267-5_43

21. Kuhbandner, C., Pekrun, R.: Joint effects of emotion and color on memory. Emotion **13**(3), 375 (2013)

22. Web Content Accessibility Guidelines (WCAG) 2.0 (2008). https://www.w3.org/TR/WCAG20/

23. ISO 15008: Road vehicles — Ergonomic aspects of transport information and control systems — Specifications and test procedures for in-vehicle visual presentation (2017)

24. Kowler, E.: Cognitive expectations, not habits, control anticipatory smooth oculomotor pursuit. Vis. Res. **29**(9), 1049–1057 (1989)

Investigating the Relationship Between a Driver's Psychological Feelings and Biosensor Data

Sara Mostowfi[1], Jung Hyup Kim[2][(✉)], and William G. Buttlar[3]

[1] Department of Architectural Studies, University of Missouri, Columbia, USA
sara.mostowfi@mail.missouri.edu
[2] Department of Industrial and Manufacturing Systems Engineering, University of Missouri, Columbia, USA
kijung@missouri.edu
[3] Department of Civil and Environmental Engineering, University of Missouri, Columbia, USA
buttlarw@missouri.edu

Abstract. Recent studies show that emotional changes can influence driving behavior. For example, positive valence could enable better takeover performance in regaining vehicle control. On the other hand, a state of anger has been shown to degrade driver situational awareness and performance compared to a neutral state. These emotional states may result from different factors like a vehicle's internal or external environment. The roadside environment is one of the external factors which might influence driver behavior and performance. Hence, it is necessary to understand how emotional conditions affect driving actions to design safer road environments. However, research involving the use of emotions can be challenging due to methodological issues associated with measuring emotions. Different methods can be used to measure emotion both subjectively and objectively. These could include the use of reliable sources for assessing evoked emotions, since subjective emotional experiences are the essence of a feeling. An objective manifestation of emotion can be captured as a representation of our inner experience. Also, the objective manifestation of emotion is the representation of our inner experience. In this study, we conducted an eye-integrated human-in- the- loop (HTIL) simulation experiment to analyze the driver's emotional state by comparing both subjective and objective data to find the relation between drivers' physiologic feelings (i.e., Kansei Engineering method) and biosensor data (i.e., facial expression and eye movement).

Keywords: Kansei engineering · Emotion · Facial expression · Eye tracking · Driving simulation

1 Introduction

Driving behavior depends on the complex relationship between various factors, and one of them is driver emotions. Different factors such as road climate, scenery, weather,

© Springer Nature Switzerland AG 2021
C. Stephanidis et al. (Eds.): HCII 2021, LNCS 13097, pp. 305–321, 2021.
https://doi.org/10.1007/978-3-030-90966-6_22

traffic density, driver attitudes, and psychological states might influence a driver's performance and behavior. An individual's mental, cognitive, and attention states are examples of internal factors that can be assessed. Traffic congestion, roads, weather, and other environmental conditions, including in-cabin ambient conditions (i.e., noise, temperature, glare, lighting, and music being played), are considered external factors [1]. Among these factors, the impacts of external environmental conditions such as road geometry and architecture on the driver's actions received a lot of attention in the literature [2, 3].

Emotional biosensing is becoming a widely used tool to assess how people feel about a given task and object [4, 5]. For instance, biosensors that can detect various signals from the human body are gaining popularity, such as capturing what a person is thinking and feeling [5]. However, previous HCI research studies have shown that biosensor data are heavily influenced by social context [5]. It is critical to define the appropriate meaning of driver behavior, performance, and decision-making corresponding to the external objects and events in the transportation context. Hence, driving simulation is vital for investigating the relationship between various driving environments and drivers' emotional states. Furthermore, a driving simulator allows for collecting data modalities that may not be practically or safely obtained in a real-world setting, such as brain activity signals [1]. One of the limitations associated with driving simulation is that a driver's behavior and the cognitive resource they devote to driving might be different from real driving. For instance, in a simulation, a driver inherently knows that a critical driving error will not lead to a severe consequence [6]. Recent research on affective computing applications and emotion sciences in driving shows that we cannot only depend on facial features to detect a person's emotional states [7]. For example, Tavakoli, Boukhechba, & Heydarian [1] demonstrate the limitations of video features on inferring a driver's condition, which can be compensated via a combination of both audio and video to characterize and quantify factors such as driver frustration. Since our anger does not always show up in our facial expressions, using various biosensing data to detect human psychological feelings was founds to be more accurate. For that reason, affective computing researchers typically deal with this problem by creating algorithms that map internal emotional states to objective, measurable signals like heart rate, skin conductivity, pupil dilation, and video and audio inputs [8].

In Calvo & D'Mello [9], two methods were implemented for emotion recognition since emotion is a complex phenomenon related to various nonverbal cues; for instance, it is hard to build an emotion recognition model based on just one modality. Integrating other modalities into a model process can result in a more robust emotion recognition model than existing unimodal [9]. In addition, gathering valid data through subjective evaluation and visually comparing design alternatives has been shown to be an effective approach. It is generally agreed that the driving environment requires both subjective and objective assessment. Subjective information typically comes from a driver self-report, including interviews and written questionnaires. The most objective information usually comes from sensor data. The combination of subjective and objective data provides the most robust situational assessment under complex driving scenarios [10]. Subjective reporting via questionnaires and interviews is generalizable, practical, and easy to analyze statistically. However, questionnaires and surveys have the disadvantage of not permitting more complicated trends to be discovered. Also, the novelty of the simulation environment to the participants can skew the participant's reaction to new environments [11]. Although behavioral tests are based on driver perceptions, the visual properties of the road are often checked directly using a questionnaire. This is because a driver's subjective opinion is closely linked to driver actions [8].To gain a general overview of driver emotion, an investigation of the role of internal and external activities is conducted, including how changes in the environment can affect driver states and behaviors. Therefore, in this study, we compare driver physiologic feelings (i.e., Kansei Engineering method) and biosensor data (i.e., facial expression and eye movement) to determine a relation between driver emotional state and physiological signals.

2   Method

2.1   Participants

Twenty-five students from the University of Missouri with normal eyesight (18–30 years in age) (Mean: 24.640, and SD: 4.663) participated in the experiment. Consent was obtained from participants before starting the experiment.

2.2   Testing Apparatus

Driving Simulator. The experiment was conducted in the ergonomics lab located in the industrial engineering department (University of Missouri-Columbia) under controlled illumination. The eye movements and facial expressions were recorded using a screen-based eye tracker (EyeTech VT3 Mini), iMotion platform on a standard PC (Asus) fitted with Logitech G920 steering wheel, brake, and gas pedal. The OpenDS driving simulation software was used to run the driving simulation (see Fig. 1) [12].

Fig. 1. The experimental setup

Eye Tracking Device. Numerous eye-tracking studies for emotion detection, such as the work done by Lu, Zheng, Li, & Lu, [13], revealed that eye movement signals detected various emotional states. However, some limitations are associated with using eye-tracking in research, such as the pupil color difference between East Asian participants and Western Caucasian participants [14]. Besides, many studies have shown that the speed for reliable emotion recognition in eye tracking is lower than both computational and human experimental investigations [15]. In addition, video-based eye trackers do not give actual physical pupil diameter; instead, relative change measures can be used as pupil dilation [16]. The eye movements were collected through a screen-based eye tracker (EyeTech VT3 Mini), with a sample rate of 60 HZ. Table 1 shows the eye movement metrics which were used to compare physiological feelings.

Table 1. Eye movement metrics [17]

Metric	Detailed description	Unit
Interpolated distance	Estimated distance between the eye-tracker and the eyes, with missing values, interpolated. Average of the eye tracker's distance to the left and right eye. Linear interpolation from the last sample before the gap until the first sample after the gap	Millimeters (mm)
Gaze velocity	Angular velocity of the gaze at the current sample point, i.e. how fast the eyes are moving at this point in time. Computation is based on a time window around the current sample. Distance between the first and last sample of this window is divided by the time lapse between them	Degrees per second (°/s)
Gaze acceleration	Angular acceleration of the gaze at the current sample point, i.e. how much the eyes increased in speed at the current sample. Computed as the difference in velocity between the current and previous sample	Degrees per second squared ($°/s^2$)

(continued)

Table 1. (*continued*)

Metric	Detailed description	Unit
Fixation index	Fixation number, counting from start of the recording	
Fixation duration	Duration of the fixation, calculated as the time difference between fixation's start and end times	Milliseconds (ms)
Saccade index	Saccade number, counting from start of the recording	
Saccade duration	Duration of the saccade, calculated as the time difference between saccade's start and end times	Milliseconds (ms)
Saccade amplitude	Amplitude of the saccade, i.e. angular distance that the eyes travelled from start point to end point	Degrees (°)
Saccade peak velocity	Peak velocity of the saccade, i.e. the maximal speed of the eyes during this saccade	Degrees per second (°/s)
Saccade peak acceleration	Peak acceleration of the saccade, i.e. the maximal increase in speed of the eyes during this saccade	Degrees per second squared ($°/s^2$)
Saccade direction	Direction of the saccade from its start point to end point, indicated as clockwise angles: 0 degrees mean a horizontal saccade from left to right, 90 degrees a vertical saccade from top to bottom	Degrees (°)

Facial Expression Recognition. The facial expressions were detected via Affectiva AFFDEX software, which detects action units derived from facial muscles and correlates them with basic emotions, such are sad, joyful, disdain, anger, fear, surprise, and disgust [18]. Test subject facial movements were recorded during driving simulations for the two study scenarios investigated. Thus, facial recognition was utilized to evaluate and analyze the test subject emotional reactions to the provided stimulus. While an experimental participant watches a stimulus on the computer screen, the software records a number of key raw indicators every frame based on biometric measures or action units, including 34 key facial landmarks (e.g., jaw, brows, nose, and others), interocular distance, and head position (yaw, pitch, and roll). A Logitech HD recording camera was mounted on top of the screen. The facial micro-expression detection mask on iMotions was then tuned to guarantee that it captured the entire face of the subjects. Participants had no information regarding the location beforehand [17, 19]. In addition to these channels, Affectiva AFFDEX export reports the (x, y) coordinates of the 34 facial landmarks measured.

Multi dimensionnel Mood Questionnaire (MDMQ). Two different questionnaires and interviews were used before and after each scenario run to capture the participants' subjective feelings, including Kansei measurement and MDMQ questionnaires. All participants were asked to fill out the MDMQ questionnaire before driving each scenario. The 12-item MDMQ was applied to assess the participant's mood on three

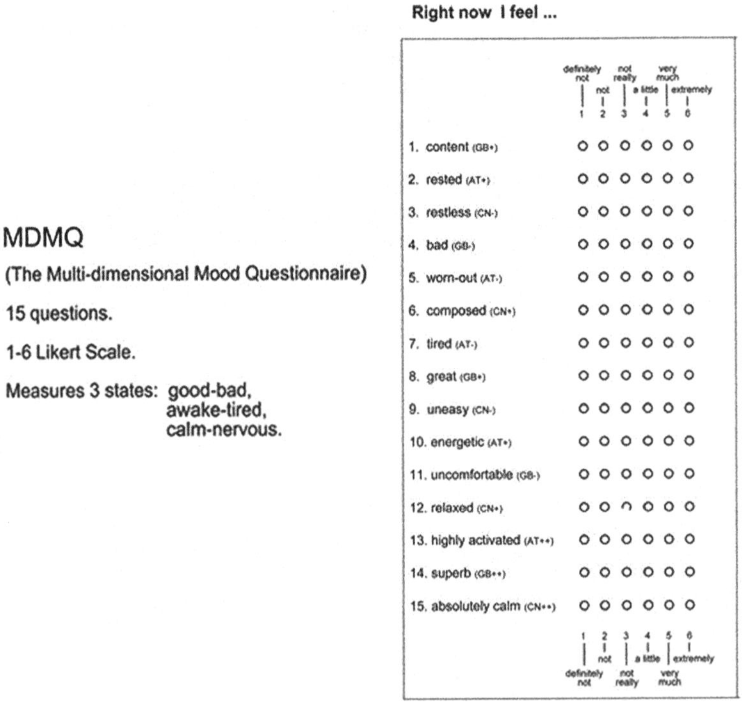

Fig. 2. Multi-dimensional mood questionnaire

dimensions ranging from good to bad (GB), awake to tired (AT), and calm to nervous (CN) [20]. The MDMQ is a self-reported tool to assess the participant's mood before starting the experiment. This method considers the individual's current mental state and is not bound to a specific object or situation [21]. (see Fig. 2). Even though we collected participants' data with this method, we did not discuss the outcomes of MDMQ in this study.

Kansei Measurements. Kansei Engineering (KE) is mainly used in product development contexts to translate human affective understanding into design features [22]. As far as we know, little work has implemented eye-tracking technology with KE methodology to analyze drivers' emotions in different road scenarios. In addition, there are various methods for extracting user subjective feelings. Among them, KE was selected due to three reasons. First, KE is a methodology for translating human psychology, such as feelings and emotions, into appropriate design features (i.e., shape, size, and other engineering characteristics). Second, KE makes possible the relation between different feelings and design characteristics [23]. Third, the subjective estimation of the concept properties is possible, which helps users express their feelings on the designs even though they are not aware [24]. In other words, the goal in Kansei is finding quantitative relationships between subjective responses and design features [25].

The method of capturing a participant's emotions or internal sensation is referred to as Kansei measurement. Physiological and psychological measurements are used in Kansei evaluations. Physiological tests are designed to capture users' behavior and reactions to a testing environment. Psychological measurement, on the other hand, is concerned with the emotional and mental states of people. In this study, two sample scenarios were selected. One is a driving environment on a highway with road signs, trees, and traffic lights (see Fig. 3. (a)). Another one is driving in the downtown urban area, including buildings, usual traffics, and advertisements (see Fig. 3. (b)).

(a) Motorway Scenario   (b) Village Scenario

Fig. 3. Driving scenarios

The Kansei questionnaire is developed on a 5-point SD scale. In Kansei, the measurement process is challenging since Kansei is the state of individuals' internal emotions. Words that describe emotional expression are mainly used in subjective evaluation to measure individuals' feelings. The semantic differential method is a popular scaling method for the quantification of personal emotions. It can be used in many forms like a 5–7-point scale; in this study, we will employ a five-point semantic differential because its more easily understood by respondents. Figure 4 shows the sample of Kansei questionnaire developed based on a 5-points semantic differential scale.

Fig. 4. Kansei engineering questionnaire

2.3 Experiment Procedure and Design

The study was conducted in three phases. Each scenario lasted about 6–8 min in the simulator (see Fig. 5). In both scenarios (Motorway and Village), the realistic traffic conditions that resemble the everyday traffic are included to extract the natural driving behavior of participants.

Training Session. Before the experiment day, an email including a PowerPoint file about the driving simulation process was sent out to every participant. In the training PowerPoint, data collection methods (Questionnaires, eye & facial recognition platform), the experiment set up, the process of eye-tracking calibration, driving scenarios, and how the participant should interact with the driving simulator were explained via image and text. The goal of this step was to make participants familiar with included devices and questionnaires in the experiment.

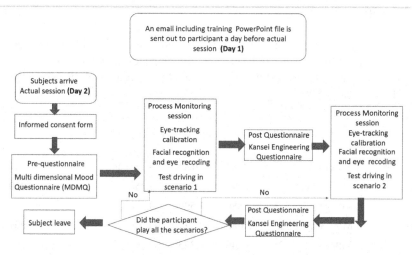

Fig. 5. Overall experiment protocol

Actual Experiment Session. The actual session was held in the ergonomics lab (industrial engineering at the University of Missouri). First, the participant filled out the MDMQ questionnaire. Then, participants sat on a chair with fixed legs behind a table with a PC screen fitted with a Logitech G920 steering wheel, brake, and gas pedal. The distance between the eye and the screen is about 50–60 cm. After the eye-tracking 9-point calibration, each participant had 3–5 min to adapt to the eye tracker. During this procedure, the experimenter instructed the participant concerning the head position and point of gaze. When the eye tracker calibration was completed, then participants were allowed to ask questions about any aspects. After a short break, the actual experiment started by driving one of the scenarios. During the test drive, participants could drive a car as usual in any direction and follow the traffic signs (which instructed them to change driving lanes). After they executed the first driving scenario, the participants completed the Kansei questionnaire. Then, another scenario was executed. Like the previous one, each participant was required to fill out a questionnaire right after the driving scenario. After all the scenarios and questionnaires were done, the experiment is over. The estimated duration for this section is about 30 mins per person upon arrival.

3 Results

Driver emotion differences between the two scenarios (motorway and village) were analyzed. For Kansei Engineering (KE) metrics, significant differences were found among the following adjectives 'Stressful', 'Tired', and 'Noisy', 'Sedative', 'Rough', 'Boring', and 'Modern'. (see Table 2).

Table 2. Statistical results for KE outcomes

KE metric	Scenario	N	Mean	StDev	SE Mean	T-Value	P-Value
Stressful	Motorway	25	3.880	1.296	0.254	2.81	**0.010**
	Village	25	2.880	1.590	0.318		
Tired	Motorway	25	2.680	1.249	0.250	−2.85	**0.009**
	Village	25	3.440	1.325	0.265		
Noisy	Motorway	25	4	1.080	0.216	2.97	**0.007**
	Village	25	3	1.323	0.265		
Sedative	Motorway	25	2.240	1.300	0.260	3.93	**0.001**
	Village	25	3.440	1.121	0.224		
Rough	Motorway	25	3.600	1.225	0.245	−2.10	0.046
	Village	25	2.960	1.428	0.286		
Friendly	Motorway	25	3.120	1.166	0.233	−1.19	0.246
	Village	25	2.800	1.155	0.231		
Emotional	Motorway	25	3.640	1.075	0.215	−0.39	0.700
	Village	25	3.520	1.194	0.239		
Nostalgic	Motorway	25	3.360	1.411	0.282	−0.41	0.683
	Village	25	3.240	1.268	0.254		
Boring	Motorway	25	2.560	1.417	0.283	3.57	**0.002**
	Village	25	3.840	1.281	0.256		
Modern	Motorway	25	2.880	1.166	0.233	3.87	**0.001**
	Village	25	3.800	1.080	0.216		
Beautiful	Motorway	25	3.120	1.236	0.255	−0.70	0.491
	Village	25	2.960	1.274	0.247		
Attractive	Motorway	25	3.200	1.155	0.231	−1.56	0.131
	Village	25	2.840	1.344	0.269		

In terms of facial expression outcomes (see Table 2), Anger and Sadness showed significant differences in response to the two external scenarios presented to the study participants. (see Table 3).

Table 3. Statistical results for facial expressions analysis

Facial expression	Scenario	N	Mean	StDev	SE Mean	T-Value	P-Value
Joy	Motorway	25	5.76	9.80	1.96	−0.07	0.943
	Village	25	5.92	10.39	2.08		
Surprise	Motorway	25	0.741	0.647	0.129	−1.26	0.220
	Village	25	1.566	3.221	0.644		
Disgust	Motorway	25	0.5423	0.4183	0.0428	−0.37	0.718
	Village	25	0.5071	0.2139	0.0428		
Fear	Motorway	25	5.76	9.80	1.96	−0.07	0.943
	Village	25	5.92	10.39	2.08		
Contempt	Motorway	25	0.741	0.647	0.129	−1.26	0.220
	Village	25	1.566	3.221	0.644		
Anger	Motorway	25	0.2510	0.4830	0.0966	2.42	**0.02**
	Village	25	0.1098	0.2252	0.0450		
Sadness	Motorway	25	0.155	0.336	0.067	2.32	**0.029**
	Village	25	0.720	1.396	0.279		

The eye movement data revealed significant differences in saccade amplitude between two scenarios (motorway: M − 12.61, SD − 11.90; village: M − 10.03, SD − 11.98; p-value = 0.041).

Furthermore, according to the Pearson correlation, a negative correlation exists between Modern − Saccade Amplitude and Noisy − Sadness in the motorway scenario. This implies that every positive change in the unit of saccade amplitude is related to decreased modern variable experience. The increment of sadness facial expression is related to a lower noisy feeling (see Table 4). However, there is no significant correlation among variables in the village scenario (see Table 5).

Table 4. Correlation coefficients between significant Kansei words and evoked emotions in motorway scenario

	Anger	Sadness	Saccade amplitude
Stressful	−.292 0.156	−0.067 0.749	−0.098 0.641
Noisy	−0.384 0.088	**−0.592 0.002**	−0.176 0.401
Tired	0.098 0.642	0.158 0.452	−0.329 0.108

(continued)

Table 4. (*continued*)

	Anger	Sadness	Saccade amplitude
Sedative	−0.021 0.919	0.095 0.653	−0.121 0.564
Boring	0.156 0.457	0.133 0.528	−0.192 0.358
Modern	0.385 0.057	0.218 0.296	**−0.413** **0.040**

Table 5. Correlation coefficients between significant Kansei words and evoked emotions in village scenario

	Anger	Sadness	Saccade amplitude
Stressful	−0.028 0.872	0.105 0.619	−0.158 0.451
Noisy	−0.171 0.415	−0.031 0.885	0.049 0.818
Tired	0.153 0.464	0.200 0.338	−0.119 0.570
Sedative	0.067 0.751	−0.218 0.295	−0.153 0.465
Boring	0.162 0.438	0.174 0.407	0.142 0.497
Modern	0.025 0.906	−0.057 0.788	0.045 0.831

4   Discussion

This study aims to find a relationship between driver's subjective emotions and biosensor data (i.e., facial expressions and eye movement). The results indicated that some KE metrics: Stressful, Tired, Noisy, Sedative, Boring, and Modern are significantly different in both scenarios. According to the results, the participants felt that the motorway scenario was more stressful and noisier than the village scenario. The participants needed to drive a closed-loop road twice in the motorway scenario (see Fig .6). Dummy vehicles were also presented on the road to increase the sense of driving on a highway for participants. As a result, high speed and traffic density can be responsible for both stressful and noisy feelings in the participants [26].

On the other hand, in the village scenario, the participants felt that this scenario was more sedative, tired, boring, and modern than the motorway scenario. The road design elements in this scenario could explain this outcome. For example, pedestrians' presence might make the participants drive slowly in crowded areas. Also, tight streets

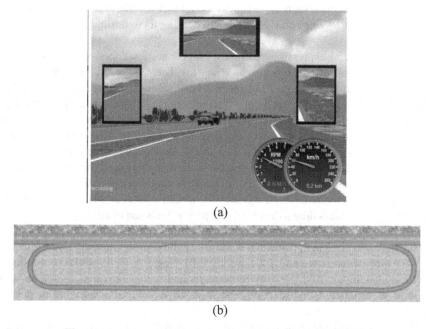

(a)

(b)

Fig. 6. Motorway scenario design (a) and (b) adopted from [26]

with buildings on both sides and lots of traffic lights make the participants careful. Those things may contribute different emotions to the participants when they drove in the village scenario (Fig. 7).

Fig. 7. Village scenario design

The evoked emotions such as 'tiredness' could increase the risk of car accidents by falling asleep while driving and slowing down or losing focus during emergency braking action.

In terms of facial expression outcomes, 'anger' and 'Sadness' showed significant differences in response to the two driving scenarios. There are several reasons associated with this. The emotions of anger and sadness have similar facial features [27]. This is supported by analyses of averaged upper and lower face halves, which show that upper facial features are most often used to distinguish sad, afraid, and angry faces. In contrast, lower facial traits are used to indicate happiness and disgust [28]. To understand emotions like sad and angry from face, the eye is also an essential facial feature used to determine such feelings. Eyebrows can convey diverse emotional cues (and they may be crucial for facial identification as the eyes). For example, in both sadness and angry emotions, eyebrows are knitted and lowered together. the mouth's features that convey angry and sad feelings are corners drawn down when a person feels sad or angry [29].

Furthermore, sadness emotion often presents when a driver's degree of attentiveness is likely to be too low. On the other hand, the anger emotion significantly impacts driving behavior such as road rage and drive swiftly [30]. Negative feelings like depression or anger can also impair driving ability Since anger and sorrow are often accompanied by passivity or resignation, and reaction time-insensitive circumstances could be delayed [31].

The facial expression results can also be explained in terms of external stimuli (roadside design). There are different visual elements such as (buildings, road signs, trees, person) on the roadside in the village scenario. However, in the motorway scenario, there is no visual element on the roadside. There is only one row of vegetation in the middle of the motorway. The only thing they should be careful of while driving is the presence of other cars. On the contrary, drivers need to react to various objects, such as other vehicles and pedestrians in the village scenario. These objects could increase their cognitive demands while reducing their attention. Furthermore, among different evoked emotions, anger and aggression are emotional states that significantly impact driving behavior and increase the likelihood of an accident [31]. Hence, the patterns, which recognize driver sadness or anger as emotional states, will find ways to increase driving pleasure and safety.

For the eye movement data result, saccade amplitude (i.e., the angular distance that the eyes traveled from start point to endpoint) yielded a significant difference between both scenarios. The participant's saccade amplitude was higher when they drove the motorway scenario. The average saccade amplitude represents the range of fixation from the beginning to the end, usually with a visual angle. This amplitude could be affected by secondary tasks, called driver distraction. It is described as diverting attention away from the primary driving task caused by the activity occurring inside or outside the car [32]. However, there was no secondary task given to the participants during the experiment. Hence, it is required for further investigation.

The current study also discovers two negative correlations (modern emotion & saccade amplitude, noisy emotion & sadness facial expression) in the motorway scenario. The correlations between evoked emotions and eye and face movement imply that the objective and reliable face and ocular movement measurements can be utilized to monitor driver's emotional state promptly. However, those correlations could not find in the village scenario. It means that the road design might significantly influence the way to interpret the meaning of facial expression and eye movement to understand a driver's psychological feelings, but further analysis is required to understand this phenomenon.

5 Conclusion

Overall, this study shows that biosensor data could capture certain subjective feelings induced in a motorist by surrounding road environments as viewed from the vehicle cab. In addition, the current study reveals that the facial expression related to sadness might capture their evoked 'noisy' emotion in some driving conditions. Also, there is a negative correlation between the Kansei word 'Modern' and saccade amplitude. More research should be done for future studies to explore how these correlations could be related to driving behaviors. The outcomes of this study will contribute to improving the future design of urban transportation environments and advanced driver-assistance systems.

References

1. Tavakoli, A., Boukhechba, M., Heydarian, A.: Personalized driver state profiles: a naturalistic data-driven study. In: Stanton, N. (ed.) Advances in Human Aspects of Transportation. AISC, vol. 1212, pp. 32–39. Springer, Cham (2020). https://doi.org/10.1007/978-3-030-50943-9_5
2. Eyben, F., et al.: Emotion on the road—necessity, acceptance, and feasibility of affective computing in the car. Adv. Hum.-Comput. Interact. 2010 (2010)
3. Groeger, J.A.: Understanding Driving: Applying Cognitive Psychology to a Complex Everyday Task, Frontiers of Cognitive Science. Routledge/Chapman & Hall, New York/ London (2000)
4. Howell, N., Chuang, J., De Kosnik, A., Niemeyer, G., Ryokai, K.: Emotional biosensing: exploring critical alternatives. In: Proceedings of the ACM on Human-Computer Interaction, 2(CSCW), pp. 1–25 (2018)
5. Merrill, N., Chuang, J., Cheshire, C.: Sensing is believing: what people think biosensors can reveal about thoughts and feelings. In: Proceedings of the 2019 on Designing Interactive Systems Conference, pp. 413–420, June 2019
6. Young, K., Regan, M.: Driver distraction: a review of the literature. In: Faulks, I.J., Regan, M., Stevenson, M., Brown, J., Porter, A., Irwin, J.D. (eds.) Distracted Driving, pp. 379–405. Australasian College of Road Safety, Sydney (2007)
7. Abdic, I., Fridman, L., McDuff, D., Marchi, E., Reimer, B., Schuller, B.: Driver Frustration Detection From Audio and Video in the Wild, vol. 9904, p. 237. Springer, Cham (2016)
8. Leahu, L., Schwenk, S., Sengers, P.: Subjective objectivity: negotiating emotional meaning. In: Proceedings of the 7th ACM Conference on Designing Interactive Systems, pp. 425–434, February 2008
9. Calvo, R.A., D'Mello, S.: Affect detection: an interdisciplinary review of models, methods, and their applications. IEEE Trans. Affect. Comput. 1(1), 18–37 (2010)
10. Huang, H., Li, Y., Zheng, X., Wang, J., Xu, Q., Zheng, S.: Objective and subjective analysis to quantify influence factors of driving risk. In: 2019 IEEE Intelligent Transportation Systems Conference (ITSC), pp. 4310–4316. IEEE, October 2019

11. Alavi, S.S., Mohammadi, M.R., Souri, H., Kalhori, S.M., Jannatifard, F., Sepahbodi, G.: Personality, driving behavior and mental disorders factors as predictors of road traffic accidents based on logistic regression. Iran. J. Med. Sci. **42**(1), 24 (2017)
12. OpenDS, March 2020. OpenDS. Welcome to opends 4.0! (2016). https://www.opends.eu/home
13. Lu, Y., Zheng, W.L., Li, B., Lu, B.L.: Combining eye movements and EEG to enhance emotion recognition. In: Twenty-Fourth International Joint Conference on Artificial Intelligence, June 2015
14. Caldara, R., Zhou, X., Miellet, S.: Putting culture under 'the spotlight' reveals universal information use for face recognition. PLoS ONE **5**, e9708 (2010). Pmid: 20305776, View ArticlePubMed/NCBIGoogle Scholar
15. Birmingham, E., Svärd, J., Kanan, C., Fischer, H.: Exploring emotional expression recognition in aging adults using the Moving Window Technique. PLoS ONE **13**(10), e0205341 (2018)
16. Tobiipro, March 2020. https://www.tobiipro.com/learn-and-support/learn/eye-trackingessentials/how-does-blinking-affect-eye-tracking/
17. iMotions, May 2021. https://help.imotions.com/hc/en-us/articles/360013734440-Fixation-and-saccade-classification-with-the-I-VT-filter
18. Pereira, M., Hone, K.: Communication skills training intervention based on automated recognition of nonverbal signals. In: Proceedings of the 2021 CHI Conference on Human Factors in Computing Systems, pp. 1–14, May 2021
19. Otamendi, F.J., Sutil Martín, D.L.: The emotional effectiveness of advertisement. Front. Psychol. **11**, 2088 (2020)
20. Meinlschmidt, G., et al.: Smartphone-based psychotherapeutic micro-interventions to improve mood in a real-world setting. Front. Psychol. **7**, 1112 (2016)
21. Steyer, R., Schwenkmezger, P., Notz, P., Eid, M.: Development of the Multidimensional Mood State Questionnaire (MDBF). Primary data. [Translated Title] (Version 1.0.0) [Data and Documentation]. Trier: Center for Research Data in Psychology: PsychData of the Leibniz Institute for Psychology Information ZPID (2004). https://doi.org/10.5160/psychdata.srrf91en15
22. Ishihara, S., Nagamachi, M., Schütte, S., Eklund, J.: Affective meaning: the Kansei engineering approach. In: Product Experience, pp. 477–496. Elsevier (2008)
23. Kittidecha, C., Yamada, K.: Application of Kansei engineering and data mining in the Thai ceramic manufacturing. J. Ind. Eng. Int. **14**(4), 757–766 (2018). https://doi.org/10.1007/s40092-018-0253-y
24. Schutte, N.S., Malouff, J.M., Thorsteinsson, E.B., Bhullar, N., Rooke, S.E.: A meta-analytic investigation of the relationship between emotional intelligence and health. Pers. Individ. Differ. **42**(921–933), 252 (2007)
25. Llinares, C., Page, A.F.: Kano's model in Kansei engineering to evaluate subjective real estate consumer preferences. Int. J. Ind. Ergon. **41**(3), 233–246 (2011)
26. Van der Heiden, R.M., Janssen, C.P., Donker, S.F., Hardeman, L.E., Mans, K., Kenemans, J.L.: Susceptibility to audio signals during autonomous driving. PLoS ONE **13**(8), e0201963 (2018)
27. Jeong, M., Ko, B.C.: Driver's facial expression recognition in real-time for safe driving. Sensors **18**(12), 4270 (2018)
28. Wegrzyn, M., Vogt, M., Kireclioglu, B., Schneider, J., Kissler, J.: Mapping the emotional face how individual face parts contribute to successful emotion recognition. PLoS ONE **12**(5), e0177239 (2017). https://doi.org/10.1371/journal.pone.0177239
29. Eisenbarth, H., Alpers, G.W.: Happy mouth and sad eyes: scanning emotional facial expressions. Emotion **11**(4), 860–865 (2011). https://doi.org/10.1037/a0022758
30. Dula, C.S., Geller, E.S.: Risky, aggressive, or emotional driving: addressing the need for consistent communication in research. J. Saf. Res. **34**(5), 559–566 (2003)

31. Colic, A., Marques, O., Furht, B.: Commercial solutions. In: Driver Drowsiness Detection: Systems and Solutions, pp. 19–23. Springer, Cham (2014). https://doi.org/10.1007/978-3-319-11535-1_3

32. McEvoy, S.P., Stevenson, M.R., Woodward, M.: The impact of driver distraction on road safety: results from a representative survey in two Australian states. Inj. Prev. **12**(4), 242–247 (2006)

Hitting the Apex Highly Automated? – Influence of Trajectory Behaviour on Perceived Safety in Curves

Patrick Rossner[✉], Marty Friedrich, and Angelika C. Bullinger

Chair for Ergonomics and Innovation, Chemnitz University of Technology, Chemnitz, Germany
patrick.rossner@mb.tu-chemnitz.de

Abstract. There is not yet sufficient knowledge on how people want to be driven in a highly automated vehicle. Currently, trajectory behaviour as one part of the driving style is mostly implemented as a lane-centric position of the vehicle in the lane, but drivers show quite different preferences, especially with oncoming traffic and in curves. A driving simulator study was conducted to investigate seemingly natural reactive driving trajectories in curves on rural roads in an oncoming traffic scenario to better understand people's preferences regarding driving styles. 46 subjects experienced different lateral offsets in curves in three different oncoming traffic scenarios either on a 3.00 m or on a 3.50 m lane width. The test track consisted of 12 right and 18 left curves with an oncoming truck, car or none oncoming vehicle in balanced order. Results show that reactive trajectory behaviour and wider lane widths lead to significantly higher perceived safety. Even though drivers tend to shift their lateral position in curves in manual driving situations, they do not want the automated vehicle to cut curves and hit the apex. On the other hand, they also do not wish to get close to the road side, as seen in manual driving, too. We recommend an adaptive driving trajectory, which modifies trajectory behaviour on different lane widths and adjusts its behaviour on type and position of oncoming vehicles. The results of the study help to design an accepted, preferred and trustfully trajectory behaviour for highly automated vehicles.

Keywords: Automated driving · Trajectory behaviour · Perceived safety · Rural roads · Curves

1 State of Literature and Knowledge

Sensory and algorithmic developments enable an increasing implementation of automation in the automotive sector. Ergonomic studies on highly automated driving constitute essential aspects for a later acceptance and use of highly automated vehicles [1, 2]. In addition to studies on driving task transfer or out-of-the-loop issues, there is not yet sufficient knowledge on how people want to be driven in a highly automated vehicle [3–5]. First insights show that preferences regarding the perception and rating of driving styles are widely spread. Many subjects prefer their own or a very similar driving style and reject other driving styles that include e.g. very high acceleration and deceleration

© Springer Nature Switzerland AG 2021
C. Stephanidis et al. (Eds.): HCII 2021, LNCS 13097, pp. 322–331, 2021.
https://doi.org/10.1007/978-3-030-90966-6_23

rates or small longitudinal and lateral distances to other road users [6, 7]. Studies show that swift, anticipatory, safe and seemingly natural driving styles are prioritized [8, 9]. In existing literature, trajectory behaviour as one part of the driving style is mostly implemented as a lane-centric position of the vehicle in the lane. From a technical point of view this is a justifiable and logical conclusion, but drivers show quite different preferences, especially in curves and in case of oncoming traffic [10, 11]. In manual driving situations without oncoming traffic, subjects drive close to the centre of the lane on straights [15, 20]. In curves, test participants show a different driving behaviour and move closer to the road centre in left turns and closer to the roadside in right turns [15, 21]. Several studies even report a tendency to cut the curve by hitting the apex, especially for left turns [22, 23, 12]. When meeting oncoming traffic in manual driving, subjects increase their lateral safety distance by moving to the right edge of the lane, both on straights [15, 20, 24] as well as in left and right curves [11, 15]. When meeting heavy traffic, subjects' reactions are even greater [13–15, 20, 25]. With the appearance of oncoming traffic in left curves, two manual driving strategies overlay: to hit the apex and to avoid short lateral distances to the oncoming traffic. In summary, the implementation of this natural driving behavior into an automated driving style includes high potential to improve the driving experience in an automated car. Previous studies [16–19] show that reactive trajectory behaviour in highly automated driving leads to significantly higher acceptance, trust and subjectively experienced driving performance on straights. This paper is based on these previous findings and focuses on trajectory behavior in highly automated driving in curves.

2 Method and Variables

A fixed-based driving simulator with an adjustable automated driving function (Fig. 1) was used to conduct a mixed-design experiment. 46 subjects experienced different lateral offsets in curves in three different oncoming traffic scenarios either on a 3.00 m or on a 3.50 m lane width. All subjects were at least 25 years old and had a minimum driving experience of 2.000 km last year and 10.000 km over the last five years (see Table 1 for details). The test track consisted of 12 right and 18 left curves with an oncoming truck, car or none oncoming vehicle. The speed of the oncoming traffic was set at 80 km/h. The lateral offset of the ego vehicle had a range from −0.4 m to +0.6 m from the middle of the lane in left curves and +0.2 m to +0.6 m in right curves in 0.2 m steps.

Fig. 1. Driving simulator with instructor centre (left) and an exemplary subject (right)

Table 1. Subject characteristics

	Number	Age		Driver's license holding [years]		Mileage last five years [km]	
	N	M	SD	M	SD	M	SD
Female	13	35.2	6.9	17.3	6.9	60,308	57,044
Male	33	33.9	7.7	15.7	7.8	87,543	69,909
Total	46	34.3	7.4	16.1	7.5	87,543	68,131

Figure 2 illustrates the different directions of the lateral offset. All in all, the different outcomes of all factors resulted in 30 different experimental conditions, as shown in Table 2. 10 sequences of these 30 conditions were preprogrammed and selected randomly for each subject. Every test participant experienced all 30 curves twice, with a short break in between. On the simulated rural road straight and curve sections were showed in alternation, so after each curve a straight section followed. The curves had a radius of 450 m and a length of 250 m, so that the ego vehicle was able to drive with 100 km/h constantly [26]. When driving through the curves, the ego-vehicle starts at a lateral offset of 0.2 m to the lane centre in direction to the right edge of the lane. The ego vehicle reaches its target lateral offset at the apex of the curve. After passing that centre point of the curve, the ego vehicle returns to the initial position of 0.2 m lateral offset to the lane centre. This trajectory behaviour is shown in Fig. 3.

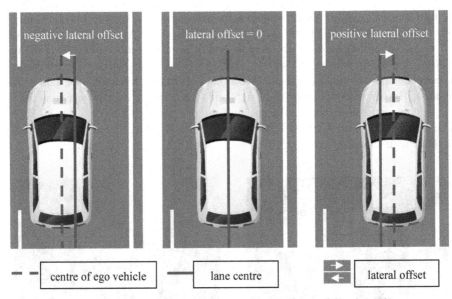

Fig. 2. Illustration of different lateral offset directions, following [29]

Table 2. Illustration of all experimental conditions

	no oncoming traffic	car	truck	no oncoming traffic	car	truck
Lateral offset (within-factor)	-0.4 m / -0.2 m / 0 m / +0.2 m / +0.4 m / +0.6 m	-0.4 m / -0.2 m / 0 m / +0.2 m / +0.4 m / +0.6 m	-0.4 m / -0.2 m / 0 m / +0.2 m / +0.4 m / +0.6 m	+0.2 m / +0.4 m / +0.6 m / +0.8 m	+0.2 m / +0.4 m / +0.6 m / +0.8 m	+0.2 m / +0.4 m / +0.6 m / +0.8 m
lane width (between-factor) 3.00 m or 3.50 m						

Oncoming traffic and lateral offset were balanced to minimize sequence and habituation effects. The participants were required to observe the driving as a passenger of an automated car. During the drive, subjects' main feedback was a verbal evaluation of perceived safety on a four-point scale after each driven curve, ranging from "1 – very unsafe" to "4 – very safe" – in accordance with the short online questionnaire evaluation of subjectively experienced driving performance of Voß & Schwalm [27]. Verbal evaluation of perceived safety of each curve took place at the beginning of the following straight section. To obtain all evaluations at the same point, an auditory signal was presented to the test participants requesting an evaluation. Subjects were trained for this procedure in an exercise round before the experiment started. At the end of the study, participants were interviewed to gain more detailed information and reasons for the assessment of the different experimental conditions.

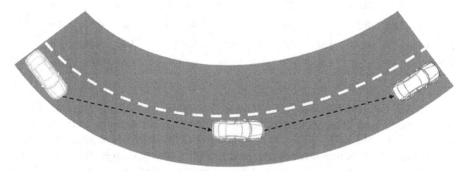

Fig. 3. Dimly illustration of the trajectory behaviour with lateral offset in a left curve

3 Results

Script-based data monitoring discovered zero invalid data recording cases, which needed to be excluded for further analysis. Left and right curves are reported separately in the following sections.

3.1 Left Curves

Table 3 and Fig. 4 give an overview of perceived safety ratings for each single scenario on both lane widths. If the lateral offset is negative, the centre of the ego-vehicle is located left from the middle of the lane. Positive lateral offset values indicate a position in direction to the right edge of the lane – see Fig. 2.

All in all, perceived safety ratings of the subjects are lower for lane width 3.00 m than for lane 3.50 m. Furthermore, perceived safety ratings for the no oncoming traffic condition were higher than for an oncoming car or truck. Without oncoming traffic, the highest ratings and therefore the preferred lateral offsets for both lane widths were between 0 m and +0.2 m. When meeting a car, the highest ratings could be determined for both lanes between +0.2 m and +0.4 m. When the oncoming traffic is represented by a truck, the evaluations of perceived safety differed between the two lane widths. On the 3.50 m lane width, that offers more lateral space to shift, the preferred lateral offset was between 0.4 m and 0.6 m. On the 3.00 m lane width, the highest rating of perceived safety was given between 0.2 m and 0.4 m.

Table 3. Mean values and standard deviations of perceived safety rating in left curves

| | Lane width of 3.50 m | | | | | | Lane width of 3.00 m | | | | | |
| | No oncoming traffic | | Car | | Truck | | No oncoming traffic | | Car | | Truck | |
Lateral offset	M	SD	M	SD	M	SD	M	SD	M	SD	M	SD
−0.4 m	3.48	0.64	2.90	0.75	2.53	1.06	3.10	0.93	2.14	1.03	1.81	0.93
−0.2 m	3.53	0.70	3.23	0.79	2.93	0.75	3.50	0.52	2.50	0.96	2.07	0.99
±0.0 m	**3.93**	**0.18**	3.53	0.57	3.28	0.79	**3.64**	**0.50**	3.36	0.59	2.79	0.93
+0.2 m	3.85	0.37	**3.73**	**0.44**	3.58	0.41	**3.86**	**0.32**	**3.67**	**0.51**	3.26	0.70
+0.4 m	3.75	0.34	**3.80**	**0.34**	3.75	0.44	3.57	0.48	**3.43**	**0.48**	**3.55**	**0.52**
+0.6 m	3.53	0.64	3.70	0.47	**3.65**	**0.49**	2.90	0.85	3.05	0.88	2.98	0.78

A rmANOVA with between-factor showed that significant main effects (considering Greenhouse-Geisser correction) exist for the within-factors oncoming traffic ($F(1.54, 60.12) = 57.49$, $p < .001$, $\eta p^2 = .60$), lateral offset ($F(2.44, 95.01) = 37.20$, $p < .001$, $\eta p^2 = .49$) and the between factor lane width ($F(1, 39) = 8.55$, $p = .01$, $\eta p^2 = .18$). Bonferroni-adjusted post-hoc analysis of the oncoming traffic factor revealed significant differences between all factors.

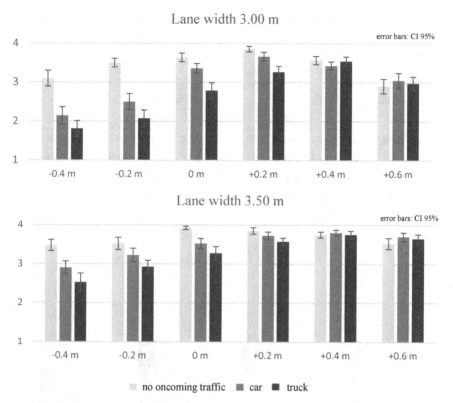

Fig. 4. Mean values and standard deviations of perceived safety rating in the left curves

3.2 Right Curves

Table 4 and Fig. 5 give an overview of perceived safety ratings for each single scenario on both lane widths. All in all, perceived safety ratings of the subjects were lower for lane width 3.00 m than for lane width 3.50 m. Furthermore, perceived safety ratings for the no oncoming traffic condition were higher than for an oncoming car or truck. Without oncoming traffic, a wide range of high perceived safety ratings existed for both lane widths. With the occurrence of an oncoming vehicle, the lateral offset of 0.2 m was assessed slightly worse for both lanes. Additionally, lateral offset of 0.8 m was rated slightly worse for the 3.00 m lane width for all oncoming traffic conditions.

The rmANOVA with between-factor (considering Greenhouse-Geisser correction) detected significant main effects for the within-factors oncoming traffic ($F(1.46, 59.51) = 21.44, p < .001, \eta p^2 = .36$), lateral offset ($F(2.04, 79.44) = 4.06, p = .02, \eta p^2 = .09$) and the between-factor lane width ($F(1, 39) = 19.64, p < .05, \eta p^2 = .10$). Bonferroni-adjusted post-hoc analysis of the oncoming traffic factor revealed significant differences between all factors.

Table 4. Mean values and standard deviations of perceived safety rating in right curves

Lateral offset	Lane width of 3.50 m						Lane width of 3.00 m					
	No oncoming traffic		Car		Truck		No oncoming traffic		Car		Truck	
	M	SD	M	SD	M	SD	M	SD	M	SD	M	SD
+0.2 m	**3.88**	**0.28**	3.40	0.60	3.23	0.68	**3.74**	**0.49**	3.14	0.82	2.86	0.92
+0.4 m	**3.73**	**0.62**	**3.63**	**0.60**	**3.53**	**0.47**	**3.76**	**0.37**	**3.50**	**0.52**	**3.38**	**0.65**
+0.6 m	**3.70**	**0.64**	**3.58**	**0.65**	**3.60**	**0.42**	**3.62**	**0.57**	**3.48**	**0.62**	**3.33**	**0.58**
+0.8 m	**3.75**	**0.50**	**3.60**	**0.62**	**3.50**	**0.56**	3.07	0.94	3.00	0.96	2.88	0.76

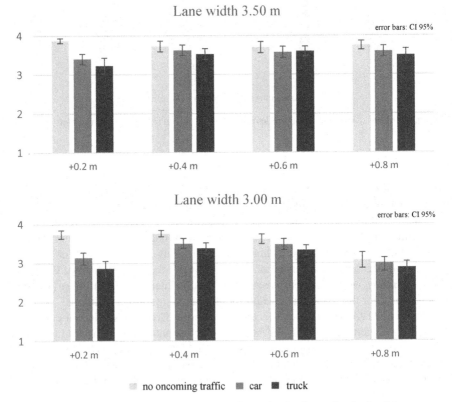

Fig. 5. Mean values and standard deviations of perceived safety rating in the right curves

4 Conclusion and Outlook

The aim of the study was to investigate seemingly natural reactive driving trajectories on rural roads in an oncoming traffic scenario in curves to better understand people's preferences regarding driving styles. The use of manual drivers' trajectories as basis for implementing highly automated driving trajectories showed high potential to increase perceived safety on straights [17–19]. Based on these previous results, it was concluded that factors which influence perceived safety in manual driving [13–15] are also factors influencing perceived safety during highly automated driving. As drivers cannot react to oncoming traffic by shifting to the right edge of the lane, the automated vehicle has to do so to increase perceived safety and driving comfort of the passenger. In addition, these new data lead to similar results. Even though drivers tend to shift their lateral position in curves in manual driving situations [12, 21–23], they do not want the automated vehicle to cut curves and hit the apex. On the other hand, they also do not wish to get close to the road side, as seen in manual driving, too [28]. Again, oncoming traffic lead to lower perceived safety ratings [17–19], especially on a narrower lane width of 3.00 m. In conclusion, keeping a lateral safety distance to oncoming traffic is very important for passengers of highly automated vehicles. A possible conclusion is an adaptive driving trajectory, which modifies trajectory behaviour on different lane widths and adjusts its behaviour on type and position of oncoming vehicles. Therefore, it seems most relevant to investigate manual trajectory behaviour in more detail to implement better reactive trajectories that include less negative side effects and lead to a better driving experience. It is important to note that a positive driving experience has the potential to improve the acceptance of highly automated vehicles [5, 9] and therefore has both ergonomic and economic benefits.

Acknowledgements. This research was partially supported by the German Federal Ministry of Education and Research (research project: KomfoPilot, funding code: 16SV7690K). The sponsor had no role in the study design, the collection, analysis and interpretation of data, the writing of the report, or the submission of the paper for publication. We are very grateful to Maximilian Hentschel for his assistance in driving simulation programming.

References

1. Banks, V.A., Stanton, N.A.: Keep the driver in control: automating automobiles of the future. Appl. Ergon. **53**, 389–395 (2015)
2. Elbanhawi, M., Simic, M., Jazar, R.: In the passenger seat: investigating ride comfort measures in autonomous cars. IEEE Intell. Transp. Syst. Mag. 7(3), 4–17 (2015). https://doi.org/10.1109/MITS.2015.2405571
3. Gasser, T.M.: Herausforderung automatischen Fahrens und Forschungsschwerpunkte. 6. Tagung Fahrerassistenz, München (2013)
4. Radlmayr, J., Bengler, K.: Literaturanalyse und Methodenauswahl zur Gestaltung von Systemen zum hochautomatisierten Fahren. FAT-Schriftenreihe, vol. 276. VDA, Berlin (2015)
5. Siebert, F.W., Oehl, M., Höger, R., Pfister, H.-R.: Discomfort in automated driving – the disco-scale. In: Stephanidis, C. (ed.) HCI International 2013 - Posters' Extended Abstracts, vol. 374, pp. 337–341. Springer, Heidelberg (2013). https://doi.org/10.1007/978-3-642-39476-8_69

6. Festner, M., Baumann, H., Schramm, D.: Der Einfluss fahrfremder Tätigkeiten und Manöver-längsdynamik auf die Komfort- und Sicherheitswahrnehmung beim hochautomatisierten Fahren. In: 32nd VDI/VW- Gemeinschaftstagung Fahrerassistenz und automatisiertes Fahren, Wolfsburg (2016)
7. Griesche, S., Nicolay, E., Assmann, D., Dotzauer, M., Käthner, D.: Should my car drive as i do? What kind of driving style do drivers prefer for the design of automated driving functions? In: Contribution to 17th Braunschweiger Symposium Automatisierungssysteme, Assistenzsysteme und eingebettete Systeme für Transportmittel (AAET), ITS automotive nord e.V., pp. 185–204 (2016). ISBN: 978-3-937655-37-6
8. Bellem, H., Schönenberg, T., Krems, J.F., Schrauf, M.: Objective metrics of comfort: developing a driving style for highly automated vehicles. Transp. Res. F: Traffic Psychol. Behav. **41**, 45–54 (2016)
9. Hartwich, F., Beggiato, M., Dettmann, A., Krems, J.F.: Drive me comfortable: customized automated driving styles for younger and older drivers. 8. VDI-Tagung "Der Fahrer im 21. Jahrhundert" (2015)
10. Bellem, H., Klüver, M., Schrauf, M., Schöner, H.-P., Hecht, H., Krems, J.F.: Can we study autonomous driving comfort in moving-base driving simulators? A Valid. Stud. Hum. Factors **59**(3), 442–456 (2017). https://doi.org/10.1177/0018720816682647
11. Lex, C., et al.: Objektive Erfassung und subjektive Bewertung menschlicher Trajektoriewahl in einer Naturalistic Driving Study. VDI-Berichte Nr. 2311, pp. 177–192 (2017)
12. Spacek, P.: Track behavior in curve areas: attempt at typology. J. Transp. Eng. **131**(9), 669–676 (2005). https://doi.org/10.1061/(ASCE)0733-947X(2005)131:9(669)
13. Dijksterhuis, C., Stuiver, A., Mulder, B., Brookhuis, K.A., de Waard, D.: An adaptive driver support system: user experiences and driving performance in a simulator. Hum. Factors **54**(5), 772–785 (2012). https://doi.org/10.1177/0018720811430502
14. Mecheri, S., Rosey, F., Lobjois, R.: The effects of lane width, shoulder width, and road cross-sectional reallocation on drivers' behavioral adaptations. Accid. Anal. Prev. **104**, 65–73 (2017). https://doi.org/10.1016/j.aap.2017.04.019
15. Schlag, B., Voigt, J.: Auswirkungen von Querschnittsgestaltung und längsgerichteten Markierungen auf das Fahrverhalten auf Landstrassen. Berichte der Bundesanstalt für Straßenwesen. Unterreihe Verkehrstechnik (249) (2015)
16. Rossner, P., Bullinger, A.C.: Drive me naturally: design and evaluation of trajectories for highly automated driving manoeuvres on rural roads. Technology for an Ageing Society, Postersession Human Factors and Ergonomics Society Europe Chapter 2018 Annual Conference, Berlin (2018)
17. Rossner, P., Bullinger, A.C.: Do you shift or not? Influence of trajectory behaviour on perceived safety during automated driving on rural roads. In: Krömker, H. (ed.) HCI in Mobility, Transport, and Automotive Systems, vol. 11596, pp. 245–254. Springer, Cham (2019). https://doi.org/10.1007/978-3-030-22666-4_18
18. Roßner, P., Bullinger, A.C.: Does driving experience matter? Influence of trajectory behaviour on drivers' trust, acceptance and perceived safety in automated driving. Understanding human behaviour in complex systems, In: de Waard, D., et al. (eds.) Proceedings of the Human Factors and Ergonomics Society Europe Chapter 2019 Annual Conference (2020). ISSN: 2333-4959
19. Rossner, P., Bullinger, A.C.: I care who and where you are – influence of type, position and quantity of oncoming vehicles on perceived safety during automated driving on rural roads. In: Krömker, H. (ed.) HCI in Mobility, Transport, and Automotive Systems. Driving Behavior, Urban and Smart Mobility. LNCS, vol. 12213, pp. 61–71. Springer, Cham (2020). https://doi.org/10.1007/978-3-030-50537-0_6
20. Rosey, F., Auberlet, J.M., Moisan, O., Dupré, G.: Impact of narrower lane width comparison between fixed-base simulator and real data. Transp. Res. Rec.: J. Transp. Res. Board **2138**(1), 112–119 (2009). https://doi.org/10.3141/2138-15

21. Spacek, P.: Fahrverhalten und Unfälle in Kurven - Fahrverhalten in Kurvenbereichen (Straßenverkehrstechnik, Bd. 2). VSS. Verfügbar unter, Zürich (1999). https://books.google.de/books?id=rCD1HgAACAAJ

22. Bella, F.: Speeds and lateral placements on two-lane rural roads: analysis at the driving simulator. In: 13th International Conference "Road Safety on Four Continents" (2005)

23. Bella, F.: Driver perception of roadside configurations on two-lane rural roads: effects on speed and lateral placement. Accid. Anal. Prev. 50, 251–262 (2013). https://doi.org/10.1016/j.aap.2012.04.015

24. Triggs, T.J.: The effect of approaching vehicles on the lateral position of cars travelling on a twolane rural road. Aust. Psychol. 32(3), 159–163 (1997). https://doi.org/10.1080/000500 69708257375

25. Räsänen, M.: Effects of a rumble strip barrier line on lane keeping in a curve. Accid. Anal. Prev. 37(3), 575–581 (2005). https://doi.org/10.1016/j.aap.2005.02.001

26. Vetters, A.: Die neuen "Richtlinien für die Anlage von Landstraßen" RAL - Stand 2012. Zugriff am 28.10.2019. Verfügbar unter (2012). http://www.vsvi-mv.de/fileadmin/Medienpool/Seminarunterlagen/Seminare_2012/Vortrag_1_-_neue_RAL_Frau_Vetters.pdf

27. Voß, G., Schwalm, M.: Bedeutung kompensativer Fahrerstrategien im Kontext automatisierter Fahrfunktionen. Berichte der Bundesanstalt für Straßenwesen, Fahrzeugtechnik Heft F 118 (2017). ISBN 978-3-95606-327-5

28. Leutzbach, W., Maier, W., Döhler, M.: Untersuchung des Spurverhaltens von Kraftfahrzeugen auf Landstraßen durch Verfolgungsfahrten. Forschungsgesellschaft für Straßen und Verkehrswesen. Straße und Autobahn, Heft 8 (1981)

29. Köhler, B.: Auswirkungen der Wahrnehmung von Markierungskonstellationen auf das Fahrverhalten in Arbeitsstellen auf Bundesautobahnen. Diss., Karlsruher Instituts für Technologie. Karlsruhe (2017)

A Systematic Review of Autonomous Taxi Service and Discussion on Its Design

Shekar Sankar Raman[✉] and Vincent G. Duffy

Purdue University, West Lafayette, IN 47907, USA
{sankarra,duffy}@purdue.edu

Abstract. The increase in speed of development in the autonomous vehicle domain has led to the conceptualization of ideas such as utilizing these autonomous vehicles for services like taxis. A key component of designing such services is the Human Computer Interaction (HCI), understanding how humans interact with the autonomous system and this taxi service can be designed keeping this in mind. This report is intended on providing a systematic literature review of recent publications by performing analysis of bibliometric data using tools such as Harzing, CiteSpace, VOS Viewer, Mendeley, BibExcel and, MAXQDA. Articles for review were chosen from several sources including Google Scholar, Web of Science, Springer-Link, ResearchGate, and even a couple of chapters from Handbook of Human Factors and Ergonomics, Fourth Edition by Salvendy. This report also provides a summarized understanding of the trending topics in this emerging area and a brief discussion on how these services are currently constructed. It also provides a step-by-step procedure explaining how this analysis was carried out.

Keywords: Shared Autonomous Vehicles (SAV) · Service design · Human computer interaction · Systematic literature review · Bibliographic data

1 Introduction and Background

1.1 Autonomous Vehicles

An Autonomous Vehicle (AV) or a driverless vehicle operates on its own and is self-reliant in operation and navigation while passengers occupy it. There are varying degrees of human interaction that determine the level of autonomy the vehicle has. The Society of Automotive Engineers (SAE) scales the autonomy of these vehicles into five levels, which range from a significant amount of human interaction (Level 0) to no human interaction (Level 5). This technology has emerged to be a hot topic of discussion and is usually discussed in conjunction with Public Transportation. Research in this area has recently become explosive, with an increase in interest in shared, on-demand, mobility services.

Shared Autonomous Vehicles (SAV) or Robo-Taxi are some of the names that this new concept has been called. Since the technology of AVs are new, SAV services are at a more primitive stage today but many aspects of this are beginning conceptualization. But

© Springer Nature Switzerland AG 2021
C. Stephanidis et al. (Eds.): HCII 2021, LNCS 13097, pp. 332–344, 2021.
https://doi.org/10.1007/978-3-030-90966-6_24

some areas have prototyped such a service, for example, Waymo has released the Early Rider Program which provides an autonomous taxi service for Valley Metro employees. There are a lot of proven upsides to this new service: According to a McKinsey Report in 2016, the nuanced business models could see revenue pools for this industry increasing by 30% translating to USD 1.5 trillion by 2030 (Kim *et al.* 2020). The SAV service could contribute to the urban mobility system of the future, for example, a simulation and study conducted about the SAV service scenario in Hamburg suggested that in a city such as Hamburg which has a flourishing Electric Vehicle (EV) market, it could significantly reduce the carbon footprint and also utilize existing charging infrastructure (Bisello *et al.* 2017).

1.2 Human Computer Interaction Element

A key portion of implementing this service is the Human Computer Interaction. Passengers interact with this automated technology in numerous stages. A study shows that there can be up to 21 critical stages in using an autonomous taxi service where the customer interacts with the technology and these stages need to be made perfect and ergonomically stable for humans to be comfortable to use. Numerous studies have been made to prototype and field test the service, the HCI, and the Human Machine Interface (HMI). Studies have also shown and have given direction in testing and prototyping methodologies (Kim *et al.* 2020). This study will try to summarize all this.

2 Purpose of Study

The objective of this study is to conduct a systematic literature review of studies on the topic of Job Design in Autonomous Taxi Services and review it from an HCI perspective. The review sought to summarize key aspects of new research in this emerging area and identify aspects of job design that are forming the basis for further research on the topic of SAVs. A study that reviewed the literature of the human aspect of Cybersecurity, (Duffy and Duffy 2020), was crucial in designing this study. The workflow of this study would be similar.

3 Research Methodologies

3.1 Data Collection

The first stage of this project was to collect the data to analyze. Keyword Search was the technique that was used, and several different databases were used in the process namely: Google Scholar, Web of Science, Scopus, and SpringerLink. Google Scholar resulted in more results than the other databases. Web of Science, Scopus, and SpringerLink were accessed from Purdue Libraries by logging into the system and performing a keyword search. To extract articles from Google Scholar, Harzing's Publish or Perish was used. Harzing can access bibliometric metadata from different databases such as Google Scholar, Pubmed, Crossref, and many other sources.

The Google Scholar search using Harzing resulted in 1000 results and bibliometric metadata was extracted, to carry out co-citation and co-author analyses, which is explained further in later sections. Metadata from Web of Science included article title, abstract, keywords, and citations. Both data sources required keyword searches and the terms used were different. In the Keyword searches conducted through Purdue Libraries in Web of Science, Scopus and SpringerLink, search words used were "Autonomous Taxi Service Design", "Transport Service Systems", "Autonomous Taxi", and "Autonomous Vehicles". In Harzing which was used in searching Google Scholar, keywords used were: "Autonomous Taxi Service Design" and "Transport Service Systems".

3.2 Data Analysis

The first analysis performed was to understand the trend of the topic in recent years to understand the emerging nature of this research topic. Web of Science allows for the visualization of the metadata obtained from keyword searches. The Web of Science database itself provides these tools to visualize and hence these inbuilt tools were used to understand the trend. The charts represent 20 results in recent years until March of 2021.

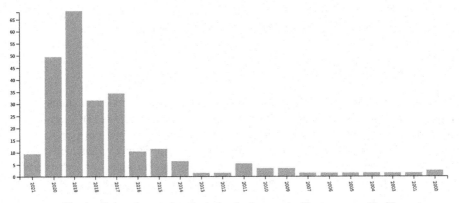

Fig. 1. Shows the trend analysis for the keywords: "Autonomous Taxi".

Figure 1 shows the trend of articles published in the Web of Science database for the search terms being "Autonomous Taxi". As we can see here, the first mention of "Autonomous Taxi" has been made as early as the year 2000 and did not have significant activity until very recently. Since 2014 there has been an exponential increase in activity in this domain. This term peaked in 2019 and is still can be considered an emerging domain regardless of the dip in mentions in the year 2020. 2021 has seen as many as 10 publications with mentions of autonomous taxis within the first three months of the year and this is a good sign that there would be more publications along the way. The dip in 2020 could be a result of the ongoing COVID 19 pandemic. Since this report focuses on the design of a taxi or a ride-hailing service, another search term was used to obtain the results shown in Fig. 2.

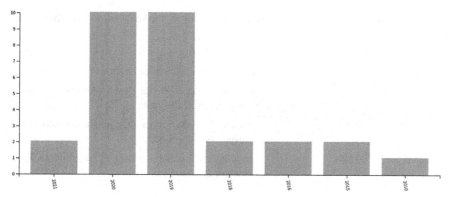

Fig. 2. Shows the results of the trend of articles using the keywords "Autonomous Taxi Service Design" in the Web of Science database.

As is evident, there are relatively fewer articles published which address the design of the service. This topic too however has seen an exponential increase in activity in recent years, more specifically from the year 2019 and onwards. The drop, in activity seen in Fig. 1 is not seen in Fig. 2 and we can conclude that regardless of the pandemic, there has been sufficient activity in prototyping and testing various designs and providing commentary on this emerging topic in recent years.

After conducting preliminary trend analysis to understand the emergence of this topic various other analyses were conducted to provide a systematic review of literature on the SAV service design domain. The first stage was to conduct co-citation and content analysis by generating clusters in the software called VOSviewer. The databases used for these analyses were Web of Science and Google Scholar through Harzing. In both cases, bibliometric metadata was extracted to perform these analyses. MAXQDA was then used to visualize keywords in these articles collected from the various sources to see which area in SAV service design has been getting a lot of attention in terms of research. CiteSpace was another software that was used to perform keyword importance and also perform citation bursts. Further bibliometric metadata was extracted from Google Scholar using Harzing to extract authorship information into leading tables and was further visualized using pivot tables and pivot charts using Microsoft Excel. Each of these analyses is explained further with commentary on them.

4 Results

4.1 Keyword Search

At the beginning of this study, a thorough keyword search was conducted in various databases. The databases used in this study are Google Scholar in the Harzing Publish or Perish 7 software; Web of Science, Scopus, and SpringerLink using the Purdue Libraries and specifically in the databases section by logging into the account. Each of these keyword searches resulted in using different keywords and the following table summarizes this information (Table 1).

Table 1. Shows the database and the number of results for the keywords used in the search.

Database	Number of articles	Keywords used
Google Scholar	1000	Autonomous Taxi Service Design, Autonomous Taxi
Web of Science	247	Autonomous Taxi Service Design, Autonomous Taxi, Transport Service Systems
Scopus	378	Autonomous Taxi Service Design, Autonomous Taxi, Transport Service Systems
SpringerLink	3234	Autonomous Taxi Service Design, Autonomous Taxi, Transport Service Systems

4.2 Co-citation Analysis

Bibliometric data with citation information was used to perform co-citation analysis. The identification, tracing, and visualization of the intellectual structure of academic papers by counting the frequency of an author of academic work who has cited the works for other authors in the references section is what one study defines as co-citation analysis. Co-Citation Analysis is used to identify, trace, and visualize the intellectual structure of an academic discipline by counting the frequency with which any work of an author is co-cited with another author in the references of citing documents (Jeong et al. 2014). Bibliometric metadata was extracted from Web of Science and imported into the VOSViewer software to perform this analysis. The keywords used in this search were "Transport Service Systems" and the final topic of SAV service design was decided upon after this (Fig. 3).

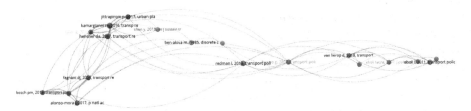

Fig. 3. Shows co-citation analysis for keywords "Transport Service Systems".

The parameter used to obtain this cluster is that the minimum number of citations on a cited reference being 6. This suggested that 20 out of a possible 25516 meet the threshold. From the visualization above and the information provided in Table 2 we can that "Kamargianni et al. 2016" has the most number of citations and hence the highest strength. Table 2 also summarizes the measures and the results that went into constructing the cluster diagram.

Table 2. Shows the authors, year of publication, number of citations, and the strength of the link of the results from the bibliometric data obtained from Web of Science

Authors	Year of publication	Citations	Link strength
Kamargianni et al.	2016	9	23
Hensher David et al.	2017	7	18
Lyons G et al.	2019	6	18
Beirao G et al.	2007	7	15
Henao A et al.	2019	6	15
..	..	..	..
..	..	..	..
..	..	..	..
..	..	..	..
..	..	..	..

4.3 Co-occurrence Keyword Analysis Using VOSViewer

This type of analysis involves co-occurrences of key words, given by words extracted from publication titles or their full text. These co-occurrences help us understand the relation between the authors in terms of research interest and also helps identify hot topics in this domain. The co-word frequency array is used to construct a co-word map that represents the intellectual content of a field (i.e., cognitive themes and their interrelations) using cluster analysis and network analysis (Tijssen and Van Raan 1994).

To perform the co-occurrence analysis of keywords data was extracted from Google Scholar using the Haring Publish or Perish 7 software. The search term used was "Transport Service Systems". Ideas from this keyword search helped finalize the final topic of this study. This resulted in over 400 results, however for study 400 results were considered. The occurrence threshold was set to 10 which resulted in 42 relevant terms with 25 relevant terms. Removing trivial words such as "pages", "the", "study", etc. resulted in the following cluster diagram from VOSviewer.

From Fig. 4 we can see the prevalence and the importance of the word service in most of these research articles. Public Transport is another term that matches very closely with transport service and hence initiated the thought of including Autonomous Taxi Service Design as the topic. Considering the increase in the trend of articles in this domain, this topic was finalized.

4.4 Word Cloud from MAXQDA

Once the topic was selected, several databases were searched for research articles. These databases included: Scopus, SpringerLink, Web of Science, ResearchGate, and Google Scholar. A selective reference list was first generated from the thousands of papers that seemed specific to the research topic and they were imported into MAXQDA. The software allowed us to visualize a select set of words in the form of a word cloud as seen

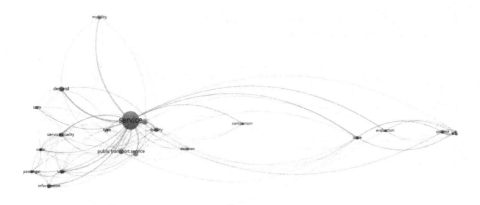

Fig. 4. Co-occurrence of keyword analysis

in Fig. 5. It should be noted that trivial words such as "The", "should", "journal", etc. were removed.

Fig. 5. Shows the word cloud obtained from a selected 8 articles, using the MAXQDA software.

Table 3 shows the list of words that were used to create this word cloud. It quantifies the frequency of the word and the number of documents each of these words was present. It must be noted that this is just an excerpt of a list of hundreds of words. From the word cloud in Fig. 5 and the frequency Table 3, we can see that automation is the most frequently used word. Other words that stand out are "demand", "time", "ergonomics", "design", "simulation" and "vol" (volume). From these words in the word cloud, we see that key issues addressed in the list of articles chosen are: demand management of taxis, waiting time for passengers, ergonomic design of the service – ease of use to passenger and simulations – since such a service is not widely adopted yet.

Table 3. Shows the frequency of words from the selected documents used to visualize the word cloud in MAXQDA.

Word	Frequency	Number of documents
Automation	626	3
Taxi	597	7
Service	428	7
Time	392	8
Vehicle	389	8
System	289	8
Autonomous	276	7
Humans	266	8
Systems	220	8
Design	219	7

4.5 Keyword Cluster Analysis Using CiteSpace

This Keyword Cluster Analysis is very similar to what was accomplished above using VOSviewer. However, the cluster analysis performed now is more focused on the Shared Autonomous Vehicle, ride-hailing service design articles that were chosen from the Web of Science database. The purpose of this analysis is to see emerging topics in Autonomous Taxi Service Design. Figure 6 below shows the emerging topic in the form of a cluster using CiteSpace.

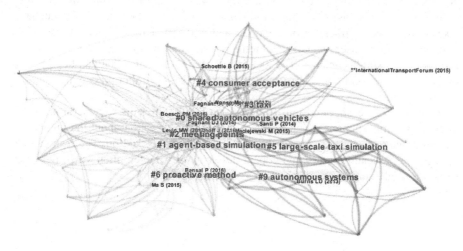

Fig. 6. Cluster analysis using CiteSpace

From the figure above we can see the emerging areas which are calculated based on the highest frequency of occurrence in multiple sources. We can see that "Agent-Based Simulation" is second to "Shared Autonomous Vehicles". This can even be seen in the chosen articles. A study, (Wen *et al.* 2018), used agent-based simulation to loop between supply and demand of on AV, public transport situation to capture the decisions of the service operator and those of the travelers to model the choices of both parties. From Fig. 6 we can see that simulation seems to be a recurring term in different forms. Another study, (Vosooghi *et al.* 2019), addresses the fleet size in a dynamically changing demand environment using a multi-agent approach. Another similar study simulated SAV allocation to passengers using a simulation model (Wilco et al. 2015). Even redistribution of these SAVs has been addressed using simulation methods (Babicheva and Burghout 2019).

Other top words addressed in this cluster are "Meeting Points". Many articles suggest scenarios and design of services where passengers meet at a designated spot to be picked up by and dropped off at by SAVs keeping the current development of the technology in mind (Kim *et al.* 2020). Another important term that can be seen is "Consumer Acceptance" which is another emerging topic of discussion. Some of the chosen articles, (Bisello *et al.* 2017; Vosooghi *et al.* 2019; Kim *et al.* 2020), address this section apart from the simulation aspect of designing the service. This is the Human Automation and Human Computer Interaction aspect of the system. (Lee et al. 2012), addresses the road safety aspect in this chapter of the Handbook of "Human Factors and Ergonomics". Another chapter from the same book, (Green 2012), talks about the issues and safety considerations that should be made in the light of road accidents.

4.6   Leading Tables in BibExcel and Visualization Using Pivot Chart

To further analyze bibliographic data BibExcel was used. For this Harzing Publish or Perish 7 software was used to extract bibliographic metadata of Google Scholar database. 2000 results were extracted from Harzing and imported into BibExcel. BibExcel is designed to assist a user in analyzing bibliographic data, or any data of a textual nature formatted in a similar manner. The idea is to generate data files that can be imported to Excel or any program that takes tabbed data records, for further processing (Persson 2009) (Fig. 7).

Once they were imported into BibExcel, all the 2000 results were scrutinized for bibliographic information which resulted in finding information about the number of articles relate to this specific topic that the authors have worked on. The results were arranged in descending order and copied into Microsoft Excel, after which the Pivot table was used to obtain the Pivot Chart as seen in Fig. 8.

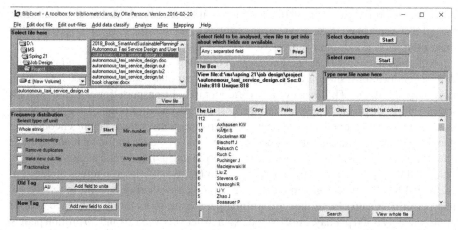

Fig. 7. Shows a screen capture of the user interface from BibExcel.

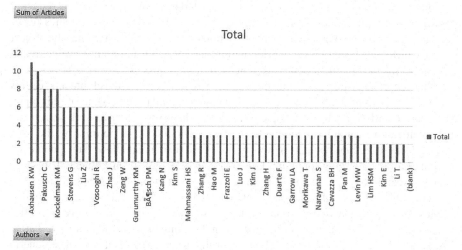

Fig. 8. Shows the leading authors organized in descending order in a Pivot Chart constructed in Microsoft Excel.

5 Discussion

People today have multiple options of means of travel from one location to another. They can take their private vehicle, use public transportation, or use a ride-hailing service such as taking a taxi. The reason why one would choose any of these options varies greatly. It could be because of the cost involved, travel time, flexibility, convenience, reliability, or perception of security. For example, public transport may cost less to get from one point to another but is strict on the flexibility in drop-off points. Whereas a taxi service would pick up and drop off passengers in many different locations but would be slightly more expensive (Furuhata *et al.* 2013). In recent years, on-demand mobility enabled through online services has recently become very popular, even more than using private and public transport (Rayle *et al.* 2016). It is purely the convenience of hailing a cab from the palm of one's hand, ease of payment (cashless), and the efficiency in the process that makes this service extremely attractive.

Ridesharing is a relatively new concept of traveling in which a few individuals going to different locations, share a vehicle, and split the cost of the travel amongst each other, such as gas, toll, etc. This is a sort of hybrid method of transportation which combines the flexibility of private transport and the cost-effectiveness of public transport. Many state or local and federal government in different countries have begun encouraging people to carpool or participate in ridesharing in a bid to reduce traffic on roads as cities are becoming increasingly congested and also from an environmental standpoint where cities and towns are being polluted more due to the use of a large number of cars. An additional motivation for governments to encourage ridesharing is a bid to reduce the number of accidents. More than 1.2 million people die in motor crashes each year or approximately 3300 per day. Furthermore, somewhere between 20 and 50 million people suffer injuries each year. Motor vehicle crashes are the ninth leading cause of death and are the leading cause of death in young adults of ages 15–29 (Green 2012).

Shared Autonomous Vehicles (SAVs) are expected to solve these issues, by reducing costs and encouraging ridesharing. Designing a service around this now becomes key as this service involves extensive interaction of Humans and Automation. Hence the project takes the different aspects of a shred ride-hailing service using autonomous vehicles and talks about the development being made in each of these processes.

This report provides a systematic literature review on the developments in this domain. First, a trend analysis was carried out to understand the emergence of this topic. The trends clearly show that this topic no longer in the primitive stages of research and that significant research has been made and continues to be made to improve the SAV service. Next, a co-citation analysis was performed to understand how many people are working on this emerging topic and how many articles have been influential in shaping the research in this domain. This was carried out in the VOSviewer software after extracting bibliometric information. Content analyses were carried out next but in different stages. First, a keyword co-occurrence cluster was generated in VOSviewer after extracting content information from Google Scholar using the Harzing Publish or Perish 7 software. Since the keyword search used for this stage in the analysis was a generic topic this cluster analysis helped identify the niche area this report would address. Once the topic was identified and a select number of research articles from different sources were collected a content analysis in the form of a word cloud was done in MAXQDA. Results from this show that topics such as "Demand", "Time", "Ergonomics" and "Design" have been highly referenced in all these articles and are repeated multiple times in the articles. After that, a cluster analysis of the content on CiteSpace gave more insight into the fact that "Simulation" has been highly used in many research. This is understood to be due to the lack of complete autonomy of vehicles and the need for significant human intervention. And finally, BibExcel was used to find the leading authors who are actively participating and conducting research in this domain.

6 Future Work

Although this report addresses the emergence of the topic and the plethora of research already made, there still is a long way to go before this service becomes a reality and comes to use to the common citizen throughout the world. Firstly, technological development is needed in terms of improving the autonomy of AVs. On the scale of earlier mentioned SAE levels of autonomy in AVs, today we stand at an early Level 3 and there is a long way to cover.

As one gets more and more attached to technology, the time spent with technology increases so does one's digital footprint. It then becomes important to keep the digital footprint in check and keep away from malicious cyber-attacks (Yağdereli et al. 2015). In the SAV taxi service scenario, the importance of cybersecurity then becomes a greater concern as the lives of passengers would be at stake, and the possibility of errors increases. This warrants the need for research in this area.

Another emerging challenge for this technology is swarm automation. This concept calls for hundreds of smaller simpler automated parts of a system to reduce the error of a single entity since the variability and uncertainty of the actions of entities are reduced. In this case, if all vehicles in an area become autonomous, the chances of road accidents or other such errors occurring would reduce (Lee et al. 2012). This is a very interesting take to implementing this technology and calls for more research in the feasibility and acceptability of such a concept. Other topics include researching human research management in the gig-economy (Duggan *et al.* 2020).

References

Babicheva, T., Burghout, W.: Empty vehicle redistribution in autonomous taxi services. EURO J. Transp. Logist. **8**(5), 745–767 (2019). https://doi.org/10.1007/s13676-019-00146-5

Bisello, A., Vettorato, D., Stephens, R., Elisei, P. (eds.): Smart and Sustainable Planning for Cities and Regions. GET, Springer, Cham (2017). https://doi.org/10.1007/978-3-319-44899-2

Duffy, B.M., Duffy, V.G.: Data mining methodology in support of a systematic review of human aspects of cybersecurity. In: Duffy, V.G. (ed.) Digital Human Modeling and Applications in Health, Safety, Ergonomics and Risk Management. Human Communication, Organization and Work. LNCS, vol. 12199, pp. 242–253. Springer, Cham (2020). https://doi.org/10.1007/978-3-030-49907-5_17

Duggan, J., et al.: Algorithmic management and app-work in the gig economy: a research agenda for employment relations and HRM. Hum. Resour. Manag. J. **30**(1), 114–132 (2020). https://doi.org/10.1111/1748-8583.12258

Furuhata, M., et al.: Ridesharing: the state-of-the-art and future directions. Transp. Res. Part B: Method. **57**, 28–46 (2013). https://doi.org/10.1016/j.trb.2013.08.012

Green, P.A.: Human factors and ergonomics in motor vehicle transportation. In: Handbook of Human Factors and Ergonomics, 4th edn, pp. 1596–1614 (2012). https://doi.org/10.1002/978 1118131350.ch58

Jeong, Y.K., Song, M., Ding, Y.: Content-based author co-citation analysis. J. Informetr. **8**(1), 197–211 (2014). https://doi.org/10.1016/j.joi.2013.12.001

Kim, S., et al.: Autonomous taxi service design and user experience. Int. J. Hum.-Comput. Interact. **36**(5), 429–448 (2020). https://doi.org/10.1080/10447318.2019.1653556

Lee, J.D., Seppelt, B.D., Madison, W.: Chapter 59 Human factors and ergonomics in automation design 2 automation promises. In: Handbook of Human Factors and Ergonomics (2012)

Persson, O.: BibExcel, International Society for Scientometrics and Informetrics (2009). https://homepage.univie.ac.at/juan.gorraiz/bibexcel/

Rayle, L., et al.: Just a better taxi? a survey-based comparison of taxis, transit, and ridesourcing services in San Francisco. Transp. Policy **45**, 168–178 (2016). https://doi.org/10.1016/j.tranpol.2015.10.004

Tijssen, R.J.W., Van Raan, A.F.J.: Technology bibliometric co-occurrence. Eval. Rev. **18**(1), 98–115 (1994)

Vosooghi, R., Kamel, J., Puchinger, J., Leblond, V., Jankovic, M.: Robo-taxi service fleet sizing: assessing the impact of user trust and willingness-to-use. Transportation **46**(6), 1997–2015 (2019). https://doi.org/10.1007/s11116-019-10013-x

Wen, J., et al.: Transit-oriented autonomous vehicle operation with integrated demand-supply interaction. Transp. Res. Part C: Emerg. Technol. **97**(October), 216–234 (2018). https://doi.org/10.1016/j.trc.2018.10.018

Wilco, B., Pierre-Jean, R., Ingmar, A.: Impacts of shared autonomous taxis in a metropolitan area. In: Proceedings of the 94th Annual Meeting of the Transportation Research Board, March 2016 (2015)

Yağdereli, E., Gemci, C., Aktaş, A.Z.: A study on cyber-security of autonomous and unmanned vehicles. J. Def. Model. Simul. **12**(4), 369–381 (2015). https://doi.org/10.1177/1548512915575803

A Deep Learning Based Road Distress Visual Inspection System Using Modified U-Net

Thitirat Siriborvornratanakul[(✉)]

Graduate School of Applied Statistics, National Institute of Development Administration (NIDA), 148 SeriThai Rd., Bangkapi, Bangkok 10240, Thailand
thitirat@as.nida.ac.th

Abstract. Nowadays the number of vehicles on road is increasing incrementally in emerging countries, and there is a need for proactive road health inspection methods that allow non-laborious and frequent road inspection with reasonable cost. Because of the nature of cheap and non-intrusive, vision-based road analysis has become a very popular topic in vision-based civil engineering researches around the world. In this paper, we discuss recent vision-based road distress detection methods, including our previous work and our presented work, for road distress visual inspection. This paper is divided into two parts. In the first part, we present non-deep learning based methods that aim to solve this problem of automatic road distress inspection. In the second part, we analyze recent deep learning based methods for road distress visual inspection and other related inspection of structure health monitoring. Finally, we propose our deep learning model called Modified U-Net whose goal is to solve the very difficult task of vision-based road's crack detection. Along this paper, we also discuss about human factors in developing vision-based solutions for automatic road distress detection.

Keywords: Road distress · Crack detection · Computer vision · Deep learning · Convolutional neural network · U-Net

1 Introduction

The essence of worldwide proactive road maintenance has triggered the needs for developing practical, automatic and non-destructive visual inspection systems. For civil engineers or experts in road health inspection, the task of manual road distress inspection is very laborious, too much time-consuming, and subjective. For computer vision based systems, the task of automate road distress detection does look easy at the first glance but turns out to be non-trivial in practice. To describe these difficulties regarding automate vision-based systems, we divide the problem into high- and low-level road distress detection. At the high-level road distress detection, not only there are many types of road distresses but also there can be many types of unrelated objects presenting in an input image; for

© Springer Nature Switzerland AG 2021
C. Stephanidis et al. (Eds.): HCII 2021, LNCS 13097, pp. 345–355, 2021.
https://doi.org/10.1007/978-3-030-90966-6_25

example, road mark, car, trash, traffic cones, pedestrian, building, etc. To recognize all these high-level objects correctly in an open environment, a very smart and complicated vision-based system is required. At the low-level road distress detection when no significant object other than road is expected in an image, it is still very difficult to categorize different types of road distresses from one another. This is because even a perfectly healthy road surface does have visual grains that exists naturally according to materials used for the construction of road. For vision-based systems, these grains are considered as salient noises that make it difficult for low-level algorithms to distinguish between healthy roads and damaged roads, particularly for very fine distress like road's cracks.

In this paper, we are interested in two groups of vision-based methods for road distress detection—classical methods (non-deep learning methods) in Sect. 2 and deep learning methods in Sect. 3.

2 Road Distress Visual Inspection Using Non-deep Learning

Before the emergence of deep learning in 2012 (before AlexNet model won the ImageNet challenge), it used to be very difficult for vision-based systems to reliably recognize many types of road distresses as well as other unrelated high-level objects all at once in an open road environment. Hence, most works discussed in this section will focus on non-deep learning methods regarding the low-level road distress inspection. Speaking of non-deep learning methods, it infers that human still plays a vital role in all processes of development, especially the process of handcrafted feature engineering.

To start with, there is a research of Miah et al. [7] that proposed a sensor fusion-based method for road pavement inspection. Their aim is to design the post processing sensor fusion system in order to perform road pavement multidimensional quality assessment and map all detected road defects on a GIS (geographic information system) map. Despite of a lot of sensors used, this research performs sensor data processing and data fusing using handcrafted vision-based algorithms. The proposed solution is in a form of road scanning vehicle that is able to detect cracks, potholes, rutting and other surface/subsurface defects and deterioration. In another research of [4], Gavilán et al. proposed a road distress detection system for fully automatic road distress assessment, using a vehicle equipped with line scan cameras, laser illumination and acquisition hardware and software. Their aim is to accurately detect road cracks which are more difficult than other types of road distresses as cracks are relatively small and can be easily confused with road's grains. In this research, the researchers use their handcrafted vision-based algorithms to process images, except for the task of road surface classification that a traditional machine learning method, multiclass SVM (supported vector machine), is employed.

From the aforementioned researches, it can be seen that previous vision-based road health inspection systems heavily rely on using some intrusive sensors that emit a specific kind of energy in order to scan road surface. These road scanning

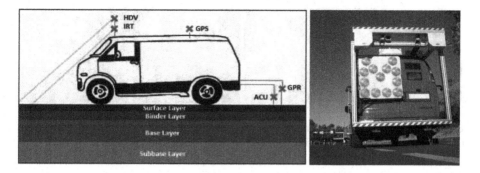

Fig. 1. Road scanning vehicles with non-deep learning vision-based algorithms as proposed by the researches of [7] and [4] from left to right respectively.

vehicles (as shown in Fig. 1) often have a lot of instructions to follow, so operating them frequently on every single road is not easy in practice. Our previous work in 2018 [11] tried to investigate this practical difficulty of road scanning vehicles by introducing a lightweight vision-based system where only one simple camera is mounted on an arbitrary car. Despite of hardware's simplicity, our previous research uses non-deep learning solutions so their usages do not generalize well to common road images shot from different camera or image settings. Besides, designing and evaluating a handcrafted vision-based road inspection system are very difficult without close cooperation from civil engineers or road inspection experts.

3   Road Distress Visual Inspection Using Deep Learning

With the power of deep learning, complicated visual patterns need not to be designed by human experts with domain expertise knowledge, but can be discovered using Convolutional Neural Network (CNN, ConvNet) as an automatic visual feature extractor. This power of vision-based deep learning means that human roles in automate road distress visual inspection development have been changed, from doing feature engineering to doing data as well as model engineering. In one of our previous works [10], even though the first author had no technical background in computer vision and image processing, she was able to develop a deep learning model for hand gesture recognition, using a self-collected dataset of 12,000 hand gesture images.

Recently, it has become common to find deep learning as part of road distress visual inspection researches. An interesting issue that we recognized during literature review is that, deep learning significantly increases the power of vision-based analysis and at the same time reduces the needs for supplementary sensing hardware (other than cameras) and fully-equipped road scanning vehicles. For example, at the high-level road distress detection where the system is expected to recognize road distresses surrounding by unpredictable non-related objects like car, pedestrian, pavement, etc., Maeda et al. [6] proposed a solution that only

Fig. 2. Experimental results regarding high-level road distress visual detection from the research of Maeda et al. [6].

one smartphone mounting inside a vehicle is all we need. This system uses a well-known deep learning architecture named SSD (Single Shot MultiBox Detector) and trains it with their proposed dataset (9,053 annotated images with 15,435 road damage instances). Using SSD, detection results are in the form of upright bounding boxes as shown in Fig. 2.

The high-level road distress visual inspection problem can possibly be solved by training state-of-the-art deep learning based object detectors with appropriate image dataset. However, at the low-level detection, even without significant unrelated objects, it is still difficult to detect some road distresses with high accuracy. This is particularly true for road crack detection where precise locations of crack pixels cannot be assumed from bounding box results of deep learning based object detectors. From our literature review, the strategy of patch-based image analysis (as illustrated in Fig. 3) seems popular for low-level crack detection using deep learning. In this strategy, a high-resolution input image is scanned and cropped/sliced to several low-resolution patches, then each patch is used as an input to a deep learning model.

There are many works that proposed deep learning solutions using patch-based strategy. In 2017, Pauly et al. [8] from University of Leed presented a crack detection system using a CNN model for patch-level image classification; each patch is a small 3-channel RGB image of size 99×99 pixels. Their experimental results show that a deeper CNN model (five convolutional layers) yields better performances in all indicators than a shallower CNN model (four convolutional layers), and the performance slightly drops if using input images taken from locations different from those of training data. In the same year of 2017, Cha et al. [1] proposed another CNN model to classify each image patch (256×256 pixels) into crack or non-crack. However, to avoid incorrect classification of cracks at the edges of images, their system is designed to scan one input image twice, leading to increase in computational time. In 2018, Fan et al. [3] from Shantou University proposed an automatic crack detection for pavements with different textures, using a 3-channel RGB image patch of size 27×27 pixels as an input to their CNN model. Unlike works mentioned earlier, the CNN model in this work is not designed for binary classification but multi-label classification where the output layer has 25 nodes forming a 5×5 probability map of pixels being crack. In addition, this work introduces modifying the proportion of positive to negative training samples in order to avoid severe imbalance in the training set.

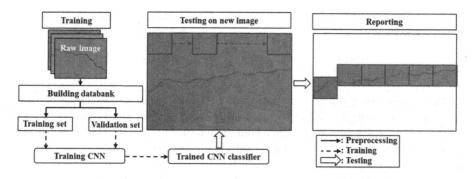

Fig. 3. Example from the research of Cha et al. [1] that uses window sliding and image patch analysis for deep learning based crack detection.

While all aforementioned deep learning works train their CNN models from scratch, there are other works that apply the popular concept of transfer learning to accelerate the training and reduce the number of training samples. For example, in 2018, Silva from Danish Technological Institute and Lucena from University of California, Irvine [2] proposed doing transfer learning on VGG16, the popular deep CNN model pretrained on ImageNet dataset, using their relatively small training dataset. In this work, an input image is sliced into patches of size 256×256 pixels and each patch is then classified into two classes–concrete surfaces with and without cracks. Another transfer learning work was recently proposed in 2019 by Jane et al. [5] from Sejong University. This work is unique in a way that it uses hybrid images from both normal vision camera and infrared camera. In the part of training a deep learning model for automate crack detection, a well-known deep CNN model called GoogLeNet (Inception v1) pretrained on ImageNet dataset is used. Authors applies transfer learning to train GoogLeNet with their concrete crack dataset so that the model is able to classify an input image into crack or intact categories. Once their CNN model is trained and ready for inference, in the step of automate crack detection, an original input image from normal vision camera is sliced with 16 different-sized non-overlapping masks and each image slice is predicted with the already-trained CNN model. The result of 16 different probability maps are then averaged for establishing a single probability map. Then, some statistical post-processing steps are applied to reduce noises and locate crack pixels in each image slice. Finally, this work uses more refinement steps that double-check the current detection result with a corresponding input image captured from infrared camera.

To end this section, we conclude that for low-level surface crack detection using deep learning, a patch-based image classification using CNN is one of the most popular solutions. Nevertheless, these patch-based solutions have some drawbacks. First, although an individual CNN prediction is not so expensive due to the small patch size, using a sliding window to crop/slice an original image and applying a CNN model repeatedly on each patch/slice is still very costly. Secondly, the step of cropping/slicing an original image into patches emphasizes human factors in the development process. This is because changing step's or patch's sizes may lead to unexpected drop in performance.

4 Proposed Method

In this paper, we want to eliminate human factor regarding the uses of sliding window technique, and at the same time we want our deep learning model to localize crack pixels by itself without depending on indirect localization via patch's location. To serve these two requirements, we propose using a deep learning model for image segmentation task, where an original input image is fed to the model and the model produces an output image showing probability of each pixel being crack.

4.1 Data Preparation, Preprocessing and Augmentation

For a deep learning model, good quality with sufficient number of training samples is one of the most important key success factors. In this paper, we use Crack-Tree dataset [12]—the image dataset consists of 206 road pavement images of size 800 × 600 pixels captured by an area-array camera under visible-light illumination. Ground truth images of the same size are included where all crack pixels are annotated as one-pixel wide curves.

Because deep learning based image segmentation models typically use lot of memory in computation, to reduce this memory consumption, input and output images of our deep learning model are set to the fixed size of 512 × 512 pixels. This means that, in model training, one input image (3-channel RGB image) and its corresponding ground truth image (1-channel binary image) are randomly cropped so that their original size of 800 × 600 pixels becomes our preferred size of 512 × 512 pixels. Note that we prefer image cropping rather than image resizing in order not to distort or disconnect one-pixel wide crack annotation in ground truth images. As for the time of model testing, any input image will be center cropped to a size of 512 × 512 pixels before being fed to the model. Apart from this preprocess of cropping, both input and output images are also scaled so that all pixel's values of range 0 to 255 are converted to the new range of 0.0 and 1.0.

To prevent overfitting, we employ several image augmentation techniques to increase the variability of training image samples. Our image augmentation includes random brightness, random contrast, random saturation, random hue, random blur, random horizontal flip, and random vertical flip; a probability of 0.5 is used to decide whether to apply each augmentation to one training sample. These data augmentations are done on the fly when loading a batch of training images to the model. This means that, same images will have different appearances in different training epochs, due to the randomness of data augmentation.

4.2 Deep Learning Model's Architecture and Training

For image segmentation tasks regarding non-natural images, U-Net [9] is perhaps one of the most popular model architectures. In this paper, we propose a modified

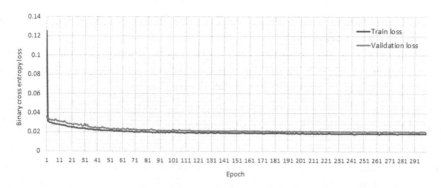

Fig. 4. Training and validation losses of our modified U-Net.

U-Net for crack detection, considering a binary classification problem regarding each image pixel (i.e., crack or non-crack pixels).

Comparing to the original U-Net, several changes are made in this paper. First, the original U-Net uses mirror padding so that an original image of size 512×512 pixels becomes an image of size 572×572 pixels when being fed to U-Net. We found that this padding significantly increases the memory usage of U-Net. Hence, we decided to feed our model with an original image of size 512×512 pixels then use padding $= 1$ in all convolutional layers. Secondly, the original U-Net is trained with batch size of 1 due to GPU's memory limitation, consequently there is no use for batch normalization. As in our work, because of our first modification, we can train our model with batch size that is bigger than 1 so batch normalization can be applied. Hence, we add 2D batch normalization after every convolutional layer, both in the contracting and expansive paths. Thirdly, the original U-Net outputs two segmentation maps of size 388×388 pixels (one map per one class) whereas our model outputs only one segmentation map of size 512×512 pixels; from our experiment, one segmentation map output provides better results. Finally, to maintain the exact input image size in the output segmentation map, we use an additional layer of adaptive average pooling as the last layer of our model.

To train the model, CrackTree dataset (prepared as explained in Sect. 4.1) is manually split to train and validation sets using 85:15 ratio, resulting in a train set of 175 images and a validation set of 31 images. Our model is then trained for 300 epochs with batch size of 3 (the maximum batch size possible for our GPU) using Stochastic Gradient Descent (SGD) optimizer (initial learning rate $= 0.01$, weight decay=0.0005, momentum $= 0.9$) in order to minimize the binary cross entropy loss. All experiments in this paper were conducted on a laptop computer running on Windows 10 operating system with one Intel Core i9-8950HK CPU (64 GB RAM) and one NVIDIA GeForce RTX 2080 GPU (8 GB RAM). Our work was developed with Python 3.8, PyTorch 1.7.1, torchvision 0.8.2, cuDNN 7.6.5 and OpenCV 4.5.1.48 in a full-precision (FP32) mode. Figure 4 shows our training graph where both training and validation losses gradually decrease and there is no sign of overfitting.

All development processes described in this section highly depend on human consideration, as all data/model settings and parameters cannot be figured out automatically by the deep learning model itself.

4.3   Deep Learning Model's Evaluation

During inference, a 3-channel input image of size 512×512 pixels is fed to our modified U-Net and the model outputs a 1-channel segmentation image whose size is the same as input image. All pixels in the segmentation image are then scaled to fit the range of 0.0 to 1.0 using the min-max normalization, where the minimum and maximum values refer to the smallest and largest pixel values of the segmentation image. Finally, the scaled segmentation image is binarized using a specific threshold value. Nevertheless, setting a good threshold value for binarization is tricky as it depends on application's requirements. In Fig. 5, each scaled segmentation image (the third row) is binarized using the threshold value that yields the maximum F1 score for that particular input.

Before proceeding to evaluation, there are two more issues to discuss—the issues of evaluation metric and thick crack. In the first issue of evaluation metric, the precision-recall curve is said to be better than the ROC (Receiver Operating Characteristic) curve for severely imbalanced dataset like our low-level crack detection. As for the other issue of thick crack, remind that ground truth images of CrackTree are all annotated with one-pixel wide curves. These one-pixel wide ground truth images introduce another problem as actual cracks may have varied widths. In this paper, if our modified U-Net model predicts crack pixels and those predicted crack pixels are no more than *trimap* pixels away from CrackTree's annotated crack edges, we will consider them as true positive.

Using the same dataset of 31 images for both validating and testing in this paper, Table 1 shows our evaluation results based on precision-recall curve with different trimap values. In the table, PR AUC refers to the area under the curve of precision-recall, and Max F1 score refers to the maximum F1 score when all predicted crack images in that particular dataset are binarized altogether with the same threshold value. From this table, it can be seen that our model's performances slightly drop when being used with unseen input images from the test set. Also, the bigger the trimap value, the better the evaluation results; this is because our current model predicts thick segmentation maps where the number of false positive pixels is high. Another model's limitation can be seen in Fig. 5 where significant misdetection occurs in the third column image of very fine cracks and there is also crack discontinuity in the fourth column image.

Table 1. Evaluation results based on our modified U-Net using different trimap values.

Indicator	Train set	Test set
PR AUC		
trimap = 0	0.0390	0.0380
trimap = 2	0.2394	0.2342
trimap = 4	0.3976	0.3913
trimap = 8	0.5984	0.5934
Max F1 score		
trimap = 0	0.0792	0.0766
	@0.5063: precision = 0.0433, recall = 0.4689	@0.5068: precision = 0.0421, recall = 0.4307
trimap = 2	0.3845	0.3766
	@0.3463: precision = 0.2523, recall = 0.8084	@0.3432: precision = 0.2492, recall = 0.7702
trimap = 4	0.5516	0.5395
	@0.2609: precision = 0.4119, recall = 0.8346	@0.2361: precision = 0.4038, recall = 0.8125
trimap = 8	0.7144	0.6995
	@0.0889: precision = 0.6197, recall = 0.8431	@0.0846: precision = 0.6114, recall = 0.8171

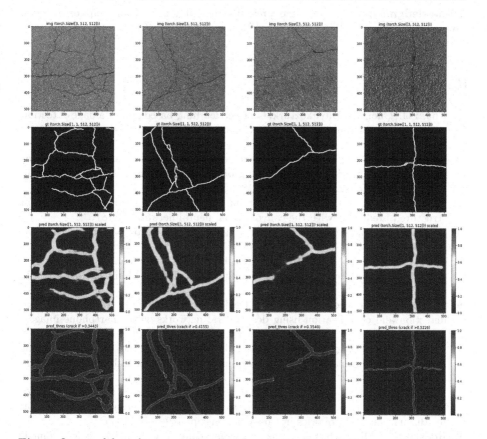

Fig. 5. Our model performance regarding four testing images. Top row shows testing images (no data augmentation). Second row shows ground truth images with trimap of 2. Third row shows scaled output images from our modified U-Net. The last row shows final crack detection results after binarization.

5   Conclusion and Future Works

Road distress visual detection using vision-based methods has been researched and studied widely over the past several years. In this paper, we review extensive methods for road distress visual inspection. Also, we analyze recent techniques and methods using both non-deep learning and deep learning to deal with the problems of vision-based road distress detection. Then, we propose our on-going work of a deep learning model for crack detection. The current model has limitations of producing thick cracks and missing very fine cracks; these limitations will be investigated in our future work. Nevertheless, we hope that this study of vision-based deep learning can be helpful not only for road distress inspection but also for the interdisciplinary knowledge of the human-computer interaction community where human roles have been changed from the recent disruption of deep learning in artificial intelligence.

Acknowledgments. This research presented herein was partially supported by a research grant from the Research Center, National Institute of Development Administration (NIDA), Bangkok, Thailand.

References

1. Cha, Y.J., Choi, W., Büyüköztürk, O.: Deep learning-based crack damage detection using convolutional neural networks. Comput.-Aided Civ. Infrastruct. Eng. **32**(5), 361–378 (2017)
2. da Silva, W.R.L., de Lucena, D.S.: Concrete cracks detection based on deep learning image classification. In: Proceeding of the 18th International Conference on Experimental Mechanics (ICEM) (2018)
3. Fan, Z., Wu, Y., Lu, J., Li, W.: Automatic pavement crack detection based on structured prediction with the convolutional neural network (2018)
4. Gavilán, M., et al.: Adaptive road crack detection system by pavement classification. Sensors **11**(10), 9628–9657 (2011)
5. Jang, K., Kim, N., An, Y.K.: Deep learning-based autonomous concrete crack evaluation through hybrid image scanning. Struct. Health Monit. **18**(5–6), 1722–1737 (2019)
6. Maeda, H., Sekimoto, Y., Seto, T., Kashiyama, T., Omata, H.: Road damage detection and classification using deep neural networks with smartphone images. Comput.-Aided Civ. Infrastruct. Eng. **33**(12), 1127–1141 (2018)
7. Miah, S., et al.: Design of multidimensional sensor fusion system for road pavement inspection. In: International Conference on Systems, Signals and Image Processing (2015)
8. Paulya, L., Peela, H., Luoa, S., Hoggb, D., Fuentesa, R.: Deeper networks for pavement crack detection. In: Proceedings of the 34th ISARC International Symposium in Automation and Robotics in Construction, pp. 479–485 (2017)
9. Ronneberger, O., Fischer, P., Brox, T.: U-net: convolutional networks for biomedical image segmentation. In: Navab, N., Hornegger, J., Wells, W.M., Frangi, A.F. (eds.) MICCAI 2015. LNCS, vol. 9351, pp. 234–241. Springer, Cham (2015). https://doi.org/10.1007/978-3-319-24574-4_28

10. Rungruanganukul, M., Siriborvornratanakul, T.: Deep learning based gesture classification for hand physical therapy interactive program. In: Duffy, V.G. (ed.) HCII 2020. LNCS, vol. 12198, pp. 349–358. Springer, Cham (2020). https://doi.org/10.1007/978-3-030-49904-4_26
11. Siriborvornratanakul, T.: An automatic road distress visual inspection system using an onboard in-car camera. Adv. Multimed. **2018** (2018)
12. Zou, Q., Cao, Y., Li, Q., Mao, Q., Wang, S.: CrackTree: automatic crack detection from pavement images. Pattern Recogn. Lett. **33**(3), 227–238 (2012)

Automation Surprises in Transportation: A Systematic Literature Review

Daniel J. Tillinghast[✉] and Vincent G. Duffy[✉]

Purdue University, West Lafayette, IN 47907, USA
{dtilling,duffy}@purdue.edu

Abstract. Within the study of human-automation or human-machine interaction, a phenomenon known as automation surprises confounds the design of semi-automated systems in the automotive setting. As automation systems grow in popularity and complexity, the nature of cooperation, shared control, and trust must be clearly defined such that both parties can dynamically transition between states of control and respond appropriately to the driving environment. To explore the emergence of automation surprises in transportation in the academic literature, this study utilizes bibliometric analysis and data mining tools to generate insights on prominent authors and sub-topics, identifying longstanding core articles in the topic. Results are shown in the form of descriptive figures created in software tools useful for bibliometric analysis. Insights from these figures and relevant articles related to automation surprises reveal an opportunity for review and reappraisal of automation surprises in transportation. A review of recent and well-established literature shows that automation surprises represent an important topic to address in the design of automotive automation systems.

Keywords: Automation · Control · Cooperation · Trust · Driver · Human-machine interaction

1 Introduction and Background

As applications of automation technology continue to take hold in transportation modes around the world, operators of vehicles like automobiles and planes experience the challenges associated with sharing control of a vehicle with a semi-automated system. When interactions between humans and automated systems break down, operators are left confused with the machine's action, omission, or intention, trying to interpret unpredictable system behavior (Woods et al. 1997, 1). Machines can thus create what are known as automation surprises, a term coined by Dr. David Woods to describe the occurrence of breakdowns in mode awareness, or "the ability...to track and to anticipate the behavior of automated systems" (1997, 6). According to Woods, "Mode errors occur when an intention is executed in a way appropriate for one mode when, in fact, the system is in a different mode" (1997, 5). When operators commit a mode error, they encounter an automation surprise when they realize the system responds differently than expected.

© Springer Nature Switzerland AG 2021
C. Stephanidis et al. (Eds.): HCII 2021, LNCS 13097, pp. 356–372, 2021.
https://doi.org/10.1007/978-3-030-90966-6_26

Especially when automated tasks become more complicated and occur in sequence without input from the operator, automation surprises can result in a number of consequences, sometimes life-threatening.

In the fields of human factors and job design, automation surprises represent an important area of study. Automation surprises are underscored by well-researched topics in the literature, including situation awareness, mental workload, and human error, each covered in depth in the core human factors knowledge base of the *Handbook of Human Factors and Ergonomics, Fourth Edition* (Salvendy 2012). The second edition of the same publication features a chapter by Woods on automation surprises, and the third edition covers human factors in automation design more generally, briefly mentioning automation surprises (Lee 2006, 1570). Automation surprises reveal gaps in operator training and the design of system communication to the user. As transportation modes such as consumer and industrial vehicles and aircraft incorporate more automated features, designers must consider the human in conjunction with automation to mitigate the occurrence of automation surprises.

2 Purpose of Study

While automation surprises in semi-automated transportation systems have represented a topic of study since the late nineties, their relevance continues to grow as consumer vehicles specifically are equipped with greater levels of automation. At the same time, proper training may be limited or unavailable for the average driver, necessitating intuitively predictable automation systems for drivers with low automation familiarity. This study applies bibliometric analysis and data mining tools to determine areas of greatest emergence and interest in the literature related to automation surprises in transportation. This study collects data for analysis from databases including Web of Science, Scopus, Google Scholar, SpringerLink, and ResearchGate. Several qualitative analysis tools are used to visualize key trends, including Vicinitas, VOSviewer, CiteSpace, and MAXQDA.

3 Procedure

To analyze the topic of automation surprises in transportation, a host of bibliometric analysis and data mining tools are used to extract insight from the current body of literature. Measures of engagement and emergence, as well as trend analysis, co-author analysis, categorization of leading authors and locales, co-citation analysis, and content analysis, will be discussed.

3.1 Identification of Emergence

To gain an initial understanding of the topic in the literature, keyword searches in the SpringerLink database and Clarivate's Web of Science database were conducted to reveal any articles of cursory interest. With no search restrictions on a keyword search for "automation surprise", 156 documents were returned, including one by a set of Swedish researchers on a concept known as driver conflict response in supervised automation (Pipkorn et al. 2020, 1). The study specifically examines the response process for a driver of a personal vehicle starting with the driver's surprise reaction, which ideally is taking control of the wheel. Some drivers were noted to commit mode errors, colliding with test objects "without even putting their hands on the wheel" (Pipkorn et al. 2020, 1). A ResearchGate query revealed that one of this publication's authors, Emma Tivesten, has been active in this topic area. In 2018, she co-authored an article studying "automation expectation mismatch", a topic very closely related to automation surprises which deals with the inconsistency between drivers' expectation of automation's capabilities and reality.

In SpringerLink, a basic search for "automation surprise transportation" restricted to the years since 2010 to narrow the results revealed an article discussing the emergence of fully automated vehicles. It details the challenges with human-automation interaction during the interim period in which full automation is not yet possible. The authors suggest a new system that promotes "both shorter transition response times and better transition quality" when a driver is asked to take manual control of a vehicle (Reilhac et al. 2017, 457). Published in 2017, this article highlights the relevance of minimizing automation surprises and human-machine conflict wherever possible.

In general, the recency of all these articles suggests that the field of study related to automation surprises in transportation is growing in popularity and relevance. The concept of automation surprises is not new, however. As aforementioned, David Woods applies the term and its related concepts to an aviation concept in 1997 with his chapter in the *Handbook of Human Factors and Ergonomics, Second Edition* and other publications. While automation surprises in aviation have long been of concern, recent research promotes the notion that automation surprises are now seeing the most relevance in automotive automation.

3.2 Data Collection

While the topic of automation surprises seems well-researched in the literature, direct queries for the term yield a dearth of results. In the Web of Science database and Elsevier's Scopus database—both of which will be used to collect data for analysis later in this paper—searches for "automation surprise" garner 156 and 213 results, respectively. These yields would not typically characterize a topic increasing in popularity, but the previously mentioned articles discovered in initial searches tend to suggest the growth and relevance of automation surprises. One potential reason for this dissonance is the fact that none of the articles found in the initial searches use the phrase "automation surprise" anywhere in their publications, with the notable exception of Dr. Woods' chapter, instead opting for discussion of related areas that are still relevant.

To address this dissonance a keyword analysis in MAXQDA proved helpful to extract search terms that would produce a greater yield of articles relating to automation surprises (n.d.). Importing Tivesten's most recent article, the SpringerLink article, and David Woods' chapter on automation surprises, a word cloud and a list of words used most frequently were generated, as seen in Fig. 1. For clarity, insignificant words such as definite articles and prepositions were removed from the list via the use of a stop list.

Word Cloud: Word frequencies   —   □   ×

In 3 documents (18271 words total)   3932 Words (TTR = 0.2152)

Display top ranks

Word	Word length	Frequency	%	Rank	Documents	Documents %
automation	10	321	1.76	1	3	100.00
driver	6	202	1.11	2	2	66.67
system	6	186	1.02	3	3	100.00
driving	7	175	0.96	4	2	66.67
automated	9	170	0.93	5	3	100.00
human	5	151	0.83	6	3	100.00
response	8	128	0.70	7	3	100.00
drivers	7	121	0.66	8	2	66.67
systems	7	120	0.66	9	3	100.00
vehicle	7	104	0.57	10	2	66.67
conflict	8	99	0.54	11	1	33.33
control	7	76	0.42	12	3	100.00
study	5	74	0.41	13	3	100.00
time	4	74	0.41	13	3	100.00
technology	10	72	0.39	15	3	100.00
steering	8	70	0.38	16	2	66.67

Fig. 1. Table of most frequent words extracted from three documents on automation surprises.

In the above table, several pertinent keywords make the top of the list, "human" and "automation" the most prominent among them. Others include "conflict," "trust," "response," and "driver". When searching the Web of Science and Scopus databases for these terms, terms lower on the list including "system," "control," and "vehicle" tended to yield the greatest number of relevant results even when varying search settings like the date. For the Web of Science and Scopus searches, the query "human automation system control vehicle" offered the best results, as summarized in Table 1. Results from these searches will be used for the following analyses. When searching in the Google Scholar database via Harzing's Publish or Perish software, the search was slightly adjusted, replacing the words "control vehicle" with "transportation" to better narrow down the search to relevant articles only (n.d.). A search was also conducted in the National Science Foundation's awards database, as will be discussed in Future Work. These searches taken together form the basis for the bibliometric methods discussed in this paper.

Table 1. Summary of keyword searches conducted to extract data in support of analyses presented in this study.

Database	Search keywords	Search settings	Number of articles
SpringerLink	"automation surprise transportation"	Year > 2010	2,292
Web of Science	"automation surprise"	None	156
Web of Science	"human automation system control vehicle"	None	554
Scopus	"human automation system control vehicle"	None	1,594
Harzing Google Scholar Search	"human automation control transportation"	None	980
National Science Foundation Award Search	"automation surprise"	None	3,000

4 Results and Discussion

4.1 Identification of Emergence

Before examining further details of bibliometric analysis, authorship trends and measures of public engagement offer important context.

Automation surprises in transportation can have an impact on the everyday driver, so the general public's engagement with the topic represents an important way to understand the topic's reach. Figure 2 details the popularity of the topic on Twitter through Vicinitas.io. Vicinitas extracts tweets with both text and rich media from Twitter based on a keyword search and displays a dashboard of engagement measures (Vicinitas n.d.). Figure 2 tracks the popularity of the "driver automation safety" keywords on Twitter. These keywords were selected as a proxy for automation surprises in transportation as academic coverage of the topic utilizes technical jargon not familiar to the general public, thus often yielding low levels of engagement. However, the word cloud generated in Fig. 3 shows that terms such as "automation", "conditional", and "responsible" appear both on Twitter and in the MAXQDA keyword list just below the keywords pictured in Fig. 1.

Though only 18 posts were made in the 7 days preceding the search, they reached an audience of roughly 60,000 users. These results show that automation surprises do garner some popularity in the public sphere, if indirect.

16	18	61	60.1K
Users	Posts	Engagement	Influence

Fig. 2. Twitter engagement measures for the keyword search "driver automation safety" obtained via Vicinitas.

Fig. 3. Word cloud from Vicinitas revealing top keywords discovered in Twitter posts related to the keyword search "driver automation safety".

4.2 Trend Analysis

In the Web of Science, Scopus, and Harzing database searches, a general upward trend of articles and authors occurs. Both Web of Science and Scopus see a drastic increase in article count after 2015. Figure 4 shows the trend by publication year for articles found through Web of Science, seeing a peak of 81 articles published in 2019. Figure 5 shows the same trend for the database search in Scopus, which includes a peak of 228 articles in 2020. Another important observation is that the outbreak of COVID-19 does not appear to have significantly affected research on this topic, as only the Web of Science database saw a reduction for 2020.

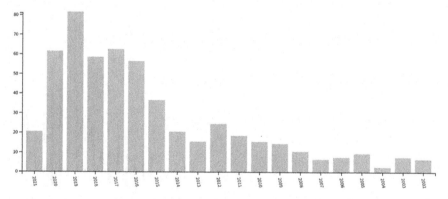

Fig. 4. Trend by year generated from Web of Science for articles found in topic search "human automation system control vehicle". The trend sees a peak of 81 articles in 2019, suggesting that the topic of automation surprises in transportation continues to grow in relevance. This trend illustrates the publication pattern for articles in the Web of Science Core Collection.

Another measure discovered in the Web of Science search was the authors' average h-index, an indicator of one's prominence in an academic field. On average, the authors from the Web of Science search held an h-index of 43, a relatively high value, with an average of 12.92 citations per article.

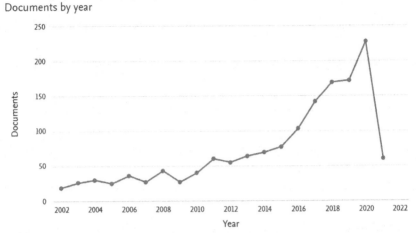

Fig. 5. Trend by year generated by the Scopus database from topic search "human automation system control vehicle". The number of articles published has increased dramatically over the past 10 years, reaching a peak at 228 articles in 2020. Already in 2021, Scopus features 60 documents that match the search terms.

As shown in Fig. 6, Google Scholar metadata from Harzing shows that the number of authors publishing work on the topic trends upward through 2018, with declines since that year. Nonetheless, the last ten years have seen the greatest increases in authorship.

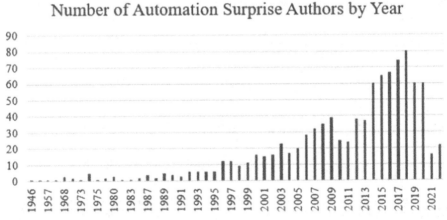

Fig. 6. PivotChart exported from Microsoft Excel using Google Scholar metadata from Harzing. This chart shows the upward trend in the number of authors releasing articles related to the search teams each year, with a peak of 80 in 2018.

4.3 Co-author Analysis

The most prominent authors tend to work with one another to some degree. Using the metadata from the Web of Science search, a co-author analysis was conducted using VOSviewer (n.d.). The threshold for the minimum number of occurrences—the number of articles on which two authors collaborated—was set to five. Here in Fig. 7 is the first indicator of specific authors' prominence in the field. Frank Flemisch appears to be well-connected with his peers, working with each one listed on the co-authorship diagram in Fig. 7.

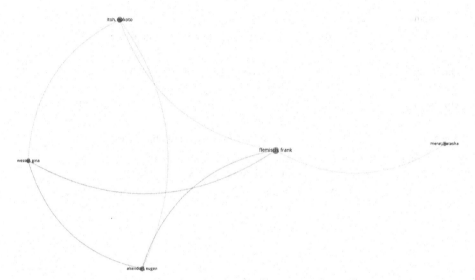

Fig. 7. Co-author analysis conducted in VOSviewer, showing the most prominent authors the topic and their relationship to other authors in the field.

These authors can be examined in more detail via search result analysis in Scopus. Table 2 shows the top ten leading authors by article count as identified by Scopus in the topic search. Top keywords from their publications are also included. Four of five authors discovered in the co-author analysis also appear in this table. These authors' presence in multiple analyses suggests their relevance to the topic area above other authors' contributions.

To identify additional top authors and articles in the field, CiteSpace was utilized for its citation burst and keyword cluster features (n.d.). Using the same Web of Science data as Fig. 7, CiteSpace identifies the top 16 most cited articles from all 554 found, showing the years with the greatest frequency of citation, known as "citation bursts", colored in red. Figure 8 illustrates this output. Note that Frank Flemisch and Natasha Merat appear in both figures and the table. Raja Parasuraman appears as a co-author on the paper by Christopher Miller listed in the citation burst.

Merat's 2014 article considers the areas of control and expectation, noting that out-of-the-loop drivers' "ability to regain control of the vehicle is better if they are expecting automation to be switched off" when resuming control of the system (Merat et al. 2014,

Table 2. Top ten leading authors from topic search as identified by Scopus among 1,594 articles. The top three leading keywords from each author's work are also featured.

Author	Years active	Leading keywords	Article count
M.L. Cummings	2005–2016	Unmanned vehicles, automation, human supervisory control	22
K. Bengler	2011–2019	Automation, automated driving, vehicles	20
F. Flemisch	2006–2019	Automation, guidance and control, man machine systems	20
N.A. Stanton	2007–2021	Automation, human, adult	19
M. Itoh	2011–2021	Automation, shared control, automated driving	14
G.L. Calhoun	2004–2019	Automation, supervisory control, human interactions	11
H.A. Ruff	2009–2019	Automation, supervisory control, human interactions	11
N. Merat	2009–2020	Automation, human, automobile driving	10
D.A. Abbink	2008–2019	Automation, automobile drivers, automobile simulators	9
E. Altendorf	2015–2019	Automation, automated driving, guidance and control	9

Top 16 References with the Strongest Citation Bursts

References	Year	Strength	Begin	End	2006 - 2021
Miller CA, 2007, HUM FACTORS, V49, P57, DOI 10.1518/001872007779598037, DOI	2007	5.73	2010	2012	
Cummings ML, 2007, INT C2 J, V2007, P1	2007	2.85	2010	2012	
Cummings ML, 2010, HUM FACTORS, V52, P17, DOI 10.1177/0018720810368674, DOI	2010	3.12	2012	2015	
Abbink DA, 2012, COGN TECHNOL WORK, V14, P19, DOI 10.1007/s10111-011-0192-5, DOI	2012	5.03	2013	2017	
Merat N, 2012, HUM FACTORS, V54, P762, DOI 10.1177/0018720812442087, DOI	2012	2.97	2014	2016	
Carsten O, 2012, HUM FACTORS, V54, P747, DOI 10.1177/0018720812460246, DOI	2012	3.55	2015	2017	
Gold C, 2013, P HUM FACT ERG SOC A, V57, P1938, DOI DOI 10.1177/1541931213571433, DOI	2013	5.18	2016	2018	
Flemisch FO, 2014, ERGONOMICS, V57, P343, DOI 10.1080/00140139.2013.869355, DOI	2014	4.98	2016	2019	
Beller J, 2013, HUM FACTORS, V55, P1130, DOI 10.1177/0018720813482327, DOI	2013	3.57	2016	2018	
Merat N, 2014, TRANSPORT RES F-TRAF, V27, P274, DOI 10.1016/j.trf.2014.09.005, DOI	2014	3.46	2016	2019	
Bengler K, 2014, IEEE INTELL TRANSP SY, V6, P6, DOI 10.1109/MITS.2014.2336271, DOI	2014	3.06	2016	2019	
de Winter JCF, 2014, TRANSPORT RES F-TRAF, V27, P196, DOI 10.1016/j.trf.2014.06.016, DOI	2014	5.11	2017	2019	
Eriksson A, 2017, HUM FACTORS, V59, P689, DOI 10.1177/0018720816685832, DOI	2017	6.03	2018	2021	
Fagnant DJ, 2015, TRANSPORT RES A-POL, V77, P167, DOI 10.1016/j.tra.2015.04.003, DOI	2015	3.39	2018	2019	
Erlien SM, 2016, IEEE T INTELL TRANSP, V17, P441, DOI 10.1109/TITS.2015.2453404, DOI	2016	4.35	2019	2021	
Nguyen AT, 2017, IEEE T IND ELECTRON, V64, P3819, DOI 10.1109/TIE.2016.2645146, DOI	2017	3.99	2019	2021	

Fig. 8. Top 16 articles with the strongest "Citation Bursts" among 489 qualified records as classified by CiteSpace. The software picks out the articles which are cited the most often and indicates the years in which they are cited. Four articles of particular relevance to automation surprises are highlighted.

274). Flemisch reports on the cooperation between drivers and highly automated systems, likely a useful reference for authors looking for background information on automation surprises. Alexander Eriksson and Neville Stanton study takeover time in highly automated vehicles, a very relevant element to the study of automation surprises (2017, 689). This study deals with noncritical scenarios but can set a baseline for researchers to study how drivers make the transition to manual control.

In addition, automation surprises are of special interest to universities around the world and aerospace research centers in the United States. Table 3 shows the location and leading keywords of the top five publishing institutions by article count.

Table 3. Top five leading institutions from topic search as identified by Scopus among 1,594 articles. The top three leading keywords from each institution's publications are also featured.

Institution	Country	Leading keywords	Article count
Delft University of Technology	The Netherlands	Automation, vehicles, man machine systems	47
Massachusetts Institute of Technology	United States	Automation, unmanned vehicles, human supervisory control	44
NASA Ames Research Center	United States	Automation, NASA, air traffic control	32
Technical University of Munich	Germany	Automation, automated driving, vehicles	32
Wright-Patterson AFB	United States	Automation, UAV, supervisory control	29

4.4 Co-citation Analysis

In addition, the Web of Science data for the search on "human automation system control vehicle" was used to develop a co-citation analysis. Co-citation analysis refers to the tracking of how two articles may co-occur as references for another article. As seen in Figs. 9 and 10, Parasuraman enjoys extensive citations on two of his papers, the first giving an overview of trust in automation, another confounding factor for operators dealing with automation surprises. Drivers with different levels of trust in automation may respond differently when posed with an automation surprise and limited time to act.

Create Map   ✕

 Verify selected cited references

Selected	Cited reference	Citations	Total link strength ⌄
☑	parasuraman r, 1997, hum factors, v39, p230, doi ...	73	308
☑	lee jd, 2004, hum factors, v46, p50, doi 10.1518/hf...	69	290
☑	parasuraman r, 2000, ieee t syst man cy a, v30, p2...	72	287
☑	bainbridge l, 1983, automatica, v19, p775, doi 10.1...	48	246
☑	endsley mr, 1995, hum factors, v37, p32, doi 10.15...	46	170
☑	endsley mr, 1995, hum factors, v37, p381, doi 10.1...	37	168
☑	sheridan t.b., 1992, telerobotics automat	39	156
☑	norman da, 1990, philos t roy soc b, v327, p585, d...	25	142
☑	de winter jcf, 2014, transport res f-traf, v27, p196, ...	30	140
☑	lee j, 1992, ergonomics, v35, p1243, doi 10.1080/0...	23	131
☑	kaber d. b., 2003, theoretical issues e, v3, p1, doi 1...	25	130
☑	michon ja, 1985, human behav traffic, p485, doi 1...	23	122
☑	endsley mr, 1999, ergonomics, v42, p462, doi 10.1...	25	118
☑	parasuraman r., 1993, int j aviat psychol, v3, p1, d...	21	118
☑	sarter nb, 1995, hum factors, v37, p5, doi 10.1518/...	25	117
☑	merat n, 2014, transport res f-traf, v27, p274, doi 1...	22	115
☑	abbink da, 2012, cogn technol work, v14, p19, doi ...	30	114
☑	flemisch f, 2012, cogn technol work, v14, p3, doi 1...	24	114
☑	flemisch fo, 2014, ergonomics, v57, p343, doi 10.1...	22	114

                    [< Back] [Next >] [Finish] [Cancel]

Fig. 9. List of references to be included in VOSviewer co-citation analysis. Co-citation analysis highlights publications with the greatest number of Citations and examines the strength of association between a publication and others revealed in the dataset, which in this case was generated from Web of Science.

The top authors in the table and VOSviewer network visualization, John D. Lee and Raja Parasuraman, report less on automation surprises in transportation than they do on the underlying human-machine interaction phenomena that drive them. Parasuraman, whose top paper is titled "Humans and Automation: Use, Misuse, Disuse, Abuse", focuses on automation in general (1997, 230). Lee takes a more specific look at an area of human-machine interaction by examining "Trust in Automation" (2004, 50). The generality of these articles is not unexpected as they are early works in the field, offering important background information from which a range of future articles are drawing.

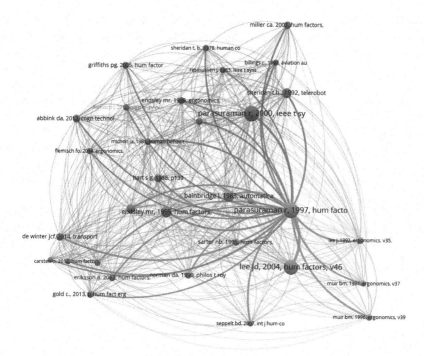

Fig. 10. Co-citation analysis conducted in VOSviewer, showing the most prominent articles on the topic search and their relationship with articles that cite them.

4.5 Cluster Analysis

Having examined authors and citation strength, which indicate relevance, content analysis becomes key to understand which specific sub-topics are emerging concerning automation surprises in transportation. Using CiteSpace, a cluster analysis, seen in Fig. 11, was generated to identify key topic clusters based on the Web of Science data. In light of the drastic increase in article count after 2015, as shown in the trend analysis, the cluster analysis was limited to include only articles from this period.

4.6 Content Analysis from MAXQDA

With the preceding measures identified and analyzed, a final analysis was completed in MAXQDA to generate a word cloud visualizing the most important keywords from leading articles on automation surprises in transportation. To accomplish this, articles were imported into MAXQDA for analysis. These included the four articles previously mentioned in Sect. 3.1, as well as Lee and Parasuraman's articles and a recently funded National Science Foundation grant, discussed in Future Work. In addition, three articles from the CiteSpace citation burst were also selected. The first article from the citation burst comes from Flemisch, who along with Klaus Bengler, also a leading author, studies cooperation between vehicle automation and humans, specifically concerning the nature of guidance and control. The authors study two main modes of control which could be useful for cutting down on automation surprises: "conduct-by-wire" and "haptic multimodal interaction", the former feeling more like typical automotive operation and the latter representing a high-tech use of a haptic interface (Flemisch et al. 2014, 343). Natasha Merat's article on resuming control, Eriksson and Stanton's article on takeover time, and an article on automation uncertainty by Klaus Bengler are also included. Eriksson and Stanton write a paper on takeover time in vehicles with high automation, a term they define as "the time it takes the driver to take back control of the vehicle from the automated system when a [takeover request] has been issued" (Eriksson and Stanton 2017, 690). To include an additional core publication in the field of automation design, Lee's chapter on "Human Factors and Ergonomics in Automation Design" in the *Handbook of Human Factors and Ergonomics, Third Edition* was featured following its discovery via a lexical search of the term "automation surprise" in the *Handbook* (Lee and See 2004, 1570). Finally, an article on bibliometric analysis by Guo et al. (2020) was included to mention bibliometric methods utilized in this paper. For clarity, insignificant words such as definite articles and prepositions were removed via the use of a stop list (Fig. 12).

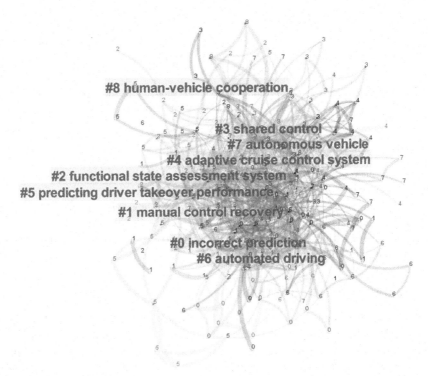

Fig. 11. Keyword clusters found via CiteSpace among 370 qualified publications published in 2015 or later. Top clusters like "incorrect prediction" have and "manual control recovery" illustrate critical elements in the study of automation surprises. Automation surprises arise when the driver fails to understand what automation will do, prompting a surprise need to recover manual control.

Fig. 12. Word cloud generated in MAXQDA from the twelve articles aforementioned. The word list aligns well with keywords discovered in CiteSpace and AuthorMapper. "Automation" naturally appears the largest, with "human", "driver", and "trust" following in size because of their frequent mention.

4.7 Discussion

Through the analysis conducted in this systematic review, a few key themes arose. The study of prominent authors and their work helped to narrow the field to a short-list of emerging themes regarding automation surprises. An extended lexical search in MAXQDA was utilized to seek out detail in the following areas. Several top keywords were considered for this analysis—"system", "driver", and "performance", to name a few—but were omitted from this discussion as their commonality precluded unique insight. Each of these themes draws from methods and applications introduced in the various articles that will be mentioned.

Cooperation: Low on the list of top keywords in MAXQDA but identified as prominent in the CiteSpace cluster analysis was the topic of cooperation between humans and vehicles. Flemisch and Bengler expand upon this idea by viewing cooperation as a "cluster concept", listing attributes that "are likely to contribute to the cooperativeness of control", including the dynamic distribution of control through delegation and the arbitration of conflicts when intentions differ between the human and the automation system. (Flemisch et al. 2014, 346). The concept of cooperation is critical to the prevention of situations in which an automation surprise could occur. Compatible goals, value systems, and representations of the vehicle's movement optimize the level of cooperation between parties.

Shared Control: Underlying the concept of cooperation is that of control. As characterized by Flemisch and Bengler, shared control between humans and vehicles involves "two entities, the driver and an automation...controlling the vehicle in varying shares and working together cooperatively" (Flemisch et al. 2014, 345). Control makes up a central consideration for understanding automation surprises as its transfer and sharing must both be well-understood by all parties involved. Tivesten and her colleagues outline two roles created by driving automation: "the delegated and the shared driving role, or unsupervised and supervised automated driving respectively" (Gustavsson et al. 2018, 1). Further, Lee in the *Handbook of Human Factors and Ergonomics, Second Edition*, divides control into multiple levels, each "supported by a different type of automation": strategic, tactical, and operational. Strategic automation deals with values and goals, tactical with "priorities and coordination", and operational with "perceptual cues and motor response" (2004, 1579). These levels of control may be continuously shared between automation and the human, as in the case of supervised automation (Pipkorn et al. 2021, 15). At each level, the system designer must carefully consider the tension between automation and human in context.

From the perspective of a job designer who must define the task of driving, clear expectations for the driver could boost job satisfaction and mitigate job enlargement. In addition, while training can prove helpful for the operator, limited monetary and time resources mean operators must determine for themselves how best to work with the system. Woods notes that "ongoing learning needs to take place during actual operations and has to be supported to help operators discover and correct bugs in their model of the automation" for routine operations (1997, 4).

Trust: Misplaced trust in automation can cultivate a breeding ground for automation surprises to occur. When a driver trusts automation to, as they view it, respond appropriately to environmental stimuli like objects in the roadway, a sense of complacency can arise, allowing "the development of a false sense of security" (Woods et al. 1997, 11). When this complacency creeps in, Woods notes that the prevailing view "seems to suggest that if the human would only try harder, it would be possible for him to perform his duties successfully" (1997, 11). However, this view fails to recognize that humans' notions of what to expect from automation should be consistent with reality. Tivesten's paper finds that drivers who expected automation not to handle a potential collision event were less likely to crash than those who had high levels of trust and did crash (Gustavsson et al. 2018, 11). At the same time, many non-crashers held a high level of trust in automation. Nonetheless, automation design should prioritize the mitigation of crash scenarios even if many trusting drivers would not crash.

5   Conclusion and Future Work

5.1   Conclusion

While automation surprises have existed as a topic of study for many years, bibliometric analysis reveals that in recent years, the topic has undergone refreshed interest as authors grapple with the human factors challenges of semi-autonomous vehicle systems. Researchers today draw upon well-established principles in human-automation interaction, such as cooperation, shared control, and trust, to help explain phenomena in the field, suggest new solutions, and fill gaps in the literature.

The topic of automation surprises in transportation seems to be encapsulated within a larger discussion of human-machine interaction, so an indirect set of search terms were used as a proxy for data collection. The results indicated that researchers have heavily pursued the topic since 2015, especially the top authors identified in the Leading Authors table and CiteSpace citation bursts. Flemisch tends to work with other authors the most, in one case co-authoring an article with Natasha Merat, another prominent author in the field. Parasuraman and Lee enjoy frequent citations over the years, offering useful background for authors that follow them. The content these authors publish also tends to follow similar trends, converging on overlapping key themes including "cooperation", "shared control", and "trust". These themes center around the driving forces that could result in automation surprise events. Drivers must understand the responsibilities and limitations of automated systems, while automated systems must dynamically respond to the varying actions of drivers who may not act predictably, especially in the case of emergencies. As long as humans are involved in the task of driving, researchers and designers should work to ensure the driver is never surprised by the actions of automation behind the wheel.

5.2 Future Work

Though much has already been discovered relating to automation surprises in transportation through the present day, academic research continues with work recently funded by the National Science Foundation (n.d.). A search tool on the NSF site allows the user to look up research projects recently deemed worthy of an NSF grant (n.d.). A grant in 2017 for $97,786 gave researcher Jing Chen at Old Dominion University the opportunity to explore the safety element of "the inclusion of human drivers in the semi-autonomous systems" (2017). The project examines "influential factors of the human driver, the vehicle sub-system, and the interaction" in the context of safety, especially given that "unanticipated input from the human driver" may confound the design of the semi-autonomous driving system in emergency situations (Chen 2017). This work appears to cover the critical element of safety in transportation automation surprises. In the direst of scenarios, automation surprises could lead to tragic consequences, making this research a pressing topic.

References

Chen, J.: Award Abstract # 1760347 CRII: CHS: Human in the Loop: Safety for Semi-autonomous Driving Systems in Emergency Situations. National Science Foundation (n.d.). https://www.nsf.gov/awardsearch/showAward?AWD_ID=1760347&HistoricalAwards=false. Accessed 29 Apr 2021

CiteSpace © 2003–2020 Chaomei Chen. CiteSpace: visualizing patterns and trends in scientific literature (n.d.). http://cluster.cis.drexel.edu/~cchen/citespace/. Accessed 1 May 2021

Eriksson, A., Stanton, N.A.: Takeover time in highly automated vehicles: noncritical transitions to and from manual control. Hum. Factors **59**(4), 689–705 (2017). https://doi.org/10.1177/0018720816685832

Flemisch, F.O., Bengler, K., Bubb, H., Winner, H. Bruder, R.: Towards cooperative guidance and control of highly automated vehicles: h-mode and conduct-by-wire. Ergonomics (2014). https://doi.org/10.1080/00140139.2013.869355

Guo, F., Li, F., Lv, W., Liu, L., Duffy, V.G.: Bibliometric analysis of affective computing researches during 1999–2018. Int. J. Hum.-Comput. Interact. **36**(9), 801–814 (2020). https://doi.org/10.1080/10447318.2019.1688985

Gustavsson, P., Victor, T.W., Johansson, J., Tivesten, E., Johansson, R., Aust, L.: What were they thinking ? Subjective experiences associated with automation expectation mismatch. In: Proceedings of the 6th Driver Distraction and Inattention Conference, no. October, pp. 1–12 (2018)

Harzing, A.W.: "Publish or Perish." Harzing.com (n.d.). https://harzing.com/. Accessed 30 Apr 2021

Lee, J.D.: Human factors and ergonomics in automation design. In: Handbook of Human Factors and Ergonomics, pp. 1570–1596 (2006). https://doi.org/10.1002/0470048204.ch60

Lee, J.D., See, K.A.: Trust in automation: designing for appropriate reliance. Hum. Factors **46**(1), 50–80 (2004). https://doi.org/10.1518/hfes.46.1.50_30392

MAXQDA. (n.d.). https://www.maxqda.com/. Accessed 1 May 2021

Merat, N., Jamson, A.H., Lai, F.C.H., Daly, M., Carsten, O.M.: Transition to manual: driver behaviour when resuming control from a highly automated vehicle. Transp. Res. Part F: Traffic Psychol. Behav. **27**(PB), 274–282 (2014)

National Science Foundation (n.d.). https://www.nsf.gov/awardsearch/simpleSearch.jsp. Accessed 30 Apr 2021

Parasuraman, R., Riley, V.: Humans and automation: use, misuse, disuse, abuse. Hum. Factors **39**(2), 230–253 (1997). https://doi.org/10.1518/001872097778543886

Pipkorn, L., Victor, T.W., Dozza, M., Tivesten, E.: Driver conflict response during supervised automation: do hands on wheel matter? Transp. Res. F: Traffic Psychol. Behav. **76**(January), 14–25 (2021). https://doi.org/10.1016/j.trf.2020.10.001

Salvendy, G. (ed.): Handbook of Human Factors and Ergonomics. Wiley, New York (2012)

Vicinitas (n.d.). https://www.vicinitas.io/free-tools/download-search-tweets. Accessed 29 Apr 2021

Visualizing Scientific Landscapes. VOSviewer (n.d.). https://www.vosviewer.com/. Accessed 30 Apr 2021

Web of Science (n.d.). https://apps.webofknowledge.com/WOS_GeneralSearch_input.do?product=WOS&search_mode=GeneralSearch&SID=6Fq7F5HAcvLG6mNPgG2&preferencesSaved=. Accessed 2 Dec 2021

Woods, D.D., Sarter, N.B., Billings, C.E.: Automation surprises. In: Salvendy, G. (ed.) Handbook of Human Factors and Ergonomics, 2nd edn, pp. 1926–1943. Wiley, New York (1997)

Research on In-Vehicle Haptic Interactions as Crucial Resources for Driver Perceptions

Xin Xin, Yiji Wang, Nan Liu, Wenmin Yang, Hang Dong, and Wei Liu[✉]

Beijing Normal University, Beijing, China
Wei.liu@bnu.edu.cn

Abstract. Multiple resource theory is currently commonly applied in human–machine interactions in vehicle design. Haptic interaction is a crucial resource for driver perceptions. This paper reviews haptic research related to haptic driving from 2008 to 2020. A total of 248 journal papers and conference proceeding papers were reviewed and analyzed in CiteSpace, and 11 key elements were clustered. This paper presents them in two domains: vibration patterns and vibration scenarios. With vibration patterns, we mainly focus on patterns and locations; within this framework, we discuss applied scenarios, such as navigation, collision warning, and eco-driving. We also discuss the main challenges and future directions for transferring the results to real driving scenes and offer a roadmap for haptic research in this area.

Keywords: Haptic · Patterns of vibration · Vibration scenario · Driving first

1 Introduction

Sensory perception is critical information that is needed for drivers to complete driving tasks. Drivers process perception information to make decisions and ensure driving safety. However, the driving task is mainly focused on visual tasks. According to multiple resource theory [1], visual display information increases the workload, leads to cognitive overload, decreases driving performance, and negative impacts traffic safety [2–4]. Researchers have performed extensive research on auditory displays, including cell phone calls and the effect of voice on driving performance, which still have adverse effects on driving performance and task completion efficiency [5–7]. Therefore, an increasing number of researchers and automobile companies have focused on how to provide a haptic modality to enhance driving performance. According to the ISO standards [8], a haptic interaction is a "sensory or motor activity on skin, muscles, joints and/or tendons as part of human-computer interaction." Therefore, compared with visual and auditory interactions, haptic interactions can present direct, intense, and continuous stimuli to the human body. There are two primary means of haptic interactions in a driving system: vibration and force. In this paper, we discuss vibration interactions.

Vibration modality plays many roles in the driving task. One of the primary purposes of vibration is to convey critical information by accessing the driver's attention. For example, Hwang and Ryu [9] gave a meaningful indication that a vibrotactile steering

© Springer Nature Switzerland AG 2021
C. Stephanidis et al. (Eds.): HCII 2021, LNCS 13097, pp. 373–388, 2021.
https://doi.org/10.1007/978-3-030-90966-6_27

wheel can provide three types of information in navigation, "turn right," "turn left" and "alert", in an effective way. In recent years, researchers have proposed maintaining situation awareness (SA) through vibrotactile seats in take-over situations [10]. Although vibration interaction can prioritize information in a specific situation, the problem is that haptic feedback cannot always give clear instructions to the driver. Participants reported that a haptic effect named Bump could not make them aware of the suggested next behavior [11]. Even if a driver has perceived the vibration feedback, there is confusion over what to do, which may have an implicit impact on the effectiveness of vibration.

In addition, inappropriate vibrotactile stimuli may lead to discomfort in the human body and a distraction from driving. Accordingly, it is a valuable to develop a haptic interface in driving situations to convey critical information. However, it is better to minimize cognitive overload and distraction.

This paper introduces vibration studies on driving situations from three aspects: vibration patterns, vibration locations, and driving situations. Driving situations are divided into three components: navigation, collision warning, and eco-driving. We focus not only on autonomous driving, which mainly discusses the L3 level because it is a significant research topic, but also on traditional driving. Through a literature review, we summarize the features of vibration, analyze the advantages and disadvantages, gain insight into the limitations of the current research, and identify future directions in automobile vibrotactile device studies.

2 Method

This literature search was performed by searching the database of the Web of Science using the keywords haptic and driving. We selected papers from 2008–2020 because papers related to haptic driving surged after 2008. We read the abstracts to select papers from scientific journals or conference proceedings. The haptic signal needs to be activated when participants drive in a real or simulated environment, and the environment should be designed for drivers in a specific driving task. Finally, we filtered 248 papers and fed the paper information into CiteSpace. The results showed that the total number of citations was 2165, the average number of citations was 8.73, the most fruitful year for publication was 2017, and the number of citations increased year by year (see Fig. 1).

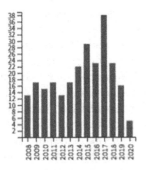 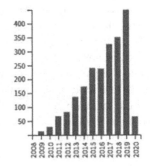

Fig. 1. Annual publication (left) and annual citation (right)

After clustering the keywords in CiteSpace, we obtained 11 key clusters: haptic perception; adjustable automation; continuous haptic feedback, frontal collision avoidance; haptic pedal; haptic information; in-vehicle eco-driving assistance system; haptic steering support; vibroacoustic communication; managing fatigue; and automotive user interface. We clustered these 11 issues into two primary domains in haptic driving research: vibration patterns and vibration scenarios (see Table 1).

Table 1. The keywords of haptic research in driving in two primary domains.

Vibration patterns	Vibration scenarios
Haptic perception	Frontal collision avoidance
Continuous haptic feedback	In-vehicle eco-driving assistance system
Haptic information	Adjustable automation
Vibroacoustic communication	Automotive user interface
Haptic steering support	Managing fatigue
Haptic pedal	

3   Patterns of Vibration

There are many parameters and variables in vibration, including frequency, amplitude, rhythm, waveform, position, direction, moving pattern, size, shape, orientation, and duration [12, 13]. It is possible to adjust parameters and change variables into different patterns to transmit information.

3.1   Patterns

Participants were able to distinguish and evaluate four kinds of amplitudes and three kinds of frequencies. Hwang et al. [9] indicated the probability that different levels of parameters may convey a critical degree of information in the driving situation. In addition, researchers designed eight patterns of vibration and compared these patterns, and the results indeed showed a preference for specific patterns that were reported by participants. In this article, different distance information was transmitted by changing the duration and rhythm of vibration [14]. Another study also uncovered that using different numbers of vibration pulses to transmit distance information is a possible approach [15].

To propose practical guidelines for vibration design, article [12] chose frequency, amplitude, position, moving pattern, and rhythm as the design variables of vibration but excluded waveform because the human body is not sensitive to variations in waveforms. The report also proposed a limitation of the varied amplitude because we probably cannot recognize small differences in amplitude because this parameter is usually not used as other parameters [13]. Therefore, we can assume that not every parameter or variable can be detected and distinguished by the driver; this can also impact the utilization of vibrotactile devices.

Although vibration patterns can influence our perception of transmitting various information in some ways, different frequencies or amplitudes can let drivers perceive the difference in information in real driving situations. Usually, vibration is measured in two dimensions: amplitude and duration (see Figs. 2 and 3), and the typical application of two kinds of patterns of vibration have different durations and amplitudes.

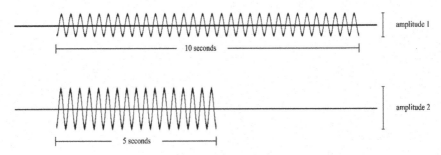

Fig. 2. Different design patterns on vibration seat

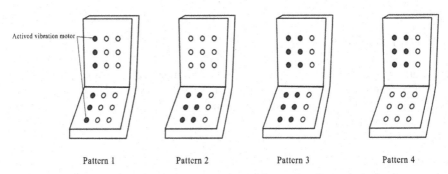

Fig. 3. Four kinds vibration patterns with different duration and amplitude

Different combinations of multiple parameters will present new experiences or opportunities in vibrotactile interactions, and there are many questions in automobile vibration devices waiting for answers but lacking in practical research.

3.2 Location

Different media can transmit vibrations in different scenes. Because a vibration signal can be better accepted by a driver, many researchers are studying which part of the vibration can transmit a message accurately. Existing research has mainly focused on steering wheels, haptic seats, and backs, haptic pedals, haptic belts (seat belts), multimodal systems, touchscreen interfaces, and human–machine physical interfaces.

Steering Wheel. Drivers need to steer the wheels all the time while driving, so many researchers have conducted various studies about vibration patterns in driving (see Figs. 4 and 5). Mars et al. [16] showed that when the visibility is weak, the steering wheel can provide vibration feedback to guide and correct the driving route. When going through tunnels, the steering wheel can provide haptic feedback to help a driver navigate curves safely [17]. A vibrating steering wheel can also provide directional information [9]. In addition to the functions listed above, the steering wheel can transmit other haptic information, such as lateral skin stretching [18], temperature [19], and steering wheel torque [20].

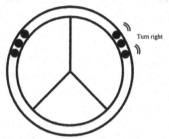
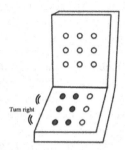

Fig. 4. Vibrational steering wheel   **Fig. 5.** Vibrational seat

In summary, transmitting vibration information by a steering wheel has some advantages: (1) a driver holds the steering wheel all the time while driving; (2) hands are extremely sensitive to tactile conditions and cannot be disturbed by other things; and (3) it is natural way to use hands to obtain feedback in driving. However, there are also disadvantages. Because hand position cannot be confirmed or predicted in different situations, the steering wheel cannot always sends alerts to the driver. Hwang et al. [9] showed that it is not appropriate to statically separate the steering wheel into two parts to transmit haptic stimuli, which means that only continuous vibration can ensure the safe operation of the driver.

Haptic Seat/Back. Because of the shortcomings of the steering wheel, some studies have focused on car seats; for instance, seat vibration can indicate direction (see Fig. 5). During either autonomous driving or manual driving, the driver and passenger have to be seated, so the car seats become an effective medium to transmit vibration. The driver cannot hold the steering wheel in autonomous driving, so in this situation, many researchers believe that it is more appropriate to use car seats as a medium to transmit vibration. An 8 × 8 matrix vibrator was embedded in a car seat, which could encode in eight different directions. This was sufficient to show the direction and distance of the turn to the driver by combining a haptic display and haptic seat [21]. In autonomous driving, the haptic seat plays a vital role in maintaining the perception of surrounding traffic situations, including changing lanes and decelerating speed excessively and optimizing the transmission between the driver and the car [22]. A haptic seat can improve the situational awareness of the driver and provide information during autonomous driving [9]. In provisional autonomous driving, a continuous haptic guide will encourage the driver to accelerate to decrease a potential security interest [23]. Grah et al. [21] introduced a reshapeable car seat back, which could allow the driver to tactilely detect obstacles in the rear. This research provided a continuous increase in surrounding perception, which can help drivers locate stimuli spatially. The participants reported a high level of satisfaction with the haptic seat. Driving performance has shown that a haptic seat will lead to faster and more effective human responses [22].

In summary, the advantages of the haptic seat are as follows: (1) the vibration stimuli can accurately act on a specific body part; (2) the vibrational elements can be combined with the seat perfectly and continuously in contact with the driver [23]. However, the shortcomings are as follows: (1) the driver can be confused by other vibrations, such as bumps caused by uneven roads; (2) depending on the texture of the seat and clothes, the tactile sensitivity may decrease; and (3) some participants thought that the tactiles were unpleasant in haptic seats.

Haptic Pedal. The most significant advantage of a haptic pedal (see Fig. 6) is that by instantly providing feedback when the threshold has been reached, the extra workload be decreased and the autonomous level of the mission will be maintained. Some researchers doubt whether haptic information can be used to assist driving while reducing energy consumption and emissions. Therefore, the haptic pedal has become a new topic of research. When the haptic pedal is active, the use of average acceleration, maximum throttle, and excess throttle will be significantly reduced, while the workload of the driver will decrease as well [19]. Geitner et al. [24] showed that the perception of haptic feedback from the accelerator pedal has no significant relationship with driver shoe size and age. However, haptic perception seems to be significantly affected by gender.

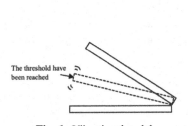

Fig. 6. Vibrational pedal

Fig. 7. Vibrational safety belt

In summary, the most valued aspect of a haptic pedal is that when the accelerator pedal has reached the set threshold, the vibration will be transmitted to the driver directly to reduce the extra workload of the driver. The disadvantages are twofold: first, when the ground is uneven, the transmission effect will be influenced. Second, the times when the driver uses the brake and accelerator pedal are not fixed. Thus, we must consider how to use the pedal to reasonably transfer information.

Haptic Belt. Research on safety belts (see Fig. 7) has emerged because drivers have to wear them when driving. Compared with traditional car navigation systems, the haptic belt, which has a different tactile coded message, has a better positioning ability [14].

Additionally, compared with the steering wheel, the participants performed better when using the safety belt as a vibration medium [25]. However, the shortcoming is that the participant reaction may be unpleasant because of the vibration position, which is too close and tight to the body. Table 2 shows the advantages and disadvantages of different sensitized location vibrations. There are other studies concerning vibration location, including multimodal systems (using multiple senses to transmit vibration) [26–30], touchscreen interfaces [31, 32], and human–machine physical interfaces (such as the buttons in the car) [33].

Table 2. Vibration location

Vibration position	Advantages	Disadvantages
Steering wheel	(1) continuous contact; (2) the hand is extremely sensitive to vibration stimuli; (3) a natural way to obtain feedback	(1) cannot predict or confirm the position of the hand
Haptic seat/back	(1) continuous contact; (2) the specific body part is accurate to the vibration stimuli; (3) natural way to combine the vibration elements and seat	(1) uneven roads influence vibration perception; (2) the texture of the seat and clothes influence the tactile sensitivity;
Haptic pedal	(1) instantly provides feedback when the threshold has been reached; (2) the foot directly perceives the vibration stimuli	(1) unsustainable contact (2) cannot predict or confirm the position of the foot; (3) uneven roads influence vibration perception
Haptic belt	(1) continuous contact	(1) the body is too close and tight to the vibration stimuli

4 Vibration Scenarios

In different driving situations, vibration feedback has different application methods and research paradigms. Based on the vibrations mentioned above in terms of both position and vibration mode, researchers have combined various specific driving scenarios and conducted numerous studies on situations such as navigation, collision warning, and economical driving. This article summarizes the independent and dependent variables in the existing research. In the following, the existing studies that applied vibration feedback to specific scenarios will be discussed in more detail. Tables 3 and 4 show the same standard independent variables and dependent variables in the navigation, collision warning, and eco-driving scenarios.

Table 3. Independent and dependent variables

Common independent variable	Common dependent variable
Vibration position Vibration parameter	Reaction time Subjective evaluation Cognitive load

Table 4. The particular dependent variable

Scenario	Particular dependent variable
Navigation	Accuracy of turning Navigation information recognition rate
Collision Warning	Minimum collision avoidance distance (MDA) Collision prevent rate
Eco-driving	Time Taken, Fuel Use, Throttle Mean, Throttle Max, Throttle SD, Brake SD, Distance, Coasting

4.1 Navigation

A common tactile navigation scenario is to transmit the direction and distance information through a tactile sensation, guiding the driver to turn left or right. Usually, a driving simulator is used to create a driving scenario. There are also a few experiments in real driving scenarios. In the study of tactile navigation, the usual positions are the steering wheel, seat, belt, and real glasses. The usual form of tactile feedback is vibration, and there are other feedback methods, such as temperature and pressure. In tactile navigation, the tactile stimulus can transmit both direction information and distance information. For example, in real glasses, the vibrator on the left side of the glasses can indicate a left turn, and that on the right side can indicate a right turn [34]. At the same time, distance information can also be transmitted. Different distance information can be transmitted by changing the duration and rhythm of the vibration, including four distances: very-far, far, near, and immediately turning [14]. Szczerba et al. [15] used different numbers of vibration pulses to transmit distance information. In tactile navigation research, the standard measurement indicators are response time, accuracy rate, recognition rate, subjective evaluation, cognitive load, and workload. In the experimental research of tactile navigation, the following research directions have been pursued:

1) Exploring the best tactile information mode for transmitting navigation information, such as changing some vibration parameters, including frequency, amplitude, duration, rhythm, etc. For example, Hwang et al. [9] put 32 vibrators in the steering wheel, and three types of vibration durations, 3 types of illusions and three vibration modes were combined to obtain many different types of vibrations as independent variables. By measuring the recognition rate and response time of different vibration

stimuli, the best tactile information mode for transmitting navigation information was obtained.

2) Finding the sensory channel that is most suitable for transmitting navigation information. In this kind of research, tactile navigation is usually compared with traditional navigation, including visual modality and auditory modality, to find the most suitable navigation method. Some use only tactile or auditory or visual navigation. In contrast, others use two or even three sensory channels for navigation at the same time, such as the combination of tactile and auditory or tactile and visual. Nukarinen et al. [34] compared three different navigation methods of haptic glasses, visual text prompts, and haptic chairs and concluded that compared with visual text cues, the response speed of haptic cues was significantly faster. Haptic cues were also evaluated as less frustrating than visual cues. Nukarinen et al. [35] compared visual navigation, a haptic seat, and the method of combining visual and haptic navigation. The response speed of all other cues was significantly faster than that of the visual cues, but the combination of multiple modes was not faster. Moreover, haptic cues alone caused the most errors but were considered the most comfortable method. Di Campli San Vito et al. [19] applied two new types of haptic feedback: thermal feedback and skin thrust. This experiment compared these two haptic navigation methods with audio navigation and concluded that the recognition rate of audio feedback and skin thrust were higher, the workload was lower, and the thermal feedback was evaluated as uncomfortable.

3) Exploring the best navigation method in high-load situations. Usually, in addition to driving, there will be other subtasks in the experiment, such as n-bank tasks, to increase the driver's cognitive load and attention resources. Ploch et al. [36] used a steering wheel that produced lateral skin extension and used the n-back task as the subtask. The performances of the haptic steering wheel and audio navigation were compared, and there was a significant difference between the accuracy rate and the n-bank accuracy rate of the haptic feedback and audio feedback. Szczerba et al. [15] also used the n-back task as a subtask, and haptic glasses were used to transmit navigation information. They concluded that haptic feedback from smart glasses could improve the performance of secondary tasks. Amna and Susanne [14] used PASAT as a secondary task, comparing the performance of the haptic belt and traditional navigation, and it was concluded that the driver showed better directional performance on the haptic display compared to traditional car navigation systems. It is worth mentioning that this experiment used different vibration durations and rhythms to transmit different distance information. The research found that tactile displays cannot decrease the workload of drivers. For example, some participants thought that haptic distance coding was demanding, and sometimes they were unable to remember different counts of pulses [14]. Therefore, the effect of haptic distance coding is worthy of further study.

In addition, other studies have concluded that driver characteristics also affect the performance of tactile navigation. Kim et al. [37] concluded that the differences in perception and cognitive ability between young and older people have an impact on driving tasks. For navigation, the combination of visual, auditory, and tactile stimuli increased the workload of older drivers, thus reducing their driving performance, while enabling young drivers to concentrate more on driving.

4.2 Collision Warning

Electronic devices and complicated road conditions make driving situations increasingly dangerous. Secondary tasks make drivers easily distracted and increase accidents. As a consequence, effective warning measures have been taken. Reducing the risk of accidents becomes even more critical. However, early warning feedback mostly adopts the audio-visual method. In early-scene scenarios, the tactile sensation has many advantages over the early audio-visual warning; for example, it does not occupy visual resources and is not easy to mask. Therefore, the application of the tactile sensation in this situation is promising. Numerous scholars have performed related research on tactile feedback in collision warnings. At present, these efforts have been mainly divided into two research directions. One is to verify the effectiveness of the early warning of each vibration position when the vibration mode is constant and to detect different vibrations. By comparing the reaction time and collision rate between positions, the second approach is to explore the corresponding vibration mode for a collision warning, that is, to explore the impact of different vibration modes on the response time and other dependent variables when the vibration position is unchanged.

In the study of collision warning situations, the independent variables are mainly different vibration positions and different vibration modes. Vibration positions include seats, seat belts, and steering wheels. Vibration modes include static vibration and dynamic vibration (dynamic vibration includes linear vibration and mobile vibration). The dependent variables include response time, collision rate, and minimum collision avoidance distance (MDA).

In verifying the effectiveness of early-warning vibration location, Chun et al. [38] used a dual-task paradigm to prove that compared to seat belts, the warning information transmitted by steering wheel vibration has a higher CRP and lower RT. However, both have significantly higher CRP and RT than no-warning conditions. The main task of this experiment was to follow a constant speed car at a distance of fewer than 40 m, and the secondary task was to let the driver enter the number displayed on the screen. Researchers used the secondary task to distract the driver from simulating the real situation. When the driver successfully performs the secondary task, the system will create a sudden forward-collision event with a 50% probability, that is, the first car suddenly decelerates, and the tactile forward collision warning (FCW) is activated when the TTC (time to collision) is less than 4 s, thus testing the RT and CPR of the driver in this situation [39]. The vibration has a specific effect on transmitting early warning information and reducing the collision rate. At present, there have been many studies on the effectiveness of tactile warnings for seats, steering wheels, and seatbelts. However, the comparison between these locations and the possibility of a linkage between these locations is still relatively weak. Additionally, the vibration locations of the existing research are based on traditional automobile structures, and it is worth discussing whether new hardware can be extended on this basis.

In terms of exploring the effects of different vibration modes, Meng et al. [39] demonstrated that the dynamic vibration reaction time is faster than the static vibration (all tractors activated simultaneously) and no-warning condition through experiments that simulate carfollowing tasks. Among them, a dynamic vibration toward the trunk has a faster RT than the vibration mode far from the trunk and the static vibration mode because the dynamic vibration toward the trunk can convey information about external events, thereby speeding up the reaction to potential collisions [40]. In addition, Ahtamad et al. [41] conducted experiments under the situation of forwarding collision warning to confirm that the RT generated by vibrotactile flow is significantly faster than the static vibration mode and no warning. However, there is no directional effect; that is, there was no significant difference between the expanding and contracting flow signals. Nevertheless, compared to the linear dynamic vibration mode toward the trunk, the vibrotactile flow reacts more slowly. Compared with static vibration, dynamic vibration can transmit more detailed information. However, currently, there are fewer studies examining the dynamic vibration mode, and designs of the dynamic vibration mode are insufficiently detailed. Many experiments either have an insufficiently realistic environment or a sample size that is too small, and the possibility of errors in the experimental results is significant, so further research is needed.

4.3 Eco-Driving

In recent years, with increasing attention given to environmental problems, energy conservation and emission reduction have become essential issues in technological development for financial and environmental savings, respectively, and eco-driving has the potential to significantly reduce greenhouse gas emissions. Eco-driving means engaging in fuel-efficient driving behaviors. Many factors affect fuel economies, such as tire inflation, drag, and vehicle maintenance. However, acceleration and deceleration behaviors are considered the most influential factors. Whether BEVs (battery electric vehicles) or gas-powered cars, drivers can significantly reduce energy consumption by engaging in different drive styles.

At present, the standard way to assist drivers in economical driving is with visual signals, such as in the Honda CRV. The primary way to promote the economic driving behavior of drivers through tactile interaction is focused on the accelerator. Moreover, there are many kinds of tactile feedback used on pedals [6, 8, 17], such as linear increase, bump, slot, continuous pulse, time pulse, linear decrease, force, and stiffness feedback. Compared with visual signals, a tactile pedal can transmit information without occupying the visual channels and can keep drivers gaze on the road when they engage in eco-driving. On the other hand, tactile feedback has more effects than visual feedback in some ways but has little effect on individual effort. Taking both a visual and tactile approach may be a compromise [8]. A study by Szczerba et al. [15] showed that adopting eco-driving support can significantly reduce drastic accelerations. However, there are no significant differences between the different modes (visual, touch, listening) and their combinations of eco-driving support information.

Moreover, there is no significant difference between the different support methods, which may be caused by the experimental environment. It is worth comparing the feedback of participants in different secondary driving tasks and interference factors of different channels in real driving conditions. Beede et al. [5] showed that tactile information could effectively promote eco-driving behavior, and this approach is more effective than visual feedback alone. However, this result is not significant and needs further verification. In addition, tactile information is more acceptable than auditory information. Another study showed that the force haptic gas pedal (FHGP) modality provides the best guidance for saving energy [17].

Haptic effects score higher in terms of attractiveness, dependability, stimulation, and novelty. The results also suggest that haptic effects can be a stimulating motivation to drive more energy efficiency. The haptic accelerator pedal was considered positive for improving perceived energy efficiency while driving [6]. Participants showed a high rating of willingness to receive haptic feedback in the explored context, which increased significantly after using the system in a driving simulation. However, another experiment by Mulder et al. [17] showed that haptic feedback was rated significantly less pleasant, helpful, desirable, and likable compared to receiving feedback visually. The evaluation of tactile feedback appears to be inconclusive, which might be caused by different experimental environments, different driving tasks of the test subjects, and different tactile feedback methods of the pedals. It is worthwhile to explore the factors caused by these evaluation differences in further research.

5   Discussion

5.1   Main Challenge

In general, drivers need semantic information and clear instructions to improve driving performance, which is transmitted through visual and auditory information [27] rather than vibration feedback. Second, inappropriate vibration feedback can distract the driver and impair driving performance. Third, the target of the vibration feedback may act on different positions of the body, and different positions of the body may be perceived differently [42]. At the same time, different positions of the body have different sensitivities to vibration. Therefore, the setting of the vibration pattern must be in a prominent position. Fourth, the meaningful information conveyed by vibration feedback is generally in the form of a vibration pattern, and it is necessary to control the frequency, interval time, and position. However, drivers need to partake in individual learning to understand the conveyed meaning, which leads to the high learning cost of using a vibration combination pattern. Different meanings require different coding forms, which have reduced mobility.

Finally, restrictions in the simulated driving laboratory environment, the driver's environment, road condition information, and trigger environment of vibration feedback are different from real scenes. This difference makes it difficult to transfer the results to real driving scenes and reduces the external evaluation of research. Improving this problem requires more effort in experimental design, and we will continue to focus on this problem in future studies.

5.2   Future Direction

In future studies, researchers should focus on two directions. In all three driving situations (navigation, collision warning, and eco-driving), it is necessary to study how to select appropriate parameters to constitute vibration patterns to transmit information more effectively, especially in collision warning studies. In navigation situations, the driver needs more meaningful information feedback (direction and distance) and explicit instructions (for example, give steering instructions at a specific time and distance) than in the other two situations. Moreover, this complex semantic information can only be fed back into the vibration pattern, and this is worthy of future study. In navigation, vibration feedback can mainly assist in direction and distance information prompts.

Moreover, distance information feedback contains richer meaning and requires more explicit and flexible instructions than directional information. The research shows that distance information transmitted by vibration patterns effectively reduces the visual burden of drivers [43]. In addition to automotive navigation applications, tactile feedback for distance cues is also being used in personal wearables to aid in extreme situations such as pedestrians, blind people, or poor visibility [44–46]. However, how to set up a more effective vibration pattern and transmit more explicit instructions has not been studied. Therefore, setting up an active vibration pattern to transmit more explicit instructions is significant, and our group will pursue this in further study.

Meanwhile, tactility as an information display has also been applied to lateral skin stretching technology and variable car seats. Ploch et al. [18] carried out experiments to stimulate subjects at higher stimulation speeds in real driving scenarios, and their results showed that the subjects' recognition accuracy for the direction of lateral skin stretching was higher than 80%. Variable car seats allow the driver to feel obstacles in the rear by deforming the seatback. Different from the existing tactile information transmission mode, the variable seat can transmit continuous spatial information through continuous deformation [21]. In future research, it is worth looking forward to the combination of lateral skin stretching technology and variable seat technology with tasks such as collision warning, navigation, and lane maintenance. Furthermore, how to assess the role of vibration to establish an effective multimodal system, including visual, auditory, and tactile feedback, and create a harmonious human–computer interaction environment is meaningful, especially in an eco-driving situations.

6 Conclusion

This paper introduces the research of vibration from two aspects: vibration patterns and vibration locations. It shows vibration parameters and vibration patterns consisting of multiple parameters to transmit information. Then, it compares the advantages and disadvantages of vibration positions and determined that the most potent and stable vibration position is the seat. Finally, it introduces studies on vibration feedback, which include research significance, measurement indexes, and development directions in three vibration scenarios. We also discuss the potential challenges of transferring the experimental results to real driving scenes. In the future, cutting-edge technology should be applied in haptic research, and how to utilize vibration to establish an effective multimodal system should be a trend for researchers.

References

1. Wickens, C.D.: Processing resources in attention, dual-task performance, and workload assessment. Transp. Res. **59**, 63–102 (1984)
2. Hibberd, D.L., Jamson, A.H., Jamson, S.: The design of an in-vehicle assistance system to support eco-driving. Transp. Res. Part C: Emerg. Technol. **58**, 732–748 (2015)
3. Muhrer, E., Vollrath, M.: The effect of visual and cognitive distraction on driver's anticipation in a simulated car following scenario. Transp. Res. F: Traffic Psychol. Behav. **14**(6), 555–566 (2011)
4. Liu, Y.: Comparative study of the effects of auditory, visual and multimodality displays on drivers' performance in advanced traveler information systems. Ergonomics **44**(4), 425–442 (2001)
5. Beede, K.E., Kass, S.J.: Engrossed in conversation: the impact of cell phones on simulated driving performance. Accid. Anal. Prev. **38**(2), 415–421 (2006)
6. Ranney, T.A., Harblu, J.L., Noy, Y.I.: Effects of voice technology on test track driving performance: implications for driver distraction. Hum. Factors **47**(2), 439–454 (2005)
7. Garrett, W., Bret, H., Zeljko, M.: Evaluating the usability of a head-up display for selection from choice lists in cars. In: Proceedings of the 3rd International Conference on Automotive User Interfaces and Interactive Vehicular Applications (AutomotiveUI 2011), pp. 39–46. Association for Computing Machinery (2011)
8. ISO 9241-940: 2017 Ergonomics of human-system interaction—Part 940: Evaluation of tactile and haptic interactions
9. Hwang, S., Ryu, J.: The haptic steering wheel: vibro-tactile based navigation for the driving environment. In: 2010 8th IEEE International Conference on Pervasive Computing and Communications Workshops, pp. 660–665. IEEE (2010)
10. Capallera, M., Barbé-Labarthe, P., Angelini, L., Khaled, O.A., Mugellini, E.: Convey situation awareness in conditionally automated driving with a haptic seat. In: Proceedings of the 11th International Conference on Automotive User Interfaces and Interactive Vehicular Applications, pp. 161–165. Adjunct Proceedings (2019)
11. Alex, R., Alonso, M.B.: Designing haptic effects on an accelerator pedal to support a positive eco-driving experience. In: Proceedings of the 11th International Conference on Automotive User Interfaces and Interactive Vehicular Applications - AutomotiveUI 2019, pp. 319–328 (2019)
12. Ji, Y., Lee, K., Hwang, W.: Haptic perceptions in the vehicle seat. Hum. Factors Ergon. Manuf. Serv. Ind. **21**(3), 305–325 (2011)
13. Self, B.P., Van Erp, J.B., Eriksson, L., Elliott, L.R.: Human factors issues of tactile displays for military environments. Tactile Displays for Orientation, Navigation and Communication in Air, Sea and Land Environments (2008)
14. Amna, A., Susanne, B.: Where to turn my car? Comparison of a tactile display and a conventional car navigation system under high load condition. In: Proceedings of the 2nd International Conference on Automotive User Interfaces and Interactive Vehicular Applications (AutomotiveUI 2010), pp. 64–71. Association for Computing Machinery (2010)
15. Szczerba, J., Hersberger, R., Mathieu, R.: A wearable vibrotactile display for automotive route guidance. Pac. Northwest Q. **59**(1), 1027–1031 (2015)
16. Mars, F., Deroo, M., Hoc, J.: Analysis of human-machine cooperation when driving with different degrees of haptic shared control. IEEE Trans. Haptics **7**(3), 324–333 (2014)
17. Mulder, M., Abbink, D.A., Boer, E.R.: The effect of haptic guidance on curve negotiation behavior of young, experienced drivers. In: 2008 IEEE International Conference on Systems, Man and Cybernetics, pp. 804–809 (2008)

18. Ploch, C.J., Bae, J.H., Ju, W., Cutkosky, M.: Haptic skin stretch on a steering wheel for displaying preview information in autonomous cars. In: IEEE/RSJ International Conference on Intelligent Robots and Systems (IROS) (2016)
19. Di Campli San Vito, P., et al.: Haptic navigation cues on the steering wheel. In: Proceedings of the 2019 CHI Conference on Human Factors in Computing Systems (CHI 2019), pp. 1–11. Association for Computing Machinery (2019)
20. Takada, Y., Boer, E.R., Sawaragi, T.: Driving assist system shared haptic human system interaction. IFAC Proc. Volumes **46**(15), 203–210 (2013)
21. Grah, T., Epp, F., Wuchse, M., Meschtscherjakov, A., Gabler, F., Steinmetz, A., Tscheligi, M.: Dorsal haptic display. In: Proceedings of the 7th International Conference on Automotive User Interfaces and Interactive Vehicular Applications (AutomotiveUI 2015), pp.100–105. Association for Computing Machinery (2015)
22. Telpaz, A., Rhindress, B., Zelman, I., Tsimhoni, O.: Haptic seat for automated driving: preparing the driver to take control effectively. In: International Conference on Automotive User Interfaces and Interactive Vehicular Applications. ACM (2015)
23. Melman, T., De Winter, J.C.F., Abbink, D.A.: Does haptic steering guidance instigate speeding? A driving simulator study into causes and remedies. Accid. Anal. Prev. **98**, 372–387 (2017)
24. Geitner, C., Birrell, S., Skrypchuk, L., Krehl, C., Mouzakitis, A., Jennings, P.: Good vibrations: driving with a haptic pedal. In: Adjunct Proceedings of the 7th International Conference on Automotive User Interfaces and Interactive Vehicular Applications (AutomotiveUI 2015), pp.100–105. Association for Computing Machinery (2015)
25. Chun, J., Han, S.H., Park, G., Seo, J., Choi, S.: Evaluation of vibrotactile feedback for forward collision warning on the steering wheel and seatbelt. Int. J. Ind. Ergon. **42**(5), 443–448 (2012)
26. Jamson, S.L., Hibberd, D.L., Jamson, A.H.: Drivers' ability to learn eco-driving skills; effects on fuel efficient and safe driving behaviour. Transp. Res. Part C: Emerg. Technol. **58**, 657–668 (2015)
27. Petermeijer, S., Bazilinskyy, P., Bengler, K., De Winter, J.: Take-over again: investigating multi-modal and directional TORs to get the driver back into the loop. Appl. Ergon. **62**, 204–215 (2017)
28. Lee, J., McGehee, D.V., Brown, T., Marshall, D.: Effects of adaptive cruise control and alert modality on driver performance. Accid. Reconstr. J. **19**(5), 10–17 (2009)
29. Beruscha, F., Krautter, W., Lahmer, A., Pauly, M.: An evaluation of the influence of haptic feedback on gaze behavior during in-car interaction with touch screens. In: 2017 IEEE World Haptics Conference (WHC), pp. 201–206. IEEE (2017)
30. Cornelio Martinez, P.I., De Pirro, S., Vi, C.T., Subramanian, S.: Agency in mid-air interfaces. In: Proceedings of the 2017 CHI Conference on Human Factors in Computing Systems, pp. 2426–2439 (2017)
31. Lassagne, A., Kemeny, A., Posselt, J., Merienne, F.: Comparing tangible and entirely virtual haptic systems for HMI studies in simulated driving situations. Science Arts & Métiers (2019)
32. Ng, A., Brewster, S. A., Beruscha, F., Krautter, W.: An evaluation of input controls for in-car interactions. In: Proceedings of the 2017 CHI Conference on Human Factors in Computing Systems, pp. 2845–2852 (2017)
33. Tian, R., Li, L., Rajput, V.S., Witt, G.J., Duffy, V.G., Chen, Y.: Study on the display positions for the haptic rotary device-based integrated in-vehicle infotainment interface. IEEE Trans. Intell. Transp. Syst. **15**(3), 1234–1245 (2014)
34. Nukarinen, T., Rantala, J., Farooq, A., Raisamo, R.: Delivering directional haptic cues through eyeglasses and a seat. In: 2015 IEEE World Haptics Conference (WHC), pp. 345–350. IEEE (2015)

35. Nukarinen, T., Raisamo, R., Farooq, A., Evreinov, G., Surakka, V.: Effects of directional haptic and non-speech audio cues in a cognitively demanding navigation task. In: Proceedings of the 8th Nordic Conference on Human-Computer Interaction: Fun, Fast, Foundational, pp. 61–64 (2014)

36. Ploch, C.J., Bae, J.H., Ploch, C.C., Ju, W., Cutkosky, M.R.: Comparing haptic and audio navigation cues on the road for distracted drivers with a skin stretch steering wheel. In: 2017 IEEE World Haptics Conference (WHC), pp. 448–453. IEEE (2017)

37. Kim, S., Hong, J.H., Li, K.A., Forlizzi, J., Dey, A.K.: Route guidance modality for elder driver navigation. In: Kay, J., Lukowicz, P., Tokuda, H., Olivier, P., Krüger, A. (eds.) Pervasive Computing. Pervasive 2012, vol. 7319, pp. 179–196. Springer, Cham (2012). https://doi.org/10.1007/978-3-642-31205-2_12

38. Chun, J., Lee, I., Park, G., Seo, J., Choi, S., Han, S.H.: Efficacy of haptic blind spot warnings applied through a steering wheel or a seatbelt. Transp. Res. F: Traffic Psychol. Behav. **21**, 231–241 (2013)

39. Meng, F., Spence, C.: Tactile warning signals for in-vehicle systems. Accid. Anal. Prev. **75**, 333–346 (2015)

40. Meng, F., Gray, R., Ho, C., Ahtamad, M., Spence, C.: Dynamic vibrotactile signals for forward collision avoidance warning systems. Hum. Factors **57**(2), 329–346 (2015)

41. Ahtamad, M., Spence, C., Ho, C., Gray, R.: Warning drivers about impending collisions using vibrotactile flow. IEEE Trans. Haptics **9**(1), 134–141 (2016)

42. Morioka, M., Griffin, M.J.: Absolute thresholds for the perception of fore-and-aft, lateral, and vertical vibration at the hand, the seat, and the foot. J. Sound Vib. **314**(1), 357–370 (2008)

43. Van Erp, J.B., Van Veen, H.A.: Vibro-tactile information presentation in automobiles. In: Proceedings of Eurohaptics, pp. 99–104. Eurohaptics Society (2001)

44. Cosgun, A., Sisbot, E.A., Christensen, H.I.: Guidance for human navigation using a vibro-tactile belt interface and robot-like motion planning. In: 2014 IEEE International Conference on Robotics and Automation (ICRA), pp. 6350–6355. IEEE (2014)

45. Ferscha, A., Zia, K.: Lifebelt: crowd evacuation based on vibro-tactile guidance. IEEE Pervasive Comput. **9**(4), 33–42 (2010)

46. Straub, M., Riener, A., Ferscha, A.: Distance encoding in vibro-tactile guidance cues. In: 2009 6th Annual International Mobile and Ubiquitous Systems: Networking and Services, MobiQuitous. pp. 1–2. IEEE (2009)

A Systematic Review of Autonomous Driving in Transportation

Zilin Xu[1]([⊠]) and Vincent G. Duffy[2]

[1] School of Mechanical Engineering, Purdue University, West Lafayette, IN 47906, USA
Xu1553@purdue.edu
[2] School of Industrial Engineering, Purdue University, West Lafayette, IN 47906, USA
duffy@purdue.edu

Abstract. With the rapid development of science and technology, some new terms, such as cloud computing, big data, and artificial intelligence, have become part of public life. Artificial intelligence is another technological revolution after human beings entered the information era, attracting more and more attention. As an extension and application of artificial intelligence technology in the automotive industry and transportation field, autonomous driving has received close attention from industry, academic, and even the national level in recent years worldwide. The self-driving car relies on artificial intelligence, visual computing, radar, monitoring devices, and global positioning systems to work in concert, which allows computers to operate motor vehicles automatically and safely without any human initiative. Autonomous driving technology will become mainstream for future cars in transportation. The review for autonomous driving in the artificial intelligent aspect was conducted using Cite Space, Harzing's Publish, VOS viewer, Mendeley, Scopus, and Web of Science. By using the data from these database websites, co-citation analysis and the leading table analysis are organized together.

Keywords: Autonomous driving · Artificial intelligence · Transportation · Harzing · VOS viewer · MaxQDA · Mendeley

1 Introduction and Background

1.1 History of Autonomous Vehicles

Self-driving cars are not a new concept; they have a long history of nearly 100 years. Autonomous vehicle technology includes video cameras, radar sensors, and laser rangefinders to understand the surrounding traffic conditions and navigate the road ahead with a detailed map (captured by a human-crewed car). This is all done through Google's data center, which processes the vast amount of information the car collects about the surrounding terrain. In this respect, self-driving cars are the equivalent of remote-controlled cars or intelligent cars in Google's data center. The information that autonomous driving vehicles are sharing is through the Internet of Things. Internet of Things is a new concept for all internet-based technology.

© Springer Nature Switzerland AG 2021
C. Stephanidis et al. (Eds.): HCII 2021, LNCS 13097, pp. 389–402, 2021.
https://doi.org/10.1007/978-3-030-90966-6_28

Ideally, humans would like to see autonomous vehicles replacing existing human driving vehicles. Still, the progression of self-driving technology suggests that there will be a transition period of 10 years or more ahead. Different types and levels of autonomous driving technologies will be developed together. This situation will cover other needs, road conditions, people, and business model situations. So autonomous driving is a technical problem that includes all aspects.

1.2 Autonomous Driving in Transportation for Safety

Safety of Traffic. In the traffic aspect of autonomous vehicles, safety is a critical issue to think about. The factor of safety issues affects the feasibility and the rationality of the system. The field of safety-critical control has received increasing attention since safety is a primary requirement for critical autonomous systems, such as autonomous cars and robots [5]. Using artificial intelligence, it becomes possible to track real-time data that, when utilized, will provide actionable insights for police officers who can predict and prevent criminal activity. This enhances passenger safety. Similarly, tracking real-time data from self-driving vehicles enables timely intervention to prevent accidents and ensure passenger safety. Artificial Intelligence in transportation that collects pedestrian and vehicle data helps reduce traffic congestion and reduce accidents by suggesting alternative routes and estimated wait times for traffic signals.

Safety of Public. Intelligent transportation systems can repeat the mistakes made in other industries. We need to be alert to the fact that in recent years, in which hacker groups have used information security vulnerabilities to get trusted access, leading to financial theft, massive data deletion, and theft of sensitive personal information, respectively. But the stakes are higher for intelligent transportation systems, namely the security and trust of ordinary people. The environment and other related location data for comprehensive perception (to achieve "human-vehicle-road" complete interconnection), full Patio-temporal traffic control for each road, and complete traffic control for each car in order to have ubiquitous, seamless travel service capabilities. The core of the construction of intelligent transportation infrastructure lies in the network of vehicles and intelligent networked vehicles with intelligent and precise control, and the network of cars with intelligent and precise control is an information-physical system (CPS) network with precise Patio-temporal location services, and accurate control of remote, Patio-temporal location is its requirement.

1.3 Autonomous Driving in Transportation for Safety

This paper shows the mainstream of autonomous driving using trend graphs. This paper also shows the importance of safety in autonomous driving by using visual analysis software such as VOS Viewer and MAXQDA. The co-citation analysis also shows the influence of the most influential authors and the future trajectory of AI in traffic. Conclusions are drawn based on the collected results, and future work on the topic is discussed in the context of the NSF.gov award.

2 Purpose of Study

The purpose of this study is to identify the trends of the relation between Artificial Intelligence and Transportation. Transportation is a vital link connecting cities and has a decisive influence on the flow of production factors and the development of town systems. The competent authorities of the intelligent transportation industry give instructions on development strategies, policies, and regulations of the intelligent transportation industry; the development plans, medium and long-term plans of the sector; and technical standards and specifications of the industry. From the viewpoint of the industry chain, all the industry chains of intelligent transportation have matured, involving communication chips, communication modules, terminal equipment, vehicle manufacturing, software development, data and algorithm provision, and high-precision positioning maps, etc. Literature reviews aim to map and evaluate the body of literature to identify potential research gaps and highlight the boundaries of knowledge [4]. A specific scale of competition and cooperation has been formed in all aspects. The main direction of research on intelligent transportation is now mainly placed in autonomous driving. This paper analyzes the impact of autonomous driving on traffic in recent years by using software such as VOS Viewer, Harzing, and Cite Space. The use of digital analytics allows for better systematic analysis and allows for very specific and valid conclusions to be drawn from the analysis.

3 Research Methodology

3.1 Data Collection

By using the bibliometric analysis method said to be used in [20], data collection was carried out in this paper through different platforms. The data were obtained by using different databases to get the papers published in recent years. Google Scholar had most articles, with 208000. The following the most significant number of articles was obtained from Research Gate, with 177450 reports. A total of 18690 articles were found in Web of Science. The least number of articles was found in Scopus, with 15929 relevant articles. The result shows in Table 1. The analysis found that the number of relevant articles included in Google Scholar was the largest, which also means that the literature data recorded by Google Scholar was the largest. The co-citation analysis through these databases is more comprehensive, and it is also more meaningful to list out the more typical literature and focus on the study.

3.2 Trend Analysis

The application of autonomous driving in traffic appeared a long time ago, but it has been in a position that is not mainstream. This paper uses co-citation analysis, Engagement timeline analysis, and other methods to determine the importance of autonomous driving. And by conducting data analysis, this paper discusses the mainstream ideas that are being carried out and the mainstream research directions that are being undertaken. Through these research directions, it is possible to analyze where the future research directions

Table 1. Search results relevant to autonomous driving on different database

Search terms	Number of articles	Database
Autonomous driving	2080000	Google Scholar
Autonomous driving	18690	Web of Science
Autonomous driving	177450	Research Gate
Autonomous driving	15929	Scopus

are directed. By conducting a literature search, it is found that autonomous driving as a mainstream hotspot occupies the main body of new intelligent transportation [7–9]. Studying autonomous driving makes it possible to analyze the future direction of brilliant transportation research and development. Therefore, this paper puts the research idea in the automatic driving of smart transportation.

The data was analyzed using trend analysis in Web of Science and Scopus, and the keyword "Autonomous Driving" was used to see the attention on artificial intelligence. The data was aggregated and integrated. The research on autonomous driving has become very hot in recent years, and the popularity of autonomous driving is increasing exponentially.

Scopus shows that have been many publications on Autonomous Driving since 2002 and the exponential increase in the next few years, indicating that Autonomous Driving in Transportation has reached a peak of activity. Figure 1 shows the trend of articles from 1962 to 2022 with the number of documents published. This also indicates that autonomous driving, as an essential core of intelligent transportation, has been in the central hot spot of contemporary society. People are beginning to pay attention to the research and development of autonomous driving.

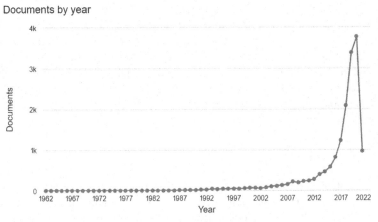

Fig. 1. Trend chart for articles released by year about autonomous driving in Scopus (1962–2021)

Another trending analysis was performed year by year through the Web of Science database shows in Fig. 2. The number of articles on autonomous driving has been increasing since 2005 and reached a peak in 2019, with 3302 articles published in a year, indicating that research on autonomous driving has become a hot topic. Extensions made to online replanning include the lazy reevaluation to account for changing environments and the repropagation to account for prediction errors [6]. After the trending analysis, the data were analyzed by using the analysis method used by [21] for data analysis, and the results are discussed in Sect. 4.

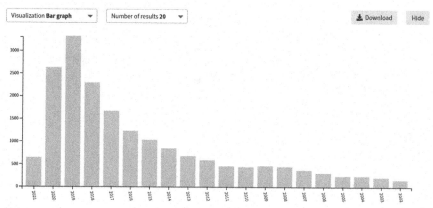

Fig. 2. Trend chart for articles released by year about autonomous driving in Web of Science (2012–2021)

4 Results

4.1 Content Analysis Based on Leading Terms

The VOS Viewer was used to organize the topics on intelligent transportation in "Autonomous Driving". The keyword map was analyzed using the Web of Science database, as shown in Fig. 3, and the leading author and the leading institution analyzed the top five key authors and institutions. A detailed analysis of the institutions and authors is presented in the following section.

The results of keyword analysis of the data in Web of Science by VOS Viewer are shown in Fig. 3. There are most references to drive and motion. Meanwhile, the concerns of autonomous movement are also huge. Also, system and control are essential indicators' reliability, safety, cost, appearance, and social acceptance are only a few legitimate concerns [7].

By discussing the principal authors, resources, keywords, and other important information about the Autonomous Driving direction, it can be analyzed that the five most influential authors are Knoll, Alois C., Cao, Dongpu, Dolan, John M., Chen, Long in Table 2. The above table examines the direction they are involved in and the institutions they belong to. All the authors are in the profession of Artificial Intelligence. Their

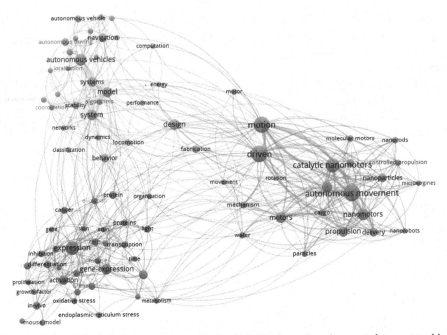

Fig. 3. Keyword analysis for autonomous driving in VOS viewer based on metadata captured in Web of Science

research areas are primarily in Motion Planning, Random Trees, and Artificial Potential fields. This indicates that those who study autonomous driving are now subordinate to the general direction of artificial intelligence and further indicates that artificial autonomous driving mainly originates from artificial intelligence.

Table 2. Leading author and their affiliated association institution with article count in autonomous driving

Author	Affiliated institution	Keywords	Article count
Knoll, Alois C.	Nanyang Technological University	Motion planning, random trees, artificial potential field	51
Tomizuka, Masayoshi	University of California, Berkeley	Motion planning, random trees, artificial potential field	46
Cao, Dongpu	Lancaster University	Plug-in hybrid vehicles; powertrains; energy management	45

(*continued*)

Table 2. (*continued*)

Author	Affiliated institution	Keywords	Article count
Dolan, John M.	Carneige Mellon University	Partially observable Markov decision process; value iteration; autonomous driving	45
Chen, Long	Sun Yat-Sen University	Object detection	39

Table 3 is the leading five affiliations in the Autonomous Driving aspect. The table shows there are two of them from the United States and two from China. The one with most documents publishing is the Technical University of Munich in Germany. The number of papers of these leading affiliations is relatively similar, indicating that their research standards are balanced, facilitating the sharing of knowledge and further promoting autonomous driving.

Table 3. Leading affiliated institution with documents count in autonomous driving

Affiliation	Country	Documents count
Technical University of Munich	Germany	277
Tsinghua University	China	268
Carnegie Mellon University	United States	231
Chinese Academy of Sciences	China	229
University of California, Berkeley	United States	208

4.2 Co-citation Analysis Reference Co-citation Analysis Reference

The data file searched from the Web of Science was analyzing into VOS Viewer. Figure 4 shows a co-citation analysis for Autonomous Driving in VOS Viewer. About Autonomous Driving, the minimum number of citations was setting to 20 for the results. As a result, there are ten papers that have been co-citation for over 20 times. Each of the two papers is closely related, indicating that the whole academic community is now in a unified pace for traffic-only research.

By conducting Co-citation Analysis, eight key articles were to be included in the subsequent analysis. The result is shown in Table 4. These eight papers illustrate the contemporary mainstream research directions of autonomous driving through different aspects. Analyzing the content, we can get that the topics related to control are still attracting more attention. The intelligent control system, the last link of the whole unmanned system, is the executor that puts into practice the conclusions of environment recognition, path planning, and machine decision making.

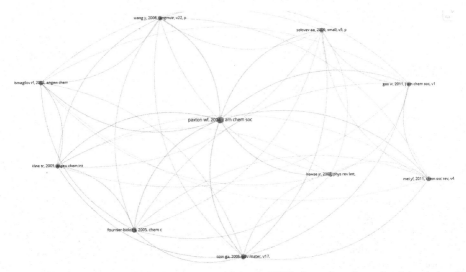

Fig. 4. Co-citation analysis for autonomous driving in VOS viewer based on metadata captured in Web of Science

Table 4. Key articles from co-citation analysis

Author	Article	Relation of inclusion
Carl Folkestad	Data-driven safety-critical control: synthesizing control barrier functions with Koopman operators	Co-citation analysis
Kanamu Takikawa	Vehicular trajectory estimation utilizing slip angle based on GNSS Doppler/IMU	Co-citation analysis
Shuo Feng	Intelligent driving intelligence test for autonomous vehicles with naturalistic and adversarial environment	Co-citation analysis
Anders Eugensson	Environmental, safety, legal and social implications of autonomous driving system	Co-citation analysis
Tove Helldin	Presenting system uncertainty in automotive UIs for supporting trust calibration in autonomous driving	Co-citation analysis
Markus Hörwick	Strategy and architecture of a SafetyConcept for fully automatic and autonomous driving assistance systems	Co-citation analysis
Junqing Wei	Towards a viable autonomous driving research platform	Co-citation analysis
Yoshiaki Kuwata,	Real-time motion planning with applications to autonomous urban driving	Co-citation analysis

4.3 Content Analysis from MAXQDA

By using the analysis of co-citation, the database of Google Scholar, Scopus, and Web of Science is used to obtain 20 papers, and MAXQDA analysis of the 20 papers is performed to generate a word cloud. Analysis of the word cloud is used to observe the prospects of autonomous driving and the current process.

From Fig. 5, systems include about 100 words, removing irrelevant words, like numbers, letters, etc. From the figure, "safety", "driver", system", "control", and "environment" are most frequency words. Technological advances have led to the development of numerous driver assistance systems such as adaptive cruise control, lane permission to make digital or hard copies of all or part of this work for personal or classroom use is granted without fee provided that copies are not made or distributed for profit or commercial advantage and that copies bear this technology [8]. The technology also influences the direction of the entire industry and positively influences the development of the industry through their efforts. By analyzing through the increasing mobility needs in passenger traffic, there are increasing demands concerning safety and comfort in automobiles [9]. The job of processing vast amounts of data provided by sensors requires high-performance microcontrollers and processors. If possible, the autonomous driving system must evaluate a wide range of information in real-time while meeting the highest safety standards and requirements. The decisions made by the system are critical to the safe operation of the vehicle. Among the obvious potential benefits for society is improved fuel economy, enhanced safety, and reduced congestion [18]. Many experts also attach great importance to artificial intelligence technology, as this technology can allow vehicles to move away from manual processes and drive intelligently. Machine learning capabilities enable driverless cars to continuously expand their knowledge base by gaining new knowledge based on the data that has been collected and prepared. Without this autonomous learning technology, programming of defined logical responses for all theoretically feasible situations would be almost unthinkable. Autonomous driving aims to improve intercity traffic travel intelligence, actively innovate in the road passenger information service mode, and enhance the residents' traffic travel experience. Aiming at the personalization, comfort, and brightness of the means of transportation, the intelligent transportation service system architecture is established with the support of the transportation cloud as a platform to form a resource-saving and environment-friendly integrated transportation system for planning, operation, and management.

4.4 Cluster Analysis

Cite Space conducted a Cluster analysis by bringing in literature from the Web of Science. The keyword for the research was "Autonomous Driving" because the topic of Artificial Intelligence in Transportation was too broad to find the correct result, so we took a further narrowing down to the field of autonomous driving and used it for professional analysis.

Fig. 5. Word cloud analysis for selected papers from MAXQDA

By conducting keyword clusters, as a result, shows in Fig. 6, few important keywords, "machine learning," "intelligent transportation," "ontology model," "risk assessment," and "laser range finder," were conducted. This result represents the current research focus of autonomous driving. These also reverse that many obstacles remain before autonomous driving can be a part of transportation on public roads [10]. From the keyword analysis, it can be concluded that the term machine learning appears most frequently. This indicates that machine learning, a core technology for autonomous driving, is becoming the mainstream of the research. One of the reasons Machine learning is becoming one of the mainstreams of the computer science aspect right now is also because it is the main technology for autonomous driving, and its development also means an increase in the reliability of autonomous driving technology. Another keyword is laser range finder. Research on sensor technology, autonomous cars, and accurate road positioning can reduce the distance between vehicles, and vehicles can move in queues, improving road capacity, which can further reduce congestion times and improve travel reliability. However, reducing traffic congestion and congestion times may lead to increased traffic volumes, which offsets some of the benefits of autonomous driving technology. Along with this problem, another core technology, "risk assessment," is being developed. By conducting risk assessment, autonomous driving technology can be developed in a more stable and reliable direction. At the same time, this reliable technology will also improve the position of vulnerable people. From the standpoint of ease of access, driverless vehicles will facilitate access for groups that cannot drive, such as the elderly, the disabled, and children, and reduce the sense of social exclusion for such groups. Highly accurate vehicular trajectory estimation has become imminently important for automated vehicles and advanced driver assistance systems that have been developed in recent years [16].

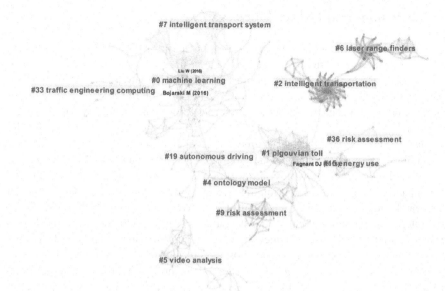

Fig. 6. Cluster for autonomous driving in keywords from cite space

By using citation burst from Cite space, articles can be obtained from the top 5 most influential documents. The result of the top 5 references shows in Fig. 7. The one with the most strength is from Urmson in 2011, with a strength of 4.24.

Top 5 References with the Strongest Citation Bursts

References	Year	Strength	Begin	End	2000 - 2021
Urmson C, 2008, J FIELD ROBOT, V25, P425, DOI 10.1002/rob.20255, DOI	2008	4.24	2011	2013	
Ziegler J, 2014, IEEE INTEL TRANSP SY, V6, P8, DOI 10.1109/MITS.2014.2306552, DOI	2014	3.82	2015	2017	
Liu W, 2016, LECT NOTES COMPUT SC, V9905, P21, DOI 10.1007/978-3-319-46448-0_2, DOI	2016	3.39	2018	2019	
Mnih V, 2015, NATURE, V518, P529, DOI 10.1038/nature14236, DOI	2015	3.18	2018	2019	
Bojarski M, 2016, ARXIV160407316, V0, P0, DOI DOI 10.1109/IVS.2017.7995975, DOI	2016	4.51	2019	2021	

Fig. 7. Top five reference by using citation burst with autonomous driving from site space

By conducting the articles from the systematic review, there are many aspects that can be mentioned [9, 19]. Research on rules, standards, and specification systems supporting interconnection of resources, efficient transportation of goods, and multiple modes of transport. The development of smart transport unit equipment for diversified multiple modal types of transport, automated multiple modal transport pickup, and unloading and transfer equipment at hubs, and integrated systems for multiple modal types of transport intelligent scheduling management. To estimate AV's safety performance, the probabilistic distributions of human driving behaviors at different driving conditions are critical [17]. Intelligent transport unit equipment is suitable for diversified multiple modal types of transport, automatic multiple modal transport pickup, drop-off transfer equipment at hubs, and an integrated multiple modal types of transport intelligent scheduling management system [3, 12].

5 Conclusions and Future Work

This paper utilizes a quantitative and visual approach to assess the development history of publications over the last decades. Some of the articles mentioned that driving intelligence tests are critical to developing and deploying autonomous vehicles [11]. However, this study still has some limitations. The direction of research deviates from country to country, and each country has its strong points. Also, within a country, different institutions research different trends. To obtain more specific data, a more specific topic analysis is required. At the same time, it is found that autonomy and control occupy the leading position in the study, which indicates that automation has become a standard of intelligence, and how to control the system is also a significant direction of development prospects. Artificial intelligence in transportation is essential; as said in the research, the driver and the speed control are redundant [1]. Only by improving artificial intelligence, including enhancing the safety of autonomous driving, will drivers be safer behind the wheel and reduce their workload of driving. Many accident cases raise questions about individuals who caused, contributed to, or were simply victims of malfunctions [2]. Suppose vehicles are controlled through intelligent transportation through automatic driving. In that case, such human-caused accidents will be greatly reduced, and people will become very safe to travel whether all these can be achieved, depending on the reliability of the intelligent system. The mainstream of autonomous driving technology, for the time being, is still to adopt the "see, hear and think," that is, to simulate the way of human driving, with a variety of electronic sensors instead of human eyes and ears to observe the environment, and then transmitted to the vehicle central electronic computer for calculation. This calculation and the past expert mode of artificial intelligence are different and are already in the deep learning-based artificial intelligence model. Whether it is electronic sensors, or artificial intelligence, its data requirements, are massive. In particular, the data collected by sensors in cars is very different from traditional data.

Autonomous driving is taking a very mainstream position in intelligent transportation. Intelligent transportation is on a rapid rise. Through the study of intelligent transportation, it is learned that the prospect of autonomous driving is excellent. At the same time, there are many researchers working in the direction of autonomous driving, which is also a hot research topic now. Through NSF awards shows from the website, the award of autonomous driving is in a hot period [14]. The future of technology companies will depend more on their level of involvement in intelligence development, which will be an important indicator of their capabilities in the future. The main objective of public lighting is to ensure people, property, and goods [13]. It is recommended to conduct timely research on market access and product access mechanisms for self-driving vehicles, focusing on proposing new solutions to liability and insurance issues, and paying attention to privacy and data protection issues related to self-driving vehicles. Research and develop a series of national and industry standards such as production and data specifications for high-precision maps for autonomous driving, interoperability standards for multi-source heterogeneous traffic big data, and safety and security standards for intelligent transportation. Accelerate the research and development of software and hardware technologies related to autonomous driving, plan the top-level design of applications, and have international market competitiveness while adapting to national conditions.

Meanwhile, intelligent transportation on railroads is also a hot spot for future research. A rail transit network usually represents the core of a city's public transportation system [15]. Therefore, the overall topological structures and functional features of a public transportation network must be fully understood to assist the safety management of rail transit and planning for sustainable development. Rail and high-speed autopilot are destined to occupy a significant position in the future market, as this is now the primary way to take the freight.

References

1. Brauer, R.L.: Chapter 31: Human behavior and performance in safety. In: Safety and Health for Engineers. Wiley, New York (2016)
2. Brauer, R.L.: Chapter 9: General principles of hazard control. In: Safety and Health for Engineers. Wiley, New York (2016)
3. Paxton, W.F., et al.: Catalytic nanomotors: autonomous movement of striped nanorods. J. Am. Chem. Soc. **126**(41), 13424–13431 (2014). https://doi.org/10.1021/ja047697z
4. Fahimnia, B., Sarkis, J., Davarzani, H.: Green supply chain management: a review and bibliometric analysis. Int. J. Prod. Econ. **162**, 101–114 (2015). https://doi.org/10.1016/j.ijpe.2015.01.003
5. Folkestad, C., Chen, Y., Ames, A.D., Burdick, J.W.: Data-driven safety-critical control: synthesizing control barrier functions with Koopman operators. IEEE Control Syst. Lett. **5**(6), 2012–2017 (2021). https://doi.org/10.1109/LCSYS.2020.3046159
6. Kuwata, Y., Teo, J., Fiore, G., Karaman, S., Frazzoli, E., How, J.P.: Real-time motion planning with applications to autonomous urban driving. IEEE Trans. Control Syst. Technol. **17**(5), 1105–1118 (2009). https://doi.org/10.1109/TCST.2008.2012116
7. Wei, J., Snider, J.M., Kim, J., Dolan, J.M., Rajkumar, R., Litkouhi, B.: Towards a viable autonomous driving research platform. In: IEEE Intelligent Vehicles Symposium, Proceedings, no. Iv, pp. 763–770 (2013). https://doi.org/10.1109/IVS.2013.6629559
8. Helldin, T., Falkman, G., Riveiro, M., Davidsson, S.: Presenting system uncertainty in automotive UIs for supporting trust calibration in autonomous driving. In: Proceedings of the 5th International Conference on Automotive User Interfaces and Interactive Vehicular Applications, AutomotiveUI, pp. 210–217 (2013). https://doi.org/10.1145/2516540.2516554
9. Hörwick, M., Siedersberger, K.H.: Strategy and architecture of a safety concept for fully automatic and autonomous driving assistance systems. In: IEEE Intelligent Vehicles Symposium, Proceedings, pp. 955–960 (2010). https://doi.org/10.1109/IVS.2010.5548115
10. Eugensson, A., Brännström, M., Frasher, D., Rothoff, M., Solyom, S., Robertsson, A.: Environmental, safety, legal and societal implications of autonomous vehicles. In: Proceedings of the International Technical Conference on the Enhanced Safety of Vehicles (ESV), pp. 1–15 (2013). http://www-nrd.nhtsa.dot.gov/pdf/esv/esv23/23ESV-000467.PDF
11. Feng, S., Yan, X., Sun, H., Feng, Y., Liu, H.X.: Intelli gent driving intelligence test for autonomous vehicles with naturalistic and adversarial environment. Nat. Commun. **12**(1), 1–14 (2021). https://doi.org/10.1038/s41467-021-21007-8
12. Guéguen, N., Meineri, S., Eyssartier, C.: A Pedestrian's stare and drivers' stopping behavior: a field experiment at the pedestrian crossing. Saf. Sci. **75**, 87–89 (2015)
13. Peña-García, A., Hurtado, A., Aguilar-Luzón, M.C.: Impact of public lighting on pedestrians' perception of safety and well-being. Saf. Sci. **78**, 142–148 (2015). https://doi.org/10.1016/j.ssci.2015.04.009
14. NSF Website. https://www.nsf.gov/awardsearch/simpleSearchResult?queryText=Autonomous+driving&ActiveAwards=true. Accessed 06 Oct 2021

15. Yang, Y., Liu, Y., Zhou, M., Li, F., Sun, C.: Robustness assessment of urban rail transit based on complex network theory: a case study of the Beijing subway. Saf. Sci. **79**, 149–162 (2015). https://doi.org/10.1016/j.ssci.2015.06.006

16. Takikawa, K., Atsumi, Y., Takanose, A., Meguro, J.: Vehicular trajectory estimation utilizing slip angle based on GNSS Doppler/IMU. ROBOMECH J. **8**(1), 1–11 (2021). https://doi.org/10.1186/s40648-021-00195-4

17. Feng, S., Yan, X., Sun, H., Feng, Y., Liu, H.X.: Intelligent driving intelligence test for autonomous vehicles with naturalistic and adversarial environment. Nat. Commun. **12**(1), 1–14 (2021). https://doi.org/10.1038/s41467-021-21007-8

18. Helldin, T., Falkman, G., Riveiro, M., Davidsson, S.: Presenting system uncertainty in automotive UIs for supporting trust calibration in autonomous driving. In: Proceedings of the 5th International Conference on Automotive User Interfaces and Interactive Vehicular Applications, AutomotiveUI, pp. 210–217 (2013). https://doi.org/10.1145/2516540.2516554

19. Simba, K.R., Uchiyama, N., Sano, S.: Real-time obstacle-avoidance motion planning for autonomous mobile robots. In: Proceedings of 2014 Australian Control Conference, AUCC 2014, no. November, pp. 267–272 (2015). https://doi.org/10.1109/AUCC.2014.7358652

20. Guo, F., Li, F., Lv, W., Liu, L., Duffy, V.G.: Bibliometric analysis of affective computing researches during 1999–2018. Int. J. Hum.-Comput. Interact. **36**(9), 801–814 (2020). https://doi.org/10.1080/10447318.2019.1688985

21. Duffy, G.A., Duffy, V.G.: Systematic literature review on the effect of human error in environmental pollution. In: Duffy, V.G. (ed.) HCII 2020. LNCS, vol. 12199, pp. 228–241. Springer, Cham (2020). https://doi.org/10.1007/978-3-030-49907-5_16

HCI in Industry and Manufacturing

Performance Comparison of User-Estimated and Learned Task Recognition Models for Maintenance Procedures

Marcus Behrendt[1]([✉]) and Bertram Wortelen[2]

[1] OFFIS – Institute for Information Technology,
Escherweg 2, 26121 Oldenburg, Germany
behrendt@offis.de
[2] Humatects GmbH, Marie-Curie-Str. 1, 26129 Oldenburg, Germany
bertram.wortelen@humatects.de
https://www.offis.de, https://www.humatects.de

Abstract. Maintenance procedures of technical installations are crucial to keep systems in a healthy state. Unfortunately, sometimes rare technical installations require certain types of maintenance that are not known to all technicians. We are investigating an idea that enables those technicians to still perform maintenance by using an assistance system (AS). An important part of such an AS, which we concentrate on in this work, is a task recognition engine. It keeps track of the tasks performed within a maintenance procedure, so that the AS can provide the technician with adequate information and help. We show how to build two types of task recognition models for this task recognition engine. The first was developed by *Honecker & Schulte* and is based on the Dempster-Shafer theory (DST). These models can be well estimated by experts, but may not represent the sequence of tasks in maintenance procedures because they are designed for parallel tasks. But still, they may be useful if there is not enough training data available. The second is based on Hidden Markov models (HMM). They are harder to estimate, but they may perform better for the sequential tasks in maintenance procedures if they are trained from a sufficient data set. Depending on the training data set's size, we investigate which kind of model performs better by evaluating them on an example maintenance procedure.

Keywords: Maintenance procedure · Task analysis · Task modeling · Task recognition · Dempster-Shafer theory · Hidden Markov models · Probabilistic reasoning · Concurrent algorithms

1 Introduction

Maintenance is a crucial part of today's industry. Neglecting maintenance of technical installations like assembly lines, wind turbines or transmission towers could lead to overall system malfunctions. Even though the direct and the

© Springer Nature Switzerland AG 2021
C. Stephanidis et al. (Eds.): HCII 2021, LNCS 13097, pp. 405–426, 2021.
https://doi.org/10.1007/978-3-030-90966-6_29

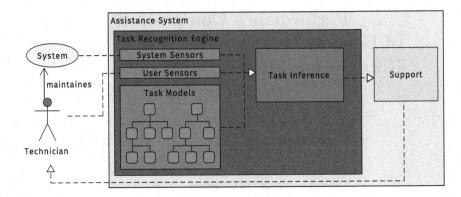

Fig. 1. Architecture of an AS that supports technicians during maintenance procedures. Based on sensor observations and task models, the currently performed task is inferred. In this way, the AS can offer contextual help to the technician or warn him if he has omitted a task.

indirect costs of maintenance may amount to 40% of a company's total costs, machine faults caused by improper maintenance could lead to follow-up costs that are five times higher [17]. This shows how important it is to properly plan and carry out maintenance.

Unscheduled maintenance occurs when an unexpected problem arises that needs urgent resolution. It often poses a particular challenge: A suitable technician with experience in this particular problem must be scheduled in time. There is now the dilemma to either wait for this experienced technician to be available or to let another technician execute the maintenance procedure, who may have received no specialized training for the system or the specific problem.

Our objective is to develop an assistance system (AS) for those technicians who have not received such specialized training. The AS will provide targeted support by sensing the technician's actions and his environment with sensors. The basic principle of the AS is shown in Fig. 1. Both sensor data and a task recognition model are used as input for recognising the task the technician is currently performing during a maintenance procedure. Then, if the AS knows what the technician is doing, it can support him accordingly. For example, the system could present important information about the task to the technician using augmented reality.

This automatic inference of tasks is a critical part of the AS, that should work as accurately as possible. There are several approaches to implementing task inference. In this paper, we evaluate two approaches to formalise and identify tasks that we find promising with respect to typical maintenance procedures. We investigate both task recognition models based on Hidden Markov Models (HTRMs) as in [4,7–10] and task recognition models based on the Dempster-Shafer theory (DTRMs) like in [11–13,23]. All of these models have been used in supervisory control missions, which (in contrast to maintenance procedures) mostly consist of parallel rather than sequential tasks. In this paper, we will therefore evaluate how these models might perform in maintenance procedures.

At first glance, HTRMs seem to be better suited to recognise the sequential tasks in maintenance procedures. This is because the underlying Hidden Markov Model (HMM) contains state transition probabilities that can be used by an HTRM to model transitions between tasks. These state transitions are not considered in the examined DTRM-based approach. However, compared to DTRMs, manual creation of HTRMs is more difficult because their parameter set is often too large to be estimated by experts. Therefore, learning from training examples is the most effective way to create HTRMs. Thus, our first hypothesis is:

Hypothesis 1 (H1). *An HMM performs better than a well-estimated DTRM in maintenance procedures if it has been trained with a sufficiently large data set.*

However, there may be the problem of not having enough data to effectively train HTRMs. So the question arises whether it is better to use a well-estimated DTRM until sufficient data is available. Consequently, our second hypothesis is a complement to our first hypothesis:

Hypothesis 2 (H2). *A well-estimated DTRM performs better in maintenance procedures than an HTRM that has been trained with little data.*

The verification of both hypotheses will form the basis for our planned AS. It allows us to define an appropriate strategy for the task inference component, i.e., which task recognition model should be used with respect to the size of the available training data. Therefore, we will evaluate both hypotheses in this paper using an example maintenance procedure in which the training data set is incrementally increased. We may find the inflection point derived from both hypotheses where the size of the training data set is sufficient for HTRMs to outperform the self-estimated DTRM.

To provide a complete description of our work, this paper is organised as follows: Sect. 2 serves as a starting point, where we briefly review related work. Section 3 demonstrates the process of creating our task recognition models for maintenance procedures. The evaluation of our two hypotheses is given in Sect. 4. Finally, Sect. 5 discusses the results obtained.

2 Related Work

Task recognition in general is a typical classification problem where all kinds of classification algorithms can be used. To the best of our knowledge, there is hardly any research for the specific problem of task recognition in maintenance procedures.

The most similar, wide field of research to mention here is activity recognition. Just like in task recognition, the human and its environment are captured by sensors. It is then estimated what activity the person is doing (walking, eating, sleeping, working, relaxing, exercising, etc.). One difference from task recognition is that activity recognition is applied over longer periods of time, typically

24/7. Another difference is that sensors used for task recognition can be more diverse and intrusive, as they are better suited for integration into technical working environments. Dynamic Basic Classifiers (DNBC) like HMMs [15,25] are methods often used for activity recognition.

Relevant works exist for recognising tasks in supervisory control missions. HMMs were used by *Hayashi* [9,10], *Boussemart & Cummings* [4], and *Donath et al.* [7,8]. *Honecker & Schulte* [11–13,23] used the Dempster-Shafer theory (DST). Tasks in supervisory control missions differ from those in maintenance procedures primarily in that they are parallel and repetitive rather than sequential and occur only once. This is mainly due to the fact that in supervisory control missions, the actual system state deviates from the desired system state over time. Therefore, the supervisor must perform both periodic system state checking tasks and the appropriate corrective tasks to steer the current system state to the desired system state. In contrast, maintenance involves working through tasks step by step to achieve the desired system state. Moreover, the tasks to be recognised in the mentioned papers are much less (3–5) than in a typical maintenance procedure that we cover in the paper. Most of the above work used task recognition as a means of assessing the operator's situation awareness and cognitive workload.

Hayashi [9,10] applied a Hidden Markov Model for task recognition (HTRM) to recognise a pilot's subtasks *"vertical flight control"*, *"horizontal flight control"*, and *"speed control"* of the overall pilot task *"manual control"*. In an experiment with pilots, their gaze fixations to six instruments were recorded and used as the input observations for the HMM.

Boussemart & Cummings [4] recognised tasks of pilots' missions including the supervision of UVs (unmanned vehicles) with HTRMs. They used manual interaction with the system as input for the HTRM. In contrast to Hayashi, the authors did not conduct an a-priori definition of the tasks. Instead, they trained optimised HTRMs and gave the resulting states a meaning a-posteriori.

Donath et al. [7,8] used an HTRM approach to recognise pilot tasks in UAV (unmanned aerial vehicle) cooperative missions for the purpose of an automatic determination of the pilot's cognitive workload. The authors used 13 observations of manual interactions as input for the HMM consisting of the three subtasks *"recognise & tag"*, *"classify"* and *"insert result"*. A high task recognition rate was demonstrated, when tasks are executed in a normative way.

Honecker & Schulte [11–13,23] considered that traditional probability-based models may have a weakness regarding false recognition of tasks, particularly in safety-critical environments like helicopter missions. In their opinion, an AS should be able to admit to being ignorant about the currently performed task if there is not enough sensor data available. They therefore developed an approach for recognising tasks in UAV cooperation missions based on the Dempster-Shafer theory (DST). The authors intended to reduce dangerous false recognition of tasks by exploiting DST's concept of *ignorance*, which is an integral part of this theory. Ignorance allows the model to not always have to know what task is being performed.

In a previous work we [2] extended Honecker's & Schulte's DST-based modelling approach for maintenance procedures. To be better suited for the sequential tasks in maintenance procedures, we kept track of already recognised tasks and excluded them for further re-recognition. But the question regarding the statistical performance of such DTRMs for maintenance procedures was left unanswered. The work just contained a demonstration of the application in an example maintenance procedure.

3 Modelling

This section describes the method of creating the two types of task recognition models for maintenance procedures. The first is based on Honecker's & Schulte's task recognition modelling approach with the DST (DTRM). The second is based on HMMs (HTRMs). Both methods rely on a formal specification of the tasks. Based on this specification, the task recognition models can be defined. In this section we present a formal specification of tasks suitable for the HTRMs and DTRMs.

Before we continue, we show the basic structure of a maintenance procedure in Fig. 2. In addition to illustrating the structure, the figure serves to clarify the terms *task* and *subtask*, which are frequently used in the paper.

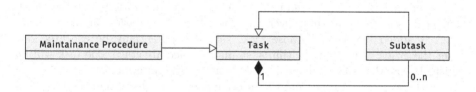

Fig. 2. Structure of a maintainence procedure: A *Maintenance Procedure* is a *Task* that can consist of several *Subtasks*. A *Subtask*, in turn, is a *Task*. In this way, a *Maintenance procedure* is structured as a tree of tasks.

3.1 Task Decomposition

A task decomposition of the maintenance procedure should be performed to obtain a formal specification for the tasks in the scenario of interest. The decomposition's purpose for task recognition is to create a task tree $T^\times$, which is defined as the tuple

$$T^\times = \langle T, K \rangle. \tag{1}$$

Here, T is the set of decomposed subtasks, and $K \subset T^2$ describes a *part-of-* relation between tasks. This means that a task is either atomic or consists of other, more fine-grained (sub)tasks. The more fine-grained a task is, the easier it is to distinguish its associated actions from those of neighbouring tasks.

This is why it makes the most sense for sensor-based task recognition that measures these actions to focus on the leaves, as these represent the atomic tasks. Therefore, the tasks to be recognised T_r are defined as

$$T_r := \{t \in T \mid \nexists t' \in T \colon \langle t, t' \rangle \in K\}, \tag{2}$$

There are some formalism that can be used for task decomposition. In our work we have used the task model description language DCoS-XML [18], which is based on CTT [19]. It is worth mentioning that DCoS-XML models extend $T^{\times}$ to include temporal relations between tasks. Our AS will later use these relations in a higher-level component to warn the technician when a task has been skipped. But this topic is not part of this research work.

3.2 Common Modelling Aspects

After the task decomposition is finished, a task recognition model can be built to enable the recognition of the tasks in T_r. Both DTRMs and HTRMs have some common features. Therefore, the following sections describe how these common features can be modelled.

Derivation of Intermediate Stages. The boundary between two tasks from T_r, where the one task begins and the other ends, is often difficult to define for the modeller and even more difficult to detect with automatic task recognition. Therefore, as a pragmatism to overcome these fuzzy boundaries, an intermediate stage is added between all those tasks that can potentially be executed one after the other. Somewhere within such an intermediate stage, one task will be finished, and the other will begin. We denote these intermediate stages as I. The tasks to be recognised, and the intermediate stages form the extended task description model $\Omega(T)$, which is defined as

$$\Omega(T) := T_r \;\dot\cup\; I. \tag{3}$$

With this extended task description model, it is possible to describe a technician's execution of a maintenance procedure from the beginning to the end as the execution sequence q defined as

$$\begin{aligned} q \colon \{1, \ldots, n\} &\to \Omega(T) \\ i &\mapsto q_i. \end{aligned} \tag{4}$$

Task recognition is then used for online prediction of $\langle q_1, \ldots, q_i \rangle$ for any time i in a maintenance procedure.

Task Recognition Input. The input for task recognition models is the state of the technician and the environment in which the tasks are performed. If a person was assigned the mission to recognise tasks, he would observe a technician and the environment with his senses and infer which task the technician is currently performing. Analogous to a person's senses, sensors are needed for task recognition models to observe the technician and the environment.

Such a sensor could for example be an eye tracker [14], a smartwatch recognising hand gestures [27], a hand position estimator [26], a RFID-based glove recognising tools [16], etc. The set of n sensors used by a task recognition model is denoted as S.

For every sensor we only consider a finite set of observations. Sensor values of a continuous domain need to be discretised first. For example, the 3-axis acceleration measured by a smartwatch had to be classified into discrete gestures like *"screwing"* or *"unscrewing"*. The finite set of observations a sensor s can make is denoted as O_s.

3.3 DST-Based Task Recognition Model (DTRM)

Honecker & Schulte developed an approach for creating task recognition models based on the DST [11–13,23]. In contrast to the classical probability theory, the general statement $P(\neg H) = 1 - P(H)$ is not applicable in the DST. This means that the counter-probability of a hypothesis H cannot be inferred from the probability of H. That is because in the DST a range is used in which it can be assumed that a hypothesis is correct. This range is restricted by a lower bound, called the belief $Bel(H)$, and an upper bound, called the plausibility $Pl(H) = 1 - Bel(\neg H)$. The authors' intention of using the DST for task recognition was to reduce false negatives in safety-critical tasks like helicopter missions.

The application of Honecker's approach enables the creation of simplified DTRMs for task recognition. The simplification has primarily the aim to decrease the traditional theory's computation effort for inference. This allows their models to be used for real-time applications. The simplification is that each task is practically represented in its own *binary* model instead of an overall model.

Binary means that a model of a task represents a complete frame of discernment, that only contains the following two hypotheses: Task is being performed and task is not being performed. A traditional DST model would preferably contain one hypothesis for each task in a single frame of discernment such that: Task t_1 is being performed, task t_2 is being performed, etc. Although it would be possible to achieve linear computation time under certain preconditions [1], the worst case would still be $O(2^{|T|})$ because in reality these preconditions cannot always be met. The disadvantage of the simplified binary model is the loss of influence hypotheses have on other tasks. Honecker & Schulte are convinced that the models still perform well despite this simplification.

One advantage of DTRMs is that they are relatively easy for humans to understand. So they can be set up by expert estimations. A DTRM is defined as the tuple

$$\lambda = \langle E, T_r, \Sigma \rangle. \tag{5}$$

The model's central component is a set of evidences defined as

$$E \subseteq T_r \times \Sigma \times H \times M \times L. \tag{6}$$

An evidence $tE\langle s,o\rangle EhEmEl$ from the set E is a relation between a task t, a sensor observation $\langle s,o\rangle$, a hypothesis h, a mass m, and a half-life l. The pairwise ordered sensor observation tuple $\langle s,o\rangle$ from the set

$$\Sigma := \{\langle s,o\rangle \mid (s \in S) \wedge (o \in O_s)\} \tag{7}$$

states whether the evidence is active and thus considered in inference. The evidence is active when observation o is measured by sensor s. An evidence's hypothesis h from the set of hypotheses defined as $H := \{0,1\}$ can either support or doubt that task t is being performed. A supporting hypothesis, that is denoted as $h = 1$, advocates that the task t is being performed. In contrary, a doubting hypothesis, that is denoted as $h = 0$, contradicts that task t is being performed. The mass m in the range $M := [0,1]$ defines the strength of the evidence. The lower it is, the less influence the evidence has for the overall statement when combining it with other evidences by the application of Dempster's Rule of Combination (see Sect. 3.3). At last, the value l from the set $L = \mathbb{R}_0^+$ defines the half-life of the evidence's mass, which is left over after the observation o has not been measured by the sensor s. The half-life therefore prevents sudden jumps in belief values.

For example, an evidence could be defined between the task $t =$ "switch off fuse", the sensor observation $\langle s =$ "eye tracker"$, o =$ "looking at fuse"$\rangle$, the hypothesis $h = 1$, the mass $m = 0.9$, and a half-life of 2s $l = 2$. By $h = 1$, this evidence would support the hypothesis with a mass of $m = 0.9$ that the task is performed when the technician is looking at the fuse. The half-life of 2 s would prevent the immediate drop of the support if the technician briefly looks elsewhere.

Inference. In order to use the model for task recognition, inference must be performed. For this purpose, similar to Honecker & Schulte, inference relies on *belief triplets*, defined as

$$B := \{\langle p,q\rangle \in [0,1]^2 \mid p+q \le 1\}. \tag{8}$$

Here, the belief value p would later support the hypothesis that a task is being performed, while the belief value q would doubt this by supporting the counter hypothesis. It is still called a *triplet* because an additional value, the *ignorance*, can be calculated by

$$r: \begin{cases} B \to [0,1] \\ \langle p,q\rangle \mapsto 1-p-q. \end{cases} \tag{9}$$

This ignorance is a residual uncertainty in which it is plausible that both hypotheses are correct. Based on the current sensor measurement, a single evidence for a task can be converted into a belief triplet by the function

$$\zeta: \begin{cases} E \to B \\ e \mapsto \begin{cases} \langle m \cdot h, m \cdot \neg h \rangle & \text{if } o \text{ is being measured by } s, \\ \left\langle m \cdot h \cdot \left(\frac{1}{2}\right)^{\frac{\Delta z}{t}}, m \cdot \neg h \cdot \left(\frac{1}{2}\right)^{\frac{\Delta z}{t}} \right\rangle & \text{if } o \text{ has been measured before,} \\ \langle 0, 0 \rangle & \text{else}. \end{cases} \end{cases}$$

$$(10)$$

Here, Δz is used for the decay of the evidence when the observation is not currently measured. It is the time difference between the current time and the last time when the observation was measured.

Those belief triplets that were converted from evidences of the same task can be combined with each other to obtain a single belief triplet for this task. To combine two belief triplets, Honecker & Schulte use a combination rule derived from Dempster rule of combination [6], which is defined as

$$\langle p, q \rangle \oplus \langle p', q' \rangle := \begin{pmatrix} \dfrac{p \cdot p' + p \cdot r(\langle p', q' \rangle) + r(\langle p, q \rangle) \cdot p'}{1 - (p \cdot q' + q \cdot p')}, \\ \dfrac{q \cdot q' + q \cdot r(\langle p', q' \rangle) + r(\langle p, q \rangle) \cdot q'}{1 - (p \cdot q' + q \cdot p')} \end{pmatrix}. \qquad (11)$$

The order in which the triplets are combined can be arbitrary, since $\langle B, \oplus, \langle 0, 0 \rangle \rangle$ reflects the algebraic structure of a commutative monoid. The set Θ containing the combined belief triplet for each task is defined as

$$\Theta := \{ \langle t_i, p, q \rangle \in T \times B \mid (j \neq k) : [t_j \neq t_k] \}. \qquad (12)$$

Using the formalism described above, we can define binary classifiers for each task and infer at each point in time whether a task is currently performed or not. Honecker & Schulte consider all tasks within a supervisory control mission as being simultaneously performed where $p > 0.5$ applies. For maintenance procedures we assume far less multitasking activity. Technicians typically do not switch back and force from one task to another – at least on small time scales of a few seconds or even minutes. Therefore, the main objective in the context of maintenance procedures is to infer which one of the tasks is performed. It is done by selecting the task prediction with the highest confidence. With respect to the belief triplets, a high confidence means a large difference between the support value p and the doubt value q. Based on this an order relation on Θ can be defined as

$$\langle t_i, p_i, q_i \rangle \leq \langle t_j, p_j, q_j \rangle :\Leftrightarrow p_i - q_i \leq p_j - q_j. \qquad (13)$$

The currently performed task t is determined by selecting the largest element in Θ. However, if the confidence is below a lower bound lb the result is *undefined* $\uparrow$:

$$\langle t_{\max}, p_{\max}, q_{\max} \rangle = \max(\Theta),$$

$$t = \begin{cases} t_{\max} & \text{if } p_{\max} - q_{\max} > lb \\ \uparrow & \text{else} \end{cases} \qquad (14)$$

3.4 HMM-Based Task Recognition Model (HTRM)

In the supervisory control settings that Honecker & Schulte investigated, they assumed a high level of multitasking and did not consider any relation between tasks in the DTRMs. However, maintenance work is typically very sequential in its nature. It would be useful to consider the order of the tasks in a model to increase the performance of task recognition. That is the reason why we investigate in Hidden Markov models (HMM) for task recognition, since each state here depends on the previous state. HMMs are used in a wide field of applications. For example in speech recognition [20,21], recognition of handwriting [5], gesture recognition [24], and DNA sequencing [22]. They are also used in activity recognition [15,25], that is a very similar field to task recognition. Several authors [4,7–10] have also used HMMs for recognising tasks in supervisory control missions.

An HMM is defined by states, input observations, initial state probabilities, state transition probabilities, and state observation probabilities [20]. So our HMM-based task recognition model (HTRM) is defined as the tuple

$$\lambda := \langle \Omega(T), O^S, \pi, \tau, \iota \rangle. \tag{15}$$

The extended task description model $\Omega(T)$ represent the HMM's states, whereas the sensor observations O^S represent the input observations of the HMM. We use a one-dimensional feature space for the input observations. It is defined as the Cartesian Product over all sensor observations, such that

$$O^S := \prod_{s \in S} O_s. \tag{16}$$

This means that a single observation in our HTRMs is always a combination of sensor observations.

Hidden Markov models can be used to encode the temporal relationships between subtasks. The execution of a maintenance procedure is defined by the execution sequence q of all subtasks (see Eq. 4). This sequence cannot be measured directly. So, as the name suggests, it is hidden. But it is hidden behind an accompanied sequence v of combined sensor observations

$$\begin{aligned} v \colon \{1, \ldots, n\} &\to O^S \\ i &\mapsto v_i. \end{aligned} \tag{17}$$

This observation sequence is measurable by the sensors from S. An HTRM can be used to infer the execution sequence given an observation sequence. For this, an HTRM makes use of the initial state probabilities, state transition probabilities, and state observation probabilities of its underlying HMM [20]. For HTRMs the initial state probability π specifies how likely it is for a state to become the first state in a sequence. Since $\Omega(T)$ represents the states in an HTRM, it can be defined as the function

$$\pi \colon \begin{cases} \Omega(T) \to [0,1] \\ t \mapsto P(q_1 = t) \end{cases}, \quad \sum_{t \in \Omega(T)} \pi(t) = 1. \tag{18}$$

A state transition probability specifies how likely it is for a state to transition to another state. This probability can be defined as the function

$$\tau: \begin{cases} \Omega(T)^2 \to [0,1] \\ \langle t,t' \rangle \mapsto P(q_i = t' \mid q_{i-1} = t) \end{cases}, \quad (\forall t \in \Omega(T)): \left[\sum_{t' \in \Omega(T)} \tau(\langle t,t' \rangle) = 1 \right]. \quad (19)$$

This assumption that the current state is only dependent on the previous state in an execution sequence is called the *Markov assumption.*

At last, a state observation probability specifies how likely an observation is emitted while being in a certain state. As O^S represent the observations in an HTRM, it can be defined as

$$\iota: \begin{cases} \Omega(T) \times O^S \to [0,1] \\ \langle t,o \rangle \mapsto P(v_i = o \mid q_i = t) \end{cases}, \quad (\forall t \in \Omega(T)): \left[\sum_{o \in O^S} \iota(\langle t,o \rangle) = 1 \right]. \quad (20)$$

The fact that an observation at a given time is only dependent on the current state and not on previous states and previous observations is called the *independence assumption.*

Inference. In order to benefit from an HTRM for task recognition, inference has to be done. We use *Evaluation* as we are interested in which task from T_r is the most likely at a given time. With Evaluation it is possible to compute $P(v|\lambda)$, the probability of the observation sequence v given the model λ. The classic inductive Forward algorithm [20] is used. It consists of

$$\alpha_1(t) = \pi(t) \cdot \iota(\langle t,v_1 \rangle) \quad (21)$$

as the initialisation step, which defines the probability that the task t is executed after only one observation v_1 is made, and

$$\alpha_{i+1}(t) = \left[\sum_{t' \in \Omega(T)} \alpha_i(t') \cdot \tau(\langle t,t' \rangle) \right] \cdot \iota(\langle t,v_{i+1} \rangle) \quad (22)$$

as the induction step for subsequent observations. The termination step to compute

$$P(v|\lambda) = \sum_{t \in \Omega(T)} \alpha_i(t) \quad (23)$$

is omitted in task recognition, as it is only calculated after v has ended. Because we are only interested in the probabilities of the tasks, we just consider the initialisation and induction step.

As the probabilities of the tasks from $\Omega(T)$ become smaller the longer the observation sequences are, it is important to normalise the probabilities of the tasks such that $\sum_{t \in \Omega(T)} \alpha(t) = 1$ to retrieve a probability distribution.

Analogous to the DTRMs, we define a lower bound lb for the selection of the currently performed task. Let the task or intermediate stage with the highest probability be defined as $t_{\max} = \max_{t \in \Omega(T)}(\alpha(t))$. The currently performed task

t is defined as either being $t_{\max}$ or being *undefined* ↑ if the probability of $t_{\max}$ is below the threshold lb:

$$t = \begin{cases} t_{\max} & \text{if } \alpha(t_{max}) > lb \\ \uparrow & \text{else.} \end{cases} \tag{24}$$

Learning. It is almost impossible to manually estimate the probability functions of an HMM as the single dimensional feature space for input observations O^S may become very large. The easiest way to build a model is by learning from tagged training examples where each state is assigned an observation. Let J be the index set of the training examples, then the training data set is defined as

$$\langle D_j \rangle_{j \in J} := \{\langle q_i, v_i, j \rangle \mid j \in J\}. \tag{25}$$

Here, $\langle q_i, v_i, j \rangle$ means: the i-th output task annotated with the i-th input observation of the j-th training example. With such a training data set, it is possible to build an HTRM using maximum likelihood estimates (MLE) [3]. The initial state probability function can then be assigned as

$$\pi(t) = \frac{|\{\langle q_1, v_1, j \rangle \in D_j \mid q_1 = t\}| + \varphi}{|\{\langle q_1, v_1, j \rangle \in D_j\}| + \varphi \cdot |\Omega(T)|}. \tag{26}$$

The state transition probability function can be assigned as

$$\tau(t, t') = \frac{|\{\langle\langle q_i, v_i, j \rangle, \langle q_{i+1}, v_{i+1}, j \rangle\rangle \in D_j{}^2 \mid (q_i = t) \wedge (q_{i+1} = t')\}| + \varphi}{|\{\langle q_i, v_i, j \rangle \in D_j \mid q_i = t\}| + \varphi \cdot |\Omega(T)^2|}, \tag{27}$$

and the initial probability function can be assigned as

$$\iota(t, o) = \frac{|\{\langle q_i, v_i, j \rangle \in D_j \mid (q_i = t) \wedge (v_i = o)\}| + \varphi}{|\{\langle q_i, v_i, j \rangle \in D_j \mid q_i = t\}| + \varphi \cdot |\Omega(T) \times O^S|}. \tag{28}$$

To prevent zero probabilities, Laplace smoothing with a smoothing parameter $\varphi > 0$ can be used. It is then possible to enable non-zero probabilities for initial states, state transitions, and state observations that do not occur in the training data set. A smoothing parameter of $\varphi = 0$ applies no smoothing to the MLE.

4   Study

We conducted a study to evaluate how an estimated DTRM performs in maintenance procedures compared to HTRMs trained from data sets of different sizes. The following section describes the planning, the implementation, and the evaluation of the study.

4.1   Task Definition

For the study, we decided to collect training and test data from participants carrying out the installation of a smart meter into a fuse box. The reason why we chose this maintenance procedure is its practical relevance. A new law on metering point operations in Germany (Messstellenbetriebsgesetz) prescribes that all analogue electricity meters have to be replaced by smart meters until 2032.

With the help of experienced technicians, we carried out a task analysis and used DCoS-XML to formalise the task. Figure 3 depicts the task tree $T\times$ of the decomposed maintenance procedure. The figure also shows the temporal relations between tasks. The 16 leaves of the tree are the tasks of T_r, which we want to recognise. They are coloured blue in the figure. Table 1 contains a name and a description for each of these tasks. As described in Sect. 3.2, we built an extended task description model $\Omega(T)$ by also deriving the set I from T_r, the intermediate stages between tasks.

4.2   Sensors

We used three sensors as input for task recognition, as shown in Fig. 4. The first was an eye tracker from Pupil Labs [14] to measure gaze fixations on surfaces defined by us. For the detection of tool usage, we used a sensor combination. It consisted of a self-developed RFID-based glove and a smartphone. The glove was able to measure the tools equipped with RFID-tags. These were, for example, a screwdriver, a spanner, and sealing pliers. The smartphone measured the use of certain applications such as the camera and the barcode scanner. These applications were also considered as tools. As a third sensor, we wanted to use a hand position estimator that we are developing. It tries to recognise the hands of a technician on the eye tracker's world camera image by means of convolutional neural networks based on [26]. It then estimates the hand position in relation to

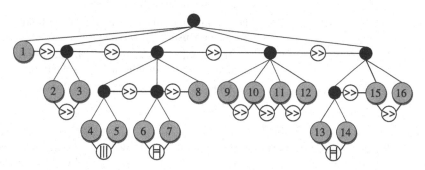

Fig. 3. The resulting DCoS-XML model of a task analysis that was done for the example maintenance procedure *"smart meter installation"*. Besides the task tree $T^\times$, it contains temporal relations between tasks: *Enabling* relations ⊗ state that the left task has to be finished to start the right task. Tasks connected by *parallel* relations ⫴ can be executed at the same time. In *order independent* relations ⊟, one of the two task has to be started first.

Table 1. The 16 tasks from T_r identified in $T'^\times$ to be recognized by our task recognition models.

$t \in T_r$	Name	Description
1	Open fuse box	The technician pulls the fuse box door open
2	Check main fuse state	The technician checks the state of the main fuse by looking at it
3	Deactivate main fuse	The technician switches the main fuse off if it is on using his/her hand
4	Check meter cross	The technician looks at the meter cross to check whether it is positioned such that the smart meter can be installed
5	Adjust meter cross	The technician adjusts the positions of the meter cross manually if needed
6	Fix meter on cross	The technician fixes the smart meter on the meter cross with screws and a screwdriver
7	Attach cables to meter	The technician attaches power cables to the smart meter and clamps them with screws
8	Activate main fuse	The technician switches the main fuse back on using his/her hand
9	Check voltage	The technician uses a multimeter to check voltage in power cabling
10	Re-deactivate main fuse	The technician switches the main fuse back off using his/her hand
11	Attach cover	The technician places a shielding cover over the smart meter and attaches it with screws
12	Attach seals	The technician seals the shielding cover using lead-sealing pliers for tampering protection
13	Take pictures of meter	The technicians takes photos of the built-in smart meter using a smartphone
14	Scan 2D code	The technician scans the barcode of the built-in smart meter using a smartphone
15	Send report	The technician sends a report with images and barcode to the head office using a smartphone
16	Close fuse box	The technician pushes the fuse box door close and locks it

the fuse box. Unfortunately, this sensor was not ready when the study was conducted. So, we decided to annotate the hand position manually by ourselves for each participant. Table 2 gives an overview of the sensors and their observations.

4.3   Participants and Study Procedure

None of the 22 participants of the study was a trained technician. We selected a simple task that is easy to learn even for a non-technician. The introduction was

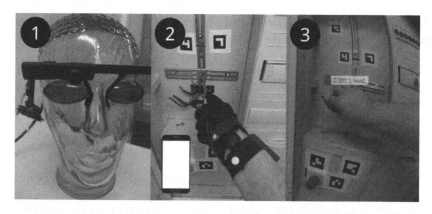

Fig. 4. The sensors used in the study: 1. an eye tracker for measuring gaze fixations on surfaces, 2. a glove with an integrated RFID reader for detecting tool usage, and 3. a hand position estimator based on convolutional neural networks (replaced by manual annotations because it was not finalised at the time).

based on a verbal explanation of the maintenance procedure without a demonstration. In this way, the introduction was kept as vague as possible so as not to influence the participants too much. In this way, we hoped that participants would behave like technicians with insufficient knowledge about the installation. This would, we expected, lead to task executions with more variance.

After the introduction, each of the participants was first equipped with the sensors and then recorded while performing the tasks. We annotated the recordings based on the world video frames of the eye tracker. In this way we created ground truth execution sequences q (see Eq. 4). Additionally, we annotated the missing hand positions for each recording.

None of the participants violated any of the temporal constraints of the maintenance procedure. However, the participants exhibited a lot of variance in the length of the execution. The executions had a mean duration of 316.4 s with a standard deviation of 95.3 s. The shortest and longest execution took 161.5 and 496.7 s, respectively. We also observed a small variance in the way participants screwed on nuts. Some participants screwed nuts on loosely by hand and only

Table 2. Sensors and their corresponding observations used for the study.

$s \in S$	$o \in O_s$
Eye tracker	Cable interface, cable cover, door handle, main fuse, smart meter, meter cross, left screw, right screw, top screw, top screw, voltage tester
Tool	Screwdriver, wrench, voltage tester, sealing pliers, mobile phone, barcode scanner, camera
Hand position	Door, top of fuse box, bottom of fuse box

later used the spanner to tighten them. Others used the spanner entirely. Lastly, we saw some variance in the execution of the few parallel and order independent tasks.

While we examined the recording, we identified three recordings in which the eye tracker slid on the participants head in such a way that pupil detection was no longer possible. After excluding these records from our study, we ended up with a data set of 19 valid records.

4.4   Evaluation

After all recording were annotated, we created our task recognition models for the evaluation. First, we estimated a task recognition model based on the Dempster-Shafer theory (DTRM) that was used to predict the execution of tasks for each participant. To make this estimate as good as possible, we observed an experienced technician performing the task in advance and then conducted an interview with him. Then, the execution of tasks for each participant was predicted with task recognition models based on Hidden Markov Models (HTRMs) trained from data sets of different sizes. As performance indicators, mean Accuracy, mean True Positive Rates (TPR), and mean Predictive Values (PPV) were collected for those predictions, that were made by models trained from data sets of the same size.

We used a leave-one-out cross validation approach for evaluation of the HTRMs. We created 19 test data sets from the 19 participants with valid recordings. For each test data set, we used the remaining 18 data sets as training data. To investigate how the number of training samples affects the model performance, we changed the amount of training data starting with just on data set up top all 18 data sets. For each test data set and each training data size, 10 random training data sets were created. This evaluation process is formally described in Listing 1.1. Figures 5 and 6 show average performance indicators over training data size.

The intermediate stages I had to be given special consideration in the evaluation. If a ground truth member was an intermediate stage, a prediction of the previous or the next task was considered as correct for both types of models. This should be considered when interpreting the result, because the intermediate stages were handled differently by the two types of models. However, as the intermediate stages accounted only for an average $\sim$15% in the ground truth data of all recorded task sequences, we assume that any effect will be small.

For the task selection in both types of task recognition models, we used a reasonable lower bound of $lb = 0.5$. Additionally, we set a very small smoothing parameter of $\varphi = 2^{-10}$ for the training of the HTRMs. For the overall evaluation, we compared the mean accuracy of predictions made by models and its standard deviation.

Figure 5 shows the findings of our study. For our estimated DTRM, the mean prediction accuracy is 0.9 for all participants. The mean accuracy of the HTRMs trained from data sets of size 1 was a bit lower at 0.884. The accuracy of the HTRMs' exceeded the accuracy of the DTRM from a training data set of size

Listing 1.1. Evaluation of HTRMs

```
algorithm evaluation is
    input: data set R
    output: set A* of an average performance indicator for
        each size of a training data set

    let A ← ∅ be the set of a performance indicator for each prediction
    for each test date r ∈ R do
        let D ← R\{r} be the training data set
        for each i ∈ {1, 2, . . . , 10} do
            let p : D → D be a random permutation of D
            let D⁺ ← ∅ be the gradually increasing training data set
            for each j ∈ {1, 2, . . . , |D|} do
                D⁺ ← D⁺ ∪̇ {p(dⱼ ∈ D)}
                λ ← train(D⁺)
                A ← A ∪̇ {⟨r, i, j, performance indicator of λ for r⟩}

    let x, y ∈ A : xξy :⟺ x₃ = y₃ be an equivalence relation
    let A* ← ∅ be the set of average metric
    for each [x]ξ ∈ A/ξ do
        A* ← A* ∪̇ {⟨x₃, (Σ_{y∈[x]ξ} y₄) ÷ |[x]ξ|⟩}
    return A*
```

2. With a data set size of 11, the HTRMs peaked in accuracy at 0.952, dropping a little to 0.949 at the end. The standard deviation of the accuracy of the DTRM was 0.047 for all participants. The standard deviation for the HTRMs was initially higher at 0.08, but undercut that of the DTRM from a training data size of 5. Overall, the standard deviation decreases monotonically over the size of training data. Based on the accuracy metric, it can be said that HTRMs are better suited for this maintenance procedure, as they outperform the DTRM with only a few training data recordings.

However, a comparison of the mean accuracy gives only a first impression of the overall performance of the models. It does not take into account how well the individual tasks are recognised. For this reason, we constructed a confusion

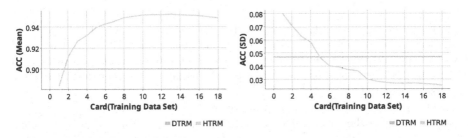

Fig. 5. Accuracy measurements of the smart meter installation procedure over a steadily increasing training data set

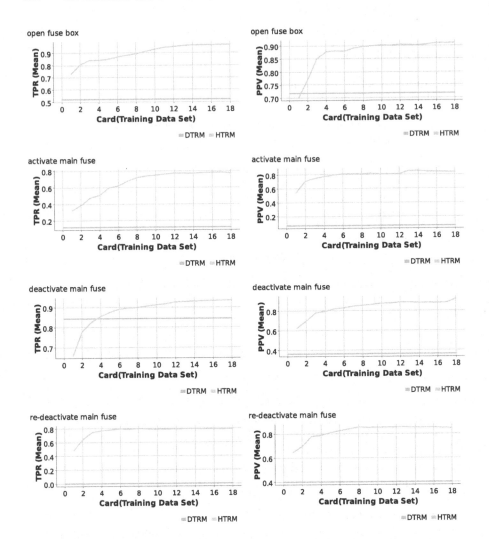

Fig. 6. Mean True Positive Rate (TPR) and mean Positive Predictive Value (PPV) for the four most important tasks from our opinion

matrix for each task $t \in T_r$. Figure 6 depicts the mean TPR and the mean PPV of the four most important tasks (in our opinion). The TPR is a meaningful value that indicates the percentage of correct predictions for a task. However, in order to illustrate how false negative predictions influence other tasks, the PPV is also considered here.

The first task, *open fuse box*, is important because it is also the first task to be performed in the smart meter installation procedure. False negatives in such an early phase in the procedure may lead to more acceptance problems on the user side. The risk of false negatives and false positives is even reinforced by the fact that this task is very similar to the task *close fuse box*, which is performed at the end of the procedure. It can be seen that the HTRMs generally perform better as the TPR and PPV values steadily increase over the training data size. The DTRM only has a small advantage with regard to PPV at the beginning. The results for this task confirmed our expectations that HTRMs would perform better, as they were better able to distinguish between this task and the task *close fuse box* due to the task transition probabilities they had learned.

The three remaining tasks are *activate main fuse, deactivate main fuse*, and *re-deactivate main fuse*. They are considered important because they are safety-critical for the further execution of the maintenance procedure. All these three tasks are very similar to each other regarding their associated actions. Additionally, because they are also short-lived, they can easily be overlooked by task recognition. The curves for the HTRMs look very promising overall, as their values increased almost steadily from an initial high value. For the DTRM, the only good performance indicator is the TPR of the task *deactivate main fuse*, which is ahead of the HTRMs up to a training data set size of 4. In summary, the DTRM struggles to classify these short-lived but safety-critical tasks. This may pose a security risk to an inexperienced technician who relies too much on an AS with task recognition. Just as with the first task considered, our expectations that HTRMs would perform better than the DTRM due to their task transition probabilities were met.

Looking at the mean values – accuracy, TPR and PPV – it can be said that HTRMs trained from a sufficient size are better suited for recognising tasks in maintenance procedures similar to the smart meter installation under study. So the first hypothesis we made, that HTRMs perform better, could be proven by this study.

The second hypothesis we put forward, that a well-estimated DTRM performs better than HTRMs trained from a data set with small size, could not be proven. Although the accuracy of the DTRM was briefly better at the beginning, the TPR and PPV for selected critical tasks were almost universally worse.

5 Discussion

In this paper we have shown how to build and use task recognition models for maintenance procedures with models developed by Honecker & Schulte, which are based on a simplified Dempster-Shafer theory, as well as with models based on Hidden Markov models. By evaluating these models in a smart meter installation as an example maintenance procedure, we have also shown how these models compare in terms of overall accuracy, TPR, and PPV. For this, we estimated a task recognition model based on the Dempster-Shafer theory (DTRM) and trained task recognition models based on Hidden Markov Models (HTRMs) from data sets of different sizes. Our first hypothesis, that HTRMs trained from a data set of sufficient size perform better than a self-estimated DTRM, could be proven. Our second hypothesis, that a well self-estimated DTRM perform better than HTRMs trained from a data set of small sizes, could not be proven. The reasons for that are manifold. First, we have only investigated in one maintenance procedure. It is possible that a self-estimated DTRM may perform better in other maintenance procedures, where different tools and sensors are used. Second, the maintenance procedure we used was perhaps too strictly specified, leaving little room for variance in executing the tasks. This was probably the reason why the HTRMs trained with small data sets were already performing so well. Third, it may be that our self-estimated DTRM was not good enough, meaning that we failed to provide accurate estimations of the model's parameters.

Even if our estimated DTRM performed worse, it might still be useful to apply them on maintenance procedures. One example is environments where data protection regulations do not allow records of maintenance procedures to be stored and analysed. In such cases, the only option for task recognition would be to use self-estimated models. Another scenario for the use of HTRMs is maintenance procedures where the tasks are easily distinguishable and not critical in a way that would pose a danger to the technician or the system.

Nevertheless, more research needs to be done to further improve the performance of task recognition. At first, more maintenance procedures need to be investigated. Then studies would have to be conducted with real technicians who do not need an introduction to the maintenance procedure under study. This would most likely lead to more variance in task execution. It should then be investigated how the difference in task execution between different technicians can be measured qualitatively. This could pave the way for building behaviour-based task recognition models, that have the potential to improve performance. Next, methods for training DTRMs should be developed and evaluated in order to compare learned DTRMs to learned HTRMs. To our knowledge, Honecker & Schulte have not presented such methods. At last, the method of task selection needs to be further explored. For example, recognition could be further improved by filtering out short-lived task changes.

References

1. Barnett, J.A.: Computational methods for a mathematical theory of evidence. In: Proceedings of the 7th International Joint Conference on Artificial Intelligence, IJCAI 1981, vol. 2, pp. 868–875. Morgan Kaufmann Publishers Inc., San Francisco (1981)
2. Behrendt, M., Osterloh, J.P.: Real-time task recognition for mechanical maintenance procedures (2018). http://www.puk-workshop.de/puk2018/paper/Real_Time_Task_Recognition_for_Mechanical_Maintenance.pdf
3. Blunsom, P.: Hidden Markov models. Lect. Notes **15**(18–19), 48 (2004)
4. Boussemart, Y., Cummings, M.: Behavioral recognition and prediction of an operator supervising multiple heterogeneous unmanned vehicles, February 2021
5. Brakensiek, A.: Modellierungstechniken und Adaptionsverfahren für die On- und Off-Line Schrifterkennung. Dissertation, Technische Universität München, München (2002)
6. Dempster, A.P.: Upper and lower probabilities induced by a multivalued mapping. Ann. Math. Statist. **38**(2), 325–339 (1967)
7. Donath, D.: Verhaltensanalyse der Beanspruchung des operateurs in der multi-UAV-Führung. Dissertation, Universität der Bundeswehr München, Fakultät für Luft- und Raumfahrttechnik, Neubiberg (2012)

8. Donath, D., Schulte, A.: Behavior based task and high workload determination of pilots guiding multiple UAVs. Proc. Manuf. **3**, 990–997 (2015). 6th International Conference on Applied Human Factors and Ergonomics (AHFE 2015) and the Affiliated Conferences, AHFE 2015
9. Hayashi, M.: Hidden Markov models to identify pilot instrument scanning and attention patterns. In: SMC 2003 Conference Proceedings. 2003 IEEE International Conference on Systems, Man and Cybernetics. Conference Theme - System Security and Assurance (Cat. No. 03CH37483), vol. 3, pp. 2889–2896 (2003). https://doi.org/10.1109/ICSMC.2003.1244330
10. Hayashi, M.: Hidden Markov models for analysis of pilot instrument scanning and attention switching (2004)
11. Honecker, F., Schulte, A.: Evidenzbasierte Pilotentätigkeitserkennung unter Berücksichtigung unterschiedlich zuverlässiger Beobachtungen. In: 57. Fachausschusssitzung Anthropotechnik der DGLR: Kooperation und kooperative Systeme in der Fahrzeug- und Prozessführung, pp. 115–130. Deutsche Gesellschaft für Luft- und Raumfahrt - Lilienthal-Obert e.V., Bonn (2015)
12. Honecker, F., Schulte, A.: Konzept für eine automatische evidenzbasierte Online-Pilotenbeobachtung in bemannt-unbemannten Hubschraubermissionen (2015)
13. Honecker, F., Schulte, A.: Kognitive und workload-adaptive Unterstützung von Hubschrauberpiloten in multi-UAV Missionen (2017)
14. Kassner, M., Patera, W., Bulling, A.: Pupil: an open source platform for pervasive eye tracking and mobile gaze-based interaction. In: Adjunct Proceedings of the 2014 ACM International Joint Conference on Pervasive and Ubiquitous Computing, UbiComp 2014 Adjunct, pp. 1151–1160. ACM, New York (2014). https://doi.org/10.1145/2638728.2641695. http://doi.acm.org/10.1145/2638728.2641695
15. Kim, E., Helal, S., Cook, D.: Human activity recognition and pattern discovery. IEEE Pervasive Comput. **9**(1), 48–53 (2009)
16. Lee, C., Kim, M., Park, J., Oh, J., Eom, K.: Development of wireless RFID glove for various applications. In: Kim, T., Stoica, A., Chang, R.-S. (eds.) SUComS 2010. CCIS, vol. 78, pp. 292–298. Springer, Heidelberg (2010). https://doi.org/10.1007/978-3-642-16444-6_38
17. März, M., Blechschmidt, N., Weck, D.L.: Projektstudie chemie und pharma: wertorientiertes instandhaltungs- und asset management. Technical report, ConMoto Consulting Group GmbH (2014)
18. Osterloh, J.P., Bracker, H., Müller, H., Kelsch, J., Schneider, B., Lüdtke, A.: DCoS-XML: a modelling language for dynamic distributed cooperative systems. In: Proceedings of the 2013 11th IEEE International Conference on Industrial Informatics (INDIN). IEEE, July 2013
19. Paternò, F.: ConcurTaskTrees: an engineered notation for task models. Handb. Task Anal. Hum.-Comput. Interact. 483–501 (2004)
20. Rabiner, L.R.: A tutorial on hidden Markov models and selected applications in speech recognition. In: Readings in speech recognition, pp. 267–296. Morgan Kaufmann Publishers Inc., San Francisco (1990)
21. Rabiner, L.R., Juang, B.H., Lee, C.H.: An overview of automatic speech recognition. In: Lee, C.H., Soong, F.K., Paliwal, K.K. (eds.) Automatic Speech and Speaker Recognition. The Kluwer International Series in Engineering and Computer Science (VLSI, Computer Architecture and Digital Signal Processing), vol. 355, pp. 1–30. Springer, Boston (1996). https://doi.org/10.1007/978-1-4613-1367-0_1
22. Schmid, S.: Single protein dynamics at steady state quantified from FRET time traces. Dissertation, Technische Universität München, München (2017)

23. Schulte, A., Donath, D., Honecker, F.: Human-system interaction analysis for military pilot activity and mental workload determination. In: 2015 IEEE International Conference on Systems, Man, and Cybernetics (SMC) (2015)
24. Tanguay, D.O.: Hidden Markov models for gesture recognition. Ph.D. thesis, Massachusetts Institute of Technology (1995)
25. Trabelsi, D., Mohammed, S., Chamroukhi, F., Oukhellou, L., Amirat, Y.: An unsupervised approach for automatic activity recognition based on hidden Markov model regression. IEEE Trans. Autom. Sci. Eng. **10**(3), 829–835 (2013)
26. Victor, D.: HandTrack: a library for prototyping real-time hand trackinginterfaces using convolutional neural networks. GitHub repository (2017). https://github.com/victordibia/handtracking/tree/master/docs/handtrack.pdf
27. Zhu, P., Zhou, H., Cao, S., Yang, P., Xue, S.: Control with gestures: a hand gesture recognition system using off-the-shelf smartwatch. In: 2018 4th International Conference on Big Data Computing and Communications (BIGCOM), pp. 72–77 (2018). https://doi.org/10.1109/BIGCOM.2018.00018

Systematic Review on How the Internet of Things will Impact Management in the Manufacturing Industry

Jordan T. Cistola[✉] and Vincent G. Duffy

Purdue University, West Lafayette, IN 47906, USA
jcistola@purdue.edu

Abstract. The Internet of Things has led to the development of new operational frameworks and models within the manufacturing industry. The emergence of advanced technologies now gives managers better quality resources and knowledge to make more improved decisions on the problems they encounter. A systematic literature review was conducted in this report over articles containing the keywords "internet of things", "manufacturing", and "management" to receive a better understanding on the relationship between them. These keywords were searched through the databases Web of Science, Scopus, and Google Scholar via Harzing to receive articles and metadata. This metadata was then analyzed through the softwares VOSviewer and CiteSpace. These softwares were able to provide co-citation analysis, co-occurrence analysis, cluster analysis, and word clouds. The co-citation analysis and searching throughout the database Web of Science is how the 9 main references used in this report were found. The co-occurrence analysis, cluster analysis, and word cloud were used to gain insight on what subtopics should receive the most attention when analyzing the references. A subtopic found to have a lot of relevance to the keywords is a term called "Industry 4.0". There are numerous new management systems and frameworks being developed from the integration of Internet of Things into manufacturing which are covered within this report.

Keywords: Internet of Things · Manufacturing · Management

1 Introduction and Background

As technology and innovation have rapidly progressed over the past decade, companies are forced to adapt and integrate these innovations if they want to stay competitive with the actively increasing global demand for consumer products. The manufacturing industry right now is experiencing a transition into the next industrial revolution which will bring forth new and improved systems as well as change the way we manage them. The Internet of Things (IoT) began this evolution and has emerged to help support manufacturing plants by giving them a better way to manage the quality of their products [14]. The Internet of Things gives us the ability to have a fully connected network of systems instead of an isolated industrial system [1]. This next industrial revolution has

© Springer Nature Switzerland AG 2021
C. Stephanidis et al. (Eds.): HCII 2021, LNCS 13097, pp. 427–443, 2021.
https://doi.org/10.1007/978-3-030-90966-6_30

been termed "Industry 4.0". Integrating IoT into the manufacturing process is said to be the most important enabler for this 4th industrial revolution we are experiencing [4]. Many challenges still have to be overcome before we see the full effect of how the Internet of Things will improve the quality and efficiency of the manufacturing process. We will see the emergence of new frameworks like Cyber-Physical Systems (CPS) which author Jay Lee defines as "transformative technologies for managing interconnected systems between its physical assets and computational capabilities" as well as the smart cloud-based production logistics synchronization (S-CPLS) mode described by author George Q. Huang [5, 9]. The future of manufacturing will highly depend on the use of big data causing manufacturing analytics to be much more important than we've seen in the past decades [6].

The emergence of these new technologies and frameworks will change the operational processes and workplace design of manufacturing facilities.

2   Purpose of the Study

The purpose of this study is to perform a systematic literature review of scientific articles based on the topic of the Internet of Things in manufacturing and how this will lead to changes in the way the manufacturing industry is managed and designed in the future. The study will also slightly cover how these new emerging ideas and technologies may affect the health of workers in the industry. For example, Chapter 60 in the Handbook of Human Factors and Ergonomics mentions how in the beginning stages of the industrial revolution physical load was an issue which then changed to more psychological stress with the arrival of industrial robots, automation, and innovative information systems needing to be learned and mastered [11]. This study was done to figure out what new management ideas and system frameworks have been introduced to integrate IoT into manufacturing and how this will impact the manufacturing workplace design.

3   Research Methodology

A literature review is ultimately a systematic way of collecting and synthesizing prior research conducted on a particular subject area [10]. These give you the ability to address research questions with much more power because of all the empirical findings and perspectives being found and integrated into one single study [10]. The main logic behind the steps in the methods section is to gain meta-data on thousands of articles all related to the 3 keywords so a literature review can be conducted. This meta-data will allow for further analysis to be complete showing the connection between these keywords as well as prove this subject area is still an increasing topic of interest in society. A brief outline of the plan used to collect and analyze the data is shown in Table 1 below, but will be described in more depth in the subsequent sections. A previous publication written by Gavin and Vincent Duffy used a similar plan to this for completing a systematic literature review [3].

Table 1. Plan used to collect and analyze data.

Step	Action	Software/Application/Database used	Data used
1	Collect data	Web of Science, Google Scholar, Scopus	N/A
2	Complete trend analysis	Vicinitas (Website)	Web of Science, Scopus
3	Complete co-citation analysis	VOSviewer	Scopus
4	Complete co-citation analysis	VOSviewer	Web of Science
5	Create author leading table	Excel	Web of Science
6	Create author leading table	Excel	Scopus
7	Create author pivot table	Scopus	Scopus
8	Complete cluster diagram of key terms	VOSviewer	Google Scholar
9	Complete cluster analysis	CiteSpace	Web of Science
10	Create keyword leading table	Excel	Scopus
11	Create word cloud	MAXQDA	9 selected references

3.1 Data Collection

Research for this report began by doing a keyword search into 3 different databases; Web of Science, Google Scholar via Harzing, and Scopus. The Web of Science and Scopus databases were able to be found through Purdue's online Library database, while Google Scholar via Harzing can be downloaded from the internet. This was done to collect a large amount of metadata on the topic of interest. The 3 keywords that were used to search throughout these databases were "Internet of Things", "Manufacturing", and "Management" which would result in thousands of articles all related and connected to those keywords. The same set of keywords was searched in each database used. The first database a keyword search was conducted on is the Web of Science. Web of Science allows you to receive and analyze metadata based on the article titles, authors, keywords, and citations which is all metadata that is needed to perform a systematic literature review. This metadata allowed a co-citation analysis from the software VOSviewer to be conducted as well as a cluster analysis from the software CiteSpace which will be talked about more in the results section. From this co-citation analysis, 1 article was retrieved to further review and is included in the reference list. 3 more articles were then retrieved from Web of Science by searching the 3 keywords by title instead of the topic. Only 10 results were shown, but after reading through each of the abstracts, the 3 articles which were selected have a lot of relevance and were worth taking a more in-depth look. Web of Science also allows you to do a trend analysis which will be talked about in Sect. 3.2.

Then, 3 keywords were searched into the Scopus database to obtain metadata. The metadata you can receive in Scopus is very similar to what you can receive in Web of Science. This data can be imported into the VOSviewer software where it conducted a co-citation and keyword analysis. 3 articles were retrieved and are present in the reference list from this co-citation analysis. Scopus also provided data that was able to be used for a trend analysis and to create leading tables based on the authors and keywords found from the search.

Next, the same keywords were searched into the Google Scholar database via Harzing. Harzing will search for articles in other databases based on your keyword and give you all the bibliometric data from the database you choose. It will only allow you to search up to 1000 articles and google scholar is the only free database available for you to search through. The metadata received from Google Scholar was used to perform a keyword analysis or also called co-occurrence analysis with the VOSviewer software.

Finally, an extended lexical search was conducted as well as a word cloud was retrieved using MAXQDA which is done by exporting the 9 articles from the reference list into the MAXQDA software. 1 chapter was added from the *Handbook of Human Factors and Ergonomics* to the reference list. The chapter is Chapter 60 which is titled "Human Factors in Manufacturing". One last reference was also added called "How smart, connected products are transforming companies" which was retrieved from a list of articles given to us by the professor and this gave the 9th and final main reference used. You will see 14 references in the reference list, but 2 of them were used to give further explanation on CiteSpace and what a co-citation analysis is. Another 2 references were used to help describe what a literature review is. The last reference was used to show a rewarded proposal in Sect. 6 which is titled "Conclusion and Future Work". These 5 references were not analyzed since they are not directly relevant to the 3 keywords.

3.2   Trend Analysis

The trend analysis is related to the data which was received in Scopus and Web of Science. A website called Vicinitas was also used to analyze twitter activity based on the three keywords. These actions were taken to further clarify the keywords that were selected are an emerging topic of interest within our society.

Figure 1 is a bar graph showing the number of articles published per year from 2001–2021 based on the keywords searched in Web of Science. This graph shows a sharp increase in the number of articles starting around the year 2016. There was virtually zero interest in this combination of keywords up until about 2013–2014. 2019 shows a peak in the number of articles. The only reason the graph looks like it declined in 2021 is because we are only 4 months into the year. There is an obvious increasing trend shown from the graph below.

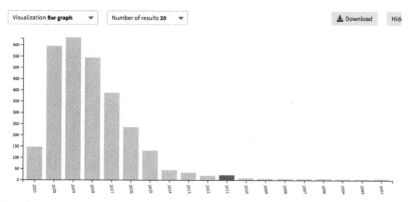

Fig. 1. Bar graph of articles per year from 2001–2021 in Web of Science using the keyword search "internet of things and manufacturing and management".

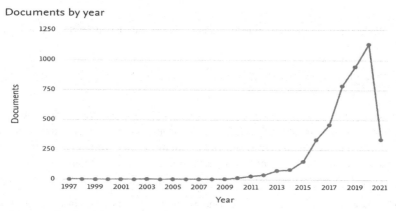

Fig. 2. Line graph of articles per year from 1997–2021 in Scopus using the keyword search "internet of things and manufacturing and management".

Figure 2 is a Line graph showing an increasing trend of articles from 1997–2021. Similarly to Fig. 1, the number of articles starts to increase exponentially around 2016 and it again peaks in 2019. Overall, both of these graphs represent there has been a steady increase of interest in these keywords over the past 20 years and a rapid increase over the past 5 or so years.

Vicinitas was used to perform the final trend analysis. The keyword "Internet of Things and Manufacturing" was only searched for this analysis. The results show the engagement of these topics via tweets from Twitter has steadily increased throughout the past year. Overall, the three trend analysis performed further solidifies the fact that this topic has people interested in them and it is emerging (Fig. 3).

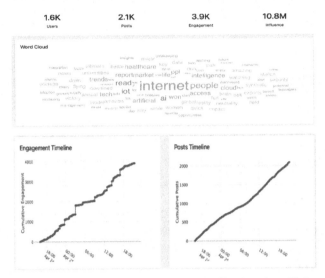

Fig. 3. Word cloud, engagement timeline, and posts timeline based on Twitter activity from Vicinitas.

4   Results

Using the three keywords and searching them in the databases; Web of Science, Scopus, and Google Scholar to collect metadata was the first step of the research conducted. Table 2, which is presented below, shows how many articles were received from each of the databases using the same three keywords that have been previously used.

Table 2. Shows database used, the corresponding number of articles obtained, and the keyword used in the search.

Database	Number of articles	Keywords
Scopus	1,133	Internet of things and manufacturing and management
Web of Science	765	Internet of things and manufacturing and managementement
Google Scholar (via Harzing)	390	Internet of things and manufacturing and managementement

4.1   Co-citation Analysis

To conduct the co-citation analysis, metadata which contains the author, keywords, article title, and citations, from Scopus and Web of Science was downloaded and exported into VOSviewer. This resulted in two separate analyses. One from the Scopus metadata which can be seen in Fig. 4, and another from the Web of Science metadata which is seen in Fig. 6. What a co-citation analysis does is "creates paradigms/clusters to reveal interdisciplinary research trends within institutions" [13]. It basically tells you what articles from your data have been cited together which lets you know there is a link between the articles. The higher number of co-citations an article acquires results in a stronger co-citation strength and leads you to believe the two articles are highly linked and related to your area of study. Figure 4 shows the co-citation analysis from the Scopus metadata by searching the 3 keywords. As seen in Table 2, Scopus gave back 1,133 articles, but the search was refined to only articles published between 2017–2021 which gave back 591 documents. The reason for this was to analyze only articles with the most recent and emerging knowledge. From these 591 documents, a total of 22,689 sources were cited amongst them. A minimum number of citations was set to 10 and only 8 out of the 22,689 articles met this threshold.

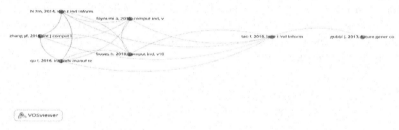

Fig. 4. Co-citation analysis using VOSviewer based on the metadata of 591 articles exported from Scopus.

Selected	Cited reference	Citations	Total link strength
✓	stock, t., seliger, g., opportunities of sustaina...	16	24
✓	lee, j., bagheri, b., kao, h.a., a cyber–physica...	13	19
✓	monostori, l., cyber–physical production syste...	16	17
✓	lee, j., kao, h.a., yang, s., service innovation a...	13	16
✓	atzori, l., iera, a., morabito, g., the internet of...	12	13
✓	qin, j., liu, y., grosvenor, r., a categorical fram...	12	13
✓	gubbi, j., buyya, r., marusic, s., palaniswami, ...	11	11
✓	xu, l.d., he, w., li, s., internet of things in indu...	10	7

Fig. 5. List of the 8 articles coming from the co-citation analysis of the Scopus metadata.

Figure 5 shows the total number of citations each of the 8 articles received as well as their total link strength. The 3 articles decided upon for the reference list had the 1st, 2nd, and 4th highest total link strength from Fig. 5 above.

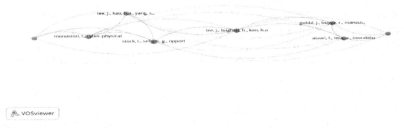

Fig. 6. Co-citation analysis using VOSviewer based on the metadata of 10 articles exported from Web of Science.

Figure 6 above shows the co-citation analysis from the Web of Science metadata. Table 1 tells you there are 765 articles from Web of Science, but a well-represented cluster diagram was not able to be formed from the articles, and none of the documents had more than 1 cited reference. So, the 3 keywords were searched into Web of Science, but by title instead of the topic which gave back 10 articles. These 10 articles were used and gave back 626 cited references. The minimum number of citations was set to 2 and only 7 articles met the threshold.

Selected	Cited reference	Citations	Total link strength
☑	bi zm, 2014, ieee t ind inform, v10, p1537, ...	2	7
☑	qu t, 2016, int j adv manuf tech, v84, p147, ...	2	7
☑	zhang yf, 2015, int j comput integ m, v28, p8...	2	7
☑	tao f, 2018, ieee t ind inform, v14, p2271, d...	2	6
☑	boyes h, 2018, comput ind, v101, p1, doi 10...	2	5
☑	fayoumi a, 2016, comput ind, v80, p54, doi ...	2	5
☑	gubbi j, 2013, future gener comp sy, v29, p1...	2	1

Fig. 7. List of the 7 articles coming from the co-citation analysis of the Web of Science metadata.

Figure 7 shows the 7 articles which came from the co-citation analysis of the Web of Science metadata. After looking through the 7 articles, only 1 was chosen for the reference list. The 2nd reference listed in Fig. 7 was the article chosen and had a total link strength of 7.

4.2   Author Analysis

Two leading tables were created based on analyzing the metadata from searching the 3 keywords into Web of Science and Scopus. The purpose of these was to identify which authors are most prevalent in this field of study. Table 3 shows you the results from the Web of Science data while Table 4 illustrates the Scopus results.

Table 3. Table of leading authors from web of science metadata

Author	Years	Count
Zhang, Yingfeng	2011, 2015, 2017–2020	16
Zhong, Ray Y.	2014–2018, 2020	16
Huang, George Q.	2014–2017, 2019–2020	13
Tao, Fei	2014–2019	13
Liu, Y.	2015, 2017–2020	9

From the keyword search of "internet of things and manufacturing and management" in Web of Science, there were a total of 2,427 authors. Table 3 shows the top 5 authors out of the 2,427 based on this combination of keywords.

Table 4. Table of leading authors from Scopus metadata

Author	Years	Count
Tao, Fei	2012, 2014–2020	11
Zhang, Yingfeng	2012, 2015, 2018–2020	9
Voigt, K.I.	2016–2020	8
Zhong, Ray Y.	2014, 2017–2018, 2020	7
Huang, George Q.	2014, 2017, 2019–2020	7

An exact number of total authors was not able to be found while analyzing the results, but Table 4 shows the top 5 authors and the years they made publications. Comparing the results from Tables 3 and 4, you will notice 4 out of the 5 authors are represented in both tables; Tao Fei, Zhang Yingfeng, Zhong Ray, and Huang George. Zhang, Yingfeng seems to be the leading author since he is ranked 1st in Table 3 and 2nd in Table 4.

A Pivot Chart was also formed from analyzing the results in Scopus. The Pivot Chart, seen in Fig. 8, shows you the top 14 leading authors rather than just the top 5. The same data used to create Table 4 was used in creating Fig. 8.

4.3 Content Analysis

To analyze the content inside all of the research articles received from Scopus, Web of Science, and Google Scholar, the softwares Harzing, CiteSpace, and VOSViewer were used. First, Harzing was used to collect metadata from Google Scholar which was then imported into VOSviewer. VOSviewer can analyze the text data that is present within

Documents by author

Compare the document counts for up to 15 authors.

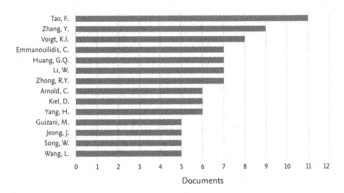

Fig. 8. Pivot chart of leading authors from Scopus search of the 3 keywords.

all of the articles and creates a cluster diagram showing the most used key terms and the linkage strength of these words. The more times the words appear together the greater amount of linkage strength they will have.

Figure 9 shows the cluster diagram made from VOSviewer of the Google Scholar via Harzing data. As you saw from Table 1, 390 results came from Harzing and all of these were imported into VOSviewer. There was a total of 2,707 terms. The minimum number of occurrences per term threshold was set to 25, and 16 out of the 2,707 terms meet the threshold. All 16 were selected to be present in the cluster diagram. The top 5 most prevalent words represented in this cluster diagram are thing, internet, manufacturing, technology, and system.

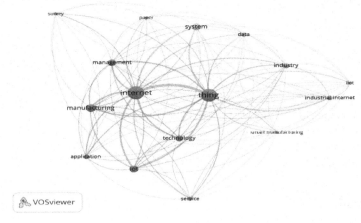

Fig. 9. Cluster diagram of key terms created in VOSviewer based on Harzing results.

To continue the content analysis, the metadata of the 765 articles received from Web of Science was exported and then imported into a software tool called CiteSpace. "CiteSpace provides various functions to facilitate the understanding and interpretation of network patterns and historical patterns, including identifying the fast-growth topical areas, finding citation hotspots in the land of publications, decomposing a network into clusters, automatic labeling clusters with terms from citing articles, geospatial patterns of collaboration, and unique areas of international collaboration" [2]. Figure 10 shows the cluster analysis created in CiteSpace of the top 8 most important and relevant subtopics from the Web of Science metadata.

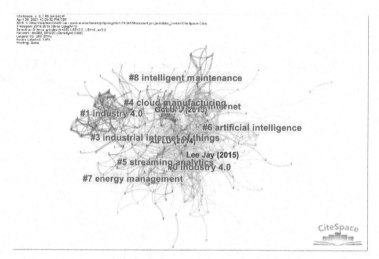

Fig. 10. Cluster analysis from CiteSpace of Web of Science metadata.

Last, a keyword leading table was created based on the 1,133 articles received by searching the keywords into Scopus. The results can be seen below in Table 5. The count column tells you how many times that keyword was used as a keyword in another article. This table provides insight into the keywords and terms which are highly related and correlated to the 3 keywords. This will be useful information to use when performing extended lexical searches throughout the articles in the reference list. The terms "Internet of Things" and "Manufacturing" were excluded from this list since those are the keywords used to get the results for Table 5. If they were not exclude from the chart, they would have been the 1st and 2nd most frequently used keywords.

4.4 MAXQDA Content Analysis

A word cloud was created using the software MAXQDA. The chapter from the *Handbook of Human Factors and Ergonomics* and the 8 articles selected from the prior analysis that was completed were imported into the MAXQDA software to receive the word cloud which is shown in Fig. 11. The word cloud allows us to see what were the most frequently used and most important words from the documents in the reference list. It

Table 5. Keyword leading table from searching "internet of things and manufacturing and management" into Scopus.

Rank	Keywords	Count
1	Industry 4.0	266
2	Information management	217
3	Embedded systems	133
4	Big data	124
5	Smart manufacturing	97

was decided to have the word cloud-only include the top 40 words. A stop list was also made to make sure only meaningful words were selected for the word cloud. Only words that were relevant to the topic of the internet of things, manufacturing, and management were included.

Fig. 11. Word cloud created from the MAXQDA software based on the 9 references.

Figure 12 displays the top 17 words used to create the word cloud in Fig. 11. You can see from the chart that "work", "data", "system", "manufacturing", and "design" were the 5 most frequently occurring words. When comparing these results to the results received in Table 4, you will notice most of the top 5 words obtained here are also present in the top 5 key terms from Table 4. "Data" is 2nd in Fig. 12 while "big data" is 4th in Table 4, "system" is 3rd in Fig. 12 while "embedded systems" is 3rd in Table 4, and "manufacturing" is 4th in Fig. 12 while "smart manufacturing" is 5th in Table 4. This gives a better understanding of what keywords and terms should be pick when completing an extended lexical search which is done next.

Lexical Search. From the word cloud created through MAXQDA, the keyword leading table created from Scopus metadata, and the citation burst made from CiteSpace, 3 key terms were picked to perform an extended lexical search in the MAXQDA software. The lexical search will search for the key term throughout the 8 articles and 1 chapter that are used in the reference list. None of the 3 key terms that was searched showed up in

Word	Word length	Frequency ▼	%	Rank	Documents	Documents %
work	4	467	0.84	1	9	90.00
data	4	337	0.60	2	10	100.00
system	6	334	0.60	3	9	90.00
manufacturing	13	310	0.56	4	10	100.00
design	6	293	0.52	5	9	90.00
smart	5	261	0.47	6	9	90.00
management	10	224	0.40	7	10	100.00
products	8	219	0.39	8	7	70.00
human	5	214	0.38	9	7	70.00
production	10	214	0.38	9	9	90.00
product	7	209	0.37	11	8	80.00
process	7	199	0.36	12	10	100.00
service	7	181	0.32	13	7	70.00
health	6	180	0.32	14	6	60.00
information	11	180	0.32	14	9	90.00
systems	7	172	0.31	16	9	90.00
resource	8	148	0.27	17	5	50.00

Fig. 12. Table of the words used in the word cloud as well as the number of times each word appears.

the chapter selected from the *Handbook of Human Factors and Ergonomics* which was not a surprise. As you saw from the trend analysis in Sect. 3.2, this subject area started to emerge around the year 2016 and the *Handbook of Human Factors and Ergonomics* was published in 2012. You will see a high degree of connectivity between these 3 key terms.

Industry 4.0: The term Industry 4.0 was found within 5 out of the 9 articles in the reference list. This key term was ranked 1st in Table 4 which showed the leading key terms from Scopus and ranked 1st in the cluster analysis created from CiteSpace. The article titled "Opportunities of Sustainable Manufacturing in Industry 4.0" had the most occurrences out of the 5 articles which were a total of 47. This article mentions how we are still in the 3rd phase of industrialization but are heading towards the 4th stage which is termed Industry 4.0. G. Seliger, the author of this document, highlights how "this development provides immense opportunities for the realization of sustainable manufacturing" [12]. In the article "Service innovation and smart analytics for Industry 4.0 and big data environment" it is said that "the actual processing of big data into useful information is then the key of sustainable innovation within an Industry 4.0 factory" [6]. This information connects with the next key term searched, "big data".

Big Data: Jay Lee emphasizes how critical the management and distribution of big data is to attaining "self-aware" and "self-learning" machines [12]. This key term is used 35 times and is seen in 5 of the articles. Big data is most frequently seen in the article called "Service innovation and smart analytics for Industry 4.0 and big data environment". Big data is highly associated with the terms "Cyber-Physical Systems" and "Smart Manufacturing" which is the next key term searched. According to a chart in the article "Design Principles for Industry 4.0 Scenarios" big data was the 10th most frequently occurring term from the identified practical publications they gathered on Industry 4.0

[4]. Also appearing in this chart was the term "Cyber-Physical systems" which was ranked 9th, "smart factory" which was ranked 5th, and one of the key terms used in this report, "internet of things" which was ranked 4th [4].

Smart Manufacturing: Smart Manufacturing comes up in 5 out of the 9 articles and makes the most occurrences in the article "A Secure Industrial Internet of Things (IIoT) Framework for Resource Management in Smart Manufacturing". This article explains how smart manufacturing will improve productivity through the use of "smart sensors, robotics, actuators, communication devices, machine learning, technologies, and data analytics", but will bring forth a plethora of challenges for us to overcome [1]. This new age of manufacturing allows us to have fully automated and interconnected machines raising the level of optimization we can have in production [8]. The article written by Yuen, J has a subsection titled "IoT for Smart Manufacturing" which highly emphasis the connection between these two terms [14].

5   Discussion

One of the emerging systems being used to integrate IoT into manufacturing is called Cyber-Physical Systems (CPS). Jay Lee defines these systems as "transformative technologies for managing interconnected systems between its physical assets and computational capabilities" [5]. The integration of the systems into production is what is transforming our factories today into Industry 4.0 factories and brings significant economic potential [5]. Jay Lee mentions a 5-level CPS structure which breaks down how you would develop and deploy a CPS for manufacturing application [5].

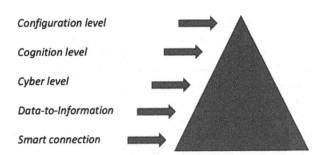

Configuration level

Cognition level

Cyber level

Data-to-Information

Smart connection

Fig. 13. A pyramid architecture for implementation of "Cyber-Physical System" [adapted from 5].

In Fig. 13, functions are shown in the form of a pyramid with 1 at the base of the pyramid and 5 at the top. It is understood that the base of the pyramid provides support for the upper level functions within the pyramid. In original article [5], functions are numbered 1–5. Associated attributes are described here. The pyramid is known as the "5C architecture for implementation of Cyber-Physical Systems" and the levels from 1 to 5 are Smart Connection, Data-to-Information Conversion, Cyber, Cognition, and

Configuration [5]. Having the ability to obtain accurate and trustworthy data is what you need to begin developing a CPS application which is what the smart connection level consists of [5]. Next the ability to transfer this data into usable information is needed which is completed during the 2nd level [5]. Also, machines will have self-awareness during this level [5]. Now moving to the cyber level, its main purpose is for it to act as the "central information hub" for the architecture as a whole [5]. This will allow for overall better and more accurate insight on the status of each machine [5]. The 4th level, cognition, provides more in depth knowledge of the system being monitored which, if presented correctly, will help expert users make the right decisions [5]. Finally, the configuration level as said by Jay Lee is the "feedback from cyber space to physical space and acts as a supervisory control to make machines self-configure and self-adaptive" [5]. CPS brings self-aware, self-maintainable, and self-organizational attributes to the machines and technologies used in factories [5]. In industry 3.0, management has to worry about things like lean operations to make sure production is running efficiently, but CPS would bring a worry-free environment where there is essentially zero downtime in production [5]. This would cause a significant change to the way managers handle operations since it is nearly impossible to find a factory today with zero downtime and no worries.

Author Yuen, J explains a model for how managers can effectively manage the risk of implementing IoT into smart manufacturing called the electronic manufacturing risk management model (EM-RMM) [14]. This model "provides a systematic procedure for risk assessment in IoT implementation" [14]. Before a model like this was created, managers would have to make decisions regarding risk purely based on their personal experience and observations, but now there is a standard process that will select any key risk factors and create a solution to help you avoid them if followed correctly [14].

Another operation framework that could impact the future management of manufacturing is the use of smart cloud manufacturing (S-CM) [9]. S-CM will allow us to "make comprehensive use of both manufacturing technologies and IT technologies to upgrade the traditional manufacturing resources into smart ones and adopt service-oriented concept to virtualize and servitize their capabilities, and finally construct cloud-based smart service pool" [9]. There are many advantages received to managers by integrating cloud manufacturing with Iot like "managing wide-range, various-resource service capability" or being able to perform "real-time, accurate, adaptive process control, and thus is able to deal with the uncertain dynamics" [9]. A lot of research is still needed to effectively integrate these together to handle the several dynamics of a production logistics process [9]. S-CM provides management with ways to overcome "plan infeasibility caused by execution dynamics" by giving them "IoT-enabled adaptive solutions" [9]. Managers are now given better solutions from the IoT to address the challenges that come with planning operations.

6 Conclusion and Future Work

The future of management in the manufacturing industry is evolving because of new systems and operational frameworks (Smart Cloud Manufacturing and Cyber-Physical Systems) which emerged because of new technologies like the IoT. From this systematic review, it was shown this is an emerging topic of interest by the surge of published articles within the past few years. The content analysis provided other highly relevant and interconnected key-terms to the IoT giving a more concise understanding of what should be focused on during research. It exemplified how important the idea of Industry 4.0 is to the IoT in manufacturing which further lead to the discovery of many interesting frameworks and management models developed by way of these new technologies being integrated into manufacturing. Managers are now able to use systems which have the ability to analyze large amounts of data leading to better more efficient solutions.

By searching the key words "internet of things" and "manufacturing" into the National Science Foundation website results in other proposals relevant to this topic. One proposal discovered which was awarded to Marion Technical College is called "Bridging the Skills Gap in Smart Manufacturing through a New Technician Education Program". This proposal highlights the need for technical education to stay up to date and on track with the continuously growing field of smart manufacturing [7]. Traditional manufacturing facilities are now becoming smart from new advanced technologies, but employees must learn the necessary skills to efficiently run them which is currently not being done at a fast enough pace [7]. This proposal aims to create a new academic pathway for instructors to adequately teach their students the needed skills to successful work in a smart manufacturing environment [7].

References

1. Abuhasel, K.A., Khan, M.A.: A secure industrial internet of things (IIoT) framework for resource management in smart manufacturing. IEEE Access **8**, 117354–117364 (2020). https://doi.org/10.1109/ACCESS.2020.3004711
2. Chen, C.: CiteSpace: visualizing patterns and trends in scientific literature. CiteSpace, 17 January 2021. http://cluster.cis.drexel.edu/~cchen/citespace/
3. Duffy, G.A., Duffy, V.G.: Systematic literature review on the effect of human error in environmental pollution. In: Duffy, V.G. (ed.) HCII 2020. LNCS, vol. 12199, pp. 228–241. Springer, Cham (2020). https://doi.org/10.1007/978-3-030-49907-5_16
4. Hermann, M., Pentek, T., Otto, B.: Design principles for industrie 4.0 scenarios. In: HICSS, pp. 3928–3937 (2016). https://doi.org/10.1109/HICSS.2016.488
5. Lee, J., Bagheri, B., Kao, H.A.: A cyber-physical systems architecture for industry 4.0-based manufacturing systems. Manuf. Lett. **3**, 18–23 (2015). https://doi.org/10.1016/j.mfglet.2014.12.001
6. Lee, J., Kao, H.A., Yang, S.: Service innovation and smart analytics for Industry 4.0 and big data environment. Procedia CIRP **16**, 3–8 (2014). https://doi.org/10.1016/j.procir.2014.02.001
7. Marion Technical College: Bridging the Skills Gap in Smart Manufacturing through a New Technician Education Program. National Science Foundation. https://www.nsf.gov/awardsearch/showAward?AWD_ID=2000177&HistoricalAwards=false. Accessed 1 May 2021
8. Michael, P.E., James, H.E.: How smart, connected products are transforming companies. Harvard Bus. Rev. **93**(10), 96–114 (2015). https://hbr.org/2015/10/how-smart-connected-products-are-transforming-companies
9. Qu, T., Lei, S.P., Wang, Z.Z., Nie, D.X., Chen, X., Huang, G.Q.: IoT-based real-time production logistics synchronization system under smart cloud manufacturing. Int. J. Adv. Manuf. Technol. **84**(1–4), 147–164 (2015). https://doi.org/10.1007/s00170-015-7220-1

10. Snyder, H.: Literature review as a research methodology: an overview and guidelines. J. Bus. Res. **104**, 333–339 (2019). https://doi.org/10.1016/j.jbusres.2019.07.039

11. Spath, D., Braun, M., Meinken, K.: Human factors in manufacturing. In: Salvendy, G. (ed.) Handbook of Human Factors and Ergonomics, 4th edn, pp. 1643–1666. Wiley, Hoboken (2012). https://onlinelibrary-wiley-com.ezproxy.lib.purdue.edu/doi/pdf/10.1002/978111813 1350.ch60

12. Stock, T., Seliger, G.: Opportunities of sustainable manufacturing in industry 4.0. Procedia CIRP **40**(Icc), 536–541 (2016). https://doi.org/10.1016/j.procir.2016.01.129

13. Surwase, G., Sagar, A., Kademani, B.S., Bhanumurthy, K.: Co-citation analysis: an overview ISBN: 935050007-8. In: BOSLA National Conference Proceedings, CDAC (2011). https://www.researchgate.net/publication/277119876_Co-citation_Analysis_ An_Overview. Accessed 9 Sept 2011

14. Yuen, J.S.M., Choy, K.L., Lam, H.Y., Tsang, Y.P.: An intelligent risk management model for achieving smart manufacturing on internet of things. In: PICMET 2019 - Portland International Conference on Management of Engineering and Technology: Technology Management in the World of Intelligent Systems, Proceedings, pp. 1–8 (2019). https://doi.org/10.23919/ PICMET.2019.8893942

Applying Design Thinking to Bring More Comfort, Agility, and Safety to the Bulk Products Sector in a Supermarket

Paulo Hermida[(⊠)], Joiceline Almeida[(⊠)], Marcos Silbermanm[(⊠)],
and Ricardo Grunitzki[(⊠)]

Mobile Innovation Lab, UX & Design Lab, Sidia Institute of Science and Technology,
Manaus, AM, Brazil
{paulo.hermida,joice.almeida,marcos.silbermann,
ricardo.grunitzki}@sidia.com

Abstract. The process of buying items in bulk in a supermarket, such as those in the fruit and vegetable sector, offers some opportunities for improvement, especially when older or very young people have to use this service. In this context, we use the Design Thinking methodology to find a comfortable, agile, and safe journey for people who use this type of service. Integrating Artificial Intelligence (AI) technology, User Experience/User Interface (UX/UI) approaches focused on people's needs, visits to supermarkets, interviews with users, among other activities, we were able to design and implement a sustainable and inclusive solution to this problem.

Keywords: Design thinking · Retail innovation · AI & Design

1 Introduction

The bulk purchase process has always been very present in retail negotiations, such as in the supermarket fruit and vegetable sectors. Recently, this type of trade has also played a very important role in reducing waste, as it allows the purchase of food and household goods by weight and without packaging or with reusable packaging.

To support this type of operation, several devices have been proposed to facilitate the identification, weighing, and pricing process of purchased items. Recently, more modern devices such as self-checkout can control the entire transaction, from purchase to payment, without the need to interact with an attendant. Such machines provide mechanisms for customers to complete their own transactions from a retailer without needing a traditional staffed checkout. The literature presents some solutions for self-checkout of bulk items, such as PC Scale Epelsa C8005A and Fox Checkout, but they are not flexible enough to deal with all the needs of both retailers and customer. The high cost of acquisition

Supported by Sidia Institute of Science and Technology http://www.sidia.com.

of such devices, the dependence of the user's input to select the item type, and the inability to add new items (such as regional fruits/vegetables) to the system combined with non-intuitive interfaces are good examples of limitations.

The present paper aim at filling this gap by providing a solution that addresses all the needs of both customer and supermarket. We applied the design thinking process in the search for a solution that allows the inclusion of people with different levels of mobility, in a fundamental activity, that is, the purchase of their food in a sector of products sold in bulk in a supermarket. The proposed solution was validated in real scenarios, where it was possible to observe: i) a reduction in the average time to purchase products, due to its intuitive interface; ii) minimization of labor cost by the seller, since our solution uses artificial intelligence to automatically identify the item; and iii) fast return on investment since the proposed solution is of low cost when compared to market competitors.

The rest of this paper is organized as follows. Section 2 presents selected existing solutions for buying items in bulk. Section 3 presents the design thinking methodology considered. The process of finding our solution is described in detail in Sect. 4. Final remarks are presented in Sect. 6.

2   Related Work

To identify the gaps and opportunities for improvements in the process of purchasing items in bulk in supermarkets, it is necessary to understand the main solutions available on the market and their characteristics. There are several solutions on the market created to assist users in their journey to purchase items in bulk. Most existing solutions are based on self-checkout systems and not specifically designed for the bulk items sector. Based on a survey of the main solutions available on the market, we selected four products based on their diversity of characteristics and nationality of the market for which they were developed. The main characteristics of the investigated products are summarized in Table 1. Due to copyright reasons, the images of these products are not presented here, but they can be found in the links presented below.

Table 1. Key features of related products

Key Features	Epelsa C6005A	SM – 5600BS CAMERA	Prix 6i AA	Fox Checkout
Item detection via camera	Yes	Yes	No	Yes
Internet Connection	Yes	Yes	Yes	Yes
Touch Screen	Yes	Yes	Yes	Yes
Audio instructions	No	Yes	No	No
Bar-code/QR-code reader	Yes	Yes	Yes	Yes
Integrated payment system	No	No	No	Yes
Shape	Scale	Scale	Scale	Totem
Supplies storage space	No	No	No	Yes
Bag support	No	No	No	Yes

The PC Scale Epelsa C6005A[1], is a compact self-service scale developed by Shenzhen Shinelong (China). Epelsa has support for integrated supermarket management, image recognition, and peripheral support. It uses image recognition for automatic detection of item type, weighing, price computing as well as payment on the scale itself. It has a built-in printer and supports WiFi to connect it to its self-service shopping system. In the absence in the absence of identification via cameras, it is also possible to use QR-code/bar-code reading for item identification.

The second product considered in this work is the SM - 5600BS CAMERA[2], which is provided by DiGi (USA). This is a compact self-recognition system scale that is fast, intuitive, and uses a built-in camera to identify fruits and vegetables. With its advanced artificial intelligence learning system, the scale can learn and improve accuracy with increased usage. Besides its connectivity via WiFi, software for management, and remote access, the main characteristic of this product is the visual and audio prompts that guide the users' journey.

The Prix 6i AA[3] is a Brazilian product provided by Toledo Brasil. This is a very simple and widely used product in Brazilian retails, which does not provide automatic recognition of items via camera, but it is designed to be a cheaper and intuitive scale that is highly dependent on human interactions to identify, weigh, and price items. The display is less intuitive than the previous products because it uses textual labels or manually typed codes for product selection.

The Fox Checkout[4] is a very complete terminal for self-checkout, developed by ELGIN (Brazil). This terminal allows the consumer to register goods, make payments and package items without the need for extra devices or furniture because all functionalities and resources are built-in in the totem.

3   Methodology

The DT choice is aligned with the way our group works to solve problems. The vision of the human being and the environment as the center of our motivation, the use of visual resources to express our ideas, and a systemic view are fundamental points to start the process of solving a problem. The union of knowledge from different areas, in a cordial and constructive way, was also fundamental so that there were no barriers or prejudices for innovative ideas and visions different from any solution. However, with all these possibilities, DT always puts us down to earth, considering the availability of technical resources and the restrictions that a solution must have when applied to a business.

According to [13], three macro processes must be present in the DT: (a) preparation, (b) assimilation, and (c) strategic control. In the preparation phase, the focus is on what is most relevant to solving the problem, this involves a detailed analysis of the scenarios, the definition of specifications and restrictions

---

[1] https://www.epelsa.cn/index.php?a=index&m=Product&id=114.

[2] https://www.digisystem.com/products/PRD00297/.

[3] https://www.toledobrasil.com/produto/prix-6i.

[4] https://www.elgin.com.br/Produtos/Automacao/AutoAtendimento/selfcheckout.

that the solution must follow, as well as the exploration of visual tools that allow understanding deeply the problem and the proposed solution. In the assimilation phase, an assessment is made of what was planned in the previous phase, through experiments, reports, and observations. In the strategic control phase, the rules, specifications, and other decisions are reviewed, and a fine adjustment is made to the solution.

Another approach used by [2,6,8], defines the focus of DT on companies and other organizations in need of innovation. Where the key objective of design is innovation. Used as key concepts, visualization, prototyping, integrative, and abductive thinking. And the nature of design problems merges with the organization's problems, and all of this applies to most alternative scenarios.

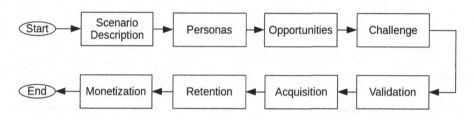

Fig. 1. The proposed methodology.

The proposed methodology is shown in Fig. 1. All elements of DT, highlighted by [2,6,8,13] are present, and follow a relative chronological order, which can be revised according to changes inherent to the innovation process. The phase is defined as **Description of the Scenario**, which aims to study the problem, always focusing on describing how it affects people, the environment, and business. At this first moment, it is already possible to detect some opportunities for improvement. In the sequence, we have the study of **Personas** who are involved in this scenario, the objective in this phase is to map the journey of these personas and to identify how they are affected by the problem. In the **Opportunities** phase, the negative effects that the problem generates, directly or indirectly, are described, and these items are considered to gain opportunities if they are eliminated with the resolution of the problem. In the **Challenge**, at this phase, the team needs to review the information previously collected, and from there propose a solution that can solve most of the problems raised. This is a moment of expansion, everyone is free to give their opinion and suggest, without technical, economic, or any other restrictions. Using techniques such as Brainstorms [17], Brain-writing [15], Rapid Ideation [4], Step-ladder technique [14], and Mind mapping [5] for example. The **Validation** phase aims to verify the effectiveness of the solutions proposed in the previous phase, for which four criteria are used: a) "Persona's journey", presenting the proposed solutions, and evaluating the positive effect they cause; b) "Technical feasibility", if the team has sufficient technical knowledge to implement the solution; c) "Commercial feasibility", comparison between the proposed solutions and those used by similar commercial products; and d) "Feedback received" from those involved in this process. In the **Acquisition** phase, the viability of the chosen solution has already been validated, and the objective now is to obtain internal or external sponsors that can invest in the creation of a prototype. This phase involves the purchase of equipment, allocation of human resources, and other investments necessary for the prototype to be assembled and tested. The **Retention** phase aims at a final round of improvements in the prototype. With the data collected and the identification of points for improvement, we justify the sponsors' final investment. In the **Monetization** phase, financial analyzes are carried out, such as ROI [12], cost-benefit ratio, indirect gains, among other financial indicators, which will serve as a basis for creating a business plan.

4   Building a Solution, Step by Step

In this Section, the process of building the solution to the proposed problem will be described in detail, which is the creation of a more agile, comfortable, and safer process for customers who use the services of selling bulk products. Following the methodology proposed in Sect. 3, each phase will be identified and associated with the corresponding actions and results.

4.1   Scenario Description

Starting with the study of the scenario, field research was carried out in three supermarkets located in Manaus/Brazil: Patio Gourmet[5], Assaí[6], and Nova Era[7]. They were chosen due to their target audience, ranging from the higher income classes to the more popular classes. The Fig. 2 presents an interview made in one of those supermarkets, where there is a partial view of the studied scenario. The basic layout normally adopted by supermarkets indent leaves a comfortable space for the customer to navigate between the products and centralizes the position of the scale, like an island in the center of the scene. The routine of workers in this area focuses on restocking and arranging products when necessary and assisting customers in the weighing and labeling process. Scales are programmed to store the product code and price in their standard base, for example, kilograms. In such a way that the calculation is already done automatically, leaving the customer only to place the items on the scale, wait for the employee to enter the product code, and generate the amount payable.

After confirming with the customer who will take the product, the label is printed and pasted on the product packaging, which is then delivered to the customer. The type of packaging varies in shape and transparency. The lighting is focused on the products, and its intensity varies a lot, especially where the products are weighed. The volume of products in this area varies widely, ranging

---

[5] https://www.patiogourmet.com.br.

[6] https://www.assai.com.br.

[7] https://www.supernovaera.com.br.

Fig. 2. A partial view of the scenario, with an interview conducted at Patio Gourmet Supermarket.

from grains to items such as pumpkins or watermelons. The diversity of products can reach hundreds, and some are visually very similar. Below the most important aspects and opportunities are found:

- **Sector layout:** The layout of the areas is similar in different supermarkets, it was noticed that the scale is in a higher position, and as the customer must place the product on the scale, this can generate discomfort for the elderly and people with some mechanical disability. In addition, the product is loose on the scale, which can lead to an accident.
- **Employee work routine:** Employees allocate part of their time to assist customers with questions about the products and the weighing and label printing process. If the number of customers increases, a queue is generated, and another employee can be moved to help.
- **Scale's setup:** The scales are programmed with the product code and the value per unit of weight, usually a kilogram. The mode of data visualization is very precarious, elderly or people with some degree of visual impairment having difficulty seeing. Only after printing the label can the value be verified in some cases.
- **Types of packaging used:** The products are packaged in transparent or semitransparent plastic bags, some products, depending on their volume, are directly labeled and do not use bags.
- **Lighting and Product Identification:** The lighting in the product area is insufficient, and the products are not always identified. This way, seniors and people who have some visual impairment will have difficulty to correctly

identify the product. This can lead to a wrong purchase and affect the health of people, who may end up consuming a different product than expected.
- **Product volume and diversity:** The volume of the products varies a lot; this creates an additional difficulty to place the product on the scale in a safe way. The number of products in this sector can reach hundreds, and in some cases, they are visually similar, creating the possibility of being chosen wrongly by customers.

With that we close the scenario description phase, this phase is especially important, here relevant information is generated that will influence all subsequent phases.

4.2   Personas

Personas are a way to synthesize many real people, creating a fictional representative. However, built on user surveys, data collection, and a lot of common sense. Getting to capture the relevant characteristics, which will contribute to the construction of a more general and inclusive solution. This more general concept and other important definitions about personas can be found in [9].

To help us, we have Maria, a retired lady who lives alone in an apartment near the supermarket and who comes at least once a week to the bulk sector. She has vision problems and motor difficulties. With average height and due to her poor health, she cannot consume certain types of food. She finds it difficult to read product information due to the small font size and lighting in the location. The weighing process is also uncomfortable for her, putting the products on the scale, evaluating the price, and deciding whether to take them or not, is an accelerated process and, depending on the queue that is formed, it can be exhausting.

4.3   Opportunities

With the data collected in the previous phases, it is already possible to list the opportunities for improvement. These items will serve as the basis for the initial construction of the solution: a) Lack of comfort in the process of taking the product on the scale to make the weighing customer make physical effort due to the height of the scale; b) Lack of safety in the process of taking the product on the scale to make the weighing, the product may come back and fall to the customer, since the scale does not have protection to prevent this situation; c) Lack of information for the customer about the items being weighed, weight, unit price, and price to pay, sometimes are informed by the employee; d) Lack of adequate lighting to identify, compare, and choose products; e) Discomfort on queue creation generated by employee's time limitation in customer service; f) Lack of flexibility in product identification, only code is used; g) Wrong product choice due to visual similarity; h) Increased supermarket costs, due to the hiring of more employees to meet the customer's demand; and i) Customer depends on the employee to carry out the weighing and label placement process.

4.4   Challenge and Validation

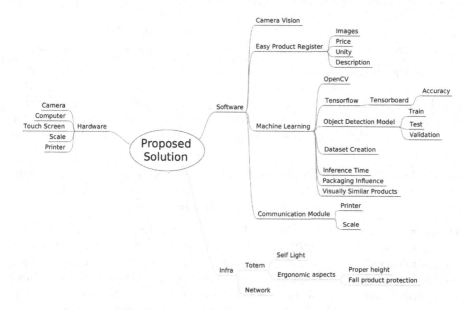

Fig. 3. Main aspects of the proposed solution.

Figure 3 illustrates the mind map of the proposed solution. This result was possible after brainstorming sessions, going through some creative ideas that ranged from the use of robots to the extinction of this sector in supermarkets. At this point, there is a small change in methodology, the validation phase that should have been done after the challenge phase was done simultaneously. This happened naturally, and everyone agreed that it would be more effective to leave this phase with a minimally viable solution.

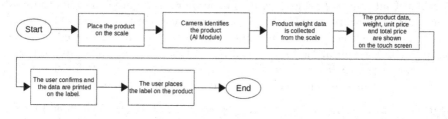

Fig. 4. The proposal flowchart.

The proposal is to introduce the use of Artificial Intelligence together with an intuitive and inclusive interface, all this being supported by an ergonomically correct structure. The Fig. 4 presents the simplified flow of the implemented solution. The process begins with the product being placed on the scale by the user, the AI system will automatically identify the type of product. At this point, the data about product weight, unit price, and total price are being shown on the touch screen, so that the user can check and confirm. After this step, the label is printed and the user places it on the product, finalizing the process.

Similar Products Visually: There are some products that are very similar, even for human beings, it is sometimes difficult to distinguish them. This will also happen with this solution, and the proposal we adopted to overcome this problem was that in the case of similar products, the products will appear on the screen with their respective descriptions, and the customer will choose the correct option.

Packaging: This is another critical point for this solution to be effective. Only transparent packaging can be used, this is not a problem, because in visits made to supermarkets, this type of packaging is already the most used.

Hardware: A notebook[8] will be used, which has two important differences for this application, it has a GPU [10] that will speed up the inference process of the neural network responsible for identifying the product, and it has a touch screen. The image will be captured by a camera[9] connected to the notebook, and the weight information will be provided by a scale[10], and the label printing is done through a thermal printer[11] also connected to a usb port on the notebook.

Software: The software development was done in the QTCreator [11] framework, using the C++ language. In Fig. 5 the user interface screens, following the flow described above.

The machine learning framework chosen to perform items identification was Tensorflow [1] combined with Transfer Learning [16] technique. The MobileNet [7] neural network has been partially retrained for the task of product identification. To carry out the training of the item identifier/machine learning model, a dataset of product images was created and processed via OpenCV [3] library.

In Fig. 6 some images of the dataset, which was created to train the neural network classifier. Experimental analysis were performed considering 13 different items of fruit and vegetables sector of supermarket. Figure 7 presents the accuracy of the trained model. The greater the accuracy, the greater the ability of the artificial intelligence model to recognize products. Our model showed ≈ 94% of accuracy in the automatic food identification task. These results are promising, since our tests consider the use of transparent plastic containers for the storage of food, and this ends up making the detection task even more difficult.

The Totem: In Fig. 8 is the initial proposal of the totem, which should receive all the equipment, and would also serve as the basis for the weighing process. In

---

[8] Samsung Spin 7.
[9] C920 HD Logitech.
[10] Prix 8217.
[11] Elgin L42.

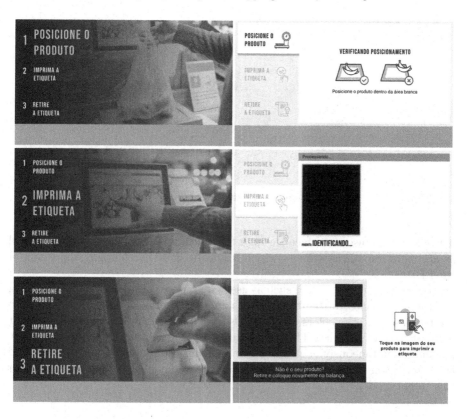

Fig. 5. The proposal user interface, in Portuguese.

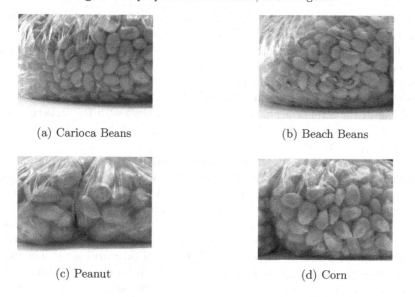

(a) Carioca Beans

(b) Beach Beans

(c) Peanut

(d) Corn

Fig. 6. Some images from the dataset.

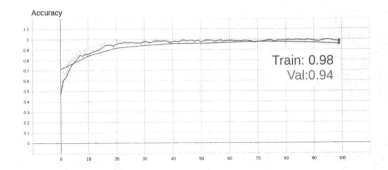

Fig. 7. The result of the model training, using Transfer Learning technique.

it would be the user interface through the touch screen of the software, as well as an operation status system, which would be done by changing the colors of the LEDs.

In this first version, issues such as user safety were considered, as the weighing environment is closed, the interface was another item considered, in addition to the touch screen, the colors of the LEDs served as a signal for the user, without a doubt it is an advance. The use of three cameras, collecting the image of the product simultaneously, can bring gains during the identification process, and the reservation of an internal space for the equipment, are positive points for this totem model.

4.5   Acquisition and Retention

After choosing the equipment, the software features, and a view of the totem structure that will centralize all items. Quotations were made and the values presented to the technical management, in addition to a first prospection in the market, which already shows the interest of supermarkets in this solution. With this information, the purchase of equipment was approved, as well as the allocation of human resources for the development of the software.

Being in the retention phase, there was a problem with the structure of the totem, in Fig. 9 the draft of the proposed totem, using common materials, just to validate some points.

At the end of the assembly, when we started to interact with the totem, some problems became evident: a) The fact that the weighing area is closed has the positive aspect of safety, but it is not practical, as it is not easy to place the product on the scale if it has a slightly larger volume. b) The touch screen is high relative to the floor, and people of average height will have difficulty accessing it. c) The tower-shaped structure proved to be unstable in case the totem is moved from the position, there is a real chance of overturning. d) The camera was designed to be on top, looking at the product from top to bottom, however it was noticed that for small volume products, the camera cannot capture the entire product, this is due to the proximity between the camera and the base of the scale. Sometimes the product may not appear in the image.

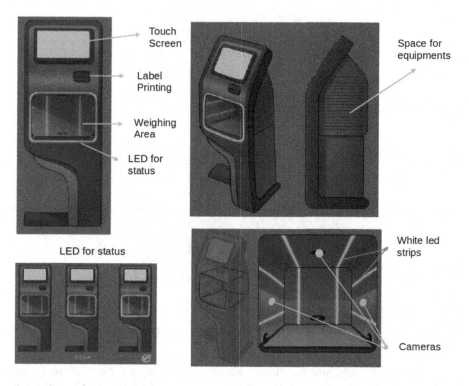

Fig. 8. The first totem model proposed for the prototype.

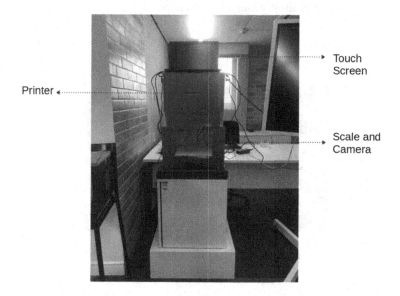

Fig. 9. Draft of the totem proposed for the prototype.

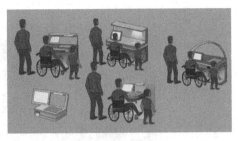

(a) Artistic concept of the new totem.

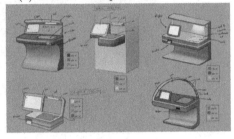

(b) Basic color draft

Fig. 10. The evolution of the new totem.

Due to the problems mentioned above, a new project for the totem was necessary. In Fig. 10 the evolution of this new idea can be seen. Sketches with new totem shapes, including ergonomic enhancements and inclusive postures regarding the physical limitations of customers.

4.6   Monetization

Fig. 11. The final modified prototype.

Figure 11 presents the new version of the totem. The problems detected in the previous version have been fixed, and now that we are producing the commercial versions, which can be seen in Fig. 12. These activities are already within the product monetization phase. Software development costs, hardware acquisition, among others, allow this product to reach the market with a value around US$ 2000, which is a very competitive price.

5 Results

After implementing the prototype, data were collected that reflect the results achieved using the Design Thinking methodology to find a sustainable solution to increase the comfort, speed, and safety of users who use the service of selling products in bulk in supermarkets.

The main results were:

1. Reduction in the average time of the weighing process for bulk products: - 20%.
2. Reduction in labor costs allocated to assist in the process of weighing bulk products: The person has been displaced to other activities.
3. ROI: 6 months.

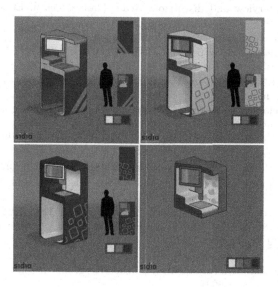

Fig. 12. The proposed commercial totem.

6 Conclusion

The use of the Design Thinking methodology was fundamental to achieve the results in this work, always maintaining a logical sequence, with measurable partial results, we managed in the end to find a sustainable solution. With a cost of approximately US\$ 2,000 and an ROI of just six months, this solution has a great possibility of being accepted in the retail market. As future work, we intend to apply our solution in a real supermarket scenario, considering the entire product line of the fruit and vegetable sector, which is approximately 200 items and to better explore the automatic identification mechanisms of items.

References

1. Abadi, M., et al.: Tensorflow: a system for large-scale machine learning. In: 12th {USENIX} Symposium on Operating Systems Design and Implementation ({OSDI} 16), pp. 265–283 (2016)
2. Bauer, R., Eagen, W.: Design thinking: epistemic plurality in management and organization. Aesthes Int. J. Art Aesthet. Manag. Organ. Life 2(3), 568–596 (2008)
3. Bradski, G., Kaehler, A.: Learning OpenCV: Computer vision with the OpenCV library. O'Reilly Media, Inc., Sebastopol (2008)
4. Clark, B., Reinertsen, D.G.: Rapid ideation in action: getting good ideas quickly and cheaply. Des. Manag. J. (Former Ser.) 9(4), 47–52 (1998)
5. Davies, M.: Concept mapping, mind mapping and argument mapping: what are the differences and do they matter? High. Educ. 62(3), 279–301 (2011)
6. Dunne, D., Martin, R.: Design thinking and how it will change management education: an interview and discussion. Acad. Manag. Learn. Educ. 5(4), 512–523 (2006)
7. Howard, A.G., et al.: Mobilenets: Efficient convolutional neural networks for mobile vision applications. arXiv preprint arXiv:1704.04861 (2017)
8. Martin, R., Martin, R.L.: The Design of Business: Why Design Thinking is the Next Competitive Advantage. Harvard Business Press, Boston (2009)
9. Nunes, J., Quaresma, M.: A construção de personas e do mapa da jornada do usuário: a delimitação de modelos mentais para o design centrado no usuário ou da interação usuário-notícia. Estudos em Design 26(2) (2018)
10. Owens, J.D., Houston, M., Luebke, D., Green, S., Stone, J.E., Phillips, J.C.: GPU computing. Proc. IEEE 96(5), 879–899 (2008)
11. Pan, Y.: Development of image processing software based on Qt creator. In: 2019 IEEE 3rd Information Technology, Networking, Electronic and Automation Control Conference (ITNEC), pp. 2667–2671. IEEE (2019)
12. Phillips, J.J.: Roi: the search for best practices. Train. Dev. 50(2), 42–48 (1996)
13. Razzouk, R., Shute, V.: What is design thinking and why is it important? Rev. Educ. Res. 82(3), 330–348 (2012)
14. Rogelberg, S.G., Barnes-Farrell, J.L., Lowe, C.A.: The stepladder technique: an alternative group structure facilitating effective group decision making. J. Appl. Psychol. 77(5), 730 (1992)
15. VanGundy, A.B.: Brain writing for new product ideas: an alternative to brainstorming. J. Consum. Market. (1984)
16. Weiss, K., Khoshgoftaar, T.M., Wang, D.D.: A survey of transfer learning. J. Big Data 3(1), 1–40 (2016). https://doi.org/10.1186/s40537-016-0043-6
17. Wilson, C.: Brainstorming and Beyond: A User-Centered Design Method. Newnes, London (2013)

An Integrated Framework Based on Fuzzy AHP-TOPSIS and Multiple Correspondences Analysis (MCA) for Evaluate the Technological Conditions of the Teleworker in Times of Pandemic: A Case Study

Leonel Hernandez-Collantes[1]([envelope]) [ORCID], Nidia Balmaceda-Castro[2],
Jiseth Guerra-Renard[3], Ana Charris-Muñoz[3], Lorayne Solano-Naizzir[3],
Carlos Vargas-Mercado[4], and Daniel Alcazar-Franco[5]

[1] Department of Telematic Engineering, Faculty of Engineering, Institucion Universitaria ITSA,
Barranquilla, Colombia
lhernandezc@itsa.edu.co
[2] Faculty of Basic Sciences, Institución Universitaria ITSA, Barranquilla, Colombia
nebalmaceda@itsa.edu.co
[3] Faculty of Human and Social Sciences, Universidad de la Costa CUC, Barranquilla, Colombia
{jguerra11,acharris29,lsolano29}@cuc.edu.co
[4] Faculty of Education Sciences, Corporación Universitaria Latinoamericana CUL,
Barranquilla, Colombia
cvargas@ul.edu.co
[5] Faculty of Engineering, Corporación Universitaria Reformada CUR, Barranquilla, Colombia
d.alcazar@unireformada.edu.co

Abstract. The COVID 19 pandemic has affected the daily routine of all people, both in their family and work environments, globally. As a result, many companies in practically all the productive sectors of the countries have required to rethink several critical aspects of the business itself so as not to be absorbed by the crisis, avoid as much as possible losses in financial, human, technological resources, etc., and even disappear. In these challenging times that we live in, the corporate technology platform must provide remote connection facilities to employees. Thus, Teleworking is facilitated in a safe, flexible way, which does not delay the processes and business goals. To define this technological roadmap, it is essential to review the current specialized components, the network infrastructure, and recommendations to improve and optimize existing processes. Concerning the application of integrated methodologies for evaluating Teleworker's technological conditions during the COVID-19, some studies have been found related to health and safety conditions, growth in the implementation of this modality, and future trends in teleworking. However, the approach to technological requirements in teleworking during the COVID-19 pandemic is still limited and not sufficiently studied. To address this challenge, this paper presents an integrated framework based on the application of Fuzzy AHP, TOPSIS, and multivariate methods for the evaluation of technological conditions of teleworkers during the COVID-19 in the construction sector. The methodology's design is based on the international guidelines

© Springer Nature Switzerland AG 2021
C. Stephanidis et al. (Eds.): HCII 2021, LNCS 13097, pp. 459–475, 2021.
https://doi.org/10.1007/978-3-030-90966-6_32

and pertinent scientific literature in Telework. The results obtained evidence that the criteria "Infrastructure," "Digital Connectivity Services," "Applications," and "Users" are relevant in the evaluation of technological conditions for Telework due to the few differences in their relative weights.

Keywords: Telework · Technological conditions · Performance evaluation · Construction industry · Multicriteria decision making · MCMD · Fuzzy analytical hierarchy process · Fuzzy AHP · TOPSIS · Multiple correspondence analysis

1   Introduction

Not only the daily lives of people globally have been affected by the COVID19 pandemic. In addition, many companies in practically all the productive sectors of the countries have required to rethink several critical aspects of the business itself, so as not to be absorbed by the crisis, avoid as much as possible losses in financial, human, technological resources, etc., and even disappear [1, 2].

One of the significant changes generated by the COVID-19 pandemic has been the adoption of changes in the work system to protect the health of employees and maintain the operating conditions of companies known as teleworking, which has existed since the end of the 1970s, but that in recent decades and especially in times of pandemic has developed and become an alternative work and business model around the world.

In this regard, more and more organizations use technology as an ally that allows them to be more competitive, so it is necessary to define a technological development path aligned with institutional policies that would enable them to fulfill both the mission and the vision entirely. In these challenging times that we live in, the corporate technology platform must provide remote connection facilities to employees. Teleworking is facilitated in a safe, flexible way, which does not delay the processes and business goals. To define this technological roadmap, it is essential to review the current specialized components, the network infrastructure, and recommendations to improve and optimize existing processes.

Various organizations have quickly implemented the teleworking model to stay in increasingly competitive markets, with restrictions and robust biosafety protocols. In this regard, [3] mention that companies must face different challenges in the face of teleworking, such as the use of guides for the development of teleworking, the adjustment of management practices for supervision and communication for teleworking, adaptations in process flows and, critical, technological conditions both in the company and in the workers' home for remote work (software, digital devices, applications [4]). These factors require a detailed study of their conditions during COVID-19 and post-pandemic, considering the growth projections of teleworking worldwide.

Concerning the application of integrated methodologies for evaluating Teleworker's technological conditions during the COVID-19, some studies have been found related to health and safety conditions, growth in the implementation of this modality, and future trends in teleworking. However, the approach to technological requirements in teleworking during the COVID-19 pandemic is still limited and not sufficiently studied. To address this challenge, this paper presents an integrated framework based on the application of Fuzzy AHP, TOPSIS, and multivariate methods for the evaluation of technological conditions of teleworkers during the COVID-19 in the construction sector.

The methodology's design is based on the international guidelines and pertinent scientific literature in Telework, which provide a common framework of high-level management for organizations through surveys applied in various departments in a construction company. First, FAHP was used to calculate the criteria and sub-criteria weights under uncertainty, considering the multi-criteria hierarchy. Then, the TOPSIS method was implemented for ranking the best department with technological conditions for Telework according to a set of indicators designed.

Subsequently, the multivariate technique of factorial analysis was used, using computational tools, prior validation process of the evaluation model's reliability, to classify the company's workers in differentiated groups considering their perception in technological conditions for Telework. Finally, proposals for improving the technical requirements to Telework in the company's various departments were raised.

The results obtained evidence that the criteria "Infrastructure" and "Users and Applications" are relevant in evaluating technological conditions for Telework due. Also, the results show that the integrated methodology allows to identify critical variables that affect the capacity of the companies to assurance the technological requirements in the company and in-home to implement the Telework, which was quantitatively demonstrated in the ranking of the departments of the company after the application of FAHP/TOPSIS techniques, and as a result of MCA method through the identification of five clusters according to the perception level in the technological conditions for Telework. Finally, weaknesses and strengths were identified, and improvement proposals were designed for future implementation.

The remainder of this paper is organized as follows. First, Sect. 2 presents the literature review. Next, Sect. 3 describes the proposed methodology. Then, Sect. 4 shows the results of the integrated framework in a construction company. Finally, conclusions and future works are presented in Sect. 5.

2 Literature Review

Global trends point towards the transformation of work environments. Among these appears teleworking as a modality that combines the policies of corporate ethics based on the fulfillment of objectives and the technological resources necessary to reach them. Looking at Fig. 1, it can be said that data networks are designed as it appears on the left of the image, with the promotion of Telework, primarily caused by the pandemic, corporate network infrastructures must be designed and implemented to support connectivity as shown on the right side:

The pandemic situation experienced throughout the world since the beginning of 2020 has led to the transformation of many processes and lifestyles, including the

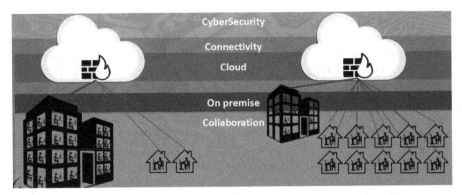

Fig. 1. Traditional use of the corporate network vs. use to facilitate teleworking.

strengthening of Telework, so it is worth analyzing the impact of a trend that in our environment does not It was widely disseminated, and today it is a fundamental pillar even to preserve jobs. The study carried out by [5] shows the influence of Telework with aspects such as job satisfaction, organizational commitment, among others. [6] analyze the implementation of teleworking as a safe practice to face the challenges of the pandemic in the work environment. [7] explains that teleworking has practically become a strategic decision for companies, even in the post-pandemic period.

[8] analyze the impact of social distancing during a pandemic in Japan, measuring how effective teleworking can be for teleworkers. A similar study by [9] presents the impact of distancing in the education sector, focused on how teachers through teleworking can enhance online learning. [10] carried out a descriptive statistical analysis in Italy to measure the impact of teleworking on productivity during the pandemic. [11] conducted a similar study in Sweden, using other tools such as ANOVA and Compositional Data Analysis, whose main conclusion is that teleworking in Sweden has allowed people to sleep a little more, benefiting their health.

Teleworking, if teleworkers do not have adequate computer security conditions, instead of representing a benefit, can become a problem. [12] present a cybersecurity awareness approach, with technologies to consider to protect the internet connection and the information. In the same sense, [13] expose the importance of cybersecurity so that Telework does not become a headache.

For the development of the study, strategies such as multiple correspondence analysis (MCA) and the FAHP-TOPSIS model have been used to evaluate the conditions of teleworkers in a company in the productive sector in Colombia. These methodologies have been widely applied in multiple fields. [14] applies MCA guidelines to determine the level of satisfaction of users of a wireless network. [15] evaluate through MCA and multi-criterion decision-making models (MCDM) to improve occupational health and safety performance, and use qualitative and quantitative techniques with actual application in the land cargo transportation sector. [16] presents another MCA application to evaluate the results of the presentation of tests in the higher education sector in mathematics, classifying those students who obtain excellent, good, fair, or bad results and the causes. [17] and [18] in their respective studies also present the application of Fuzzy MCDM and

AHP approaches to design industrial maintenance plans and the management of human talent, respectively. Other studies also combine techniques to assess the conditions of teleworkers in the pandemic, such as the work carried out by [19].

3 Methodology

The research methodology aims to evaluate the technological conditions of the Teleworker in times of pandemic by integrating Multiple Correspondence Analysis (MCA) and Fuzzy AHP-TOPSIS model. In this regard, the following four-phase methodology is proposed, as seen in Fig. 2:

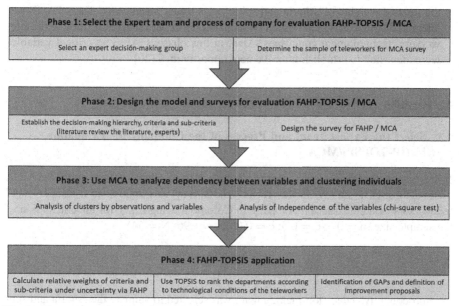

Fig. 2. The methodological framework to evaluate the technological conditions of the Teleworker in times of pandemic.

- **Phase 1 (Select the Expert team and process of company for evaluation FAHP-TOPSIS/MCA):** A decision-making group is selected according to their experience in information and communication technologies (ICT) and Teleworker. The experts will be invited to be part of the decision-making process through Fuzzy AHP-TOPSIS method. Subsequently, a sample of teleworkers of a construction company was selected to apply the MCA method.

- **Phase 2 (Design the model and surveys for evaluation FAHP-TOPSIS/MCA):** The decision hierarchy was established in this phase. The criteria and sub-criteria are determined considering the expert's opinion and the pertinent scientific literature. Subsequently, the surveys for the application of the FAHP and MCA methods were designed.
- **Phase 3 (Application of MCA):** The Multivariate Correspondence Analysis (MCA) method was applied to identify the significance of a set of key variables associated with teleworking and the classification of individuals in clusters according to the similarity in their answers for each variable. For this objective, a survey was applied in 47 teleworkers of a construction company, and then, data collected were analyzed using R 4.0.5 software.
- **Phase 4 (FAHP-TOPSIS application):** In this step, FAHP was applied to calculate the relative weights of criteria and sub-criteria under uncertainty. Then, FAHP was integrated with TOPSIS to rank the organization's departments according to the teleworkers' technological conditions. Also, in this phase, GAPs and critical variables were identified to establish improvement opportunities [20].

4 Results

4.1 Select the Expert Team and Process of the Company for Evaluation FAHP-TOPSIS/MCA

In this phase, first were determined the sample size of teleworkers to apply the MCA method through a survey. In this regard, the survey was applied to a sample of 47 teleworkers of a construction company in Colombia using Eq. 1 for the calculation of the sample size (p = 0,5; q = 0,5; e = 0,05; k = 1.96; N = 54).

$$n = \frac{k^2 * p * q * N}{(e^2 * (N-1)) + k^2 * p * q} \tag{1}$$

Subsequently, a decision-making team was selected to validate the criteria and sub-criteria for evaluating technological conditions of teleworkers using the Fuzzy AHP method. In this regard, the group comprised seven participants experts in Computer Science, Engineering, teleworking, and multi-criteria decision-making methods.

4.2 Design the Model for Evaluation MCA/FAHP-TOPSIS

In this step, a survey of 16 questions was designed to identify the critical variables in evaluating physical, technological, and support conditions for the Telework under the pandemic Covid-19 scenario (refer to Table 1). The survey was based on telework guidelines and the pertinent literature and was applied to the sample of workers selected in item 4.1. On the other hand, the survey allowed the identification of clusters of individuals considering the similarity in their responses via the MCA method.

Table 1. Structure of the survey for technological conditions of telework in pandemic Covid-19 situation (MCA methodology)

Question	Code of variable	Answer options
What is the Internet service provider that you have in your home?	V1	C: Claro: 1 M: Movistar: 2 E: ETB: 3 TU: Tigo/Une: 4 K: Kuatro: 5
What bandwidth do you have contracted?	V2	MB: 1–5 MB (very low) B: 6–10 MB (low) M: 11–20 MB (medium) A: 21–50 MB (high) MA: 51–100 MB (very high) N: NS/NR
Connects to the Internet through	V3	C: Wire: 1 I: Wireless: 2
If you connect wirelessly, which device do you use most often?	V4	P: Laptop: 1 C: Cell phone: 2 T: Tablet: 3 O: Other: 4
How many devices are connected to the network in your home?	V5	B: 1 M: 2 A: From 3 onwards
During quarantine, you had internet connection problems	V6	CP: With little frequency: 1 F: Frequently: 2 CM: Very often: 3
Rate the level of importance you place on the security of information and Internet connection	V7	N: It's not important: 1 MI: It is more or less important: 2 SI: It's important: 3 EI: It's very important: 4
For you, to carry out your daily work from home, technology is an aspect	V8	NI: It's not important.: 1 RI: Relatively important I: Important: 2 MI: Very important: 3

(continued)

Table 1. (*continued*)

Question	Code of variable	Answer options
How satisfied are you with the settings and organization you currently have for working from home?	V9	MS: Very satisfied: 1 AS: Somewhat satisfied: 2 I: Indifferent: 3 AI: Somewhat Dissatisfied: 4 MI: Very unsatisfied: 5
Do you have all the necessary equipment to do work from home?	V10	S: Yes N: No
Are you satisfied with your current connection speed provided by the service provider?	V11	S: Yes N: No
Do you think that your home Internet connection's current speed and reliability would make it easier for you to carry out your daily office work?	V12	TI: The current connection is totally insufficient: 1 I: Current connection is insufficient: 2 S: The current connection is sufficient: 3 TS: The current connection is totally sufficient: 4
How often do you use corporate applications when connecting to the Internet?	V13	B: Once a week: 1 D: Two to four times a week: 2 T: Every day of the week: 3 N: I do not use corporate apps: 4
What have been the main technological inconveniences you have had when connecting to the business network from home?	V14	PI: Internet connection problems (slowness in the local network, provider problems, etc.): 1 PE: Power supply problems: 2 PC: Computer equipment problems: 3
During the quarantine, have you required technical support from the company's IT team?	V15	S: Yes N: No
If you have required technical support, the response time has been	V16	B: Less than 24 h: 1 R: 24 to 36 h: 2 A: Greater than 36 h: 3 N: I have not required support: 4

Afterward, an MCDM model was designed according to the expert's opinion, Telework guidelines, and the relevant literature review. In this regard, the multi-criteria decision hierarchy is comprised of 3 criteria and 15 sub-criteria. The hierarchy is presented in Fig. 3:

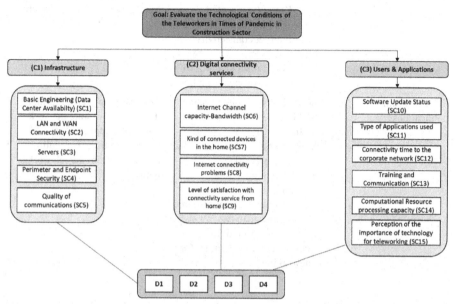

Fig. 3. Multi-criteria decision-making model to evaluate the technological conditions of teleworkers in times of pandemic in the construction sector.

In Table 2, the criteria and sub-criteria are described.

Table 2. Description of criteria

Criterion (C)	Sub-criteria (SC)	Criterion description
C1. Infrastructure	SC1. Basic engineering (data center availability) SC2. LAN and WAN CONNECTIVITY SC3. Servers SC4. Perimeter and endpoint security SC5. Quality of communications	This criterion refers to the main dimensions or critical points to consider when evaluating the technological infrastructure of any company. Although there are other essential aspects, the company under study believes those exposed as the most relevant

(continued)

Table 2. (*continued*)

Criterion (C)	Sub-criteria (SC)	Criterion description
C2. Digital connectivity services	SC6. Internet channel capacity-bandwidth SC7. Kind of connected devices in the home SC8. Internet connectivity problems SC9. Level of satisfaction with connectivity service from home	This criterion refers to the main technological aspects to consider from the teleworker perspective
C3. Users and applications	SC10. Software update status SC11. Type of applications used SC12. Connectivity time to the corporate network SC13. Training and communication SC14. Computational resource processing capacity SC15. Perception of the importance of technology for teleworking	This criterion seeks to evaluate the use of corporate network resources (applications, connection time, computing resources) from the teleworker network

Finally, a survey was elaborated to collect the experts' opinions via paired comparisons among criteria and sub-criteria. In this regard, for each pairwise judgment, the experts answered this question: Concerning the objective /criteria, ¿how important is each element on the leftover item on the right? Fig. 4 shows an example of the survey for FAHP applied by the experts.

According to your experience with respect to "Infrastructure" sub-criterion, ¿how important is each sub-criterion on the left concerning the sub-criterion on the right when evaluating the overall performance in occupational health and safety management in companies of land cargo transportation?

		1	2	3	4	5		
Basic Engineering (Data Center Availability)	is	O	O	O	O	O	Important than	LAN and WAN Connectivity
Basic Engineering (Data Center Availability)	is	O	O	O	O	O	Important than	Servers
Basic Engineering (Data Center Availability)	is	O	O	O	O	O	Important than	Perimeter and Endpoint Security
Basic Engineering (Data Center Availability)		O	O	O	O	O	Important than	Quality of Communications

① Much less	③ Equally	⑤ Much more
② Less	④ More	

Fig. 4. Survey for FAHP evaluation

4.3 Application of Multivariate Correspondence Analysis (MCA)

In this phase, the MCA method was applied, using software R version 4.0.5. to evaluate the technological conditions for teleworking from the perception of the workers. Initially, a factorial map was obtained, representing the relative positions of the variables proposed in the measurement of technological conditions for teleworking under the Covid-19 scenario (see Fig. 5). The factorial map allowed the classification of the surveyed individuals, considering the similarity in the answers given by the workers. The two dimensions of the questionnaire collect 25.76% of the variability in the responses obtained. Considering the results of the factorial map, five clusters or differentiated groups can be identified considering the correspondences in the workers' reactions who participated in the survey.

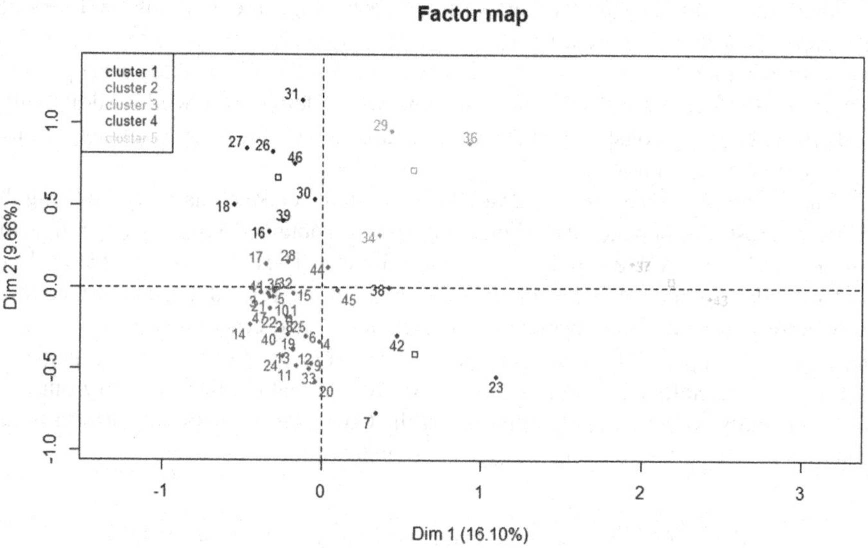

Fig. 5. Factor map

The first cluster (C1) is workers with acceptable technological conditions for Telework, which comprises eight individuals, representing 17% of the sample. Among the characteristic variables for this group is the type of connection through a wired network, having frequently presented internet connection problems, and the need for technical support from the company's systems team, with a response time in support of fewer than 24 h.

The second cluster (C2) is grouped workers with good technological conditions for Telework, made up of 28 workers, representing 59.57% of the total surveyed. This group is characterized by connecting to the Internet wirelessly and using the laptop computer as the most widely used device, having the necessary equipment to carry out their work from home, feeling satisfied with the current speed of their internet connection provider. Service, having high bandwidths (between 21 and 50 MB) and stating that they had presented internet problems infrequently during the pandemic, so they did not require technical support from the company.

The third cluster (C3) is that of workers with normal technological conditions for teleworking, made up of 6 workers representing 12.76% of the sample. This group is characterized by having a level 3 internet provider on the scale of service providers and having low bandwidths (between 6 and 10 MB), which affects their low satisfaction with the service provider—current internet connection speed.

In the fourth cluster (C4), there are workers with low technological conditions for teleworking, made up of 3 workers representing 6.38% of the sample. This group has low or very low bandwidths in their Internet connections (between 1 and 10 MB), making users perceive low speed and current reliability of the same at the time of doing their job. Additionally, the workers of this group consider that they do not have all the necessary equipment to carry out the work remotely from home.

The fifth cluster (C5) are workers with low technological conditions for Telework, made up of 3 workers representing 6.38% of the sample. This group has low or very low bandwidths in their Internet connections (between 1 and 10 MB), making users perceive low speed and current reliability of the same when doing their work. Additionally, workers in this group consider that they do not have all the necessary equipment to carry out remote work from home.

Finally, the independence of the variables within the cluster was analyzed using the Chi-square test. The dependent or significant variables obtained a p-value lower than the significance level (p-value < 0.05), as shown in Table 3. These results showed that 11 of the 16 variables proposed in the survey are significant and related to aspects of connectivity, information security, availability of equipment, and conditions for teleworking and technical support. The preceding raises the design of multifactorial strategies to improve the technological requirements of workers that allow them to carry out their work efficiently from home, not only during the Covid-19 pandemic but also in future scenarios involving teleworking management model of the companies.

Table 3. Chi-squared test for independent analysis in software R 4.0.5.

Code	Variable	p-value
V1	Type of home internet service provider	3.396216e−5
V2	Contracted bandwidth	3.506645e−15
V5	Number of devices connected to the home network	2.310960e−3
V7	Level of importance of information security and Internet connection	2.357089e−2
V10	Availability of equipment necessary to perform work from home	7.207625e−5
V11	Satisfaction with the current speed of your internet connection provided by the service provider	9.991729e−7

(*continued*)

Table 3. (*continued*)

Code	Variable	p-value
V12	Perception of the speed and current reliability of the home Internet connection for the proper development of daily work from home	3.040563e−6
V13	Frequency of use of corporate applications when connecting to the Internet	6.365357e−10
V14	Main technological disadvantages presented when connecting to the business network from home	6.181746e−4
V15	Need for technical support from the company's IT team during the pandemic	2.361388e−6
V16	Response time of the technical support team	1.119931e−4

4.4 Identification of the Improvement Opportunities via FAHP-TOPSIS Application

In this last phase, the results obtained after applying the FAHP-TOPSIS methods are described to evaluate the level of technological conditions for teleworking in the scenario of the Covid-19 pandemic. Initially, the Fuzzy AHP method was applied to calculate the relative weights of the criteria and sub-criteria, considering the uncertainty in the experts' opinions given the complexity of Covid-19 and the consistency indices between the experts' judgments were calculated. In this sense, the criterion "Infrastructure" (GW = 53.6%) was the most crucial criterion in evaluating technological conditions for teleworking, which denotes the importance of guaranteeing technical and specialized needs so that users can perform their work activities efficiently from home. The second most important criterion was "Users and Applications" (GW = 31.6%), which shows the relevance in developing strategies to adapt workers to Telework in training, use of applications, and security. Finally, the criterion "Digital Connectivity Services" (GW = 14.8%) was third in importance for evaluating technological conditions, considering mainly the bandwidth capacity of the Internet channel, connectivity problems, and user satisfaction. The previous raises the design of multifactorial strategies that include technological aspects and interaction with users to adapt to Telework. In addition, consistency ratios (CR) for criteria and sub-criteria were calculated as shown in Table 4. All consistency ratios, evidencing consistent judgments (CR < 0.1).

Table 4. Local and global weights of criteria and sub-criteria

Cluster	GW	LW	CR
Criteria			**0.011**
C1. Infrastructure	**0.536**		**0.057**
SC1. Basic Engineering (Data Center Availabilty)	0.136	0.254	
SC2. LAN and WAN Connectivity	0.077	0.144	
SC3. Servers	0.139	0.259	
SC4. Perimeter and Endpoint Security	0.088	0.165	
SC5. Quality of communications	0.095	0.178	
C2. Digital Connectivity Services	**0.148**		**0.050**
SC6. Internet Channel Capacity-Bandwidth	0.050	0.339	
SC7. Kind of connected devices in the home	0.016	0.109	
SC8. Internet connectivity problems	0.030	0.204	
SC9. Level of satisfaction with connectivity service from home	0.052	0.348	
C3. Users and Applications	**0.316**		**0.067**
SC10. Software Update Status	0.022	0.069	
SC11. Type of Applications used	0.029	0.092	
SC12. Connectivity time to the corporate network	0.046	0.145	
SC13. Training and Communication	0.046	0.145	
SC14. Computational Resource processing capacity	0.059	0.188	
SC15. Perception of the importance of technology for teleworking	0.114	0.361	

Finally, the TOPSIS method was applied to evaluate and rank the technological conditions for teleworking in 4 departments (D1: Business Development, D2: IT, D3: Human Talent, D4: Financial) of establishing improvement Actions for each department. To apply this methodology, a set of indicators associated with the sub-criteria found in the FAHP hierarchy described in Fig. 3 was designed with the support of experts and the company. Within the indicators, the performance variables of the network were analyzed, which influence their behavior, such as delay, jitter, throughput [18]. Subsequently, they generate the TOPSIS decision matrix, the normalized decision matrix R, the weighted and normalized TOPSIS decision matrix V, the separations of the positive and negative solution, and the Closeness Coefficient calculation. This study was called the Coefficient of Technological Condition section. The Technological Conditions Coefficient allowed ranking the company's departments according to the preference order of CC_i (Very low conditions: $0 \leq CCi \leq 0,25$ ‖ Low conditions: $0,25 < CCi \leq 0,5$ ‖ Medium conditions: $0,5 < CCi \leq 0,75$ ‖ High conditions: $0,75 < CCi \leq 1$). The calculation of the closeness coefficient and the separation from Negative Ideal Solution (NIS) and Positive Ideal Solution (PIS) are shown in Table 5.

Table 5. Ranking of departments in the evaluation of technological conditions for teleworking in scenario of Covid-19 via TOPSIS method

Company	CC_i	S_i^+	S_i^-	Rank	Level
D2	0.714	0.038	0.096	1	Medium
D4	0.575	0.056	0.076	2	Medium
D3	0.543	0.064	0.076	3	Medium
D1	0.158	0.106	0.029	4	Very low

The results show that Department D2 is the one with the best level of technological conditions ($CC_i = 71.4\%$), although with opportunities for improvement in the level of actual use of the link or throughput. On the other hand, departments D4 and D3 have coefficients of technological conditions between 54 and 57%, which are mainly affected by indicators of digital connectivity services and indicators in users and applications' criteria. Finally, Department D1 was identified as having poor technological conditions for teleworking ($CC_i = 15.8\%$), which is why the development of a multi-criteria improvement plan is required to increase the technical, support, and skill capacity of the users for teleworking, considering that this department is responsible for the development and maintenance of new businesses for the company.

5   Conclusions and Future Work

To evaluate the telework conditions of a company in the construction sector in Colombia, a framework was designed that integrates the guidelines given by the Fuzzy AHP-TOPSIS methodology and the MCA multiple correspondence analysis. In general terms, the results show that the company's technological infrastructure is prepared for the Telework connectivity scheme, allowing users to connect without significant inconveniences. The pandemic enhances this situation. Precisely, the "Infrastructure" criterion, one of those analyzed by FAHP, is critical for the company because the efficient connectivity of teleworkers depends on it. Through the TOPSIS method, it is concluded that the IT department is the one with the best technological conditions, given that its users are connected to the best specification equipment on the network. The MCA analysis allowed segmenting the 47 employees of the company into five clusters, each one with related variables. After applying the chi-square test, it is concluded that 11 of the 16 variables are significant and are related to aspects of connectivity, information security, availability of equipment, and conditions for teleworking and technical support, among others.

The approach proposed in this study, the integrated framework, can be applied in any company in the productive sector, adapting without inconvenience to companies' criteria and sub-criteria. Likewise, the MCA can identify key business variables relevant to teleworking and the classification of individuals in clusters.

Finally, as future work, the proposed methodology will be extended to other sectors. In addition, further research can improve the methodology's performance considering different techniques of MCDM such as DEMATEL, VIKOR, and intuitionistic methods to analyze the interdependency and interrelations between criteria and sub-criteria and evaluate future events influence teleworking.

References

1. Lopez-Leon, S., Forero, D.A., Ruiz-Díáz, P.: Recommendations for working from home during the COVID-19 pandemic (and beyond). Work (2020). https://doi.org/10.3233/WOR-203187
2. Riva, G., Mantovani, F., Wiederhold, B.K.: Positive technology and COVID-19. Cyberpsychol. Behav. Soc. Netw. (2020). https://doi.org/10.1089/cyber.2020.29194.gri
3. Fana, M., Milasi, S., Napierala, J., Fernandez-Macias, E., Vazquez, I.G.: Telework, work organisation and job quality during the COVID-19 crisis: a qualitative study. In: J RC Working Papers Series on Labour, Education and Technology (2020). https://ideas.repec.org/p/ipt/lae dte/202011.html. Accessed 29 June 2021
4. Hernandez, L., Jimenez, G., Baloco, C., Jimenez, A., Hernandez, H.: Characterization of the use of the internet of things in the institutions of higher education of the city of barranquilla and its metropolitan area. In: Stephanidis, C. (ed.) HCI 2018. CCIS, vol. 852, pp. 17–24. Springer, Cham (2018). https://doi.org/10.1007/978-3-319-92285-0_3
5. Garcia-Contreras, R., Muñoz-Chavez, P., Valle-Cruz, D., Rubalcaba-Gomez, E., Becerra-Santiago, J.: Teleworking in times of COVID-19. some lessons for the public sector from the emergent implementation during the pandemic period: teleworking in times of COVID-19. In: ACM International Conference Proceeding Series, pp. 376–385 (2021). https://doi.org/10.1145/3463677.3463700
6. Belzunegui-Eraso, A., Erro-Garcés, A.: Teleworking in the context of the Covid-19 crisis. Sustainability 12(9), 1–18 (2020). https://doi.org/10.3390/su12093662
7. Lopez, M.R.: Telework decision strategy: a systematic review. Dissertation Abstracts International Section A Humanities and Social Sciences, vol. 82, no. 1-A (2021)
8. Kawashima, T., et al.: The relationship between fever rate and telework implementation as a social distancing measure against the COVID-19 pandemic in Japan. Publ. Health (2020). https://doi.org/10.1016/j.puhe.2020.05.018
9. Suranti, N.M.Y.: Variations of models and learning platforms for prospective teachers during the COVID-19 pandemic period. Indones. J. Teach. Educ. (2020)
10. Tokarchuk, O., Gabriele, R., Neglia, G.: Teleworking during the COVID-19 crisis in Italy: evidence and tentative interpretations. Sustainability 13(4), 1–12 (2021). https://doi.org/10.3390/su13042147
11. Hallman, D.M., Januario, L.B., Mathiassen, S.E., Heiden, M., Svensson, S., Bergstrom, G.: Working from home during the COVID-19 outbreak in Sweden: effects on 24-h time-use in office workers. BMC Publ. Health 21(1) (2021). https://doi.org/10.1186/s12889-021-105 82-6
12. Wang, L., Alexander, C.A.: Cyber security during the COVID-19 pandemic. AIMS Electron. Electr. Eng. 5(2), 146–157 (2021). https://doi.org/10.3934/ELECTRENG.2021008
13. Medina-Rodríguez, C.E., Casas-Valadez, M.A., Faz-Mendoza, A., Castañeda-Miranda, R., Gamboa-Rosales, N.K., López-Robles, J.R.: The cyber security in the age of telework: a descriptive research framework through science mapping. In: 2020 International Conference on Data Analytics for Business and Industry: Way Towards a Sustainable Economy (ICDABI), pp. 1–5 (2020). https://doi.org/10.1109/ICDABI51230.2020.9325633
14. Hernandez, L., et al.: Optimization of a WiFi wireless network that maximizes the level of satisfaction of users and allows the use of new technological trends in higher education institutions. In: Streitz, N., Konomi, S. (eds.) HCII 2019. LNCS, vol. 11587, pp. 144–160. Springer, Cham (2019). https://doi.org/10.1007/978-3-030-21935-2_12

15. Jimenez-Delgado, G., Balmaceda-Castro, N., Hernández-Palma, H., de la Hoz-Franco, E., García-Guiliany, J., Martinez-Ventura, J.: An integrated approach of multiple correspondences analysis (MCA) and fuzzy AHP method for occupational health and safety performance evaluation in the land cargo transportation. In: Duffy, V.G. (ed.) HCII 2019. LNCS, vol. 11581, pp. 433–457. Springer, Cham (2019). https://doi.org/10.1007/978-3-030-22216-1_32

16. Rueda, D., Balmaceda, N.: Analisis de Correspondencias Multiples aplicado a la prueba Saber Pro 2017 en el programa de matematicas de las universidades del Departamento del Atlantico (2019)

17. Abdulgader, F.S., Eid, R., Rouyendegh, B.D.: Development of decision support model for selecting a maintenance plan using a fuzzy MCDM approach: a theoretical framework. Appl. Comput. Intell. Soft Comput. (2018)

18. Abdullah, L., Zulkifli, N., Integration of fuzzy AHP and interval type-2 fuzzy DEMATEL: an application to human resource management. Expert Syst. Appl. 42(9), 4397–4409 (2015)

19. Duque Porras, J., Fonseca, L.A.P.: Reward, social support and general health in Colombian teleworkers. a mixed study. In: Black, N.L., Neumann, W.P., Noy, I. (eds.) IEA 2021. LNNS, vol. 219, pp. 123–130. Springer, Cham (2021). https://doi.org/10.1007/978-3-030-74602-5_19

20. Hernandez, L., Jimenez, G.: Characterization of the current conditions of the ITSA data centers according to standards of the green data centers friendly to the environment. In: Silhavy, R., Senkerik, R., Kominkova Oplatkova, Z., Prokopova, Z., Silhavy, P. (eds.) CSOC 2017. AISC, vol. 574, pp. 329–340. Springer, Cham (2017). https://doi.org/10.1007/978-3-319-57264-2_34

Integration of Internet of Things Devices in Manufacturing Workspaces: A Systematic Literature Review

Theodore A. Hipsher[✉] and Vincent G. Duffy[✉]

Purdue University, West Lafayette, IN 47906, USA
{thipshe,duffy}@purdue.edu

Abstract. The manufacturing workspace has evolved rapidly alongside the advancement of information technology. This has led to significant improvements in not only manufacturing output, but also safety and quality standards tracking. The integration of Internet of Things (IoT) technologies into the manufacturing workspace has been a major component in this evolution and contributes to Industry 4.0. This article looks to conduct a bibliometric analysis of IoT technologies and their increasing relevance as it relates to Safety Monitoring and Industry 4.0. This is accomplished through the use of readily available software tools such as MAXQDA, Harzing, CiteSpace and VOSviewer. Through use of these tools, key topics like Internet of Things, Safety Monitoring, Industry 4.0 can be readily analyzed and compiled into easy to interpret figures and data collectives. This report includes examples of the outputs of these tools as they relate to IoT, safety monitoring, and Industry 4.0. Through this analysis, it can be concluded that IOT integration into manufacturing is growing in popularity and will have a major effect on monitoring in the manufacturing workspace for the foreseeable future.

Keywords: Internet of Things · Manufacturing · Safety monitoring · Industry 4.0 · VOSviewer · MAXQDA · Harzing · CiteSpace · Web of Science · Google Scholar

1 Introduction and Background

With the world becoming increasingly interconnected and technology ever-evolving, there is a significant need for manufacturing workforces to adapt through the use of software and interconnected systems. This need arises from a desire for manufacturing facilities to stay competitive along with the diversified demand of consumers (Escobar and Morales-Menendez 2018). This creates a challenge that requires the manufacturing industry to adapt and embrace new technology. The Internet of Things (IoT) has the potential to transform the manufacturing sector (Kantarci and Mouftah 2014) and meet the demands of this challenge.

The term "Internet of Things" dates back more than 20 years and was previously referred primarily to radio-frequency identification (RFID) infrastructure developed by the Massachusetts Institute of Technology (MIT) (Wortmann and Flüchter 2015). In

© Springer Nature Switzerland AG 2021
C. Stephanidis et al. (Eds.): HCII 2021, LNCS 13097, pp. 476–493, 2021.
https://doi.org/10.1007/978-3-030-90966-6_33

Fig. 1. Visualization of the Internet of Things influencing everyday life (Cass 2018).

more recent years, IoT refers to a much broader range of applications and industries. The International Telecommunication Union (ITU) defines IoT as "a global infrastructure for the information society, enabling advanced services by interconnecting (physical and virtual) things based on existing and evolving interoperable information and communication technologies" (Union 2015). While there are broad applications for IoT devices, one of the most prominent is the "Smart Industry," where the development of intelligent production systems and connected production sites is often discussed under the heading of Industry 4.0 (Wortmann and Flüchter 2015).

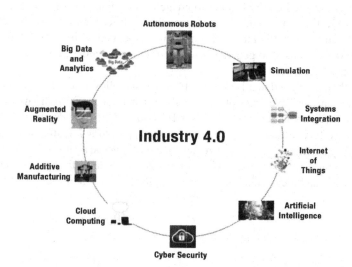

Fig. 2. Visualization of the aspects of Industry 4.0 (Rolfes et al. 2019).

2 Purpose of Study

The objective of this study is to conduct a systematic literature review of articles, research, and publications based on the Internet of Things in the manufacturing sector. Specifically, this is to review IoT as it applies to safety monitoring and Industry 4.0. Through this systematic review, this study will show the increasing relevance of Internet of Things devices in the manufacturing sector. Tools such as Harzing's Publish or Perish (Harzing n.d.), VOSviewer (VOS n.d.), and MAXQDA (Max n.d.) are used to generate collections of data and analysis. Mendeley (Mendeley n.d.) was used to cite the relevant studies and generate references (see references section).

3 Procedure

Beginning with the basis of a key word search of "Internet of Things" in Google Scholar (Google Scholar n.d.) and Web of Science (Web of Science n.d.) a total of ten articles with relevant abstracts were analyzed in-depth. From this in-depth analysis, two key search terms were derived, these are "Safety Monitoring" (to drive focus on safety related improvements in the space) and "Industry 4.0". These three search terms, "Internet of Things", "Safety Monitoring", and "Industry 4.0" were used to compile meta data. Critically the refinement of "Safety Monitoring" with the term "Internet of Things", was necessary to ensure that the data and trends associated with "Safety Monitoring" are relevant to the bibliometric analysis.

The three search keywords were used to obtain metadata in Web of Science including article title, author, abstract, keywords, and references. Along with this Web of Science tools were used to perform trend analysis referenced in later sections. The metadata collected was exported to VOSviewer to create cluster diagrams of key terms and co-citations. MAXQDA was also used in conjunction with fifteen relevant articles to conduct a lexical search to show the most relevant terms associated with these related articles. MAXQDA was also used to generate a word cloud for the most frequently used terms in the fifteen articles.

The method employed in this bibliometric analysis follows examples seen in similar bibliometric analyses. Examples of these analyses can be seen in "Bibliometric analysis of simulated driving research from 1997 to 2016" (Guo et al. 2019), "Systematic literature review on the effect of human error in environmental pollution" (Duffy et al. 2020), and "Green supply chain management: A review and bibliometric analysis" (Fahimnia et al. 2015). While these analyses use different tools and include differing information, the overall methods and ideas guide the method employed in this analysis.

4 Research Methodology

4.1 Source Information

Information for this study was primarily collected from Google Scholar and Web of Science. This was accomplished through the use of keyword searches in each of the corresponding engines. Scopus (Scopus n.d.) and Harzing's Publish or Perish used to confirm the relevance of search terms.

Table 1 shows searches performed using several different databases for the "Internet of Things." These results are used to show that there is significant interest in IoT along with serving as a basis of information for this analysis.

Table 1. Searches were performed for the "Internet of Things" using various databases.

Database	Result
Google Scholar (Google Scholar n.d.)	476,000 results
Web of Science (Web of Science n.d.)	55,000 results
Scopus (Scopus n.d.)	101,000 documents
Harzing's Publish or Perish (Harzing n.d.)	1000 publications (limited by software)

Tables 2 and 3 show searches performed on "Safety Monitoring" refined by "Internet of Things" and "Industry 4.0," respectively. These serve as examples of the integration of Internet of Things devices being incorporated into safety applications along with the manufacturing industry as a whole.

Table 2. Searches performed for "safety monitoring" refined by "Internet of Things" using various databases.

Database	Result
Google Scholar (Google Scholar n.d.)	4,400 results
Web of Science (Web of Science n.d.)	445 results
Scopus (Scopus n.d.)	220 documents
Harzing's Publish or Perish (Harzing n.d.)	250 publications

Table 3. Searches performed for "Industry 4.0" using various databases.

Database	Result
Google Scholar (Google Scholar n.d.)	133,000 results
Web of Science (Web of Science n.d.)	8,568 results
Scopus (Scopus n.d.)	14,806 documents
Harzing's Publish or Perish (Harzing n.d.)	1000 publications (limited by software)

4.2 Trend Review

Web of Science provides powerful and readily available tools for macro-analysis of published information. Keyword searches return results which can then be graphed by year of publication and broken down by category. Regarding macro-analysis of publications, this study will exclude any information from 2021, as there is not a full year of information to collect.

Figure 3 shows the macro-analysis for the "Internet of Things" as it relates to the publication of information over time. This shows that, while IoT has been around for over 20 years, there was not a significant increase in publication until 2010. Since then, there has been a significant increase in the number of publications on IoT, increasing from 251 records in 2010 to a peak in 2019 at 12,790 records. This is a near 5,000% increase in relevance in published work. Reports predict an increase in usage of IoT devices of over 400% from 2019 to 2027 (Newman 2020). Overall, this analysis shows a clear and steady increase in interest in IoT technologies, with an exception to 2020. However, due to a reduction in the manufacturing workforce because of a worldwide pandemic, this exception may be an outlier as a result of extenuating global circumstances. Figure 4 shows a breakdown of categories for the same set of publication information.

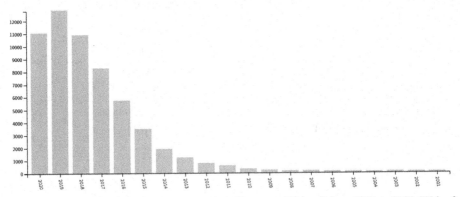

Fig. 3. Trend analysis of publications related to "Internet of Things" from 2001 to 2020 (Web of Science n.d.).

Figure 5 shows the macro-analysis for "Safety Monitoring" when refined by "Internet of Things" as it relates to the publication of information over time. This refined analysis

Field: Web of Science Categories	Record Count	% of 57,057	Bar Chart
ENGINEERING ELECTRICAL ELECTRONIC	25,236	44.229 %	
TELECOMMUNICATIONS	18,251	31.987 %	
COMPUTER SCIENCE INFORMATION SYSTEMS	16,414	28.768 %	
COMPUTER SCIENCE THEORY METHODS	12,502	21.911 %	
COMPUTER SCIENCE HARDWARE ARCHITECTURE	5,255	9.210 %	
COMPUTER SCIENCE INTERDISCIPLINARY APPLICATIONS	4,697	8.232 %	
COMPUTER SCIENCE ARTIFICIAL INTELLIGENCE	4,684	8.209 %	
COMPUTER SCIENCE SOFTWARE ENGINEERING	3,479	6.097 %	
INSTRUMENTS INSTRUMENTATION	2,644	4.634 %	
AUTOMATION CONTROL SYSTEMS	2,395	4.198 %	

Fig. 4. Breakdown of top 10 publication categories for "Internet of Things" (Web of Science n.d.).

looks at a year range from 2001 to 2020 and shows a similar trend to Fig. 3. The increase in relevance of "Safety Monitoring" from 2010 to its peak in 2019 is the same order of magnitude as that found in Fig. 1 in the same time range. Overall, this analysis also shows a clear and steady increase in interest in safety monitoring. It shows a similar exception for 2020, likely for the same reason as previously discussed. Figure 6 shows a breakdown of categories for the same set of publication information.

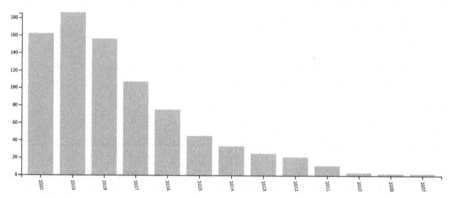

Fig. 5. Trend analysis of publications related to "Safety Monitoring" refined by "Internet of Things" from 2001 to 2020 (Web of Science n.d.).

Figure 7 shows the macro-analysis for "Industry 4.0" as it relates to publication information over time. This analysis looks at a year range from 2001 to 2020 and shows a similar trend to Figs. 3 and 5. An interesting aspect of this graph compared to others is that the term "Industry 4.0" did not appear until 2012. While it has a late appearance compared to the search terms used in Figs. 3 and 5, it does show a similar trend to both

Field: Web of Science Categories	Record Count	% of 815	Bar Chart
ENGINEERING ELECTRICAL ELECTRONIC	310	38.037 %	
COMPUTER SCIENCE INFORMATION SYSTEMS	197	24.172 %	
TELECOMMUNICATIONS	160	19.632 %	
COMPUTER SCIENCE THEORY METHODS	157	19.264 %	
COMPUTER SCIENCE INTERDISCIPLINARY APPLICATIONS	70	8.589 %	
COMPUTER SCIENCE ARTIFICIAL INTELLIGENCE	62	7.607 %	
INSTRUMENTS INSTRUMENTATION	58	7.117 %	
ENGINEERING MULTIDISCIPLINARY	52	6.380 %	
AUTOMATION CONTROL SYSTEMS	49	6.012 %	
MATERIALS SCIENCE MULTIDISCIPLINARY	49	6.012 %	

Fig. 6. Breakdown of top 10 publication categories for "Safety Monitoring" refined by "Internet of Things" (Web of Science n.d.).

with a higher order of magnitude in increasing relevance. Similar to Figs. 3 and 5, 2020 continues to establish itself as an ongoing outlier affliction of the global pandemic on the manufacturing industry. Figure 8 shows a breakdown of categories for the same set of publication information.

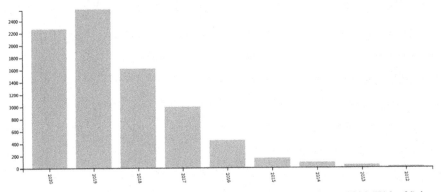

Fig. 7. Trend analysis of publications related to "Industry 4.0" from 2001 to 2020 (Web of Science n.d.).

Field: Web of Science Categories	Record Count	% of 8,568	Bar Chart
ENGINEERING ELECTRICAL ELECTRONIC	1,441	16.818 %	▆▆
ENGINEERING INDUSTRIAL	1,330	15.523 %	▆▆
ENGINEERING MANUFACTURING	1,294	15.103 %	▆▆
AUTOMATION CONTROL SYSTEMS	1,072	12.512 %	▆▆
COMPUTER SCIENCE INFORMATION SYSTEMS	950	11.088 %	▆
COMPUTER SCIENCE THEORY METHODS	852	9.944 %	▆
COMPUTER SCIENCE INTERDISCIPLINARY APPLICATIONS	743	8.672 %	▆
TELECOMMUNICATIONS	668	7.796 %	▆
COMPUTER SCIENCE ARTIFICIAL INTELLIGENCE	667	7.785 %	▆
OPERATIONS RESEARCH MANAGEMENT SCIENCE	593	6.921 %	▆

Fig. 8. Breakdown of top 10 publication categories for "Industry 4.0" (Web of Science n.d.).

4.3 Summary of Research Methodology

The three data sets, "Internet of Things," "Safety Monitoring Internet of Things," and "Industry 4.0" show very similar trends. Each of these terms results in a significantly different number of articles. However, it is apparent that year after year, there is increasing interest in each topic. "Industry 4.0" is a significant standout since it has gone from no relevance before 2012 to over 2,500 articles in 2019. It is expected that this interest and the resulting articles introduced will continue to rise for several years in the future.

5 Bibliometric Analysis

5.1 Co-citation Analysis

A useful tool used in the bibliometric analysis is co-citation analysis. "Co-citation analysis is demonstrated as a way to help identify key literature for cross-disciplinary ideas" (Trujillo and Long 2018). The tools used in creating the analysis for this section include Web of Science, Google Scholar, Herzing's Publish or Perish, VOSviewer, and MAXQDA. Information collected for each analysis was reduced to ensure that only the most relevant data is presented for each search phrase.

Using Web of Science, 3,000 articles were analyzed for the co-citation analysis of "Internet of Things." This can be seen in Fig. 9. These articles were reduced to those including at least 20 citations of a cited reference, which left a total of 57. The strongest of these cited references were related to authors Atzori, Al-Fuqaha, Gubbi, and Xu, each with a minimum of 60 citations.

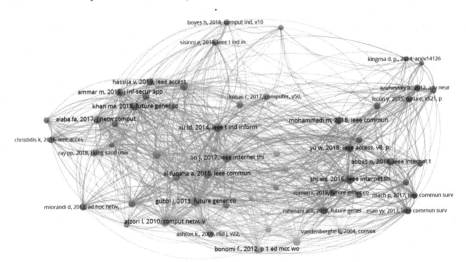

Fig. 9. Co-citation analysis network for "Internet of Things" (VOS n.d.).

Using Web of Science, a total of 861 articles were analyzed for the co-citation analysis of "Safety Monitoring Internet of Things." This can be seen in Fig. 10. These articles were reduced to those that included at least 7 citations of a cited reference, which left a total of 32. The strongest of these cited references were related to authors Atzori, Gubbi, Xu, and Zanella.

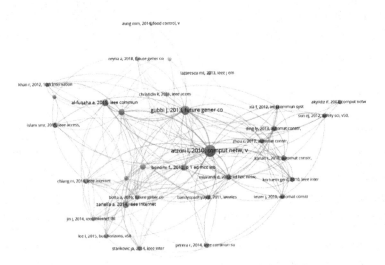

Fig. 10. Co-citation analysis network for "safety monitoring Internet of Things" (VOS n.d.).

Using Web of Science, a total of 3000 articles were analyzed for the co-citation analysis of "Industry 4.0," as detailed in Fig. 11. These articles were reduced to those that included at least 75 citations of a cited reference, which left a total of 32. The strongest of these cited references were related to authors Liao, Xu, Lasi, and Kagermann, with a minimum of 200 citations.

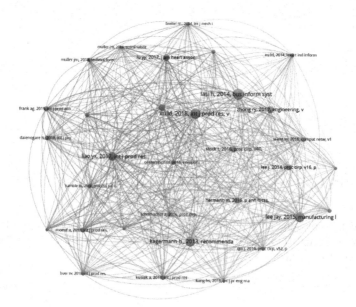

Fig. 11. Co-citation analysis network for "Industry 4.0" (VOS n.d.).

5.2 Content Analysis

Analysis of content was accomplished through a multistep process. Research article information was first collected through Harzing's Publish or Perish data collection tool. VOSviewer was then used to create a map based on text information. Terms had to occur 250 times to be part of the map in Fig. 12. A total of 40 terms meet this requirement, 24 of which are mapped.

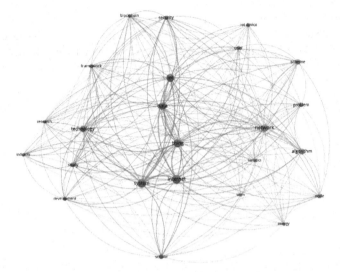

Fig.12. Content analysis network for "Internet of Things" (VOS n.d.).

Figure 13 shows the content analysis for "Safety Monitoring Internet of Things." Terms had to occur 100 times to be part of the network map. A total of 31 meet this requirement, 19 of which are mapped.

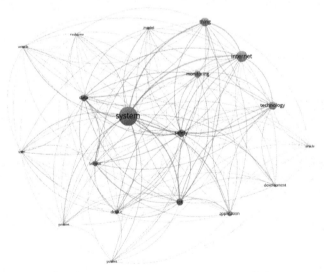

Fig. 13. Content analysis network for "safety monitoring Internet of Things" (VOS n.d.).

Figure 14 shows the content analysis for "Industry 4.0." Terms had to occur 275 times to be part of the network map. A total of 46 meet this requirement, 28 of which are mapped.

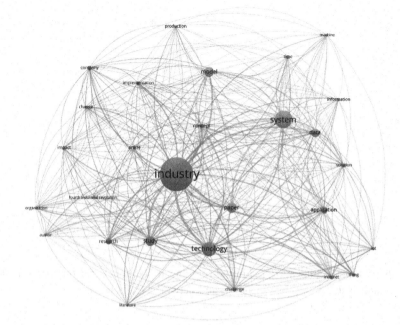

Fig. 14. Content analysis network for "Industry 4.0" (VOS n.d.).

5.3 Key Word Analysis

MAXQDA (Max n.d.) is a powerful analysis tool that can be used to pull terms along with other information from documents. MAXQDA was used to compile a word cloud of relevant keywords used in the research articles referenced in this document. Articles were selected based on relevance to the previously analyzed phrases and terms. These relevant articles were uploaded to MAXQDA with "filler words" removed to leave only relevant keywords. This gives a useful visualization of the terms in Fig. 15 that are most important.

5.4 Bibliometric Analysis Summary

The analysis performed in this section shows strong interconnections between publications for their respective search phrases. Each co-citation analysis included a similar number of articles. However, the requirements for these articles to be present, based on the number of times referenced, varied wildly. It is expected that "Safety Monitoring Internet of Things" would have the lowest overall references, which is supported to be the case. However, it would be expected that the "Internet of Things" would have the potential for the most co-citations, but, in fact, "Industry 4.0" has the most. "Industry 4.0" produced a similarly sized network to "Internet of Things," but had a requirement of 100 references to "Internet of Things" 20 required references. The content analysis showed similar results with "Industry 4.0," suggesting that there are more shared terms in the analyzed documents compared to the "Internet of Things." The keyword analysis

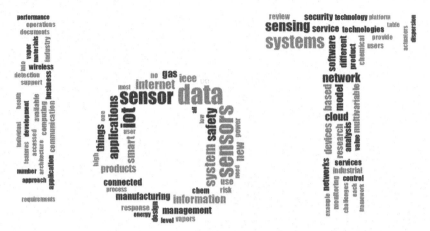

Fig. 15. Word cloud of most relevant terms from MAXQDA (Max n.d.).

shows that the most relevant terms in the referenced documents for this paper include "sensor, data, systems, applications, IoT, and network" (Max n.d.).

6   Discussion

6.1   Primer

Through use of the methods applied in this bibliometric analysis many concerns present themselves as they relate to the search terms. These methods create these concerns through exposure of relevant and linked terms from tools such as MAXQDA and VOSviewer. From this, other relevant articles and analyses can be found putting forward or addressing the concerns raised.

6.2   Internet of Things

The desire to become more connected with everyday life has never been higher. Phrases like "smart home" and "smart transport" can be partially attributed to the increasing prevalence of IoT devices (Wortmann and Flüchter 2015). This has led to an extremely diverse range of fields of application for IoT technologies, creating the possibility for IoT solutions to reach everyday life. These IoT solutions range from smart thermostats to networked industrial machines and smart vehicles (Michael and James 2015). This inevitably bleeds into other aspects of life, including safety and industry.

Concerns
There are major concerns present with IoT devices that need to be addressed. Many of these concerns are focused largely on the security of interconnected devices. Malicious users have the possibility of causing failure of IoT systems or gathering sensitive information. This is being addressed through cloud data collection through trustworthy sensing for cloud management (Kantarci and Mouftah 2014), among other tools.

6.3 Safety Monitoring

IoT devices have the possibility of making significant improvements to safety not only in manufacturing spaces but in every aspect of life. Safety-critical systems, systems that have the potential and may cause accidents directly or indirectly (Srinivas Acharyulu and Seetharamaiah 2015), are a prime consideration for interconnectivity using IoT devices. Examples of devices that fall under the classification of "safety-critical" include weapon delivery systems, manufacturing controls, maintenance and use of robotics, power generation, road traffic control systems, dispatch systems, medical diagnostics systems, and medical robots (Srinivas Acharyulu and Seetharamaiah 2015).

Safety monitoring ultimately leads to the possibility of safety automation in critical systems where the integration of "smart" systems can lead to a significant or virtual elimination of hazards (Wu et al. 2019). This type of monitoring and automation has the possibility of reducing failures, an event where a system or subsystem component does not exhibit the expected external behavior (Srinivas Acharyulu and Seetharamaiah 2015), which reduces safety concerns along with increasing quality in output for the system in question.

Concerns

While these connected devices have the possibility of providing real-time data of safety-related operations alongside creating robust hazard reduction in safety-critical systems, major concerns inhibit rapid adoption. Due to the nature of IoT devices, there is a concern for overreliance on the features they provide. Interconnectivity provides major benefits but has the drawback of a potential breakdown of the system in question if a link is broken. This breakdown could cause failure that, if not caught by backup safety systems, could cause negative effects that lead to harm to the end-user, when looking at safety-critical systems.

6.4 Industry 4.0

Industry 4.0, otherwise referred to as "Smart Industry" (Wortmann and Flüchter 2015) or as part of the "4th Industrial Revolution" (Lasi et al. 2014), is a topic of discussion that is increasing at an exceptional rate (see Fig. 7). While the term "Industry 4.0" refers to a collection of technologies that include IoT devices (see Fig. 2), IoT plays a major part in several aspects that define Industry 4.0. These aspects Influenced by IoT include flexibility, decentralization, and resource efficiency (Lasi et al. 2014).

Future applications of IoT devices in manufacturing workspaces are broad. Due to IoT collecting real-time data from factory floors (e.g., machinery vehicles, materials, and environments), on-demand changes can be made to optimize systems without human intervention (Yang and Shen 2016). Energy benefits can be derived from the use of IoT devices through facility-wide monitoring (see Fig. 16) via the deployment of sensors at locations of interest along with dynamic on-line energy control in IoT-enabled closed loops. This is significant due to manufacturing accounting for approximately one-third of global energy demand (Karnouskos et al. 2009). IoT devices have the potential to contribute to preventative maintenance by providing early diagnostics and reduce unscheduled downtime and unexpected breakdowns, which can come at significant cost (Yang and Shen 2016; Lee et al. 2006).

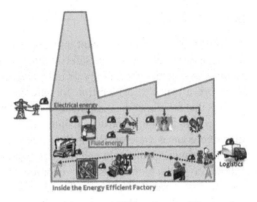

Fig. 16. Visualization of energy-efficient factory (Karnouskos et al. 2009).

Supply Chain Management

IoT can assist in supply chain management, allowing the ability to collect real-time information on shop floors, inventory, purchasing and sales, and logistics (Yang and Shen 2016). These can be correlated with one another to increase production rate and reduce information inconsistencies between different parties. This supply chain management capability contributes to the implementation of lean manufacturing, which looks to maximize resource utilization through the minimization of waste (Sundar et al. 2014). Lean manufacturing is reliant on accurate data and the ability to rapidly change to varying circumstances, which is contributed to through the use of IoT devices.

Concerns

There are severe limitations that exist in the implementation of Internet of Things devices in manufacturing. It is necessary for modern manufacturing that facilities readily adapt to new technologies and ever-evolving customer demands. However, manufacturing facilities often implement or have implemented hardware that may be outdated and inflexible to change. This lack of flexibility can be limited by software as well, whereas physical hardware, such as robots, can be readily changed to meet demand, although typically require a new program to be created. Smart industrial devices would ideally take input data from several sources and change programming automatically to meet desired tasks (Bi et al. 2014).

This leads to an overall issue with IoT as it exists today in manufacturing. IoT is currently designed to simply collect and show information for the equipment in question. However, it is not designed to act on that information to create the possibility of autonomous decision-making (Bi et al. 2014). This detracts from the agility a company can exhibit concerning evolving demands.

Standardization is another major hurdle to system integration (Jiang et al. 2012). For IoT devices to be readily accessed and implemented, standards must be established. While there have been some standards identified and application scenarios developed, there is a necessity to meet requirements of heterogeneity, dynamicity, and evolution (Bi et al. 2014).

Ultimately, manufacturing companies must weigh the risks of the implementation of IoT devices in facilities with the benefits they provide. Between security risks of connected devices that are remotely accessible and collect data via cloud tools, along with the quickly outdated nature of connected hardware and software, companies must strike a balance between cost and agility to meet consumer and stakeholder demands (Boyes et al. 2018).

7 Conclusion

Undoubtedly, there is a long future ahead for the research, development, and implementation of IoT devices. There is clear evidence in research articles and other written works which, through qualitative works, shows that this future is clear (Mukhopadhyay et al. 2014). The potential use cases for IoT devices are consistently evolving. While this paper only focuses on safety monitoring and industry 4.0 to relate IoT to modern-day manufacturing, there is an incredible range of other use cases currently present. These use cases range from improving everyday life at home to homeland defense for entire countries.

It can be concluded that the implementation of IoT devices in manufacturing workplaces has and will lead to massive improvements for those willing to embrace the technologies. Though several potential drawbacks exist, primarily due to the relatively new nature of the technology, how it is implemented, there is significant backing to remediate these issues. This backing comes from the research sector highlighted by this report to have become increasingly involved over recent years, along with backing from the implementation sector that seeks to receive a major return on investment for this emerging technology.

8 Future Work

This paper focuses on a very narrow aspect of the Internet of Things. While there are several other applications mentioned, these can be explored in more depth using similar bibliographic analysis tools. There is also significant work and information that could be gathered on the general development of IoT devices such as the development of the ability to perform analysis in a scalable and reliable fashion. A clear indication of the importance of this other work can be seen in the continuing grant funding given to Rensselaer Polytechnic Institute through the National Science Foundation (NSF n.d.).

References

Escobar, C.A., Morales-Menendez, R.: Machine learning techniques for quality control in high conformance manufacturing environment. Adv. Mech. Eng. **10**(2), 1–16 (2018). https://doi.org/10.1177/1687814018755519

Kantarci, B., Mouftah, H.T.: Trustworthy sensing for public safety in cloud-centric Internet of things. IEEE Internet Things J. **1**(4), 360–368 (2014). https://doi.org/10.1109/JIOT.2014.2337886

Cass, J.: Internet of things: what it is, how it works, examples and more. Just Creative (2018). https://justcreative.com/internet-of-things-explained/

Wortmann, F., Flüchter, K.: Internet of things. Bus. Inf. Syst. Eng. **57**(3), 221–224 (2015). https://doi.org/10.1007/s12599-015-0383-3

Union of IT: Internet of Things Global Standards Initiative (2015). https://www.itu.int/en/ITU-T/gsi/iot/Pages/default.aspx

Rolfes, K., Perry, L., Shunk, D.: Industry 4.0 and People-Centric Leadership. Association for Manufacturing Excellence (2019). https://www.ame.org/target/articles/2019/industry-40-and-people-centric-leadership

Harzing: Harzing's Publish or Perish (n.d.). https://harzing.com/resources/publish-or-perish

VOSviewer: VOSviewer Visualizing Scientific Landscapes (n.d.). https://www.vosviewer.com/

MaxQDA: MaxQDA the Art of Data Analysis (n.d.). https://www.maxqda.com/

Mendeley (n.d.). https://www.mendeley.com/reference-management/reference-manager/

Google Scholar: Google (n.d.). https://scholar.google.com/

Web of Science (n.d.).https://apps-webofknowledge-com.ezproxy.lib.purdue.edu/UA_GeneralSearch_input.do?SID=3Fjf1Hph1yQNuJ6Flcl&product=UA&search_mode=GeneralSearch

Guo, F., Lv, W., Liu, L., Wang, T., Duffy, V.G.: Bibliometric analysis of simulated driving research from 1997 to 2016. Traffic Inj. Prev. **20**(1), 64–71 (2019). https://doi.org/10.1080/15389588.2018.1511896

Duffy, G.A., Duffy, V.G.: Systematic literature review on the effect of human error in environmental pollution. In: Duffy, V.G. (ed.) HCII 2020. LNCS, vol. 12199, pp. 228–241. Springer, Cham (2020). https://doi.org/10.1007/978-3-030-49907-5_16

Fahimnia, B., Sarkis, J., Davarzani, H.: Green supply chain management: a review and bibliometric analysis. Int. J. Prod. Econ. **162**, 101–114 (2015). https://doi.org/10.1016/j.ijpe.2015.01.003

Scopus (n.d.). https://www-scopus-com.ezproxy.lib.purdue.edu/search/form.uri?display=basic&zone=header&origin=resultslist#basic

Newman, P.: The internet of things 2020. Insider (2020). https://www.businessinsider.com/internet-of-things-report?IR=T

Trujillo, C.M., Long, T.M.: Document co-citation analysis to enhance transdisciplinary research. Sci. Adv. **4**(1), 1 (2018). https://doi.org/10.1126/sciadv.1701130

Michael, P.E., James, H.E.: How smart, connected products are transforming companies. Harvard Bus. Rev. **93**(10), 96–114 (2015). https://hbr.org/2015/10/how-smart-connected-products-are-transforming-companies

Srinivas Acharyulu, P.V., Seetharamaiah, P.: A framework for safety automation of safety-critical systems operations. Saf. Sci. **77**, 133–142 (2015). https://doi.org/10.1016/j.ssci.2015.03.017

Wu, F., Wu, T., Yuce, M.R.: An internet-of-things (IoT) network system for connected safety and health monitoring applications. Sensors (Switzerland) **19**(1) (2019). https://doi.org/10.3390/s19010021

Lasi, H., Fettke, P., Kemper, H.-G., Feld, T., Hoffmann, M.: Industry 4.0. Bus. Inf. Syst. Eng. **6**(4), 239–242 (2014). https://doi.org/10.1007/s12599-014-0334-4

Yang, C., Shen, W.W.X.: Applications of internet of things in manufacturing. Comput. Support. Coop. Work Des. **2** (2016)

Karnouskos, S., Colombo, A.W., Lastra, J.L.M., Popescu, C.: Towards the energy-efficient future factory. In: IEEE International Conference on Industrial Informatics (INDIN), pp. 367–371 (2009). https://doi.org/10.1109/INDIN.2009.5195832

Lee, J., Ni, J., Djurdjanovic, D., Qiu, H., Liao, H.: Intelligent prognostics tools and e-maintenance. Comput. Ind. **57**(6), 476–489 (2006). https://doi.org/10.1016/j.compind.2006.02.014

Sundar, R., Balaji, A.N., Satheesh Kumar, R.M.: A review on lean manufacturing implementation techniques. Procedia Eng. **97**, 1875–1885 (2014). https://doi.org/10.1016/j.proeng.2014.12.341

Bi, Z., Xu, L.D., Wang, C.: Internet of things for enterprise systems of modern manufacturing. IEEE Trans. Industr. Inf. **10**(2), 1537–1546 (2014). https://doi.org/10.1109/TII.2014.2300338

Jiang, H., Zhao, S., Zhang, Y., Chen, Y.: The cooperative effect between technology standardization and industrial technology innovation is based on Newtonian mechanics. Inf. Technol. Manag. **13**(4), 251–262 (2012). https://doi.org/10.1007/s10799-012-0133-x

Boyes, H., Hallaq, B., Cunningham, J., Watson, T.: The industrial internet of things (IIoT): an analysis framework. Comput. Ind. **101**(March), 1–12 (2018). https://doi.org/10.1016/j.compind.2018.04.015

Mukhopadhyay, S.C., Suryadevara, N.K.: Internet of things: challenges and opportunities. In: Mukhopadhyay, S.C. (ed.) Internet of Things. SSMI, vol. 9, pp. 1–17. Springer, Cham (2014). https://doi.org/10.1007/978-3-319-04223-7_1

National Science Foundation (n.d.). https://www.nsf.gov/awardsearch/showAward?AWD_ID=1553340

A Systematic Literature Review of Potential and Emerging Links Between Remote Work and Motivation

Labiba Imdad[1](✉) and Vincent G. Duffy[2](✉)

[1] School of Psychological Sciences, Purdue University, West Lafayette, USA
limdad@purdue.edu
[2] School of Industrial Engineering, Purdue University, West Lafayette, IN 47906, USA
duffy@purdue.edu

Abstract. With the sudden shift from in-person to remote settings in the workplace and various other institutions as triggered by the lockdowns during the COVID-19 pandemic, this paper sought to examine the prevalence of research on the link between remote work and motivation. Two time periods were observed using VOSviewer and Harzing to determine whether a shift in focus on these topics took place as a result of the pandemic and what the overall insights were. In addition, a co-citation analysis was done in two parts. One part gave consideration of the references from a search using terms "motivation" and "remote work". The other considered the same search terms with constraints on the dates of articles for the analysis to emphasize prior research that was more recently emphasized. Upon further analysis, it was found that a shift did take place with earlier research focusing on combating low motivation of healthcare workers in remote regions and the latest research focusing on potential solutions for reduced motivation levels of individuals who had to work from home. In both instances, it was seen that work in remote regions and work done remotely, that is from home, were associated with low motivation levels. While the area of remote work and motivation are highly relevant to job design, it also implicates human-computer interaction as an increase in the number of remote jobs may imply more time spent with computers which in turn may have potential connections with human motivation.

Keywords: Remote work · Motivation · Rural regions · Worker retention · Healthcare

1 Introduction and Background

Research on the areas of motivation and remote work has been on the rise over the past couple of years as demonstrated by the trend diagrams in this paper. The prevalence of research in the area of motivation is hardly astounding given its reaching impacts on various areas in job design such as workplace productivity and job satisfaction (Whitfield 1988). From content theories of motivation to process models, a lot has been proposed to understand and enhance work motivation with popular theories being Herzberg's

© Springer Nature Switzerland AG 2021
C. Stephanidis et al. (Eds.): HCII 2021, LNCS 13097, pp. 494–508, 2021.
https://doi.org/10.1007/978-3-030-90966-6_34

Two-Factor Theory, Maslow's Hierarchy of Needs, and Hackman and Oldham's Job Characteristics Model (Whitfield 1988). Moreover, as the struggle of remote regions to retain workers, especially in healthcare, continues to remain dire with a significant part of the problem linked to low motivation (Dolea et al. 2010), it can easily be speculated as to why there has been a persistent pattern of research in the link between remote work and motivation.

Taken in another sense, remote work can also mean work that is done from one's place of residence instead of a common physical place where employees meet. The study of the relationship between this sense of the phrase "remote work" and motivation has also seen a rise in the number of documents published in the year 2020 when measures were beginning to take place for the COVID-19 pandemic. A common problem faced by the workplace worldwide as a result of this was reduced levels in motivation as individuals were forced to transition from engaging in in-person work to remote work due to enforced lockdowns (Kulikowski et al. 2021). As an increasing number of jobs are being converted to remote work, it becomes highly important to understand exactly what the implications of this will be and its ties to working motivation. This can lead to further understanding of what the future of work looks like.

2 Purpose of Study

The purpose of this literature review was to understand the dominating and emerging areas of research in links between motivation and remote work. The purpose can be divided into twofold with one being understanding what the dominating area of research has been in the intersection of remote work and motivation in the overall literature, and another being how it varies within specific periods as major crises such as the COVID19 pandemic are introduced. Taken together, this can be used to enhance our current understanding of prevalent problems in motivation within the context of remote work, and the implications of future work on the individual as a substantial number of jobs become remote as projected by an Upwork survey (Remoters, "Remote Work Trends & Stats for 2021").

As mentioned previously in this paper, remote work here is at one instance taken to mean work done in rural regions, and at other instances to mean work that is done from one's place of convenience or synonymously, work-from-home.

3 Methods

3.1 Data Collection

The articles chosen for this literature review were taken from two databases: Web of Science, and Scopus. The keyword searches that were conducted on these databases were "motivation", "remote work", and "motivation and remote work." To account for the latest and most up-to-date information, the date range was set to include all articles from 1980 to March 2021 on all databases. The range was limited to March 2021 as this review was conducted during the end of March utilizing the data before then, and 2021 is still an ongoing year as of the time of this paper. Information including abstract and cited references, authors, title, and the source was utilized from the Web of Science database. The data was primarily collected through Harzing after which it was taken into VOSviewer for further analysis.

3.2 Trend Analysis

A trend analysis was done on the Web of Science and Scopus databases using articles from 1980 to 2020. The year 2021 was excluded as research in this year is still ongoing. Keyword searches for motivation, remote work, and the combination of motivation and remote work were done. The Figures below show the results for the Web of Science Database. As can be seen, the number of documents published per year has been on a constant rise for all the keyword searches (Figs. 1, 2 and 3).

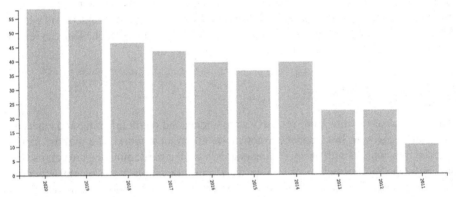

Fig. 1. Trend analysis of articles on *motivation* AND *remote work* (*Web of Science* n.d.)

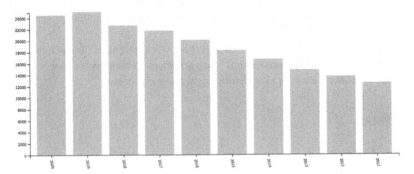

Fig. 2. Trend analysis of articles on motivation (*Web of Science* n.d.)

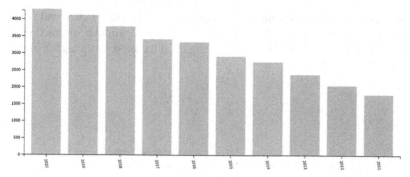

Fig. 3. Trend analysis of articles on remote work (*Web of Science* n.d.)

Additionally, a keyword search for the combination of motivation and remote work was done on Scopus to ensure that the rise in the number of published documents was not something exclusive to the Web of Science Database. The Figure below shows that the same consistency in the rise of the number of articles can be found in the Scopus database providing evidence of its emerging relevance (Fig. 4).

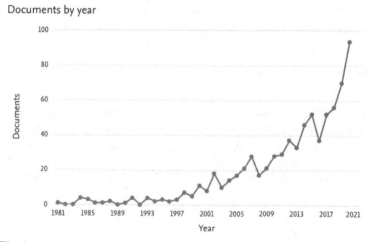

Fig. 4. Trend analysis of articles on motivation and remote work (*Scopus* n.d.)

4 Results

4.1 Co-citation Analysis 1

A co-citation analysis was done with VOSviewer using data from the Web of Science database with the date range set to 1980 to 2020 to account for the latest information. The purpose of this was to determine the degree of connectivity between papers and their link strength, that is, the number of times each of the papers cited and referenced one another. This was then used to establish which papers would be deemed important for this literature review with the papers being cited the most given higher importance (Fig. 5).

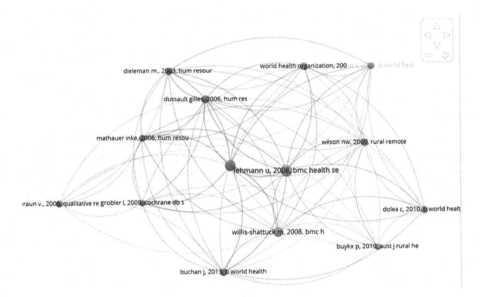

Fig. 5. Co-citation analysis for motivation and remote work (*VOSviewer* n.d.).

The latest 500 records were selected from the assigned date range to be imported into VOSviewer from the Web of Science database. Full Record and Cited References were recorded with the unit of analysis being cited references. The minimum number of cited references was set to 7 to account for sufficient information. Of the 15304 cited references that appeared, 15 met the threshold of which, 10 were then selected for this literature review.

4.2   Co-citation Analysis 2

A further co-citation analysis was done using VOSviewer to mainly collect the papers between 2020 to March 2021 from the Web of Science database. The purpose of this was to examine links between motivation and remote work that were likely inspired by the COVID-19 pandemic. As mentioned previously, the range was limited to March as 2021 is still an ongoing year, and this work was done by the end of March. The link strength between these papers was then used to determine which papers would be included as with the same procedure in the previous co-citation analysis (Fig. 6).

80 records appeared within the time range of 2020 to March 2021. The Full Record and Cited References of these documents were recorded and then imported into VOSviewer to conduct a co-citation analysis. The minimum number of citations of

Fig. 6. Co-citation analysis for motivation and remote work of articles published within 2020–2021 (*VOSviewer* n.d.). The articles were taken from the Web of Science database through Harzing. Afterward, they were imported into VOSviewer to conduct a co-citation analysis.

a cited reference was set to 2. Of the 3719 cited references, 33 met the threshold. Of the 33 cited references, the 10 most prevalent were selected.

4.3 Content Analysis

Content from the research articles (taken from Web of Science) was analyzed using Harzing and VOSviewer. Two content analyses were conducted using data from 1980 to 2020 and 2020 to March 2021. For each of these sets, a map was created using text data to display words that appeared with the greatest frequency as well as the strength of links of these words, that is, the frequency with which they appeared together. A final content analysis was done through MAXQDA using the combination of articles that have been selected for this paper.

Content Analysis 1: Motivation and Remote Work. A content analysis was done with the keyword search "*Motivation* AND *Remote Work*" on the Web of Science database from Harzing. For this analysis, the date range was set to 1980 to 2020. The purpose of this was to identify which words appeared together with the greatest frequency in the overall literature from 1980 to 2020. After obtaining the data from Harzing, it was imported to VOSviewer where a content analysis was done. The fields from which the terms were selected were Title and Abstract Fields with the minimum number of occurrences of a term set to 15. With this parameter, 51 items out of 5516 met the threshold. Out of these 51 terms, 35 of the most occurring were selected to be displayed. The figures below show the final products.

Content Analysis 2: Constrained Search 2020–2021. For the second content analysis, the same procedure as the previous one was followed except with the date range being set to 2020 to March 2021. The minimum number of occurrences of a term was set to 7 which resulted in 59 items meeting the threshold out of 2347 ones. Of these 59 ones, 35 of the most occurring terms were selected.

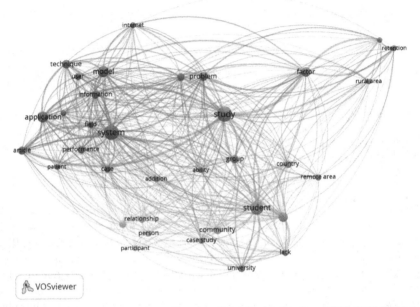

Fig. 7. Content Analysis for remote work and motivation with data from 1980–2020 (*VOSviewer* n.d.). The articles chosen for this analysis were taken from the Web of Science database. Words that appeared with the greatest frequency are "study", "system", and "student" (Table 1).

Table 1. The table here displays the most frequently occurring keywords along with the number of times they appeared. This was found from the results of the content analysis shown in Fig. 7.

Keyword	Occurrences
Study	126
System	117
Student	95
Application	68
Model	65

The purpose of including a different date range was to examine the strength of links between words in the period of the covid-19 pandemic and see what areas emerged in the study of the relationship between motivation and remote work. As can be seen in Fig. 8 below, numerous differences in words can be found when compared with the previous content analysis.

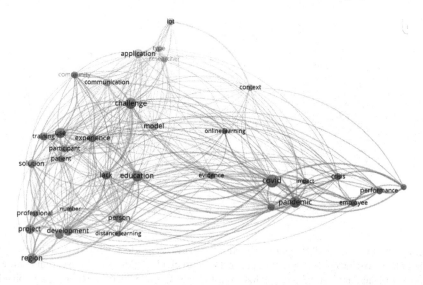

Fig. 8. Content Analysis for remote work and motivation with data from 2020–March 2021 (VOSviewer n.d.). The articles chosen for this analysis were taken from the Web of Science database. Words that appeared with the greatest frequency are "covid", "challenge", and "pandemic" (Table 2).

Table 2. The table here displays the most frequently occurring keywords along with the number of times they appeared in the selected articles within the time range of 2020–March 2021. This was found from the results of the content analysis shown in Fig. 8.

Keyword	Occurrences
Covid	34
Challenge	26
Pandemic	25
Education	23
Project	20

Content Analysis with MAXQDA. A final content analysis was done using MAXQDA. For this analysis, all articles referenced in this paper have been used. The minimum frequency of words was set to five and seventy-five of the most occurring were selected to be displayed. The figure below shows the results (Fig. 9).

Fig. 9. The figure here displays the content analysis that was done with MAXQDA using the articles that have been selected for this paper. The most cited articles from the overall literature on remote work and motivation in the period from 1980 to 2021 and 2020 to 2021 were combined to perform this analysis. The most important keywords from the combination of these articles appear to be "health", "rural", and "learning".

5   Discussion

5.1   The Recurring Link Between Motivation and Remote Work in the Period of 1980 to 2021

The most cited articles within the time range of 1980 to 2020 focus on a common overarching theme which is the problem of retaining and motivating healthcare workers in remote areas. The World Health Organization reported that the imbalanced distribution of healthcare workers is a worldwide problem that needs to be addressed (Buchan et al. 2013). This is such a prevalent problem that measures that could be considered extreme such as "withholding degree and salary" and "imposing large fines" have commonly been implemented (Frehywot et al. 2010) after which it was found that such methods solve part of the problem only in the short-term rather than the long-term (Wilson et al. 2009). Research done by Shattuck and colleagues found that a large part of the problem of lacking healthcare workers in areas of need was tied to the failure of being able to motivate healthcare workers in remote areas (Willis-Shattuck et al. 2008). Moreover, it was mainly remote places that faced the problem of experiencing shortages in healthcare workers as these areas lack the resources needed to motivate and retain current workers in addition to attracting new ones (Dussault and Franceschini 2006). Africa is one such area where the low motivation of healthcare workers was found to be a serious problem along with the shortage of qualified professionals (Mathauer and Imhoff 2006).

In addition to the lack of resources, political factors such as policy and incentivization from governments of developing countries were found to be a significant contribution to this problem (Lehmann et al. 2008). Given the instability of government policies and decisions in developing countries, healthcare workers experience tension as several of these constantly changing decisions are tied to their outcomes. (Dussault and Franceschini 2006). This further exacerbates the problem of the shortage of healthcare workers in remote regions.

With all that being said, however, it is important to note that low motivation is only one of several factors that affect retention of healthcare workers in remote regions as events such as the high population of family-oriented women in healthcare, the desire for better work-life balance, and high mobility of doctors were found to be contributors to the problem as well (Buykx et al. 2010).

To address this problem of the shortage of healthcare workers in remote regions, several initiatives have been taken with a lot more strategies and recommendations suggested as consistent with the literature. Shattuck and colleagues suggest placing a heavy emphasis on career development, financial rewards, and hospitality management as these are common factors among countries in motivating healthcare workers (Willis-Shattuck et al. 2008). On the other hand, researchers such as Mathauer and Imhoff suggest focusing on non-financial incentives such as showing high appreciation to healthcare workers and paying attention to the individual goals of workers (Mathauer and Imhoff 2006). Dieleman and colleagues also report that non-financial incentives such as "appreciation by managers, colleagues, and the community" play a critical role in motivating healthcare workers in remote areas (Dieleman et al. 2003).

5.2 The Recurring Link Between Motivation and Remote Work in the Period of 2020 to March 2021

As expected, the most cited articles within the time range of 2020 to March 2021 had a dominant focus on challenges brought on by the COVID-19 pandemic to remote workspaces, more specifically in education, and as they relate to motivation. Kulikowski and researchers report that of the numerous challenges brought on by the pandemic in education, an outstanding one was the low job motivation of teachers after the transition to remote work and e-learning (Kulikowski et al. 2021). This is compounded by the effects of unreliable internet access for both students and teachers which have been shown to disrupt the teaching and learning process (Yusuf 2020). Moreover, it has been seen that while education systems, in general, have been impacted, it was mostly ones in remote regions that took the biggest hit as access to the internet is limited in these areas (Omodan 2020).

Other challenges brought on by forced remote work and e-learning were loss of participation and engagement of students in online classes, and additional effort required on the part of teachers to develop and restructure content to make it highly engaging while at the same time being able to cover everything in the curriculum (Dhawan 2020).

Dr. Vlachopoulos of Amsterdam University reports that 400 million students from various countries including China, Spain, and the Netherlands stopped attending classes due to the virus and forced remote classes (Vlachopoulos 2020).

Given that the pandemic has had negative impacts on motivation levels, the most frequently cited articles also had a dominant focus on enhancing motivation in remote contexts. Articles such as "Self-Determination Theory and the Facilitation of Intrinsic Motivation, Social Development, and Well-being" (Ryan and Deci 2000) and "Motivation through the Design of Work: Test of a Theory" (Hackman and Oldham 1976) were frequently cited. Trend Analyses conducted on Scopus on the topics of motivation and remote work showed these areas to have increased in focus in the year 2020 adding further relevance to these topics (Figs. 10 and 11).

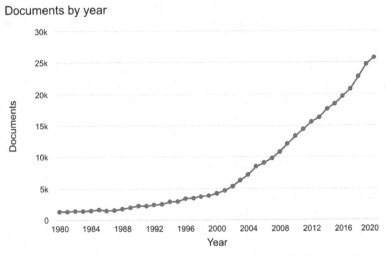

Fig. 10. Content Analysis of Motivation from 1980 to 2020 (*Scopus* n.d.).

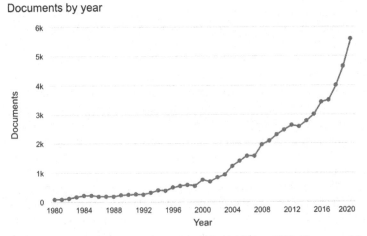

Fig. 11. Content Analysis of Remote Work from 1980 to 2020 (*Scopus* n.d.).

On an optimistic note, however, a paper by Zimmerman titled "Investigating Self-Regulation and Motivation" was cited frequently as it provides useful insights on how the problem of low motivation during remote learning and work can be tackled. In this paper, it is mentioned that individuals who were provided with self-regulation training experienced heightened levels of motivation along with improved time-management and self-reflection skills (Zimmerman 2008). Given that there is lower authority monitoring in remote work as a teacher or a boss is not physically present to keep track of individuals' progress, self-regulation becomes crucial in maintaining motivation and making progress. Thus, it is hardly surprising why this paper was frequently cited during this period as its insights can be used to boost motivation in remote work settings. Another frequently cited paper by Ryan and Deci titled "Self-Determination Theory and the Facilitation of Intrinsic Motivation, Social Development, and Well-being" suggests creating "conditions supportive of autonomy and competence" while avoiding "conditions that controlled behavior" as these have been shown to be beneficial for intrinsic motivation (Ryan and Deci 2000).

5.3 Final Thoughts

Putting this into observation, it can be seen that the results of the same keywords drastically differ between the 1980 to 2020 time period to the 2020 to March 2021 time period showing that the link between remote work and motivation is rising.

6 Conclusion

The dominant theme in the links between remote work and motivation within the years of 1980 to 2020 is the problem of being able to retain and motivate healthcare workers in remote regions with considerable research being done in the area of combatting this problem. The articles in this literature review reveal a negative connection between the motivation of healthcare workers and remote regions with a common obstacle is having to compete with urban regions that have more resources. However, when the links between motivation and remote work are observed in isolation within the period of 2020 to March 2021 during which the COVID-19 pandemic struck, the dominant theme appears to be reduced motivation levels among individuals taking part in online classes and to some extent, employees doing their work from home. The articles considered solely within this time range show there to be a connection between low motivation and remote work, that is work done online. Given this, it can be seen that while the overarching area pervading the literature of motivation and remote work is in the focus of combating low motivation levels of healthcare workers in remote regions, the theme has the potential to vary within specific periods, especially as new crises are introduced such as the COVID-19 pandemic.

7 Future Work

As the analyses which were done here show there to be a shift in the dominant link between motivation and remote work after observing a portion of the overall period between 1980 and 2021 and comparing it to the entire period between 1980 and March 2021, this reveals many new areas for further research. For instance, it was uncovered here that a major crisis such as the COVID-19 pandemic caused detrimental effects which dominated the overall research direction on remote work and motivation. The research done in this area revealed that sudden shifts to remote work from in-person settings can have a detrimental impact on motivation. Given this, it would be recommendable to reconsider making sudden shifts in work settings from in-person ones to remote ones. This area can further be researched with control studies to explore the exact relationship between motivation and remote work, and pinpoint causes.

Additionally, by observing links between remote work and motivation in other periods and crises that occurred within those periods, insights can be released on what crises have affected motivation in remote work settings and how job design can be enhanced to combat factors that reduce motivation in remote settings. Along with job design, the area of remote work and motivation also implicates human-computer interaction as an increase in the number of remote jobs may imply more time spent with computers at home. This brings in new factors to consider and research such as health and safety risks of having to work long hours in front of computers, and optimization of humancomputer interaction for long periods of remote work.

Aside from the above, further insights can be revealed through a lot of the work that is currently being done on motivation and remote work. One such prominent piece of work that is currently being done is by the University of Maryland which focuses on investigating factors such as motivation and grit that affect individuals' decisions on pursuing and remaining in STEM fields (NSF 2021). The shift to remote settings from in-person ones could potentially lead to a decrease in motivation, with those within the STEM fields being hit the most. This is because more motivation may be required to remain in such fields due to the difficulty associated with them.

Another article related to this is "Associations between grit, motivation, and achievement in high school students" by Muenks, Yang, and Wigfield. The work done by Muenks and colleagues shows that there is a distinction to be drawn between motivation and grit as some components of the former have weak and negative associations with the latter (Muenks 2018). Hence, for future work, it is worth investigating whether particular attention needs to be given to motivation independently of grit to boost workplace productivity and efficiency, especially in remote contexts.

References

Buchan, J., et al.: Early implementation of WHO recommendations for the retention of health workers in remote and rural areas. Bull. World Health Organ. **91**(11), 834–840 (2013). https://doi.org/10.2471/blt.13.119008

Buykx, P., Humphreys, J., Wakerman, J., Pashen, D.: Systematic review of effective retention incentives for health workers in rural and remote areas: towards evidence-based policy. Aust. J. Rural Health **18**(3), 102–109 (2010). https://doi.org/10.1111/j.1440-1584.2010.01139.x

Dieleman, M., Cuong, P.V., Anh, L.V., Martineau, T.: Human resources for health glossary. Hum. Resour. Health **1**, 1–10 (2003). http://www.hrhresourcecenter.org/node/1080

Dolea, C., Stormont, L., Braichet, J.M.: Evaluated strategies to increase attraction and retention of health workers in remote and rural areas. Bull. World Health Organ. **88**(5), 379–385 (2010). https://doi.org/10.2471/BLT.09.070607

Dussault, G., Franceschini, M.C.: Not enough there, too many here: understanding geographical imbalances in the distribution of the health workforce. Hum. Resour. Health **4**, 1–16 (2006). https://doi.org/10.1186/1478-4491-4-12

Frehywot, S., Mullan, F., Payne, P.W., Ross, H.: Compulsory service programmes for recruiting health workers in remote and rural areas: do they work? Bull. World Health Organ. **88**(5), 364–370 (2010). https://doi.org/10.2471/BLT.09.071605

Lehmann, U., Dieleman, M., Martineau, T.: Staffing remote rural areas in middle- and low-income countries: a literature review of attraction and retention. BMC Health Serv. Res. **8**, 1–10 (2008). https://doi.org/10.1186/1472-6963-8-19

Mathauer, I., Imhoff, I.: Health worker motivation in Africa: the role of non-financial incentives and human resource management tools. Hum. Resour. Health **4**, 1–17 (2006). https://doi.org/10.1186/1478-4491-4-24

Whitfield, D.: Handbook of Human Factors. Displays, vol. 9 (1988). https://doi.org/10.1016/0141-9382(88)90068-6

Willis-Shattuck, M., Bidwell, P., Thomas, S., Wyness, L., Blaauw, D., Ditlopo, P.: Motivation and retention of health workers in developing countries: a systematic review. BMC Health Serv. Res. **8**, 1–8 (2008). https://doi.org/10.1186/1472-6963-8-247

Wilson, N.W., Couper, I.D., De Vries, E., Reid, S., Fish, T., Marais, B.J.: A critical review of interventions to redress the inequitable distribution of healthcare professionals to rural and remote areas. Rural Remote Health **9**(2), 1060 (2009)

Dhawan, S.: Online learning: a panacea in the time of COVID-19 crisis. J. Educ. Technol. Syst. **49**(1), 5–22 (2020). https://doi.org/10.1177/0047239520934018

Dryselius, A.: Motivation in the Remote Workplace (2021)

Hackman, J.R., Oldham, G.R.: Motivation through the design of work: test of a theory. Organ. Behav. Hum. Perform. **16**(2), 250–279 (1976). https://doi.org/10.1016/0030-5073(76)90016-7

Kulikowski, K., Przytuła, S., Sułkowski, Ł: The motivation of academics in remote teaching during the Covid-19 pandemic in polish universities—opening the debate on a new equilibrium in e-learning. Sustainability (switzerland) **13**(5), 1–16 (2021). https://doi.org/10.3390/su13052752

Omodan, B.I.: The vindication of decoloniality and the reality of COVID-19 as an emergency of unknown in rural universities. Int. J. Sociol. Educ. **1** (2020). https://doi.org/10.17583/rise.2020.5495

Ryan, R.M., Deci, E.L.: Self-determination theory and the facilitation of intrinsic motivation, social development, and well-being. Am. Psychol. **55**(1), 68–78 (2000). https://doi.org/10.1037/0003-066X.55.1.68

Vlachopoulos, D.: Covid-19: threat or opportunity for online education? High. Learn. Res. Commun. **10**(1), 16–19 (2020). https://doi.org/10.18870/hlrc.v10i1.1179

Yusuf, B.N.: Are we prepared enough? A case study of challenges in online learning in a private higher learning institution during the Covid-19 outbreaks. Adv. Soc. Sci. Res. J. **7**(5), 205–212 (2020). https://doi.org/10.14738/assrj.75.8211

Zimmerman, B.J.: Investigating self-regulation and motivation: historical background, methodological developments, and future prospects. Am. Educ. Res. J. **45**(1), 166–183 (2008). https://doi.org/10.3102/0002831207312909

NSF Award Search: Award # 1534846 - an examination of grit in relation to diverse high school students' stem motivation, self-regulation, and outcomes: a longitudinal validation study. https://nsf.gov/awardsearch/showAward?AWD_ID=1534846&HistoricalAwards=false. Accessed 24 April 2021

Muenks, K.: Supplemental material for associations between grit, motivation, and achievement in high school students. Motivat. Sci **4**(2), 158–176 (2018). https://doi.org/10.1037/mot0000076. supp

Remote Work Trends & Statistics for 2021: Remote Work Status & Future After Covid. Remoters, 4 February 2021. https://remoters.net/remote-work-trends-future-insights/

Modern Workplace Ergonomics and Productivity – A Systematic Literature Review

Jiachen Jiang and Vincent G. Duffy[✉]

Purdue University, West Lafayette, IN 47906, USA
{jiang518,duffy}@purdue.edu

Abstract. With the development of remote collaboration platforms, the word 'workplace' is no longer limited to offices. With the impact of COVID-19, more and more people bring their workplaces out of the corporate office. With that said, moving workplaces to different places has offered researchers opportunities to study the impact on productivity and ergonomics on traditional office workers in various environments. This study is a systematic literature review of the topic of workplace ergonomics and productivity. The review was conducted using platforms such as Scopus, VOSviewer, MAXQDA, Vicinitas, and Web of Science. Bibliometric and co-citation analyses were performed using these tools to show the relationship between diseases caused by bad posture and habits, such as Musculoskeletal Disorders and Computer Vision Syndrome, and productivity. Additionally, environmental and cognitive ergonomics, such as room humidity, room temperature, brightness, also play important roles in worker productivity. It is crucial to understand these issues so that employers can offer better support for their employees in all sorts of working environments without sacrificing much productivity.

Keywords: Workplace · Ergonomics · Productivity

1 Introduction and Background

Computers play an important role in modern workplace. It is increasingly uncommon to spot office workers without the help of a computer. According to NTIA (National Telecommunications and Information Administration) [2], 80.5% of the people in managerial and professional specialty occupations use computers, and 70.5% of the people in technical, sales, and administrative support roles use computers. Although computers have brought convenience to work with faster calculation and communication abilities, they have introduced new problems, namely ergonomic disorders such as musculoskeletal injuries and eyestrains [3]. Back, arm, hand, and shoulder pain are common posture-related injuries. Some of the musculoskeletal pain can be caused by poor workstation design, bad posture, or remaining static for long periods of time. Holding parts of the body for long period of time in the same posture reduces blood circulation to muscles, bones, tendons, and ligaments, leading to pain. For heavy computer users, it is also likely

© Springer Nature Switzerland AG 2021
C. Stephanidis et al. (Eds.): HCII 2021, LNCS 13097, pp. 509–524, 2021.
https://doi.org/10.1007/978-3-030-90966-6_35

for overuse injury to occur in the elbow and wrist area due to excessive typing and usage of mouse. Eye strain is also another contributing factor to various disorders that office workers may experience. Focusing the eyes at the same distance point for long periods of time can cause fatigue. The human eyes structurally prefer to look at objects six meters away, and most office workers place their computers less than one meter away. The lights from computer screens also cause fatigue by causing symptoms such as blurred vision, temporary inability to focus on further objects, and headaches. All these issues are not uncommon on office workers with computers, and many of them causes permanent or long-term injuries.

When employees suffer from these injuries, their performance may be affected. Multiple human resources websites [1] have suggested that work environment and employee wellness are among five most important factors affecting employee productivity. A worker suffering from ergonomic injuries requires more time and effort to complete the same amount of work than a perfectly healthy worker. Meanwhile, a healthy worker also possesses more physical and mental resources to invest in their tasks, which ultimately benefits the company. It is also possible to infer that employees who exercise more often tend to demonstrate higher productivities, and those who do not exercise tend to have relatively reduced productivity. Companies should use these as guidelines to modify their workplace environments to create more friendly offices in order to boost employee productivity.

2 Purpose of Study

The purpose of this study is to perform a systematic literature review of publications involving modern office ergonomics and office productivity to determine if these articles can be used in increasing workers' productivity at workplace. With actions taken by the employers, it is possible to boost worker productivity with office ergonomic improvements, such as modification of office furniture and hardware, office temperature and humidity control, and office background music. This literature review aims to discover what efforts have been made to identify relationships between ergonomics and productivity, as well as the findings, if any. Platforms such as Harzing's Publish or Perish, Web of Science, VOSviewer, and MAXQDA have been used to collect data for this literature review.

3 Data Collection

3.1 Database Search

This is one of the very first steps of conducting this literature review. A wide variety of publications were collected from various databases. Across all the databases, similar search terms were utilized. One thing to note is that sometimes the phrase 'efficiency' can be swapped with 'productivity', and the search results are similar.

Table 1 shows a table of various databases utilized in this search as well as the search terms associated with each database and results.

Table 1. Results of database search

Database name	Search term	Results
Scopus	Office AND ergonomics AND productivity	222 documents
Web of Science	Ergonomics AND productivity	947 publications
Google Scholar	Office ergonomics and productivity	57800 results
Harzing's Publish or Perish	Office ergonomics AND productivity	980 publications

3.2 Trend Analysis

The trend analysis for this topic is completed on Scopus and Harzing's Publish or Perish. When analyzing search results, the publishing year was filtered to up to 2020. Year 2021 was not used because, as of the completion of this literature analysis, it is still halfway into 2021. The results from Scopus are shown in Fig. 1, and the results for Harzing's Publish or Perish are shown in Fig. 2.

Figure 1 shows the results from Scopus search. Although the x-axis goes up to 2021, actual data points end in 2020. As illustrated in the graph, there was not a lot of interest on the topic prior to the 1980s. There was a peak around 1985, which eventually turned into a fluctuating but steady increase since then. It would be rational for one to predict that the number of publications will go up after 2020 due to COVID-19. A lot of companies announced work from home policies during 2020, causing a large portion of office workers to work from their residences [4], which motivates researchers to conduct study on the impact of productivity while employees work from home.

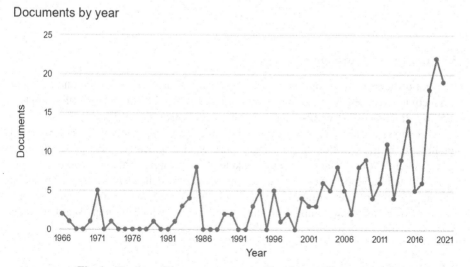

Fig. 1. Number of documents per year from Scopus (*Scopus*, n.d.)

Figure 2 below shows a graphic representation of the pivot table on the number of authors summarized by year exported from Harzing's Publish or Perish. The general trend shows a steady increase, although also with slight fluctuations. The increase initiated at around 1985, which is relatively consistent as what Fig. 1 shows in terms of number of publications.

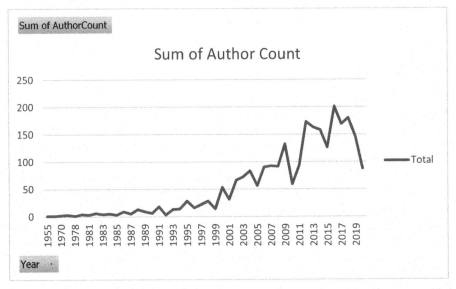

Fig. 2. Sum of number of authors per year from Harzing's Publish or Perish (*Harzing's Publish or Perish*, n.d.)

3.3 Emergence Indicator

It is not difficult to see from the above two figures that the topic of ergonomics and productivity has been an emerging area since late 1980s. MAXQDA was utilized in this step to extract some keywords related to this topic, shown in Fig. 3.

Of course, certain words such as 'ergonomics' and 'productivity' were expected to show up in the word cloud. Other key phrases also appeared, such as 'computer', 'environment', 'performance', 'musculoskeletal'. The appearance of 'computer' further validated the importance of a modern workplace, which often involves computers. The appearance of 'performance' further indicated that the ergonomic issues among office workers may have impact on their productivity, which ultimately affects their performance.

3.4 Engagement Measure

To further examine the emergence and the engagement of the topic of ergonomics and productivity, Vicinitas was utilized. The keyword in the Vicinitas search was 'ergonomics

Fig. 3. Word Cloud generated in MAXQDA for keywords from sample articles related to the topic.

and productivity'. Vicinitas is a tool that analyzes contents on Twitter. In a modern world like today, Twitter is widely used to transmit information. As a result, it is necessary to examine the engagement of the general population on Twitter.

Figure 4 below shows the timeline of various recent tweets related to the topic. Although there wasn't large number of tweets, it is safe to say that the trend has been increasing steadily, meaning the general population has been increasingly aware of the potential relationship between ergonomics and productivity.

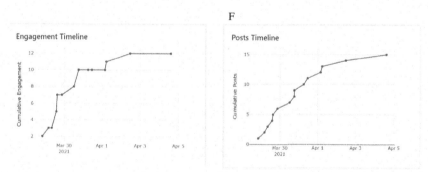

Fig. 4. Timeline generated from Vicinitas related to ergonomics and productivity. (*Vicinitas*, n.d.)

4 Result

4.1 Co-citation Analysis

Co-citation analysis is a semantic similarity measure for documents that makes use of citation relationships. Co-citation is defined as the frequency with which two documents are cited together by other documents [5]. By conducting a co-citation analysis, it would be able to determine the most important publications and authors.

Figures 5 and 6 below shows a result of co-citation analysis by CiteSpace with the search results from Web of Science. The text in red are names of the authors. Attempts were made to create cluster bursts from this analysis, but no keywords were extracted. One of the possible reasons might be that this topic is so new and fresh that there has not been a lot of attention to it. Previous Vicinitas search supports this view, as there has been only a dozen of tweets related to this topic. Another possible reason is that keywords do exist, but none of them are repetitive. In this case, authors might be tackling this topic via different perspectives. As we have discussed earlier and would discuss later in this literature review, factors affecting productivity range from physical ones to cognitive ones, from office environment to work out frequency. It is entirely possible to have nonrepetitive keywords, given that this topic is relatively new and supports multiple approach perspectives.

With that said, in order to examine the cluster bursts related to this topic, a wider range of articles were selected to import into CiteSpace. The search criteria were expanded to all fields, including abstract, title, keywords, etc. The results are shown in Fig. 5.

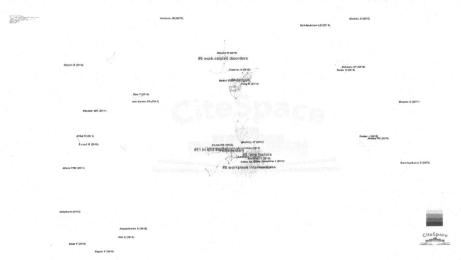

Fig. 5. Co-citation analysis by CiteSpace with Web of Science search results

Fig. 6. Co-citation analysis by CiteSpace with Web of Science search results

Figure 7 is the co-citation analysis result from VOS viewer with the document exported from Web of Science. Since this is a relatively new emerging area, the minimum number of citations of a cited reference was reduced to 10 from the default value 20.

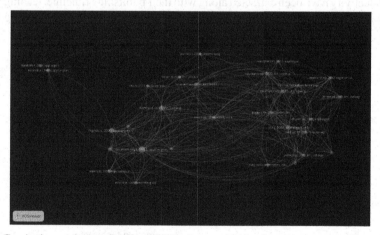

Fig. 7. Co-citation analysis result from VOS viewer with the document exported from Web of Science.

Figure 8 shows the list of publications used to generate the above cluster diagram. It shows the number of citations and numeric link strength.

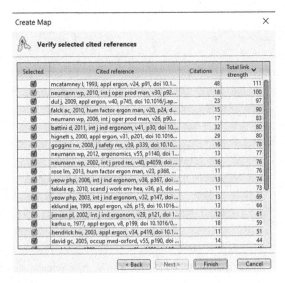

Fig. 8. List of publications used to generate Fig. 7.

The next step in co-citation analysis was to examine leading authors from search results of Scopus. As shown in Table 2, top 5 leading authors in this topic of ergonomics and productivity have been extracted along with their publishing timeline, leading words, and publication counts. Note that Ishii and Shimoda had extremely similar leading words, suggesting that their research areas were highly related.

Table 2. Leading authors from Scopus search (*Scopus,* n.d.)

Author name	Publishing year	Leading words	Publication count
Hedge, Alan	1993, 1995, 1998–2000, 2009–2018, 2020–2021	Sedentary lifestyle, sitting position, office workers, computer workstations, office chair	61
Ishii, Hirotake	1997–1999, 2001, 2004–2009, 2011–2021	Office buildings, thermal comfort, interaction techniques, pose estimation	82
Shimoda, Hiroshi	1988, 1991, 1995, 1997–2000, 2002–2009, 2011–2021	Office buildings, thermal comfort, interaction techniques, pose estimation	94

(continued)

Table 2. (*continued*)

Author name	Publishing year	Leading words	Publication count
Johnston, Venerina	2004, 2007–2021	Work disability, sick leave, musculoskeletal disease, computer workstations, neck pain	109
Robertson, Michelle M	1990–1992, 1994–1998, 2000, 2002–2010, 2012–2021	Health management, safety estimate, musculoskeletal disease, sitting position, office workers	104

Table 3 shows a table of top 5 leading institutions, including institution name, their country, leading keywords, and publication count. There is a variety of institutions around the world focusing on this area. The top 5 institutions are located in North America, Europe, Asia, and Australia (continent name). The leading keywords are associated mainly with workplace, human, and ergonomics.

Table 3. Leading institutions from Scopus search (*Scopus*, n.d.)

Institution name	Country	Leading words	Publication count
Cornell University	USA	Human, ergonomics, productivity, workplace	100
Kyoto University	Japan	Ergonomics, productivity, intellectual productivity, concentration-time, office buildings	22
The University of Queensland	Australia	Human, workplace, controlled study, occupational health, ergonomics	130
Curtin University	Australia	Human, workplace, controlled study, occupational health, ergonomics	154
Zürcher Hochschule Winterthur	Switzerland	Ergonomics, productivity, human, workplace, efficiency	16

Table 4 shows the leading publications from the Scopus search. The table contains authors, article title, and year published. One of the articles was published by a company, Steelcase Inc. It is not difficult to see that ergonomics and productivity has been a topic among firms in the United States around 1980s, right around the time that the steady increase of number of publications initiated. Some of the authors also appeared in Table 2.

Table 4. Leading publications from Scopus search (*Scopus,* n.d.)

Author	Title	Year
Hedge, Alan	Quantifying office productivity: an ergonomic framework	1998
Vimalanathan, K; Ramesh Babu, T.	The combined effect of environmental and cognitive ergonomics factors on the office workers' productivity in India	2012
Johnston, Venerina; Pereira, Michelle Jessica; Comans, Tracy A.; Sjøgaard, Gisela; Straker, Leon; Melloh, Markus; O'Leary, Shaun Patrick Chen, Xiaoqi	The impact of workplace ergonomics and neck-specific exercise versus ergonomics and health promotion interventions on office worker productivity: a cluster-randomized trial	2019
Steelcase Inc., USA	Ergonomics and productivity in the electronics office	1984
Fernández, Juan M. Dulce; Carbonell, Laura M. Pimienta	Design and construction of a prototype of ergonomic pad controlled through electronic sensors to correct bad postures on office workers and its impact on productivity	2012

4.2   Content Analysis

Content analysis can be used to examine patterns in communication in a replicable and systematic manner [6]. Following the co-citation analysis, the content analysis part is completed at this step. Platforms and tools used were similar to that of co-citation analysis. However, VOSviewer proved to me the most efficient one.

Figure 9 below shows the VOSviewer cluster of the keywords extracted from Web of Science search results. The logic of this diagram is similar to that of co-citation analysis. Instead of showing the authors' names, it shows the keywords in each publication. As expected, 'ergonomics' and 'productivity' are the most stood-out ones. It can be seen that ergonomics is related to keywords such as musculoskeletal disorders, health, productivity, performance, safety, environment, fatigue, etc. Productivity is related to items such as low-back pain, neck pain, disorders, comfort, etc.

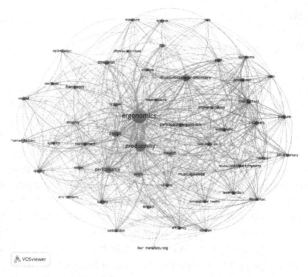

Fig. 9. VOSviewer cluster of the keywords extracted from Web of Science search results.

Figure 10 here shows the word cloud generated from Vicinitas in terms of keywords. Again, productivity and ergonomics are the two most obvious ones, followed by keywords such as chair, office, comfort, which all relates back to ergonomics.

Word Cloud

Fig. 10. Word cloud generated from Vicinitas keywords.

We can also refer back to Fig. 3 for the word cloud generated by MAXQDA. Those keywords came from the publications hand-picked by examining the abstracts, which should make them more relevant to the topic. Although there is not as many keywords as the one generated by Vicinitas, these words should be more essential to the topic. Of course, when generating both word clouds, prepositions and other non-related words have been manually de-selected.

5   Discussion

5.1   Modern Workplace Ergonomics

When thinking about workplace ergonomics, most people think about the unhealthy habits or postures that workers keep at a long time, or various inappropriate ways to use certain hardware. For instance, holding the mouse for a long time is one of the most common unhealthy postures in modern offices. Additionally, putting the computer monitor too close to the eyes is an inappropriate usage of hardware. Indeed, these behaviors would definitely cause various physical disorders all over the body – neck, back, wrist, waist, leg, etc. Consequently, these disorders will impact individual worker productivity. Workers suffer from disorders, and they may take sick leave, thus lowering the productivity for the company as well. Various studies have indicated that physical discomfort lower worker productivity, both in short term and in long term [20]. Meanwhile, environmental and cognitive ergonomics also play important roles in office worker's productivity [19]. Environmental factors may include climate, lighting, and noise. The temperature, humidity, brightness, sound levels will affect how employees work in the office in terms of their perception, learning, memory, thinking, and execution functions. Various studies have indicated that temperature, illumination, complexity of tasks and interaction effect of temperature, illumination, complexity of tasks have significant effects on the office workers' productivity [19]. The degree of how these factors would impact the productivity varies with each other.

5.2   Productivity and COVID-19

Productivity at workplace can be impacted by multiple factors at workplace, and some of which are rather surprising to traditional readers. It is already known that ergonomic factors such as posture, office equipment, lighting, temperature, humidity influence workers' productivity. However, other factors, such as background music, exercise, employee satisfaction can also alter productivity.

Companies in general have a common goal to maximize employer performance at work, and some innovative proposals have already surfaced. In pre-COVID era, some companies offer amazing gym benefits in order to encourage employees to work out more often, aiming to improving productivity at workplace. For instance, Apple's current corporate headquarters, the spaceship-like Apple Park in Cupertino, California, has amazing fitness facilities. The facility consists of weights and a two-story yoga room, a 100,000-square-foot Fitness & Wellness Center, and dental & medical service center [21]. Studies have also proven that workplace intervention combining ergonomics and area-specific exercise offers possible benefits for sickness presenteeism and health-related productivity loss among a general population of office workers and sickness absenteeism for office workers with area-specific pain in the longer-term [20]. Although there is yet any study on how Apple's fitness facility could improve their employee's performance at work, Apple CEO Tim Cook did claim that 'It's (fitness is) something that makes them (employees) feel better and more energetic.' It is yet inconclusive to determine what background music increases productivity, but some studies have shown that background music could block off some of the disturbing noise in the office, reducing the chance that workers being disrupted by a far less pleasant sound. This reduces the possibility for a worker to become unproductive, which, in turn, improves their productivity. In contrast to the ergonomic factors, the effect of background music on productivity is largely subjective. One may need to experience different types of music to determine the optimal type of music (classic, jazz, rock, ambient, natural sound, etc.) that helps boost their productivity.

COVID-19 has had a profound impact on worker productivity. According to a journal published on Frontiers in Communication [27], productivity has increased on average. However, those who do not feel comfortable with e-work tend to be less productive. It is yet conclusive to say whether the productivity has been lowered or not due to COVID, since it largely depends on the individual's working style. However, it is not to say that there is no way to promote productivity on a company level. There are many measures that companies can take to help maintain productivity in a remote work era. For instance, companies can develop counseling programs or work from home routines to help those who do not feel comfortable with work from home get used to the new normal.

5.3   Association with "List of Ten Ways"

In this review, the list of ten ways to conduct systematic review, shown in Fig. 11 below, is implemented when appropriate. Sections 1 and 2 listed the background and purpose of this review. Sections 3.2 and 3.3 demonstrated trends from recent literature and publications. The rest of Sects. 3 and 4 showed the methodologies used and results obtained, including co-citation analysis and content analysis, leading to the conclusion in the next section.

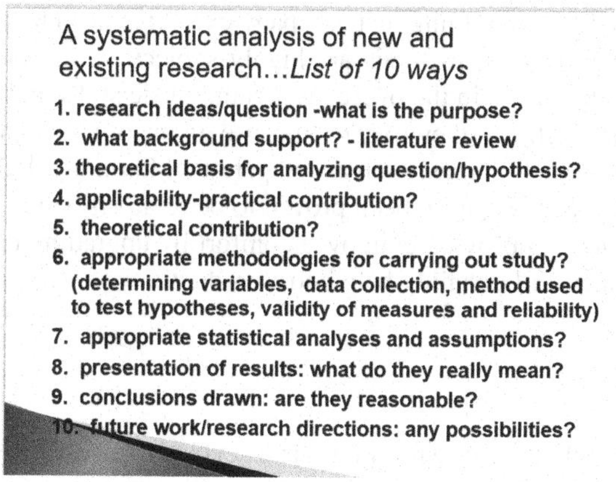

A systematic analysis of new and
existing research...*List of 10 ways*

1. research ideas/question -what is the purpose?
2. what background support? - literature review
3. theoretical basis for analyzing question/hypothesis?
4. applicability-practical contribution?
5. theoretical contribution?
6. appropriate methodologies for carrying out study?
   (determining variables, data collection, method used
   to test hypotheses, validity of measures and reliability)
7. appropriate statistical analyses and assumptions?
8. presentation of results: what do they really mean?
9. conclusions drawn: are they reasonable?
10. future work/research directions: any possibilities?

Fig. 11.   List of ten ways.

5.4   In Relation to Safety Engineering

At the first glance, this topic may not relate to "safety" very much. Indeed, most of the modern workplace are scenes such as offices in skyscrapers in central business districts. However, in some occupations, ergonomics and workstation design can have an impact on whether the operators would be able to perform their duties accordingly. For instance, evidence has shown that workstation design and ergonomics, in addition to intense workload, are related to some incidents caused by air traffic controllers [24]. This can also be extended to other public transport operators, such as bus drivers, train operators, etc.

6   Conclusion

COVID-19 has brought a number of changes that could affect worker productivity to the workplace. According to Pew Research Center [26], 20% of American workers worked from home before coronavirus outbreak, and 71% of American workers are working from home after the outbreak. In other words, there has been approximately a 225% increase in the number of American workers working from home. Not only in America, but companies around the world have also been taking measures to provide employees with better workplaces at home. Salesforce India, for example, provided its employees with workstations just like the ones in the office [25]. These measures can help workers maintain their productivity level in home offices. The range of topics covered by modern workplace ergonomics have exceeded traditional ergonomics on a physical level. Environmental and cognitive ergonomics should also be taken into account. In addition to disorders happening on the human body caused by incorrect posture, unhealthy habits, and improper usage of equipment, outside environmental factors such as lighting, humidity, brightness, may also impact productivity. It is also possible to alter worker productivity by engaging employees with activities outside of work, such as offering gym memberships with compensation package, or building company fitness centers. One thing that company executive need to keep it mind is that the results for some of these methods are highly subjective. It would not be wise to introduce background music in the office, as certain music styles not only provide zero help in boosting productivity, they may even cause distraction to some population, It is safe to implement methodologies, such as temperature, humidity, lighting-related ones across the company, as these have been proven to be relatively objective to the general population. Of course, improving employee comfort by upgrading office equipment to more ergonomic ones will certainly help boost productivity.

7   Future Work

As of today, there has been quite a few literatures devoted to investigating the relationship between workplace ergonomics and productivity, as shown in the search results demonstrated above. With that said, this is still a relatively new emerging area indicated by the lack of keyword clusters in Figs. 5 and 6. Although the interest in this topic may mainly come from companies that aim to improve employee performance at work, the research results can be applied in other fields as well, namely education and automation. During COVID-19, more and more educational institutions started to offer remote instruction in addition to in-person instruction. Studies have indicated that online learning have caused reduction in productivity and motivation for some students [22]. It could be beneficial to implement ergonomic methodologies on students and investigate the effect on productivity based on academic achievements. Human monitoring still plays a crucial role in automation, especially in occupations like automated air traffic control. Fatigue could happen during monitoring stage, lowering the effectiveness of human monitoring. It could be valuable to investigate whether ergonomic changes could improve monitoring activities on human operators. Additionally, there have been a number of future works published on National Science Foundation, one of which focuses on the use of a Whole-Body Powered Exoskeleton to assist in certain tasks, and how this could affect worker productivity [23].

References

1. Author, Guest: 5 Critical Factors Affecting Employee Productivity at Work - Sage HR Blog. Sage HR Blog—Easy to implement HR tips!, 24 October 2019. https://blog.sage.hr/5-critical-factors-affecting-employee-productivity-at-work/
2. CHAPTER 6: The Digital Workplace. https://www.ntia.doc.gov/legacy/ntiahome/dn/html/Chapter6.htm#:~:text=The%20proportion%20of%20people%20using,sales%2C%20and%20administrative%20support%20occupations. Accessed 27 Mar 2021
3. Computer-Related Injuries. Better Health Channel (n.d.) https://www.betterhealth.vic.gov.au/health/healthyliving/computer-related-injuries
4. Global Workplace Analytics: Work-at-Home After Covid-19-Our Forecast. Global Workplace Analytics, 12 April 2020. https://globalworkplaceanalytics.com/work-at-home-after-covid-19-our-forecast
5. Small, H.: Co-citation in the scientific literature: a new measure of the relationship between two documents. J. Am. Soc. Inf. Sci. **24**, 265–269 (1973). https://doi.org/10.1002/asi.4630240406
6. Alan., B.: Business Research Methods.(Ed. By, Bell, E., 1968), 3rd edn. Oxford University Press, Cambridge (2011). ISBN 9780199583409. OCLC 746155102
7. Haynes, B.P.: An evaluation of the impact of the office environment on productivity. Facilities **26**(5–6), 178–195 (2008). https://doi.org/10.1108/02632770810864970
8. Ranasinghe, P., et al.: Computer vision syndrome among computer office workers in a developing country: an evaluation of prevalence and risk factors. BMC. Res. Notes **9**(1), 1–9 (2016). https://doi.org/10.1186/s13104-016-1962-1
9. Smith, M.J., Bayehi, A.D.: Do ergonomics improvements increase computer workers' productivity?: an intervention study in a call centre. Ergonomics **46**(1–3), 3–18 (2003). https://doi.org/10.1080/00140130303522
10. Reznik, J., Hungerford, C., Kornhaber, R., Cleary, M.: Home-based work and ergonomics: physical and psychosocial considerations. Issues Mental Health Nurs. 1–10 (2021). https://doi.org/10.1080/01612840.2021.1875276
11. Robertson, M.M., Huang, Y.H., Lee, J.: Improvements in musculoskeletal health and computing behaviors: effects of a macroergonomics office workplace and training intervention. Appl. Ergon. **62**, 182–196 (2017). https://doi.org/10.1016/j.apergo.2017.02.017
12. Pickson, R.B., Bannerman, S., Ahwireng, P.O.: Investigating the effect of ergonomics on employee productivity: a case study of the butchering and trimming line of pioneer food cannery in Ghana. Mod. Econ. **08**(12), 1561–1574 (2017). https://doi.org/10.4236/me.2017.812103

13. Robertson, M.M., Ciriello, V.M., Garabet, A.M.: Office ergonomics training and a sit-stand workstation: effects on musculoskeletal and visual symptoms and performance of office workers. Appl. Ergon. **44**(1), 73–85 (2013). https://doi.org/10.1016/j.apergo.2012.05.001

14. Vink, P., Koningsveld, E.A.P., Molenbroek, J.F.: Positive outcomes of participatory ergonomics in terms of greater comfort and higher productivity. Appl. Ergon. **37**(4 SPEC. ISS.), 537–546 (2006). https://doi.org/10.1016/j.apergo.2006.04.012

15. Mossa, G., Boenzi, F., Digiesi, S., Mummolo, G., Romano, V.A.: Productivity and ergonomic risk in human based production systems: a job-rotation scheduling model. Int. J. Prod. Econ. **171**, 471–477 (2016). https://doi.org/10.1016/j.ijpe.2015.06.017

16. Davis, K.G., Kotowski, S.E., Daniel, D., Gerding, T., Naylor, J., Syck, M.: The home office: ergonomic lessons from the "new normal." Ergon. Des. **28**(4), 4 (2020). https://doi.org/10.1177/1064804620937907

17. Resnick, M.L., Zanotti, A.: Using ergonomics to target productivity improvements. Comput. Ind. Eng. **33**(1–2), 185–188 (1997). https://doi.org/10.1016/s0360-8352(97)00070-3

18. Ranasinghe, P., et al.: Work related complaints of neck, shoulder and arm among computer office workers: a cross-sectional evaluation of prevalence and risk factors in a developing country. Environ. Health Glob. Access Sci. Source **10**(1), 1–9 (2011). https://doi.org/10.1186/1476-069X-10-70

19. Vimalanathan, K., Ramesh Babu, T.: The combined effect of environmental and cognitive ergonomics factors on the office workers's productivity in India. J. Appl. Sci. Res. **8**(8), 4222–4226 (2012)

20. Pereira, M., et al.: The impact of workplace ergonomics and neck-specific exercise versus ergonomics and health promotion interventions on office worker productivity: a cluster-randomized trial. Scand. J. Work Environ. Health **45**(1), 42–52 (2019). https://doi.org/10.5271/sjweh.3760

21. Murphy, M.: Apple's New $5 Billion Campus Has a 100,000-Square-Foot Gym and No Daycare. Quartz. Accessed 5 Apr 2021. https://qz.com/984785/apples-new-5-billion-apple-park-campus-has-a-100000-square-foot-gym-and-no-daycare-aapl/

22. Beaver, B.: Online school causing less productivity and motivation for one college student. The Talisman. 28 May 2020. https://www.ballardtalisman.org/a-features/online-school-causing-less-productivity-and-motivation-for-one-college-student

23. Kim, S., Lawton, W., Nussbaum, M.A., Srinivasan, D.: Effects of using a prototype whole-body powered exoskeleton for performing industrial tasks. In: Proceedings of the Human Factors and Ergonomics Society Annual Meeting, vol. 63 (2019). https://doi.org/10.1177/1071181319631469

24. Stager, P., Hameluck, D.: Ergonomics in air traffic control. Ergonomics **33**, 493–499 (1990)

25. Menon, R.: Companies provide home office upgrade to make WFH better. 22 May 2020. https://www.livemint.com/companies/news/companies-offer-home-office-upgrade-to-make-work-from-home-comfortable-11590149589007.html

26. Parker, K., Menasce Horowitz, J., Minkin, R., How coronavirus has changed the way Americans work. In: Pew Research Center's Social and Demographic Trends Project. Pew Research Center, 25 May 2021. https://www.pewresearch.org/social-trends/2020/12/09/how-the-coronavirus-outbreak-has-and-hasnt-changed-the-way-americans-work/

27. Beno, M., Hvorecky, J.: Data on an Austrian company's productivity in the pre-Covid-19 era, during the lockdown and after its easing: to work remotely or not?" Front. Commun. **6** (2021). https://doi.org/10.3389/fcomm.2021.641199

Evaluating the Performance in the Environmental Management and Reverse Logistics in Companies of Plastic Sector: An Integration of Fuzzy AHP, DEMATEL and TOPSIS Methods

Genett Jimenez-Delgado[1]([⊠]) [iD], Daniel Alcazar-Franco[2], Diana García-Tamayo[3], Pedro Oliveros-Eusse[4], and Melissa Gomez-Diaz[3]

[1] Department of Industrial Engineering, Engineering Faculty, Institucion Universitaria ITSA, Barranquilla, Atlántico, Colombia
gjimenez@itsa.edu.co
[2] Faculty of Engineering, Corporación Universitaria Reformada CUR, Barranquilla, Colombia
d.alcazar@unireformada.edu.co
[3] Faculty of Economic Sciences, Universidad de La Costa CUC, Barranquilla, Colombia
{dgarcia34,mgomez24}@cuc.edu.co
[4] Department of Humanities, Universidad de La Costa CUC, Barranquilla, Colombia
polivero@cuc.edu.co

Abstract. The plastic industry is considered one of the most dynamic industries with the highest competitive projection in the country [1]. Thanks to the advances of this industry, new products have been developed with various applications at industrial, commercial, service levels, and society's daily lives. Plastics are highly demanded their chemical and physical properties, versatility, and low cost. However, many challenges are arising from the growth in consumption and the dynamics of the plastics industry, such as the prices of raw materials, substitute products of plastic, the demands of consumers, government, and other interested parties with the impact of plastics on the environment during the different stages of their life cycle. Concerning the life cycle of the plastic products is especially determinant the post-consumption, where plastic waste presents a low percentage of recycling and a prolonged period of degradation, being a product questioned for its negative environmental implications. In this sense, companies in the sector must implement different strategies and tools to evaluate their environmental performance, considering the product life cycle. In the world, there are various government regulations for the responsible use of plastics. International methodologies focused on sustainable environmental management in the products, processes, and organizational level have also been developed, such as the product life cycle approach, reverse logistics, and the ISO 45001 standard. However, it is necessary to create objective and analytical methodologies for evaluating environmental management and reverse logistics that provide solutions for the plastic industry, helping companies comply with applicable legal requirements and standards, and supporting decision-making processes. Concerning the decision-making is a complex process given the complexity of the sector and the multiple criteria taken into account when evaluating and establishing improvement strategies. In the literature

© Springer Nature Switzerland AG 2021
C. Stephanidis et al. (Eds.): HCII 2021, LNCS 13097, pp. 525–545, 2021.
https://doi.org/10.1007/978-3-030-90966-6_36

review, we found several studies with the application of a multicriteria combined approach focused on selecting plastic recycling methods, location of plastic processing centers, eco-design of plastic products, and selection of suppliers. Despite these considerations, the research-oriented on applying integrated methodologies for evaluating performance in the environmental management and reverse logistics in the plastic industry, under multiple criteria and uncertainty, are mostly limited and with the exciting potential of development. Therefore, this document presents a hybrid methodology for evaluating the performance in the environmental management and reverse logistics in the plastic industry by applying two techniques of Multi-criteria Decision Methods (MCDM) uses in environments under uncertainly. First, the fuzzy Analytic Hierarchy Process (FAHP) is applied to estimate the initial relative weights of criteria and sub-criteria. The fuzzy set theory is incorporated to represent the uncertainty in the judgments of decision-makers. Then, the Decision-making Trial and Evaluation Laboratory (DEMATEL) was used for evaluating the interdependences between criteria and sub-criteria. FAHP and DEMATEL are later combined for calculating the final criteria and sub-criteria weights under vagueness and interdependence. Subsequently, the Technique for Order of Preference by Similarity to Ideal Solution (TOPSIS) was used to rank the companies of the plastic industry. Finally, we detect improvement opportunities for the companies of the plastic sector.

Keywords: Environmental management · Reverse logistics · Performance evaluation · Plastic industry · Multicriteria decision making (MCMD) · Fuzzy analytical hierarchy process (Fuzzy AHP) · DEMATEL · TOPSIS

1   Introduction

The plastic industry is one of the productive chains of higher evolution, both in the production growth as economic and social. According to Arandes et al. [1] and Nones [2], the growth rate in plastic materials consumption will be 4% up to 2030. This growth in the consumption of plastic materials has occurred in parallel with the development of new materials, processes, and technologies to manufacture new products that are now used in sectors such as packaging, automotive, housing, textiles, and other goods of consumption.

However, different factors such as the prices of raw materials, the needs and expectations of consumers, government regulations, and concern about the impact of plastics on the environment could affect the growth dynamics of the sector [3]. In this sense, companies do not develop and implement improvement strategies and innovations in their processes, products, and organizational systems [4–6]. Therefore, the challenge for companies to be competitive and sustainable is finding the balance between the design and development of products and services that satisfy their customers and interest groups, generate profits, and contribute to sustainable development. It is then necessary that the companies of the plastic sector implement strategies of environmental management, reverse logistics, and circular economy as drivers of opportunities for sustainable development [7].

Regarding environmental management, there are different methodologies, techniques, and standards such as ISO 14001, product life cycle analysis, evaluation of environmental aspects and impacts, reverse logistics, among others that can help companies design, implement and evaluate their performance concerning the actions carried out in the prevention of pollution. However, although there are several techniques, legal regulations, and management standards in environmental, evaluating performance can become a challenging and subjective process due to the complexity of the plastic sector and the different interest groups involved.

In this sense, the use of the practical approaches based on the integration of qualitative and quantitative techniques as Multi-criteria Decision Methods (MCDM) can facilitate the performance evaluation and improvement in the environmental management and reverse logistics, with a systematic and objective process, with actual application in the companies of the plastic sector.

Concerning the application of integrated methodologies in the performance evaluation of environment management and reverse logistics, different investigations with multicriteria combined approaches were found for the plastic industry in general, focused on the selection of plastic recycling methods [8], location of plastic processing centers [9], design of support systems for decision making applied to the eco-design of plastic products [10], and selection of suppliers and sustainable orders [11]. However, hybrid methodologies that provide solutions for the industry in the performance evaluation of environmental management and reverse logistics are still limited and not sufficiently studied.

This paper presents a hybrid methodology based on the integration of Fuzzy AHP, DEMATEL, and TOPSIS methods to evaluate performance in environmental management and reverse logistics in the plastic industry to address this challenge.

The design of the methodology is based on the approach of the ISO 14001 standard and literature review in reverse logistics, which provide a common framework of high-level management for organizations, through the design of a performance evaluation instrument, which was applied in 4 companies of the plastic industry. First, FAHP was used to calculate the criteria and sub-criteria weights under uncertainty, considering the multicriteria hierarchy designed (4 factors and 12 sub-factors). Then, the Decision-making Trial and Evaluation Laboratory DEMATEL was implemented for evaluating the interrelations and feedback among criteria and sub-criteria. Subsequently, TOPSIS is applied to rank the plastic companies to select the company with the best performance evaluation (the alternative with the higher closeness coefficient).

In the remainder of this work, a literature review on the reported studies in the field is analyzed in Sect. 2; a description of the method is provided in Sect. 3. In Sect. 4, the discussion of results is presented. Finally, Sect. 5 presents the conclusions and future works.

2   Literature Review

Environmental management is defined as "part of the management system used to manage environmental aspects, comply with legal requirements and other requirements, and address risks and opportunities" [12]. Environmental management helps companies reduce pollution, reduce environmental impacts, and contributing to sustainable development through the development of environmentally friendly products, processes, and technologies and the recovery of value from waste through reverse logistic practices. In this respect, reverse logistics support the environmental management of organizations and sustainable development to maximize the value of products, integrating strategies for recycling, product return, remanufacturing, repair, and waste disposal. The impacts of reverse logistics include environmental, social, and economic improvement [13, 14]. The plastics industry is called to implement different standards, tools, and methodologies such as reverse logistics to manage and evaluate its commitment to the environment in its activities and the life cycle of its products, including its final and post-consumption disposition. The above, due to the complexity of this industry and the high impact generated by its processes and products on the environment and stakeholders.

One of the critical elements in environmental management and reverse logistics is performance evaluation, which, according to ISO 14001 [12], is performance related to environmental aspects. In this sense, performance evaluation includes compliance with the environmental policy, legal requirements, risk assessment, the effectiveness of operational controls, the progress in achieving objectives, indicators, and other criteria in environmental management.

Regarding the evaluation of performance in environmental management and good practices in reverse logistics, is a complex process, with the participation of different stakeholders (workers, managers, clients, government, suppliers, experts, among others), multiple criteria involved in the evaluation, and uncertainty environments that make it difficult to determine the most appropriate actions in the prevention of pollution. In this regard, companies can use different qualitative and qualitative methodologies to identify performance gaps, their causes, and establish improvement actions, such as the product life cycle approach, reverse logistics, and the ISO 14001 standard, among others. However, Multi-criteria Decision-Making Methods (MCDM) can underpin companies in the plastic industry to develop the performance evaluation considering the sector's complexity, the relationships between multiple criteria, and under uncertain environments in organizations.

At state of the art, exciting studies were found to apply methodologies for evaluation and decision-making in environmental management and reverse logistics. For a better comprehension of the scientific evidence concerning this topic, a recent literature review (January 2008–June 2021) was developed using the search code "environmental management" AND "reverse logistics" AND "MCDM" in the Scopus database. After a detailed reviewing, only ten articles published in indexed journals were identified, mainly in Engineering, Environmental Science, Business, Management and Accounting, Energy, Computer Science, and Decision Sciences (refer to Fig. 1).

The first studies were oriented towards selecting reverse logistics projects, reverse logistics systems, and models of reverse logistics operations through the application of MCDM techniques such as ANP, Fuzzy set theory, and AHP [15–17]. The impacts of these investigations include the development of return policies, design of reprocessing facilities, selection of operation models, and implementation of reverse logistics projects appropriate to the nature, products, and resources of the companies. Another of the studies found presents a model for evaluating performance in the management of the supply chain incorporating fuzzy MCDM technique (F-DEMATEL, F-ANP, and F-TOPSIS) for decision-making considering multiple attributes in environments of uncertainty [18].

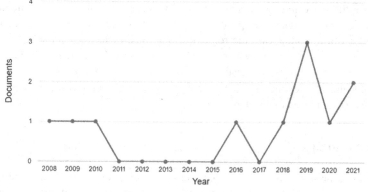

Fig. 1. Documents by year – MCDM-research focused on environmental management and reverse logistics (source: Scopus).

Recent studies propose the use of hybrid techniques and fuzzy methods such as F-ANP in conjunction with multiobjective mixed-integer linear programming (MILP) for the configuration of reverse logistics networks in the electronic sector [19], the application of Combined Gray-DEMATEL and Fuzzy-VIKOR methods in the selection of the return pattern of reverse logistics of vehicles in China [20], sustainable modeling in reverse logistics strategies and their environmental, economic and social impact using fuzzy MCDM based on the VIKOR and Gray relational analysis (GRA) techniques [21], the evaluation of green supply chain management practices in an environment of uncertainty in the battery industry using the F-DEMATEL technique [22] to find the critical methods that affected the performance of the green supply chain management and the implementation of green practices. Other approaches used include applying step-wise weight assessment ratio (SWARA) methods in a hybrid way with the MOORA and WASPAS techniques to select third-party reverse logistics service providers [23]. The most recent study developed a decision support system to choose and evaluate third-party reverse logistics providers (3PRLP) for e-commerce retailers using a fuzzy hybrid approach based on F-AHP and F-TOPSIS incorporating economic, environmental, social, and risk criteria [24].

Considering the reported literature, the evidence from research aiming to evaluate environmental management performance and the good practices in reverse logistics is scarce. Therefore, this research contributes to the scientific literature proposing a hybrid methodology for overall performance evaluation in environmental management and reverse logistics and providing managers procedures and techniques to generate a culture of prevention of pollution and environmental impacts, generating added value for companies and the environment. More research concerning hybrid MCDC applications are then required adapted to dynamics and complexities of the plastic sector context characterized by the increase of economic, social, and environmental demands, which raises continuous improvement in operations, use of resources, products with less polluting life cycles, and more excellent value for society. In this regard, the novelty of the present study is based on the integration of the FAHP, as a derived method of the Analytical Hierarchy Process method (AHP) with the DEMATEL technique and TOPSIS method to evaluate the performance in environmental management and the implementation of strategies in reverse logistics in plastic companies. In particular, FAHP was chosen due to its capability of calculating the relative importance of factors and subfactors under uncertainly. On the other hand, we proposed integrating the FAHP to DEMATEL method to provide a robust approach to evaluation taking into account the vagueness in the judgments and the interdependence between factors and subfactors [25], with the aim to design realistic improvement plans.

3   Methodology

The proposed approach aims to evaluate the plastic industry's environmental management and reverse logistics performance by the integrated methodology using FAHP, DEMATEL, and TOPSIS. In this regard, the methodology is comprised of four phases (refer to Fig. 2):

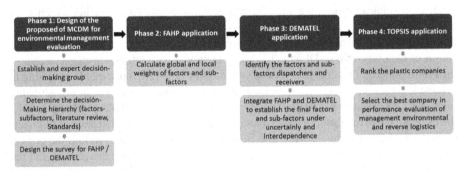

Fig. 2. Methodological approach for evaluating the performance in the environmental management and reverse logistics in the plastic industry

- **Phase 1 (Design of the model for performance evaluation in Environmental Management and Reverse Logistics FAHP/DEMATEL):** A decision-making team is selected based on their experience in environmental management and reverse logistics in the plastic industry. The experts will be invited to be part of the decision-making process through FAHP and DEMATEL methods. Then, the factors and subfactors are defined to establish a decision hierarchy considering the expertise of the decision-makers, the review of the literature, regulations, and good practices in environmental management and reverse logistics [12, 14]. Subsequently, the surveys for the application of the FAHP and DEMATEL methods were designed.
- **Phase 2 (FAHP application):** In this phase, FAHP it's applied to estimate the global and local weights of factors and sub-factors under vagueness in the ponderation. Besides, the experts were invited to perform pairwise comparisons, and then it's developed the process following the FAHP method, as detailed in Sect. 3.1.
- **Phase 3 (DEMATEL application):** In this phase, DEMATEL is used to establish the interdependence between factors and sub-factors (described in Sect. 3.2) to identify the

factors and sub-factors receivers and dispatchers. Additionally, it is applied to assess the strength of each influence relation [26]. Subsequently, FAHP and DEMATEL are combined to obtain the factors and sub-factors weights, taking into account uncertainty and interdependence.

- **Phase 4 (TOPSIS application):** In this step, the Technique for Order Preference by Similarity of an Ideal Solution (TOPSIS) method was implemented to rank the companies of the plastic industry from highest to lowest based upon their closeness coefficient (described in Sect. 3.4). Subsequently, the best company is selected (the alternative with the higher closeness coefficient) based on performance evaluation in environmental management and reverse logistics. Finally, the GAPs and critical variables were identified to improve environmental management and reverse logistics performance through the definition of improvement proposals [27].

3.1 Fuzzy Analytic Hierarchy Process (FAHP)

Fuzzy AHP is an extension of the Analytic Hierarchy Process (AHP) method developed by Thomas L. Saaty as an integrated approach between AHP and fuzzy logic to improve the decision-making process due to the incapability of the AHP method to represent the inaccurate data and vagueness of human judgments in decision-making processes [25]. The fuzzy logic theory was introduced to express the uncertainly in comparison ratios [28].

In FAHP, the uncertain judgments are expressed in a matrix using fuzzy triangular numbers [29]. This matrix of fuzzy numbers "M" is denoted by three real numbers (a, b, c). A triangular fuzzy number, a, and c represent the lower and upper limits, respectively, while b denotes the mean [30]. Concerning the literature review, the decision-makers adopted a reduced AHP scale when making comparisons [25] (Refer to Table 1).

Table 1. Linguistic terms and their fuzzy triangular numbers

Reduced AHP scale	Definition	Fuzzy triangular number
1	Equally important	[1, 1, 1]
3	More important	[2, 3, 4]
5	Much more important	[4, 5, 6]
1/3	Less important	[1/4, 1/3, 1/2]
1/5	Much less important	[1/6, 1/5, 1/4]

The steps of the FAHP algorithm is described as follows:

- Step 1: Perform pairwise comparisons between criteria/sub-criteria using the linguistic terms and the corresponding fuzzy triangular numbers established in Table 1. With this data, a fuzzy judgment matrix $\tilde{A}^k (a_{ij})$ is obtained as described below in Eq. 1:

$$\tilde{A}^K = \begin{bmatrix} \tilde{d}_{11}^k & \tilde{d}_{12}^k & \cdots & \tilde{d}_{1n}^k \\ \tilde{d}_{21}^k & \tilde{d}_{22}^k & \cdots & \tilde{d}_{2n}^k \\ \cdots & \cdots & \cdots & \cdots \\ \tilde{d}_{n1}^k & \tilde{d}_{n2}^k & \cdots & \tilde{d}_{nn}^k \end{bmatrix} \tag{1}$$

$\tilde{d}_{ij}^k$ indicates the *kth* expert's preference of *ith* criterion over *jth* criterion via fuzzy triangular numbers.

- Step 2: In this phase, GAPs and critical variables were identified, and improvement strategies were defined to improve overall performance in evaluating occupational health and safety management.
- Step 3: In the case of a focus group, the judgments are averaged according to Eq. 2, where K represents the number of experts involved in the decision-making process. Then, the fuzzy judgment matrix is updated, as shown in Eq. 3.

$$\tilde{d}_{ij} = \frac{\sum_{k=1}^{K} \tilde{d}_{ij}^k}{K} \tag{2}$$

$$\tilde{A} = \begin{bmatrix} \tilde{d}_{11} & \cdots & \tilde{d}_{1n} \\ \vdots & \ddots & \vdots \\ \tilde{d}_{n1} & \cdots & \tilde{d}_{nn} \end{bmatrix} \tag{3}$$

- Step 4: Calculate the geometric mean of fuzzy judgment values of each factor by using Eq. 4. Here, $\tilde{r}_i$ denotes triangular numbers.

$$\tilde{r}_i = \left(\prod_{j=1}^{n} \tilde{d}_{ij} \right)^{1/n}, i = 1, 2, \ldots, n \tag{4}$$

- Step 5: Determine the fuzzy weights of each factor ($\tilde{w}_i$) by applying Eq. 5.

$$\tilde{w}_i = \tilde{r}_i \otimes (\tilde{r}_1 \oplus \tilde{r}_2 \oplus \cdots \oplus \tilde{r}_n)^{-1} = (lw_i, mw_i, uw_i) \tag{5}$$

- Step 6: Defuzzify ($\tilde{w}_i$) by performing the Centre of Area method applying Eq. 6. M_i is a non-fuzzy number. Then, normalize M_i applying Eq. 7.

$$M_i = \frac{lw_i + mw_i + uw_i}{3} \tag{6}$$

$$N_i = \frac{M_i}{\sum_{i=1}^{n} M_i} \tag{7}$$

3.2   Decision Making Trial and Evaluation Laboratory (DEMATEL)

DEMATEL is an MCDM method technique that identifies causal relationships between factors and sub-factors in complex multicriteria decision models [26]. The DEMATEL technique's fundamental approach is based on the graph theory with a visual representation named impact-digraph map categorizing the factors into two groups: dispatchers and receivers [31]. Dispatchers are the factors or sub-factors that influence other factors or sub-factors, while the receivers are affected by factors or sub-factors [25]. In addition, the DEMATEL method indicates the influence level of each element so that significant interdependences can be determined [32].

The procedure of DEMATEL method is described as follows [25]:

- Step 1: Make the matrix of direct influence: The decision-makers are asked to compare criteria/sub-criteria to measure their causal relationship. With these comparisons, an average n x n matrix called the direct relationship matrix is generated. In this matrix, each element bij represents the average degree to which the criterion/sub-criterion i affect the criterion/sub-criterion j. For this, the experts, based on their personal experience, point out the direct impact that each element i exerts on each of the other elements j using this four-level comparison scale: nonexistent impact (0), low impact (1), medium impact (2), high impact (3) and very high impact (4).
- Step 2: Normalize the direct influence matrix: The normalized direct relation matrix N is calculated using Eqs. 8–9:

$$N = k \cdot B \tag{8}$$

$$k = min \left(\frac{1}{\max_{1 \leq i < n} \sum_{j=1}^{n} |b_{ij}|}, \frac{1}{\max_{1 \leq j < n} \sum_{i=1}^{n} |b_{ij}|} \right) i, j \in \{1, 2, 3, \ldots, n\} \tag{9}$$

- Step 3: Obtain the total relation matrix: After normalizing the direct relation matrix N, the full relation matrix S is obtained by implementing Eq. 10, where I is the identity matrix:

$$S = N + N^2 + N^3 + \cdots = \sum_{i=1}^{\infty} N^i = N(I - N)^{-1} \tag{10}$$

- Step 4: Develop a causal diagram: Using the $D + R$ and $D - R$ values, where R_i represents the sum of the *j-th* column of the matrix S (see Eqs. 11–12) and D_i Criteria/Sub-criteria with positive values of D-R, have a high influence on the other criteria/sub-criteria and are called dispatchers. represents the sum of the *i -th* row of the matrix S (see Eqs. 11 and 13), dispatchers and receivers can be identified. The negative values of D−R indicate that the criteria/sub-criteria are significantly influenced by others (receivers). In addition, the D+R values indicate the degree to which the criteria/sub-criteria i affect or are affected by others.

$$S = \left[s_{ij} \right]_{nxn}, i, j \in \{1, 2, 3, \ldots, n\} \tag{11}$$

$$R = \sum_{j=1}^{n} s_{ij} \tag{12}$$

$$D = \sum_{i=1}^{n} s_{ij} \tag{13}$$

- Step 5: Establish the threshold value and obtain an impact-digraph map: The threshold value is calculated to identify the significant interrelationships between criteria or sub-criteria (see Eq. 14). Suppose the influence degree of a criterion/sub-criterion in the matrix S is bigger than the threshold value (p). In that case, this criterion/sub-criterion is included in the map of impact digraphs. This graph is done by assigning the data set $(D + R, D - R)$.

$$p = \frac{\sum_{i=1}^{n} \sum_{j=1}^{n} s_{ij}}{n^2} \qquad (14)$$

3.3 The FAHP-DEMATEL Method

An integrated FAHP-DEMATEL method is proposed to provide more realistic results [25, 32]. The combined technique considers the limitations of FAHP to assess the feedback and interdependence between decision elements. For the considerations above, it is necessary to complement the FAHP method with DEMATEL as a robust approach that can underpin decision-maker professionals in environmental management to design short-term and long-term plans that increase performance evaluation in occupational health and safety the positive impacts on the stakeholders and sustainable development. The relative weights of factors and sub-factors (w_j) considering the interdependence are obtained by multiplying the weights outcomes from FAHP and the normalized direct relation matrix N (refer to Eq. 15).

$$wi_j = \begin{matrix} SC_1 \\ SC_2 \\ SC_3 \\ . \\ SC_z \end{matrix} \begin{bmatrix} SC_1 & SC_2 & . & . & . & . & SC_z \\ n_{11} & n_{12} & . & . & . & . & n_{1z} \\ n_{21} & n_{22} & . & . & . & . & n_{2z} \\ n_{31} & n_{32} & . & . & . & . & n_{3z} \\ . & . & . & . & . & . & . \\ . & . & . & . & . & . & . \\ n_{z1} & n_{z2} & . & . & . & . & n_{zz} \end{bmatrix} * \begin{bmatrix} w_1 \\ w_2 \\ w_3 \\ . \\ . \\ w_z \end{bmatrix} \qquad (15)$$

3.4 Technique for Order of Preference by Similarity to Ideal Solution (TOPSIS)

TOPSIS is an advantageous method in multicriteria decision-making. This ranking technique it's based on the fact that the preferred alternative should have the shortest distance from the positive ideal solution (PIS) and the farthest from the perfect negative solution (NIS) through the calculation of the closeness coefficient [33].

TOPSIS technique can be described as follows:

- Step 1: Create a decision matrix X with "m" gynecobstetrics departments and "n" sub-criteria (See Eq. 16). X_{ij} is the value of the sub-criterion $S_j (j = 1, 2, 3, \ldots, n)$ in each gynecobstetrics department $GD_i(i = 1, 2, \ldots, m)$.

$$
X = \begin{array}{c} GD_1 \\ GD_2 \\ GD_3 \\ \vdots \\ GD_m \end{array}
\begin{bmatrix}
S_1 & S_2 & \cdots & \cdots & S_n \\
x_{11} & x_{12} & \cdots & \cdots & x_{1n} \\
x_{21} & x_{22} & \cdots & \cdots & x_{2n} \\
x_{31} & x_{32} & \cdots & \cdots & x_{3n} \\
\cdot & \cdot & \cdot & \cdot & \cdot \\
\cdot & \cdot & \cdot & \cdot & \cdot \\
\cdot & \cdot & \cdot & \cdot & \cdot \\
x_{y1} & x_{y2} & \cdots & \cdots & x_{yn}
\end{bmatrix}
\tag{16}
$$

- Step 2: Calculate the normalized decision matrix R using Eq. 17. Let n_{ij} be the norm used by TOPSIS (Eq. 18). Besides, r_{ij} is defined as the element of this matrix.

$$
R = X \cdot n_{ij} \tag{17}
$$

$$
n_{ij} = \frac{x_{ij}}{\sqrt{\sum_{i=1}^{y} x_{ij}^2}} \tag{18}
$$

- Step 3: Obtain the weighted normalized decision matrix V (See Eq. 19). The sub-criteria weights (w_j) are calculated from the hybrid FAHP-DEMATEL method.

$$
V = \left[w_j r_{ij} \right] = \left[v_{ij} \right] \tag{19}
$$

- Step 4: Establish the ideal (C^+) and anti-ideal (C^-) scenarios by Eqs. 20 and 21 respectively:

$$
C^+ = \left\{ \left({}^{max}_i c_{ij} | j \in J \right), \left({}^{min}_i c_{ij} | j \in J' \right) for\ i = 1, 2, \ldots, m \right\} = \left\{ c_1^+, c_2^+, \ldots, c_j^+, \ldots, c_n^+ \right\} \tag{20}
$$

$$
C^- = \left\{ \left({}^{min}_i c_{ij} | j \in J \right), \left({}^{max}_i c_{ij} | j \in J' \right) for\ i = 1, 2, \ldots, m \right\} = \left\{ c_1^-, c, \ldots, c_j^-, \ldots, c_n^- \right\} \tag{21}
$$

Considering that,

$$J = \{j = 1, 2, \ldots, n | j\ associated\ with\ the\ benefit\ sub\text{-}criterion\}$$

$$J' = \{j = 1, 2, \ldots, n | j\ associated\ with\ the\ cost\ sub\text{-}criterion\}$$

- Step 5: Compute the separation measures of each plastic company to C^+ and C^- using Euclidean separation (Eqs. 22–23).

Euclidean separation from ideal scenario

$$
d_i^+ = \sqrt{\sum_{j=1}^{n} \left(c_{ij} - c_j^+ \right)^2} \quad i = 1, 2, \ldots, m \tag{22}
$$

Euclidean separation from the anti-ideal scenario

$$
d_i^- = \sqrt{\sum_{j=1}^{n} \left(c_{ij} - c_j^- \right)^2} \quad i = 1, 2, \ldots, m \tag{23}
$$

– Step 6: Calculate the relative closeness coefficient (CC_i) by implementing Eq. 24. If $CC_i = 1$, the performance of the plastic company performs according to Positive Ideal Solution (PIS).

$$CC_i = \frac{d_i^+}{\left(d_i^+ + d_i^-\right)}, \quad 0 < CC_i < 1, \quad i = 1, 2, \ldots, m \tag{24}$$

– Step 7: Rank the companies of the plastic industry, considering the closeness coefficient CC_i in the following levels: (Very low performance: $0 \leq CCi \leq 0{,}25$ ‖ Low performance: $0{,}25 < CCi \leq 0{,}5$ ‖ Medium performance: $0{,}5 < CCi \leq 0{,}75$ ‖ High performance: $0{,}75 < CCi \leq 1$).

4 Results and Discussion

4.1 Design of the Model for Performance Evaluation in Environmental Management and Reverse Logistics FAHP/DEMATEL

In this phase, a multicriteria decision model was structured to evaluate performance in environmental management and reverse logistics in the plastic industry based on integrating the F-AHP, DEMATEL, and TOPSIS techniques. First, a team of experts in environmental management, reverse logistics, and multicriteria decision techniques were formed to validate the model's hierarchy of criteria and sub-criteria. The expert profiles are as follows:

- Participants 1, 2, and 3 are Managers in Environmental management departments in companies in the chemical and plastic sector, with more than five years of experience leading environmental management systems and reverse logistics processes.
- Participant 4 is a consulting engineer in Environmental Management with more than ten years of experience implementing the ISO 14001 standard in manufacturing companies.
- Participant 5 is a professional in industrial engineering with a master's degree in Logistics and five years of experience as a consultant in reverse logistics processes in manufacturing companies.
- Participants 6 and 7 are industrial engineers and Associate researchers with expertise in designing assessment models and applying MCDM techniques in the practical scenario, including F-AHP, DEMATEL, and TOPSIS.

Then the multicriteria decision hierarchy was designed composed of 4 criteria and 12 sub-criteria, which were identified taking into account the opinion of the team of experts, the ISO 14001 standard and current environmental regulations, and the related scientific literature shown in Fig. 3.

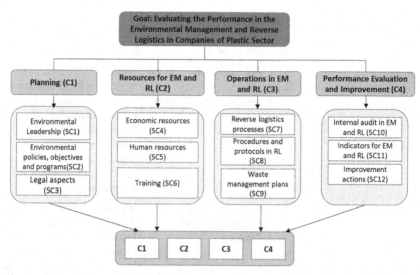

Fig. 3. Decision-making model for evaluating the performance in the environmental management and reverse logistics in companies of the plastic sector

The description of each of the criteria included in the model is detailed in Table 2.

Subsequently, a survey was designed to collect the experts' opinions via paired comparisons between criteria and sub-criteria. In this respect, for each pairwise comparison, the experts answered this question: Concerning the objective/criteria, ¿how important is each element on the leftover item on the right? An example of the F-AHP survey is shown in Fig. 4.

On the other hand, a survey for applying the DEMATEL technique was elaborated (refer to Fig. 5) for analyzing the interdependence between factors and sub-factors and identifying the criteria and sub-criteria dispatchers and receivers via Eqs. 8–14.

4.2 Importance and Interdependence Between Criteria and Sub-criteria: The Integration of F-AHP/DEMATEL

In this stage, the F-AHP and DEMATEL methodologies were integrated to determine the importance between criteria and sub-criteria, considering the vagueness in the experts' judgments and the interdependence relationships between the evaluation factors of the model. In the first instance, the relative weights of the criteria and sub-criteria were calculated via F-AHP. Considering the results obtained (refer to Table 3), the criterion "Planning" (GW = 51.6%) was identified as the most relevant criteria in the performance evaluation of environmental management and reverse logistics. However, the weights of the criteria "Resources" (GW = 23.0%), "Performance evaluation and improvement" (GW = 14.6%), and "Operations" (GW = 10.8%) suggest the development of multifactorial strategies focused on reducing pollution and the life cycle of products with environmental, economic and social impacts. In addition, the consistency ratios of the criteria and sub-criteria were calculated, which show consistency in the experts' judgments (CR < 0.1).

Table 2. Description of criteria

Criterion (C)	Sub-criteria (SC)	Criterion description
C1. Planning	SC1. Environmental leadership SC2. Environmental policies, objectives, and programs SC3. Legal aspects	This criterion evaluates the capacity of the companies to assume leadership, establish policies, objectives, and programs in environmental management and/or reverse logistics, and comply with the applicable environmental legislation [12–14]
C2. Resources	SC4. Economic resources SC5. Human resources SC6. Training	It Evaluates the availability of economic and human resources for environmental management and reverses logistics and personnel training on these topics [12–14]
C3. Operations	SC7. Reverse logistic processes SC8. Procedures and protocols SC9. Waste management plans	It considers the incorporation of reverse logistics processes, adherence to environmental protocols, and waste management plans resulting from manufacturing operations [12–14]
C4. Performance evaluation and improvement	SC10. Internal audit S11. Indicators for EM and RL S12. Improvement actions	This criterion measures the capacity for continuous improvement in environmental management and/or reverse logistics by developing internal audits, monitoring indicators, and implementing action plans [12–14]

According to your experience with respect to "Planning" sub-criterion, ¿how important is each sub-criterion on the left concerning the sub-criterion on the right when evaluating the performance in occupational health and safety management in the companies of electric sector?

		1	2	3	4	5		
Environmental leadership	is	O	O	O	O	O	Important than	Environmental policies, objectives and programs
Environmental leadership	is	O	O	O	O	O	Important than	Legal aspects
Environmental policies, objectives and programs	is	O	O	O	O	O	Important than	Legal aspects

① Much less	③ Equally	⑤ Much more
② Less	④ More	

Fig. 4. Survey for FAHP evaluation

According to your experience with respect to "Planning" sub-criterion, ¿how much influence each sub-criterion on the left has over the sub-criterion on the right when evaluating the performance in occupational health and safety management in the companies of electric sector?

		0	1	2	3	4		
Environmental leadership	has	O	O	O	O	O	Influence over	Environmental policies, objectives and programs
Environmental leadership	has	O	O	O	O	O	Influence over	Legal aspects
Environmental policies, objectives and programs	has	O	O	O	O	O	Influence over	Legal aspects

(0) Nonexistent impact (1) Low impact   (2) Medium impact (3) high impact (4) Very high impact

Fig. 5. Data-collection instrument implemented for DEMATEL comparisons

Table 3. Local and global weights of criteria and sub-criteria

Cluster	GW	LW	CR
Criteria			**0.053**
C1. Planning	**0.516**		**0.022**
SC1. Environmental leadership	0.299	0.580	
SC2. Environmental policies, objectives, and programs	0.071	0.137	
SC3. Legal aspects	0.116	0.283	
C2. Resources	**0.230**		**0.035**
SC4. Economic resources	0.108	0.468	
SC5. Human resources	0.063	0.276	
SC6. Training	0.059	0.256	
C3. Operations	**0.108**		**0.012**
SC7. Reverse logistic processes	0.064	0.590	
SC8. Procedures and protocols	0.018	0.163	
SC9. Waste management plans	0.027	0.247	
C3. Performance evaluation and improvement	**0.146**		**0.035**
SC10. Internal audit	0.052	0.354	
SC11. Indicators for EM and RL	0.035	0.239	
SC12. Improvement actions	0.059	0.406	

Then, the DEMATEL technique was used to calculate the prominence (D+R) and relation (D−R) and identify the criteria and sub-criteria dispatchers and receivers (refer to Table 4). According to the outcomes, "Planning" and "Performance evaluation and Improvement" were classified as dispatchers, while "Resources" and "Operations" were identified as receivers. In addition, "Planning" (C4) has the highest D+R-value (14.13). This criterion is the principal generator of impacts and the most relevant element in environmental management and reverse logistics performance evaluation.

Table 4. Dispatchers and receivers via DEMATEL

Cluster (Criteria/sub-criteria)	Prominence (D+R)	Relation (D−R)	Dispatcher	Receiver
C1. Planning	14.13	1.115	X	
SC1. Environmental leadership	0.995	−0.024		X
SC2. Environmental policies, objectives, and programs	1.047	−0.116		X
SC3. Legal aspects	0.940	0.141	X	
C2. Resources	13.83	−0.06		X
SC4. Economic resources	1.043	0.025	X	
SC5. Human resources	0.965	−0.017		X
SC6. Training	0.992	−0.007		X
C3. Operations	13.51	−1.170		X
SC7. Reverse logistic processes	0.981	0.081	X	
SC8. Procedures and protocols	1.000	−0.099		X
SC9. Waste management plans	1.008	0.017	X	
C4. Performance evaluation and improvement	13.68	0.080	X	
SC10. Internal audits	0.963	−0.008		X
SC11. Indicators	0.990	0.000	X	
SC12. Improvement actions	1.048	0.008	X	

In addition to identifying dispatchers and receivers criteria and sub-criteria, an impact-digraph was developed to analyze the interdependencies between each cluster. Figure 6a) the diagram for the criteria is observed, and in Fig. 6b) an example for the cluster "Planning" is shown. It is evident that "Planning" impacts the other criteria of the model at the criteria level. On the other hand, in the cluster of sub-criteria associated with "Planning," feedback relationships are observed between the sub-criteria "Environmental leadership," "Environmental policies, objectives and programs," and "legal aspects."

Finally, F-AHP and DEMATEL methods are combined using Eq. 15 to calculate the global and local weights of criteria and sub-criteria considering the uncertainty in the experts' judgments and the interdependence between criteria and sub-criteria. The final global and regional weights were shown in Table 5. The results show that the

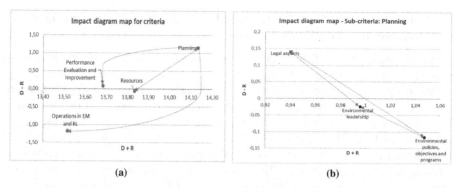

Fig. 6. Impact digraph maps for a) criteria and b) improvement

requirements incorporated in the model present few differences concerning the relative weights, so the design of strategies to improve environmental management and reverse logistics must consider the different criteria proposed.

Table 5. Local and global contributions of criteria and sub-criteria resulting from FAHP-DEMATEL integration

Cluster	GW	LW
C1. Planning	**0.181**	
SC1. Environmental leadership	0.037	0.206
SC2. Environmental policies, objectives, and programs	0.080	0.443
SC3. Legal aspects	0.064	0.352
C2. Resources	**0.267**	
SC4. Economic resources	0.078	0.291
SC5. Human resources	0.090	0.335
SC6. Training	0.100	0.374
C3. Operations	**0.264**	
SC7. Reverse logistic processes	0.056	0.211
SC8. Procedures and protocols	0.105	0.397
SC9. Waste management plans	0.103	0.392
C4. Performance evaluation and improvement	**0.287**	
SC10. Internal audits	0.087	0.303
SC11. Indicators	0.107	0.373
SC12. Improvement actions	0.093	0.324

4.3 Calculation of Performance Level and Identification of Improvement Opportunities via TOPSIS Application

In this last phase, the TOPSIS method was applied to rank the level of performance in environmental management and reverse logistics in 4 companies in the plastic industry to identify opportunities for improvement for each company. Initially, a set of evaluation indicators was designed for each of the sub-criteria of the model and then Eqs. 16–24 to generate the TOPSIS decision matrices, the normalized matrix R, the weighted and normalized TOPSIS decision matrix V, the separations of the positive and negative solution, and the closeness coefficient is calculated, which for this investigation was called Coefficient of Performance. Through the Performance coefficient, the companies were classified according to the preference order of CC_i (Very low performance: $0 \leq$ CCi ≤ 0.25 ∥ Low performance: $0.25 <$ CCi ≤ 0.5 ∥ Medium performance: $0.5 <$ CCi ≤ 0.75 ∥ High performance: $0.75 <$ CCi ≤ 1). Table 6 shows the closeness coefficient and the separation from Negative Ideal Solution (NIS) and Positive Ideal Solution (PIS).

Table 6. Ranking of plastic companies in performance evaluation of environmental management and reverse logistics using TOPSIS method

Company	CC_i	S_i^+	S_i^-	Rank	Level
PC2	0.773	0.080	0.096	1	High
PC1	0.547	0.044	0.148	2	Medium
PC3	0.265	0.138	0.050	3	Low
PC4	0.146	0.152	0.026	4	very low

The results show that company 2 was the one with the best performance in environmental management and reverse logistics (CCi = 77.3%), although with opportunities for improvement in internal audits. On the other hand, company one was classified with a medium performance level (CCi = 54.7%), with options for improvement in the availability of economic and human resources, staff training, and internal auditing processes. Finally, companies 3 and 4 obtained performance levels lower than 26.5%, which is why multifactorial improvement plans are required to increase performance in environmental management and reverse logistics, impacting sustainable development and the generation of economic and social value.

5 Conclusions and Future Work

This study presents an integrated approach F-AHP, DEMATEL, and TOPSIS to evaluate the performance in environmental management and reverse logistics in companies in the plastic sector. The Proposed methodology consisted of 4 phases: Design of the multicriteria model, application of the F-AHP and DEMATEL techniques to calculate the weights of the criteria and sub-criteria under conditions of uncertainty and interdependence, and finally, the use of the TOPSIS method to classify plastic companies and identify opportunities for improvement.

The results obtained show that the criteria incorporated in the model have relative weights with few differences between them, being "Performance evaluation and improvement" the most relevant, which implies the focus of continuous improvement in environmental management and reverse logistics. On the other hand, company two was identified as the best performance with a closeness coefficient of 77.7% with identified improvement opportunities for all the companies evaluated. The proposed approach allows managers to improve environmental management and reverse logistics performance from a comprehensive approach that considers the companies' technical, economic, and human capacities to generate minor environmental impacts and add value to customers and stakeholders [34].

Future studies will consider other sectors and the analysis of scenarios in other countries to compare the results. Besides, future works may include criteria associated with the interested parties as links of cooperation to improve environmental performance and reverse logistics. In addition, other research can enhance the performance of the methodology considering different techniques of MCDM such as DEA, VIKOR, and intuitionistic methods.

References

1. Arandes, J., Bilbao, J., Lopez, D.: Reciclado de residuos plásticos. Revista Iberoamericana de Polímeros 5(1), 28–45 (2004)
2. Nones, C.: Gestión y técnicas de reciclaje polimérico: Estudio del escenario actual, aplicaciones y nuevas tendencias. Universidad Politécnica de Cataluña (2019)
3. Jimenez, G., Hernandez, L., Hernandez, H., Cabas, L., Ferreira, J.: Evaluation of quality management for strategic decision making in companies in the plastic sector of the Colombian Caribbean region using the TQM diagnostic report and data analysis. In: Stephanidis, C. (ed.) HCI 2018. CCIS, vol. 852, pp. 273–281. Springer, Cham (2018). https://doi.org/10.1007/978-3-319-92285-0_38
4. Jimenez, G., Novoa, L., Ramos, L., Martinez, J., Alvarino, C.: Diagnosis of initial conditions for the implementation of the integrated management system in the companies of the land cargo transportation in the city of Barranquilla (Colombia). In: Stephanidis, C. (ed.) HCI 2018. CCIS, vol. 852, pp. 282–289. Springer, Cham (2018). https://doi.org/10.1007/978-3-319-92285-0_39
5. Jimenez, G., Zapata, E.: Metodologia integrada para el control estratégico y la mejora continua, basada en el Balanced Scorecard y el Sistema de Gestión de Calidad: aplicacion en una organizacion de servicios en Colombia. In: 51a Asamblea Anual del Consejo Latinoamericano de Escuelas de Administracion CLADEA 2016, Medellin, Colombia, pp. 1–20 (2016)
6. Jimenez, G.: Procedimientos para el mejoramiento de la calidad y la implantación de la Norma ISO 9001 aplicado al proceso de asesoramiento del Centro de Investigaciones y Desarrollo Empresarial y Regional en una Institucion de Educacion Superior basados en la gestión por procesos. In: Congreso de Gestion de la Calidad y Proteccion Ambiental GECPA 2014, Habana, Cuba, pp. 1–22 (2014)
7. Singh, N., Hui, D., Singh, R., Ahuja, I., Feo, L., Fraternali, F.: Recycling of plastic solid waste: a state of art review and future applications. Compos. B Eng. 115, 409–422 (2017)
8. Vinodh, S., Prasanna, M., Hari Prakash, N.: Integrated Fuzzy AHP–TOPSIS for selecting the best plastic recycling method: a case study. Appl. Math. Model. 38(19–20), 4662–4672 (2014)

9. Fidelis, R., Ferreira, M., Colmenero, J.: Selecting a location to install a plastic processing center: network of recycling cooperatives. Resour. Conserv. Recycl. **103**, 1–8 (2015)

10. García, C., Herva, M., Roca, E.: A decision support system based on fuzzy reasoning and AHP–FPP for the ecodesign of products: application to footwear as case study. Appl. Soft Comput. **26**, 224–234 (2015)

11. Cheraghalipour, A., Farsad, S.: A bi-objective sustainable supplier selection and order allocation considering quantity discounts under disruption risks: a case study in plastic industry. Comput. Ind. Eng. **118**, 237–250 (2018)

12. ISO 14001:2015 Environmental management systems—requirements with guidance for use (2015)

13. Jayant, A., Gupta, P., Garg, S.K.: Reverse logistics network design for spent batteries: a simulation study. Int. J. Logist. Syst. Manag. **18**(3), 343–365 (2014)

14. Jimenez, G., Santos, G., Félix, M., Hernández, H., Rondón, C.: Good practices and trends in reverse logistics in the plastic products manufacturing industry. Procedia Manuf. **41**, 367–374 (2019)

15. Ravi, V., Shankar, R., Tiwari, M.K.: Selection of a reverse logistics project for end-of-life computers: ANP and goal programming approach. Int. J. Prod. Res. **46**(17), 4849–4870 (2008). https://doi.org/10.1080/00207540601115989

16. Wadhwa, S., Madaan, J., Chan, F.T.S.: Flexible decision modeling of reverse logistics system: a value-adding MCDM approach for an alternative selection. Robot. Comput. Integr. Manuf. **25**(2), 460–469 (2009). https://doi.org/10.1016/j.rcim.2008.01.006

17. Sasikumar, P., Haq, A.N.: A multicriteria decision-making methodology for the selection of reverse logistics operating modes. Int. J. Enterp. Netw.Manag. **4**(1), 68–79 (2010). https://doi.org/10.1504/IJENM.2010.034477

18. Uygun, Ö., Dede, A.: Performance evaluation of green supply chain management using integrated fuzzy multicriteria decision-making techniques. Comput. Ind. Eng. **102**, 502–511 (2016). https://doi.org/10.1016/j.cie.2016.02.020

19. Tosarkani, B.M., Amin, S.H.: A multiobjective model to configure an electronic reverse logistics network and third-party selection. J. Clean. Prod. **198**, 662–682 (2018). https://doi.org/10.1016/j.jclepro.2018.07.056

20. Tian, G., et al.: Selection of take-back pattern of vehicle reverse logistics in china via grey-DEMATEL and fuzzy-VIKOR combined method. J. Clean. Prod. **220**, 1088–1100 (2019). https://doi.org/10.1016/j.jclepro.2019.01.086

21. Asees Awan, M., Ali, Y.: Sustainable modeling in reverse logistics strategies using fuzzy MCDM: case of China Pakistan economic corridor. Manag. Environ. Qual. Int. J. **30**(5), 1132–1151 (2019). https://doi.org/10.1108/MEQ-01-2019-0024

22. Faris, H.M., Maan, H.Y.: Evaluation of green supply chain management practices under uncertainty environment: a case study in the company for batteries industry. Paper presented at the IOP Conference Series: Materials Science and Engineering, vol. 881, no. 1 (2020). https://doi.org/10.1088/1757-899X/881/1/012085. www.scopus.com

23. Jayant, A., Singh, S., Walke, T.: A robust hybrid multicriteria decision-making approach for selection of third-party reverse logistics service provider (2021). https://doi.org/10.1007/978-981-15-5519-0_32. www.scopus.com

24. Wang, C., Dang, T., Nguyen, N.: Outsourcing reverse logistics for e-commerce retailers: a two-stage fuzzy optimization approach. Axioms **10**(1) (2021). https://doi.org/10.3390/axioms10010034

25. Ortiz-Barrios, M.A., Kucukaltan, B., Carvajal-Tinoco, D., Neira-Rodado, D., Jiménez, G.: Strategic hybrid approach for selecting suppliers of high-density polyethylene. J. Multi-Crit. Decis. Anal. **24**, 1–21 (2017). https://doi.org/10.1002/mcda.1617

26. Jimenez-Delgado, G., et al.: Improving the performance in occupational health and safety management in the electric sector: an integrated methodology using fuzzy multicriteria approach. In: Duffy, V.G. (ed.) HCII 2020. LNCS, vol. 12199, pp. 130–158. Springer, Cham (2020). https://doi.org/10.1007/978-3-030-49907-5_10

27. Hernandez, L., Jimenez, G.: Characterization of the current conditions of the ITSA data centers according to standards of the green data centers friendly to the environment. In: Silhavy, R., Senkerik, R., Kominkova Oplatkova, Z., Prokopova, Z., Silhavy, P. (eds.) CSOC 2017. AISC, vol. 574, pp. 329–340. Springer, Cham (2017). https://doi.org/10.1007/978-3-319-57264-2_34

28. Izquierdo, N.V., et al.: Methodology of application of diffuse mathematics to performance evaluation. Int. J. Contr. Theory Appl. (2016). ISSN 0974-5572

29. Jimenez-Delgado, G., Balmaceda-Castro, N., Hernández-Palma, H., de la Hoz-Franco, E., García-Guiliany, J., Martinez-Ventura, J.: An integrated approach of multiple correspondences analysis (MCA) and fuzzy AHP method for occupational health and safety performance evaluation in the land cargo transportation. In: Duffy, V.G. (ed.) HCII 2019. LNCS, vol. 11581, pp. 433–457. Springer, Cham (2019). https://doi.org/10.1007/978-3-030-22216-1_32

30. Halbach, P., et al.: Investigating key factors for social network evolution and opinion dynamics in an agent-based simulation. In: Duffy, V.G. (ed.) HCII 2020. LNCS, vol. 12199, pp. 20–39. Springer, Cham (2020). https://doi.org/10.1007/978-3-030-49907-5_2

31. Su, C.M., Horng, D.J., Tseng, M.L., Chiu, A.S., Wu, K.J., Chen, H.P.: Improving sustainable supply chain management using a novel hierarchical grey-DEMATEL approach. J. Cleaner Prod. **134**, 469–481 (2016)

32. Wei, P.L., Huang, J.H., Tzeng, G.H., Wu, S.I.: Causal modeling of web-advertising effects by improving SEM based on DEMATEL technique. Int. J. Inf. Technol. Decis. Making **9**(05), 799–829 (2010)

33. Jiménez-Delgado, G., Santos, G., Félix, M.J., Teixeira, P., Sá, J.C.: A combined AHP-TOPSIS approach for evaluating the process of innovation and integration of management systems in the logistic sector. In: Stephanidis, C., et al. (eds.) HCII 2020. LNCS, vol. 12427, pp. 535–559. Springer, Cham (2020). https://doi.org/10.1007/978-3-030-60152-2_40

34. Azevedo, J., et al.: Improvement of production line in the automotive industry through lean philosophy. Procedia Manuf. **41**, 1023–1030 (2019). https://doi.org/10.1016/j.promfg.2019. 10.029

Use of Simulation Technology in Transportation Training: A Systematic Literature Review

Seanan C. Lee[1]([⊠]) and Vincent G. Duffy[2]

[1] College of Engineering, Purdue University, West Lafayette, IN 47906, USA
seananlee@purdue.edu
[2] School of Industrial Engineering, Purdue University, West Lafayette, IN 47906, USA
duffy@purdue.edu

Abstract. Simulators are widely used in training aircrew and seafarers as they provide a safer and more affordable alternative to training in an operational environment. In this study, a systematic literature review is conducted to review their usage in air, sea, rail, and road transportation, though the information available on rail simulation is extremely limited, despite it being a vital means to transport passengers and cargo globally. With tools such as VOSviewer and CiteSpace, it is possible to identify articles with the most impact and highest relevance to simulation training. Studies show that training effectiveness is affected by both the equipment and instruction quality. Fidelity – a simulator's ability to replicate the real world – of the equipment determines what levels of training can be achieved, and its ability to enable the suspension of disbelief directly contribute to the students' success. Instructors must also facilitate positive training transfer by attaining the best performance possible from the student and provide them with scenarios representative of actual conditions. Effective crew training and proper human-computer interface design are critical for accident mitigation, as the increased system complexity can take away the crew's attention and overload training needs. Despite their popularity in air and sea transportation, simulator training for land transportation is extremely underutilized. Cost and fidelity are the primary hurdles it must overcome to achieve popularity for rail and road transportation, and further studies are required to determine its effectiveness in reducing the accident rate of novice drivers.

Keywords: Simulation training · Simulator fidelity · Knowledge transfer · Training relevancy · Simulation reliability · Training methodology · Interface design

1 Introduction

Simulation is widely used in transportation for crew certification as it can effectively replicate conditions that are dangerous or impractical to practice in an operational environment. Flight simulators were integrated into aviation training since the second world war, where rudimentary Link Trainers were used extensively by the United States Army Air Forces to reduce training accident rates [1]. In the 1950s, maritime education and

© Springer Nature Switzerland AG 2021
C. Stephanidis et al. (Eds.): HCII 2021, LNCS 13097, pp. 546–561, 2021.
https://doi.org/10.1007/978-3-030-90966-6_37

training institutions adopted simulation to train seafarers in navigation, and its uses today include bridge operation, engine control, and damage control [2]. The use of simulators in the two industries is governed internationally by Annex 1 to the Convention on International Civil Aviation and the International Convention on Standards of Training, Certification, and Watchkeeping for Seafarers respectively. High-fidelity simulations have superseded parts of the costly on-site training in air and sea transportation, but they cannot completely replace experiences gained by operating in real-world conditions [2].

The use of simulation in air and marine transportations is more prevalent than its usage in rail and road transportations. In this study, an attempt will be made to compare the industry environment and determine the cause behind the slow adoption of simulation technology by land transportation. This study will also review simulators and simulation training used in different modes of transportation and how their use can be expanded beyond crew certification. The problem of human-computer interaction arises with technology adoption as the increased system complexity can take away the crew's attention and overload training needs. By emphasizing positive training transfer through effective simulator training, transportation safety can be improved in an increasingly interconnected world [1].

2 Purpose of Study

The purpose of this study is to determine what factors impact simulator training effectiveness in transportation and discover the reason behind its slow adoption for land transportation through a systematic literature review. The increased system complexity in modern transportation calls for a holistic review of existing training methodologies and examining whether the use of simulator training can be extended without sacrificing crew performance. Tools such as Vicinitas, VOSviewer, CiteSpace, and MAXQDA will be used to analyze existing literature and to conclude whether there is sufficient data available to determine the effectiveness of simulator training currently available to transportation professionals.

3 Research Methodology

3.1 Data Collection

The data required for this study is primarily gathered from two databases: Scopus and Web of Science. Two databases are used as they survey different journals, and the larger collection of sources is beneficial for gaining a better understanding of the topic. Both sources contain information on the article's title, authors, year, source, citation, and abstract, and that information will be used for co-citation, co-authorship, cluster, and content analyses. searching for "simulator training", together with "flight", "ship", "road", or "rail" yielded 3,754 and 1,638 results in Scopus and Web of Science respectively. However, it is worth mentioning that not all the results are directly relevant to this study, as computer simulations are also used during the development of land vehicles, watercraft, and aircraft.

3.2 Trend Analysis

Information from Scopus and Web of Science are used to study how the topic of transportation simulator training evolved over the years. The entries in Scopus are from 1958–2021, and the entries from Web of Science are from 1966–2021. The data from 2021 is excluded as the year has not ended at the time of writing for this paper, and the entries before 1990 are not listed due to their age and possible obsolescence.

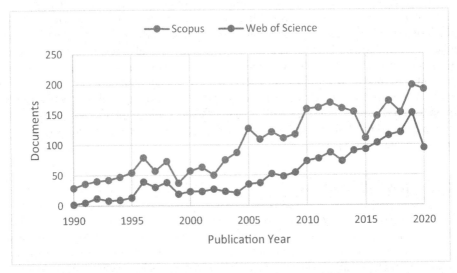

Fig. 1. Trend analysis from Scopus and Web of Science

Figure 1 shows an upward trend for research in transportation simulator training between 1990 and 2020. The upward trend in research corresponds with the increasing popularity of simulator training in the last 30 years. The maximum number of entries can be found in 2019 for both databases, with 198 entries in Scopus and 152 entries in Web of Science. It is worth noting that the research interest in the field increased between 1996–1998 before the notable increase in the early 2000s. Additionally, the results from Scopus decreased dramatically in 2015, whereas those from Web of Science continued its increasing trend. The decreased trend in 2020 can potentially be attributed to the COVID-19 pandemic, as research activities were limited due to public health concerns and the associated downturn in passenger transportation. Simulator training in transportation is an emerging field as the number of articles published per year on the topic increased by 72% between 2015 and 2019. Additionally, the field experienced significant growth in the last 30 years as the number of publications per year increased tenfold between 1990 and 2019.

Figure 2 identifies the authors' organizational affiliation using the data from Scopus. From that information, it is concluded that flight simulation is the dominant form of transportation simulation training, as five of the top ten author affiliations – NASA Ames Research Center, Boeing Corporation, Wright-Patterson Air Force Base, German Aerospace Center, and Cranfield University – are organizations specializing in aerospace

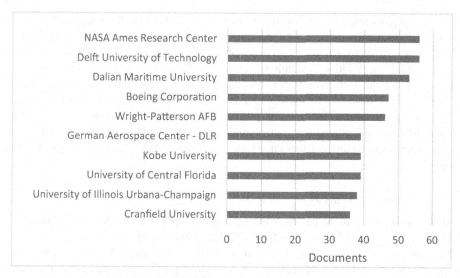

Fig. 2. Affiliation analysis from Scopus

research. For the remaining five organizations, one is focused on maritime affairs – Dalian Maritime University – and the other four are comprehensive universities with a variety of research interests.

Table 1. Source titles analysis from Web of Science

Source titles	Record count	% of 1,638
Aviation Space and Environmental Medicine	44	2.686
Transportation Research Part F: Traffic Psychology and Behaviour	37	2.259
Accident Analysis and Prevention	33	2.015
Human Factors	32	1.954
IEEE International Conference on Systems Man and Cybernetics Conference Proceedings	27	1.648
Proceedings of the Society of Photo-Optical Instrumentation Engineers (SPIE)	24	1.465
International Journal of Aviation Psychology	22	1.343
Aerospace Medicine and Human Performance	20	1.221
TransNav: International Journal on Marine Navigation and Safety of Sea Transportation	19	1.160
Aeronautical Journal	17	1.038

The information from Web of Science shown in Table 1 further supports the claim that flight simulation is the most conducted form of transportation simulation training. Four of the top ten source titles – Aviation Space and Environmental Medicine, International Journal of Aviation Psychology, Aerospace Medicine and Human Performance, and Aeronautical Journal – are aerospace publications. TransNav and Transportation Research Part F discusses issues related to marine and land-based transportation respectively, and the remaining four journals pertain to human factors in various fields. The top source titles further indicate that transportation simulation training is an interdisciplinary issue that requires human factors knowledge, technical expertise, as well as operational knowledge.

3.3 Engagement Analysis

Analyzing tweets with the hashtag #FlightSimulator on Twitter via Vicinitas shows that 398 users have made 598 posts with this hashtag between April 5 and April 15, 2021. The 598 posts received 1,600 likes and retweets, and of those 598 posts, 285 were original tweets, 263 were retweets, and the remaining 20 were replies. From the word cloud in Fig. 3, it is evident that many of them are referring to titles in the Microsoft flight simulator series, with limited references on full-motion simulators used in aircrew certification. That can potentially be attributed to the airline hiring slow-down due to the COVID-19 pandemic and the reduced need for simulator training. Another use for simulator training outside of transportation that could gain popularity in the public domain is in the classroom. The same amateur flight simulators being tweeted about can also now be found in some primary and secondary classrooms as means to solidify mathematics and science lessons. Grants from the national science foundation support the use of low-level simulators to encourage the development of programs for students and offer them a hands-on introduction to careers in science, technology, engineering, and mathematics [3].

Fig. 3. Twitter word cloud from Vicinitas

4   Results

4.1 Co-citation and Co-authorship Analyses

A co-citation analysis was used to determine how the various sources relate to one another. Papers being cited and co-cited often suggests that they might be of higher importance, and they are grouped into clusters to indicate their connection. The information from web of science was used to generate a co-citation map of relevant works. The 1,638 documents found on Web of Science have a total of 13,825 cited references. Figure 4 shows the 17 most cited articles, which are cited by at least 12 other publications.

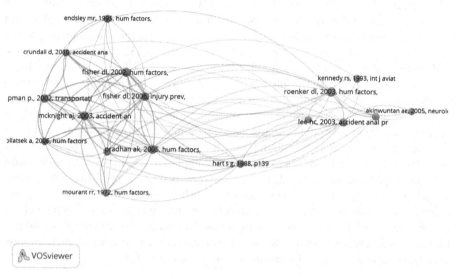

Fig. 4. Co-citation Analysis from VOSviewer

Co-authorship analysis looks at the involvement of authors in different articles, and they can be used to identify leading authors and to assess collaboration trends in the field. The 3,754 articles found in Scopus were analyzed, and only authors with more than six documents and six citations were shown. Of the 7,959 authors, 115 meet the requirements, and 43 of them formed a connected network shown below in Fig. 5.

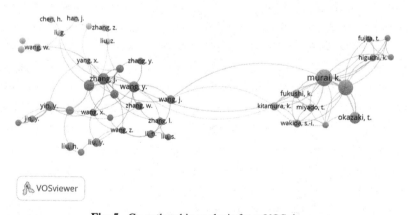

Fig. 5. Co-authorship analysis from VOSviewer

4.2 Cluster Analysis

Information was extracted from the documents' titles and abstracts to create a word cluster representing key terms used and how they interconnect. A large circle represents a word that appears frequently in the documents, and the lines indicate how they are connected across documents. Due to Scopus' limitation on exporting information in abstracts, only information from Web of Science is used. To emphasize the most important keywords, the cutoff for the cluster in Fig. 6 was set to a minimum of 150 occurrences for each term, which encompasses 23 of the 34,332 terms found in the title and abstract of 1,638 papers. Those keywords can be correlated with the documents from co-citation and co-authorship analyses to determine whether they are relevant to the study.

Table 2 shows the five most relevant keywords with regards to transportation simulator training while overlooking words with similar meanings (i.e., simulator and flight simulator) or are commonly found in abstracts of all topics (i.e., participant). The analyses show that "system" and "performance" are important considerations for simulator training as they ranked third and sixth in occurrences respectively. This makes sense, considering the importance of a systematic approach when designing training programs to maximize knowledge transfer. Additionally, the performance of the simulators must facilitate those efforts. Simulator training in marine and air traffic ranking second and fourth respectively, and "driver" is also identified as the keyword with high relevance, suggesting simulation in road transportation is an emerging field.

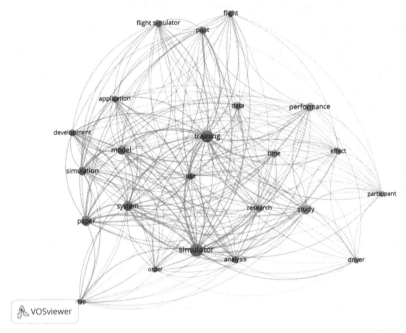

Fig. 6. Cluster analysis from VOSviewer

Table 2. Most relevant keywords from VOSviewer

Keyword	Occurrences	Relevance (%)
Driver	248	3.05
Ship	231	1.91
Simulator	1109	1.76
Pilot	359	1.44
Training	959	1.23

4.3 Citation Burst

The search results from Web of Science were analyzed in CiteSpace to identify articles that caused a surge of citations by attracting interest from the human-computer inter-action community. The search results are from the years 1966 to 2021, but the earliest article found with a citation burst is from 1996. Co-citation and co-authorship analyses identified one high-impact source – Fisher et al. 2006 – that brings valuable insight into simulation training for novice drivers. Another high-impact article – Casutt et al. 2014 – was identified by the citation burst, and it pertains to the driving performance of older motorists. Additional cited references are selected via a manual review of lexical search results from Scopus and Web of Science, with web search results supplementing them when necessary (Fig. 7).

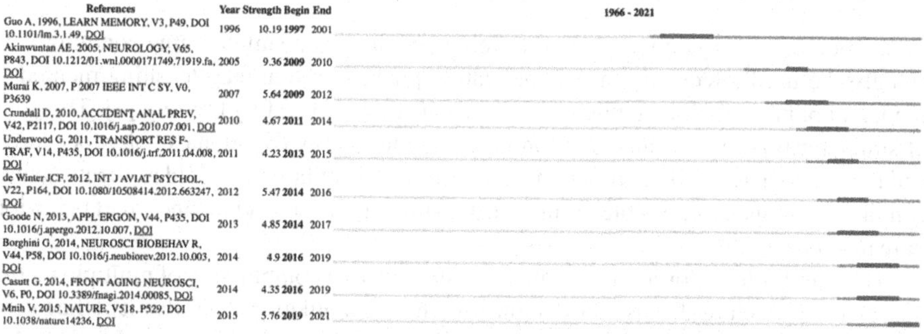

Fig. 7. Top ten references with the strongest citation bursts from CiteSpace

4.4 Content Analysis

MAXQDA is used to create a word cloud for all the articles referenced, which are a subset of the results from the co-citation analysis, co-authorship analysis, citation burst, and lexical search. The word cloud in Fig. 8 contains 100 keywords that are important for understanding the use of simulator training across different modes of transportation. Keywords from the word cloud and cluster analysis such as "initial training", "assessment", and "certification" represent the terms used in lexical searches to identify additional sources not represented in co-citation analysis, co-authorship analysis, and citation burst.

Fig. 8. Word cloud from MAXQDA

5   Discussion

Simulation can be used in structured training activities that simulate line conditions. It can also be used effectively in the application phase in a four-step teaching method – preparation, presentation, application, and evaluation – for safety training [4]. The goal of simulator training in transportation is similar but places its emphasis on procedures and rules associated with their operating conditions. Simulations should replicate actual conditions as much as possible, as unrealistic simulation can lead to "incorrect behavior in real contexts" [5].

Training for transportation operations often utilizes a combination of multiple methods, including lecture-discussion, demonstration, and simulation. The advent of the internet allows for online delivery of some content but diminishes the interaction between the student and the instructor. Lecture-discussion and online training are effective ways to deliver the required procedural and systems knowledge to the student, but their one-way nature limits the transfer of operational knowledge [4]. Demonstration and simulation allow the students to observe and gain hands-on experience, and simulation has the additional advantage of allowing situational training that deviates significantly from normal operations [5].

5.1   Types of Simulators Used in Transportation Training

There are three categories of simulators available for aircrew training: full flight simulators, flight training devices, and aviation training devices. The three differ in cost, performance, and what Levels of training can be accomplished in them. Full flight simulators are the most sophisticated of them all, and they incorporate motion to enhance the training experience. They range from Level A to D, with Level A being the least sophisticated and Level D being virtually indistinguishable from an actual aircraft [6]. Type ratings – additional authorization required for flying large aircraft – can be completed in their entirety in Level C or D simulators, greatly reducing the cost and risk associated with initial training [7].

Flight training devices are stationary devices that are more affordable, and they range between Levels 1 and 7. The higher the number, the more they resemble an actual aircraft. Levels 4 through 7 are the only ones that can be certified after 2008, with Levels 1 through 3 replaced by aviation training devices [8]. Levels 4 through 6 provide training for airplane operations, and Level 7 is used exclusively for helicopter training. Level 4 flight training devices are part-task training that does not require a control yoke, Level 5 represents a class of airplane, and Level 6 can provide model-specific training.

Unlike the other two categories, aviation training devices – both basic and advanced – are not intended for training in visual conditions as it lacks the sophisticated visual component used to enhance fidelity, even though some manufactures incorporate motion into their offerings [6]. The different devices are used in various combinations within training organizations to maximize knowledge transfer and training capacity [9].

Different simulator fidelity Levels can be used in conjunction with one another to facilitate effective and affordable training of seafarers. Low-cost, standalone workstation simulators can be used for asynchronous refresher training, and networked workstation simulators allow for interactions between trainees under instruction supervision. Full mission simulators maximize realism by containing hardware specific to the ship's class, and it is used for advanced training and crew certification [10]. On the other hand, most land-based transportation simulators are less sophisticated and typically do not incorporate motion even though kinesthetic feedback plays a significant role, and incorporating them improves training relevancy [11].

5.2 Simulation Training in Air Transportation

Flight simulation is by far the most prevalent form of transportation simulator training, and technology has improved greatly since the days of the Link Trainer. Fidelity is a continued concern in flight simulation, especially for visual maneuvers and primary training. It is found that pilots respond "more rapidly, with more authority, and in a more precise manner" in full flight simulators where there are visual and somatosensory cues. Flight training devices and aviation training devices lack motion cues and the patterns of control response observed within it deviate from those employed in flight [12]. The elevated cost associated with full flight simulators limits their use to large training organizations, with most primary flight training done in small aircraft or training devices.

Instructors must facilitate positive training transfer, as this will contribute significantly to training outcomes. Following the crash of American Airlines Flight 587 in 2001, investigators learned that the flight crew received improper training and the simulator had significantly different control responses compared with the aircraft. These two factors led to the First Officer over-controlling the aircraft, leading to "surprise and confusion" [13].

Simulator instructors must "obtain the highest performance possible from the student for a task while optimizing the time in the simulator period to do so", even when the students vary in "attitude, hands-on skill level, and cognitive ability" [1]. Training should replicate real-world operating conditions in a safe environment where mistakes become learning experiences and should be used to develop crew resource management techniques. One way to effectively prepare students for real-world conditions is to conduct Line-Oriented Flight Training after the students have achieved a degree of competence in aircraft handling. Line-Oriented Flight Training shifts the focus from flying the aircraft to simulating flights representative of line operations to develop communication, management, and leadership skills [14]. It emphasizes non-pre-briefed abnormal situations, in contrast with a standard training session where pre-briefs will cover the flight's profile [1]. Systematic training that engages the student will yield the best outcome when combined with a quality instructional program.

5.3 Simulation Training in Sea Transportation

The two primary uses for simulation in the maritime industry are bridge simulators and engine room simulators. Bridge simulators are used to train deck officers responsible for navigating the ship, and engine room simulators are used to train engineering officers responsible for the ship's propulsion plants. Both instructors and assessors require additional knowledge to ensure training uniformity between different institutions. Cultural backgrounds and different interpretations of the model course guidelines from the international maritime organization can affect training outcomes. Instructors must have training awareness, training skills, and managerial skills & aptitudes to support positive instructor-student knowledge transfer [15]. Complete ships can be simulated by connecting bridge and engine room simulators, and they have been used to train new seafarers and conduct experimental training on the energy-efficient operation of vessels [16].

The U.S. Navy has been using USS *Trayer*, a 210-foot-long replica of an Arleigh Burke-class destroyer, to train recruits at Naval Station Great Lakes since 2007. It uses virtual reality and special effects to form an immersive training environment for Navy recruits. Built-in measures allow for realistic training in flooded compartments and with fire with limited risk factors. The simulator also facilitates 12-h exercises on ship handling, combat, and damage control [17]. More effective training can be delivered through simulators for both civil and military applications, as they allow for practicing potentially dangerous procedures in a controlled environment, lower training cost, and enable the rapid repetition of events.

5.4 Simulation Training in Rail Transportation

Traditional railroad training emphasized on-the-job learning with an assigned tutor driver and repeated route exposure. While this model is proven to be a way to cultivate expertise in train driving, it is "expensive, consumes resources, takes time to mature, and limits the trainee to the knowledge of the tutor" [11]. The long training process has been cited as a critical constraint for expanding rail capacity, and simulators are currently an extremely underutilized and unproven tool in the railroad industry. Beyond increasing training throughput, as simulator sessions do not require network access, they can also facilitate training on hazardous scenarios without real-world consequences [18].

Three factors significantly influence end-user evaluation for simulator utility: reality, relevancy, and reliability. While replicating the driver-cab accurately and having an accurate visual environment is important, inaccurate simulation models that fail to replicate how the train handles and feels will cause the users to reject simulation as a valid training aid. Similarly, if simulator training cannot deliver relevant content for actual routes, the training is not effective, as fictional routes can deliver a false impression of security [11]. Psychological unreliability stems from the perceived lack of motivation to perform in a controlled environment, and it can be alleviated by adopting an integrated training model where simulators are used in conjunction with actual equipment on the tracks.

5.5 Simulation Training in Road Transportation

Driving simulator training has been observed to increase performance on the road for healthy older drivers and people with disabilities. Many driving errors are caused by age-related cognitive performance reduction, as the driver is called upon to process a large volume of information simultaneously with tasks like "traffic observation, speed control, scanning for hazard events, traffic rules, [and] car handling". Overall driving performance in the elderly increased by 7% after ten simulator training sessions, and their overall cognitive performance improved as well [19]. For people with disabilities learning to drive with adaptive devices, simulators provide a "safe environment to evaluate driving skills and to safely practice within hazardous situations that would be difficult to practice on the road". It also provides a safe environment to experiment with various forms of driving aids, and some were able to complete their road test without additional on-road training [20].

However, the effectiveness of simulator training for novice drivers was not consistent across five studies [21]. Only one study reported a significantly lower infractions rate in the experimental group compared to the control group [22], and the number of training sessions made little impact on driving performance. The remaining four studies reported no significant difference between the rate of road crashes between the two groups [21]. The lack of evidence supporting or refuting the efficacy of simulator driving training programs calls for additional studies in a more uniformly controlled environment.

5.6 Human-Computer Interaction in Simulators

Effective crew training and proper human-computer interface design are critical for accident mitigation. Intuitive and simple interfaces facilitate decisive action when the crews are under great psychological stress, and automation mismanagement due to improper training has been cited as a probable cause in multiple accidents.

The crash of Asiana Airlines Flight 214 in 2013 highlights pilots' reliance on automation and how it "reduces monitoring and decreases the likelihood that a human operator will detect signs of anomalous or unexpected system behavior involving the processes under automatic control." The pilots inadvertently deactivated automatic airspeed control provided by the auto-throttle due to their "faulty mental model" of the airplane's flight control modes. They were unaware of the flight control system's state until seven seconds before impact, and the accident report cited system complexities and inadequate training as probable causes [23]. The use of transportation simulators could have provided the crew a venue to familiarize themselves with increasingly complex systems and automation logic. The pilots in Asiana Airlines Flight 214 were unaware of their mistake due to their inadequate automation management training and the lack of computerized alert. A context-dependent low energy alerting system can provide pilots with additional aural and visual warnings to potentially unsafe conditions, but as of 2021, such systems are still only in the development phase [24].

On the other hand, the collision between USS *John S. McCain* (DDG-56) and MV *Alnic MC* in 2017 showcases how crew training cannot mitigate the dangers posed by improperly designed interfaces. The Integrated Bridge and Navigation System on the *McCain*, an Arleigh Burke-class destroyer, had the throttles actuated via touch screens rather than mechanical controls, taking away the operators' ability to confirm its settings either visually or by touch [25]. Following the accident, the United States Navy began installing physical throttles on ships previously only fitted with touch-screen throttle control. The Naval Sea Systems Command also began studying the impact of variance in bridge and systems designs within ship classes, as standardized designs facilitate greater training commonality and reduce confusion among sailors [26]. Usability testing conducted within simulators can identify these kinds of shortcomings in the proposed user interface's ability to support the users in completing their tasks. Information integration onto multi-function displays enables a significant reduction in crew workload, but the interface must enable high learnability, high efficiency, high memorability, high satisfaction, and low errors [27].

6 Conclusion

Simulations are widely used for aircrew and seafarer training, but their use in rail and road transportation training is limited. Through surveying different sources, it is believed that cost and efficacy are the two major barriers preventing widespread simulator adoption. Stationary training devices are available at lower prices than full-motion simulators, but their utility is limited for land transportation, as kinesthetic feedback plays a larger role [11]. The on-the-job training model currently in use with rail and road transportations disincentivizes simulation training adoption as its effectiveness is not yet proven with the simulators currently in use. Full flight simulators and full mission simulators have documented success in air and sea transportation, but they are expensive to acquire and operate. The high cost further disincentivizes early adopters in rail and road transportation as their investment might make little impact on training quality. Additionally, the effectiveness of simulator training for novice drivers is not uniform across studies, with results ranging from significant improvement to practically no change [22].

The use of simulator training is well documented in air and sea transportation as their operations are more procedure-oriented and they operate under relatively consistent conditions. However, fidelity continues to be a concern even for high-end full flight simulators and full mission simulators. More cost-efficient training can be accomplished by using simulators with various fidelity levels, but they must meet the requirements for the work tasks [2]. Proper instructor-student knowledge transfer and realistic scenarios are prerequisites for effective simulator training [1]. Increasingly complex systems and automation logic can take away the crew's ability to detect unexpected system behavior; on the other hand, intuitive and simple human-computer interfaces can reduce the need for extensive automation management training and facilitate reductions in crew workload [27]. Even though simulator technology has come a long way from the 1930s Link Trainer, simulation training is still not infallible. Simulation training does not dismiss the need to gain operational experience in actual conditions, and the two should be used in conjunction to maximize training effectiveness.

7 Future Work

The effectiveness of simulator training for novice drivers is unclear right now as different studies have made claims that are contradictory with one another. Some have concluded that driving performance improves greatly, and others have observed very little behavior change [21]. The five experimental, quasi-experimental, and cohort studies surveyed by Martín-Delosreyes in 2019 are all conducted under different conditions, and there is a need for a large-scale, uniform study to determine if simulator training should be incorporated into driver education. It is believed that with proper equipment at an affordable price and well-trained instructors, it is possible to increase simulation use in rail and road transportation.

Primary and secondary classrooms are another location where simulators could gain popularity. Its use for reinforcing concepts in mathematics and science among students is an emerging field studied with support from the National Science Foundation. Simulators can motivate students to pursue a career in science, technology, engineering, or mathematics by engaging them in hands-on experiences otherwise cost-prohibitive to many students [3].

References

1. Myers, P., Starr, A.W., Mullins, K.: Flight simulator fidelity, training transfer, and the role of instructors in optimizing learning. Int. J. Aviat. Aeronaut. Aerospace. **5**, 1–27 (2018)
2. Sellberg, C.: Simulators in bridge operations training and assessment: a systematic review and qualitative synthesis. WMU J. Maritime Affairs **16**(2), 247–263 (2016). https://doi.org/10.1007/s13437-016-0114-8
3. Affane Aji, C.: NSF award # 1614249 - fly high your math and science skills. https://nsf.gov/awardsearch/showAward?AWD_ID=1614249
4. Goetsch, D.L.: Safety and health training. In: Occupational Safety and Health for Technologists, Engineers, and Managers, pp. 259–287. Pearson, New York, NY (2019)
5. Brauer, R.L.: Procedures, rules, and training. In: Safety and Health for Engineers, pp. 449–460. Wiley, Hoboken, NJ (2016)
6. Marsh, A.K.: ABCs of simulators - a tangled web we weave. https://www.aopa.org/news-and-media/all-news/2011/may/01/abcs-of-simulators

7. Federal Aviation Administration: Use of a flight simulator and flight training device. 14 C.F.R. § 61.64. (2021)
8. Federal Aviation Administration: FAA approval of basic aviation training devices (BATD) and advanced aviation training devices (AATD). Advisory Circular, pp. 61–136. (2008)
9. Templeton, M.: Purdue aviation adds full flight simulator to suite of training devices. https://polytechnic.purdue.edu/newsroom/purdue-aviation-adds-full-flight-simulator-suite-of-training-devices
10. Wärtsilä Voyage Solutions: Engine Room Simulator. https://cdn.wartsila.com/docs/default-source/product-files/optimise/simulation-and-training/engine-room-simulator-brochure.pdf?sfvrsn=3477cf44_6
11. Naweed, A.: Simulator integration in the rail industry: the Robocop problem. Proc. Instit. Mech. Eng. Part F J. Rail Rapid Trans. **227**(5), 407–418 (2013)
12. Caro, P.W.: The relationship between flight simulator motion and training requirements. Human Factors J. Human Factors Ergon. Soc. **21**(4), 493–501 (1979)
13. National Transportation Safety Board: In-Flight Separation of Vertical Stabilizer, American Airlines Flight 587, Airbus Industrie A300–605R, N14053, Belle Harbor, New York, November 12, 2001 U.S. Government Washington, DC (2004)
14. SKYbrary: Line oriented flight training. https://www.skybrary.aero/index.php/Line_Oriented_Flight_Training
15. Nazir, S., Jungefeldt, S., Sharma, A.: Maritime simulator training across Europe: a comparative study. WMU J. Maritime Affair **18**(1), 197–224 (2018). https://doi.org/10.1007/s13437-018-0157-0
16. Jensen, S., Lützen, M., Mikkelsen, L.L., Rasmussen, H.B., Pedersen, P.V., Schamby, P.: Energy-efficient operational training in a ship bridge simulator. J. Clean. Prod. **171**, 175–183 (2018)
17. Lawlor, M.: Simulation makes the virtual a reality. https://www.afcea.org/content/simulation-makes-virtual-reality
18. Tichon, J.G.: The use of expert knowledge in the development of simulations for train driver training. Cogn. Technol. Work **9**(4), 177–187 (2006)
19. Casutt, G., Theill, N., Martin, M., Keller, M., Jäncke, L.: The drive-wise project: driving simulator training increases real driving performance in healthy older drivers. Front. Aging Neurosci. **6**, 1–14 (2014)
20. Couture, M., Vincent, C., Gélinas, I., Routhier, F.: Advantages of training with an adaptive driving device on a driving simulator compared to training only on the road. Disabil. Rehabil. Assist. Technol. **16**(3), 309–316 (2019)
21. Martín-delosReyes, L.M., et al.: Efficacy of training with driving simulators in improving safety in young novice or learner drivers: a systematic review. Transport. Res. F Traffic Psychol. Behav. **62**, 58–65 (2019)
22. Fisher, D.L., Pollatsek, A.P., Pradhan, A.: Can novice drivers be trained to scan for information that will reduce their likelihood of a crash? Injury. Prevent. **12**(Suppl. 1), i25–i29 (2006)
23. National Transportation Safety Board: Descent Below Visual Glidepath and Impact with Seawall, Asiana Airlines Flight 214, Boeing 777–200ER, HL7742, San Francisco, California, July 6, 2013 U.S. Government Washington, DC (2014)
24. Avionics Systems Harmonization Working Group: Low Energy Alerting - Proposed Requirements for Context-Dependent Low Energy Alerting Systems for Airplanes Engaged in Commercial Operations U.S. Government Washington, DC (2021)
25. National Transportation Safety Board: Collision Between US Navy Destroyer John S. McCain and Tanker Alnic MC, Singapore Strait, 5 Miles Northeast of Horsburgh Lighthouse, August 21, 2017. U.S. Government, Washington, DC (2019)

26. Eckstein, M.: Navy reverting DDGs back to physical throttles, after fleet rejects touch-screen controls. https://news.usni.org/2019/08/09/navy-reverting-ddgs-back-to-physical-thr ottles-after-fleet-rejects-touchscreen-controls

27. Shi, Y., Ouyang, D.: Usability evaluation of the flight simulator's human-computer interaction. In: Huang, D.S., Jo, K.-H. (eds.) ICIC 2016. LNCS, vol. 9772, pp. 693–702. Springer, Cham (2016). https://doi.org/10.1007/978-3-319-42294-7_62

Safety Management and Challenges Associated with Industry 4.0 on Transportation and Logistics: A Systematic Literature Review

Chien-Hsien Lin[1](✉) and Vincent G. Duffy[2]

[1] School of Aeronautics and Astronautics, Purdue University, West Lafayette, IN 47906, USA
lin1197@purdue.edu
[2] School of Industrial Engineering, Purdue University, West Lafayette, IN 47906, USA
duffy@purdue.edu

Abstract. "Industry 4.0" has become the most significant subject of the emerging fields in manufacturing and industrial practices over the decade. It leverages the new smart technologies, including Artificial Intelligence, the Internet of Things, Autonomous Vehicles, Advanced Robots, etc. for the high involvement of automation. Such highly automated processes may raise different concerns from the traditional industry. They should have impacts on the safety management with adaption to the current development. Here we narrow down to the role of Industry 4.0 in the aspects of transformation and logistics and conducted a systematic literature review of the associated topics. We used various tools, such as CiteSpace and VOSviewer to analyze the metadata as well as several collected articles from the databases for trend, co-citation, and content analyses. We found that there is still an apparent lack of studies to incorporate the safety issues in Industry 4.0. And we suggest that safety management for Industry 4.0 on transportation and logistics should consider system design, data communication (as cybersecurity), and integration of intelligent technologies. Subjects of health and sustainability should be also included as challenges related to safety. Though many challenges are needed to be handled, emerging technologies can play significant roles to improve the safety of the work environment in the era of Industry 4.0.

Keywords: Industry 4.0 · Transportation · Logistics · Safety management · Bibliometric analysis · Artificial Intelligence · Autonomous vehicles · Cyber-physical systems · Manufacturing

1 Introduction and Background

The "Fourth Industrial Revolution", so-called "Industry 4.0" was officially introduced by German scientists for the nation's strategies for leading technology and manufacturing in 2013 [1]. Since then, this modern term of industrial practices and manufacturing has drawn significant attention by worldwide scientists, enterprises, investors, governments, etc. The driver of revolutionizing industrial operations is the emerging technologies within the decades, including Additive Manufacturing, Cloud Computing, Smart

© Springer Nature Switzerland AG 2021
C. Stephanidis et al. (Eds.): HCII 2021, LNCS 13097, pp. 562–575, 2021.
https://doi.org/10.1007/978-3-030-90966-6_38

sensors, Big Data, Internet of Things (IoT), Artificial Intelligence (AI), Robotics, and Autonomous Vehicles, etc. Also, the concept of Cyber-Physical Systems (CPS) is the core function of Industry 4.0, integrating the digital space with the physical world [2]. The main object of implications of Industry 4.0 is to promote high automation of manufacturing, increase productivity, establish safer workplaces, decrease environmental impacts, and innovate product customization.

The new technologies associated with the framework of Industry 4.0 could change the landscape of transportation and logistics to create a new term of "Logistics 4.0" [3]. For example, IoT platforms that connect devices all over logistics and supply chain could improve the work of vehicle tracking, predictive maintenance, and safe transportation without human factors. Thanks to Big data and AI, they also enable decision-decentralized management in real-time and autonomous vehicles for transport.

While developing and implementing emerging technologies, such as CPS to the sector of transportation and logistics, the strategic role of them related to safety in industry 4.0 become more essential and may be necessary to be modified with respect to the conventional ones [4]. For instance, will it be a challenge for the adoption of autonomous deliveries with safety? Will the diversity of workers' culture be the concern of human-automation interaction? The following is to explore such impacts and engagements.

2 Purpose of Study

This study aims to perform a systematic literature review of the scientific articles publishing issues associated with Industry 4.0 as well as safety strategies mainly within the sector of transportation and logistics. We would like to explore the emerging safety challenges and modified management addressing the impacts of Industry 4.0 on transportation and logistics. Likewise, Badri et al. (2018) have also conducted a review of several related articles to provide recommendations due to the occupational health and safety concerns in industry 4.0 [5]. We will compare our results with theirs further in the discussion section.

3 Research Methodology

3.1 Data Collection

The data required for the systematic literature review of this study is acquired from three different databases, including Web of Science [37], Google scholar [39], and Springer-Link [40]. The combined keywords used to search for the relevant articles are "Industry 4.0", "transportation", "logistics", "safety". However, the keywords used for the search in Web of Science are only two, "Industry 4.0" and "safety". It is because we got a small number (less than 40) of articles found in this database if we used the intended four keywords. Since the term "industry 4.0" was just introduced in 2013, we searched for the data within a range of years, from 2013 to up to date. The data set exported from Web of Science consists of authors, titles, sources, abstracts, and cited references, while those from Google scholar via a software, Harzing's Publish or Perlish [33] do not have cited references, and those from SpringerLink do not have abstracts and cited references either. Table 1 lists all the brief information of metadata from the various databases.

Table 1. The number of extracted articles and their inputted keywords to search for the three databases. (Last access on Apr. 22, 2021)

Databases	Number of articles	Keywords
Web of Science	368	Industry 4.0, safety
Google scholar (via Harzing)	479	Industry 4.0, safety, transportation, logistics
SpringerLink	640	Industry 4.0, safety, transportation, logistics

3.2 Procedures and Tools

According to the information of data, we utilized the metadata of Web of Science and SpringerLink which has the largest samples of articles for trend analyses. The data of Google Scholar does not have complete information of years of publication, so it was used for content analysis merely by VOSviewer [36]. And that of Web of Science was used for both content and co-citation analyses via the tools of VOSviewer and CiteSpace and to find the leading authors by BibExcel [38]. Finally, we have selected several articles that have the closest relevance to the topic of this study or are the most cited within the search of the databases to perform a content analysis of mapping keywords as well by MAXQDA [34]. Following we will discuss the results and identify the future work. The references are arranged by Mendeley [35].

4 Analyses and Results

4.1 Trend Analysis

As described before, the trend analyses are performed with two databases. The sources of articles are both within the range from 2013 to this year (2021). Figures 1 and 2 are the trend analyses of the metadata from the same database, Web of Science, but Fig. 2 utilized a narrower topic searched by "industry 4.0" and "safety" while Fig. 1 only used just "industry 4.0". The emerging trends of both figures are quite similar, showing the studies correlating safety with industry 4.0 also emerge with the field of industry 4.0. Figure 3 is the trend analysis of the metadata from SpringerLink based on the four full keywords mentioned above, and the trend is also similar to the previous two. The numbers of articles all grow exponentially after the year 2015. Note that the number in 2021 of Fig. 3 is almost the same as that in 2019 while it has just passed the first quarter this year. This means that it will likely surmount the number last year largely.

Emergence Indicators (EI). Table 2 exhibits the EIs of three metadata as the same in the bar charts above. We can see that the EIs of both the metadata from Web of Science are quite close, and that of the data sources with the keyword "safety" is a little bit higher than that without it. The indicator for the data sources from SpringerLink is higher than the previous two. Nonetheless, all the values are over 4.0 that is significantly large for EIs.

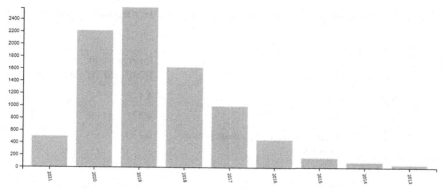

Fig. 1. The bar chart of the number of articles searched for the keyword, "Industry 4.0" by years from Web of Science. The diagram was plotted by the online analyzing tools of Web of Science.

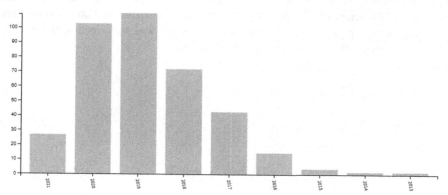

Fig. 2. The bar chart of the number of articles searched for the combined keywords, "Industry 4.0" and "safety" by years from web of science. The diagram was plotted by the online analyzing tools of Web of Science.

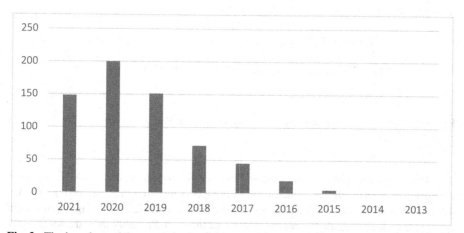

Fig. 3. The bar chart of the number of articles searched for the combined keywords, "Industry 4.0", "transformation", "logistics", and "safety" by years from SpringerLink.

Table 2. The table shows the emergence indicators of the same three metadata from the bar charts, respectively.

Databases	Keywords	Emergence indicator [(2018~2020)/(2015~2017)]
Web of Science	Industry 4.0	4.110
Web of Science	Industry 4.0, safety	4.831
SpringerLink	Industry 4.0, safety, transportation, logistics	6.130

4.2 Co-citation Analysis

Co-citation analysis can provide an investigation of the intellectual development and structure of the scientific discipline by tracking pairs of articles that are cited together in other source papers [6]. The co-citation of this study was performed with the set of metadata from the Web of Science by using CiteSpace.

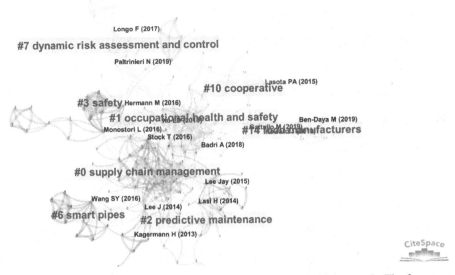

Fig. 4. The map of co-citation analysis with the clusters labeled with keywords. The figure was created by CiteSpace.

Figure 4 displays the cluster map of co-citation analysis as the result. There are 8 clusters labeled in the figure, indicating the key aspects and subtopics connecting industry 4.0 and OHS issues. Notice that a couple of the most cited articles in the original metadata is not shown here, outside the central domain of the map. Probably they are not directly relevant to our topic of study with less cross-citation strength. Table 3 lists the top 10 articles with the highest centralities of the cluster map in Fig. 4. We note that the article with the largest centrality here is to study sustainable manufacturing in Industry 4.0 by Stock et al. in 2016 [7]. We will also include all of these articles for a content analysis visualized as a word cloud in the next part.

Table 3. The top 10 articles with the highest centralities to the cluster map from the co-citation analysis are listed in the table. The titles are listed in the order of higher to lower values of centralities.

Titles	Authors	Publication year
Opportunities of Sustainable Manufacturing in Industry 4.0 [7]	Stock, T., et al.	2016
When Titans meet–Can industry 4.0 revolutionize the environmentally-sustainable manufacturing wave? The role of critical success factors [8]	Jabbour, A.B.L.D., et al.	2018
Cyber-physical systems in manufacturing [9]	Monostori, L., et al.	2016
Implementing Smart Factory of Industrie 4.0: An Outlook [10]	Wang, S.Y., et al.	2016
Sustainable Industrial Value Creation: Benefits and Challenges Of Industry 4.0 [11]	Kiel, D., et al.	2017
Digital Twin Reference Model Development to Prevent Operators' Risk in Process Plants [12]	Bevilacqua, M., et al.	2020
A Cyber-Physical Systems architecture for Industry 4.0-based manufacturing systems [13]	Lee, Jay, et al.	2015
Design Principles for Industries 4.0 Scenarios: A Literature Review [14]	Hermann, M. et al.	2015
Industry 4.0 implications in logistics: an overview [15]	Barreto, L. et al.	2017
Service innovation and smart analytics for Industry 4.0 and big data environment [16]	Lee, Jay, et al	2014

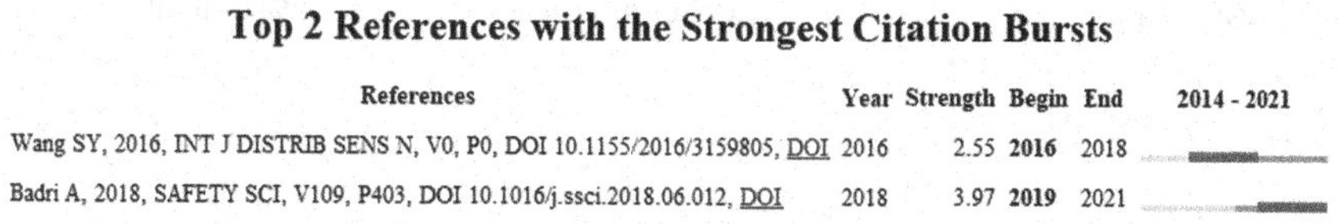

Top 2 References with the Strongest Citation Bursts

References	Year	Strength	Begin	End	2014 - 2021
Wang SY, 2016, INT J DISTRIB SENS N, V0, P0, DOI 10.1155/2016/3159805, DOI	2016	2.55	2016	2018	
Badri A, 2018, SAFETY SCI, V109, P403, DOI 10.1016/j.ssci.2018.06.012, DOI	2018	3.97	2019	2021	

Fig. 5. The citation bursts within the metadata from web of science are derived by CiteSpace.

There are only two references with the strongest citation bursts from the co-citation analysis via CiteSpace here (see Fig. 5). They are both published within the recent five years, indicating that the topic of interest is relatively fresh and emerges quickly within these years.

Table 4 lists the leading authors of the papers searched from the Web of Science as well. They are analyzed and extracted by BibExcel. The ranked number one is Vidoni, R. However, there is no significant leading author that is way above others.

Table 4. The leading authors of the metadata from Web of Science are analyzed by BibExcel.

Authors	Number of articles
Vidoni, R	5
Lau, H.K	4
Li, C.H	4
Fumagalli, L	3
Rauch, E	3
Barata, J	3
Gualtieri, L	3
Huh, J.H	3
Vignali, G	3
Bottani, E	3
da Cunha, PR	3

We also extracted the leading countries of the same metadata by the online tool of Web of Science (See Table 5). We can see that there are 3 countries/regions in Europe within the top 5 in Table 5. The number of articles from Italy is almost twice that from the USA. It seems that the subjects of safety in Industry 4.0 have been studied and published more in the European area.

Table 5. Here is to list five leading countries with the most publications relating both industry 4.0 and safety topics from the metadata of Web of Science.

Countries/Regions	Number of articles	% of total
Italy	62	16.67
Germany	46	12.37
USA	33	8.87
Peoples of Republic China	30	8.07
England	25	6.72

4.3   Content Analysis

Here we performed two types of content analyses to statistically derive the occurrences of meaningful terms for our topic of interest.

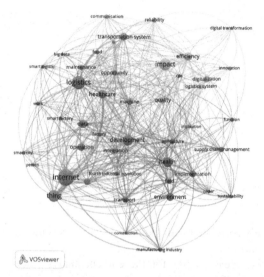

Fig. 6. This figure presents the clusters of content analysis by using VOSviewer with metadata exported from google scholar via Harzing's publish or perish.

Figure 6 shows the cluster map of the co-occurrence of terms within the titles and keywords of articles, which are included in the metadata exported from Google Scholar via Harzing's Publish or Perish. By analyzing and visualizing this content analysis with VOSviewer, we set the minimum number of occurrences as being 10 to collect the new keywords. Therefore, there are 81 terms meeting the threshold, and we presented 45 out of them after ignoring the auxiliary and non-relevant words. We listed the top ten keywords with the larger numbers of times in Table 6. Initially, we bypassed the word, "Industry" which originally occurred the most times in the map since the whole data should be inside the scope of "Industry". It gives us a clearer way of exploring the terms or insights that are specific to our topic.

Word Cloud. We have collected 10 papers from the co-citation analysis previously (See Table 3). And then we manually selected 16 more articles that are closely related to the topic, which should include either subtopic of transportation/logistics or safety or both in Industry 4.0. Two relevant chapters about safety facts and strategies applied in automated workplaces and transportation from the textbooks [17, 18] are also added in our source library. Then we performed the content analysis comprehensively to establish a word cloud (see Fig. 7) via MAXQDA for these 28 articles in total. We have filtered the nonrelevant terms as stop words and showed the top 50 words with the highest frequencies. (Again, we also bypassed the term, "Industry".) The top 10 words in Fig. 7 are listed in Table 7 with their percentages of occurrences. These words may have insights

Table 6. Keywords with the top ten numbers of occurrences in the content analysis by VOSviewer

Keywords	Occurrences
Internet	50
Logistics	46
Impact	40
Thing	36
Development	35
Health	31
Efficiency	27
Data	27
Healthcare	26
Environment	25
Operation	25

into our topic, closely correlated with Industry 4.0, transportation, and safety challenges in the developing state.

The manually selected articles for the content analysis here are cited from the references: [1, 4, 5, 19–30], and [8].

Fig. 7. The word cloud resulted from the content analysis of 26 papers plus two chapters from the textbooks [17, 18].

Table 7. Here to list the top 10 words with the highest percentages of total words from the content analysis by MAXQDA.

Keywords	% of total terms
Manufacturing	0.90
Systems	0.86
Data	0.77
Management	0.51
Smart	0.49
Production	0.48
Safety	0.47
Research	0.45
Logistics	0.44
Information	0.42

5 Discussion

Results Discussion. Following we will discuss the results in the previous section.

Trend Analysis. The trend analysis in Sect. 4.1 proved that the topic of Industry 4.0 is indeed a rapidly emerging field within the decade and the number of publications increased exponentially when the term has been introduced in 2013. Industry 4.0 highly involves data-driven technologies, intensive sensors, and robots, etc. to raise the level of automation of factories. It also largely changed the way of transportation and logistics in the traditional industry. The utilization of automated vehicles could both increase the efficiency of transportation and decrease the affection of human factors to accident causation. However, changes in technology without accompanying strategic and cultural changes can cause more problems than they solve [31]. We have to contribute more safety efforts to meet these coming challenges that we would like to explore in this study.

We compared the trend of articles including the topic of Industry 4.0 only with those involving both topics of Industry 4.0 and safety. It is apparent that awareness of safety issues related to Industry 4.0 also emerges along with that within the researchers. However, the number of articles addressing safety topics is still way lower than the total number of all publications related to industry 4.0 alone. We calculated the fraction of the quantities of articles from 2018 to 2020 for the two metadata, the ratio of safety-related papers is only 4.47% within the total base of industry 4.0 in this study. In addition, we noticed that the number of articles in 2020 from the data set of Web of Science is a little lower than that in 2019, which should have been larger than the previous year. It may be affected by the pandemic situation last year impeding the research progress. But the number of articles in 2020 from the data set of Google Scholar is still higher than the previous year. Maybe it is also that the two databases have different searching bases.

Co-citation Analysis. From the co-citation, we found that many articles in Table 3 or others in the top list were studied about sustainability in Industry 4.0. It seems that safety challenges and management may be highly overlapped with the topic of sustainable strategies in Industry 4.0. Almost all the keyword clusters labeled on the map (Fig. 4) are closely correlated to the safety issues of this study except for the one with "food manufacturer". It indicates that it is a successful and meaningful co-citation analysis for the topic. We can also infer some applications or adaption for the safety management from the cluster keywords, for instance, dynamic risk assessment and control, and development of smart pipeline and predictive maintenance in the places.

We also found the leading authors and the citation bursts. Nevertheless, the counts of articles of each author and the citation bursts are both relatively small. It implies that the topic of safety related to transportation in Industry 4.0 is indeed fresh while it is still emerging within the decade by the trend analysis above. Moreover, we also found that counties in the European area have more studies in the safety topics with Industry 4.0. Maybe they have more consideration about the safety challenges or have a bit more advance of research in such topics than the nations of other continents.

Content Analysis. We have two main results (Fig. 6 and 7) for the content analysis from the metadata and literature contents. The first result of the cluster map just includes terms appearing in titles and keywords. We can outline four aspects from Table 6, IoT, health, environment, and operations. Note that here we only search for the term of safety in this study. It seems that many articles also consist of the subject of health or healthcare in their topics. Also, the operation of IoT could be a challenge to the safety issues involving the environment. The second result of the word cloud includes the terms from more comprehensive contents but with fewer samples of literature. From the insights of the word cloud, we can imply that the safety topic in transportation is all around manufacturing and systems. And data plays an important role in the field.

Literature Review and Reappraisal. We will also briefly provide a review and reappraisal of a couple of literature of our choices from the paper list in this study.

Tang et al. have published work to discuss the strategic role of logistics in industry 4.0 [4] and they mentioned many aspects of safety concerns and strategies. We may relate their conclusion to our result. One is that they recommended that the private and public sectors can collaborate with the government to develop standard safety guidelines and regulations that suitable for the new technologies. It is correlated to one of the clusters in the co-citation map, which is represented by the term, "cooperative". We believe it is an essential way to address the safety challenges of our topic.

Both content analyses in Sect. 4 reveal lots of occurrences in terms of data, information, the internet, and digitalization. They present another aspect of safety management in Industry 4.0, probably beyond the topic of transportation. This aspect is about security or cybersecurity management in Industry 4.0. Somehow hackers have already become the main risk of corporate assets and technologies especially involving the internet and internal network. It was mentioned in the article of Forcina and Falcone (2021) [19] as well. Almost 80% is related to security within the recent researches about safety management in Industry 4.0. This should be a difficult challenge for the emerging subject. Everything is connected and it probably needs to evolve into a completely different level of safety strategies and system design.

Although the workers may have to learn about and adapt to the new technologies around the manufacturing workplaces in the era of Industry 4.0, such innovation can provide a safer environment of occupation, which is the purpose of the sociotechnical system theory [17]. All the content analyses have high frequencies of occurrences of the terms, like "smart" and "intelligent", which could represent smart sensors and AI systems. They have the features of automatic risk control and decentral decision-making for quick response to suspend operations to prevent disaster from taking place. For example, if a worker runs into the path of an automated cart while transporting cargo, the vehicle will detect in advance and stop operating immediately. Moreover, such new technologies can be integrated to form systems to better protect the environment and address manufacturing waste [21]. That will be both "safe" for labor and the environment.

6 Conclusion

The topic here is to try to find out the specific challenges and adaption of safety management with the impact on transportation and logistics in the era of Industry 4.0. From the sources collection, we realized that there are not too many articles to explore how to incorporate these disciplines together (OHS and Industry 4.0) while the publications with the subject of Industry 4.0 are quite effervescent. This scenario is the same as the conclusion of Badri et al. (2018) [5]. Several keywords from the content analyses may imply that safety management in Industry 4.0 should consider system design, data communication (as cybersecurity), and integration of intelligent technologies. Meanwhile, issues of health and sustainability should be also included as challenges related to occupational safety. Although there are many challenges needed to be handled, emerging technologies can play essential roles to improve the safety of the work environment in the epoch of Industry 4.0.

7 Future Work

Although we know that automated vehicles and other robotic systems can reduce the risks of human factors that could induce accidents, there are still large opportunities for human-automation interaction for the employees relying on the part of transportation and logistics in the state of Industry 4.0. In future work, both human factors, such as stress and feeling uselessness and integration of management should be studied further to explore their impact and modification on the safety issues in the manufacturing field. The safety processes should take the physical, mental, and emotional needs of employees into account [17]. For example, an awarded project within the National Science Foundation (NSF.gov) [40] has been found to conduct studies to explore methods of worker training for the intelligent manufacturing environment. To help to minimize the release of hazardous materials, employees in the entire transportation chain or logistics must receive training and retaining as a constant [17, 18]. However, the training contents must be also adjusted from the conventional industries. As mentioned above, there is still an obvious lack of research reports in the topics of safety management and engineering along with the new technologies developed for Industry 4.0. To adapt efficiently to the new era, researchers may have to study further human factors and management of human resources to see how they could affect safety strategies in Industry 4.0.

References

1. Kagermann, H., Wahlster, W., Helbig, J: Recommendations for Implementing the Strategic Initiative Industrie 4.0: Final Report of the Industrie 4.0 Working Group. Acatech-National Academy of Science and Engineering, Germany (2013)
2. Da Xu, L., Xu, E.L., Li, L.: Industry 4.0: state of the art and future trends. Int. J. Prod. Res. **56**(8), 2941–2962 (2018)
3. Diez, C.M.: Logistics 4.0: The New Transportation Era (2018). https://medium.com/iot-security-review/logistics-4-0-the-new-transportation-era-672ff08e958c. Accessed 22 Apr 2021
4. Tang, C.S., Veelenturf, L.P.: The strategic role of logistics in the industry 4.0 era. Transp. Res. Part E Logist. Transp. Rev. **129**(July), 1–11 (2019)
5. Badri, A., BoudreauTrudel, B., Souissi, A.S.: Occupational health and safety in the industry 4.0 era: a cause for major concern? Saf. Sci. **109**, 403–411 (2018). https://doi.org/10.1016/j.ssci.2018.06.012
6. Surwase, G., Anil Sagar, B., Kademani, S., Bhanumurthy, K: Co-citation analysis: an overview. In: BOSLA National Conference Proceedings, pp. m179–185 (2011)
7. Stock, T., Seliger, G.: Opportunities of Sustainable Manufacturing in Industry 4.0. Procedia CIRP **40**, 536–541 (2016). https://doi.org/10.1016/j.procir.2016.01.129
8. Jabbour, S., Lopesde, A.B., Chiappetta Jabbour, C.J., Foropon, C., Filho, M.G.: When Titans meet – can industry 4.0 revolutionise the environmentally-sustainable manufacturing wave? The role of critical success factors. Technol. Forecast. Soc. Chang. **132**(February), 18–25 (2018)
9. Monostori, L., et al.: Cyber-physical systems in manufacturing. CIRP Ann. **65**(2), 621–641 (2016)
10. Wang, S., Wan, J., Li, D., Zhang, C.: Implementing smart factory of industrie 4.0: an outlook. Int. J. Distrib. Sensor Netw. **12**(1), 3159805 (2016). https://doi.org/10.1155/2016/3159805
11. Kiel, D., Müller, J.M., Arnold, C., Voigt, K.I.: Sustainable industrial value creation: benefits and challenges of industry 4.0. Int. J. Innov. Manage. **21**(8), 1–22 (2017)
12. Bevilacqua, M., et al.: Digital twin reference model development to prevent operators' risk in process plants. Sustainability **12**(3), 1088 (2020). https://doi.org/10.3390/su12031088
13. Lee, J., Bagheri, B., Kao, H.A.: A cyber-physical systems architecture for industry 4.0-based manufacturing systems. Manuf. Lett. **3**(December), 18–23 (2015)
14. Hermann, M., Pentek, T., Otto, B.: Design principles for industrie 4.0 scenarios: a literature review. Techn. Univ. Dortmund **1**(1), 4–16 (2015)
15. Barreto, L., Amaral, A., Pereira, T.: Industry 4.0 implications in logistics: an overview. Proc. Manuf. **13**, 1245–1252 (2017)
16. Lee, J., Kao, H.A., Yang, S.: Service innovation and smart analytics for industry 4.0 and big data environment. Proc. CIRP **16**, 3–8 (2014)
17. Goetsch, D.L.: Computer, automation, and robots. In: Occupational Safety and Health for Technologists, Engineers, and Managers, New York, NY, pp. 526–537. Pearson, 9th Edition (2019). (Chapter 23)
18. Brauer, R.L.: Transportation. In: Safety and Health for Engineers. John Wiley & Sons, Inc., pp. 375–409. 3rd Edn., (Digital Ed.) (2016). (Chapter 14)
19. Forcina, A., Falcone, D.: The role of industry 4.0 enabling technologies for safety management: a systematic literature review. Proc. Comput. Sci. **180**(2019), 436–445 (2021)
20. Kans, M., Galar, D., Thaduri, A.: Maintenance 4.0 in railway transportation industry. In: Koskinen, K.T., et al. (eds.) Proceedings of the 10th World Congress on Engineering Asset Management (WCEAM 2015), pp. 317–331. Springer International Publishing, Cham (2016). https://doi.org/10.1007/978-3-319-27064-7_30

21. Abdul, M.M., Ali, S.M., Kusi-Sarpong, S., Shaikh, M.A.A.: Assessing challenges for implementing industry 4.0: implications for process safety and environmental protection. Process. Saf. Environ. Prot. **117**, 730–741 (2018)
22. Kayikci, Y.: Sustainability impact of digitization in logistics. Proc. Manuf. **21**, 782–789 (2018)
23. Polak-Sopinska, A., Wisniewski, Z., Walaszczyk, A., Maczewska, A., Sopinski, P.: Impact of industry 4.0 on occupational health and safety. In: Karwowski, W., Trzcielinski, S., Mrugalska, B. (eds.) AHFE 2019. AISC, vol. 971, pp. 40–52. Springer, Cham (2020). https://doi.org/10.1007/978-3-030-20494-5_4
24. Min, J., Kim, Y., Lee, S., Jang, T.W., Kim, I., Song, J.: The fourth industrial revolution and its impact on occupational health and safety, worker's compensation and labor conditions. Saf. Health Work **10**(4), 400–408 (2019)
25. Werner-Lewandowska, K., Kosacka-Olejnik, M.: Logistics 4.0 maturity in service industry: empirical research results. Proc. Manuf. **38**(2019), 1058–1065 (2019)
26. Makarova, I., Shubenkova, K., Buyvol, P., Mavrin, V.: Safety features of the transport system in the transition. Arch. Autom. Eng. **86**(4), 79–99 (2019)
27. Oztemel, E., Gursev, S.: Literature review of industry 4.0 and related technologies. J. Intell. Manuf. **31**(1), 127–182 (2020)
28. Kamble, S.S., Gunasekaran, A., Gawankar, S.A.: Sustainable industry 4.0 framework: a systematic literature review identifying the current trends and future perspectives. Process. Saf. Environ. Prot. **117**, 408–425 (2018)
29. Liu, Z., Xie, K., Li, L., Chen, Y.: A paradigm of safety management in industry 4.0. Syst. Res. Behav. Sci. **37**(4), 632–645 (2020)
30. Hofmann, E., Rüsch, M.: Industry 4.0 and the current status as well as future prospects on logistics. Comput. Ind. **89**, 23–34 (2017)
31. Mathis, T.L.: Safety 4.0: Updating Safety for Industry 4.0. EHSToday (2018). https://www.ehstoday.com/safety-technology/article/21919570/safety-40-updating-safety-forindustry-40. Accessed 22 Apr 2012
32. Harzing's Publish or Perish. https://harzing.com/resources/publish-or-perish. Accessed 22 Apr 2021
33. MAXQDA. https://www.maxqda.com/. Accessed 22 Apr 2021
34. Mendeley. https://www.mendeley.com/?interaction_required=true. Accessed 22 Apr 2021
35. VOSviewer. https://www.vosviewer.com/. Accessed 22 Apr 2021
36. Web of Science. https://wcs-webofknowledge-com.ezproxy.lib.purdue.edu/RA/analyze.do?product=WOS&SID=5BPc6ylRdVDGq3F3Du9&field=CU_CountryTerritory_CountryTerritory_en&yearSort=false. Accessed 22 Apr 2021
37. BibExcel. https://homepage.univie.ac.at/juan.gorraiz/bibexcel/. Accessed 22 Apr 2021
38. Google Scholar. https://scholar.google.com.tw/. Accessed 22 Apr 2021
39. SpringerLink. https://link.springer.com/. Accessed 22 Apr 2021
40. Bratlie, K.: PFI:BIC: iWork, a Modular Multi-Sensing Adaptive Robot-Based Service for Vocational Assessment, Personalized Worker Training and Rehabilitation, NSF.gov. https://nsf.gov/awardsearch/showAward?AWD_ID=1719031&HistoricalAwards=false

The Influence Mechanism of Terminal Demand Fluctuation on Service Quality of Digital Supply Chain

Caihong Liu[1], Hannah Ji[2], and June Wei[3(✉)]

[1] Department of Business, Jiaxing University, Jiaxing 314001, China
rainbowliu@zjxu.edu.cn
[2] Carey Business School, Johns Hopkins University, Baltimore, MD 20723, USA
[3] College of Business, University of West Florida, Pensacola, FL 32514, USA

Abstract. Due to the Terminal demand fluctuation in the open market environment, the structure stability of digital supply chain will be affected, resulting in the instability of service quality. Based on the T-JIT theory, a conceptual model should be constructed from the change of market demand, the flow of service information on the nodes of digital supply chain, the quality of service information of nodes in the chain and the digital capability of enterprises. Then, the model hypothesizes are to be verified by the survey data of digital supply chain for Chinese manufacturing. The results show that: under certain market demand disturbance, the stronger the enterprise's digital technology capability, the higher the service information flow and service information quality of digital supply chain, and the stronger the enterprise's digital technology capability, the more significant the positive regulation effect.

Keywords: Terminal demand fluctuation · Service quality · Digital supply chain · Digital technology capability · Total Just in Time

1 Introduction

At present, Major enterprises have begun to use digital technology to help enterprises transform and upgrade to modern manufacturing [1]. A large number of studies have shown that the success of all companies' digital transformation lies in the digital transformation of the supply chain [2]. The digitalization of supply chain aims to create an intelligent network system through the application of new technologies, thereby realizing new value creation for the enterprise. Under the impact of COVID-19, the world has realized the importance of supply chain digitalization. At the same time, the service capability of the digital supply chain in the abnormal environment will also face more challenges. This paper will study the influence of market demand fluctuations on it and the dependence of digital supply chain service quality on digital technology will also be ascertained.

© Springer Nature Switzerland AG 2021
C. Stephanidis et al. (Eds.): HCII 2021, LNCS 13097, pp. 576–584, 2021.
https://doi.org/10.1007/978-3-030-90966-6_39

2   Theory and Research Model

2.1   The Connotation of Digital Supply Chain

Xu (2014) first proposed the concept of supply chain digitization. Since then, some scholars have continuously expanded its connotation from different perspectives [4]. The digital supply chain can to improve business performance, minimize risks, and integrate digital supply chain The framework is divided into digital planning, digital procurement, digital production and digital logistics [5]. The digitalization of the supply chain is an intelligent process that drives the upgrade of the supply chain system through technological innovation and creates new value for the organization [6]. Therefore, this paper holds that the digitalization of supply chain is the digitalization upgrade of each link and each participant driven by digital technology, so as to improve the responsiveness and operational intelligence of the supply chain.

2.2   The Conceptual Model Based on T - JIT Theory

With the development of production servitization, production service quality and supply service quality have been paid more and more attention, and Just In Time (JIT) has also been favored in service management. Hu Lili et al. [7] analyzed the existing problems of logistics enterprises' JIT logistics service from two aspects of material supply and operation management, put forward corresponding improvement strategies to solve the problems, and evaluated the implementation effect of the improvement strategy from the service quality index and logistics cost index. Gao Jie [8] conducted a research on the inbound logistics operation mode of JIT-based automobile manufacturing enterprises, and compared three operating modes: JIT logistics mode undertaken by the carrier, JIT logistics mode undertaken by 3PL, and self-operated auto manufacturing enterprises. The JIT logistics operation model finally concluded that the JIT logistics model undertaken by 3PL was the optimal model. Some scholars take D company as the research object, take improving the logistics service quality of customers as the research goal, starting from the concept of service quality, logistics service quality and the domestic and foreign literature research of logistics service quality, comprehensively use the questionnaire survey method, process analysis method and fuzzy comprehensive evaluation method, adopt the combination of qualitative and quantitative, theoretical analysis and empirical research Methods to study the logistics service quality of D company under JIT distribution of auto parts [9]. Therefore, Kenneth (2014) proposed the total just in time (T - JIT) theory.

   T - JIT strategy incorporates JIT-production, JIT-purchasing, JIT-selling and JIT-information [10]. T-JIT can more comprehensively and accurately reflect the optimization problems of supply chain management, which has a positive impact on the competitiveness of the whole enterprise, the capability of SC and organizational performance[11]. Under the environment of T-JIT, enterprises should achieve the goal of high quality JIT through advanced IT factors. Based on this, referring to the existing t-jit theoretical model [12], the paper puts forward the following T-JIT model as Fig. 1.

   The innovation of the model lies in highlighting the mission, dependent conditions and operation purpose of digital supply chain.

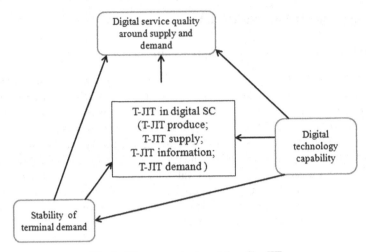

Fig. 1. The conceptual model on T – JIT

2.3 Research Hypotheses

According to the Fig. 1, some research hypotheses should be provided as following.

J1: the greater the fluctuation of the end consumer demand, the worse the digital supply and demand service quality of the supply chain.

J2: The digital technology capability of enterprise has a positive effect on its supply and demand service quality.

J3: The stronger the digital technology capability of enterprises adapting to the change of terminal demand is, the more certain the terminal demand is.

J31: The more the terminal demand matches with the digital technology capability of the enterprise, the stronger the positive influence of their combined force on the service quality of the digital supply chain is. And the vice versa is.

3   Research Design and Questionnaire Measurement

3.1   Research Design

(1) The questionnaire design.

According to the Fig. 1 and research hypotheses, the literature reference method was adopted in this paper to design the questionnaire items (Table 1).

Table 1. Questionnaire items

Unobservable variable	Observable indicators	References
Terminal demand certainty (TD)	a. How much does the terminal demand change every week? (TD1) b. How much does the product mix of terminal demand change every week? (TD2) c. How strong is the enterprise's ability to predict the terminal demand? (TD3)	[13]
Digital technology capability (DC)	a. The supply chain digital platform is further integrated and expanded; (DC1) b. The collaborative innovation of internal and external business of enterprise supply chain is enhanced; (DC2) c. Businesses are becoming more responsive to the market (DC3)	[14, 15]
Supply and demand service quality (SQ)	a. Humanity and speed in handling complaints; (SQ1) b. High efficiency of service resource supply and demand allocation; (SQ2) c. High customer service satisfaction; (SQ3) d. Obvious service value-added effect (SQ4)	[16–18]
T-JIT of digital SC (JT)	a. Digital production; (JT1) b. Digital logistics; (JT2) c. Digital marketing; (JT3) d. Digital information coverage (JT4)	[19, 20]

(2) Sample

The digitization of China's manufacturing supply chain is not yet high. In order to increase the effectiveness of the study and considering the inconvenient field research under the influence of the epidemic, this paper selects some enterprises in China's economically developed Yangtze River Delta region as the research objects to conduct telephone survey., this time selected 230 enterprises, the type of enterprise distribution is wide, including electrical manufacturing, textile industry, machinery manufacturing, pharmaceutical manufacturing, etc., the number of all kinds of enterprises distribution is relatively equal. Secondly, considering that the middle and senior leaders of the enterprise have a relatively comprehensive understanding of the organizational strategy and the use of information technology, this research mainly focuses on them. The survey finally collected 210 valid questionnaires, with the effective rate of 92.0%.

3.2 Questionnaire Measurement and Testing

In this paper, SPSS22.0 was used for the data analysis, and the variance maximization orthogonal rotation method was adopted. The reliability coefficient value is 0.933, which is greater than 0.9, which indicates that the reliability of the research data is of high quality. The KMO statistics were all greater than 0.80, and the Bartlett spherical test passed the test at the significance level of 0.001. The variance interpretation rate values of the four factors were 21.813%,20.359%,18.849% and 13.671% respectively, and the cumulative variance interpretation rate after rotation was 74.692% > 50%, indicating that the information of the research items could be extracted effectively. The whole factor structure was clear and initially met the basic criteria of validity, as shown in Table 2.

Table 2. Validity analysis

item	factor loadings				variance of common
	factor1	factor2	factor3	factor4	
TD11	0.117	0.736	0.427	0.124	0.753
TD12	0.357	0.715	0.116	0.263	0.722
TD13	0.249	0.777	0.237	0.19	0.759
DC11	0.504	0.604	0.116	0.16	0.658
DC12	0.154	0.305	0.161	0.86	0.882
DC13	0.304	0.15	0.336	0.733	0.765
SQ11	0.712	0.142	0.169	0.447	0.755
SQ12	0.638	0.334	0.211	0.242	0.622
SQ13	0.15	0.215	0.779	0.291	0.76
SQ14	0.204	0.236	0.809	0.234	0.807
JT11	0.662	0.221	0.551	0.01	0.791
JT12	0.522	0.206	0.665	0.09	0.766
JT13	0.677	0.434	0.363	0.125	0.794
JT14	0.577	0.446	0.147	0.263	0.623
Eigenroot value (before rotation)	7.638	1.067	0.965	0.787	-
Cumulative variance interpretation	54.559%	62.180%	69.070%	74.692%	-
Eigenroot value	3.054	2.85	2.639	1.914	-
Cumulative variance interpretation	21.813%	42.172%	61.021%	74.692%	-
KMO	0.898				-
Bartlett'test ?	1722.604				-
df?	91				-
p	0				-

In order to further test the rationality of the items, the discrimination test of the data is shown in Table 3.

Table 3. Validity analysis.

Factor	TD	DC	SQ	JT
TD	0.778			
DC	0.677	0.724		
SQ	0.67	0.696	0.788	
JT	0.711	0.672	0.718	0.801

It can be seen from Table 3 that the correlation coefficient of each index in each factor is greater than 0.6, and the AVE value of each factor is greater than the absolute value of the correlation coefficient between this factor and other factors, indicating that the data construct has good aggregation and discriminative validity.

4 Path Analysis and Hypothesis Testing

This paper is based on AMOSS 22.0 software for data analysis (Table 4).

4.1 The Path Analysis

Table 4. Model regression coefficient

X	→	Y	SE	z	p	Normalized path coefficient
DC	→	TD	0.126	7.839	0	0.843
TD	→	JT	0.129	3.066	0.002	0.494
JT	→	SQ	0.098	4.753	0	0.636
DC	→	JT	0.154	2.41	0.016	0.393
DC	→	SQ	0.113	2.639	0.008	0.433
TD	→	SQ	0.092	-0.402	0.688	-0.063

These conclusions clarifies that the research hypotheses J1, J2 and J3 are valid.

The influence relationship between unobservable variables and the influence relationship between observable indexes and unobservable variables can be shown in Fig. 2.

Obviously, in Fig. 2, CD should have some moderating effect on the effect of JT on SQ. How do these moderating effects behave? The problem is unavoidable for enterprises to carry out targeted digital supply and demand service management.

4.2 The Mediating Effect of DC

Regarding TD as the control variable and CD as the moderating variable, the force of JT on SQ is observed as shown in Table 5.

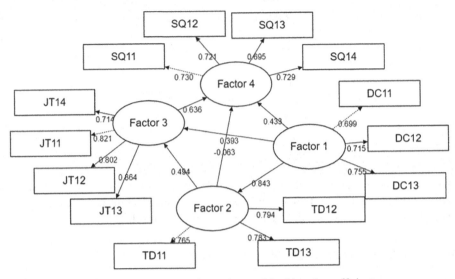

Fig. 2. Amos structural equation model with path coefficient

Table 5. Control variable and CD

Model	Model1	Model2	Model3
Cons	3.092 (14.105**)	3.471 (15.134**)	3.442 (15.229**)
TD11	0.049 (1.259)	0.037 (1.002)	0.027 (0.732)
TD12	0.125 (2.289*)	0.069 (1.272)	0.078 (1.463)
TD13	0.024 (0.532)	-0.004 (-0.092)	-0.013 (-0.294)
JT	0.571 (10.051**)	0.482 (8.235**)	0.490 (8.489**)
DC		0.206 (4.120**)	0.198 (4.009**)
JT*DC			0.123 (2.587*)
N.sample	185	185	185
R²	0.649	0.679	0.691

Models 1, 2, and 3 respectively represent the influence of independent variables on dependent variables under the three situations of not considering the moderating variable, only adding the moderating variable and adding the interaction term of the independent variable and the moderating variable.

This not only confirms the moderating effect of CD, but also indirectly verifies the validity of the research hypothesis J31.

5   Conclusion

The conclusions are as follows: firstly, the digital technology capability of enterprises is positively correlated with the formation of digital supply chain under T-JIT. Secondly, the certainty of terminal market demand is positively correlated with the formation of digital supply chain under T-JIT. Thirdly, there is a positive correlation between the digital technology capability of enterprises and the digital service quality of supply chain; fourthly, there is no direct positive correlation between the certainty of end market demand and the digital service quality of supply chain. Fifthly, the digital supply chain formed under t-JIT is directly proportional to its digital service quality. Sixth, with the change of terminal market demand, different digital technology capabilities of enterprises have significant differences in the relationship between digital supply chain and digital service quality of supply chain.

Acknowledgments. This research was supported by the Natural Science Foundation of Zhejiang Province in China (Grant No. LY18G010011).

References

1. Chen, C., Xu, J.: Manufacturing enterprise digital transformation ability evaluation system and application. Sci. Technol. Manage. Res. **40**(11), 46–51 (2020). https://doi.org/10.3969/j. issn.1000-7695.2020.11.007
2. Longji, T., Yonggang, P., Ting, Z.: Research on empowering digital transformation of supply chain by industrial internet. Supply Chain Manage. **1**(7), 53–77 (2020). https://doi.org/10. 19868/j.cnki.gylgl.2020.07.005
3. Guo, H., Gong, J., Zang, M.: Digital supply chain: creating value with wisdom. North. China. Power. **5**, 78–80 (2020)
4. Xu, J.: Managing Digital Enterprise. Atlantis Press, Paris (2014). https://doi.org/10.2991/ 978-94-6239-094-2
5. Rogo Research Institute, Jingdong Logistics: Comprehensive research report on digital supply chain (2018)
6. Büyüközkan, G., Göçer, F.: Digital supply chain: literature review and a proposed framework for future research. Comput. Indus. **97**, 157–177 (2018). https://doi.org/10.1016/j.compind. 2018.02.010
7. Lili, H., Yong, L., Jingbo, Z.: The study of authentic proof on strategies of upgrading JIT logistics service level——taking Rongfeng logistics company as an example. J. Huaihua Univ. **29**(8), 30–32 (2010). https://doi.org/10.3969/j.issn.1671-9743.2010.08.011
8. Gao, J.: Research on the inbound logistics operation mode of automobile manufacturing enterprises based on JIT. Xi'an: Master's thesis of Xi'an University of Technology (2010). https://doi.org/10.7666/d.D294446
9. Xu, J.: Research on logistics service quality management under JIT distribution of auto parts of D company. Master's thesis of Donghua University, Shanghai (2013)
10. Green, K.W., Anthony Inman, R., Birou, L.M., Whitten, D.: Total JIT (T-JIT) and its impact on supply chain competency and organizational performance. Int. J. Prod. Econ. **147**, 125–135 (2014). https://doi.org/10.1016/j.ijpe.2013.08.026
11. Hao, L., Hu, D., Li, C.: Supplier selection and order allocation of purchasing management for enterprise supply chain in T-JIT environment. J. Highway. Transp. Res. Dev. **35**(1), 149–158 (2018). https://doi.org/10.3969/j.issn.1002-0268.2018.01.020
12. Hao, L., et al.: Study on cooperative risk optimization of dual-channel supply chain based on background of T-JIT theory. J. Highway. Transp. Res. Dev. **37**(2), 146–158 (2020). https:// doi.org/10.3969/j.issn.1002-0268.2020.02.019

13. Xuan, Z., Jun, Z.: Inter-organizational collaboration, supply chain electronic integration capacity and supply chain performance ——the moderating role of demand uncertainty and intra-organizational IT. J. Bus. Econ. **8**, 5–19 (2019). https://doi.org/10.14134/j.cnki.cn33-1336/f.2019.08.001

14. Zhang, L.C., Shu, B., Bian, Q., Hua, L.J.: Rapid response to manufacturing-oriented digital platform for complicated product in aerospace industry. Comput. Integr. Manuf. Syst. **14**(4), 722–730 (2008)

15. Lu, Y., Ramamurthy, K.R.: Understanding the link between information technology capability and organizational agility: an empirical examination. MIS Q. **35**(4), 931–954 (2011). https://doi.org/10.1007/s11575-011-0104-1

16. Huang, W.: Research on the supply chain service quality improvement strategy of Hangzhou re Lian Group. Master's thesis of Shanghai International Studies University, Shanghai (2016)

17. Li, J.: Research on service quality evaluation and improvement of container shipping enterprises based on supply chain flexibility. Master's thesis of Dalian Maritime University, Liaoning (2010). https://doi.org/10.7666/d.y1696812

18. Esbjerg, L., et al.: An integrative conceptual framework for analyzing customer satisfaction with shopping TNP experiences in grocery retailing. J. Retail. Consum. Serv. **4**(19), 445–456 (2012). https://doi.org/10.1016/j.jretconser.2012.04.006

19. Ma, Q.: Total JIT (T-JIT) and its impact on supply chain competency and organizational performance. Logist. Eng. Manage. **37**(10), 70–71 (2015). https://doi.org/10.3969/j.issn.1674-4993.2015.10.028

20. Bortolotti, T., Danese, P., Romano, P.: Assessing the impact of just-in-time on operational performance at varying degrees of repetitiveness. Int. J. Prod. Res. **51**(3–4), 1–14 (2012). https://doi.org/10.1080/00207543.2012.678403

Digital Intrapreneurship: A Work Climate Perspective

Ivan D. Ortiz Sandoval, Tehauaroga Tehiva, Mikay Parsons, and Kaveh Abhari[(⊠)]

San Diego State University, San Diego, CA, USA
kabhari@sdsu.edu

Abstract. Digital intrapreneurs (DIs) act and behave in a similar way to typical digital entrepreneurs without the risk of the venture. Digital Intrapreneurship, however, is under the influence of different organizational factors. This study is meant to focus on the relationship between digital intrapreneurship behavior and the workplace climate—specifically, how the workplace climate can influence DIs' ability to innovate and exploit digital technologies. Our study revealed that three key workplace climate dimensions play into the formation of digital intrapreneurship behavior: individual, situational and organizational factors. The individual factors are represented by motivations, digital literacy, goals, needs, and the DI's mindset. The individual factors are affected by the different situational factors that consist of collaborative norms, workplace culture, and group dynamics. The situational factors are in close relationship with organizational factors: mission, core values, and the reward system. The study also concludes that technological factors like digital infrastructure play a key role in the relation of the DI work climate and DI activity enabled said factors.

Keywords: Entrepreneurship · Digital intrapreneurship · Intrapreneurs · Work climate

1 Introduction

For years, entrepreneurs have driven the creation and success of businesses. However, the release of the term "intrapreneurship" by Gifford Pinchot 35 years ago has opened new ways to approach the entrepreneurial world. Digital intrapreneurs (DIs) are intrapreneurs who act and behave in a similar way to typical digital entrepreneurs (DEs), except without the risk of the venture [1]. This means that, while DIs perform entrepreneurial behaviors, they do so both at a smaller scale and as an employee within an organization [2]. Thus, DIs' behaviors fall under the influence of different organizational factors [1, 3]. This study focuses on the relationship between digital intrapreneurship behavior and workplace climate, specifically how workplace climate can influence DIs' abilities to innovate and exploit digital technologies.

While current innovation literature highlights the role of employees in innovation, it falls short in explaining the behavioral aspects of digital intrapreneurship affected by work climate [4]. Digital innovation has created new norms around uncertainty in

C. Stephanidis et al. (Eds.): HCII 2021, LNCS 13097, pp. 585–595, 2021.
https://doi.org/10.1007/978-3-030-90966-6_40

organizations striving for innovation [5]. As the key tool used by DIs, digital innovation allows for intrapreneurs to explore new ideas sans risk, while also providing a competitive advantage to withstand the inconsistencies in the DE climate [5]. The importance of DIs speaks to the need to nurture their ability to innovate within their organizational framework and constraints [6].

In this paper, after providing necessary background information about digital intrapreneurship, we model the relationship between the success of DIs and the digital intrapreneurship work climate (DIWC). The conceptual model proposed by this research focuses on three key dimensions of work climate and the relationships between them that nurture said digital intrapreneurship behavior: individual, situational, and organizational factors. The paper then concludes with a discussion of the model's practical applications and possibilities for future studies.

2 Background

2.1 Nourishing Digital Intrapreneurship

Digital intrapreneurs (DIs) behave like digital entrepreneurs (DEs) without the risk of capital loss or personal failure. While DIs innovate within the business, they have an entrepreneurship mindset. This mindset is what defines DIs as they engage, act, and make decisions like DEs [7]. Expanding on the subject of intrapreneurs, Gifford Pinchot wrote *Intrapreneuring* in 1985 discussed the traditional approach to intrapreneurship and provided simple conceptualizations of intrapreneurs [1]. One of the definitions provided by Pinchot defines intrapreneurs as "the dreamers that do, they don't just come up with ideas, their core role is turning ideas into [successful] business realities," [8]. This definition signifies the role of intrapreneurs in successful businesses, and thus the present study identifies the key mechanisms to nourish DI activities in order to drive innovation and success within organizations.

In this paper, we refer to "nourishing" as all of the activities and resources, from a work climate perspective, that are required to encourage and develop successful DIs. Like other positions in the business world, DIs have both internal and external motives influencing their level of participation. Employee driven innovation is positively influenced by both external, structural support as well as intrinsic, psychological empowerment [9]. This relationship means that in order for employee driven innovation to occur in an organization, employers and managers must empower the ordinary employee to create ideas and participate in the development and implementation process. Through this, external forces increase the internal motivation of DIs to push further, increasing innovation productivity and success overall. However, in this study, we mainly focus on the internal factors due to their relative manageability, compared with external factors, to best optimize the DI activity output.

2.2 Work Climate: Digital Intrapreneurship Perspective

A work climate is a set of perceived properties of a work environment that influences the motivation and behavior of individuals who work in that environment [10]. These perceptions influence employees' intrapreneurial productivity, motivation, and creativity [1]. However, DIs differ from entrepreneurs as they require digital tools to create values [11]. As a result of this need, DIs require their workplaces to provide the proper technical infrastructure and support to succeed in their efforts to innovate [12, 5].

Despite certain personality features that define DIs, digital intrapreneurs are 'social actors' and thus are impacted by their social environment. According to the social exchange theory developed by the sociologist George Homans, social interactions are made of social exchanges [13]. This theory argues that people weigh the pros and cons of every relationship such that, when the cons outweigh the pros, people will terminate that relationship. We argue that the social exchange theory helps to maximize the benefits that digital intrapreneurs get out of their workplace relationships, increasing their innovation activities like collaboration, ideation, and experimentation.

As part of the workplace climate, collaborative norms and group dynamics play important roles in encouraging innovation behavior amongst DIs. Collaborative norms, made up of social norms, are defined by the interactions that a person has with another [14]. Social norms, more broadly, are expectations about what behaviors, thoughts, or feelings are appropriate within a given context, situation, or society. Work climates can thus include a set of collaborative norms that help increase employee productivity and creativity. There are seven norms of collaboration: pausing, paraphrasing, posing questions, proposing ideas, providing data, paying attention to self and others, presuming positive intentions [14]. Collaborative norms also help workers become more creative due to their increase in interaction and deliberation amongst employees [14]. The present study focuses on collaborative norms related to DI, meaning we primarily consider the relationships that DIs have with other coworkers in their work environments. When implemented in a work environment, collaborative norms help develop an environment that specifically increases DI productivity and well-being [2, 5].

In tandem with collaborative norms, we need to talk about group dynamics because they play a role in a group setting. Group dynamics, conceptualized by Kurt Lewin, represent the effects of the roles individual members play in a group setting [15]. A positive group dynamic includes high levels of trust in each other, a common goal, a collective decision-making process, and efforts to hold each other accountable [16]. For DIs, a positive group dynamic is necessary to both boost their individual creativity as well as the creativity of the group [2]. The present study argues the importance of avoiding poor group dynamics, which often include negative behaviors that disrupt the flow of work, collaboration, and decision-making in an organization, decreasing its overall success and effectiveness [16]. To avoid a negative group dynamic, organizations must carefully plan to avoid things like weak leadership, excessive deference to authority, blocking, groupthink, free riding, and evaluation apprehension. If these behaviors are avoided, a positive group dynamic can be established to increase a positive work climate in which DIs can thrive.

3 Theoretical Framework

Our proposed model explains the relationships between work environment components including work climate and DI behaviors and outcomes. We theorize these relationships based on four interrelated concepts: *environmental factors, digital intrapreneurship experience, digital intrapreneurship infrastructure,* and *digital intrapreneurship outputs.* As a result of this model, we hypothesize that digital intrapreneurship outputs increase within an organization if the digital intrapreneurship is supported by intrapreneurial work practices, digital technology and positive digital intrapreneurship experience. While there are external factors encouraging or demanding DI such as competition, customer demand/needs, digital innovation trends, new technologies, political changes, and the economy [12], we emphasize the direct influence of the individual factors, situational factors, and organizational factors on DI behavior and output. A work climate in which a digital intrapreneur can thrive must include collaborative norms and group dynamics. DIs require an environment that psychologically and structurally empowers them to engage in employee driven innovation (EDI). These factors highlight the relationship between the individual DI, the situation they are in and the organizational culture that influences them [17]. As a cluster, these factors form the DI experience. Moreover, the DI should fall in a continuous learning cycle in order to revisit and improve the work climate and the key enablers (work practices and digital technology). The rest of this section discusses the importance of these components and their relationships (Fig. 1).

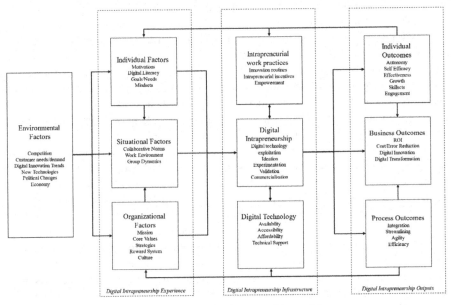

Fig. 1. A digital intrapreneurship model

3.1   Digital Intrapreneurial Experience

The individual factors are represented by individual motivations, digital literacy, goals, needs, and mindsets. The motivations associated with DIs are both extrinsic and intrinsic motivations [18]. For example, we argue that internal motivation increases both the productivity and creativity of DIs. In addition, digital literacy enables DIs to fully utilize innovation technologies, increasing their ability to engage in effective innovation themselves [7]. We also found that the goals/needs of a DI are positively influenced by the risk-free nature of their positions as DIs [19]. Finally, DIs are known to be self-sufficient [9]. This is due to the nature of the role of an intrapreneur. Similar to an entrepreneur, minus the risk of the venture, they do not conform to regular employee roles and take ownership in their activities DIs [19]. Finally, DIs are known to be self-sufficient [9]. This is due to the nature of the role of an intrapreneur. Similar to an entrepreneur, minus the risk of the venture, they don't conform to regular employee roles and take ownership in their activity [6], in other words, a mindset in which they will have to lead and make decisions for the company. [6], in other words, a mindset in which they will have to lead and make decisions for the company.

Successful DIs share a certain set of skills and traits including autonomy, intrinsic motivation, digital literacy, and attitude toward technology [20, 21]. Autonomy, the ability for employees to work independently and make their own decisions, is necessary as it increases interest in the organization's industry. By being autonomous, DIs develop intrinsic motivations vital to the success of an organization through their persistence and greater productivity [22]. A workplace with people that are animated by intrinsic motivations will motivate each other through their relationships with each other and a sense of unity. It is easier to nurture something that is already created than create it. That being said, it is easier to increase someone's existing intrinsic motivation than to nurture it from scratch, [23] hiring or empowering DIs based on their inherent motivation increases their likelihood of success. This can provide an organization a competitive edge in terms of innovation productivity. In terms of other organizational factors, the work environment must include access to up-to-date digital technologies to support the DI's use of technology to increase effectiveness and productivity [3].

In addition to autonomy and intrinsic motivation, successful DIs have high digital literacy. According to the ALA task force [24], digital literacy is "the ability to use information and communication technologies to find, evaluate, create, and communicate information, requiring both cognitive and technical skills." (p.1). For DIs, digital literacy involves familiarity and expertise with new digital tools [7]. This is relevant to our context because digital literacy is related to innovation and the field of digital intrapreneurs. Related to digital literacy, attitude towards technology is also important to digital intrapreneurship. A positive attitude toward and comfort with ever-changing technologies increases a DI's ability to effectively innovate in a digital environment. Successful DIs keep an open mind when working with new technological tools. This means that, when working in an environment where digital technology is the primary tool used for innovation, a positive attitude towards technology is a prerequisite [11, 25].

These individual factors have two-way relationships with various situational factors, including collaborative norms, work climate, and group dynamics. Collaborative norms refer to the ways a DI will interact with its coworkers while working in a digital environment, such as pausing, paraphrasing, asking questions, etc. [14]. To create an atmosphere that encourages positive collaborative norms, a warm and welcoming workplace climate allows DIs to thrive in their overall creativity [14]. Contributing to the workplace culture, group dynamics include the relationships between DIs and their coworkers [15].

Situational factors are also related to the organizational factors identified in the present study: the organization's mission, core values, and reward systems. First, the mission of a company has an impact on DIs as it improves their effectiveness, consequently the organization's effectiveness too [26] This mission is also linked to an organization's core values as these guiding principles ensure consistency amongst employees' mindsets and beliefs about their shared goals. In particular, DIs must be the first to embody these values as a central aspect of their job is to represent their company. An organization's mission pertaining to digital innovation cannot be accomplished without hiring the right people and motivating them in an effective way. Therefore, the last organizational factor explored in this study is the types of reward systems or reward philosophies employed by an organization.

3.2 Digital Intrapreneurial Infrastructure

Workplace programs and practices that encourage DI innovation and success are referred to as DI infrastructure in this paper. DI infrastructure includes intrapreneurial work practices, digital intrapreneurship, and digital technologies, all elements that allow DIs to engage in the innovation process.

Technological factors like digital technology infrastructure and support play a key role in DI activity and success [5]. Digital infrastructure refers to the physical and organizational structures and the facilities needed for the practice and operations of digital innovation. Workplace practices comprising this infrastructure (i.e., innovation routines, incentives, and empowerment) encourage innovation activity amongst DIs [27]. Infrastructure in an organization stimulates innovation through increasing DIs' interactions, engagements, collaboration, and exploration, and thus work practices motivate and increase positive DI activity. Effective infrastructure influences the entire process of digital intrapreneurship, including exploration, ideation, experimentation, validation, and commercialization [4]. The ability for DIs to experiment sans risk allows the DEs to increase innovation while minimizing the risks associated with typical trial and error processes. However, their effectiveness and success rely on the availability, accessibility, affordability, and technical support of digital technologies provided to DIs by their organizations [3]. Allowing DIs, the optimal use of such technologies supports and encourages their progress and success. Workplace environments in tandem with the individual factors of DIs and powerful technological tools provide the motivation, collaboration, encouragement, and infrastructure needed for DIs to engage in effective innovation activities. Technological factors like digital technology infrastructure and support play a key role in DI activity and success [5]. Digital infrastructure refers to the physical and organizational structures and the facilities needed for the practice and operations of digital innovation. Workplace practices comprising this infrastructure (i.e., innovation routines, incentives, and empowerment) encourage innovation activity amongst DIs. Infrastructure in an organization stimulates innovation through increasing DIs' interactions, engagements, collaboration, and exploration, and thus work practices motivate and increase positive DI activity. Effective infrastructure influences the entire process of digital intrapreneurship, including exploration, ideation, experimentation, validation, and commercialization [4]. The ability for DIs to experiment sans risk allows the DEs to increase innovation while minimizing the risks associated with typical trial and error processes. However, their effectiveness and success rely on the availability, accessibility, affordability, and technical support of digital technologies provided to DIs by their organizations [3]. Allowing DIs, the optimal use of such technologies supports and encourages their progress and success. Workplace environments in tandem with the individual factors of DIs and powerful technological tools provide the motivation, collaboration, encouragement, and infrastructure needed for DIs to engage in effective innovation activities.

While individual factors clearly play a vital role in the success of DIs in an organization, situational factors influence the behaviors of DIs and their outputs. Bandura's social cognitive theory [28] explains that DIs are influenced by other people's behavior, roles, and relationships, the factors that comprise their work climate. In the case of DIs, this theory explains the influence a work climate can have on their DI behavior as well as how they can learn through their observations of others in the digital field.

Bandura's social learning theory argues that learning happens during observation and through mediational processes [28]. For DIs, observing others engage in collaborative activities or utilize new technologies may motivate their own efforts to collaborate more or experiment with novel tools. Various mediational processes occur that help determine whether or not an individual will imitate a behavior they have observed/are currently observing. The four mediational processes involved in the social learning theory are attention, retention, reproduction, and motivation [29]. Work environments that discourage these processes prevent DI's from successfully learning from the behaviors and successes of those around them, a key avenue for increasing productivity and effectiveness in innovation efforts.

In order to learn from others' behaviors, we should pay attention to the behavior itself. Thus, a DI's work climate must highlight positive behaviors through programs like reward systems. This suggestion draws employee attention toward the most effective and favorable behaviors, increasing the overall ability of the team [26]. However, in order to perform a new behavior, an individual must retain the information they pay attention to recreate the behavior later. Thus, retention is one of the most important mediation processes involved in social learning theory [30]. After retaining information about a new behavior, individuals must be able to reproduce the information they have processed. For DI's to properly reproduce new behaviors, their work climate must effectively demonstrate, explain, and model favorable and positive behaviors. In order to learn from others' behaviors, we should pay attention to the behavior itself. Thus, a DI's work climate must highlight positive behaviors through programs like reward systems. This suggestion draws employee attention toward the most effective and favorable behaviors, increasing the overall ability of the team. However, in order to perform a new behavior, an individual must retain the information they pay attention to recreate the behavior later. Thus, retention is one of the most important mediation processes involved in social learning theory [31]. After retaining information about a new behavior, individuals must be able to reproduce the information they have processed. For DI's to properly reproduce new behaviors, their work climate must effectively demonstrate, explain, and model favorable and positive behaviors.

Reproduction, the third mediational process in the theory, can only occur if the observer has the capacity to reproduce the behavior. For DI's, the work environment must provide them the tools and resources necessary to successfully learn the new behaviors they observe from others [11]. Given the proper tools and support, the final process identified by social learning theory is motivation [31]. This stage occurs after DIs conclude that the rewards of performing the behavior outweigh the costs. In a work environment for DI's, this could include increasing employee perceptions of the positives of new, innovative behaviors. Social cognitive theory helps explain the necessary attributes of a work climate in which Dis may thrive. If the work environment does not fulfill these processes, DIs will likely not reproduce novel behaviors that drive productivity and effectiveness in their positions.

3.3 Digital Intrapreneurs Outputs

The outcome of successful and effective DIs is conceptualized as DI activity output. It includes individual outcomes, business outcomes, and process outcomes. Workplaces that prioritize the success of their DIs help employees to increase their self-efficacy, provide a greater return on investment (ROI), and streamline processes for successful innovation. Nourishing DIs increases their overall output and value. At an individual level, when DIs develop more effective behaviors and skills, they add a competitive advantage to the success of digital ventures. The DI's continuous ability to practice and improve their skillset with less risk enables them to prepare for more effective and innovative DE activity.

With the proper environmental and individual factors, DIs are more likely to experiment with and successfully utilize digital innovation technologies. The ability to experiment freely and test innovative ideas sans risk strengthens a company's ability to withstand inconsistencies in its environment/market [5]. The encouragement of DI activity generates a competitive advantage for DEs by strengthening talent within the organization. We argue that the individual outcomes produced by successful DIs route directly through their own autonomy, self-efficacy, effectiveness, personal growth, skillset, and increased engagement.

Robust infrastructures provided by organizations allow DIs to further develop their capabilities to engage in digital intrapreneurship activities. Through observations of others and a supportive work environment, DIs engage in a continuous learning experience that strengthens their ability to withstand and endure the challenges in the field, such as keeping up with the rapid developments in digital innovation technologies [32]. Individual outcomes influence business outcomes through ROI, cost/error reduction, increased digital innovation, and productive transformation [33]. By allowing DIs to grow and fortify their capabilities, risk levels and error reduce while innovation productivity increases. Finally, individual and business outcomes influence the overall process outcomes. DI will engage with the digital technologies to exploit the resource and transform it into an output such as digital innovation. This digital innovation would then have a process such as integration that would have to be streamlined and maintained for efficiency. This repetitive action would then influence the individual outcome reflective in their skillset. Business outcomes refer to the ROI, the digital innovations created by the DI. The DI would innovate go through the digital intrapreneurship process for efficiency in which would result in a lower cost of error for the organization.

4   Discussion and Recommendations

We began our work by understanding digital innovation as the crux of digital intrapreneurship. As we went through our literature review, we identified a connection to DI behaviors and their workplace environment. The work climate affects the motivation and behavior of the DIs. There are many factors that come into play such as internal, environmental, organizational. The act of "nurturing" DI refers to ensuring that all possible influential factors are positively encouraging individuals to fail and try again until they succeed. To narrow our study to a specific approach out of the many avenues available, we created a conceptual model.

Our conceptual model shows how DI is encouraged through different mechanisms. There are four key concepts within our model which include: environmental factors, digital intrapreneurship experience, digital intrapreneurship infrastructure, digital intrapreneurship outputs. Within digital intrapreneurship experience, we identified individual, situational and organizational factors. Under digital intrapreneurship infrastructure is intrapreneurial work practices, digital intrapreneurship, and digital technologies. Under digital intrapreneurship outputs are the individual outcomes, business outcomes, and process outcomes. The model represents the work climate necessary for digital intrapreneurship to flourish. The "nurturing" perspective is to have all factors working to positively influence the DI to engage in DI activities with the hopes of a positive outcome. In the case of negative outcomes such as failure, it is the work climate that "nurtures" again to the DI to try again until success. The feedback loops in this model should result in an increase within all the factors in the model, specifically the digital intrapreneur experience and activity output.

In order to increase successful digital intrapreneurship, we have provided a list of recommendations for organizations to follow. One important way to encourage digital intrapreneurship is to reinforce positive behaviors in the workplace. According to Luthans, there are different types of organizational behavior modifications (O.B. Mod.) that can improve employee performance [34]. In a digital intrapreneurship context, an O.B. Mod. approach is one strategy that could increase the likelihood that DIs adopt positive behaviors modeled by other team members or encouraged by management.

These rewards increase employee motivation to experiment and learn new skillsets. Organizations should provide opportunities for employees to be promoted and receive meaningful recognition for their hard work. Well-designed reward systems encourage employees to strive for more than the minimum expectation. Further, improvements to an organization's culture can improve DIs' innovation and performance [17]. The culture of the organization needs to encourage DIs to strive for a central goal informed by the organization's mission and values. Making these explicit can help focus employee efforts and increase successful collaboration. In a digital environment, promoting a culture of innovation is uniquely key to the success of DIs. This is a set of shared beliefs and risk-taking behaviors that lead to openness towards innovation. A culture of openness provided by the creation of an innovation culture also has a positive impact on collaboration.

DIs must be nourished through internal and external motivating factors. These factors must promote both psychological and structural empowerment through internal and external factors. The internal locus of control in an individual is a primary concern, as individuals must be motivated to learn and open to learning from mistakes in order to engage in effective digital intrapreneurship activities. The ideal DI work climate is a complex environment in which everyone has an important role to play. Simple positive shifts in a work climate can have powerful effects on the success of DIs and their work. Individual, situational, and organizational factors must all be taken into consideration when planning a work climate for higher and more effective digital intrapreneurship.

References

1. Pinchot, G., Soltanifar, M.: Digital Intrapreneurship: The Corporate Solution to a Rapid Digitalisation, pp. 233–262. Springer, Cham (2021)
2. Reibenspiess, V., Drechsler, K., Eckhardt, A., Wagner, H.T.: Tapping into the wealth of employees' ideas: design principles for a digital intrapreneurship platform. Inf. Manage. 1, 103287 (2020). https://doi.org/10.1016/j.im.2020.103287
3. Soltanifar, M., Hughes, M.: Digital Entrepreneurship: Impact on Business and Society. Springer, Cham (2005)
4. Opland, .L., Jaccheri, L., Pappas, I.O., Engesmo, J.: Utilising the innovation potential-a systematic literature review on employee-driven digital innovation. In: European Conference on Information Systems (2020)
5. Vassilakopoulou, P., Grisot, M.: Effectual tactics in digital intrapreneurship: a process model. J. Strateg. Inf. Syst. 29, 1 (2020). https://doi.org/10.1016/j.jsis.2020.101617
6. Seshadri, D.V.R., Tripathy, A.: Innovation through intrapreneurship: the road less travelled. Vikalpa 31, 17–29 (2006). https://doi.org/10.1177/0256090920060102
7. Young, R., Wahlberg, L., Davis, E., Abhari, K.: Towards a theory of digital entrepreneurship mindset: the role of digital learning aptitude and digital literacy. In: AMCIS 2020 Proceedings, pp 1–10 (2020)
8. Pinchot, G.: The Pinchot Perspective. In: Pinchot.com (2013). http://www.pinchot.com/
9. Echebiri, C., Amundsen, S., Engen, M.: Linking structural empowerment to employee-driven innovation: the mediating role of psychological empowerment. Adm. Sci. 10, 42 (2020). https://doi.org/10.3390/admsci10030042
10. Barroso, D.B.R., et al.: stakeholder perception in the organizational environment focusing on behavior. Int. J. Adv. Eng. Res. Sci. 5, 44–54 (2018). https://doi.org/10.22161/ijaers.5.2.5
11. Baptista, J., et al.: Digital work and organisational transformation: emergent digital/human work configurations in modern organisations. J. Strateg. Inf. Syst. 29, 101618 (2020). https://doi.org/10.1016/j.jsis.2020.101618
12. Honig, B., Samuelsson, M.: Business planning by intrapreneurs and entrepreneurs under environmental uncertainty and institutional pressure. Technovation 99, 102124 (2021). https://doi.org/10.1016/j.technovation.2020.102124
13. Homans, G.C.: Social Behavior as Exchange. Am. J. Sociol. 63, 597–606 (1958). https://doi.org/10.1086/222355
14. Climer, A.: Seven Norms of Collaboration (2015)
15. Gençer, H.: Group dynamics and behaviour. Univ. J. Educ. Res. 7, 223–229 (2019). https://doi.org/10.13189/ujer.2019.070128
16. Feisal, F.: Corporate innovation: democratizing decision-making. In: Noviaristanti, S., Hanafi, H.M., Trihanondo, D. (eds.) Understanding Digital Industry, pp. 18–19. Routledge (2020). https://doi.org/10.1201/9780367814557-6
17. Amaechi, E.: Understanding culture and success in global business: developing cultural and innovative intrapreneurs in small businesses. In: Thakkar, B.S. (ed.) Culture in Global Businesses: Addressing National and Organizational Challenges, pp. 205–224. Springer International Publishing, Cham (2021). https://doi.org/10.1007/978-3-030-60296-3_9

18. Cnossen, B., Loots, E., van Witteloostuijn, A.: Individual motivation among entrepreneurs in the creative and cultural industries: a self-determination perspective. Creat. Innov. Manage. **28**, 389–402 (2019). https://doi.org/10.1111/caim.12315
19. Schlaegel, C., Engle, R.L., Richter, N.F., Taureck, P.C.: Personal factors, entrepreneurial intention, and entrepreneurial status: a multinational study in three institutional environments. J. Int. Entrep. **25**, 1–42 (2021). https://doi.org/10.1007/s10843-021-00287-7
20. Nambisan, S.: Digital entrepreneurship: toward a digital technology perspective of entrepreneurship. Entrep. Theory Pract. **41**, 1029–1055 (2017). https://doi.org/10.1111/etap.12254
21. Martiarena, A.: What's so entrepreneurial about intrapreneurs? Small Bus. Econ. **40**, 27–39 (2013). https://doi.org/10.1007/s11187-011-93481-1
22. Koe, W.-L.: The motivation to adopt e-commerce among Malaysian entrepreneurs. Organ. Mark. Emerg. Econ. **11**(1), 189–202 (2020). https://doi.org/10.15388/omee.2020.11.30
23. Ryan, R.M., Deci, E.L.: Self-determination theory and the facilitation of intrinsic motivation, social development, and well-being. Am. Psychol. **55**, 68–78 (2000)
24. ALA: Report of the ALA Special Task Force on Digital Literacy (2017)
25. Abhari, M., Abhari, K.: Ambient intelligence applications in architecture: factors affecting adoption decisions. In: Arai, K., Kapoor, S., Bhatia, R. (eds.) FICC 2020. AISC, vol. 1129, pp. 235–250. Springer, Cham (2020). https://doi.org/10.1007/978-3-030-39445-5_18
26. Choon, T.T., Patrick, K.C.: The impact of goal setting on employee effectiveness to improve organisation effectiveness: empirical study of a high-tech company in Singapore. J. Bus. Econ. Policy **3**, 1–16 (2016)
27. Njoroge, N., Yazdanifard, R.: The impact of social and emotional intelligence on employee motivation in a multigenerational workplace. Int. J. Inf. Bus. Manage. **6**, 163 (2014)
28. Bandura, A.: Social foundations of thought and action : a social cognitive theory/Albert Bandura, Vol. 16, pp. 2–9, 617. Prentice-Hall, New Jersey (1986)
29. Wood, R., Bandura, A.: Social cognitive theory of organizational management university of New South Wales. Acad. Manage. Rev. **14**, 361–384 (1989)
30. Bandura, A.: Social learning theory, pp. 1–46 (1971)
31. Bandura, A.: Social learning theory. Gr. Organ. Stud. **2**, 384–385 (1977). https://doi.org/10.1177/105960117700200317
32. Bäckström, I., Bengtsson, L.: A mapping study of employee innovation: proposing a research agenda. Eur. J. Innov. Manage. **22**, 468–492 (2019)
33. Shahi, C., Sinha, M.: Digital transformation: challenges faced by organizations and their potential solutions. Int. J. Innov. Sci. **13**, 17–33 (2021). https://doi.org/10.1108/IJIS-09-2020-0157
34. Luthans, F., Stajkovic, A.D.: Reinforce for performance: the need to go beyond pay and even rewards. Acad. Manage. Exec. **13**, 49–57 (1999). https://doi.org/10.5465/ame.1999.1899548

Design Requirements for Crop-Specific Online and Web-Based Portals

Isaac Nyabisa Oteyo[1,2]($\boxtimes$) ⓘ, Philip Apodo Oyier[2] ⓘ, and Stephen Kimani[2] ⓘ

[1] Software Languages Lab, Vrije Universiteit Brussel, Pleinlaan 2,
1050 Brussels, Belgium
isaac.nyabisa.oteyo@vub.be
[2] School of Computing and IT, Jomo Kenyatta University of Agriculture
and Technology, P.O. Box 62000, 00200 Nairobi, Kenya
oyier@itc.jkuat.ac.ke, skimani@scit.jkuat.ac.ke

Abstract. Legumes such as common beans (*Phaseolus vulgaris L.*) continue playing a critical role in making developed and developing economies food sustainable as alternative sources to animal proteins. The crops bring together different stakeholders in their value chain such as farmers, service providers, researchers and policymakers. Web-based portals are emerging as important tools that these different stakeholders can use to perform various tasks, access, and share vital information pertaining to common beans. However, designing portals that are specific to common beans has not been given adequate consideration in the literature. In this study, we administered a survey to profile challenges and design requirements for web-based portals that are specific to common beans. We present the survey findings in this paper. The findings provide useful insights to researchers and industry in developing future agricultural web-based portals, and can be applied to portals on other crops or different domains.

Keywords: User requirements · User interface design · Online portals · Food security

1 Introduction

Sustainable access to information is vital in agricultural activities [2,9]. Recently, web-based portals have received a lot of attention from research and industry as important sources of agricultural information such as information on pest control and management for common beans [3,4,10]. Common beans (*Phaseolus vulgaris L.*) is an important crop in developing regions since it serves as an alternative source to animal proteins. Subsequently, different stakeholders for common beans including those in agriculture, service providers, research, and policy making rely on the web-based portals to access and share valuable information that can help farmers in managing their crops well based on up-to-date crop management practices. However, from the literature, existing portals are

ⓒ Springer Nature Switzerland AG 2021
C. Stephanidis et al. (Eds.): HCII 2021, LNCS 13097, pp. 596–615, 2021.
https://doi.org/10.1007/978-3-030-90966-6_41

not specific and particular to common beans. As such, the existing agricultural portals are cluttered with a lot of information that can make it difficult for farmers to get important information on common beans at a glance. Additionally, designing portals that are specific to common beans has not received adequate attention in the literature. This can be a problem in developing regions where farmers operate in rural areas and accessing web-based portals in such areas is faced with various challenges such as Internet access issues. Addressing this gap can help in advancing adoption of information and communication technologies (ICTs) in performing agricultural activities in both developed and developing regions.

In this study, we administered a survey to: (1) profile internet usage by stakeholders of common beans, (2) document the challenges faced by stakeholders when accessing online information on legumes such as common beans, (3) identify preferred portal services and features, (4) identify preferred document formats and portal subscription modes, and (5) determine design requirements for crop-specific web-based portals. We used the survey findings to model design requirements as a function of different portal features. The overall findings can be used by researchers and industry when implementing agriculture related information portals.

Research Questions: The study was guided by the following research questions:

- What are the challenges faced when accessing legume portals?
- What are the preferred services and features for legume portals?
- What are the design requirements for legume portals?
- What features can be used to attract users to visit legume portals?
- What document formats are preferred on legume portals?
- What subscription modes are preferred on legume portals?

Contributions: This study makes the following two contributions: (1) the study documents challenges faced by stakeholders when accessing online information on common beans, and design requirements for online portals on common beans, and (2) the study proposes a model for grouping design requirements for online portals on common beans. The model can be applied to other crops and other domains.

In the subsequent sections, we present and discuss materials and methods in Sect. 2, survey results in Sect. 3, requirements model and preliminary prototype portal in Sect. 4, key findings in Sect. 5, related work in Sect. 6, and finally, conclusions and directions for future work in Sect. 7.

2   Materials and Methods

An online questionnaire was sent to different stakeholders for portals on common beans: (1) farmers, (2) researchers and policymakers, and (3) service providers.

The purpose of the questionnaire was to collect data that could help in answering the research questions described in Sect. 1. In order to identify the questionnaire items, we studied related research articles and related portals such as LegumePlus[1], Legume Information System[2] etc. From this study, we noted the type of users, common portal features and services. We used this knowledge to inform and design the items of our questionnaire. This process went through several iterations before being digitised into an online questionnaire. The questionnaires were applied between September 10 and October 19 2020 to respondents in Nairobi-Kenya, which is a developing region in East Africa. A total of 27 respondents were purposively selected (9 farmers, 13 researchers and policymakers, and 5 service providers) based on their participation in agricultural research and technology transfer projects in one of the leading agricultural university in the region and government agencies. The questionnaire items were grouped according to the research questions. The questions were both closed-ended and open-ended to solicit more feedback from the respondents. An ordinal scale (such as "not important, slightly important, important, very important") was used on the questionnaire items to guide the responses received. The online questionnaires were sent to the email addresses of the target respondents. Weekly email reminders were sent to the unresponsive respondents to motivate them to complete the survey. The data collected was analysed and the results are presented in this paper.

3   Results and Discussion

In this section, we present and discuss the results of the survey that was administered in this study as follows:

3.1   Demographics

This section shows the distribution of survey respondents in terms of gender, academic qualifications, crops focused on, access to the internet, means of accessing the internet, and years of internet access and usage.

Gender and Academic Level Distribution: 79.3% of the respondents were male while 20.7% were female. Note that in this study, we do not focus on any specific gender and as such our findings are not gender specific. In terms of academic levels, 57.5% of the respondents were doctorate degree holders, 31.4% had masters level education, 7.4% had undergraduate and finally, 3.7% had diploma level education. On average, there were more respondents with postgraduate academic qualifications. This was important to reduce errors that could arise when providing responses to the survey questions.

---

[1] http://legumeplus.eu.

[2] https://legumeinfo.org.

Focus Crops and Role Played: Most farmers grow peas, lentils, cowpeas, and beans; fewer farmers grow soybeans. The farmers played different roles in the farm with 44.4% being farm owners, 11.1% as chief farm managers, 22.2% as agricultural instructors, 11.1% as farm supervisors, 11.1% as consultants, and another 11.1% as research assistants. Majority of the service providers handled desmodium followed by beans. 20% of the service providers handled beans and another 20% handled chickpeas. For researchers and policymakers, the main fields of professional engagement were agriculture at 30.8%, food nutrition, food science and technology, social science and humanities (all at 15.4% each), and computing and information technology at 7.6%.

Access and Means of Accessing the Internet: 96.3% of the respondents had access to the Internet. This is an important statistics that emphasises the need for online portals with information on particular crops. As mentioned before, such portals can make information access and sharing among users easy. The means of accessing the Internet were grouped into four main categories as shown in Table 1. On average, most of the stakeholders accessed the Internet from their mobile phones or tablets using either cellular or WiFi connections. With the increased adoption of smartphones in developing regions, we anticipated to get this kind of results for an urban area setting. Accessing the Internet directly from mobile phones or tablets is more flexible especially to farmers that spend most of their time in farm fields. We believe that accessing the Internet on mobile phones can save on time and effort spent visiting Internet cafés, and hence the low response on Internet cafés as a means of accessing the Internet.

Table 1. Means of accessing the Internet.

Category	Farmers	Researchers and policymakers	Service providers	Average
Internet access directly from mobile phone or tablet	75.0%	69.2%	80%	74.7%
WiFi connectivity at the place of residence or work	37.5%	84.6%	80%	67.4%
Wired connectivity/LAN at the place of residence or work	37.5%	53.8%	60%	50.4%
Internet café	12.5%	0.0%	0.0%	4.2%

Years of Internet Access and Usage: From Table 2, most of the respondents have used the Internet for more than 10 years. This tallies with the academic levels where most respondents were doctorate degree holders that encompasses a huge component of research. In modern times, the Internet is a big source of research materials and information. Also, the spread of smartphones started experiencing peaks about a decade ago and changed access to information in the developing world [1]. As such, with smartphones, Internet access was brought closer to the end-user.

Table 2. Numbers of years of accessing and using the Internet.

	Farmers	Researchers and policymakers	Service providers	Average
<1 year	0.0%	0.0%	0.0%	0.0%
1–5 years	25.0%	23.1%	0.0%	16.0%
6–10 years	50.0%	0.0%	0.0%	16.7%
>10 years	25.0%	76.9%	100.0%	67.3%

3.2   Knowledge on Existing Legume Portals and Challenges Faced

Table 3 shows the knowledge the respondents had on existing legume portals. Most respondents had knowledge on IFPRI[3] portal. This portal has a food price watch section which is useful to most of the respondents. However, the average percentage of respondents with knowledge on existing portals was less than 40%. This is despite the fact that most respondents had access to the Internet. We believe, this situation is occasioned by the information on existing legume portals not being entirely focused on common beans. As such, we think that some users did not spend enough time on those portals to get the kind of information they were expecting or looking for on those portals. From a user experience perspective, failing to get the expected information on the first visit to the portal can be a barrier to return to the same portal the second time or recommend the portal to other users.

Table 3. Knowledge on existing online legume portals.

	Farmers	Researchers and policymakers	Service providers	Average
http://legumeplus.eu	11.1%	7.7%	0.0%	6.3%
https://www.glnc.org.au/	33.3%	23.1%	0.0%	18.8%
https://www.ildis.org/	11.1%	0.0%	0.0%	3.7%
https://legumeinfo.org/	11.1%	0.0%	0.0%	3.7%
http://www.legato-fp7.eu/	0.0%	0.0%	0.0%	0.0%
http://tropicallegumes.icrisat.org/	11.1%	15.4%	0.0%	8.8%
https://www.foodsecurityportal.org/	33.3%	61.5%	20.0%	38.3%

Table 4 shows the challenges cited when accessing resources on common beans online. Lack of portals on common beans was the most cited challenge followed by irrelevant portal content. This resonates with the findings in Table 3 that shows that less than 40% of the stakeholders had knowledge on existing portals

---

[3] https://www.foodsecurityportal.org/.

for common beans. We believe that this is because the existing portal are generic to agriculture and not specific to common beans. On irrelevant portal content, we believe that this challenge is occasioned by cluttering of information on existing portals that can make it difficult to get relevant information at a glance.

Table 4. Challenges faced when accessing legume portals.

Challenges	Farmers	Researchers and policymakers	Service providers	Average
Lack of Internet	11.1%	0.0%	0.0%	3.7%
Slow Internet	11.1%	23.1%	20%	18.1%
Lack of portals on common beans	66.7%	23.1%	80%	56.6%
Irrelevant portal content	22.2%	15.2%	40%	25.8%
Online privacy and trust concerns	11.1%	7.7%	20%	12.9%

3.3 Portal Features and Design Requirements

This section presents the preferred portal features and design requirements.

Preferred Portal Document Format(s): Figure 1 shows the average preferred document formats by legume stakeholders. In order of preference, video content is most preferred followed by audio content, presentations, PDF, HTML, text file documents, and finally XML documents. Video content is preferred since it can provide demonstrations with audio explanations that users can easily watch and follow on mobile phones. XML and HTML document formats are not preferred because they require translation into a form that can be understood. Such translation requires experiences in computer programming which can be difficult to non-programmers. Text file (word) documents are not preferred because they are perceived to transmit computer viruses that can be a threat to security and privacy.

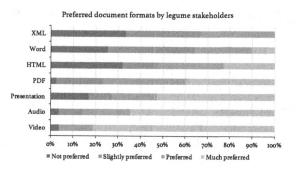

Fig. 1. Average preferred portal document format by legume stakeholders.

Preferred Portal Subscription Mode(s): Figure 2 shows the average preferred portal subscription mode by legume stakeholders. Most respondents prefer free content access on portals for common beans. A small fraction of the respondents agrees to monthly, semi-annual, and annual subscriptions. This can be as a result of the perceived costs that are associated with subscribing for premium content. We believe that annual subscription is preferred after the free content because of the perceived longer period of content access. Some content like video and audio can have a cost implication to prepare. Having such content on common bean portals may require a sustainable financial model. Our recommendation is that portal designers and owners can consider a mix (hybrid) of both free and premium content.

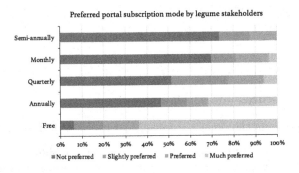

Fig. 2. Average preferred portal subscription mode by legume stakeholders.

Portal Style and Placement of Menus: Farmers prefer portals with horizontal or vertical text, sub-menus and dropdown menus (Table 5). Similarly, service providers prefer portal that use icons or graphics, while researchers and policymakers prefer portals with horizontal text, sub-menus with icons or graphics. In terms of placing major links or menus, service providers prefer menus on the right, while researchers and policymakers prefer menus either on top or left (Table 6). Finally, farmers prefer menus on top, right or left side of the portal. On average, most respondents prefer right menus followed by top menus.

Table 5. Portal style and placement of menus.

	Horizontal text	Submenus	Vertical text	Drop down menus	Icons or graphics
Researchers and policymakers	31%	23%	15%	8%	23%
Farmers	33%	0%	33%	22%	11%
Service providers	0%	0%	20%	20%	60%
Average	21.3%	7.7%	22.7%	16.7%	31.3%

Table 6. Portal style and placement of menus.

	Left menu	Right menu	Top menu	Bottom menu
Researchers and policymakers	38%	0%	54%	8%
Farmers	22%	33%	33%	11%
Service providers	0%	100%	0%	0%
Average	20.0%	44.3%	29.0%	6.3%

Services and Features: Figure 3, Fig. 4, and Fig. 5 show the rating for the preferred portal services and features by researchers and policymakers, farmers and service providers respectively. In general, researchers and policymakers prefer information on food composition and documentary series such as seed systems, processing and marketing, breeding, and crop management as important features and services to have on portals for common beans. On the other hand, farmers prefer market information (such as crop prices) and information on legume food composition. Finally, service providers prefer weather information and crop calendars, policy analysis tools, funding information, and online resources for local legume markets.

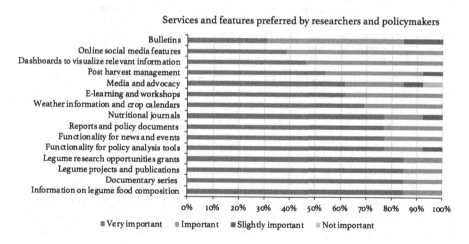

Fig. 3. Services and features preferred by researchers and policymakers.

Design Requirements: Figure 6, Fig. 7, and Fig. 8 show the rating for the design requirements by different stakeholders for common beans. In general, portals for common beans should be easy to navigate and access (or locate and get) items of interest (e.g., documents, menu items, links of interest), efficient (i.e., the portal should be fast). In addition, for researchers and policymakers, the

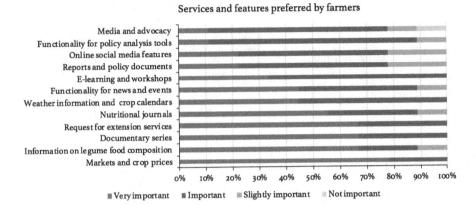

Fig. 4. Services and features preferred by the farmers.

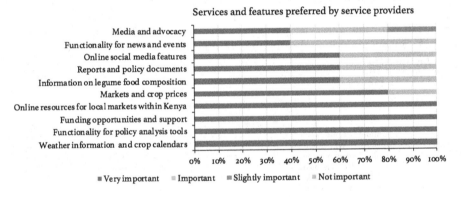

Fig. 5. Services and features preferred by service providers.

portal should be able to respond to end-user instructions through appropriate feedback mechanisms, protect end-user's privacy, be easy to reverse or cancel actions, and also be easy to understand and use. For farmers, the portal should be easy to understand and use, be personalised to specific needs, be consistent in design and layout, provide multiple ways of doing things, and be efficient (i.e., fast). For service providers, in addition to the above, the portal should provide mechanisms for error prevention, provide help facilities, and be visually appealing.

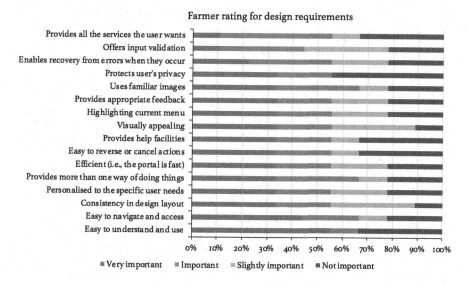

Fig. 6. Design requirements as rated by the farmers.

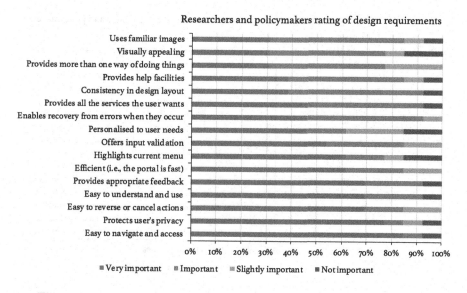

Fig. 7. Design requirements as rated by the researchers and policymakers.

Portal Attraction Methods and Features: Figure 9, Fig. 10, and Fig. 11 show the rating for different methods and features that can attract users to portals for common beans. Researchers and policymakers consider updated portal content, efficient and effective customer support, supporting users to reset or remember forgotten usernames and passwords as key attracting methods/

Service providers rating of design requirements

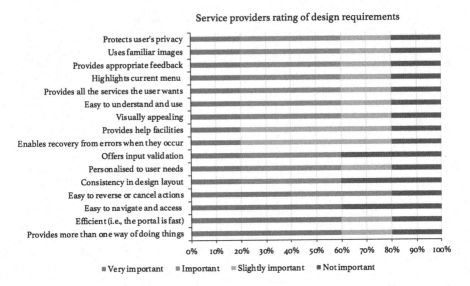

Fig. 8. Design requirements as rated by the service providers.

Portal attraction methods and features for researchers and policymakers

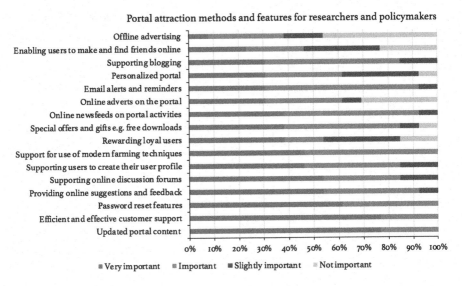

Fig. 9. Portal attraction methods and features for researchers and policymakers.

features to portals for common beans (Fig. 9). Farmers consider support for use of modern farming techniques, supporting users to reset or remember forgotten usernames and passwords, and updated portal content as key attracting methods/features to portals for common beans (Fig. 10). Finally, service providers consider personalising portal features, rewarding royal customers, special offers

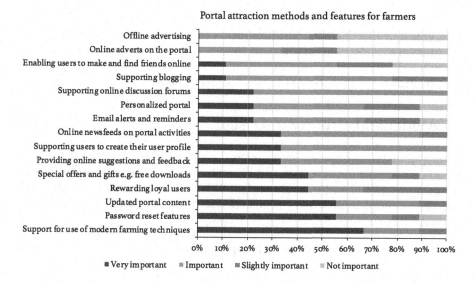

Fig. 10. Portal attraction methods and features for farmers.

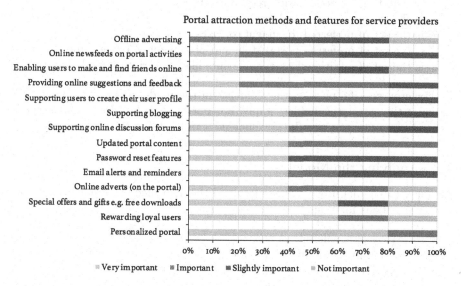

Fig. 11. Portal attraction methods and features for service providers.

and gifts (e.g., free content downloads) as key attracting methods and features to portals for common beans (Fig. 11).

Study Bias and Limitations: Open questions such as "Other: ..." were included in the online questionnaire to collect new requirements. The data collection questionnaire was circulated on email. As such, this implied that only respondents with Internet access could respond to the questionnaire. Moreover, with online questionnaire, it was difficult to ascertain the sample providing the information was the right person. Nonetheless, the received information provides useful insights that can be used in implementing portals for common beans. The insights drawn can be extended to the design of portals in other domains.

4   Model and Prototype Design

From the analysis of the survey responses, we propose the model illustrated in Eq. (1) for legume portal design requirements. We base the proposed model on: (1) preferred portal features, (2) preferred document formats, (3) portal style and placement of menus, and (4) non-core features like subscription modes for content.

$$D_r = \Gamma + \Upsilon + \Phi + \Psi \tag{1}$$

where,

D_r refers to the portal design requirements,
Γ is the set of preferred features,
Υ is the set of preferred document formats,
Φ is the set of preferred portal style and placement of menus, and
Ψ is the set of additional portal elements like subscription mode for content.

For crop specific portals, the elements in the model will often remain similar since the same stakeholders apply. For portals in other domains, the model elements can change since the stakeholders can be different.

4.1   Applying the Model

To apply the model in Eq. (1), we grouped the identified requirements from the survey results as follows;

$\Gamma = \{\gamma_1, \gamma_2, \gamma_3\}$, where;
γ_1 = section for news and events for dynamically updated content,
γ_2 = media and advocacy section,
γ_3 = stakeholder specific sections.
$\Phi = \{\phi_1, \phi_2, \phi_3\}$, where;
ϕ_1 = horizontal text,
ϕ_2 = drop down menus,
ϕ_3 = use of images.
$\Upsilon = \{\upsilon_1, \upsilon_2\}$, where;
υ_1 = section for free resources,
υ_2 = section for free datasets that can motivate users to visit the portal.

$\Psi = \{\psi_1, \psi_2, \psi_3\}$, where;
ψ_1 = responsive design to foster accessibility from different devices,
ψ_2 = consistent layout,
ψ_3 = links to social media and blogging platforms to keep users updated.

Then, using the *union* property of sets, Eq. (1) becomes Eq. (2).

$$D_r = \Gamma \sqcup \Upsilon \sqcup \Phi \sqcup \Psi \tag{2}$$

which results to;

$$= \{\{\gamma_1, \gamma_2, \gamma_3\}, \{\upsilon_1, \upsilon_2\}, \{\phi_1, \phi_2, \phi_3\}, \{\psi_1, \psi_2, \psi_3\}\}$$

This model transforms D_r into a set of portal design requirements with subsets Γ, Υ, Φ and Ψ. The model holds under the following conditions:

1. if $(\forall i \in D_r, i > 0) \wedge (D_r \neq \emptyset)$ and,
2. if $\forall i \in D_r, \exists j, k, m$, and n, such that $(j \in \Gamma, j > 0) \vee (k \in \Upsilon, k > 0) \vee (m \in \Phi, m > 0) \vee (n \in \Psi, n > 0)$ is *true*.

Note that the lower bound for the elements in each set Γ, Υ, Φ and Ψ can be zero, but at least one set should have at least one element, while the upper bound for the set elements is not limited. The above grouping, yielded a set of design requirement that we used to generate the prototype described in Sect. 4.2 and Sect. 4.3. This model can be used to identify, classify, and group requirements for portals in other domains or for other crops.

4.2   Portal Architecture

Figure 12 shows the overall prototype architecture. This architecture portrays three key portal actors: users, content providers, and the portal administrator(s). The administrator performs administrative tasks such as updating menu items or adjusting the portal design layout. The content provider gives useful information that is relevant to the different portal stakeholders. Finally, the users (farmers, service providers, researchers and policymakers) access the portal to consume the information provided. All portal content is stored in the portal database from where it is retrieved for display on portal pages.

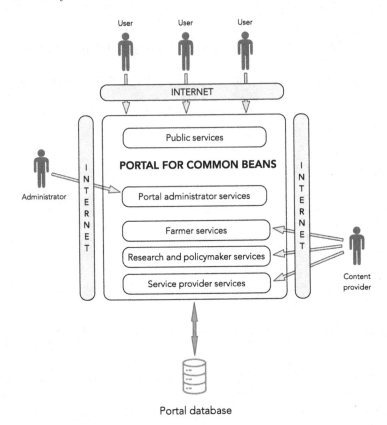

Fig. 12. Overall architecture of the prototype web portal.

4.3   Design Decisions

We based our prototype on the following design decisions:

- *Text alignment:* From the survey findings, farmers, researchers and policy-makers prefer horizontal text. All the stakeholders prefer vertical text alignment. In our prototype design, we employ a mixture of the two approaches.
- *Menu type:* From the survey findings, farmers, service providers, researchers and policymakers prefer drop-down menus, while only farmers prefer sub-menus. Similarly, all the stakeholders prefer infographics such as icons and images. In our design, we selectively use icons and images that are relevant to the target crop.
- *Menu placement:* From the survey findings, farmers, researchers and policy-makers prefer left, top, and bottom menus, while service providers prefer right menus. As such, in our prototype design, we utilised a mix of different menu placements. Moreover, most of the existing portals have top menus that are based on the top-down techniques for reading web pages.

We believe that the above design decisions can apply to other crop portals or different domains. The resulting prototype is as illustrated in Fig. 13(a), Fig. 13(b), and Fig. 13(c). Figure 13(a) shows the portal attraction features such as food composition, bulletins, publications, nutritional journals etc. Figure 13(b) shows the drop-down menus that were preferred by most survey respondents. Figure 13(c) shows some of the resources that will be availed on the portal such as datasets, policy analysis tools, price watch, and visualisation tools. These features and resources can be replicated in portals that focus on different crops or domains.

4.4   Comparison to Other Portals

Table 7 shows how the prototype portal compares to other agricultural portals. Most of the existing portals that we considered in this study use: (1) top menus with horizontal text alignment, (2) drop down menus, (3) icons or graphics. The prototype conforms to what other portals support i.e., making use of icons or graphics, drop down menus, horizontal text alignment, and having dedicated sections for news and events. The news and events form part of the changing content to keep the portal "fresh" and updated. To improve navigation through the legume portal, we employed a mix of different menu placement styles. As such, we have consistent top and bottom menus, while we use right and left menus on specific portal pages such as on the pages for news and events.

5   Findings

This study was based on six research questions as described in Sect. 1. In this section, we present the findings that provide answers to the research questions.

Finding 1: Challenges Faced. Broadband and cellular network access are now available in most developing regions. However, in these regions the Internet connection speeds can be slow due to poor quality network signals in some areas that are far away from urban centres. Often, this phenomenon can lead to intermittent network connections. The challenges associated with Internet access can lead to a perceived lack of portals on common beans since accessing them becomes a problem. Moreover, from the literature, existing portals are general and not specific to particular crops. As such, their content can be perceived as irrelevant, and hence the need for methods and features to attract users to legume portals. We believe that stakeholders will visit crop specific online portals that are tailored to provide specific crop information. Finally, some of the existing agricultural portals require subscription for premium content that users can perceive to be costly.

Finding 2: Preferred Services and Features. Farmers prefer portals that provide information on market prices, food composition, and documentary series on agricultural information. Moreover, they require portals that can allow them to request for services such as extension services. Researchers prefer portals that

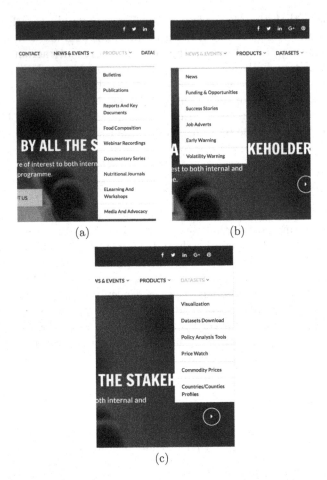

Fig. 13. (a) Portal attraction features, (b) Drop down menus, and (c) Some datasets to be availed to stakeholders on the portal.

Table 7. Comparing the preliminary portal prototype to other portals.

	Text alignment	Menu type	Menu placement	Icons and graphics
https://www.glnc.org.au/	HT	DDM	TM	✓
https://www.ildis.org/	HT	–	TM	✓
https://legumeinfo.org/	HT	DDM	TM	✓
http://www.legato-fp7.eu/	HT	–	LM, RM	✓
http://tropicallegumes.icrisat.org/	HT	DDM	TM, BM	✓
https://www.foodsecurityportal.org/	HT	–	TM, BM	✓
Preliminary portal prototype	HT	DDM	TM, BM, LM, RM	✓

HT:- Horizontal text; DDM:- drop-down menus; IG:- LM:- left menus; RM:- right menus; TM:-top menus; BM:- bottom menus provide information on food composition, documentary series e.g., on seed systems, research opportunities such as project grants, and functionalities for policy analysis. Finally, they require functionalities on news and events, and policy documents. Service providers prefer portals with weather information and crop calendars. This is important to schedule market campaigns or inform farmers about market conditions. Farmers can use such information to plan for crop harvesting, processing, and storage.

Finding 3: Design Requirements. Online portals for common beans should be consistent in design in terms of portal layouts and use of colours. The content they provide should be personalised to user needs. In recent times, there is a growing concern for privacy and confidentiality. Portal designers should reassure users that the information they provide will not be used outside the intended purpose. The portals should also be efficient and easy to reverse or cancel actions. The above requirements can also apply to portals in other domains.

Finding 4: Portal Attraction Methods and Features. Portals that address particular needs can be more attractive to specific groups of users. For instance, portals that address modern farming issues can attract farmers. From the portal administrative perspective, effective customer support (e.g., using chatbots) and rewarding royal users with incentives such as discounts on premium content can attract more users. Also, consistent email reminders on new information or content updates with pointers where to find it on the portal can attract users. Updated portal content makes the portal "fresh" from the perspective of the user.

Finding 5: Preferred Document Formats. From the survey findings, video and audio content are most preferred because they can easily be accessed via smartphones. In addition, PDF and presentation documents are preferred. These documents can easily be accessed using smartphones and tablets as well. Though not preferred by the survey respondents, XML documents can be useful to portal designers especially when providing frequently changing portal content such as newsfeeds.

Finding 6: Preferred Portal Subscription Modes. Portal subscription by users can be done monthly, quarterly, semi-annually, annually or portal content can be provided for free. Free subscription mode is preferred because of the associated costs on premium content. As mentioned before, having free content on legume portals may require a sustainable financial model. As such, we recommend portal designers and owners to consider a mix (hybrid) of both free and premium content.

6   Related Work

Several studies in the literature have documented research on online agricultural portals. Thanopoulos *et al.* [8] document an online web portal for training users in organic agriculture. The portal is used to organise, classify and publish digital informative, educational, and scholarly resources for organic farmers. Masner *et al.* [7] describe Agris which is a unified online information space for agriculture, food industry, forestry, water supply and distribution in rural areas. Jothi and Neelamalar [2] document the impact of portals in communicating agricultural information to farmers. The study focuses on analysing communication necessity via the Internet to farmers in underdeveloped regions. Though not directly linked to portals, the study elaborates the importance of using the Internet in rural communication especially to farmers. Marimuthu *et al.* [6] discuss about a persuasive technology method developed to help farmers adopt technology supported farming. The developed technology has a portal component to share information on marketing and farming accessories like dairy, organic products, and farm machineries. Walisadeera *et al.* [9] investigate how to create a knowledge repository for agricultural information while taking into account the context in which the information is needed. Finally, Li *et al.* [5] analyse the feasibility and necessity of a public platform that can be used in agricultural information services. A micro website was established to realise the information transition from a PC website to the mobile web site. To the best of our knowledge, none of these studies focuses on crop-specific portals.

7   Conclusion and Future Work

In this study, we profile challenges stakeholders face when accessing legume information online. These challenges can hinder adoption of ICTs in farming. As such, we document design requirements for online legume portals. We use the identified requirements to prototype a crop-specific legume portal. In the future, the preliminary prototype will be subjected to heuristic evaluation. The evaluation results will be used to inform subsequent refinements to realise an improved version that will be subjected to a user-based evaluation. The user-based evaluation will assess the design and placement of menus, and also assess the effectiveness of the methods/features used to attract users to the portal. Finally, online portals compliment mobile applications in information dissemination. As such, future efforts will be channeled towards developing a companion mobile application that can be used with the refined online portal for common beans.

Acknowledgement. This work is supported by the Legumes Centre for Food and Nutrition Security (LCEFoNS) programme which is funded by VLIR-UOS. The programme is a North-South Collaboration between the Katholieke Universiteit Leuven, Vrije Universiteit Brussel (both in Belgium) and Jomo Kenyatta University of Agriculture and Technology (Kenya).

References

1. Aker, J., Fafchamps, M.: How Does Mobile Phone Coverage Affect Farm-Gate Prices? Evidence from West Africa. Technical report, Department of Economics and the Fletcher School, Tufts University (2010)

2. Jothi, P.S., Neelamalar, M.: A study on the impact of websites in communicating science and technology information: with special reference to agricultural resources to farmers. In: 2011 International Conference on Electrical and Control Engineering, pp. 5714–5717. IEEE (2011). https://doi.org/10.1109/ICECENG.2011.6057187

3. Krishna, A., Naik, G.: Use of information quality concepts to improve effectiveness of agricultural information delivery: some empirical evidence. In: Proceedings of the 10th International Conference on Theory and Practice of Electronic Governance, pp. 610–612. ICEGOV 2017, Association for Computing Machinery, New York, NY, USA (2017). https://doi.org/10.1145/3047273.3047349

4. Krishna, A., Naik, G.: Addressing crisis in Indian agriculture through agricultural information delivery. IIMB Manag. Rev. **32**(2), 217–229 (2020). https://doi.org/10.1016/j.iimb.2020.09.004

5. Li, Z., Luo, C., Zhang, J.: Research on the development and preliminary application of 12396 new rural sci-tech service hotline WeChat public platform. In: 2015 International Conference on Network and Information Systems for Computers, pp. 453–456. IEEE (2015). https://doi.org/10.1109/ICNISC.2015.33

6. Marimuthu, R., Alamelu, M., Suresh, A., Kanagaraj, S.: Design and development of a persuasive technology method to encourage smart farming. In: 2017 IEEE Region 10 Humanitarian Technology Conference (R10-HTC), pp. 165–169. IEEE (2017). https://doi.org/10.1109/R10-HTC.2017.8288930

7. Masner, J., Šimek, P., Jarolímek, J., Hrbek, I.: Mobile applications for agricultural online portals - cross-platform or native development. AGRIS on-line Pap. Econ. Inform. **7**(2), 1–8 (2015). https://doi.org/10.22004/ag.econ.207065

8. Thanopoulos, C., Protonotarios, V., Stoitsis, G.: Online web portal of competence-based training opportunities for organic agriculture. AGRIS on-line Pap. Econ. Inform. **4**(1), 1–15 (2012). https://doi.org/10.22004/ag.econ.131357

9. Walisadeera, A.I., Ginige, A., Wikramanayake, G.N.: User centered ontology for Sri Lankan agriculture domain. In: 2014 14th International Conference on Advances in ICT for Emerging Regions (ICTer), pp. 149–155. IEEE (2014). https://doi.org/10.1109/ICTER.2014.7083894

10. Zhang, Y., Wang, L., Duan, Y.: Agricultural information dissemination using ICTs: a review and analysis of information dissemination models in China. Inf. Process. Agric. **3**(1), 17–29 (2016). https://doi.org/10.1016/j.inpa.2015.11.002

Assessing the Impact of Lean Tools on Production and Safety by a Multicriteria Decision-Making Model and Statistical Analysis: A Case Study in Textile Sector

José Carlos Sá[1]([✉]) [iD], Joni Pinto Jorge[1], Gilberto Santos[2] [iD], Maria João Félix[2] [iD], Luis Barreto[3] [iD], Genett Jiménez-Delgado[4] [iD], Carlos Rondón-Rodriguez[5], and Carlos Vargas-Mercado[6]

[1] Polytechnic of Porto, School of Engineering (ISEP), Porto, Portugal
cvs@isep.ipp.pt
[2] Design School, Polytechnic Institute Cavado Ave, Barcelos, Portugal
{gsantos,mfelix}@ipca.pt
[3] Instituto Politécnico de Viana do Castelo, ESCE, Valença, Portugal
lbarreto@esce.ipvc.pt
[4] Department of Industrial Engineering, Engineering Faculty, Institucion Universitaria ITSA, Soledad, Atlántico, Colombia
gjimenez@itsa.edu.co
[5] Department of Economic Sciences, Universidad de la Costa CUC, Barranquilla, Colombia
crondon1@cuc.edu.co
[6] Department of Education Sciences, Corporación Universitaria Latinoamericana CUL, Barranquilla, Colombia
cvargas@ul.edu.co

Abstract. The global competitiveness creates an enormous pressure on companies as they need to reduce production costs in order to increase productivity. In this sense, the SMED and 5S tools appear as competent tools to reduce the waste associated with these processes. This work aims to study and assess some processes in a company in the textile sector. Improvement proposals supported in the SMED and 5S methodology are presented in different areas of the company. Advantages, investments and respective return times are presented. Regarding to SMED, reductions in setup time in the order of 30–40% were obtained with investment return times between 6 and 7 months. The implementation of the 5S allowed to reduce the time and distance traveled for a given task. The reorganization of the area, it was possible to obtain a space gain of about 58 m^2. For this purpose, a multi-criteria decision model was designed to diagnose the critical areas for the implementation of Lean tools. Then, a questionnaire was also applied to the workers, with the goal to assess the impact of the implementation of lean philosophy in the field of occupational safety.

Keywords: Lean · Lean safety · 5S · SMED · Lean tools · MCDM · Fuzzy AHP · TOPSIS

© Springer Nature Switzerland AG 2021
C. Stephanidis et al. (Eds.): HCII 2021, LNCS 13097, pp. 616–638, 2021.
https://doi.org/10.1007/978-3-030-90966-6_42

1 Introduction

The Lean concept emerged through the Toyota Production System (TPS), developed by Taiichi Ohno in the middle of the 1940s. This production system is based on a set of principles that aim to reduce costs by eliminating activities that do not add value [1]. TPSs was a strategy adopted by Ohno to overcome the difficulties resulting from World War II. due to the scarcity of resources (material, financial and human), he was forced to focus on reducing waste as the main strategy [2]. The concept of waste is something that exists in organizations, but that is in general not identified by managers, who focus on obtaining results, ignoring the associated costs [3]. It is increasingly important to eliminate them, as they are sources of costs and productivity losses within companies, endangering their sustainability [4]. In the waste identification approach, the main goal is to reach a condition where capacity and load are the same. In companies there are people, processes, materials and technology to produce the right amount of product / service that was requested by the customer. The situations that there is not a balance between load and capacity result in losses for organizations [5]. To improve process performance, Toyota Motor Corporation (TMC) has identified three major causes of any operations system: waste (Muda), variations (Mura) and overloads (Muri), the most famous of which is Muda. In the Lean philosophy principles, the concepts of continuous elimination of waste are referred to as Muda, Mura and Muri (3M or 3M's) [6]. The novelty of this research is the development of an integrated methodology for the diagnosis and evaluation of the improvements through Lean tools in processes of the textile industry, through the design of a Fuzzy AHP-TOPSIS multi-criteria decision model for the diagnostic phase and statistical analysis for the evaluation phase focused on productivity, quality, and safety in operations.

2 Literature Review

The Behrouzi and Wong [2] refer to value as a starting point for lean thinking in which it is quantified through end customer satisfaction of the product supplied. They consider that waste are all activities that do not add value, making that the products or services made available on the market have higher costs compared to their competitors. With a different view, Caldera et al. [7] preset lean thinking as a dynamic, knowledge-oriented, customer-focused process that allows all workers to continuously reduce waste and create value.

Regarding to lean philosophy, it refers as waste (Muda) the overproduction, the halts on the production process, the transportation, the movement, the defects, the stocks and the rework [8]. Currently, two new types of waste are considered that organizations should take into account, they are safety and talent [9].

The way of thinking addressed by Toyota allows practices and lean tools to become popular among large companies. However, small and medium-sized enterprises (SME) can also learn to benefit from that thinking to reduce costs and become more competitive [10]. Although it is true that this philosophy was originated within industry, many service organizations can also implement this paradigm very effectively [11]. Melton [12] states that the main lean techniques and tools adopted by Toyota included: Kanban – Visual signaling to support organizations to implement pull production systems, allowing them to synchronize their production with the needs of their customers; 5S - Tool for organization and standardization of the workplace; Visual Management - Method of measuring performance on the shop floor; SMED (Single Minute Exchange of Die) - Quick tool exchange; Poka-Yoke - Error-proof system.

2.1 SMED

Based on the work developed by Shingo it is possible to recognize the main benefits that emerge from the implementation of the SMED methodology. The advantages that come from it can be classified as direct or indirect advantages, as referred by Moreira and Pais [13]. Table 1 shows the advantages referred by those authors.

Table 1. Advantages of the SMED methodology. Adapted from Moreira and Pais [13]

Direct advantages	Indirect advantages
Setup time reduction	Stock Reduction
Adjustment time reduction	Increased production reliability
Error reduction	Standardization of operations
Increased product quality	
Increased security	

As a result of the advantages presented, Karam, Liviu, Cristina, and Radu [14], mention that the economic gains associated with the implementation of SMED can be observed in different perspectives. Thus, the proper implementation of the improvement system can be an important factor, such as the reduction in labor and management costs. From the management of lots and the reduction and flexibility of their dimensions, it is intended to ensure the flow of the product in the manufacturing area. In this way it is possible to respond more quickly and effectively to market variations, producing accordingly to the orders and with more competitive prices. The authors report that the benefit of increasing equipment availability by decreasing downtime, increases the overall equipment effectiveness indicator [14].

The examples shown in Table 2 can prove adaptability of SMED to different types of industry. In the analysis performed in each described example, it is possible to observe the reduction in setup times resulting from the simple reorganization of workspaces and/or tools. In some cases, the existence of transformations from internal setup operations to external setup has been considered. In addition, to cost reduction and increased productivity, another relevant advantage is being able to increase the OEE, essentially by increasing equipment availability.

2.2 5S

The most remote origin of the historical 5'S is essentially based on the principles of Shinto, Buddhism (self-discipline) and Confucianism (order), these being related to the

Table 2. Analysis of some case studies of the Benefits of Implementing SMED.

Reference	Analysis
[15]	This example of SMED implementation was carried out in a line of CNC machining of a company in the area of electronic components. With the application of this new system, it was possible to fix several products in the same bushing, which allowed to reduce the time from 108 min to 16 min, with a reduction of setup time by approximately 85%. The economic benefit obtained was €7,100/year
[16]	Work developed in a stamping line in a textile company. The authors intended to demonstrate the benefit of SMED in eliminating setup times. With the implementation of the new system, the tool change time was significantly reduced by about 25.62% (from 300 min. to 223 min)
[17]	Also, positive results were achieved in an automotive industry dedicated to welding parts. With the implementation of the SMED methodology, the external work was separated from the internal work. To convert the internal work in external work, the standardization of tools and the use of templates was performed. Some adjustments were also made to the tools to reduce internal working time. The setup time was reduced by 33% with cost savings of around €13,200/year
[18]	This case study addresses the SMED implementation in a PVC pipe/profile extrusion line and intended to demonstrate that the reduction in preparation time allows to increase productivity and flexibility. The time required for the change of the matrix and consequently change of products before the improvement was 145 min, and was performed once a day. After the implementation of the new system, was obtained a reduction from 130 to 34 min in the exchange of the matrix and from 15 to 7 min in the change of products (pipes or profiles). With the implementation of the improvement applied to the matrix, it was achieved a reduction in setup time of approximately 73.8%. The benefits presented include the flexibility of the production line and the company's ability to exchange matrix or change production type (pipes or profiles) twice a day
[19]	A study was carried out in a multinational company related to the production of parts for the automotive industry. The SMED methodology was applied, which allowed reducing the set up time by 11%, and the 5'S tool to organize the change in production activities. With the application of these tools, an increase in the OEE was obtained by more than 90%
[20]	The aim of this study was to conclude that there is the possibility of simultaneously reducing set up time and improving ergonomic conditions. This research was conducted in an area of production of lathes in a metallurgical factory, in which there were numerous complaints from workers due to shoulder pain, essentially due to incorrect postures and high efforts in manual tasks. In addition, setup time was high (105 min) causing productivity problems and delays in the customer delivery time. With the SMED tool and the improved of the ergonomic conditions, setup time was reduced by 46%

Japanese culture [21]. The 5S is a continuous improvement tool, developed in Japan based on five stages whose initials are presented by the letter "S". The method was created shortly after World War II, around the year 1950, and was first developed by Hiroyuki Hirano [22]. It includes five words Seiri, Seiton, Seiso, Seiketsu, and Shit-suke, which mean Use, Organization, Cleanliness, Standardization, and Discipline. This methodology was part of the country's reconstruction effort, in the 1950s, and emerged in industries, contributing to the quality of Japanese-made products. The method is one of the Lean thinking tools, which is governed in the search for discipline and rigor at work, in order to identify problems in an agile way that allows a quick resolution and that generates opportunities for future improvements. The methodology is also included in "Kaizen", which means "change for the better", allowing the improvement of efficiency and productivity, based on a structured program to systematically achieve organization and standardization in the workplace. The 5'S aims to reduce the waste of raw materials and space in order to increase organizational efficiency [23].

Patel and Thakkar [22] report that the successful implementation and execution of the 5'S principles bring several advantages such as:

- Simplicity and understanding by all as it requires only knowledge of the discipline and commitment concepts. This practice can be implemented at all levels;
- Promotion of team spirit, discipline and increased sense of responsibility and compassion for the company;
- Creation of clean and organized work environments, ensuring a pleasant environment for visiting customers, thus helping to promote new business;
- The continuous commitment between management and involvement is the pillar of all workers for the successful implementation of the method's practices;
- To have a continuous need to maintain an excellent level of service;
- Internal audits typically allow that quality and effectiveness of customer service to be improved;
- Activities are planned and ongoing audits helping to prepare workers for true 5S audits to obtain and maintain certification.

From the advantages mentioned above, it is possible to observe that the 5S can involve self-organization behaviors, being above all a process that should involve all the people within organizations, where habits, attitudes and behaviors should be changed, ending with adverse behaviors, favoring change and continuous improvement.

The examples presented Table 3 underline the transversality of the 5S applicability in different types of industry. In the synthesis made of the described examples it is possible to conclude the decrease in times and the increase of spaces due to the reorganization of layouts and visual management. In some cases, productivity increases and mone-tary gains are obtained. In addition to the quantitative approach, other relevant aspects with positive impact were presented, e.g. safety and cleanliness that contributed to the improvement of the process and to the working environment.

Table 3. Analysis of some case studies of the Benefits of Implementing 5S

Reference	Analysis
[24]	This example of implementation of the 5S methodology was carried out in a line of looms on a company in the textile sector. The actions defined in this work allowed to reduce four hours per operator weekly, which corresponds to a gain of 10% of the total available time per week
[25]	This research work was carried out to apply the 5S methodology for problem solving in a ceramics industry. With this implementation there was an improvement in the use of space with reduction of 12.91% square meters in the storage area. Safety, increased productivity, improved inventory system, cleaning and maintenance of equipment, among other improvements contributed for a better efficiency in the production system, improving indirectly workers morale with the improvement of the work environment
[26]	This case study was conducted in a food and beverage industry in Bangladesh. The case study implements the 5S methodology in an industrial food and beverage production environment. The results obtained were considered satisfactory given that productivity increased from 59,500 products to 82,498, which was reflected in an increase of approximately 36.85%. By comparison the rejected products rate, decreased from 19.4% to 13.3%, corresponding to a reduction of rejected products by about 6.1%
[27]	This presents the implementation of the 5S in a sheet metal manufacturing company, where there are processes, such as cutting, pressing and welding. As a result, the company's productivity increased by about 91%
[28]	This research addresses the implementation of the 5S methodology in a plastics manufacturing company. The results after the implementation of the 5S showed that the efficiency of the production system increased from 67% to 88.8%
[29]	This study reports the application of the 5'S methodology in a welding company, standing out the significant contribution of its application to the organizational progress, both in terms of quality, productivity and safety. After the implementation, there was a reduction in demand activity by 18.75% and in the distance covered by 11.20%

2.3 Lean Safety

The basic premises of lean philosophy offer some possibilities to further improve safety. Safety aims to eliminate occupational risks, thus requiring dynamic and proactive processes. Such management establishes concepts that fit the philosophy of continuous improvement [30]. There are some lean tools, such as 5S, SMED, Visual Management, that help to identify improvement opportunities and to develop them. In this way, the concept of lean philosophy can be linked to security. The tools have an impact on safety, since their application reduces the possibility of work accidents.

Lean philosophy strategies encourage material reduction in the workplace area, providing an organized, clean and systematic workflow location. Therefore, it can be expected that the normalization of production processes ensures a safer working environment [30]. For the workers, considering ergonomic issues related to the design of the workplace, such as access to materials, equipment, tools and communication between workers, is decisive for their safety [31, 32]. In a similar way, Arezes, Dinis-Carvalho, and Alves [33] report that many researchers in advocating the implementation of lean philosophy, are also promoting people's involvement, establishing with them a connection with ergonomics and safety.

For Howell, Ballard, Abdelhamid, and Mitropoulos [34], the loss or injury of workers and the consequent stoppage of the production process represents the waste in performance. The authors argue that minimizing waste and continuously improving is the result of the combination of lean and safety.

In a research project developed by Prakash [35], some problems encountered in the construction industry were pointed out. These include lack of communication between work teams, lack of documentation, deficiency in decision-making and negative iterations during the project. According to Mitropoulos, Abdelhamid, and Howell [36] a working system needs to be developed to achieve high levels of productivity and safety. Nahmens and Ikuma [31] questioned, during an investigation, whether the implementation of lean principles would result in greater security. On the other hand, Main, Taubitz, and Wood [37] underline the importance of demonstrating that safety and lean concepts need to be addressed simultaneously.

Lean thinking suggests that activities carried out to promote occupational safety and health should be improved, waste produced can be identified and eliminated, so that negative impacts on the process can be reduced or even eliminated. As all accidents at work involve waste of time and resources, lean and safety have as the common basis waste and risks reducing [38]. In the basic principles of lean philosophy, as mentioned by Cirjaliu and Draghic [6], it is possible to find concepts such as the continuous elimination of waste, called elimination of the Moul, as well as the elimination of Muri. Since safety focuses on human factors, the main action is focused on the Muri's concept of elimination. In Japanese the word Muri means physical tension or overload. Actions such as: 1 – To Shaping up while working; 2 – To Push hard; 3 – To Lift weights; 4 – To Repeat tiring actions and 5 – To Waste a traveled distance, are considered Muri and, consequently, and accordingly to the principles of lean philosophy should be eliminated. Any implementation that does not reduce Muri, as mentioned in some publications, should not be regarded as the "true spirit" of lean implementation [32].

As mentioned before, any lean philosophy implementation should reduce Muri, which is one of the introductory principles for Lean Safety. Thus, Lean tools should serve as a basis to support the development of a safer working environment, as the studies presented in Table 4 state. However, Hasle et al. [40] refer to lean as an open tool that can have positive or negative effects on security depending on the cause and the actual value of its implementation.

3 Methodology

The research methodology followed in his work was the action-research methodology, intended to interactively explore the reality on the shop floor, thus identifying the problems and testing solutions in real situations [43, 44]. Thiollent [45] states that such methodology allows the use of knowledge and the sharing of information. According to

Table 4. Analysis of some case studies on the benefits of applying Lean tools in the safety

Reference	Analysis
[39]	This work studied the SSM (Safety Stream Mapping) methodology, which is a methodology based on VSM (Value Stream Mapping) and WID (Waste Identification Diagram). This methodology served to understand the safety level of a textile industry. The authors of this work addressed two themes: the Lean philosophy, in order to reduce costs and increase turnover by eliminating waste and activities without added value and the concept of security since its lack does not bring any advantage to the company
[40]	The objective of this work was a systematic scientific literature review on the effects of lean on the workers' health and safety. The results were analyzed in order to obtain information about the effects of lean on the work environment. The authors obtained negative evidence of lean in terms of worker health and safety in the cases where the work performed was manual and with low complexity. However, results of positive effects were also obtained. The authors highlighted the importance of moving from a simple cause and effect to a more comprehensive model that compromises lean as an open philosophy and ambiguous concept, which can have positive or negative effects, depending on the actual value of its implementation on the shop floor level
[41]	This work consisted in the implementation of some Lean tools (5S, Visual Management and OPL (One Point Lesson)) in a service provider company, in order to promote the change of habits, improve the work environment and consequently the safety conditions. Another objective was to analyze the impact of those lean tools on the safety and the perception of the workers. The authors concluded that lean was an important tool to improve working conditions and workplaces. Regarding the organization of the warehouse and its location, it was possible to achieve a reduction of about 80% in the route and in the travel time. Improvements were achieved between 38% and 41% in the results of 5S audits. A study was conducted on the perception of workers regarding the implementation of lean tools and their impact on the workplace, revealing that 83.4% of the workers agreed that the work environment was improved
[42]	The main goal of this case study was to determine the impact of lean tools on the concept of safety management in a company. The first stage consisted of the identification and registration of accidents at work over a period of two years. For that purpose, a set of lean tools (Kaizen, 5S, TPM (Total Productive Maintenance)) was selected to be applied on the work environment. This implementation allowed suggesting safety improvement measures in all areas of the production plant. The study stated that lean management methods and tools clearly have impact on safety at work. It was concluded that the tools contributed to the reduction of accidents, nothwithstanding the authors also concluded that it was pertinent to implement a 6S system, in which safety must be one of the factors of improvement

the author's, this plan is divided into three main actions that are: observing the reality to gather information and build a scenario; think how to explore it, analyzing and interpreting the facts; implement and evaluate the actions. Tripp [46] mentions the importance of planning as monitoring of the implemented situations, allowing the evaluation of the results in order to plan and define an adequate improvement in the first cycle of the action-research. Concerning addressing the problem, this needs to be quantitative because variables are measurable and it needs to address conclusive situations. Its main goal is aims to quantify problems and understand their dimension.

The methodological design of the study considered the integration of a fuzzy multi-criteria model based on Fuzzy AHP and TOPSIS for the evaluation of the areas of the organization, considering criteria and sub-criteria associated with the improvement of processes through the Lean philosophy, identifying the improvement potential of each of the areas for the implementation of Lean tools. Subsequently, a questionnaire was applied among the analyzed processes to evaluate the implementation of Lean solutions in safety and productivity, complemented with a statistical analysis of the data collected. In this regard, the methodology is comprised of three phases (refer to Fig. 1):

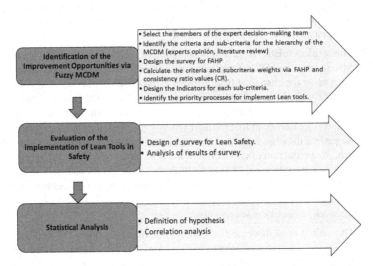

Fig. 1. The methodological approach assessing the impact of Lean Tools on Production and Safety by a Multicriteria decision-making model and Statistical in textile sector

4   Results

4.1   Identification of the Improvement Opportunities via Fuzzy Multicriteria Decision-Making Model

In this first phase, an MCDM model was designed based on Fuzzy AHP and TOPSIS techniques to evaluate three processes in a textile organization (multifilament area, raffia area, and raffia raw materials storage area) and their improvement potential taking into account different criteria for the implementation of Lean tools. In the first place, a team of experts was formed to identify and validate the criteria and sub-criteria of the model, made up of leaders from the areas of the textile company and experts in Lean methodology and multi-criteria decision making. Then, based on the opinion of the experts and the review of the relevant scientific literature, the multi-criteria decision hierarchy was constructed, consisting of 3 criteria and 9 sub-criteria. The hierarchy is shown in Fig. 2.

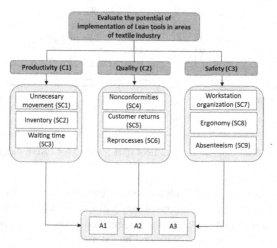

Fig. 2. Multi-criteria decision-making model to evaluate the potential of implementation of Lean tools in textile industry.

The criteria and sub-criteria were labeled and described in Table 5.

Table 5. Description of criteria

Criterion (C)	Sub-criteria (SC)	Criterion description
C1. Productivity	SC1. Unnecesary movement SC2. Inventory SC3. Waiting time	This criterion addresses the main types of waste that affect the ability of the process to optimize its resources in terms of time, movements, and materials. [47–49]
C2. Quality	SC4. Nonconformities SC5. Customer returns SC6. Reprocesses	This criterion refers to the losses generated in the processes due to quality problems, including non-conformities, customer returns, and reprocesses. [50–53]
C3. Safety	SC7. Workstation organization SC8. Ergonomy SC9. Absenteeism	This criterion evaluates the waste in the processes associated with problems in occupational health and safety, such as workstation organization, Ergonomy aspects, and absenteeism [54–56]

Subsequently, a survey was designed to collect the experts' judgments through paired comparisons between the criteria and sub-criteria. In this respect, for each pairwise evaluation, the experts respond the following question: According to the goal /criteria, ¿how important is each element on the leftover the item on the right? The experts used Fig. 3 to represent their judgments until finalizing all the criteria and sub-criteria.

According to your experience with respect to "Safety" sub-criterion, ¿how important is each sub-criterion on the left concerning the sub-criterion on the right when evaluating the potential of implementation of Lean tools in areas of textile industry?									
		1	2	3	4	5		
Workstation organization	is	O	O	O	O	O	Important than	Ergonomy
Improvement actions	is	O	O	O	O	O	Important than	Absenteeism
Investigation of incidents	is	O	O	O	O	O	Important than	Absenteeism

① Much less		③ Equally		⑤ Much more
② Less		④ More		

Fig. 3. Data-collection instrument implemented for FAHP judgments

After applying the Fuzzy AHP methodology, the relative weights of the criteria and sub-criteria were obtained and the consistency ratios between the expert judgments. In this sense, productivity (GW = 49.4%) was identified as the most important criterion in the implementation of Lean tools, followed by safety (GW = 29.1%) and quality (GW = 21.5%). This raises the design of multifactorial strategies focused on reducing waste that affects the efficiency of the process and the generation of value. Table 6 shows the relative weights of criteria and sub-criteria and their consistency ratios, which yielded CR < 0.1, evidencing consistent judgments.

Table 6. Local and global weights of criteria and sub-criteria

Cluster	GW	LW	CR
Criteria			**0.003**
C1. Productivity	**0.494**		**0.015**
SC1. Unnecesary movement	0.058	0.118	
SC2. Inventory	0.246	0.499	
SC3. Waiting time	0.189	0.382	
C2. Quality	**0.291**		**0.001**
SC4. Nonconformities	0.092	0.431	
SC5. Customer returns	0.086	0.401	
SC6. Reprocesses	0.039	0.167	

(continued)

Table 6. (*continued*)

Cluster	GW	LW	CR
C3. Safety	**0.215**		**0.025**
SC7. Workstation organization	0.049	0.168	
SC8. Ergonomy	0.042	0.144	
SC9. Absenteeism	0.199	0.686	

Finally, the TOPSIS technique was applied to rank the processes with the most waste and prioritize the implementation of Lean tools, for which a set of indicators was designed for each evaluation sub-criterion and the subsequent calculation of the closeness coefficient for the identification of the most critical areas for the implementation of the Lean philosophy. Table 7 shows the calculation of the closeness coefficient and the separation from Negative Ideal Solution (NIS) and Positive Ideal Solution (PIS).

Table 7. Ranking of processes in evaluation of potential implementation of Lean Tools via TOPSIS method

Area	CC_i	d_i^+	d_i^-	Rank
A3	0,754	0,042	0,139	1
A2	0,454	0,096	0,080	2
A1	0,398	0,134	0,089	3

The results show that areas 1 (multifilament area) and 2 (area raffia) are the priority areas for the implementation of Lean tools because they present the lowest proximity coefficients, 39.8%, and 45.4%, respectively, while area 3 (raffia raw materials storage area) has the lowest priority. In addition, opportunities for improvement were identified in all areas of the company, which are described in Sect. 4.1.1.

4.1.1 Implementing Lean Tools for Improvement Opportunities

The first phase considered the development of an agile wrench that would allow the release/tightening of the pre-stretch oven pulley in a more efficient and fast way, thus replacing the Swedish tool wrench used in the operations. The Swedish tool wrench had some limitations and required some dexterity to handle it. In view of the problem presented and the shape of the tool, an oversight during the change of the pulley caused irreversible damage to the ceramic coating of the pulley. In order to avoid this type of occurrence, two nylon covers were also developed for the new wrench in order to mitigate it.

The second phase consisted of the organization of the workstation through the implementation of the 5S methodology. Next to the workstation there is a workbench where different tasks are performed, such as packaging of reels, registration of manufacturing orders, placement of some tools, among others. In the replacement of pulleys operations', forwarding the damaged pulley to the workshop and returning with a repaired one is a very inefficient task. It was then developed a workbench restructuring. This development consisted of the creation of two drawers with slides in the center of the table with the shape of a matrix (5×5), lined with high density foam for the storage of the pulleys. In one of the drawers will be stored the damaged pulleys and in the other the repaired ones. In this development also arose the need to meet the operators' ergonomic needs, in the high of the workbench and the introduction of two side shelves for the packaging of the reels. A bottom shelf it was also introduced along the entire workbench length to allow the storage of materials and tools.

In the raffia area, in order to avoid waste and production losses, a solution was presented for reducing the time in the change of lines. Thus, a new extraction system was studied, using the available space inside the winder to replace the existing pneumatic cylinder. The extractor base was kept and the guides were replaced by longer ones allowing to support the pneumatic cylinder rod during the extraction of the reel. With this design it was necessary to purchase flow regulators and a pressure multiplier to ensure the stability of the cylinder during the extraction. 3D modeling was also performed allowing a better visualization and understanding of the new system.

Regarding the areas of raw materials storage and movement of people and materials, were identified improvement opportunities in one of the raffia areas. The results presented include areas organization and cleaning, processes improvement, allowing the reduction of workers' movements when production change was needed. A study was carried out concerning the areas layout. After this study, new layouts were designed regarding how the raw materials were placed to supply the extruders in the raffia area. This configuration includes the appropriate positioning of the shelves, as well as the differentiation, organization and identification of the materials. An area was delimited for the storage of necessary pallets and tubes required in the daily process. A scale for weighing reels when a change of production is need was also installed, thus avoiding unnecessary displacement and avoiding manual weighing registration. It is important to refer that the scale was connected to the industry monitoring system 4.0, allowing to register the produced kilograms in each machine, and generating a label that allows to identify when the reel is used as an intermediate product. This system allows to control the production for the required needs, streamlining the entire production system in this extrusion area.

4.2   Evaluation of the Implementation of Lean Tools in Occupational Safety (Lean Safety Questionnaires)

After the lean implementations, questionnaires were carried out with the goal of register the opinions of workers, therefore collecting information on the occupational safety of their workplaces. The questionnaires aimed to measure the impact on occupational safety of the improvements defined in the production process. The questionnaires were based on a set of statements with a measurement scale, considering a group of interconnected opinions, as an introspective indicator. The measurement was based on the Likert scale, and as a research requirement the decision focused on the 5-point scale with information collection, as presented in a brief historical review by Lucian (2016).

The study was carried out in the areas where the procedural improvements occurred. The answers were given by the workers of the respective areas on a scale of 1 to 5 being: 1 = Totally disagree; 2 = Partially disagree; 3 = Not agree or disagree; 4 = Partially agree; 5 = Totally agree. Thirteen generic and in the scope of occupational safety statements were created.

The statements were:

Q1 - The workplace has improved.

Q2 - The physical effort developed in the workplace improved.

Q3 - The workplace is safer.

Q4 - Improvement in the level of daily stress.

Q5 – Now you have more autonomy.

Q6 - Better motivation to develop work with safety.

Q7 - Greater participation to contribute to the improvement of working methods.

Q8 - Easier to identify the occupational risks to which he was exposed.

Q9 - Decreased in the absence days due to health problems.

Q10 - Safety knowledge has improved.

Q11 – Lean tools have improved the integration of security with the work activities developed.

Q12 – More readiness to respond to emergencies.

Q13 – Overall, you consider that the Lean tool has improved your working conditions.

The questionnaires were individually answered by the workers from the different areas in order to obtain a better perception of the impact of Lean tools on occupational safety. During the completion of the questionnaires follow-up to the employees was carried out and improvement suggestions were registered. The results obtained through the questionnaire were analyzed with the Excel©. For each question, the average results obtained on the scale from 1 to 5 were converted into % and presented in graphically presented.

4.2.1 Multifilament Area

In the multifilament area, 6 workers, who often work at the process improvement site were, interviewed. Concerning Q1 two of the six workers fully agreed that the working environment has been improved, while the remaining four partially agree. These four workers presented as a suggestion for future work, the implementation of a reels bagging system in their own benches. In general, workers agree that the work environment has been improved, and that this improvement should be replicated in the remaining extruders. The workers fully agree that the physical effort, safety and daily stress in the workplace has been improved, especially in the operation of tightening/ unscrewing the pulley and regarding the distance traveled and needed to do that task. The increase in the height of the workbench and the side shelves contributed positively for the ergonomic level. The new workbench also allows to storage a larger amount of materials, preventing them from being scattered throughout the factory (and outside the workplace).

Regarding the autonomy and decrease of absence days due to health problems, the procedural improvement did not have an impact on the workers' autonomy and there are not enough data to perceive the evolution of the absenteeism days. All workers are now motivated to develop the work safely, namely in the way the pulley is removed, the distance traveled to replace it and the increased ergonomics of the new workbench. Nevertheless, all workers agree that they contributed to the improvement of the working methods and have gained greater perception of the occupational risks to which they were exposed. This is due to the fact that as the changes were made, workers were contributing with new ideas, such as wrench length, number and size of shelves and drawers. With the introduction of the new tool for tightening/untightening the pulley and the workbench change, workers recognized the ergonomic risks to which they were exposed before the implementation of those improvements. The level of knowledge and integration of Lean tools related to the safety of work activities has also been improved by all workers, considering the previously presented reasons. On the other hand, all workers are more prepared to respond to emergencies. This is related to the time gain associated with the elimination of unnecessary movements, allowing workers to be more available and to react more efficiently to the emergencies. Similarly, workers agree that overall Lean tools have improved job conditions based on observations of the previous issues.

4.2.2 Raffia Area

In the extrusion sector, eight workers who often work on the site of the implementation of the improvement procedures were interviewed. Regarding Q1, half of the workers fully agree that the work environment has been improved, while the other half partially agrees. During the collection of information, the workers stated that it would be appropriate to improve the lifting control of the stacker forks with a pressure adjustment system. They reported the importance of replicating the improvement in the remaining three pieces of equipment. On the Other Hand, All Workers Fully Agree that Physical Effort, Safety and Daily Stress in the Workplace Have Been Improved. The improvement allowed to removed effort and work in the most laborious operation of the safety has also increased mainly because it is no longer needed to use a cardboard tube to assist in the extraction of the reel, reducing the risk of crushing the upper limbs. it is also no longer needed a second work to perform the extraction of the reel. Before the improvements, it was required to ask for assistance from workers who would be busy in other tasks. The autonomy of workers has increased as there is no longer a second worker. All the workers are motivated to develop work safely because the new system does not have the need to use the cardboard tube, allowing also to increase the level of confidence when performing the reel extraction, because the new system is more robust and safer.

The workers fully agree that they contributed to the improvement of the working methods and gained greater perception of the occupational risks to which they were exposed. As the new system was implemented, some ideas emerged from the production collaborators, namely in the tuning of the system. With the implemented improvement, workers immediately recognized the high risks to which they were previously exposed. The risks consist of the probability of crushing an upper limb as well as the hard effort that was needed to pull the reel to the stacker. Regarding the decrease in the number of absence days due to health problems, the results don't show any improvement. Due to the project timeline there isn't, yet enough data to measure the number absence days. The level of knowledge and integration of Lean tools related to the safety of work activities has also been improved by all workers, for the reasons previously presented in occupational risks. On the other hand, all workers agreed they are more prepared to respond to emergency situations, especially due to the fact that it is no more necessary to ensure a second worker for reel extraction. Similarly, workers agree that overall lean tools have improved job conditions based on previous observations.

4.2.3   Raffia Raw Materials Storage Area

In the raw material storage area, eight workers who often work on the site where the procedural improvement implementation was carried out were interviewed. Only two of the eight workers fully agree that the work environment has improved (Q1). The remaining six workers only agree partially. from the observations obtained, workers mentioned that the workplace was cleaner and more organized. As a suggestion for a future improvement, they referred that it would be pertinent to install casters in the materials drums and boxes in order to facilitate their transport. Nevertheless, all workers fully agreed that physical effort, safety and daily stress in the workplace has been clearly improved. They also reported that the reorganization and identification of materials alongside the extruders allowed to reduce the distance traveled whenever there is a need for a new material. However, they manifested the importance of not Having badly overlapped pallets, with a high risk of fall, as well as the creation of an access ladder to the new material area (shelves), thus allowing to reduce the risk of injuries.

Once more, and regarding the decrease in the number of absence days due to health problems the results don´t show any improvement. The improved process has no impact on their autonomy, and because of the timeline of the project there are not enough data to perceive the evolution of the number of absence days due to absenteeism. Workers are motivated to develop work safely because the workspace and storage area are clean and organized. All workers agreed that they contributed to the improvement of the working methods, and they have more perception of the occupational risks to which they were exposed. All changes and limitations were made together with production workers. They all increased their insight about occupational risks, especially in the case of poor stacking of material pallets and bags. The knowledge of all workers has improved in terms of knowledge and integration of lean tools in the safety of the work activities carried out by them, allowing them to understand that they must keep the materials in their places, reducing the risk of tripping over a bag, for example, or of a pallet falling to the ground. On the other hand, all workers are more prepared to respond to emergencies, due to the fact they can more easily recognize the materials or the lack of them, thus allowing them to be replaced in advance and with safety. In the same way, workers agree that lean tools have improved their overall job conditions.

4.3   Statistical Analysis of Data

A statistical study of correlation between two statements was carried out, allowing to support the investigation. The population was made up of the different workers of the different areas where the Lean implementations were applied. Twenty-two workers were interviewed; thus, a population size was equal to the sample (n = 22). To answer to the statements, the Likert scale was used as mentioned before, in which 1 –T otally disagree; 2 - Partially disagree; 3 - Do not agree or disagree;4 - Partially agree; 5 - Totally agree.

For the data collection, the following statements were studied (Q1 and Q2):

Q1: Overall I am satisfied with the Lean methodologies implemented in my work area.

Q2: I am currently satisfied with the security level of my job.

The research question is: "Is the satisfaction of occupational safety levels correlated with the degree of satisfaction of the implementation of Lean methodologies?".

Hypothesis test:

H0 – There is no association between Lean and Security, i.e., Security and Lean are independent.

H1 - There is an association between safety and Lean (bilateral test).

The test was performed was the Spearman-Bivariate test, and it was used the IBM SPSS Statistics 23 computer suite, considering monotonous data and small samples. Spearman is a nonparametric test that aims at a correlation between two or more ordinal variables. This test is performed with a confidence interval CI = 95% and with its significance level at 5%.

To perform the statistical test, the computer suite mentioned above was used. Table 8 shows the result obtained in the correlation test.

Table 8. Spearman-Bivariate correlation test result (SPSS 23)

Correlation			Implementations Lean	Occupational safety
Spearman's rho	Lean Implementations	Correlation coefficient	1.000	.516*
		Sig. (2-tailed)	-	.014
		N	22	22
	Occupational safety	Correlation coefficient	.516*	1.000
		Sig. (2-tailed)	.014	-
		N	22	22

* Correlation is significant at the 0.05 level (2-tailed).
As p-value = 0.014 (1.4%) < 0.05 (5%), H0 is rejected.

There is sufficient statistical evidence to state that occupational safety is correlated with the degree of satisfaction of the implemented Lean methodologies. More specifically, the greater the degree of satisfaction of Lean implementations, the greater impact it will have on the level of job security. This is because the correlation factor $\rho = 0.516$, meaning that there is a positive linear correlation (more Lean satisfaction implies more safety) and moderate intensity (between 0.5 and 0.7), between implementation and occupational safety. In conclusion, there is a moderate correlation, where $\rho = 1$ is a strong correlation and $\rho = 0$ is no correlation.

5 Discussion

Through the first two improvements presented in this work, it is possible to observe a clear decrease in the duration of production changes/tools and reduced recovery times. The last improvement implemented, referring to the layout organization, is possible to observe a great reduction of time in unnecessary movements when a change of production occurs. It is also possible to observe from the study performed that exists a correlation between lean and safety.

In the case of a pulleys change in a multifilament extruder, the reorganization of the operations and investment for improving the workbench and the construction of a wrench for the pulley replacement, allowed to avoid unnecessary displacement, obtaining savings of about 41% of time. The investment associated with this improvement is around 726€ generating the maximum profit after 6.5 months. For a number of pulley changes equivalent to that observed in 2019, this improvement may allow annual profits in the order of 1,334 €. In view of the implemented improvement in the screw/tighten pulley wrench and comparing with 2019 history, the company can achieve a cost reduction in maintenance services for ceramic pulley coating in the order of 50%, corresponding annually to 1,518€.

The new extraction system for switching the reels set allowed the elimination of an internal operation. The new pneumatic cylinder/system is robust and allows the worker to perform an autonomous extraction of the reel in a convenient and safe way. An investment of 3,426.76€ was made in the total of the four existing winders in the extruder. Due to this investment, it was possible to obtain, in this process, savings of about 34% in terms of time needed. With the investment made it will be possible to generate a maximum profit after approximately 7.2 months. For a number of changes of reels' sets like in 2019, this improvement may allow an increase of the annual billing in the order of 5,725€.

Regarding the raw material supply area, the use, reorganization of layouts and standardization contributed to a notable gain of 58 m^2. This gain made it possible to store raw materials close to the equipment, thus reducing unnecessary displacements when a production change takes place. The distance traveled was reduced by approximately 85.9% and the travel time by 83.3%. Considering the time gain and the number of production changes observed before the project, as the average productive gain of the four extruders in the sector, it will be possible to obtain annual profits in the order of 20,692€. The final goal for the implementation of the 5S program was achieved in this area, reaching the goal of 65% in the internal audit global assessment. The improvements observed were mainly due to the sense of use, organization and standardization.

However, the task of maintaining the program is more demanding, requiring systematic follow-up, guaranteeing that old habits and routines do not return. For this reason, there is a continuing need to raise awareness and train workers. In general, the improvements implemented contributed to the increase in the workers' morale. With regard to the impact of lean on workers' safety, for example, the excessive effort to remove the reel from the sleeve, the unsuitable pulley wrench and workbench, that placed the ergonomic conditions of the workplace at risk and the unnecessary displacements were a cause of increased daily stress. The improvement in autonomy had a special impact on the raffia extrusion winders, as there is no longer needed a second worker to assist in the extraction of the reels. In general, workers agree that the implementations of the lean tools have improved the safety conditions in the workplace. Finally, they concluded that the improvements should be replicated for the remaining equipment and manufacturing areas. The second questionnaire made it possible to conclude about the statistical correlation between the satisfaction of the implemented Lean tools and the satisfaction of the occupational safety level in the workplace. In view of the available sample (n = 22) and with the non-parametric Spearman test, it was possible to conclude with a confidence interval CI = 95% that there is a dependency between the two statements, that is, the null hypothesis is rejected (H0). This dependence implies a positive and moderate intensity correlation factor, presenting a $\rho = 0.516$.

6 Conclusion

This study presents an integrated methodology based on FAHP-TOPSIS and statistical analysis to assess the potential of improvement opportunities for implementing Lean tools in the textile sector. The proposed methodology includes three phases: Design of the MCDM model, application of FAHP method to calculate the relative weights of criteria and sub-criteria, rank the priority areas and definition of lean solutions via TOPSIS method, and finally, the evaluation of the impact on Lean tools in safety and productivity via survey and correlation analysis.

From a global perspective, the improvements presented in this research may allow an annual billing increase in the order of 29,269€. To obtain these results, it was necessary an investment of approximately 4,152€ corresponding to the first two improvement actions. Regarding the last action no investment was needed, it was simply used materials and resources available in the company, such as paints for the floor delimitation, workers for the materials organization and materials identification and internal labor (mainly maintenance workers) for making the small changes in the layouts.

In what concerns to the impact of lean on workers' safety, questionnaires were applied to assess it. The obtained results allowed to conclude that, in general, the workplace improved significantly, however the workers also mentioned some improvement opportunities allowing to continue what was developed. Some of the statements, such as improvement in physical effort, safer work and daily stress improvement were all classified with great enthusiasm by the workers. Their awareness to identify the occupational risks to which they were exposed in their jobs prior to implementations also increased. Throughout the research project, it was identified a great motivation by the production and maintenance workers, which greatly facilitated the implementation of the improvement's procedures.

References

1. Lander, E., Liker, J.K.: The Toyota production system and art: making highly customized and creative products the Toyota way. Int. J. Prod. Res. **45**(16), 3681–3698 (2007). https://doi.org/10.1080/00207540701223519
2. Behrouzi, F., Wong, K.Y.: Lean performance evaluation of manufacturing systems: A dynamic and innovative approach. Procedia Computer Science **3**, 388–395 (2011). https://doi.org/10.1016/j.procs.2010.12.065

3. Rodrigues, J., De Sá, J.C.V., Ferreira, L.P., Silva, F.J.G., Santos, G.: Lean management "Quick-Wins": results of implementation. a case study. Qual. Innov. Prosp. **23**(3), 3 (2019). https://doi.org/10.12776/qip.v23i3.1291

4. Oliveira, J., Sá, J.C., Fernandes, A.: Continuous improvement through "Lean Tools": an application in a mechanical company. Procedia Manuf. **13**, 1082–1089 (2017). https://doi.org/10.1016/j.promfg.2017.09.139

5. Santos, G., Sá, J.C., Oliveira, J., Ramos, D.G., Ferreira, C.: Quality and safety continuous improvement through lean tools. Lean Manuf. Implement. Opportun. Challenges, 165–188 (2019)

6. Cirjaliu, B., Draghici, A.: Ergonomic issues in lean manufacturing. Procedia. Soc. Behav. Sci. **221**, 105–110 (2016). https://doi.org/10.1016/j.sbspro.2016.05.095

7. Caldera, H.T.S., Desha, C., Dawes, L.: Exploring the role of lean thinking in sustainable business practice: a systematic literature review. J. Clean. Prod. **167**, 1546–1565 (2017). https://doi.org/10.1016/j.jclepro.2017.05.126

8. El-Namrouty, K.A.: Seven wastes elimination targeted by lean manufacturing case study "Gaza strip manufacturing firms." Int. J. Econ. Finan. Manage. Sci. **1**(2), 68 (2013). https://doi.org/10.11648/j.ijefm.20130102.12

9. Wyrwicka, M.K., Mrugalska, B.: Mirages of lean manufacturing in practice. Procedia Eng. **182**, 780–785 (2017). https://doi.org/10.1016/j.proeng.2017.03.200

10. Womack, J., Jones, D.: Beyond Toyota: how to root out waste and pursue perfection. Harv. Bus. Rev. **74**(5), 140–151 (1996)

11. Cuatrecasas, L.: A lean management implementation method in service operations. Int. J. Serv. Technol. Manage. **5**(5–6), 532–544 (2004). https://doi.org/10.1504/IJSTM.2004.006283

12. Melton, T.: The benefits of lean manufacturing: what lean thinking has to offer the process industries. Chem. Eng. Res. Des. **83**(6A), 662–673 (2005). https://doi.org/10.1205/cherd.04351

13. Moreira, A.C., Pais, G.C.S.: Single minute exchange of die: a case study implementation. J. Technol. Manage. Innov. **6**(1), 129–146 (2011). https://doi.org/10.4067/S0718-27242011000100011

14. Karam, A.A., Liviu, M., Cristina, V., Radu, H.: The contribution of lean manufacturing tools to changeover time decrease in the pharmaceutical industry. SMED Project. Procedia Manuf. **22**, 886–892 (2018). https://doi.org/10.1016/j.promfg.2018.03.125

15. Timasani, R., Doss, K., Mahesh, N.S.: Reducing the set-up time in a CNC machining line using QCO methods. SASTECH **10**(2), 56–62 (2011)

16. Ibrahim, M.A., et al.: Enhancing efficiency of die exchange process through single minute of exchanging die at a textile manufacturing company in Malaysia. J. Appl. Sci. **15**(3), 456–464 (2015). https://doi.org/10.3923/jas.2015.456.464

17. Ferradás, P.G., Salonitis, K.: Improving changeover time: a tailored SMED approach for welding cells. Procedia CIRP **7**, 598–603 (2013). https://doi.org/10.1016/j.procir.2013.06.039

18. Almomani, M.A., Aladeemy, M., Abdelhadi, A., Mumani, A.: A proposed approach for setup time reduction through integrating conventional SMED method with multiple criteria decision-making techniques. Comput. Ind. Eng. **66**(2), 461–469 (2013). https://doi.org/10.1016/j.cie.2013.07.011

19. Ferreira, L.P., Silva, F.J.G., Campilho, R.D.S.G., Casais, R.B., Fernandes, A.J., Baptista, A.: Continuous improvement in maintenance: a case study in the automotive industry involving Lean tools. Procedia Manuf. **38**, 1582–1591 (2019). https://doi.org/10.1016/j.promfg.2020.01.127

20. Brito, M., Ramos, A.L., Carneiro, P., Gonçalves, M.A.: Combining SMED methodology and ergonomics for reduction of setup in a turning production area. Procedia Manuf. **13**, 1112–1119 (2017). https://doi.org/10.1016/j.promfg.2017.09.172

21. Randhawa, J.S., Ahuja, I.S.: 5S – a quality improvement tool for sustainable performance: literature review and directions. Int. J. Qual. Reliab. Manage. **34**(3), 334–361 (2017). https://doi.org/10.1108/IJQRM-03-2015-0045

22. Patel, V.C., Thakkar, H.: Review on implementation of 5S in various organization. J. Eng. Res. App. **4**(3), 774–779 (2014) www.ijera.com

23. Falkowski, P., Kitowski, P.: The 5S methodology as a tool for improving the organisation of production. J. Achiev. Mater. Manuf. Eng. **24**, 1–4 (2007)

24. Neves, P., Silva, F.J.G., Ferreira, L.P., Pereira, T., Gouveia, A., Pimentel, C.: Implementing Lean tools in the manufacturing process of trimmings products. Procedia Manuf. **17**, 696–704 (2018). https://doi.org/10.1016/j.promfg.2018.10.119

25. Patel, V.C., Thakkar, H.: A case study: 5s implementation in ceramics manufacturing company. Bonfring Int. J. Indust. Eng. Manage. Sci. **4**(3), 132–139 (2014). https://doi.org/10.9756/bijiems.10346

26. Ashraf, S., Rashid, M., Rashid, A.R.M.: Implementation of 5S methodology in a food & beverage industry: a case study. Int. Rese. J. Eng. Technol. **4**(3), 1791–1796 (2017)

27. Kakkar, V., Dalal, V.S., Choraria, V., Pareta, A.S., Bhatia, A.: Implementation of 5S quality tool in manufacturing company: a case study. Int. J. Sci. Technol. Res. **4**, 2 (2015)

28. Rojasra, P.M., Qureshi, M.N.: Performance improvement through 5S in small scale industry: a case study. Int. J. Modern Eng. Res. **3**(3), 1654–1660 (2013)

29. Rizkya, I., Syahputri, K., Sari, R.M., Siregar, I.: 5S implementation in welding workshop – a lean tool in waste minimization. IOP Conf. Ser. Mater. Sci. Eng. **505**, 012018 (2019). https://doi.org/10.1088/1757-899X/505/1/012018

30. Silveira, F., Neto, I.R., Machado, F.M.: Occupational and environmental safety and health. In: Arezes, P.M. (eds.), Occupational and Environmental Safety and Health. SSDC, vol. 202. Springer, Cham (2019). https://doi.org/10.1007/978-3-030-14730-3

31. Nahmens, I., Ikuma, L.H.: An empirical examination of the relationship between lean construction and safety in the industrialized housing industry. Lean Constr. J. **2009**, 1–12 (2009)

32. Firore, C.: An execution. In: Andrade, T. (ed.) Lost Colony: The Untold Story of China's First Great Victory over the West, pp. 3–18. Princeton University Press (2011). https://doi.org/10.1515/9781400839537-003

33. Arezes, P.M., Dinis-Carvalho, J., Alves, A.C.: Workplace ergonomics in lean production environments: a literature review. Work **52**(1), 57–70 (2015). https://doi.org/10.3233/WOR-141941

34. Howell, G.A., Ballard, G., Abdelhamid, T.S., Mitropoulos, P.: Working near the edge: a new approach to construction safety. In: Proceedings 10th Annual Conference of the International Group for Lean Construction, 1–12 (2002)

35. Prakash, R.: Framework for understanding the relationship between lean and safety in Construction. J. Constr. Eng. Manag. 1–52 (2010) http://hdl.handle.net/1969.1/ETD-TAMU-2010-05-7966

36. Mitropoulos, P., Abdelhamid, T.S., Howell, G.A.: Systems model of construction accident causation. J. Constr. Eng. Manage. **131**(7), 816–825 (2005). https://doi.org/10.1061/(ASCE)0733-9364(2005)131:7(816)

37. Main, B., Taubitz, M., Wood, W.: You cannot get lean without safety understanding the common goals. Prof. Safety. **53**, 01 (2008)

38. Prakash, R.: Framework for understanding the relationship between lean and safety in Construction. J. Constr. Eng. Manage. 1–52 (2010)

39. Gonçalves, I., Sá, J.C., Santos, G., Gonçalves, M.: Safety stream mapping—a new tool applied to the textile company as a case study. In: Arezes, P.M., et al. (eds.) Occupational and Environmental Safety and Health. SSDC, vol. 202, pp. 71–79. Springer, Cham (2019). https://doi.org/10.1007/978-3-030-14730-3_8

40. Hasle, P., Bojesen, A., Jensen, P.L., Bramming, P.: Lean and the working environment: a review of the literature. Em Int. J. Oper. Prod. Manage. **32**(7), 829–849 (2012). https://doi.org/10.1108/01443571211250103
41. Cordeiro, P., Sá, J.C., Pata, A., Gonçalves, M., Santos, G., Silva, F.J.G.: Correction to: the impact of lean tools on safety—case study. In: Arezes, P.M., et al. (eds.) Occupational and Environmental Safety and Health II. SSDC, vol. 277, pp. C1–C1. Springer, Cham (2020). https://doi.org/10.1007/978-3-030-41486-3_88
42. Furman, J.: Impact of selected lean management tools on work safety. Multidiscip. Aspects Prod. Eng. **2**(1), 253–264 (2019). https://doi.org/10.2478/mape-2019-0025
43. Robertson, J.: The three RS of action research methodology: reciprocity, reflexivity and reflection-on-reality. Educ. Action Res. **8**(2), 307–326 (2000). https://doi.org/10.1080/09650790000200124
44. Souza, I., Tereso, A., Mesquita, D.: Communication in project management: an action research approach in an automotive manufacturing company. In: Rocha, Á., Adeli, H., Reis, L.P., Costanzo, S., Orovic, I., Moreira, F. (eds.) WorldCIST 2020. AISC, vol. 1159, pp. 64–73. Springer, Cham (2020). https://doi.org/10.1007/978-3-030-45688-7_7
45. Thiollent, M.: Metodologia da Pesquisa-ação. Coleção Temas básicos de pesquisa-ação (Cortez (ed.); 16.a ed). Editora Autores Associados, Brasil (2008)
46. Tripp, D.: Pesquisa-ação: uma introdução metodológica. Educ. Pesqui. **31**(3), 443–466 (2005). https://doi.org/10.1590/s1517-97022005000300009
47. Rodrigues, J., Sá, J.C., Silva, F.J.G., Ferreira, L.P., Jimenez, G., Santos, G.: A rapid improvement process through "quick-win" lean tools: a case study. Systems. **8**(4), 55 (2020). https://doi.org/10.3390/systems8040055
48. Jimenez, G., et al.: Improvement of productivity and quality in the value chain through lean manufacturing – a case study. Proc. Manuf. **41**, 882–889 (2019). https://doi.org/10.1016/j.promfg.2019.10.011
49. Azevedo, J., et al.: Improvement of production line in the automotive industry through lean philosophy. Proc. Manuf. **41**, 1023–1030 (2019). https://doi.org/10.1016/j.promfg.2019.10.029
50. Jimenez, G., Novoa, L., Ramos, L., Martinez, J., Alvarino, C.: Diagnosis of initial conditions for the implementation of the integrated management system in the companies of the land cargo transportation in the city of Barranquilla (Colombia). In: Stephanidis, C. (ed.) HCI 2018. CCIS, vol. 852, pp. 282–289. Springer, Cham (2018). https://doi.org/10.1007/978-3-319-92285-0_39
51. Jimenez, G., Zapata, E.: Metodología integrada para el control estratégico y la mejora continua, basada en el Balanced Scorecard y el Sistema de Gestión de Calidad: aplicación en una organización de servicios en Colombia. In: 51a Asamblea Anual del Consejo Latinoamericano de Escuelas de Administración CLADEA 2016, Medellín, Colombia, pp. 1–20 (2016)
52. Jimenez, G., Hernandez, L., Hernandez, H., Cabas, L., Ferreira, J.: Evaluation of quality management for strategic decision making in companies in the plastic sector of the Colombian Caribbean region using the TQM diagnostic report and data analysis. In: Stephanidis, C. (ed.) HCI 2018. CCIS, vol. 852, pp. 273–281. Springer, Cham (2018). https://doi.org/10.1007/978-3-319-92285-0_38
53. Jimenez, G.: Procedimientos para el mejoramiento de la calidad y la implantación de la Norma ISO 9001 aplicado al proceso de asesoramiento del Centro de Investigaciones y Desarrollo Empresarial y Regional en una Institucion de Educación Superior basados en la gestión por procesos. In: Congreso de Gestión de la Calidad y Protección Ambiental GECPA 2014, Habana, Cuba, pp. 1–22 (2014)

54. Jimenez-Delgado, G., Balmaceda-Castro, N., Hernández-Palma, H., de la Hoz-Franco, E., García-Guiliany, J., Martinez-Ventura, J.: An integrated approach of multiple correspondences analysis (MCA) and fuzzy AHP method for occupational health and safety performance evaluation in the land cargo transportation. In: Duffy, V.G. (ed.) HCII 2019. LNCS, vol. 11581, pp. 433–457. Springer, Cham (2019). https://doi.org/10.1007/978-3-030-22216-1_32

55. Jiménez-Delgado, G., Santos, G., Félix, M.J., Teixeira, P., Sá, J.C.: A combined AHP-TOPSIS approach for evaluating the process of innovation and integration of management systems in the logistic sector. In: Stephanidis, C., et al. (eds.) HCII 2020. LNCS, vol. 12427, pp. 535–559. Springer, Cham (2020). https://doi.org/10.1007/978-3-030-60152-2_40

56. Jimenez-Delgado, G., et al.: Improving the performance in occupational health and safety management in the electric sector: an integrated methodology using fuzzy multicriteria approach. In: Duffy, V.G. (ed.) HCII 2020. LNCS, vol. 12199, pp. 130–158. Springer, Cham (2020). https://doi.org/10.1007/978-3-030-49907-5_10

Ergonomics Training and Evaluations in a Digital World Using Collaborative Technologies: A Bibliometric Analysis

Asra Sheikh[1]([⊠]) and Vincent G. Duffy[2]

[1] Purdue University, West Lafayette, IN 47907, USA
sheikh9@purdue.edu
[2] School of Industrial Engineering, Purdue University, West Lafayette, IN 47907, USA
duffy@purdue.edu

Abstract. Ergonomics training is an essential element for maintaining occupational health and safety. With the world rapidly digitizing, it is important to adopt new methods to accommodate computer-supported learning while keeping the same level of efficiency and collaboration as in-person training sessions. Emerging collaborative technologies can be a potential means to conduct training over a virtual platform. In this systematic literature review, publications for ergonomics training and collaborative technologies were analyzed using tools such as Harzing's Publish or Perish, VOS Viewer, MAXQDA, Mendeley, CiteSpace and BibExcel. Through content and co-citation analyses, emerging trends were identified. Various databases such as Google Scholar, Web of Science, SpringerLink, and ResearchGate served as the primary sources for references. From this study, it was assessed that there was significant research on the topic of interest, however, there is immense potential for growth particularly in the context of collaborative robots and virtual reality. Performing a literature review will help bring awareness to the importance of being able to conduct ergonomics training through a virtual collaborative technology.

Keywords: Ergonomics training · Collaborative technologies · Ergonomic intervention · Evaluations · Virtual platform · Systematic literature review

1 Introduction and Background

The purpose of ergonomics training is to educate workers and employers on ergonomic hazards that may be associated with the job, their prevention, and possible medical effects (Goetsch, 2018, 205–242). Traditional ergonomic training methods often involved on-site workspace assessments or in-class lecture sessions. In the advancing world of technology, this may not be a feasible option as many workers may be working remotely or are a part of organizations spanning numerous geographical locations. Similarly, in specialized industries, using virtual collaborative environments for training allows workers to simulate complex designs, situations, and equipment, and thereby prepare them for

© Springer Nature Switzerland AG 2021
C. Stephanidis et al. (Eds.): HCII 2021, LNCS 13097, pp. 639–652, 2021.
https://doi.org/10.1007/978-3-030-90966-6_43

ergonomic risks (Markopoulos et al., n.d.). Early ergonomic intervention is key to safe workspace design and occupational health.

Collaboration with ergonomists, designers, employers, and workers can be facilitated with virtual or digital platforms to reduce the need of manual labor, and to expand the learning capabilities. Additionally, using collaborative technologies can be more cost efficient as the designer can collaborate with the user without having to travel (Freire et al. 2012). Such new technologies can range from cutting-edge virtual environments and game engines, to simple video conferencing and learning management systems.

1.1 Relation to Safety Engineering

Ergonomics is a major aspect of safety engineering, and many safety professionals emphasize the importance of having training programs to ensure occupational wellbeing. Ergonomics training helps inform workers on factors that affect their health, performance, satisfaction, and personal preferences. Analyses can be conducted to include the type of labor, anthropometric data, and the degree of interaction with machines (Brauer, 2016). To assess whether all these aspects of ergonomics are within guidelines, safety professionals can benefit from emerging collaborative technologies.

Training and virtual collaboration can also help improve team communication and thus reduce errors, particularly in high-risk industries such as healthcare, aviation, and maritime (Kolbe et al., 2014). In healthcare industries, it was often found that major oversights were a result of several human factors rather than a single person's mistake (Härgestam et al., 2013). In such cases, 'simulation-based team training' could aid healthcare workers who have fast moving jobs be better prepared for emergencies and high stress situations (Rybing et al., 2016).

1.2 Relation to Human-Computer Interaction

Collaborative technologies are extremely beneficial "since people often do not share the same organizational and physical environments with their direct work associates, they have to rely on technology to create shared virtual work environments" (Riemer et al., 2009). Therefore, conducting worker ergonomics training over virtual work environments, may involve web-based applications, software, or gadgets that require human-computer interaction to successfully operate.

In human-computer interaction design, the degree of user involvement with a machine can be at three different levels: physical, cognitive, and affective (Karray et al., 2008). Ergonomics training on virtual environments may be designed to involve physical, hands-on aspects to operate and navigate the system, cognitive so that the user can understand the system, and offer a pleasurable experience so that the user continues using the system (Karray et al., 2008).

2 Purpose of Study

The purpose of this study is to conduct a systematic literature review on emerging collaborative technologies and ascertain whether they can be a suitable means to provide effective digital ergonomics training to workers and designers. This literature review will provide insight to the existing research and future potential of using collaborative technologies for conducting ergonomics training. Success and limitations of existing research can also be examined. A variety of software such as VOS Viewer, Harzing's Publish or Perish, CiteSpace, BibExcel, Mendeley, and MAXQDA enabled a thorough literature evaluation.

3 Research Methodologies

3.1 Data Collection

For this research, data was collected from two databases: Web of Science and Google Scholar. Web of Science provided information on the article's authors, titles, abstract, cited references, and source. It is important to note that the Web of Science database could be further refined to conduct searches in 'All databases' or the 'Web of Science Core Collection'. Using 'All databases' in Web of Science produced more results, however, it is not effective for co-citation analyses as it does not give the option to export 'Full record and cited references' for record content. Searches in Google Scholar were conducted using Harzing's Publish or Perish as Harzing is a powerful tool to pull data from multiple databases. Google Scholar was selected as it easily generated a large number of results and had a much broader scope of publications. The keywords used for the lexical search in both databases were "ergonomics training" AND "collaborative technologies". This produced 38 results in Web of Science All Databases, and 9 results in the Web of Science Core Collection. For the purposes of this literature review, only the Web of Science Core Collection results will be considered. In Harzing, the maximum number of results are limited to 1000 as a default (*Harzing's Publish or Perish,* n.d.). In this case, the results were stopped at 980, and the collection time took about 8 min.

3.2 Trend Analysis

Using data from Web of Science, a trend analysis was conducted. Web of Science offered multiple categories such as source titles, countries, publication years etc. to conduct a trend analysis. The analyses can be displayed as a bar chart or tree map.

Figure 1 presents the publication years trend analysis for articles on both "ergonomics training" and "collaborative technologies". It can be seen that growth is relatively stagnant, with no more than two articles. There appears to have been a slight increase in 1995 and 2018. It is also interesting to note that certain recent years like 2019, 2016, and 2014 have had no articles published.

This analysis indicates a shortage of existing research in the usability of collaborative technologies for conducting ergonomics training. However, this also indicates that there is substantial potential for progress.

Figure 2 shows the sum of times cited per year analysis obtained from the citation report in Web of Science. This chart shows promise that there is growing interest in this field of using digital collaborative tools to promote ergonomics training. There have been fluctuations till 2015, after which there was a spike in 2017 and 2019 and a slight drop in 2020. 2021 can be ignored as it is the current year.

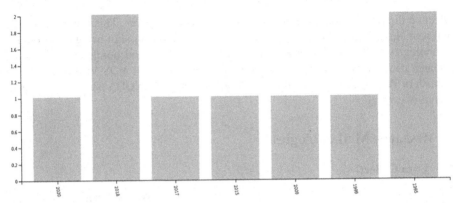

Fig. 1. Trend analysis for publication years on "ergonomics training" AND "collaborative technologies" (*Web of Science*, n.d.)

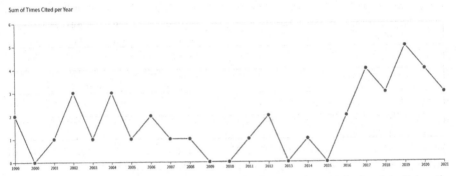

Fig. 2. Trend analysis for sum of times articles for 'ergonomics training' and 'collaborative technologies' were cited per year (*Web of Science*, n.d.)

3.3   Relevant Statistics

'Leading' lists can provide valuable insight on the most influential authors, journals, universities, etc. that publish articles related to a topic of interest. To obtain such lists, BibExcel software was used with metadata exported from Google Scholar via Harzing. BibExcel was selected as it "can be used to analyze the frequency of occurrence of text in different fields of bibliometric data" (Fahimnia et al., 2015), and it is compatible with Google Scholar, thus allowing for a much larger bibliometric database. Using the keywords 'ergonomics training' and 'collaborative technologies', leading lists were generated for authors and journals.

Leading Authors. The top 15 authors with the greatest number of published articles were identified and presented in Table 1. To present the results visually, a trend chart (PivotChart) was generated as shown in Fig. 3. It can be seen that Stanton NA and Carayon P are at the top of the list with 18 and 14 published articles respectively.

Leading Journals. The top 6 journals with the greatest number of published articles relevant to the keywords were identified and presented in Table 2. To present the results

Table 1. Top 15 leading authors for publications related to ergonomics training and collaborative technologies (*BibExcel*, n.d.)

Author	Number of published Articles
Stanton NA	18
Carayon P	14
Robertson MM	12
Salmon PM	11
Fiore SM	10
Wilson JR	10
Walker GH	9
Cuevas HM	8
Salas E	8
Neumann WP	7
Karwowski W	7
Montague E	6
Duffy VG	6
Waterson P	6
Cooke NJ	6

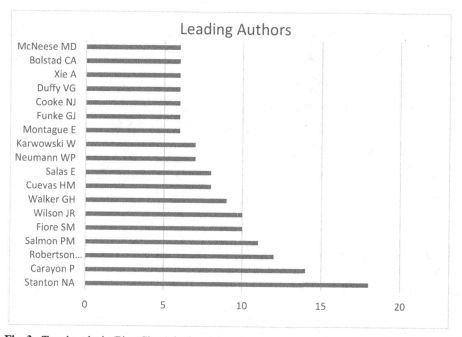

Fig. 3. Trend analysis (PivotChart) for leading authors for number of papers published related to ergonomics training and collaborative technologies (*BibExcel*, n.d.)

Table 2. Top 6 leading journals for publications related to ergonomics training and collaborative technologies (*BibExcel*, n.d.)

Journal	Number of Articles
Applied ergonomics	63
Ergonomics	58
Proceedings of the Human Factors and Ergonomics Society Annual Meeting	28
Organization science	15
Work	9
Human Factors and Ergonomics in Manufacturing & Service Industries	9

visually, a trend chart (PivotChart) was generated as shown in Fig. 4. It can be seen that the Applied Ergonomics and Ergonomics journals have the highest count with 63 and 58 published articles respectively. This shows that Harzing collected metadata from major ergonomics journals that explored the topic of ergonomics training and collaborative technologies. Therefore, the Google Scholar results via Harzing can be used as appropriate reference material for this systematic review.

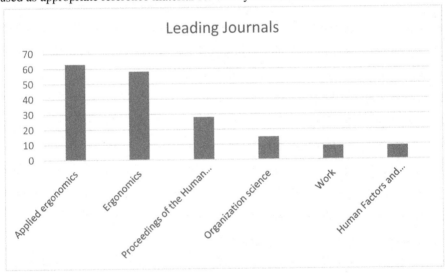

Fig. 4. Trend analysis (PivotChart) for leading journals for number of papers published related to 'ergonomics training' and 'collaborative technologies' (*BibExcel*, n.d.)

4 Results

4.1 Co-citation Analysis

A co-citation analysis was performed using the 9 articles from Web of Science in VOS Viewer software. A co-citation map is an extremely useful tool as it can visually display any co-cited publications, i.e. if they can be seen concurrently in the reference list of other articles (Fahimnia et al., 2015). Web of Science data was exported in the form of a text file and uploaded to VOS Viewer. The VOS Viewer parameter was set to 1 minimum number of cited references, for which 235 references met the threshold. The minimum number could not be changed, indicating only one co-citation. When selecting the number of cited references, the largest set of connected items included 60 items (*VOS Viewer*, n.d.). The resulting co-citation map can be seen in Fig. 5.

When analyzing co-citations for 'ergonomics training' and 'collaborative technologies', a single major cluster was formed with 1770 links and 60 items as seen in Fig. 5. This indicates that while the relation between ergonomics training and collaborative technologies is apparent with strong linkage, having only 1 citation reveals the need for more investigation of the topic. Also, most of the articles shown in Fig. 5 were from the 1990's which indicates that the citations are not recent.

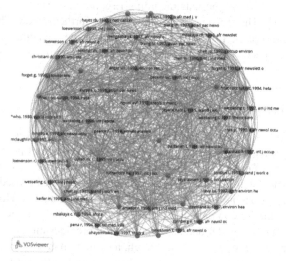

Fig. 5. Co-citation analysis for Web of Science articles on ergonomics training and collaborative technologies (*VOS Viewer*, n.d.)

In an effort to obtain more relevant articles, the co-citation analysis was repeated with the same 9 articles from Web of Science on CiteSpace. CiteSpace is a much more exhaustive and effective tool to allow cluster analysis. The co-citation can be seen in Fig. 6.

Through the CiteSpace analysis, 34 far more recent cited references were identified which were pertinent to ergonomics training and collaborative technologies. They

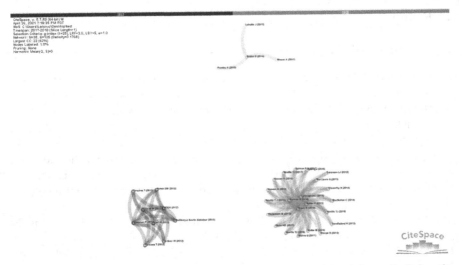

Fig. 6. Co-citation analysis for Web of Science articles on ergonomics training and collaborative technologies (*CiteSpace*, n.d.)

originated from established journals including Ergonomics, Applied Ergonomics, and Applied Psychology. These articles were collected for further review. Though three distinct clusters can be seen in Fig. 6, identifying cluster names and citation bursts was not achievable in CiteSpace. This could be due to the limited number of articles available for the analysis.

4.2   Content Analysis

Content analysis aids in identifying keywords related to the topic of interest. Results from a keyword search for 'ergonomics training' and 'collaborative technologies' in Harzing's Publish or Perish from Google Scholar were extracted and imported to VOS Viewer. One particular limitation of Harzing is that it cannot be used for co-citation analysis because it does not export the cited references metadata. However, Harzing proved to be valuable for content analysis because it can gather references from Google Scholar which is a much wider database and thereby provides more content.

Using 980 results from the Harzing search, a content map was created as shown in Fig. 7. The minimum number of occurrences was set to 22 which resulted in 55 terms meeting the threshold. The total number of terms were 7157 (*VOS Viewer*, n.d.). The VOS Viewer software automatically filtered the remaining words to 60% relevance, resulting in 33 terms to be selected.

As seen in Fig. 7, four major clusters were produced in green, red, blue, and yellow. The main themes that can be identified from the clusters appear to be ergonomic, training, human factors, and education. It is interesting to note that 'collaborative technology' is not an independent theme but falls under the training cluster. This could be indicative of research on collaborative technologies like 'simulation' and 'virtual reality' (connected

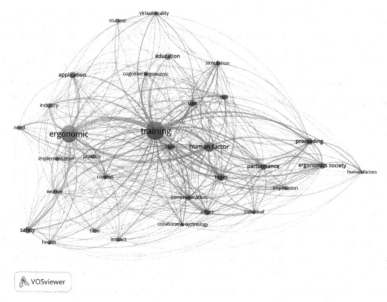

Fig. 7. Content analysis for Google Scholar articles (from Harzing) on ergonomics training and collaborative technologies (*VOS Viewer*, n.d.)

in the same cluster) is conducted for various types of training, but not specifically for ergonomics training and education.

Table 3. Applicable keywords for ergonomics training and collaborative technologies (*VOS Viewer*, n.d.)

Term	Occurrences	Relevance
Training	614	0.72
Ergonomic	577	1.38
Human Factor	190	0.49
Team	104	0.52
Education	89	0.38
Safety	85	1.71
Ergonomic society	70	2.76
Simulation	43	0.84
Cognitive Ergonomic	43	1.01
Health	42	1.61
Virtual Reality	32	0.52
Collaborative Technology	25	0.91

Important keywords, their occurrences, and % relevance to the topic of ergonomics training and collaborative technologies were analyzed and presented in Table 3. It can be seen that 'training' and 'ergonomic' occurred the highest number of times, whereas 'collaborative technology' had a fairly lower occurrence. This can be justified by the fact that that training and education has been a long-standing health and safety practice in many organizations for injury/hazard prevention (King, 1995). However, application of virtual collaborative technologies in ergonomics is still an emerging field (Pontonnier et al., 2013).

4.3   MAXQDA Content Analysis (Word Cloud)

MAXQDA is a software that enables content visualization (MAXQDA, n.d.). Major keywords with the highest frequencies were extracted from the references utilized in this systematic literature review. The relevant articles were obtained from database searches and co-citation analyses. Importing the articles to MAXQDA resulted in the word cloud shown in Fig. 8. The word cloud presents the top 50 frequent terms after irrelevant words were removed. It can be seen that "ergonomics", "training", "interaction", and "technology" are the largest, meaning they have the highest occurrence.

Fig. 8. Content analysis (Word Cloud) generated from selected articles on ergonomics training and collaborative technologies (MAXQDA, n.d.)

5   Discussion

Ergonomics training and intervention are fundamental to reduce occupational risks. Whether the worker sits in front of a computer or they are performing manual labor such as machine operation or heavy lifting, being aware of ergonomic risk factors can prevent various musculoskeletal disorders. Originally, ergonomics training would be conducted onsite and revolve around the specific person or workspace design. However, the availability of ergonomic professionals can be limited, thereby hindering ergonomic education or intervention in a workspace (Baker and Jacobs, 2013, 163–74).

Interestingly, certain large factories and corporations are providing 'train-the-trainer' trainings to offer support to new and emerging ergonomics specialists. In regard to ergonomics training for worker's occupational health on the other hand, ergonomics professionals usually work only with organizational stakeholders, but employees are often the most aware of flaws in their workspace. Therefore, collaboration of all parties will allow for establishing sustainable ergonomics measures (Labuttis, 2015).

In the present day, the optimum solution is to bring together "traditional knowledge and modern technologies" (Gašová et al., 2017). Digital tools are the new future for ergonomics (Gašová et al., 2017). Such tools must simulate a collaborative environment to achieve maximum user experience. By using a collaborative technology, employers can improve their employee's working conditions regardless of their geographical location. A computer-based collaborative ergonomic training session can prove to be inexpensive and beneficial particularly to educate a large volume of workers. The more well-trained workers are on knowing how to make correct ergonomic adjustments, the lesser is any job or mental stress; hence tremendously improving productivity and satisfaction of both employee and employer (Lubkowska et al., 2017).

Another emerging aspect of this topic is COVID-19 which resulted in a surge of teleworkers and the desire to limit physical proximities among strangers. Due to the sudden move from offices to home, many employees have been grossly unprepared, resorting to unconventional and creative workspace practices. For example, stacking books to improve laptop height or using dining table chairs to sit on, regardless of its ergonomic feasibility. Workers may have received ergonomics training on-the-job, but at home, they may not be aware of potential risks in their home office set up. Collaborative technologies should be explored and promoted to allow proper ergonomic intervention in a remote environment. Similarly, with social distancing, successful collaboration over a digital platform can uphold area-specific health guidelines and restrictions. This further establishes how ergonomics training carried out using collaborative technologies can be an extremely useful practice as it not only supports many health and safety practices but is also convenient and timesaving.

6 Conclusion

The systematic literature review included various analyses to successfully reexamine ergonomics training and collaborative technologies. Using different databases such as Google Scholar and Web of Science, a wide variety of articles were referenced and collected in Mendeley for accurate citation. Using CiteSpace, articles from lexical searches in the databases could be used for a co-citation analysis to determine relevant references and the links between citations. In depth review of these articles provided direction on the emergence and amount of work presently done on the topic of interest. From VOS Viewer and MAXQDA, a content analysis could be conducted to extract relevant keywords which could be used for further database searches and enhancing understanding of the topic. Finally, BibExcel provided valuable information on leading authors and journals and how prominent their work is.

Ergonomics training is a highly encouraged practice in many organizations. With technological advancements, it is evident through the co-citation analysis that research is being conducted to utilize technologies that will allow workers to collaborate with designers and ergonomists to allow for a much more efficient and flexible delivery of training. It should be noted that the sports industry is actively looking into ways to promote ergonomics evaluations and system design as there is "little crossover of these concepts into the sporting domain" (Neville and Salmon, 2016). As human-computer interactions become increasingly apparent in everyday life and is a rapidly emerging topic, the need to adapt and use collaborative virtual platforms to achieve the same results as a traditional ergonomic training also grows.

7 Future Work

With the rise of human-computer interaction and industry 4.0, virtual environments (VE) and game engines (GE) are being explored as potential means to conduct collaborative ergonomics training. The goal is to simulate a workspace and allow researchers to examine the working conditions (Paravizo and Braatz, 2019). Using gamification theories, the virtual environment could be developed to support complex interaction creation and have advanced visual graphics. However, factors such as anthropometry must be taken into account, but may be challenging. Users could interact virtually about their available resources and tasks which could be presented in game format (Paravizo and Braatz, 2019). Using game-based interactive virtual platforms can increase worker engagement and enjoyment during training. This collaborative technology is something that can be investigated further.

The National Science Foundation (NSF) of USA also presents notable awards and grants for potential research. The award granted to Virginia Polytechnic Institute and State University is called "Collaborative Research: A Robotic Platform for Body-Scale Human Physical Interaction in Embodied Virtual Reality". This research was initiated in 2020 indicating it is new and emerging with high potential for future success. The abstract discusses the use of a 'cobot' (short for collaborative robot) and virtual reality to allow users to feel forces and movements on respective body parts. Such a robotic system would be operated via a virtual reality platform. This technology, also termed as 'ForceBot' is especially promising because it enhances understanding of "how robotics can be used to identify potential risks of human worker/robot collaborations, and for training towards reducing workplace risk exposures" (NSF Library, 2021, 3–5).

A comparable study in 2014 discusses 'real-time ergonomics evaluation'. By using sensors and magnetic interference, a full-body system can be used for providing real-time ergonomic assessment and intervention to workers. Since the system covers all body parts, it is easier to locate specific areas of ergonomics concern and provide immediate feedback (Battini et al., 2014). Though this study was focused for warehouse workers involved in heavy manual labor, the concept of real-time ergonomics can be explored for implementation in other industries. It is evident that there is a wealth of information for conducting future research on ergonomics training and collaborative technologies.

References

1. Baker, N.A., Jacobs, K.: Tele-Ergonomics, pp. 163–74 n.d. https://doi.org/10.1007/978-1-4471-4198-3
2. Battini, D., Persona, A., Sgarbossa, F.: Computers & industrial engineering innovative real-time system to integrate ergonomic evaluations into warehouse design and management. Comput. Ind. Eng. **77**, 1 (2014). https://doi.org/10.1016/j.cie.2014.08.018
3. BibExcel (n.d.). https://homepage.univie.ac.at/juan.gorraiz/bibexcel/
4. CiteSpace (n.d.). https://citespace.podia.com/
5. Fahimnia, B., Sarkis, J., Davarzani, H.: Green supply chain management: a review and bibliometric analysis. Int. J. Prod. Econ. **162**, 101–114 (2015). https://doi.org/10.1016/j.ijpe.2015.01.003
6. Freire, L.L., Arezes, P.M., Campos, J.C.: A literature review about usability evaluation methods for e-learning platforms. Work **41**, 1038–1044 (2012). https://doi.org/10.3233/WOR-2012-0281-1038
7. Gašová, M., Gašo, M., Štefánik, A.: Advanced industrial tools of ergonomics based on industry 4.0 concept. Procedia Eng. **192**, 219–224 (2017). https://doi.org/10.1016/j.proeng.2017.06.038
8. "Google Scholar," n.d. https://scholar.google.com/.
9. Härgestam, M., Lindkvist, M., Brulin, C., Jacobsson, M., Hultin, M.: Communication in interdisciplinary teams: exploring closed-loop communication during in situ trauma team training. BMJ Open **3**(10), e003525 (2013). https://doi.org/10.1136/bmjopen-2013-003525
10. "Harzing's Publish or Perish: https://harzing.com/resources/publish-or-perish
11. Karray, F., Alemzadeh, M., Saleh, J.A., Arab, M.N.: Human-computer interaction: overview on state of the art. Int. J. Smart Sensing Intell. Syst. **1**(1), 137–159 (2008). https://doi.org/10.21307/ijssis-2017-283
12. King, P.M.: Employee ergonomics training: current limitations and suggestions for improvement. J. Occup. Rehabil. **5**(2), 115–123 (1995). https://doi.org/10.1007/BF02109914
13. Kolbe, M., et al.: Monitoring and talking to the room: Autochthonous coordination patterns in team interaction and performance. J. Appl. Psychol. **99**(6), 1254–1267 (2014). https://doi.org/10.1037/a0037877
14. Labuttis, J.: Ergonomics as element of process and production optimization. Procedia Manuf. **3**, 4168–4172 (2015). https://doi.org/10.1016/j.promfg.2015.07.391
15. Library, Document, and About NSF. "NRI : INT : Collaborative Research : A Robotic Platform for Body-Scale Human Physical Interaction in Embodied Virtual Reality FUNDING AWARDS DOCUMENT LIBRARY General ABOUT, pp. 3–5 (2021)
16. Lubkowska, W.: The potential of computer software that supports the diagnosis of workplace ergonomics in shaping health awareness. In: AIP Conference Proceedings 1906 November (2017). https://doi.org/10.1063/1.5012461
17. Markopoulos, E., Goonetilleke, R.S., Ho, A.G., Luximon, Y. (eds.): Advances in Creativity, Innovation, Entrepreneurship and Communication of Design: Proceedings of the AHFE 2020 Virtual Conferences on Creativity, Innovation and Entrepreneurship, and Human Factors in Communication of Design, July 16-20, 2020, USA. Springer International Publishing, Cham (2020)
18. MAXQDA. https://www.maxqda.com/
19. Mendeley. https://www.mendeley.com/?interaction_required=true
20. Neville, T.J., Salmon, P.M.: Never blame the umpire – a review of situation awareness models and methods for examining the performance of officials in sport. Ergonomics **59**, 1–14 (2015). https://doi.org/10.1080/00140139.2015.1100758

21. Paravizo, E., Braatz, D.: Using a game engine for simulation in ergonomics analysis, design and education: an exploratory study. Appl. Ergon. **77**, 22–28 (2019). https://doi.org/10.1016/j.apergo.2019.01.001

22. Pontonnier, C., Duval, T., Dumont, G.: Sharing and bridging information in a collaborative virtual environment: application to ergonomics. In: 4th IEEE International Conference on Cognitive Infocommunications, CogInfoCom 2013 - Proceedings, 2013, pp. 121–26 (2013). https://doi.org/10.1109/CogInfoCom.2013.6719226

23. Riemer, K., Steinfield, C., Vogel, D.: ECollaboration: on the nature and emergence of communication and collaboration technologies. Electron. Mark. **19**(4), 181–188 (2009). https://doi.org/10.1007/s12525-009-0023-1

24. Rybing, J., Nilsson, H., Jonson, C.-O., Bang, M.: studying distributed cognition of simulation-based team training with DiCoT. Ergonomics **0139**, 1–12 (2016). https://doi.org/10.1080/00140139.2015.1074290

25. VOS Viewer. https://www.vosviewer.com/

26. Web of Science. https://apps-webofknowledge-com.ezproxy.lib.purdue.edu/WOS_GeneralSearch_input.do?product=WOS&search_mode=GeneralSearch&SID=5EDrgaN6A3gV4ZXsIoq&preferencesSaved=

A Systematic Literature Review of Wireless Sensor in Safety Application

Zichen Zhang[1]($\boxtimes$) and Vincent G. Duffy[2]

[1] School of Mechanical Engineering, Purdue University, West Lafayette, IN 47906, USA
zhan3719@purdue.edu
[2] School of Industrial Engineering, Purdue University, West Lafayette, IN 47906, USA
duffy@purdue.edu

Abstract. With the rapid development of wireless sensor technology, wireless sensors have the potential to be applied in various fields. The introduction of wireless sensors in safety application is one of the feasible applications. The wireless sensors can be used to monitor human and environment to avoid potential safety issues. In this study, a systematic literature review was conducted by software like VOSviewer, CiteSpace, Harzing's Publish or Perish, MAXQDA and Mendeley. A trend analysis was conducted. It was found that the wireless sensors in the safety application are becoming increasingly popular. However, compared with a large number of wireless sensor papers, there is still a lot of research space in the safety application. The engagement measurement by Vicintas showed there is a lot of room for popularization of wireless sensors for safety in daily life. A co-citation analysis demonstrated the three clusters of wireless sensors in the safety application: wireless sensor network, location privacy and communication protocol. The citation burst analysis showed the trend has shifted from sensor network design to location privacy, Internet of Things (IoT) and applications. The Content Analysis listed the most frequent words from 15 selected key articles (such as data, node, network, monitoring). It can be concluded that safety applications of wireless sensors are increasing, and there is still a lot of work to be done.

Keywords: Wireless sensor · Safety engineering · Safety system · Sensor network

1 Introduction and Background

With the recent rapid development of micro-electro-mechanical systems (MEMS) technology, analogue electronics, digital electronics, and wireless communications, more and more low-cost, low-power, multifunctional wireless sensors that are small in size and communicate untethered in short distances have been developed (Akyildiz et al. 2002). It has led to the continuous expansion of monitoring of the human, environments, systems, vehicles, etc.

Currently, there is still much room for safety improvement. According to the data from the National Safety Council, about 4,500 work-related deaths occurs each year, and the death rate exceeds 0.03‰ in all industries. More than 3.5 million people are injured

© Springer Nature Switzerland AG 2021
C. Stephanidis et al. (Eds.): HCII 2021, LNCS 13097, pp. 653–667, 2021.
https://doi.org/10.1007/978-3-030-90966-6_44

each year, resulting in a day or less of work (Roger L. Brauer 2016). Wireless sensors can effectively monitor human and environment to prevent potential safety issues. With the rapid development of wireless sensors, there is still much room for the introduction of wireless sensors in the safety application.

2 Purpose of Study

The purpose of this research is to conduct a systematic literature review of safety-related papers on wireless sensors. With the rapid development of wireless sensors, there is a chance to improve safety. This study tries to find out the progress achieved in introducing wireless sensors into safety application. A variety of bibliometric mapping software tools are implemented to give results.

3 Research Methodology

3.1 Data Collection

Several databases are utilized to conduct the literature review of the wireless sensor in the safety application. Articles and data are mainly collected from Web of Science, Google Scholar and Springer Link. The results of Google Scholar are exported by Harzing's Publish and Perish.

Search terms in each database are similar: the topic should include both wireless sensor term and safety term. Table 1 shows the search result from each database and the corresponding search terms.

Table 1. Search result from each database with corresponding search terms.

Database	# of Articles	Search term
Web of Science	1,644	TOPIC: ("wireless sensor") AND TOPIC: (safety)
Google scholar (via Harzing's Publish and Perish)	1,000	Keywords: "wireless sensor" AND safety
Springer Link	7,945	"wireless sensor" AND (safety)

3.2 Trend Analysis

Figure 1 shows the trend analysis result between 1997 and 2021 from Web of Science database. The number of articles increased rapidly from 1995 to 2015 and reached a peak in 2015. From 2015 to 2020, the number of articles dropped slightly, probably because of the lag in the database.

As the topic is wireless sensors in safety application, a trend analysis about the wireless sensor is carried out. Figure 2 shows the trend analysis result about wireless

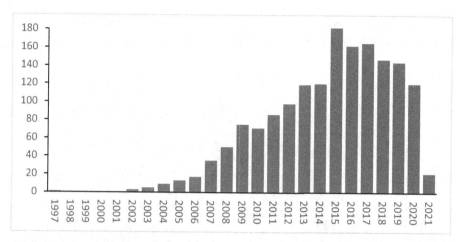

Fig. 1. Trend analysis of articles about wireless sensor and safety per year from Web of Science

sensor between 1997 and 2021 from Web of Science. The number of articles on wireless sensors is similar to the trend of articles on wireless sensors in safety. The number of articles increased rapidly before 2015 and reached a peak in 2015. Then, the articles maintained a high level between 2015 and 2017. The number dropped slightly after 2017. It can be concluded that with the development of wireless sensors, more and more wireless sensors are introduced to the safety application.

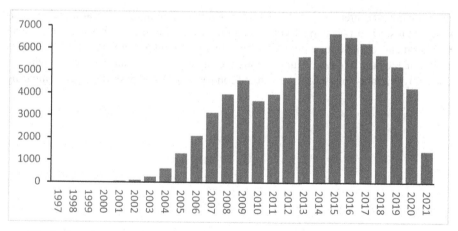

Fig. 2. Trend analysis of articles about wireless sensor per year from Web of Science

Since MEMS (micro-electro-mechanical system) technology is the basis of wireless sensor, a trend analysis about MEMS technology is carried out in the Web of Science database. Figure 3 shows the trend analysis result of MEMS from 1997 to 2021 on Web of Science. The number of articles increased rapidly before 2007 and remains at a high level after 2007. It shows MEMS technology is 8 years ahead of wireless sensor, which confirms the relation between MSMS technology and wireless sensor.

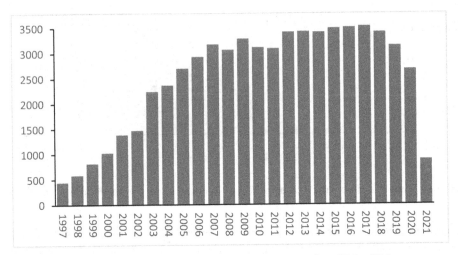

Fig. 3. Trend analysis of articles about MEMS per year from Web of Science

3.3 Engagement Measurement

Engagement measurement is carried out by Vicintas. Vicintas can track and analyze real-time and historical tweets on Twitter (Vicinitas 2020). Figure 4 shows the engagement measurement result about wireless sensor safety by Vicintas. Only a post was found on Twitter in the past 10 days. Figure 5 shows the engagement measurement of the wireless sensor by Vicintas. 634 posts were found on Twitter in the past 10 days. Comparing

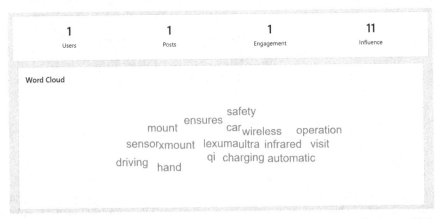

Fig. 4. The engagement measurement result of wireless sensor safety in Twitter in the past 10 days by Vicintas

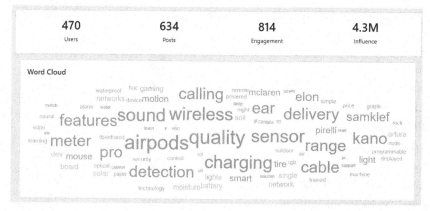

Fig. 5. The engagement measurement result of the wireless sensor in Twitter in the past 10 days by Vicintas

these two Vicintas results, only about 1.5‰ of the posts about wireless sensors include safety.

According to the result in Sect. 3.1 Data Collection, 1,644 articles on wireless sensors and safety were collected in the Web of Science database, comparing with 104,988 articles about wireless sensors, about 1.5% of the articles contain safety. The ratio of containing safety in Web of Science is 10 times higher than that in Twitter. It shows the wireless sensors in the safety application are still in the laboratory stage and far from popularization.

3.4 Source Analysis

A source analysis about the wireless sensor in the safety application was conducted by Web of Science. Table 2 shows the source analysis result of wireless sensor and safety. Sensors is the main source of wireless sensors and safety.

3.5 Countries/Regions Analysis

A countries and regions analysis about the wireless sensor in safety application is conducted by Web of Science. Table 3 shows the result of countries and regions analysis of wireless sensor and safety in the Web of Science database. China is a leading country in the safety application of wireless sensor.

3.6 Funding Agencies Analysis

A funding agencies analysis about the wireless sensor in safety application was conducted by Web of Science. Table 4 shows the result of funding agencies analysis of wireless sensor in safety application. National Natural Science Foundation of China (NSFC) is the leading agency in the field of wireless sensor and safety. The result is consistent with the result in Sect. 3.5 Countries/Regions Analysis that China is the leading country in the field of wireless sensors and safety application.

Table 2. Source analysis result of wireless senor and safety in Web of Science database

Source titles	Record count	% of 1,644
Sensors	76	4.54%
Proceedings of SPIE	29	1.73%
IEEE Access	28	1.67%
IEEE Sensors Journal	25	1.49%
Lecture Notes in Computer Science	24	1.44%
International Journal of Distributed Sensor Networks	22	1.32%
Wireless Personal Communications	22	1.32%
Applied Mechanics and Materials	20	1.20%
Advanced Materials Research	17	1.02%
Procedia Engineering	13	0.78%

Table 3. Countries/regions analysis result of wireless senor and safety in Web of Science database

Countries/Regions	Record count	% of 1,644
Peoples R China	509	30.96%
USA	210	12.77%
Inida	180	10.95%
South Korea	116	7.06%
Italy	91	5.54%
England	75	4.56%
Taiwan	59	3.59%
Spain	53	3.22%
Canada	48	2.92%
Germany	48	2.92%

Table 4. Funding agencies analysis result of wireless senor and safety in Web of Science database

Funding agencies	Record count	% of 1,644
National natural science foundation of China NSFC	148	9.00%
European commission	52	3.16%
Fundamental research funds for the central Universities	41	2.49%
National science foundation NSF	27	1.64%
Ministry of science and technology Taiwan	20	1.22%

4 Results

4.1 Co-citation Analysis by VOSviewer

The co-citation analysis was based on the result from Web of Science by the VOSviewer. The minimum number of citations for cited references was set to 20 to get the top 12 articles with the most citations. Table 5 shows the co-citation analysis result of the 1,644 papers in the Web of Science database. Figure 6 shows the co-citation analysis result diagram.

Table 5. Co-citation analysis result table of top 12 articles from 1,644 papers in Web of Science database.

Title	Cluster	Weight < Citations >
akyildiz if, 2002, comput netw, v38, p393, https://doi.org/10.1016/s1389-1286(01)00302-4 Akyildiz et al. 2002)	1	91
akyildiz if, 2002, IEEE Commun mag, v40, p102, https://doi.org/10.1109/mcom.2002.1024422 (Ian et al. 2002)	1	59
yick j, 2008, comput netw, v52, p2292, https://doi.org/10.1016/j.comnet.2008.04.002 (Yick et al. 2008)	1	43
atzori l, 2010, comput netw, v54, p2787, https://doi.org/10.1016/j.comnet.2010.05.010 (Atzori Iera, and Morabito 2010)	1	28
lynch j. p., 2006, shock and vibration digest, v38, p91, https://doi.org/10.1177/0583102406061499 (LYNCH, Jerome P; LOH 2006)	1	26
perrig a, 2002, wirel netw, v8, p521, https://doi.org/10.1023/a:1016598314198	1	26
chong cy, 2003, p ieee, v91, p1247, https://doi.org/10.1109/jproc.2003.814918 (Chong and Kumar 2003)	1	20
heinzelman wb, 2002, ieee t wirel commun, v1, p660, https://doi.org/10.1109/twc.2002.804190 (Heinzelman et al. 2002)	2	34
heinzelman w. r., 2000, p1, doi [https://doi.org/10.1109/hicss.2000.926982, https://doi.org/10.1109/hicss.2000.926982] (Heinzelman et al. 2002)	2	29
akkaya k., 2005, ad hoc networks, v3, p325, https://doi.org/10.1016/j.adhoc.2003.09.010 (Akkaya and Younis 2005)	2	21
kamat p, 2005, int con distr comp s, p599, https://doi.org/10.1109/icdcs.2005.31 (Kamat et al. 2005)	3	32
Trappe w., sasn 04 p 2 ACM work, p88, doi [https://doi.org/10.1145/1029102.1029117, https://doi.org/10.1145/1029102.1029117] (Ozturk et al. 2004)	3	20

These 12 articles belong to three clusters: wireless sensors network, wireless sensor communication protocol and wireless sensor location privacy. Papers on wireless sensor

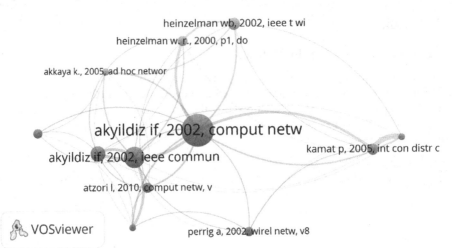

heinzelman wb, 2002, ieee t wi

heinzelman w r., 2000, p1, do

akkaya k., 2005, ad hoc networ

akyildiz if, 2002, comput netw

akyildiz if, 2002, ieee commun

kamat p, 2005, int con distr c

atzori l, 2010, comput netw, v

VOSviewer

perrig a, 2002, wirel netw, v8

Fig. 6. Co-citation analysis with cluster diagram of top 12 articles by VOSviewer from 1,644 papers in Web of Science database.

network cluster account for more than half of the most cited papers, indicating that it is a leading topic in the field of wireless sensor and safety. A wireless sensor network has a great number of wireless sensors which are densely deployed either inside the phenomenon or very close to it (Ian et al. 2002). This allows wireless sensors to monitor human and conditions with loose location restrictions and cooperative effort of wireless sensor nodes. In this way, the wireless sensors network technology improves the feasibility of safety improvement by simplifying the human and environment monitoring. The wireless sensor communication protocol is a method to design and manage the networks in consideration of energy supply limitation and bandwidth limitation. It enables wireless sensors to maximize the lifecycle (Akkaya and Younis 2005). In this way, the wireless sensors can monitor human and environment more efficiently, and improve safety with lower energy consumption. As sensor privacy is becoming more increasingly important, wireless sensor location needs to be protected from being backtracked, especially when the wireless sensors are used to monitor human.

4.2   Co-citation Analysis and Citation Burst Analysis by CiteSpace

Co-citation Analysis by CiteSpsace

Another software for Co-Citation Analysis is CiteSpace. Citespace analysis only focused on the papers from 2017 to 2021, so it provides the latest trend in wireless sensors and safety. Figure 7 shows the results of the Co-Citation Analysis.

"#1 correlation analysis" shows that the statistical method is increasingly popular in wireless sensor and safety. The statistical approach is a useful method to determine the effectiveness of the safety projects and provides an overview of safety performance (Roger L. Brauer 2016a). "#2 safety monitoring" and "#3 environmental monitoring"

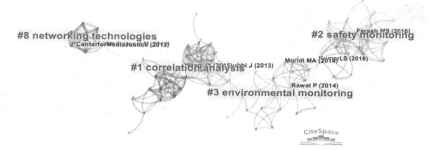

Fig. 7. Co-citation analysis with cluster diagram with title label by CiteSpace from papers in Web of Science database between 2017 and 2010.

indicates the practical applications of wireless sensors in safety improvement is monitoring the environment and human. "#8 networking technologies" represents one of the basic technologies of wireless sensors.

Citation Burst Analysis by CiteSpace

Citation Burst Diagram shows the trend of research burst events in the research area (Chaomei Chen 2020). Figure 8 shows the citation burst diagram generated by Citespace. 12 burst items were found in the diagram. It shows the focus in the field of wireless sensor and safety was wireless sensor network (Akyildiz et al. 2002). Nowadays, the focus has shifted to wireless sensor location privacy (Long et al. 2014), Internet of Things (IoT) (Xu et al. 2014; Gubbi et al. 2013) and safety applications such as the railway industry (Hodge et al. 2015) and coal mines (Kumari and Om 2016). It is reasonable that the focus shifted from topics about the wireless sensor prototype (such as the design and establishment of sensor network) to safety-related topics (such as sensor node location privacy and application in the field of safety engineering).

Top 12 References with the Strongest Citation Bursts

References	Year	Strength	Begin	End	1995 - 2021
Akyildiz IF, 2002, COMPUT NETW, V38, P393, DOI 10.1016/S1389-1286(01)00302-4, DOI	2002	4.76	2002	2006	
Akyildiz IF, 2002, IEEE COMMUN MAG, V40, P102, DOI 10.1109/MCOM.2002.1024422, DOI	2002	4.75	2004	2007	
Sun LM, 2005, WIRELESS SENSOR NETW, V0, P0	2005	3.61	2009	2010	
Lynch J P, 2006, Shock and Vibration Digest, V38, P91, DOI 10.1177/0583102406061499, DOI	2006	4.21	2010	2011	
Gungor VC, 2009, IEEE T IND ELECTRON, V56, P4258, DOI 10.1109/TIE.2009.2015754, DOI	2009	3.38	2011	2014	
Yick J, 2008, COMPUT NETW, V52, P2292, DOI 10.1016/j.comnet.2008.04.002, DOI	2008	3.59	2012	2013	
Conti M, 2013, IEEE COMMUN SURV TUT, V15, P1238, DOI 10.1109/SURV.2013.011413.00118, DOI	2013	3.87	2015	2016	
Long J, 2014, IEEE ACCESS, V2, P633, DOI 10.1109/ACCESS.2014.2332817, DOI	2014	3.61	2016	2019	
Xu LD, 2014, IEEE T IND INFORM, V10, P2233, DOI 10.1109/TII.2014.2300753, DOI	2014	4.63	2017	2018	
Gubbi J, 2013, FUTURE GENER COMP SY, V29, P1645, DOI 10.1016/j.future.2013.01.010, DOI	2013	4.11	2017	2018	
Hodge VJ, 2015, IEEE T INTELL TRANSP, V16, P1088, DOI 10.1109/TITS.2014.2366512, DOI	2015	4.08	2017	2019	
Kumari S, 2016, COMPUT NETW, V104, P137, DOI 10.1016/j.comnet.2016.05.007, DOI	2016	3.9	2018	2019	

Fig. 8. Co-citation analysis with citation burst diagram by CiteSpace from 1,644 papers in Web of Science database.

4.3 Content Analysis by MAXQDA

To get more intuitive results on the content of wireless sensors and safety, a content analysis is conducted by MAXQDA. The MAXQDA can generate a word cloud based on several documents. Table 6 shows the 15 articles that are imported to MAXQDA to do content analysis. The criteria for the key articles are (the article is closely related to the wireless sensor in safety application) OR (the article is cited over 30 times from the 1,644 papers results in Web of Science database) OR (Citation burst strength is over 4).

Table 6. 15 key articles for content analysis.

Author	Title	Reason
Ki, Song Do	A study on cloud-based safety ESS watchdog system using ultra-compact wireless sensor (Ki et al. 2021)	Related topic
Tayeh, Gaby Bou	A Wearable LoRa-Based Emergency System for Remote Safety Monitoring (Tayeh et al. 2020)	Related topic
Hodge, Victoria J	Wireless Sensor Networks for Condition Monitoring in the Railway Industry: A Survey (Hodge et al. 2015)	Related topic Citation Burst
Akkaş, M. Alper	Using wireless underground sensor networks for mine and miner safety (Akkaş 2018)	Related topic
Lara, Óscar D.	A survey on human activity recognition using wearable sensors (Lara and Labrador 2013)	Related topic
Lande, Shilpa	An efficient implementation of wireless sensor network for performing rescue safety operation in underground coal mines (Lande et al. 2020)	Related topic
McGrath, Susan P	Improving Patient Safety and Clinician Workflow in the General Care Setting with Enhanced Surveillance Monitoring (McGrath et al. 2019)	Related topic
Akyildiz, I. F	A Survey on Sensor Networks (Ian et al. 2002)	Co-citation analysis Citation burst
Akyildiz, I. F	Wireless sensor networks: A survey (Akyildiz et al. 2002)	Co-citation analysis Citation burst

(continued)

Table 6. (*continued*)

Author	Title	Reason
Yick, Jennifer	Wireless sensor network survey (Yick et al. 2008)	Co-citation analysis Citation Burst
Heinzelman, Wendi B	An application-specific protocol architecture for wireless microsensor networks (Heinzelman et al. 2002)	Co-citation analysis
Kamat, Pandurang	Enhancing source-location privacy in sensor network routing (Kamat et al. 2005)	Co-citation analysis
Xu, Li Da	Internet of things in industries: A survey (Xu et al. 2014)	Citation burst
LYNCH, Jerome P	A Summary Review of Wireless Sensors and Sensor Networks for Structural Health Monitoring (Lynch 2006)	Co-citation analysis Citation burst
Gubbi, Jayavardhana	Internet of Things (IoT): A vision, architectural elements, and future directions (Gubbi et al. 2013)	Citation burst

Figure 9 shows the word cloud result from the 15 key articles by MAXQDA. Non-informative words have been excluded and only the top 70 frequently occurring words are retained. These words occurred at least 147 times in the 15 articles.

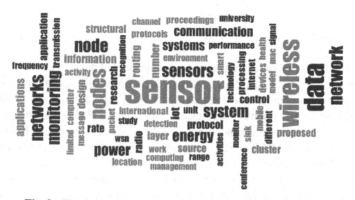

Fig. 9. Word cloud generated from 15 key articles by MAXQDA

Table 7 shows the top 10 frequently occurring words among 15 key articles by MAXQDA. The 1,501 occurrences of "data" proved the importance of data in wireless sensor and safety. The sensors collect data and the control unit process data. Data is tightly related to monitoring the human and conditions. The "network" and "networks" appeared 1,603 times. Consistent with the result in Sect. 4.1 Co-citation Analysis by VOSviewer, wireless sensor network is a popular technology nowadays and it simplifies the monitoring of human and conditions. Each sensor acts as a node in the wireless sensor network. Therefore, it can be explained that "nodes" and "node" appeared 1,776 times in the 15 key articles. "monitoring" occurred 725 times, probably because the main function of the sensor is to monitor human and environment to prevent potential safety issues. "system" occurred 654 times, indicating that the monitoring projects were considered systematically.

Table 7. Top 10 frequently occurring words in 15 key articles by MAXQDA

Word	Frequency	%	Rank	Documents %
Sensor	2114	1.75	1	100.00
Data	1501	1.24	2	100.00
Wireless	1375	1.14	3	100.00
Nodes	1017	0.84	4	73.33
Network	809	0.67	5	100.00
Networks	794	0.66	6	86.67
Node	759	0.63	7	80.00
Monitoring	725	0.60	8	100.00
Sensors	704	0.58	9	100.00
System	654	0.54	10	100.00

5 Discussion

The literature review provides trends analysis, engagement measurement, source analysis, country analysis, funding agency analysis, co-citation analysis, citation burst analysis and content analysis from several databases. MaxQDA generates the word could of keywords in this topic. VOSviewer analyzes the data from the Web of Science to generate a map to illustrate the connections between citations. Citespace imports full record and references data from the Web of Science database. Then, cluster result and citation burst figure are generated by Citespace.

The wireless sensors are powerful tools to monitor human and conditions, which can be used to improve safety. Trend analysis shows that wireless sensors in the safety application are becoming increasingly popular. The engagement measurement concludes that more wireless sensors is far from popularization in safety application. Countries and funding agency analysis show that China has become the leading country in this field. Co-citation analysis shows that wireless sensor network, wireless sensor communication protocol and sensor privacy are three main research areas. Citation burst analysis shows that the trend has shifted from sensor network design to privacy and safety applications.

Content analysis shows the importance of data, nodes and monitoring in this area. Monitoring human and environment is an important safety application. In short, research about wireless sensors and safety is increasing, and there is still a lot of room for further research and generalization.

6   Future Work

As mentioned in Sect. 4.2 Co-Citation Analysis and Citation Burst Analysis by CiteSpace, as wireless sensor technology matures, more and more researchers turn to the safety application of the wireless sensors. The wireless sensor in safety engineering is one of the leading applications. The National Science Foundation has shown awarded multiple projects related to the introduction of wireless sensors into the field of safety by searching "wireless sensor" AND "safety" on www.nsf.gov.

"SBIR Phase I: SmartNet Applications for Mobility and Safety (SAMS)" by Pravin Varaiya at Sensys Networks, Inc. in 2012 is a research project about improving traffic mobility and safety based on the wireless sensor network platform. The wireless sensors can detect vehicles, bicycles, pedestrians and parked vehicles; locate vehicles; input traffic signals. These data are combined and innovative application is developed to improve transportation safety and efficiency (National Science Foundation 2012). It is a meaningful research project since most transportation-related accidents, injuries, and deaths involve motor vehicles. According to World Health Organization, about 1.2 million people die on roads every year. Improving the facilities is a practical way to improve transportation safety (Roger L. Brauer 2016). Therefore, wireless sensors can improve transportation safety by monitoring the traffic and making the facilities more intelligent.

High confidence active safety control by cyber-physical system (CPS) medium in automotive cyber-physical systems by Radhakisan Baheti at the University of California-Berkeley in 2009 is a research project implementing wireless sensor in the safety analysis area. The project treated the vehicle-driver-road system as a cyber-physical system (CPS) and studied the safety performance of advanced vehicle dynamics control systems. The study focused on the interaction between tire and road, the interaction between driver and design of the vehicle and advanced controller. The wireless sensors embedded in the tires played an important role in measuring the interaction between tire and road. Body wireless sensor is introduced into the system to real-time monitor driver's behavior and uncertainty bounds to study the driver-vehicle interaction. The wireless sensors played an important role in getting real-time data of tire and driver so that the researchers can evaluate the safety performance based on these data (National Science Foundation 2009).

Prescribed fire management by implementing self-configuring in situation wireless sensor networks by Richard Han at the University of Colorado in 2003 is one of the research projects about wireless sensor and safety. It emphasized the importance of weather data to the forest and public land fire management. Richard recognized the limitation of current weather data collection equipment. The research project proposed a self-configuring wireless fire weather sensor network to provide real-time data. The wireless sensor network has the following characteristics: low maintenance, adaptive and automatically self-organizing network; analysis of fault-tolerant; low power operation;

time-synchronized duty cycles; energy harvesting and remote dynamic reprogramming. These characteristics can effectively monitor the environment and improve in the safety management process of prescribed wildland fires (National Science Foundation 2003).

In addition to the projects on the National Science Foundation website, researchers around the world have also carried out many meaningful research projects. Researchers at the National Pingtung University of Science & Technology have developed a wireless sensor that detects the degree of human attention by detecting electroencephalography (EEG) signals (Liu et al. 2013). The human factor theory of accident causation points out the human error is the root cause of every accident event (Goetsch 2019). The project can be used to monitor the attention of operators to avoid safety issue. Therefore, the application of wireless sensors in the safety application would be a good direction for future work.

References

Ki, S.D., Cho, S.H., Lee, H.S., Kim, D.K.: A study on cloud-based safety ESS watchdog system using ultra-compact wireless sensor. Turkish J. Comput. Math. Educ. **12**(6), 573–578 (2021)

CiteSpace: Visualizing Trends and Patterns in Scientific Literature. https://sites.google.com/site/citespace101/first-example/4-3-interpret-results. Accessed 28 Apr 2020

National Science Foundation: Award Abstract # 0931437 CPS:Medium: High Confidence Active Safety Control in Automotive Cyber-Physical Systems https://www.nsf.gov/awardsearch/showAward?AWD_ID=0931437&HistoricalAwards=false. Accessed 29 Apr 2020

Tayeh, G.B., Azar, J., Makhoul, A., Guyeux, C., Demerjian, J.: A wearable LoRa-based emergency system for remote safety monitoring. In: 2020 International Wireless Communications and Mobile Computing, IWCMC 2020, pp. 120–25. IEEE, Limassol, Cyprus (2020)

Xu, L.D., Wu, H., Li, S.: Internet of Things in Industries: A Survey. IEEE Trans. Indust. Inf. **10**(4), 2233–2243 (2014)

National Science Foundation Award Abstract # 1142381 SBIR Phase I: SmartNet Applications for Mobility and Safety (SAMS). https://www.nsf.gov/awardsearch/showAward?AWD_ID=1142381&HistoricalAwards=false. Accessed 29 Apr 2020

Yick, J., Mukherjee, B., Ghosal, D.: Wireless sensor network survey. Comput. Netw. **52**(12), 2292–2330 (2008)

Chandel, A., Chouhan, V.S., Sharma, S.: A survey on routing protocols for wireless sensor networks. In: Goar, V., Kuri, M., Kumar, R., Senjyu, T. (eds.) Advances in Information Communication Technology and Computing. LNNS, vol. 135, pp. 143–164. Springer, Singapore (2021). https://doi.org/10.1007/978-981-15-5421-6_15

Ian, F., Akyildiz, W.S., Yogesh, S., Erdal, C.: A Survey on Sensor Networks. IEEE Commun. Mag. **40**(8), 102–114 (2002)

National Science Foundation Award Abstract # 0330466 SENSORS: Collaborative Research: Self-Configuring. In: Situ Wireless Sensor Networks For Prescribed Fire Management. https://www.nsf.gov/awardsearch/showAward?AWD_ID=0330466&HistoricalAwards=false. Accessed 29 Apr 2020

Alper Akkaş, M.: Using wireless underground sensor networks for mine and miner safety. Wirel. Netw. **24**(1), 17–26 (2016). https://doi.org/10.1007/s11276-016-1313-0

Atzori, L., Iera, A., Morabito, G.: The internet of things: a survey. Comput. Netw. **54**(15), 2787–2805 (2010). https://doi.org/10.1016/j.comnet.2010.05.010

Heinzelman, W.R., Chandrakasan, A., Balakrishnan, H.: Energy-efficient communication protocol for wireless Microsensor networks. In: the 33rd Annual Hawaii International Conference on System Sciences on Proceedings, pp. 1–10. IEEE, Maui, HI (2000)

Kamat, P., Zhang, Y., Trappe, W., Ozturk, C.: Enhancing source-location privacy in sensor network routing. In: The 25th IEEE International Conference on Distributed Computing Systems (ICSCS'05) on Proceedings, pp. 599–608. IEEE, Columbus, OH (2005)

Kumari, S., Om, H.: Authentication protocol for wireless sensor networks applications like safety monitoring in coal mines. Comput. Netw. **104**, 137–154 (2016). https://doi.org/10.1016/j.com net.2016.05.007

Long, J., Dong, M., Ota, K., Liu, A.: Achieving source location privacy and network lifetime maximization through tree-based diversionary routing in wireless sensor networks. IEEE Access **2**, 633–651 (2014). https://doi.org/10.1109/ACCESS.2014.2332817

Goetsch, D.L.: Occupational Safety and Health for Technologists, Engineers, and Managers, 9th edn. Pearson, New York (2019)

Heinzelman, W.B., Chandrakasan, A.P., Balakrishnan, H.: An application-specific protocol architecture for wireless Microsensor networks. IEEE Trans. Wirel. Commun. **1**(4), 660–670 (2002). https://doi.org/10.1109/TWC.2002.804190

McGrath, S.P., Perreard, I.M., Garland, M.D., Converse, K.A., Mackenzie, T.A.: Improving patient safety and clinician workflow in the general care setting with enhanced surveillance monitoring. IEEE J. Biomed. Health Inf. **23**(2), 857–866 (2019). https://doi.org/10.1109/JBHI.2018.283 4863

Chong, C.Y., Kumar, S.P.: Sensor networks: evolution, opportunities, and challenges. In: 2003 IEEE, vol. 91, pp. 1247–56. IEEE (2003)

Lande, S., Chabukswar, P., Bhope, V.: An efficient implementation of wireless sensor network for performing rescue safety operation in underground coal mines. In: 2020 International Conference for Emerging Technology, INCET 2020 on Proceedings, pp. 1–6. INCET, Belgaum, India (2020)

Hodge, V.J., O'Keefe, S., Weeks, M., Moulds, A.: Wireless sensor networks for condition monitoring in the railway industry: a survey. IEEE Trans. Intell. Transp. Syst. **16**(3), 1088–1106 (2015). https://doi.org/10.1109/TITS.2014.2366512

Akyildiz, I.F., Su, W., Sankarasubramaniam, Y., Cayirci, E.: Wireless sensor networks: a survey. Comput. Netw. **38**(4), 393–422 (2002)

Lynch, J.P.: A summary review of wireless sensors and sensor networks for structural health monitoring. Shock Vibr. Digest. **38**(2), 91–128 (2006). https://doi.org/10.1177/058310240606 1499

Gubbi, J., Buyya, R., Marusic, S., Palaniswami, M.: Internet of Things (IoT): a vision, architectural elements, and future directions. Future Gener. Comput. Syst. **29**(7), 1645–1660 (2013). https://doi.org/10.1016/j.future.2013.01.010

Brauer, R.L.: Safety and Health for Engineers, 2nd edn. John Wiley & Sons Incorporated, New York (2016)

Liu, N.-H., Chiang, C.-Y., Chu, H.-C.: Recognizing the degree of human attention using EEG signals from mobile sensors. Sensors **13**(8), 10273–10286 (2013). https://doi.org/10.3390/s13 0810273

Author Index

Printed in the United States
by Baker & Taylor Publisher Services